Crimes Against Humanity

GEOFFREY ROBERTSON QC

Crimes Against Humanity

THE STRUGGLE FOR GLOBAL JUSTICE

THE NEW PRESS
NEW YORK

Originally published in the United Kingdom by
Allen Lane, The Penguin Press, 1999

Published in the United States by
The New Press, New York, with a new introduction, 2000
Distributed by W. W. Norton & Company, Inc., New York

LIBRARY OF CONGRESS CATALOGING-IN-PUBLICATION DATA

Crimes against humanity : the struggle for global justice / Geoffrey Robertson.
p.   cm.
Includes bibliographical references.
ISBN 1-56584-597-8 (hc.)
1. Crimes against humanity.   2. Human rights.   I. Title.
K5301.R63   2000
323'.09'04—dc21   00–021344

The New Press was established in 1990 as a not-for-profit alternative to the
large, commercial publishing houses currently dominating the book publishing
industry. The New Press operates in the public interest rather than for private
gain, and is committed to publishing, in innovative ways, works of educational,
cultural, and community value that are often deemed insufficiently profitable.

The New Press, 450 West 41st Street, 6th floor, New York, NY 10036
www.thenewpress.com

Printed in the United States of America

9 8 7 6 5 4 3 2 1

For Julius and Georgina

And here, over an acre of ground, lay dead and dying people. You could not see which was which except perhaps by a convulsive movement, or the last quiver of a sigh from a living skeleton, too weak to move. The living lay with their heads against the corpses, and around them moved the ghastly procession of emaciated, aimless people, with nothing to do, and no hope of life, unable to move out of your way, unable to look at the terrible sights around them . . . Babies had been born here, tiny wizened things that could not live. A mother, driven mad, screamed at a British sentry to give her milk for her child, and thrust the tiny mite into his arms and ran off, crying terribly. He opened the bundle, and found the baby had been dead for days. This day at Belsen was the most horrible day of my life.

Richard Dimbleby
BBC broadcast from Belsen, 13 May 1945

Contents

CONTENTS

Preface

The notion that individuals, wherever in the world they live, possess a few basic powers which no political order can remove, has had a momentous impact at two points in modern history. The first, in the last quarter of the eighteenth century, was in every way revolutionary: it inspired and justified both the American battle for independence from Britain and the overthrow of the despotic monarchy in France. It endowed these upheavals with a political meaning far beyond the republics which were their immediate object, by establishing the liberty of the individual as a precondition of and restriction on the power of the State. This was not unique to America and France: in other societies limitations had been imposed by tradition or cultural convention, or (most notably in Britain) by compact and common law, but what was truly groundbreaking was the constitutional enumeration of rights which the citizen could enforce against the government by taking it to court. But the notion that 'rights' might belong to anyone, anywhere, as a human inheritance was ridiculed by nineteenth-century philosophers and when the majority of Western powers agreed to outlaw slavery, this was attributed to shared moral generosity rather than to any recognition of an inalienable individual right not to be held in bondage or servitude. It dawned on no political leader, even after the carnage of the First World War, that international institutions might tell states how to treat their nationals – the League of Nations and the Permanent Court of International Justice were untroubled by 'human rights' until Hitler rendered them irrelevant. At this point, the individual had no rights in international law, which dealt with treaties and agreements between states and was completely inaccessible to their citizens.

The Holocaust was a revelation that was to change this for ever. It crystallized the Allied war aims, and called forth an international tribunal – the court at Nuremberg – to punish individual Nazis for the barbarities they had authorized against German citizens. These charges – called, for the first time, 'crimes against humanity' – were distinct from the 'war crimes' the Axis partners had inflicted upon Allied soldiers and prisoners-of-war. The logic of the crime against humanity, first defined in Article 6(c) of the Nuremberg Charter, was that future state agents who authorized torture or genocide against their own populations were criminally responsible, in international law, and might be punished by any court capable of catching them. For the first time, it could be said that individuals had a 'right' to be treated with a minimum of civility by their own governments, which 'right' all other governments had a correlative duty to uphold by trying the torturers who fell into their hands, or else by setting up international courts to punish them. This was the legal legacy of Nuremberg, supplemented by a United Nations system which promised institutional support for a 'Universal Declaration of Human Rights', approved by the General Assembly of the United Nations. The second great moment for human rights – the creation of a process by which it could emerge from the domestic laws and constitutions of a few countries into a universal system affording some minimum protection to everyone, everywhere – had arrived. At the Palais Chaillot in Paris, on 10 December 1948, the president of the General Assembly, Dr H. V. Evatt (the Australian Foreign Minister), announced the advent of a new international law of human rights, for the first time transcending the laws and customs of independent sovereign states: 'millions of men, women and children, all over the world, many miles from Paris and New York, will turn for help, guidance and inspiration to this document'.

But this moment was short-lived. The evolutionary process for international human rights law, commenced so confidently, was frozen almost to a standstill by the Cold War. The power blocs did not deny the idea of universal human rights – with shameless hypocrisy, they contentedly signed convention after convention on the subject – so long as no meaningful enforcement action could ever be taken. 'Human rights' became a phrase incorporated into insults traded between the

Great Powers, as they secretly vied for the support of dictatorships which comprehensively violated them. The four decades between 1948 and the collapse of communism may be characterized – and stigmatized – as the lipservice era for human rights, when diplomats strove to ensure that they could never be meaningfully asserted against a nation state. There were times – the early days of Jimmy Carter's presidency, for example – when the idea resonated before succumbing to *realpolitik*, and undoubtedly the 'help, guidance and inspiration' of human rights was an important factor in the ultimate failure of some regimes notorious for denying them: the military juntas of Latin America, the apartheid system in South Africa, the USSR and its puppet states of eastern Europe. But all that happened to human rights *law* over those four decades was a series of academic exercises, honing and refining and putting in place international conventions – most notably the twin Covenants on Civil and Political Rights and on Economic and Social Rights – which were marvels of modern diplomacy: none of the states which signed them intended them to work.

The only progress in this regard was regional, and confined to western Europe, where a human rights court at Strasbourg gradually made guarantees of 'fundamental freedoms' more meaningful to citizens across a dozen or so harmonious continental borders. Come the communist collapse, the European Convention and its Strasbourg court were sufficiently impressive for the newly liberated nations of eastern Europe to sign up for membership, and by the time of the UN's triumphalist talk-fest at Vienna in 1993 there was a much more genuine desire to put human rights at the centre of the 'New World Order' proclaimed after the apparent defeat of Saddam Hussein. It seemed possible to extrapolate the Strasbourg experiment to a global level, most optimistically by having all 185 member nations ratify the UN Covenant on Civil and Political Rights and accept the jurisdiction of the Human Rights Committee established under its protocol, so creating a forum for individuals to complain about and obtain redress, as a matter of law, against their governments. In the meantime, a start was at last made to capitalize on the Nuremberg legacy – international tribunals were established, in The Hague and at Arusha, to punish the perpetrators of crimes against humanity during the genocidal conflicts in former Yugoslavia and Rwanda.

But evolution of international law is never a linear progress: there are backwards steps, and recessive genes. These came at Vienna, in the form of belated but vehement Third World objections, not so much to the very idea of human rights as to its elucidation in the UN Declaration and the twin Covenants. These were said to embody 'Western' perceptions of freedom at odds with those in Asia and Africa, and antipathetic to states governed by religious (especially Islamic) law. This ushered in a new 'universality' debate, rekindled and rephrased from the nineteenth century when objections to the notion of 'natural' or 'inalienable' rights had successfully called into question the philosophical truth of the French and American Declarations. Human rights were said, in the *fin de siècle* buzzphrase, to be 'culturally relative' – by such statesmen as Dr Mahathir (who found an independent judiciary inconvenient to his own aspirations in Malaysia), President Suharto (the incarnation of nepotistic corruption) and Lee Kuan Yew (whose assaults on freedom of speech in Singapore had been designed to maintain his electoral hegemony). The championship of 'Asian values' has weakened with Asian economies, and in 1998 Dr Mahathir's behaviour over Anwar Ibrahim – gloating after he was beaten up in police custody – made many of his countrymen protest in favour of old-fashioned Western values asserted by the Indonesian protesters who had just swept Suharto from power. The idea of human rights was in the ascendant, the stage was set for their third historical period: the age of enforcement.

My personal interest in this subject derives from the happenstance of being born on 30 September 1946 – the day of the judgment at Nuremberg. The length of my life may thus be taken as a precise temporal measure of the inability of international institutions to deliver on the promise of that momentous day, namely that crimes against humanity would be deterred in the future by the simple expedient of punishing their perpetrators. In my lifetime I have observed – for Amnesty International, for clients who were victims, or merely as a television viewer – endless and undiminishing breaches of civil liberties in most countries of the world. Of late, there has been a dramatic change in the rhetoric of politicians and plenipotentiaries who always wring their hands over these human rights blackspots around the globe, a shift from that bootless phrase 'something should be done' to an undertaking: 'something *will* be done'. On 17 July 1998, in Rome, 120 nations voted in support of a statute creating an international criminal court, to punish those guilty of flagrant violations of fundamental freedoms wherever such violations occur. The promise of Nuremberg suddenly, and for the first time since 1946, seemed capable of realization. It seemed even more capable on 24 March 1999, that extraordinary day which began with the English Law Lords ruling that the Torture Convention had destroyed General Pinochet's sovereign immunity, and ended with NATO's bombing campaign against the sovereign state of Yugoslavia in response to Serbian atrocities in Kosovo. When in September a UN force landed on the shore of East Timor, to protect its people from massacre by Indonesian troops and to enforce their right to self-determination, the era of human rights enforcement seemed to have dawned.

But there are many reasons for caution, indeed for cynicism, about the resolve of states to enforce international human rights law, notwithstanding the fact that it is currently in fashion in diplomatic discourse and has become the United Nation's catchcry for the twenty-first century. It is popular, certainly, in the West, where decent peoples do want their governments to intervene to stop the slaughter in far-off countries of which they know something from the television news (although this wish for action is tempered – certainly in the United States – by a refusal to countenance any casualties). But the project still remains in the care of diplomats who throughout the Cold War used human rights opportunistically, as a propaganda weapon against the other side. Diplomacy is the antithesis of justice: it brokers trade-offs which always allow oppressors to escape punishment. Since global enforcement of human rights standards will for the most part be entrusted to the United Nations, with its lamentable record of doing so little to staunch gross abuses by countries of any significance (or even by insignificant countries, if they are protected by powerful alignments), my babyboom birthright is still a long way off. After all, the very action which revived the idea of an international criminal court, namely the establishment in 1993 of the Hague Tribunal to punish crimes against humanity in former Yugoslavia, was conceived as a figleaf to cover the UN's early reluctance to intervene in the

Balkans, and has been blighted by NATO's refusal to arrest the most important of the Bosnian Serb leaders wanted for trial in The Hague.

Nevertheless, the very possibility that nemesis will one day strike the perpetrators of crimes against humanity, as it threatened to catch up with General Pinochet, means that international human rights law can be said to exist in the real world as well as in the rhetoric of politicians and the pipe-dreams of professors. I hold to the modified positivist position that a rule is one of law not because it has been laid down with clarity in a treaty or a textbook, but because there is at least a slim prospect that some day, someone will be arrested for its breach. I have set out to write a book which distinguishes between rules of law thus defined, and rules of thumb or of diplomatic etiquette. The world has suffered in the last half-century an endless avalanche of repetitious and overlapping rules, cascading from UN conferences and commissions and conventions. It is time to enforce a few of them, with the help of international tribunals sufficiently learned and independent to be accredited with judicial wisdom. There are examples at regional level: the European Court of Human Rights, the Inter-American Court and the Privy Council, and there are some splendid decisions on human rights issues delivered by constitutional courts of the leading nations. It is now possible to synthesize a simple body of rules potentially enforceable throughout the world, properly described as 'international human rights law' because states publicly recognize that they should never be breached – however frequently or secretly they are.

The movement for global justice has been a struggle against sovereignty – the doctrine of non-intervention in the internal affairs of nation states asserted by all governments which have refused to subject the treatment they mete out to their citizens to any independent external scrutiny. That it will remain a struggle well into the millennium is clear from the behaviour of the United States, the one true superpower, in voting (with Libya and China) against the creation of an International Criminal Court, out of an arrogant concern that it may one day take jurisdiction to try an American alleged to be a war criminal. A small mind in a great country is a matter for regret, especially in light of the crucial role the US can – and occasionally does – choose to play in keeping that peace which is a precondition for human rights enjoyment.

The position of the US will change – more quickly, I suspect, than that of Libya and China – as the communications revolution continues its work of making human beings everywhere respond with simultaneous outrage to the images of genocide and torture it has the capacity to download into every corner of the planet. CNN has in this way served as recruiting officer for the human rights movement. Amnesty International was founded by a few English do-gooders in 1961: by the century's end, it boasted over a million members, and there were more than 900 other non-government organizations sharing aspects of its work. Twelve million people from all over the world signed a petition presented to the UN's General Secretary on the fiftieth anniversary of the Universal Declaration of Human Rights, demanding that its promises be made good in the millennium.

But, as this book will demonstrate, the United Nations system is not structurally or psychologically geared to deliver on these promises – other than by setting up institutions independent of its internal politics, which might make adjudicative decisions which require the enforcement powers of the Security Council (ranging from trade sanctions to armed intervention) to be deployed against violating states. Any such system would challenge both the shibboleth of the sovereignty of nation states and the obsessive neutrality ingrained in UN personnel and procedures. Such challenges have been permitted in the case of pariah states like South Africa, Iraq and Libya and criminal justice has been imposed on those in a state of disintegration (former Yugoslavia and Rwanda) but these cases are *ad hoc* – a weasel Latin phrase used in UN resolutions as a coded diplomatic signal that the action will not be used as a precedent to threaten other members. Obeisance to member state sovereignty is the UN's systemic defect, and it accounts for the pathetic performance of the Human Rights Commission and that toothless tribunal, the Human Rights Committee. If the promises of the Universal Declaration are to be realized, we must look to bodies independent of the UN, to regional treaty systems and their courts, to forge an international human rights law sufficiently understood and respected to be enforced in municipal courts throughout the world.

It is this last objective, the most readily achievable since it calls for a consensus of principles and not an accommodation with political power, which has in fact become unnecessarily elusive. This is because human rights have been pigeonholed by academics as a subset of international law, that most airyfairy of disciplines, at worst a mirage and at best a hostage to international politics. Its rules have to be extrapolated from dozens of overlapping conventions, from explanations contained in the mindnumbing tomes and indigestible treaties which count as 'sources' of customary law, along with the interminable debates and resolutions of the UN General Assembly, not to mention the obscure *travaux préparatoires* of all the conferences which led to all the conventions. Many of the current human rights textbooks are incomprehensible to non-lawyers, full of extinct Latin phrases and those alphabet-soup acronyms which stand for the profusion and confusion of UN conventions and committees. So in this book I have used as few acronyms as possible, and kept the Latin *de minimis*. I have tried to avoid the common textbook pretence that conventions and UN committees and General Assembly declarations reflect reality. For example, they tell students about the Human Rights Committee as if it is a large and respected organization, not a group of underfunded part-timers. They prate portentously about 'The African Commission of Human Rights' as though it were a serious body, not a twice-yearly week of slapstick. Many scholars maintain with a straight face that the Universal Declaration embodies universal law, although some of its provisions are universally ignored. Optimism is an eye disease which inflicts many who expound human rights law in university lecture halls or the expensive hotel suites of Geneva where UN diplomats hold their conferences. It is perceived differently from political prison cells and unmarked police cars. I cannot forget standing on a Belfast street shortly after 'Bloody Sunday', as an armoured car passed, and it dawned upon me that there was an exact point in its passing at which, in the event of any crossfire, I would be hit by a bullet to the head. It is that point I have tried to keep in mind while writing this book.

Today, human rights is much in fashion, which makes it the subject of a certain amount of humbug. In a world where virtue is no longer its own reward, there are plenty of human rights prizes, many funded by corporations exposed for exploiting the poor, awarded to dinner-jacketed lawyers, journalists and politicians who have never had to risk their careers in a course perceived by national authorities as subversive. The UN cheapens the human rights cause by recruiting voguish but vapid models and pop stars as 'goodwill ambassadors', while transnational corporations make it more expensive by hiring accountants to produce 'ethical auditing' reports (based more on public relations principles than economics) to show that the good business they do in Third World countries is business that is good. It would be churlish to decry the fashionability of human rights, but premature to think that this means the struggle to have them enforced – the crucial third phase of the human rights revolution – has in any sense been won. I have written this book not merely to relate how, at the turn of the twenty-first century, the human rights movement is at last going on the offensive, but in an effort to warn how far it has yet to go.

I am especially grateful to Amnesty International for inviting me to conduct missions which gave me experience of the sharp end of this subject, to Rosanne van Alebeek for her research on sovereign immunity and to Graham Blewitt for his help with my not-uncritical survey of the Hague Tribunal for the Former Yugoslavia. My thanks also to Stefan McGrath, Caroline Pretty and Sally Holloway, my patient editors, and to Chris Whitehouse, Anthony Hudson, Patrick Okonmah and Nicolas Burton for their work on the manuscript. My wife, Kathy Lette, and my young children have done their best to remind me, with some force, that the most fundamental human right begins at home.

Doughty Street Chambers
1 March 2000

Introduction

This book should be a wake-up call to the United States government. It warns Washington that it stands on the wrong side of one of the most important international developments of our time: the emergence of an international system of justice for the world's worst human rights criminals.

The man sounding this warning is hardly a wild-eyed radical or alien thinker. Indeed, it would be difficult to imagine a more sympathetic critic than Geoffrey Robertson. A successful London barrister steeped in the Anglo-American legal tradition, Robertson openly admires the United States and accepts its powerful position in today's world. Robertson also maintains an independent distance from the human rights movement. For example, he spares no criticism of the tactics behind the movement's recent campaigns to abolish anti-personnel land mines, end the use of child soldiers, and establish an International Criminal Court. If any informed non-American shares Washington's distrust of the emerging international system of justice, Robertson would seem to be the one.

Yet Robertson presents a powerful endorsement of this emerging legal system for redressing genocide, war crimes, and crimes against humanity. That he enthusiastically embraces a system that the US government is doing everything it can to subvert demonstrates how far Washington has moved from even its closest intellectual kin overseas. If there was ever a signal that the US government is out of step with the rest of the world, this book is it.

The emerging international system of justice is a response to the problem of impunity that lies behind so many atrocities. For nearly fifty years, the tensions of the Cold War froze efforts to build on the

Nuremberg precedent. For every world-class despot—from Pol Pot to Saddam Hussein—there was one or another of the permanent five members of the United Nations Security Council willing to use its veto to block the establishment of an international tribunal. Meanwhile, with rare exception, national efforts to bring abusive dictators to justice crumbled under the murderous pressure that these despots were able to bring to bear. The bigger the crime, it seemed, the less likely it was that a ruler would be held to account. A squeegee man on the streets of New York City stood a better chance of being punished than did a genocidal killer or a big-time war criminal.

This impunity was an insult to the victims of atrocities. It signaled that their fate did not matter, that their plight could be forgotten, that no one cared enough to see their persecutors brought to justice. It also encouraged other would-be tyrants to embark on similar paths. If there was little or no chance of paying for their crimes, many reasoned, why not commit whatever atrocities were necessary to maintain or strengthen their grip on power?

The emerging international system of justice is designed to break that deadly logic. It pays tribute to the victims of abuse by demonstrating new resolve to bring their tormentors to justice. It also offers great promise as a deterrent because it targets not an entire people, the way broad trade sanctions do; not front-line conscripts, the way military intervention often does; but the tyrant himself, the man who orders and directs the killing.

Of course, given the rudimentary state of this emerging justice system, arrest, prosecution, and trial are hardly certainties. For the time being, many more tyrants will escape justice than will find themselves in the dock. But even if only an occasional despot is deterred—even if a single genocide is averted—that is reason enough to embrace this new prospect of justice.

Yet Washington is profoundly ambivalent about this new justice system, despite the system's great promise. On the one hand, the US government has been the principal supporter of the new methods. Partly in response to the world's failure to stop genocide in the past decade, and partly out of commitment to the principle that mass murderers should be arrested, tried, and punished, Washington helped to create, fund, staff, and provide the military muscle behind the war-crimes tribunals for Rwanda and the former Yugoslavia. On the other hand, the US government has done everything it could to prevent these country-specific precedents from being built upon to create a legal system that might extend globally and thus impact US military commanders or internal and foreign affairs.

One example of this distrust of the emerging justice system was Washington's lukewarm response to the arrest in Britain, at Spain's request, of the former Chilean dictator General Augusto Pinochet. This was the first time since Nuremberg that a former head of state faced international justice for his crimes. As Robertson eloquently explains, 'The *Pinochet Case* was momentous because, for the first time, sovereign immunity was not allowed to become sovereign impunity'. Yet the US foreign policy establishment openly fretted about the implications of this revived form of justice.

The Pinochet case proceeded under the UN Convention Against Torture, which requires state parties to prosecute or extradite torturers whenever they are found. The convention codifies the principle of 'universal jurisdiction', which similarly empowers courts worldwide to proceed against anyone brought before them who is responsible for such offenses as genocide, war crimes, or crimes against humanity. If under these legal theories those responsible for the most heinous human rights crimes could be arrested and tried anywhere, Washington worried, might not US officials who were complicit in serious human rights abuse overseas risk apprehension if they traveled abroad? Even though Britain's courts presumably could be trusted to provide a fair trial, what would happen if an American faced trial in a country that is less attentive to the requirements of due process?

Part of the solution to this problem lies in the creation of a permanent international tribunal that would be dedicated to ensuring the highest fair-trial standards and that would be available whenever national governments fail to investigate or prosecute their own citizens accused of genocide, war crimes, or crimes against humanity. In July 1998, the governments of the world gathered in Rome to adopt a treaty for the establishment of such a court, the International Criminal Court (ICC). The court was endorsed by 120 nations, including virtually all of the world's democracies. But Washington was in an uncomfortable minority of seven that opposed the court, along with such committed "defenders" of human rights as China, Libya, and Iraq.

At first, Washington's opposition might seem puzzling. After all, the US government says that its forces are firmly committed to avoiding the atrocities for which the ICC is designed to seek retribution. Indeed, the list of crimes subject to ICC jurisdiction closely resembles that in the Pentagon's own military manuals. Moreover, should a rogue US service member commit a war crime, the US government's official policy is that it would launch a vigorous investigation and prosecution.

Washington thus claimed that its opposition was due not to disagreement with the goals of the ICC but to fear that the court could be misused to launch unjustified, politically motivated prosecutions of Americans. But the court's statute contains numerous safeguards against unwarranted prosecutions, including several inserted by the US delegation. Most important is the principle of 'complementarity', which deprives the court of jurisdiction so long as a national government conscientiously investigates and, if appropriate, prosecutes any of its citizens accused of these serious crimes. Moreover, even if a government fails to pursue such a case in good faith, both the suspect and his state of nationality are entitled to numerous appeals before different panels of judges to guard against any possible injustice.

Once Washington's excuses and justifications are peeled away, what remains is its naked unwillingness to subject its citizens to the emerging international system of justice, regardless of how reprehensible their deeds may be. For some on the right wing of the American political spectrum—the Jesse Helms school—arrogant nationalism lies behind this rejection of international justice: they simply refuse to countenance any international or foreign tribunal judging US conduct. But even the more moderate Clinton Administration does not want the US government's unique international security responsibilities constrained by the possibility that a tribunal might find its conduct criminal.

Either way, most other governments naturally do not accept a conception of 'justice' that applies to them but not to the United States. The nationalist rejection of international justice is dismissed as the worst of American parochialism. And even though Washington does have special responsibilities for global security, few outside the United States see that as justifying effective impunity for genocide, war crimes, or crimes against humanity. Indeed, the US government's refusal to countenance an international tribunal that would only have jurisdiction over American war-crime suspects if the US government failed to proceed against these suspects calls into question Washington's supposed commitment to prosecuting its own war criminals.

Although the ICC would clearly be a stronger institution with US support, the United States is not an indispensable member of the new court. Sixty governments must ratify the ICC treaty for the court to be established. Already, over ninety governments have signed the treaty, and ratifications are proceeding apace. Among those likely to ratify the treaty are many countries with substantial economic and military resources to give the court the backing it will need, including the entire European Union. But the US government, with its considerable international clout, could still make life difficult for this fledgling institution.

Written from a lawyer's perspective on these developments, Robertson's book serves as a useful reminder to human rights activists that they aspire to a system of law. The modern human rights movement grew up focusing on countries that lacked reliable legal institutions for enforcing rights. The movement thus developed alternative enforcement tools, such as public shaming, diplomatic appeals, and calls for economic sanctions. These forms of pressure, by raising the cost of abuse, could often be quite effective in curtailing or preventing violations. But, Robertson reminds us, they should not be confused with the enforcement of rights under the rule of law.

There are 'no rights without remedies; no human rights without remedies for human rights', he asserts with the conviction of a practicing lawyer. Legal remedies, he explains, are the touchstone of a right. Robertson thus has no patience for 'the common textbook pretense that conventions and UN committees and General Assembly resolutions reflect reality'. Rather, at least for the most heinous human rights abuses, 'a rule is one of law not because it has been laid down with clarity in a treaty or a textbook, but because there is at least a slim prospect that some day, someone will be arrested for its breach'.

That is why Robertson rightly sees such promise in the emerging international system of justice. The Pinochet case, for example, showed that 'international human rights had acquired the quality of law; it had become, in some small degree, enforceable in the courts of the world'. With the appearance of courts and international tribunals willing at least sometimes to enforce international human rights standards, it becomes possible, for the first time, to contemplate moving from a paradigm of pressure to uphold human rights standards to one of enforcement of human rights law.

This development is of revolutionary importance because, until now, so many governments have counted on human rights standards being unenforceable. Governments were quite content to sign convention after human rights convention, Robertson points out, 'so long as no meaningful enforcement action could ever be taken'. The emerging international system of justice provides the best chance of moving beyond this 'lip-service era for human rights' to 'a future international order based more on law than on diplomatic expediency'. 'The great achievement of international law', Robertson explains, will be 'to lift the veil of sovereign statehood far enough to make individuals responsible for . . . crimes against humanity'.

Does this sound the death knell for state sovereignty? Does Robertson foretell an era when international courts will try every national transgressor of human rights law? Hardly. Despite the exaggerated fears of many right-wing American opponents of the emerging international system of justice, Robertson recognizes that for the foreseeable future the Westphalian system of government is here to stay. Governments will always be reluctant to constrain one anothers' latitude, particularly when that means spilling blood for the welfare of others. So we are nowhere near the day when the enforcement of international human rights standards will be as normal as is, say, the enforcement of domestic criminal law.

But Robertson would draw the line at crimes against humanity—the widespread or systematic commission of the most severe atrocities, such as torture or summary execution. When a crime is so heinous that it is deemed to be committed not just against its victims but against all of humanity, then all of humanity has an interest—indeed, a duty—to see it remedied. Any tyrant who crosses this line should rightly risk indictment, arrest, prosecution, and punishment. Lesser human rights offenses might be left to national legal systems, but in the case of national neglect of the most serious human rights crimes, we should aspire to a system in which international courts are available to try the perpetrators, and in which the world's governments are willing to enforce the courts' judgments.

Washington should not be allowed to justify its opposition to recent trends in international justice via demagogic denunciations made by American service members who appear before distant, foreign tribunals. Being the 'sole remaining superpower' should hardly carry this prerogative. Rather, it must explain why sovereignty should be seen as license to commit crimes against humanity.

Refreshing as his lawyerly vision is in raising the aspirations of the human rights movement, Robertson is not a legalist in the sense of promoting blind adherence to the law regardless of its content. Instead, he shows himself to be a true jurist, attentive to his moral compass and willing, when necessary, to override international law in its current inchoate state to achieve a result that he finds morally defensible. Two interesting examples are his discussions of humanitarian intervention and amnesty.

Robertson meets head-on the argument that NATO's intervention in Kosovo was illegal because it had not been authorized by the UN Security Council, as the UN Charter would seem to require. He condemns as 'anachronistic' the Charter's 'bias toward sovereign independence' and decries a mechanism for authorizing humanitarian intervention that 'depend[s] upon the unanimous approval of five nations [the permanent members of the Security Council] with their own diplomatic games to play'.

Similarly, Robertson differs with those who contend that, because

Yugoslav and Serb troops did not begin large-scale killings and forcible displacement until NATO's bombers were preparing to take off, NATO's intervention was premature. Recalling the role these same Yugoslav and Serb troops played in Croatia and Bosnia, he sees the NATO campaign in Kosovo as a proportionate response to an ongoing conspiracy to commit crimes against humanity. Given Serbian president Slobodan Milosevic's history of crimes against humanity, he argues in essence, there was no need to allow a new round of such crimes before acting to halt the pattern.

Robertson also makes an important conceptual contribution to one of the most perplexing problems facing the human rights movement as it attempts to build an international system of justice: when should those who commit crimes against humanity be granted amnesty for their offenses as the price of peace or a democratic transition? On one side of the debate are those who fear that refusing to grant amnesty risks perpetuating bloodshed or repression by giving a tyrant an incentive to cling to power by whatever means. On the other side are those who fear that granting amnesty both does a disservice to the victims of past atrocities and creates a precedent of impunity that only encourages more bloodshed.

The argument that amnesty is necessary to convince tyrants to step down is often overstated. Tyrants tend to cling to power for as long as they can. By the time their power wanes and they confront forced retirement, they have little capacity to insist on amnesty, as Ferdinand Marcos, Jean-Claude Duvalier, the Shah of Iran, Mobutu Sese Seko, Mengistu Haile Mariam, Alfredo Stroessner, and a host of other dictators have discovered. Pinochet secured an amnesty only by granting it to himself at the height of his power, over a decade before he was to step down, and even then, when faced with a plebiscite rejecting his continued rule and the military's growing disinclination to keep him in power, he was unable to close key loopholes in the amnesty that have since been exploited in the pursuit of his fellow officers.

As for the argument that the failure to grant amnesty might prolong war, the Bosnian conflict provides the most recent counterexample. As Robertson points out, the Yugoslav Tribunal's indictment of Bosnian Serb political and military leaders Radovan Karadzic and

Ratko Mladic actually facilitated the Dayton peace accord by leading to 'their gradual loss of power and position' and their absence from the Dayton negotiations. Even Milosevic, whose indictment was at least foreseeable at the time of the Dayton talks, did not insist on amnesty. As Robertson observes, 'The Dayton Accord, which required all parties to cooperate in the arrest and surrender of persons indicted by the Tribunal, was negotiated without this condition becoming a sticking point'.

Still, even the remote possibility of prolonging war or dictatorship can generate intense pressure to grant amnesty which, in turn, has given birth to elaborate justifications for why justice might be dispensable. Robertson firmly rejects the most common of such justifications: the argument that truth might be an adequate alternative to justice for the most serious human rights crimes; that the victims and their families might settle for an accounting of the crimes they suffered rather than trial and punishment of their persecutors.

This theory largely grew out of the experience of Latin America in the 1970s and 1980s, where a strong legal tradition, coupled with the great lengths to which governments went to cover up their human rights crimes, meant that significant stigma was attached to the exposure of official complicity in these atrocities. But the meaning of truth wanes when killers boast of or publicize their crimes, as so often happens with today's civil wars and ethnically motivated conflicts. When, for example, soldiers of the rebel Revolutionary United Front in Sierra Leone chop off victims' limbs and then carve their 'RUF' initials in their chests to 'send a signal' to the government, truth becomes superfluous unless accompanied by justice.

Robertson notes a parallel problem with truth-telling divorced from justice—it tends to reinforce rather than replace demands for justice. That is because 'revelation of the details of official depravity only makes the demands for retribution by victims and their sympathizers more compelling'. Governments in such places as Chile and Argentina have learned the wisdom of Robertson's warning that 'time wounds all heals'; he explains that, with time, 'democratic governments become more confident, prosecutors more daring, the public more inclined to do something about old men whose behavior in uniform has brought their country international contempt'.

Robertson thus concludes that 'the balm applied by truth commissioners is short-lived: reconciliation cannot happen without some measure of justice'.

As for the most widely admired institutional truth-telling process—post-apartheid South Africa's Truth and Reconciliation Commission (TRC)—Robertson sees it less as an example of truth substituting for justice than as a form of plea bargaining in which truth was traded for leniency. The TRC granted amnesty for political offences, but only on the condition that those involved testified truthfully about what they and their accomplices had done. Robertson sees conditional amnesties of this sort as 'an exercise in *realpolitik*, a crude accommodation which avowedly subordinates justice to political expediency'. He faults the TRC, however, for 'attempt[ing] to dress up [this] expediency as justice'.

Instead, for Robertson, the solution to the problem of amnesty lies in distinguishing the responsibilities of national and international authorities. He recognizes that national authorities may well feel compelled to grant amnesty, and suggests that it may be unfair to ask them to weigh more than the fate of their own country. But the international community, in his view, must consider the precedential effect of amnesty for tyrants elsewhere. It should never grant amnesty, and if an amnesty is issued by national authorities, it should refuse to recognize it. Robertson thus would endorse the compromise that the UN struck in 1999 in Sierra Leone, where it brokered a peace agreement under which national authorities felt they had little choice but to grant amnesty to a group of rebels known for butchering and mutilating their victims, but to which it attached a footnote indicating that it would not recognize the amnesty.

This solution may not be immediately satisfying since, at least for a time, a beneficiary of a national amnesty can avoid punishment by simply staying in his own country. But if he ever travels abroad, he risks arrest and prosecution, either by a court exercising universal jurisdiction over crimes against humanity or by the soon-to-be-operative International Criminal Court. As Robertson explains, 'The concept of universal jurisdiction for crimes against humanity is the solution that international law offers to the spectacle of impunity for tyrants and torturers who cover themselves with domestic immunities and amnesties and pardons. They can still hide, but in a world where jurisdiction over their crimes is universal, they cannot run'. With time, health concerns or changes in domestic politics may make flight inevitable—a reality discovered in 1999 by former Ethiopian dictator Mengistu Haile Mariam, Kurdish rebel leader Abdullah Ocalan, and Izzat Ibrahim al-Douri, Saddam Hussein's second-in-command. Only Ocalan was apprehended; as pressure built for their arrest, Mengistu and al-Douri were able to escape their home countries because the South African and Austrian governments were slow in responding. As governments grow more comfortable exercising universal jurisdiction, the best solution to impunity at home may well be patience—and an attentive eye to tyrants' travel plans.

As powerful a defense of the international system of justice as Robertson offers, there are parts of this book with which I must respectfully disagree. For example, he properly criticizes the ICC's governmental supporters for succumbing to US pressure and accepting restrictions on the court's jurisdiction without first securing the commitment of Washington to support the court. A widely popular proposal at Rome would have given the court direct jurisdiction—that is, jurisdiction without a referral from the Security Council—in any one of four circumstances: whenever the crime in question was allegedly committed by a national of a state party, on the territory of a state party, or against victims who were nationals of a state party, or whenever the suspect was in the custody of a state party. In the vain hope of securing US support for the court, the delegates in Rome dispensed with both victim-based and custodial jurisdiction, leaving only nationality and territorial jurisdiction.

If compromise was necessary, states Robertson, he would have gone one step further to secure US support. He faults the court's backers for insisting on retaining territorial jurisdiction, which could be used to pursue UN peacekeepers who might be involved in atrocities even if their government objected. In Robertson's view, such jurisdiction should have been a low priority, given how it has 'inflamed

American paranoia'. Here, I beg to differ. Far from the 'petty' concern that Robertson describes, I believe that territorial jurisdiction is a necessary component of the court's legitimacy, because it is key to allowing the court to scrutinize not only forces that commit atrocities at home (which today occurs mostly though not exclusively in the global south) but also troops who commit abuses outside their borders (a form of jurisdiction more likely to embrace the global north).

Robertson also, in my view, undervalues the compromised court that emerged from Rome. The only cases the court is likely to see, he claims, are those sent by the UN Security Council or delivered by governments that are too weak to bring a toppled dictator to trial. But he neglects the ICC's role as an insurance policy against abusive coups. Democratic governments might legitimately fear that a weak national judiciary could effectively encourage a restive military to launch a coup out of the belief that the military could then insist on a national amnesty. A functioning ICC would undercut this rationale, since it would be immune to the threats and coercion used to secure amnesty at the national level.

These quibbles aside, Robertson offers a thoughtful, provocative, lively defense of the merits of the emerging international system of justice. It is sad testament to American parochialism that so few in the US government today would endorse his views. As these ideas gain a global following—and they inevitably will—the United States risks more than diplomatic embarrassment and isolation by failing to embrace them. It risks being on the wrong side of an historic evolution of the defense of our most basic rights. Let us hope that this book can lead a process, long overdue, of reconsideration in Washington.

KENNETH ROTH
Executive Director, Human Rights Watch

Crimes Against Humanity

I

The Human Rights Story

'Establish the Rights of Man; enthrone equality . . . let there be
no privileges, no distinctions of birth, no monopolies; make safe
the liberty of industry and trade, the equal distribution of family
inheritances.'   Thomas Paine[1]

IN THE BEGINNING: NATURAL RIGHTS

Any system of law – including the first written Hammurabi code,
several thousand years before Christ – inferentially confers 'rights' on
the citizens to whom it applies, at least in the negative and residual sense
of entitling them to behave in any manner which it does not specifically
prohibit. The ancient codes of the Greek city states and of imperial
Rome conferred such 'rights', but went on to bestow positive powers on
certain classes of citizens, over and distinct from other classes. Religions,
similarly, enforced within theocratic communities rules and taboos
from which positive entitlements might be deduced. Christianity goes
further and applies its rules to all living persons, irrespective of status or
nationality: from the commandment 'Thou shalt not steal', for example,
one might infer a moral right for everybody to enjoy private property.
But the closest the lawyers of the ancient world came to the idea that
some special rights were *universal* was in the Roman concept of *jus
gentium*, those rules which they discovered to be common to all civilized
societies, and which might therefore be catalogued specially as a kind
of international law. Laws were thus categorized, not because of their
intrinsic or self-evident merit or validity, but simply because they were
in service in every civilized society.

I

This 'lowest common denominator' approach of *jus gentium* – these laws have a special quality because they are approved by rational men and regarded as binding by all civilizations – was picked up two thousand years later to justify the assertion of jurisdiction over crimes against humanity, wherever and by whomsoever committed. But in ancient times, when rules of battle were rudimentary, when the greatest of crimes were punished by the gods and extradition was unknown, the notion that *jus gentium* might reflect and even protect inalienable human rights was never coherently propounded. What did emerge, however, through the church-dominated Middle Ages, was the quasi-theological notion that there were 'laws of nature': rules ordained by God, to be observed by all His human creations on peril of divine punishment. This theory was highly attractive to the crowned heads of Europe – to princes and to popes with princely ambitions – for the first law of nature invariably imposed unquestioning obedience to the prince, as God's regent on his own little patch of the earth. The 'Divine Right of Kings' was part of the natural order of things, and from it flowed a number of legal consequences (such as the immunity from prosecution of heads of state) which international human rights law is still in the process of extirpating.

Essential to this feudal conception was *sovereignty* (the power of the divinely approved ruler over all his or her subjects), the exercise of which – however barbaric – could not be questioned either by those subjects or by other sovereigns. There could, of course, be treaties between two or more states, giving rise to international law, but they could only be invoked by the sovereigns who had signed them (or their heirs and successors). The only 'rights' an individual could possess, in such a world, other than *vis-à-vis* his own sovereign, was if he happened to be visiting a foreign country. Then, as a temporary 'alien', he was entitled to call on the protection of his own sovereign against infringements on his liberty threatened by the state in which he was sojourning. This had the consequence, for several centuries, of giving aliens abroad more 'rights' than the citizens of their host country.

The appearance of 'rights' as a set of popular propositions limiting the sovereign is usually traced to Magna Carta in 1215, although that document had nothing to do with the liberty of individual citizens: it was signed by a feudal king who was feuding with thuggish barons,

2

and was forced to accede to their demands. It had two symbols of a constitutional settlement, however: firstly, it limited the power of the State (in a very elementary way, since the King *was* the State), and secondly it contained some felicitous phrases which gradually entered the common law and worked their rhetorical magic down the centuries. For example, in Article 40 of Magna Carta, the King promised, 'To no man will we sell, to no man will we deny or delay justice or right.' This was the forerunner – what might be called the King John version – of Article 6 (1) of the European Convention on Human Rights, 'Everyone is entitled to a fair and public hearing within a reasonable time.'

The first appearance of 'rights' in the modern sense, declared as such and enforceable in the courts, was in the 1688 Bill of Rights which emerged in England from the so-called 'Glorious Revolution'. 'Glorious' it certainly was not at the time, for it was popularly fuelled by a vicious anti-Catholicism and resulted in the infliction of many other disabilities upon followers of that religion. It did, however, mark in England the end of the King's claims to absolute rule by Divine Right and imposed upon him a measure of accountability to Parliament. The 'rights' which it declared were for the most part those of parliamentarians, to veto royal decisions to raise new taxes and to enjoy freedom of debate without prosecution before the King's judges. But by declaring themselves 'a full and free representative of this nation' assembled 'for the vindicating and asserting of their ancient rights and liberties', the Lords and Commons purported to state rights which had been acquired by prescription – i.e. by custom and tradition – and which were capable of being upheld by the courts. Chief of these were: the right of subjects to live under the law as approved by Parliament without arbitrary royal interference; the right to due process in the selection of jurors; the right not to lose liberty through excessively high fixing of bail; and the right not to be inflicted with 'cruel or unusual punishment'. In 1679 the first Habeas Corpus Act had provided the most valuable and enduring right of all: to have the lawfulness of detention tested promptly by the courts.

These 'rights' still have resonance today, although they are understood in ways which would have bewildered seventeenth-century parliamentarians. For example, the prohibition on 'cruel or unusual punishment' was inserted because of public outrage at the treatment of Titus Oates, the popular clergyman and perjuryman whose lies sent dozens of Catholics to the scaffold. Oates was sentenced to be defrocked, whipped and set in the pillory – indignities thought cruel and unusual for a Church of England minister by his fanatical fellow Protestants. The idea that the death penalty *per se*, or the genital mutilation, bowel-burning and drawing and quartering which then attended it, might be 'cruel' never entered seventeenth-century heads. Hence the first rule of interpreting a bill of rights: the concepts have evolved to a meaning which reflects modern humanitarian usage rather than the contemporary understanding when they were first formulated.

What makes the English Bill of Rights the first 'modern' step towards the human rights revolution was its philosophical foundation in the work of Thomas Hobbes and its subsequent explication by John Locke. Hobbes, whose major work *Leviathan*, published in 1651, is often quoted in support of state tyranny, in fact broke the nexus between God and the State, because he identified the true source of political power in the consent of the people. He rolled back civil society to its most primitive and brutal and warlike manifestation, and deduced that its terrified denizens would authorize a ruler to lay down laws for their own protection, against the environment and each other. For Hobbes, an implacable opponent of individual freedom, this was a once-and-for-all surrender of individual power. For John Locke, however, the people's consent to government was continuous and capable of being withdrawn if that government broke the purpose of the compact, which was to further their majority interests. Writing in 1690, two years after the 'Glorious Revolution' and with the object of celebrating and justifying it, he was the first political philosopher to venture the principle that government was by popular consent, and was contingent upon a commitment to protect liberty:

Men, by nature all free, equal and independent, no-one can be put out of this estate and subjected to the political power of another without his own consent. The only way whereby anyone divests himself of his natural liberty and puts on the bonds of civil society is by agreeing with other men to join and unite into a community for their comfortable, safe and peaceable living one among another, in a secure enjoyment of their properties . . .[2]

4

The compact, by which men gave up certain freedoms to join a body politic, meant that they were left with those freedoms which the State did not need to take away in order to maintain and protect the public good. Since the whole object and purpose of the compact was the public good, the State 'can never have a right to destroy, enslave or designedly to impoverish the subjects'. It followed that there could be circumstances when subjects were entitled to revolt, breaking the compact and renegotiating it:

The end of government is the good of mankind. And which is best for mankind: that the people should be always exposed to the boundless will of tyranny, or that the rulers should be sometimes liable to be opposed when they grow exorbitant in the use of their power and employ it for the destruction and not the preservation of the properties of their people?

With this rhetorical flourish, although he could scarcely admit it, Locke was providing a justification not merely for the revolution of 1688 but for Cromwell's short-lived republic which in 1649 had executed Charles I on these very grounds, i.e. for warring with and murdering his own subjects. The King's trial was an unsatisfactory precedent – his refusal to participate denied the Parliament faction the opportunity to argue the jurisprudential case for tyrannicide – but Locke drew upon the written submissions of the King's prosecutor, John Cook, for his demonstration that rulers were not above the law that protected the liberty of their subjects.[3] The argument was a threat to other absolute monarchs, like Louis ('L'État, c'est moi') XIV. They might be deposed, if their governance was so arbitrary and tyrannical that it cut down rather than protected the residual rights of their people. As the eighteenth century progressed, Locke's philosophy was embraced and developed by leading European intellectuals, who found in England a constitution which seemed to guarantee political liberty through the supremacy (although it was far from that) of Parliament. By the middle of the century they had begun to identify 'universal' rights: to person and property, and hence not to be held in slavery (Rousseau: 'Man is born free; and everywhere he is in chains'); the liberty of the press (Voltaire: 'I know many books that fatigue, but none which have done real evil'); and the right not to be subjected to torture (as Cesare Beccaria argued, the liberty which men had been

5

forced by necessity to yield to the State was the very minimum required for the State to defend what remained: 'Punishments that exceed what is necessary for the protection of the deposit of public security are by their very nature unjust'). It was Beccaria, in his *Of Crimes and Punishments* of 1764, who first enunciated the credo of the modern human rights lawyer:

. . . if, by defending the rights of man and of unconquerable truth, I should help to save from the spasm and agonies of death some wretched victim of tyranny or of no less fatal ignorance, the thanks and tears of one innocent mortal in his transports of joy would console me for the contempt of all mankind.[4]

REVOLUTIONS AND DECLARATIONS

This was heady stuff to find in philosophy, but it required politicians and propagandists and indeed revolutionaries to give it any legal force. Man was born free, but at the time of Rousseau's observation was everywhere in chains. The first to break them were the American Founding Fathers, in 1776, making, in the potent prose of Thomas Jefferson, their claim to re-acquire their inalienable human rights from the government of George III:

We hold these truths to be self-evident, that all men are created equal; that they are endowed by their Creator with certain inalienable rights; that amongst these are life, liberty, and the pursuit of happiness. That, to secure these rights, governments are instituted among men, deriving their just powers from the consent of the governed; that, whenever any form of Government becomes destructive of these ends, it is the right of the people to alter or abolish it, and to institute a new government, laying its foundations on such principles, and organizing its powers in such form, as to them shall seem most likely to effect their safety and happiness.

This was, of course, an act of defiance and not an act of law: it was the preamble to a litany of complaints against the 'tyranny' of George III, reminiscent of those made in the 1688 Bill of Rights against the Stuart kings. There were complaints about the unfairness of trials and lickspittle judges, although taxation without consent was the motivating grudge and the clarion cry that 'all men are created equal' hardly squared with the slaves owned (in Jefferson's case, impregnated) by many of the signatories. But it is Jefferson's preamble which resonates through subsequent centuries, identifying the denial of human rights as the *justification* for the revolution foreshadowed by John Locke. The fundamental rights to life, equality, liberty and the pursuit of happiness are not drawn from any empirical source or discovered through rational argument; they may be given by God but the proof of their existence is that we all feel and think them – they attach 'inalienably' to the human person, like a shadow. They are not the end product of philosophical inquiry but the starting point for it, imposing a duty on government to order itself in a way which will maximize opportunities for individual fulfilment.

It was the oppressive human rights record of the government, its 'history of repeated injuries and usurpations', which absolved the colonials from their duty of allegiance to the British Crown. With this reasoning, the Declaration of Independence identified that moment 'when in the course of human events' the boundless will of tyranny entitled the people to depose their ruler: this was straightforward Locke, dressed in gripping prose. It is this Declaration which has been more profound in its consequences than any other in history. It is the barest of statements, eliciting a pity for the oppressed which turns into righteous anger and becomes a clarion call to recover their dignity. Its 'inalienable rights' were identified by the US constitution of 1789 (guarantees of habeas corpus and fair trial) and the amendments which followed two years later. The First Amendment provided that Congress (i.e. the State) 'shall make no law' prohibiting the free exercise of religion, or abridging the freedom of speech, or freedom of the press, or the right of peaceful assembly. The Fourth Amendment secured the people in their homes and persons 'against unreasonable searches and seizures' and the Fifth and Sixth enshrined 'due process', i.e. rights against self-incrimination and double jeopardy and expropriation of property, and the rights to speedy and public and impartial trial, with advance disclosure of prosecution evidence, the right to cross-examine hostile witnesses and to call defence witnesses, and the right to counsel. Although protection from slavery and forced servitude was not added to the US constitution until 1865 (following a civil war fought over the right of the Southern slave-owning states to secede from the Union), America had in place by the end of the eighteenth century a functioning domestic court system in which basic human rights could be enforced as such, by individual citizens. This had come about more as an act of faith than of philosophy: as the great legal architect of the American constitution, Alexander Hamilton, wrote in 1787: 'The sacred rights of mankind are not to be rummaged for amongst old parchments or musty records. They are written, as with a sunbeam, in the whole volume of human nature by the hand of divinity itself, and can never be erased or obscured.'[5]

At an intellectual level, however, this achievement owed much, and itself gave impetus, to the dissatisfactions in France which were to culminate in that 'hour of universal ferment'. Enthusiasm for the American colonists in their war against France's historic foe gave an inspirational quality to their victory and made Lafayette, who had helped to achieve it, a national hero: his popularity on his return to Paris was rivalled only by that of the American ambassador, the charismatic lightning-conductor Ben Franklin, who was succeeded in that post by Thomas Jefferson. In January 1789, Jefferson wrote to James Madison from Paris, 'Everybody here is trying their hands at forming declarations of rights.'[6] In August, during the parliament called to solve a cash-flow crisis itself partly caused by French support for the American war, it was Jefferson who helped Lafayette with the draft of 'The Declaration of the Rights of Man and the Citizen' – a detailed description of 'natural, inalienable and sacred rights' which any citizen could advance against an oppressive government. These were birthrights, which the State was constituted to protect up to the point at which their exercise might harm others, a point which had to be defined by law rather than through arbitrary exercises of government power. The Declaration was followed in 1791 by the French constitution, providing for poor relief and free public education – the first sign of what today are called 'economic and social rights'.

Up to his neck in every revolutionary movement of this incandescent era was Thomas Paine, the first writer to fuse outraged polemic and constitutional philosophy to produce a distinctive literature of human rights. This former English customs official ignited the American

Revolution with his incendiary pamphlet 'Common Sense', explaining (in January 1776, when the talk was of appeasement with the Crown) why it was ineluctable that the colonists fight for their liberty. Paine helped Jefferson to draft the Declaration of Independence, fought alongside Washington and then returned to London to write (at the Angel Tavern, Islington) one of the most influential books of all time: *The Rights of Man*. This is a classic liberal text – Paine's idea was minimal government, limited to protecting individual liberty, equality and enterprise – but his fervour for free market individualism was leavened by his novel and detailed plans for social security, family benefits, and public education, not out of charity, but as a right derived from membership of society. He scorned as a contradiction in terms the notion of an 'unwritten constitution', and refuted Edmund Burke's argument for monarchies as a legitimate inheritance from our forefathers: 'The vanity and presumption of governing beyond the grave, is the most ridiculous and insolent of all tyrannies.' The book came peppered with attacks on Britain's hereditary establishment sufficiently savage to have Paine prosecuted for sedition. He fled to France before being convicted *in absentia* by a rigged jury, whereupon crowds thronging the streets outside the Old Bailey set up the chant, 'Paine and the Liberty of the Press'. In France he was elected to the National Assembly and to the committee which drafted the constitution, and spent some months in prison for failing to match the bloodthirstiness of his comrades. He wrote *The Age of Reason* – a book for which many courageous printers and booksellers would be jailed for blasphemy in nineteenth-century Britain. Tom Paine is on postage stamps in America and there is a gold statue of him in Paris (Napoleon said there should be a gold statue of Paine in every city of the universe) but the prophet has been without honour in his own country. It took two centuries before the abolition of hereditary peers finally gave acknowledgement of Paine's point that, 'The idea of hereditary legislators [is] as absurd as an hereditary mathematician . . . as absurd as an hereditary poet laureate.'[7]

The American declarations were shaped by the colonial experience of indignity at the hands of British soldiers and sedition laws. Dissident Frenchmen had suffered imprisonment and confiscation of property, without trial (or any other legal process), through the system of *lettres de cachet* – warrants for arrest, search and seizure signed at the whim

9

of the Bourbon kings. Hence the French Declaration emphasizes the presumption of innocence and the need for legal process before arrest and detention. It elevates the possession of private property to a 'sacred and inviolable right' to be expropriated only upon proof of public necessity, and then with just compensation. Freedom of speech, 'one of the most precious of the rights of man', was given special protection ('No one is to be disquieted because of his opinions') – testimony to the influence of Voltaire and reaction to the regular use of *lettres de cachet* against critics of the King and his government. This removal of censorship had a most immediate and striking effect, releasing what Simon Schama describes as a 'polemical incontinence that washed over the whole country', propelling it to a republic within two years, and thereafter inciting each increasingly bloody phase of the Terror. Unfortunately, the class-crazed and bloodthirsty Jacobins did not see human rights as universal – as one leader wrote, 'the rights of man are made, not for the counter-revolutionaries, but only for *sans-culottes*'.[8]

As the Terror became the order of the day and brought wave after wave of revolutionaries tumbrilling to the guillotine after the aristocrats, so 'The Rights of Man and the Citizen', which had started it all, appeared a sick joke. The good old days of the King's *lettres de cachet* were contrasted with the killings ordered by the Committee for Public Safety, notwithstanding the device to reduce the length of pain invented by one assemblyman, the kindly Dr Guillotine. Victims were first put on show trial by the public prosecutor, Antoine Fouquier-Tinville. There was no 'due process' in his Revolutionary Tribunal: suspects were denied advance notice of the case against them, the right to defence counsel and the right to call witnesses; the biased jury normally convicted whenever Fouquier-Tinville asked whether they had heard enough evidence. Although blame for the barbarities of the Revolution is always fixed on its political leaders, Fouquier-Tinville emerges as the first of modern history's monster lawyers, rivalling Andrei Vyshinsky, the choreographer of Stalin's show trials. At least Fouquier-Tinville met his own fate shortly after the fall of Robespierre, appealing in vain to his judges as a 'mild-mannered family man who had always obeyed the law and done his duty'.[9] What he had done, like so many state servants who only follow orders, was to deny to citizens the most fundamental of liberties guaranteed them by a law which, lacking at that time independent judicial enforcement, was just not worth the parchment on which it was written.

That was a problem for France, precisely because it left the 'rights' in the Declaration to be enforced by politicians in the National Assembly and their representatives on the Committee for Public Safety. In America, by contrast, the constitution and its Bill of Rights were enforceable by an independent judiciary, empowered to strike down government orders and even congressional legislation which violated the rights they guaranteed. This development in legal theory, achieved in 1803 by Chief Justice Marshall in the great case of *Marbury* v. *Madison*, provided human rights in the US with a set of teeth, by endorsing courts rather than legislatures as their enforcement machinery:

The very essence of civil liberty certainly consists in the right of every individual to claim the protection of the laws, whenever he receives an injury . . . (the) government of the United States has been emphatically termed a government of laws, and not of men. It will certainly cease to deserve this high appellation, if the laws furnish no remedy for the violation of a vested legal right.[10]

These French and American documents became models for many constitutions drafted over the next two centuries containing human rights guarantees: the struggle has always been for independent courts to enforce them, at national and now at international levels.

THE NINETEENTH CENTURY: BENTHAM, MARX AND THE HUMANITARIAN IMPULSE

The Terror that enveloped France a few years after the Declaration provided a practical refutation of its claim that 'rights' were natural, let alone inalienable and sacred. 'When I hear of natural rights,' snapped Jeremy Bentham, 'I always see in the background a cluster of daggers and pikes introduced into the National Assembly . . . for the avowed purpose of exterminating the King's friends.'[11] It was Bentham who led the attack on 'natural rights' as vague and abstract nonsense – 'nonsense upon stilts' – which, by encouraging the obliteration of socially useful distinctions, tends to produce political anarchy exemplified by the Terror. Bentham's attack on the Declaration was logical – all the rights, he pointed out, including the right to liberty, were to be limited by law, thereby begging the question of what content the law should have to be compatible with liberty. He was also pragmatic. No one was in fact 'born free' – all were born helpless, and subject for years to parental authority. Men were not equal in rights: there was the master and the apprentice, the genius and the lunatic. Moreover, 'natural rights' were of uncertain provenance: if from God, their content (apart from biblical injunctions) was unknowable; if from 'nature' they were unprovable and unpredictable. The force of Bentham's arguments was partly responsible for 'natural rights' falling out of fashion in the nineteenth century and the first half of the twentieth century. When they returned, it would be as '*human* rights' rather than 'natural rights', sourced in the nature of humans rather than in the laws of God or the seasons.

The next formidable critic of 'the rights of man' was Karl Marx. In 1844 he wrote an essay, 'On the Jewish Question', which questioned whether the French Declaration could provide a way forward for Jews like himself, who were suffering from discrimination in Germany. His dismissive conclusion was that 'the so-called rights of man . . . are nothing but the rights of egotistic man, of man separated from other men and from the community'. The Declaration focused, not on man as citizen, but on man as bourgeois – an individual withdrawn from the community, motivated only by whim and self-interest. For example, the right to property was 'the right to enjoy possessions and dispose of the same arbitrarily, without regard to other men, independently from society: the right of selfishness'. The 'political emancipation' produced by the Revolution was the reduction of man to an egocentric and independent individual: true emancipation would rather enlarge him as a citizen, 'a moral person' – a theme Marx was to take up a few years later in *The Communist Manifesto*.

The force of this early critique led Marxist thinkers in the next century to characterize human rights as a device to universalize capitalist values, notably freedom of enterprise without social responsibility. Hence socialist governments were silent or suspicious of the concept, until it proved useful to rally support for leftist causes in the later stages of the Cold War. But Marx was actually supportive of the Declaration's identification of *citizen's* rights: citing Rousseau with approval, he perceived these communal rights as new resources which could assist social transformation to a 'moral existence'.[12] This level of abstraction always infuriated Bentham, although some content would subsequently be found in the idea of 'second generation' or 'social and economic' rights of citizens to education, housing and work, and later still in the notion of a *third* generation of rights, belonging to citizens of the world, to peace and development and a clean environment. But Lenin derided the English and French revolutions as uprisings of the bourgeoisie, with freedom of speech a fraud enabling the rich to control propaganda in their interests. 'The capitalists have always used the term "freedom" to mean freedom for the rich to get richer and the poor to starve to death.'[13] Shortly after the Bolshevik accession to power, Lenin was presented by his favourite lieutenant with a set of draft guarantees of liberty, the 'Anti-Thermidorian Catechism', as an insurance against the revolution degenerating into terror. He waved it away: 'Comrade, I see no need to circulate this ... It is a childish idea ... that we could stop or forestall so fatal a development with the help of this sheet of paper.' The comrade in question was Nikolai Bukharin, who in 1936 was ordered by Stalin to put his catechism into the new Soviet constitution, which did not save him two years later from being wrongly arrested, dishonestly tried and peremptorily shot.

The nineteenth century did see three humanitarian impulses which were in due course to assist the development of international law. Most notable was the legislative attack on the slave trade in England in 1807 and in America after the Civil War. It was finally acknowledged by European nations, in the Berlin Treaty on Africa in 1885, that 'trading in slaves is forbidden in conformity with international law'. This breakthrough only applied to inter-state trading, however, and did not require states to outlaw the practice locally: the slavery convention, which did, came into force much later, in 1926, and not until 1970 did the last state – Oman – announce formal abolition of the status. None the less, this was progress – attempts made by Jefferson and Robespierre respectively to abolish slavery by the

American and French declarations had signally failed. Although an international law rule did not begin to crystallize until 1885, for most of the century the British navy took upon itself a novel enforcement role, liberating victims of slavers around the African coast. Its actions in intercepting slave ships, freeing victims and even educating them in schools on the Seychelles and other islands must rate as the first example of a humanitarian enforcement mission.

Secondly, there came the notion of 'a right of humanitarian intervention' in the internal affairs of a state if its rule over some of its citizens was perceived as barbaric. Pressure was put on the Ottoman sultans in the 1880s to promulgate measures to protect Christian minorities from discrimination; when these failed, Gladstone obtained parliamentary approval to allocate ships, men and money to protect Christians from slaughter by Turks in Bulgaria. In 1898, the US declared war on Spain because its oppressive rule in Cuba 'shocked the moral sense of the people of the United States'. It was government behaviour 'shocking to the conscience of mankind' which might justify intervention, but only as a matter of conscience and not of legal obligation. International lawyers adamantly refused to admit that 'the so-called rights of mankind' existed. As late as 1912, a leading textbook opined that 'should a State venture to treat its own subjects or part thereof with such cruelty as would stagger humanity' public opinion might demand intervention, but this could only happen out of Christian charity and could not be defended on grounds of international law.[14]

None the less, in Theodore Roosevelt's 1904 State of the Union message, the right, and indeed the duty, to intervene in the affairs of sovereign states which were committing what he almost called 'crimes against humanity' was persuasively articulated:

. . . there are occasional crimes committed on so vast a scale and of such peculiar horror as to make us doubt whether it is not our manifest duty to endeavour at least to show our disapproval of the deed and our sympathy with those who have suffered by it . . . in extreme cases action may be justifiable and proper. What form the action shall take must depend upon the circumstances of the case; that is, upon the degree of the atrocity and upon our power to remedy it. The cases in which we could interfere by force of arms as we interfered to put a stop to intolerable conditions in Cuba are necessarily very few. Yet . . . it is inevitable that such a nation should desire eagerly to give expression to its horror on an occasion like that of the massacre of the Jews in Kishenef, or when it witnesses such systematic and long-extended cruelty and oppression of which the Armenians have been victims, and which have won for them the indignant pity of the civilized world . . .[15]

Of course, it helped that the interests of humanity coincided with the interests of the United States – Roosevelt was retrospectively justifying US intervention against oppressive Spanish dominion over Panama and Cuba – but his inclusion of Jews in eastern Europe and Armenians in Asia Minor as within the potential protection of the world's 'indignant pity' is worthy of note. But his promise did not save the Jews from the pogroms of 1905 or the Armenians from the genocidal attacks of Turkey in 1916.

The third nineteenth-century advance was not taken for the sake of indignant pity, but rather to reduce the cost of killing soldiers in wars. The expense of new weaponry was the reason why the major powers attended a conference in St Petersburg in 1868 and later ones in The Hague in 1899 and 1907, agreeing limits on the development of poison gases and explosive and 'dum-dum' bullets. That these rules of war came to be dressed up in the language of humanity was due to the influence of the International Committee of the Red Cross, founded in 1863 by Henri Dunant, a wealthy Swiss who had been appalled at the bloody array of bodies left on mid-European battlefields after the armies moved on. His object, and indeed the object of the 1907 Hague Convention (which forty-four nations signed), was not in any way to restrict the right of sovereign states to go to war, but simply to make these wars more humane for injured soldiers and prisoners. The futility of this exercise was demonstrated in the trenches of the First World War, where a million dead bodies would mock the notion that modern war could be made humane by laws which tinkered with methods of killing.

BETWEEN WARS: THE LEAGUE OF NATIONS
AND STALIN'S SHOW TRIALS

After four years of a pointless war of unprecedented ferocity and carnage, in which 8.5 million lives were lost, it might have been thought that any new world order would aspire to some protection of human rights. But the concept was never mentioned at the Versailles Peace Conference in 1919, nor in the Covenant of the League of Nations. The closest that document came was in Article 23, whereby members promised 'just treatment' to natives in Trust territories and that they would 'endeavour to secure and maintain fair and humane conditions of labour'. This gesture, inspired more by fear that badly treated labourers would turn to Bolshevism than by any acceptance of workers' rights, at least led to the establishment of the International Labour Organization (ILO), the first rights-related global agency. There was some talk at Versailles of prosecuting war crimes, but this was vigorously opposed by the US on the basis that 'the laws of humanity' were uncertain and violations were punishable only by God. One article of the Versailles Treaty proposed an international tribunal to try the Kaiser for a crime against 'international morality' but this was inserted to placate public opinion in Britain and France and was never intended to take effect (see page 210).

The only lasting significance of the peace process after the First World War was the inclusion by the Allies, in peace treaties signed with some enemy states, of 'minorities clauses' by which they were required to guarantee civil and political rights and religious and cultural toleration to groups (minorities) who by race or language differed from the rest of the population. These treaties were supervised by the Council of the League of Nations (which could be petitioned by individuals or associations) and were monitored through the compulsory jurisdiction of the Permanent Court of International Justice, activated by any state member. The League took this idea one step further, and in the case of several states with bad records for maltreating minorities (e.g., Albania, Latvia, Iraq) made their admission to the League conditional upon a similar obligation to safeguard the rights of minorities within their borders.

These minorities clauses bound only a few countries, and after 1922 the League lacked the resolve to extend them any further. Yet they are of some historic importance, as the first human rights limitation on sovereign states enforced by a global institution and an international court. The Permanent Court of International Justice showed an early awareness of the need to protect minority cultures in its advisory opinion on *Minority Schools in Albania* (1935), which condemned Albania's decision to close down private schools serving its Greek minority, and other judgments which were supportive of German settlers in Poland and of Polish nationals in Danzig (see page 142). In 1933, shortly after Hitler's accession to power, the League received an individual petition from Franz Bernheim (its first from a victim of Nazism), whose sacking on the grounds that he was Jewish contravened a minorities treaty for Upper Silesia. Bernheim and several other Jews were awarded compensation for discrimination by a League commission – prompting Germany to withdraw from the League.[16] In 1939, the League's Minorities Section was disbanded, although at least the experiment had served to disprove the American claim at Versailles that 'laws of humanity' were too vague and subjective to be justiciable.

From 1936 to 1938 there was presented in Moscow a series of 'show trials' which were to prove, in time, second only to the Holocaust in their impact on post-war human rights thinking. These were the public tip of Stalin's iceberg of terror, the means by which he sought to justify the purge of his leading opponents, and then, less publicly, of their followers. The victims of these purges are now estimated, incredibly but reliably, to outnumber the six million Jews lost in the Holocaust.[17] This is without precedent in human history at a time of peace: in Nazi Germany, only a few thousand lives were lost in concentration camps before the war, and in the French Revolution the Terror at its pre-Thermidorian height claimed no more than 17,000. But between 1936 and 1938, in Moscow alone, 30,000 defendants were tried in the Supreme Court and sentenced to death by firing squad. And these were the trials reserved for important people: in the provinces, millions were killed after summary proceedings or through beatings and starvation in the gulag.

Andrei Vyshinsky, like Fouquier-Tinville, was a hard-working lawyer devoid of any moral scruple. It was his evil genius to produce the main show trials as forensic spectacles which persuaded many in the West that they were genuine applications of criminal law. The prosecution case – that most of the old Bolsheviks were spies for foreign powers – was incredible enough, as was the theory that the moderate groups led by Bukharin had secretly joined forces with their main enemies, the Trotskyites, to sabotage the country and the communist revolution. What made these preposterous conspiracy theories seem credible in the West was simply that the conspirators confessed, in public proceedings overseen by a judge. It was not until 1956 that Khrushchev admitted what should have been obvious to observers at the time: the defendants had all been subjected to months of torture by the NKVD until they agreed to sign and speak the script prepared for them by Vyshinsky.[18] They were put on 'the conveyor' – a disorientation procedure which alternated psychological pressures of sleeplessness and starvation with interrogation to enhance suggestibility and acquiescence. This was interspersed with beatings and physical torture, such as burning the body with a molten knife. As each victim agreed to 'confess' he was confronted with others who had broken, and together they were encouraged to elaborate further hypothetical scenarios in the basic prosecution fantasy. The few who held out were shot in the secret cellars of the Lubyanka prison, while VIP defendants were required to repeat their false confessions in public, as the price exacted for saving the lives of their wives and children. (One of Stalin's first decrees in this terror period was to give the secret police special powers over the families of convicted traitors.)

The trials were held in an auditorium in front of several hundred specially invited observers from around the world – fellow travellers like the influential English QC D. N. Pritt, who could be relied upon to write dishonest propaganda pamphlets with titles like 'The Moscow Trial was Fair'. The defendants were allowed counsel, but only to speak *after* their convictions, in mitigation of their confessed crimes. Vyshinsky occupied centre stage, eliciting from the dozen or so defendants their self-lacerations around which he wove his fantastical plots. The transcripts typically read like this extract, in which the old

Bolsheviks Zinoviev and Kamenev play the Rosencrantz and Guilden-stern of the Russian Revolution:

KAMENEV: I, together with Zinoviev and Trotsky, organized and guided this terrorist conspiracy. I had become convinced that Stalin's policy was successful and victorious . . . yet we were motivated by boundless hate and by lust for power.

VYSHINSKY: You expressed your loyalty to the Party in various articles and statements. Was all this deception on your part?

KAMENEV: No, it was worse than deception.

VYSHINSKY: Perfidy?

KAMENEV: Worse than that!

VYSHINSKY: Worse than deception? Worse than perfidy? Then find a word for it. Treason?

KAMENEV: You have found the word.

VYSHINSKY: Zinoviev, do you confirm this?

ZINOVIEV: Yes, I do. Treason, perfidy, double-dealing.

Nikolai Bukharin (who designed that 'Anti-Thermidorian Cat-echism' precisely to prevent this turn of events) was the only one of the defendants to offer any resistance, or to show any self-control after his year on 'the conveyor'. Although he pleaded guilty to treason (to save his wife and baby son) he managed to blurt out that his confession had been obtained by 'medieval methods'. He tried to explain that his treason consisted in feeling his own powerlessness before the totalitarian state he had helped to construct, and the impossibility of beating it at the game it chose to play with his own life.[19] When Bukharin tried to question one of the lying prosecution witnesses, the presiding judge ruled cross-examination irrelevant. This judge was V. Ulrich, head of the military section of the Supreme Court, who reported throughout the trials to Stalin and followed his orders in respect to passing the death sentences which were imposed on most defendants. He is the archetypal scoundrel judge, but was acting in accordance with the textbook *Judicial Organization in the USSR*, written by public prosecutor Vyshinsky:

The laws of the Soviet power are a political directive and the work of the judge amounts not just to the application of the law in conformity with the needs of bourgeois judicial logic, but to the application of the law as a political expression of the Party and the Government . . . the judge must be a political worker, rapidly and precisely applying the directives of the Party and the Government.

Stalin's show trials came to haunt later generations because they proved how a system of law, with procedural forms and rituals calculated to impress, could be vulnerable to political manipulation by an all-powerful state. Vyshinsky perverted the trial process so that Stalin could rewrite history by eliminating those who made it. These 'purge' trials with their inevitable conclusion for 'enemies of the people' – a bullet in the head, followed by burial in an unmarked grave – cast a long historical shadow. The rights of defendants which later appeared in the UN Conventions and which are now written in the Statute of the International Criminal Court (the right, for example, even in the face of compelling evidence, to refuse to testify without fear of any adverse inference being drawn) may be traced to the reaction to Vyshinsky's colossal frame-ups. No account of human rights in the twentieth century can ignore the Moscow trials: they became the model for political trials to the present day (and not only in communist countries). The truth about them that only novelists could at first tell, like George Orwell in *Animal Farm* and Arthur Koestler in *Darkness at Noon*, followed by Khrushchev's belated acknowledgement that they were monstrous perversions of justice, did much to persuade the European left that, *pace* Marx and Lenin, human rights was not such a bad idea after all. (The fact that Vyshinsky's ashes still occupy a place of honour in the Kremlin wall may be evidence that, in Russia, the lesson has not fully been learned.)

H.G. WELLS: WHAT ARE WE FIGHTING FOR?

One of the great mysteries of the twentieth century is why, for its first forty years, there was virtual silence on the subject of universal human rights from European intellectuals, politicians and public figures. Even as Jews in Germany were forced out of jobs and professions and then into labour camps, even as kulaks, then old Bolsheviks and later millions of innocent citizens were exterminated in the Soviet gulag, still the notion of protecting human rights was not raised either at the League of Nations or in academic journals or the popular press. This may at a theoretical level owe much to the demolition of 'natural rights' by Bentham and Marx, but more pragmatically those nations which might have embraced the idea, such as Britain and France, were concerned lest it might make the natives restless in their far-flung colonial domains. For that reason, they squashed a proposal made at the League in 1934 by Haiti for a treaty to guarantee the human rights of ethnic minorities. Astonishingly, this was the League's only reference to the subject before its demise at the onset of the Second World War, and the idea does not appear to have been seriously advanced by any major thinker or statesman of the period.[20]

The revival of the human rights idea in the twentieth century really began at the instigation and inspiration of the British author H. G. Wells, in the months immediately following the declaration of the Second World War. It can be traced to letters he wrote to *The Times* in October 1939, advocating the adoption by 'parliamentary peoples' of a Declaration of Rights – a fundamental law defining their rights in a democracy and drafted to appeal 'to every responsive spirit under the yoke of the obscurantist and totalitarian tyrannies with which all are in conflict'. The League of Nations had been too conservative, half-hearted and diplomatic throughout 'the tortuous Twenties and the frightened Thirties': now, the only sane alternative was to declare 'the fundamental law for mankind throughout the world'. It is a remarkable tribute to Wells and a few of his friends (English socialists ranging from former Labour Lord Chancellor Sankey to Barbara Wootton, J. B. Priestley and A. A. Milne, creator of Winnie the Pooh) that they were able to distil into nine short and readable principles a declaration that came to attract support throughout the world. In their modest English way, they eschewed the messianic preambles of the French and American declarations in favour of the simple observation that 'since a man comes into this world through no fault of his own' he is in justice entitled

(1) Without distinction of race or colour to nourishment, housing, covering, medical care and attention sufficient to realize his full possibilities of physical and mental development and to keep him in a state of health from his birth to his death.

(2) Sufficient education to make him a useful and interested citizen, easy access to information upon all matters of common knowledge throughout his life, in the course of which he would enjoy the utmost freedom of discussion.

(3) That he and his personal property lawfully acquired are entitled to police and legal protection from private violence, deprivation, compulsion and intimidation . . .

And so it went on, in fine and only occasionally dated style, promising *inter alia*: 'There shall be no secret dossiers in any administrative department'; 'a man's private house or apartment or reasonably limited garden enclosure is his castle'; 'no man shall be subjected to torture, beating or any other bodily punishment, or to imprisonment with such an excess of silence, noise, light or darkness as to cause mental suffering or in infected, verminous or otherwise insanitary quarters'.

Here, for the first time since the eighteenth-century revolutions, was an attempt – by well-meaning middle-class socialists – to restate human rights in a homely way, as a talisman against the coming cataclysm. In the first months of the 'phoney war' it attracted extraordinary support in England: the *Manchester Guardian* and the *Daily Herald* took up the issue, and tens of thousands flocked to hear H. G. Wells speak under the banner 'The New World Order – The Fundamental Principles'. What gave his campaign further momentum was the swift publication of a Penguin Special, *H. G. Wells on the Rights of Man*, which sold many thousands of copies in the UK and was translated into thirty languages and syndicated in newspapers throughout the world. For the first few months of 1940, this was the idea whose time had come – in an act of utter optimism the War Ministry even had copies of Wells's booklet translated into German and dropped on SS divisions, although they continued to overrun France. It had more impact on President Franklin D. Roosevelt, a friend of Wells who was much taken by his new book: it influenced his famous appeal in 1941 for a world 'formed upon four essential freedoms' – freedom of speech and worship, and freedom from want and fear. And on 1 January 1942, a few weeks after American entry into the war, H. G. Wells secured his objective: the Allied powers declared that 'complete victory over their enemies is essential . . . *to preserve human rights* and justice in their own lands *as well as in other lands*' (my italics). Human rights was henceforth a war aim, emphasized in the rhetoric of politicians while lawyers in the back rooms of the State Department and the common rooms of Oxbridge tried their hands at drafting something that was now definitely on the post-war agenda: an international bill of rights.

They did so, inevitably, in language that lacked the passion and simplicity of H. G. Wells. His achievement was to make human rights relevant to a world from many parts of which they had vanished with the secret policeman's knock on the door, and to include in his list the social and economic rights which Western governments had refused to acknowledge during the Great Depression. His Penguin Special, which must be accounted one of the twentieth century's most influential books, was a far-sighted demand for what he was the first to call a 'New World Order', in which fundamental human rights, enforced by law, would protect individuals against governments of whatever political complexion. What made this slim volume of 128 pages so powerful was the way its author was able to mix unassuming idealism with a devastating attack on Stalin, and especially upon 'the young Germany of Hitler, wearing its thick boots (that have stamped in the faces of Jewish women), its brown shirts, that recall the victims smothered in latrines and all the cloacal side of Hitlerism; its swastika – ignorantly stolen from the Semitic Stone-age peoples; oafish and hysterically cruel, they remind us all how little mankind has risen above the level of an exceptionally spiteful ape'. Wells was the first to argue from 'those outrages upon human dignity' in the concentration camps – outrages that others only felt after seeing the pictures of the corpse-strewn Belsen, six years later.

But these examples were used to illustrate a broader thesis, namely that Western tradition required, as a response to totalitarianism, a reassertion of individual liberty, and for that liberty to be protected by an international order that relied on law rather than diplomacy.

This was the prescience of Wells's vision, as astonishing, in its way, as his first novel *The Time Machine* half a century before. Wells's grasp of international law was negligible, and he offered no answer to the problem of how his declaration, which was to be incorporated in the domestic law of every state, might be enforced in states without independent legal systems. He was, however, positive that it would take more than diplomacy to bring them into line, and that pleas of state sovereignty must not be allowed to prevail: 'There was an extraordinary mass of foolish talk after 1918 about not interfering in the internal affairs of this, that or the other member of the League of Nations. It is time we recognized fully that the making of any lethal weapon larger than what may be required for the control of big animals, is a matter of universal concern . . .'

Universal concern would call forth a universal legal order, but when war aims began to crystallize as defeat loomed for the Axis powers, this was too radical for the Allied governments to contemplate. It was to a strengthened League of Nations model that they turned, at the four-power conference at Dumbarton Oaks in late 1944 which led to the Charter of the United Nations, signed by forty-four nations in San Francisco on 26 June 1945. The original 'Great Power' plan was to leave the promotion of 'respect for human rights and fundamental freedoms' as merely an incidental aspiration of the new organization: that this was elevated into one of the Charter's primary purposes was due to last-minute pressure exerted on the US delegation by a group of American non-governmental organizations (notably, the American Jewish Congress and the National Association for the Advancement of Colored People). It was the US, then, which took the lead in giving human rights its prominent position in the UN Charter, both in its preamble (which evinces a determination 'to reaffirm faith in fundamental human rights, in the dignity and worth of the human person, in the equal rights of men and women') and in Article 1, which sets out as a chief purpose of the UN:

To achieve international co-operation in solving international problems of an economic, social, cultural or humanitarian character, and in promoting and encouraging respect for human rights and for fundamental freedoms for all without distinction as to race, sex, language or religion.

The Charter established an Economic and Social Council with power to set up a Human Rights Commission. Significantly, Article 55 says that 'universal respect for, and observance of, human rights' is essential for 'conditions of stability and well-being which are necessary for peaceful and friendly relations among nations'. To achieve this, members pledge themselves in Article 56 to take 'joint and separate action' in co-operation with the UN. But members must never forget Article 2(7), which sets up the rule which H. G. Wells identified as the road block for human rights, and at whose barrier their progress was halted for much of the remaining century:

Nothing contained in the present Charter shall authorize the United Nations to intervene in matters which are essentially within the domestic jurisdiction of any State or shall require the members to submit such matters to settlement under the present Charter; but this principle shall not prejudice the application of enforcement measures under Chapter VII.

By reference to this crippling rule, the UN and its instrumentalities declined to act against any state which objected to having its internal repression investigated or condemned. It was a restriction over which diplomats could wring their hands, whilst having no desire at all to intervene to stop barbarities perpetrated by their allies or to create precedents which might later justify intervention in the affairs of their own governments. It was not until 1993, after the Cold War was over and as the spectre of 'ethnic cleansing' returned to Europe, that there was sufficient superpower resolve to apply the *proviso* to Article 2(7), namely that it could be overridden by Chapter VII. This is the chapter of the Charter which permits the Security Council to order armed intervention against any state once it has determined that such a response is necessary to restore international peace and security. Since Article 55 expressly makes the observance of human rights a condition necessary for peaceful relations, the appalling crimes against humanity which occurred after 1945 could have been forcibly combated by the UN under its Chapter VII power, but until the Balkan atrocities in the 1990s the Security Council never sought or even thought to invoke military action upon human rights grounds.

Nevertheless, the UN Charter was the first treaty to make human rights a matter for global concern. By identifying violations as a danger

25

to world peace and security it provided a mechanism for international intervention, as a last resort, in the affairs of nation states. What it did not do was to impose any *legal* duty on member states to comply with human rights standards. This could have been accomplished, as several small countries urged, by incorporating a bill of rights in the Charter: the move was opposed by all the major powers, conscious of the motes in their own eyes (France and the UK had no desire at the time to grant any form of democracy to their colonies; all the Southern states in the US had 'Jim Crow' laws discriminating against blacks; there were millions still consigned without trial to Soviet gulags). For this reason the Charter pledges on human rights were circumscribed: the duty was to *promote* human rights, not to guarantee them as a matter of law for all citizens. This vagueness was quite deliberate: no Great Power was prepared in 1945 to be bound by international law in respect of the treatment of its own subjects. The only positive rule of law to which they committed themselves was to refrain from threatening or using force against the territory or independence of any other state (Article 2(4)), subject to their 'inherent right of individual or collective self-defence if an armed attack occurs against a member' (Article 51). It was the application of this formula which was mostly to exercise the Security Council in its efforts to broker peace, until the internecine bloodbaths in former Yugoslavia and Rwanda caused it to exercise a power to punish crimes against humanity that it had actually possessed from the outset.

THE UNIVERSAL DECLARATION OF HUMAN RIGHTS

In closing the San Francisco conference, President Truman had promised that under the newly minted UN Charter 'we have good reason to expect the framing of an international bill of rights (which) will be as much a part of international life as our own Bill of Rights is a part of our own Constitution'.[21] The momentous task of drafting this constitution for humankind was allotted to the newly formed Commission on Human Rights, set up by the Economic and Social Council pursuant to Article 68 of the Charter. It was chaired by

Eleanor Roosevelt and served by a secretariat headed by a Canadian law professor, John Humphrey, who over the next two years was instrumental in putting before the delegates drafts he culled from many sources – notably the American Law Institute, the constitutions of Latin American countries (which contained social and economic rights); drafts by Sir Hersch Lauterpacht, H. G. Wells and the Sankey Committee, and the eighteenth-century declarations.[22] The Commission's most severe division turned on whether the bill should be legally enforceable (either as an annex to the UN Charter or as a multilateral human rights convention) or merely take the form of a declaration – of principles without powers of implementation, other than by the slow process of acceptance as customary international law. The Soviet Union and its puppets were implacable foes of enforceability, while Britain and Australia led the demand for a binding document. Australia's delegates were the first to propose an international court of human rights, pointing out the obvious: 'a mere declaration of principles would not offer assurance against the revival of oppression'. The Americans blew hot and cold. Roosevelt initially inclined to the American Bar Association call for 'a new Bill of Rights that will be a part of law enforceable against governments which deny human rights' but she shifted towards the Soviets' position the more that US relations with them worsened: neither of those sparring superpowers wanted rules, or even a referee, when the gloves had to come off.[23] The idealistic nations gave in, and this had, with hindsight, two negative advantages: the declaration was agreed, with superpower involvement, by the end of 1948 (it might not have been agreed at all thereafter), and it came with no enforcement machinery to be discredited (as discredited it would undoubtedly have been) during the years of the Cold War.

What emerged was not a legal guarantee but a 'declaration' made by the General Assembly, putting beyond doubt the nature and meaning of the pledge to respect human rights contained in Article 55 of the Charter. The Universal Declaration of Human Rights was adopted by forty-eight members of the General Assembly on 10 December 1948. It is poignant to recall the eight member states which abstained from voting: the USSR, Czechoslovakia, Poland and two communist satellites, Yugoslavia, South Africa and Saudi Arabia.

(The six communist abstentions were opportunistic – these countries had played an important part in the drafting and insisted on a non-binding declaration, then abstained on the grounds that it would have little effect. South Africa could not square the non-discrimination clauses with its apartheid laws, and Saudi Arabia – unlike other Muslim countries – objected that the right to change religion prevented it from punishing apostasy.) It was to be a measure both of the triumph of human rights as an idea, and of the failure to make it a reality, that these nations came in later years consistently to endorse the Declaration, as did well over a hundred countries which emerged to independence after 1948. This is the Declaration's achievement of sorts, that no state has ever been prepared to boast of its breach.

Although it was the first modern human rights text to be drafted in the pedestrian prose of a UN committee, there is anger flashing from the Charter's preamble. After the briefest of natural law nods towards 'inherent dignity' and 'inalienable rights' (and a welcome non-sexist substitution of 'human family' for 'man'), it recites as its rationale that contempt for human rights results in 'barbarous acts which have outraged the conscience of mankind' and so human rights 'should be protected by the rule of law' in order to avoid the need to revolt against tyranny. For members of the drafting committee, and speakers in the General Assembly debate, the Holocaust had supplied human rights with the most utilitarian of justifications: the alternative to them is war.

It is possible to find, behind the adoption of most of the articles, some reference to the perversions of Nazism. Thus 'master race' ideology is refuted by Article 2, which entitles everyone to rights 'without distinction of any kind, such as race, colour, sex, language, religion, political or other opinion, national or social origin, property, birth or other status'. The Declaration was drafted by the Human Rights Commission after receiving a detailed report on the prosecution evidence at the Nuremberg trials. The killing of 'useless eaters', the *Einsatzgruppen* orders to kill indiscriminately, the gas chambers, Mengele experiments, 'night and fog' decrees and the extermination projects after *Kristallnacht* were at the forefront of their minds and provided the examples to which they addressed their drafts.[24] Thus the first draft of Article 3 ('Everyone has a right to life, liberty and security of person') originally went on 'except in cases prescribed by law' – until it was realized how many had been put to death under perfectly valid laws passed by the Nazis. (The African Charter, drafted many years later, also makes this mistake (see pp. 62–3).) The Article 19 guarantee of freedom of expression and Article 20 guarantee of freedom of peaceful assembly were incorporated by reference to Hitler's crackdown on dissent after the Reichstag fire, and Article 21 – the right to participate in government through secretly balloted and free elections – was an attempt to address the fascist habit of rule through decree, without reference to any democratic body. The addendum to the right to education in Article 26, which reads as a controversial support for private schooling ('Parents have a prior right to choose the kind of education that shall be given to their children') was a heartfelt reaction to Nazi brainwashing: as Roosevelt explained, it was 'designed to avert situations such as prevailed in Nazi countries where education, which was entirely under state control, tended to atrophy children's intellectual facilities'.[25] The rights to an effective remedy (Article 8) and to a fair hearing by an independent tribunal (Article 10) were reactions to the puppet courts, packed with Nazi judges, established to enforce the Party's decrees.

Of course, many of these rights are to be found in similar language in H. G. Wells's draft and in the eighteenth-century declarations, but the Nazi record and the even more indiscriminatingly brutal Japanese record (which was also before the Commission in digests of the Tokyo trials) gave an emphasis to those individual rights which seemed incompatible with totalitarianism. What amazes today is the contemporaneity of the document, over half a century on. Roosevelt and her drafting committee produced an imperishable statement that has inspired more than 200 international treaties, conventions and declarations, and the bills of rights found in almost every national constitution adopted since the war. There were, in retrospect, a few errors: it was not necessary to spell out as a universal right 'periodic holidays with pay' (Article 24); and the special copyright provision for the profits of scientists and authors in Article 27(2) is surely out of place (it was probably inserted because a conference on the Berne Copyright Convention coincided with the main drafting session). These are quibbles: more serious is the failure (thanks to communist objection) to make political rights depend upon democracy, and the failure to provide any protection at all for minority rights. This was largely due to the prevailing fallacy that if you look after individual rights, group rights will take care of themselves (see p. 143), and by way of reaction to Hitler's exploitation of German minorities as an excuse for invading Poland and Czechoslovakia. But colonial attachments and racist assumptions played a part: for example, Australia argued that 'the principle of assimilation of all groups was in the best interests of all in the long run'[26] – a principle of white superiority for which indigenous people in that and other countries would tragically suffer. Otherwise, the Universal Declaration has stood time's test, and what resonates most loudly today is Article 28:

Everyone is entitled to a social and international order in which the rights and freedoms set forth in this declaration can be fully realized.

This was a right without precedent in the eighteenth-century declarations. It called for some international enforcement system, harking back to the provisions of the Charter which permitted Security Council intervention under Chapter VII in the event of human rights violations on a scale which threatened world peace. The French delegate, René Cassin (who played an important part in drafting the Declaration), was aware that the Charter made it possible to penetrate the sovereignty of the State: 'This was specifically put into the Charter in the hope of avoiding a repetition of what happened in 1933, when Germany began to massacre her own nationals and when other nations refused to consider this a matter of international concern.'[27]

At this point, the true significance of the Charter and the Universal Declaration for the still-distant human rights movement can with hindsight be appreciated. It lies in the nexus both these documents assert between grave human rights violations and international insecurity: atrocities within a sovereign state are a matter for international law because they upset neighbouring states in a manner likely to disturb world peace. This was the assumption of Article 55 of the Charter (promotion of respect for human rights helps create 'conditions of stability and well-being') and the preamble of the Universal Declaration ('recognition of . . . equal and inalienable rights of all members of the human family is the foundation of . . . peace in the world'). Today the rationale for humanitarian intervention might be stated differently – with more sophistication (in terms of the psychological necessity to eradicate behaviour that diminishes everyone's humanity) or less (a crime-free global village). But in 1948, US Secretary of State George Marshall explained the link that the framers had in mind:

Governments which systematically disregard the rights of their own people are not likely to respect the rights of other nations and other people and are likely to seek their objectives by coercion and force.[28]

This was true of Hitler, of course, and of Saddam Hussein: it describes Libya and Iran and Afghanistan in the grip of the Taliban, but not Singapore or Nigeria or Burma, where domestic repression to a lesser or greater extent does not coincide with an aggressive foreign policy or a desire to export revolution. None the less, by making the somewhat questionable assumption that a state's respect for human rights was a precondition of international peace, the Charter and the Declaration provided the legal mechanism which could later be triggered to challenge the sovereign right of states to oppress groups of their own people.

Although a product of Allied war aims, with an intellectual provenance described above, the final draft of the Universal Declaration emerged from a geographically and culturally mixed committee on which major contributions were made by delegates from India, China and Lebanon, with further input from representatives of Chile, Iran and Egypt. Many of today's African and Asian countries had not at this stage been granted independence, but fourteen members of the 56-state General Assembly were Asian, four were African and twenty came from Latin America. The communist abstainers had given assent to the individual freedom provisions: what they feared was the Declaration's bias towards democracy (to assuage them, the word itself is only mentioned once, in Article 29). So there is little historical merit in the criticism raised decades later, that the Universal Declaration embodies only liberal Western values. On the contrary, it vouchsafed economic, social and cultural rights of enormous importance to developing countries. These included the right to work and to basic standards of health, housing and education. The drafting committee, conscious of the need to avoid 'cultural imperialism', took evidence from anthropologists who warned of ethnocentrism, the assumption of the superiority of one's own cultural values. The actual drafting history reveals very few cultural divides, other than over the rights to marry and to change religion – a sticking point for the Saudis but not for other Muslim nations like Syria, Iran and Pakistan. The USSR and its henchstates championed the non-discrimination clauses and the rights to work and housing, whilst it was the bloc of Latin American states, supported by delegates from China, India and the Philippines, which successfully insisted on the inclusion of the 'new' or 'second generation' social and economic rights, despite opposition from the US and its 'liberal' Western allies. These communitarian rights are made in some cases contingent upon 'national effort' or 'the organization and resources of each state', but their inclusion was at the behest of representatives of poor and underdeveloped countries. The Australian Labour government, with its strong trade union ties, first broke Western ranks, pointing out (to the embarrassment of his widow, who chaired the session) that the third of President Roosevelt's 'four freedoms' was freedom from want.[29]

There is nothing in the Declaration that is hostile to developing countries, or to Asian and African countries, or to the culture and aspirations of ethnic groups or tribes. It sets bedrock standards, beyond which diversity is encouraged. As a matter of history, the allegation that the Declaration was intended to be an instrument of Western hegemony fails: it was a righteous and at the time largely uncontentious response to the horrors of concentration camps in Europe and of Japanese military occupation in Asia, pithily defining the freedoms which would have to be upheld to prevent any repetition of this intolerable state behaviour. At the time, these rights were not perceived as Western or Eurocentric, but as obvious. That over the following half-century the Declaration would be flouted without regard to geography, by governments of every creed and colour and often by or with the connivance of the US and its European allies, amply demonstrates that its guarantees are not 'Western' in any meaningful sense. 'Liberal' the Declaration is not, in any consistent way: philosophically it embodies a lowest common denominator of post-war decency, imbued with the dour moral conservatism of the time (adopting, for example, the family as 'the natural and fundamental group unit of society') allied to some emerging socialist ideals such as a basic wage, favourable conditions of work and the right to join trade unions. As for the individual freedom clauses, these were all made subject to the sweeping exceptions of Articles 29 and 30, which embody the communitarian philosophy that 'Everyone has duties to the community in which *alone* the free and full development of his personality is possible.' So the real failure is not to be found in a perspective skewed towards Western values, as Asian leaders like Mahathir, Suharto and Lee Kuan Yew were much later to allege, but in its lack of enforcement machinery: that could only come from progressive incorporation of its clauses into treaties and in due course into customary international law. Its orginal purpose was to serve as 'the measuring rod of illegitimacy and illegality of practices of power' and without it, as the leading Indian legal scholar Upendra Baxi concludes, 'there would have been no objective way of measuring and combating State-caused human deprivation and suffering'.[30]

The Declaration was proclaimed by the General Assembly as 'a common standard of achievement for all peoples and all nations', to be promoted by education and, more optimistically, by 'progressive measures, national and international, to secure their universal and effective recognition and observance'. This coy phraseology conceals the awkward fact that this proclamation lacks legal force, whilst articulating the hope that it might come to possess such force through 'progressive measures' by states and through its adoption by international law. Although its drafters had drawn heavily on the eighteenth-century declarations, they had wisely refrained from incorporating appeals to God and to nature. Instead, they invoked the 'categorical imperative' familiar from the moral philosophy of Immanuel Kant: 'Act so that you treat humanity, whether in your own person or in that of another, always as an end and never as a means only.'[31] Kant located the seat of universal laws in national respect for intrinsic human worthiness, which he termed 'dignity' — the key word in the preamble, which opens by recognizing 'the inherent dignity of all members of the human family' and goes on, by secular and rational argument, to affirm faith in 'the dignity and worth of the human person' which needs protection (a) because securing the 'four freedoms' is the highest international aspiration and (b) because of the empirical evidence that violating human rights conduces to war and barbarism. The preamble advances, through seven powerful propositions, the logical and moral argument that human rights are universal, and proceeds to state their content: it is an exercise in persuasion rather than law. Eleanor Roosevelt prophesied that the Universal Declaration 'might well become the international Magna Carta of mankind'. But she warned the General Assembly that it would not initially have that status: 'It is not a treaty; it is not an international agreement. It is not and does not purport to be a statement of law or legal obligation.' What *was* intended to have precisely that status was the accompanying Convention on the Prevention and Punishment of Genocide, which was presented for signature the following day (it entered into force in 1951). This required states to punish, either domestically or 'by such international criminal tribunal as may have jurisdiction', acts which were intended to destroy, in whole or part, a national ethnic or racial group, committed by anyone 'whether they are constitutionally responsible rulers, public officials or private individuals'.

These two documents – the convention placing an international law obligation on every state to act against genocide and the inspirational Universal Declaration – provide the UN with its finest historical moment. (The Geneva Conventions, presented in March 1949, completed the post-war human rights triptych.) But the starry eyed delegates and self-congratulating diplomats present at the Palais Chaillot, in the shadow of the Eiffel Tower, at the birth of the first New World Order in December 1948 failed to heed the lesson of the Berlin airlift, made necessary by Stalin's petulant decision to seal the city against road and rail transport. The USSR, for no good reason, was threatening two million West Berliners with starvation, having just abstained from voting for a declaration that every man has the 'right to a standard of living adequate for the health and well-being of himself and of his family, including food'. The Soviet ambassador to the UN gave a tight, abstemious smile as he explained the Soviet abstention to newsmen: the Declaration, he said, was 'just a collection of pious phrases'. This was Andrei Vyshinsky, the century's most polished legal liar, who had commenced his new career as communism's arch-diplomat.

2

The Post-war World

'Count up the results of fifty years of human rights mechanisms, thirty years of multibillion dollar development programmes and endless high-level rhetoric and the general impact is quite underwhelming . . . this is a failure of implementation on a scale that shames us all.'   Mary Robinson, UN Human Rights
Commissioner, 10 December 1998

The Universal Declaration was adopted by the UN General Assembly on 10 December 1948: 'Human Rights Day', as it was thereafter annually celebrated, with as much enthusiasm as the times would permit. The Declaration and the Genocide Convention had been the high-water marks of a movement which was not so much for human rights as against the tyranny and racist ideology of Nazism: its force was spent in its culmination. Thereafter, it proved powerless to move politicians or diplomats to do anything much about genocide, or any other of the multiple and massive breaches of human rights which took place over the next fifty years. This appalling failure occupied a period when over a hundred international treaties and conventions and declarations were promulgated, invariably preceded by preparatory commissions and conferences taking diplomats to the world's most pleasant and expensive cities: Geneva (incessantly), The Hague, Vienna, Rome and New York. (It may be no coincidence that the only conference of much value to the cause took place, briefly, in Tehran.) The result has been to define and extend human rights on paper – endless reams of paper – but never seriously to discomfit a single torturer until Duško Tadić was put behind bars for twenty years by the Hague Tribunal in May 1997. He was, however, just a thug; the following year General Pinochet, architect of the 'disappearances' in South America which claimed thousands of lives, became a much more significant candidate for international justice after his arrest in London. The fact that Pinochet *was* arrested in 1998 – he had been a frequent visitor in previous years – was an achievement made possible by a development in a parallel universe to that occupied by politicians and diplomats and UN bureaucrats, namely the real world, where people are coming to believe in the principles to which these functionaries have for too long given lipservice.

This has been mainly achieved by the moral force of the principles themselves, promulgated by the hundreds of non-government organizations (NGOs) like Amnesty International and Human Rights Watch which have sprung up to promote them. Political leaders have on occasion given genuine commitment (e.g. President Carter in 1977) and inspiration has come from victims whose struggles provoke anger throughout a world that is now instantaneously informed of human rights violations by satellite television. The pictures are as important as ever: just as the pitiable skeletons of Belsen haunted in flickering black and white the architects of the 1948 Declaration, so television's colour coverage of the piled-up bodies in Bosnia and Rwanda produced a public response which forced the UN to establish a court to convict those responsible for the carnage. The television pictures from the Kosovo borders initially swung public support behind the NATO bombing of Serbia in 1999, although had it bombed the Bosnian Serbs at Srebrenica in 1995, or demonstrated any resolve to arrest their leaders indicted by the Hague Tribunal (see p. 206), then the later tragedy may have been avoided. Equally, had the world worked out a way of putting Pinochet and other tyrants of the 1970s behind bars within a decade of their crimes against humanity, Milošević may have been deterred from following their example.

This chapter explains the post-war evolution of systems aiming to protect human rights. Firstly, there are the institutions – courts (so called if their decisions are binding on states) – then there are the commissions and committees which receive and rule upon petitions from individuals, sometimes encouraging a government to change its mind. The treaties which set up these adjudicatory bodies, and the adjudications themselves, are 'sources' for emerging international human rights law, along with custom and state practice: if all such 'sources' point in the same direction, or a great preponderance of authority is in favour of a particular principle, it may be said to have crystallized into a 'rule' of international law. But international law, unlike municipal law, cannot be said to 'rule': it lays down a standard which independent states may in practice ignore, and often do, without suffering anything more than diplomatic embarrassment. However, sufficient sources have congealed for international human rights to be stated in terms of the elemental liberties described in chapter 3. Some of the most vexing topical issues, such as the rights of minorities and of prisoners condemned to death, receive separate treatment in chapter 4.

1946–76: THIRTY INGLORIOUS YEARS

The promise of a New World Order was ushered in by the Universal Declaration and the Genocide Convention in December 1948, followed a few months later by the final part of the human rights triptych, the four Geneva Conventions requiring civilized treatment for civilians and prisoners and sick and wounded victims of war. In 1950, in the temporary absence of the Soviet Union, the Security Council took the momentous decision to commence military action under the UN Charter against North Korea. This war ebbed and flowed until 1953, costing almost a million lives. The most appalling atrocities were committed, in complete defiance of the Geneva Conventions, by the North Koreans allied with Chinese forces under the brutal and dictatorial Kim-Il Sung and by the UN-supported South Koreans led by the brutal and corrupt Syngman Rhee. The US air force carpet-bombed civilian targets with almost as much tonnage as had devastated Nazi Germany, and its soldiers (so a few confessed fifty years later) massacred hundreds at the hamlet of No Gun Ri, while North Koreans left their prisoners to die of starvation and later (when the Chinese took over the camps) introduced a technique new to the human rights lexicon: 'brainwashing'.

Any prospect of a New World Order based on the Universal Declaration was swiftly shattered. Stalin's terror made a comeback: show trials played to capacity radio audiences throughout eastern Europe, with confessions rehearsed at gunpoint. László Rajk in Hungary and Rudolf Slánský in Czechoslovakia took the Nikolai Bukharin part, without any ambiguity in their script. Stalin remained in place until his death in 1953, as did his gulag, which devoured millions and provided slave labour to build the vast scientific complexes needed for the Soviet nuclear industry. The arms race began in 1949 when the Soviet Union first tested its bomb: the Great Powers vied to develop weapons of mass destruction in complete defiance of all Hague Conventions on this subject. Just for a moment, in February 1956, a ray of hope for human rights briefly shone, when, at the Twentieth Congress of the Soviet Communist Party, Khrushchev condemned Stalin and admitted that the show trial confessions had been obtained by torture. But the moment was lost, partly through a last gasp of colonialism by the British government, leading France and Israel into a racist war with Egypt over the Suez Canal. With UN and US attention diverted by the misbehaviour of these foolish allies, the cries for freedom sweeping Hungary (excited by Khrushchev's apparent denunciation of Stalinism) went unheeded by the West, and Soviet tanks rolled into Budapest to make mockery of the Universal Declaration promise that 'the will of the people shall be the basis of the authority of government'. Tens of thousands of Hungarians were arbitrarily detained, and hundreds were executed without any pretence at fair trial. The determination of the Soviet Union to destroy any freedom which might be asserted against the interests of communism reached its apotheosis in 1961 with the building of the Berlin Wall. Those brutal apparatchiks Walter Ulbricht and later Erich Honecker directed that anyone seeking to exercise the universal right of freedom of movement by crossing it, should be shot on sight.

Liberty took a bashing in the West as well. In the US, Senator McCarthy and his ambitious helper, Congressman Nixon, poisoned the wells of free speech, while the electrocution in 1953 of Ethel Rosenberg – a mother of young children – was a signally cruel event. Discrimination against blacks was endemic, and in some American states there was what amounted to apartheid as petty as that which was imposed by law in South Africa. US intervention in its 'spheres of influence' was as frequent as that of the Soviet Union, although much less heavy-handed: the Americans worked their will through

CIA-financed fronts rather than by sending in their own tanks. When a democratic election threw up a socialist regime in Guatemala, for example, which confiscated land owned by the United Fruit Company and redistributed it to peasants, the CIA trained and supported an insurrectionary force which overthrew the government and installed a military junta. The junta restored the land to United Fruit and began a process of secretly kidnapping, torturing and killing its left-wing opponents (a prelude to the 'disappearances' under US-backed dictators in the 1970s). A CIA operation against Cuba notoriously failed at the Bay of Pigs in 1961, after which Fidel Castro let the Soviet Union defend his country with nuclear-tipped ballistic missiles aimed at Washington and New York. The Cuban Missile Crisis of October 1962 came very close to triggering a third world war in which hundreds of millions would have died in a nuclear holocaust. If President Kennedy had taken the advice of the Pentagon to bomb the Cuban missile sites, provoking retaliation and counter-retaliation between the two superpowers and their European surrogates (NATO and the Warsaw Pact), mutual destruction would have been assured. Civilization would have started again, probably in Tasmania.[1]

So what had happened in the meantime to the systems for protecting human rights so confidently put in place by the UN Charter, which had created an Economic and Social Council with the duty, under Article 68, to establish a commission 'for the promotion of human rights'? This Human Rights Commission met for a few weeks each year, riven by bloc-voting and by the refusal of member states to allow themselves or other members to be criticized. It resolved at its inception in 1947 that it had 'no power to take any action in regard to any complaints concerning human rights' – a resolution which pretty much summed up its impact over the next twenty years. All that was achieved in this period was paperwork – in particular, the paper upon which the two main Covenants were drafted, prior to their presentation to the General Assembly in 1966. It took a further decade for the International Covenant on Civil and Political Rights and the International Covenant on Economic, Social and Cultural Rights to attract ratification from the minimum number of states (thirty-five) to come into operation. The Human Rights Commission for all this time remained tight-lipped about breaches of the Universal Declaration, or the Genocide and Geneva Conventions, by any government which was a member of the UN.

At last, in the 1960s, there appeared a pariah state that the UN could do something about, especially when it withdrew its membership. That state was South Africa, with its system of apartheid which had united the other African countries in condemnation, egged on by the Soviet Union. Drs Verwoerd and Vorster found few defenders in the West at a time when the civil rights movement was forcing the US to take minority rights seriously and when the UK was furious at the white separatists who had declared themselves the minority rulers of Rhodesia. It was in 1960 that South Africa first provoked that horrified international response which is the hallmark of crimes against humanity, when its police massacred sixty-nine peaceful protesters in the black township of Sharpeville. This state was an easy (as well as a proper) target because it had few powerful supporters besides Israel (itself a pariah in Arab eyes). In 1963 other African countries prevailed upon the Security Council to urge a trade boycott, and in 1967 the General Assembly condemned apartheid as a 'crime against humanity', calling for economic sanctions. The Economic and Social Council ordered the Human Rights Commission to make 'a thorough study of situations which reveal a consistent pattern of violations of human rights, as exemplified by the policy of Apartheid as practised in the Republic of South Africa'.[2] For the first time, the prospect of *doing something* about human rights violations was on the agenda of the Human Rights Commission.

There was, comparatively speaking, quite a lot of idealism swirling around the world again in early 1968, when the UN convened a conference in Tehran specifically to review the first twenty years of the Universal Declaration. In the West, much of it was a spill-over from the civil rights movement and protests against the Vietnam War, orchestrated by the 'peace and love' themes that had captured popular music. It helped that China was temporarily out of the power game, in the process of self-devastation at the hands of the Gang of Four. (The Cultural Revolution killed over a million citizens, a matter of human rights that every other country was happy to ignore.) Against this background, the Proclamation of Tehran in May 1968 won unanimous support. Its second principle was portentous:

The Universal Declaration of Human Rights states a common understanding of peoples of the world concerning the inalienable and inviolable rights of all members of the human family and constitutes an obligation for the members of the international community.

Here we go again. Only three months after the Tehran Proclamation, Soviet tanks rolled through Czechoslovakia, to nip the Prague Spring in the bud by replacing the Dubček government with hardline Stalinists. The UN Human Rights Commission did and said nothing. The General Assembly was also useless – an idle forum for diplomats, occasionally galvanized by a set-piece speech from the leader of the US or the USSR (Khrushchev's petulant behaviour in taking off a shoe and banging it on the podium was its most memorable moment). Its most damaging action, for international law, was when it decided to make a unanimous 'Friendly Declaration' in 1970 which became a tyrant's charter:

No State or group of States has the right to intervene, directly or indirectly, for any reason whatever, in the internal or external affairs of any other State. Consequently armed intervention and all other forms of interference or attempted threats against the personality of the State or against its political, economic and cultural elements, are in violation of international law.[3]

The Human Rights Commission had nothing to say about the CIA's provocations in Chile, where the Nixon administration sponsored the military overthrow of a long-standing democracy and its elected leader, Dr Salvador Allende. The century's most vicious human rights violation – the 'disappearance' – followed in the wake of General Pinochet's coup. Although Pinochet only killed about 4,000 in this way, 'Operation Condor' was a conspiracy he masterminded with other military juntas in Latin America to secure the disappearance of left-wingers and liberal elements throughout the region.

During the 1960s, and until the final victory of the North in 1975, Vietnam proved another graveyard for the good intentions of the 1949 Geneva Conventions. It had been America's lamentable mistake to shore up the vicious Catholic dictator Ngo Dinh Diem, whose political perversity led him to offend his religious *majority* by persecuting Buddhist monks, several of whom brought their plight indelibly to world attention by setting themselves alight in front of news photographers. President Johnson began the bombing of North Vietnam in 1964, which in due course visited eighteen million gallons of 'Agent Orange' on forests and rice fields. Napalm was used against villagers – mainly women and small children – suspected of supporting the Vietcong. A few firefight atrocities were brought to account: Lieutenant Calley was convicted over My Lai, although Ernest Medina, who had greater responsibility as his commanding officer, was acquitted. Dr Henry Kissinger recommended the bombing of neutral Cambodia, which only served to rally support behind the Khmer Rouge.[4] Under Pol Pot's guidance, 1.7 million Cambodians (20 per cent of the population) were killed, in a genocidal mania which not only went unpunished, but was actually rewarded by the Khmer Rouge being given a place in the anti-Vietnam coalition supported by the UN at the prompting of Reagan doctrinaires. The move to end the Vietnam War came after America wearied of television pictures of its boys being brought home in bodybags from a country where ragged children ran screaming with the pain of napalm in their eyes and where a police chief could shoot suspects in the head in full view of press photographers.

The behaviour of the superpowers in this era was motivated entirely by national and ideological interests, but some sneaking respect for the idea of international justice required aggression to be dressed in the language of legality. When the US wanted to serve its strategic or economic interests by invading a country, it took care to solicit an 'invitation' first. Makeshift principles were invented: to justify the US invasion of Dominica in 1965, for example, President Johnson declared he was merely enforcing a regional rule that communist governments were incompatible with the Inter-American system. Even more risible was the 'Brezhnev Doctrine' (hastily formulated in 1968 to excuse the invasion of Czechoslovakia) that international socialist law which permitted 'fraternal military assistance' to any country whose socialist system was under threat. This bogus doctrine too could be triggered by a convenient 'request' from any apparatchik in a general's uniform or clinging to a ministerial post. The best that can be said for Cold War law was that superpowers felt obliged to resort to such fictions, covering up as best they could the atrocities committed by their own allies in order to accuse more loudly the other side. Action against

South Africa excepted, it was not until the end of the Vietnam War, and the emergence in Chile of a dictator who was so confident of American support that he would openly resort to mass torture, that some states began to take human rights seriously.

It was largely in response to Pinochet's excesses (see chapter 10) that the General Assembly passed the Declaration Against Torture in 1975, the year which marked the end of the Vietnam War. About this time, also, the modern human rights movement gathered a certain strength, formally through the Helsinki Accords of 1975 in Europe and the entry into force, with thirty-five ratifying states, of the UN's twin Covenants in 1976 and the adoption of human rights as a foreign policy objective by the Carter administration in 1977. In 1976, the Security Council declared that apartheid was 'a grave threat to the peace' and urged states to support the ANC. The following year, it took the unprecedented step of imposing mandatory trade sanctions on South Africa and Rhodesia under Chapter VII of the Charter. At last, one widespread and systematic violation of human rights had been found to justify interference in a state's internal affairs, albeit that the interference amounted only to a ban on trade. The ban was not policed, however, and was easily circumvented by multinational corporations.

It was during this period that the conspicuous courage of individuals in standing up to state abuses began to matter. Andrei Sakharov, for example, gained immense moral stature. This ascetic scientist, one of the 'fathers of the Russian bomb' and hence a respected member of its privileged *nomenklatura*, put principles before preferment by publishing criticisms of Soviet policies and trenchant attacks on the abuse of psychiatry to silence dissidents. His personal clout protected him as he masterfully exploited the media to draw attention to the plight of political prisoners, through hunger strikes and letters to the US Congress urging trade sanctions. Behind the scenes, his courage was deplored by Western diplomats almost as much as by the Soviet government – Kissinger raged that he damaged *détente*. But Sakharov always and steadfastly took his stand on human rights instruments – the Universal Declaration, the Civil Covenant and the Helsinki Final Act.[5] He was the first dissident to demonstrate the counterproductive effect of censorship, through the cachet it gave to his publications in the

West and their consequent popularity when they received a *samizdat* circulation back in Russia. It was noteworthy that Sakharov bypassed the UN system completely, deriding its partisan politics and its 'quiet diplomacy'.

The next valiant figure to emerge was Václav Havel, spokesman for Charter 77, a document prepared by leading Czech intellectuals which argued that their country's ratification of the Civil Covenant imported its 'rights' into municipal law, according to the promises made by parties (including hardline Czechoslovakia) to the Helsinki Agreement. This was to give Helsinki (essentially a rudimentary blueprint for political co-operation between eastern and western Europe) a legal importance it did not possess. Indeed, it was specifically made non-binding so that the Americans could sign it without the Senate's consent and the Soviet Union could agree to human rights in return for a Western promise (equally unenforceable) to respect its borders. What was significant, though, was that appeals of this kind could now gather public momentum by taking such international instruments at their face value, however little intention the diplomats who signed them had of honouring them.

The other important development was that the US, so wary of overseas entanglements, was now prepared to give the Universal Declaration its due, as a force in foreign policy. The Soviet Union responded that 'we will never tolerate interference in our internal affairs', but this formula was becoming frayed. What the entry into force of the twin Covenants had done in 1976 was to make human rights abuses a legitimate subject of international concern. There was growing acceptance of Sakharov's argument, in his 1973 open letter to the US Congress calling for trade sanctions against Russia until it abandoned its policy of refusing Jews the right to emigrate to Israel. Such a sanction, he contended persuasively, 'does not represent interference in the internal affairs of socialist countries, but simply a defence of international law, without which there can be no mutual trust'.

THE HUMAN RIGHTS COMMISSION:
A PERMANENT FAILURE?

Most of the states that belong to the Human Rights Commission have no wish to create precedents for investigations or enforcement procedures which might next be used against an ally, or against themselves. South Africa had been a different matter, however, because the country had few allies and its racism – three million whites suppressing a 17-million black majority – was so egregious. The Commission continued to meet only for a few weeks each year, and to avoid any breath of criticism of states or state rulers, whether of Pol Pot's genocide or of Emperor Bokassa's primitive savagery or of mass murder by Idi Amin. Its votes come in power blocs which play games with each other on west–east, now north–south, divides. At its fifty-first session in April 1995, all Third World country members irresponsibly cast their votes to defeat a resolution critical of Nigeria, despite the military government's overthrow of democracy and its grotesquely unfair treason trials of dissidents like Ken Sara-Wiwa. A few months later, he was executed – by a military command that knew it could get away with murder at the UN's Human Rights Commission.

This commission even lacked the courage, at its 1990 session, to condemn China after the shootings of dissidents in Tiananmen Square. It pretends to work through the 'quiet diplomacy' of its 'Resolution 1503 procedure' which encourages confidential dialogue with representatives of violating states. There is no evidence that this procedure, derided by Sakharov and human rights campaigners, has ever achieved any concrete results, although it has certainly served to protect violating states which make great play of their 'co-operation' with those UN emissaries who parachute in for a few days once the massacre is over. UN 'fact-finding' in such circumstances is superficial and heavily influenced by officials of the host state who 'look after' the emissary and determine whom he meets – usually military commanders, rehearsed prisoners and paid propagandists.

The record of the Human Rights Commission, ever since its initial resolution not to act on human rights violations, has been woeful. It has never taken economic or social rights seriously, and has largely confined itself to studying breaches of civil rights in those countries which lack lobbying influence at the UN – and even with them its responses have been dilatory and ineffectual. The Commission's 'fact-finding' procedures have failed to find the facts which would discomfit powerful member states or their allies. It appointed 'Special Rapporteurs' to report on critical situations, but as Philip Alston (the fairest of the UN's appraisers) concludes, 'the selection of rapporteurs has been a quintessentially political process, the mechanics of which do little to ensure that expertise and competence will be the principle qualities sought . . . the range of people is unduly narrow . . . nominees are usually diplomats, and expertise in human rights law is often not prominent among their attributes'.[6]

This instrumentality of the United Nations is crippled by that organization's instinctive deference to its own members and by its bureaucratic commitment to 'neutrality' in any fact-finding or adjudication. The crucial defect of the Commission is that its members (over fifty of them) are representatives of *governments* rather than appointed as independent experts. They are diplomats, time-servers of states (including military juntas and feudal dictatorships) who regard their part-time job – most representatives are fully employed in departments of their national government – as political rather than judicial. The Commission sits for only six weeks a year and, although it sometimes sends missions to human rights blackspots, it has no power to insist that they can range freely and investigate fully, or even that they should be allowed entry. It cannot take on the superpower violators and equally it cannot tackle the small states which ally themselves for protection to regional or political blocs. Notoriously, the Commission failed to confront Idi Amin over his years of butchery in Uganda: as president of the Organization of African Unity, he mobilized African state support in order to keep his own murders off its agenda. UN members could have agreed to set up an independent appointments body to nominate members of the Commission, but this did not suit the self-interest of governments which were determined from the outset that this commission should be kept under diplomatic control.

A full-time post of Commissioner of Human Rights was created after the Vienna Conference in 1993, but its first occupant was an undistinguished diplomat who refused to criticize any member state. Now an individual of high repute – Mary Robinson – has been recruited, but the Commission still lacks the personnel, powers and procedures to make much impact on violators. The best way forward is to bring non-government organizations (which do most of the real human rights fact-finding) into the appointments process, thereby providing some guarantee that members are true experts in human rights, rather than experts in defending governments accused of violating them. Member states chosen as targets for fact-finding missions should be bound (on peril of Security Council sanctions) to permit entry for as long as necessary for thorough investigation, and to give access to whichever places and prisoners the mission requests. The Human Rights Commission, if ever it can be distanced from UN politicking, could then usefully become an international 'truth commission', conducting examinations of a human rights emergency, with an objectivity and urgent authority that even the best NGOs, like Amnesty, cannot aspire to because their missions have no power to open the doors of prisons and police stations. The Commission's reports could then go quickly to the Security Council, which might decide to intervene under Chapter VII, or refer the report to an international court prosecutor for further investigation if there is evidence of crimes against humanity. This reform will remain utopian until state parties are prepared to give the UN the power to condemn the conduct of its own members, i.e. themselves.

THE CIVIL COVENANT AND ITS HUMAN RIGHTS COMMITTEE

States voting in favour of the Universal Declaration in 1948 did not anticipate for a moment that their vote meant they were assuming any obligation to enforce the rights declared. None the less, Article 28 momentously decreed that 'Everyone is entitled to a social and international order in which the rights and freedoms set forth in this Declaration can be fully realized'. So the General Assembly directed the Human Rights Commission to proceed with the drafting of a treaty which would, upon ratification, oblige states to guarantee human rights to their citizens as part of their domestic law and would set up some mechanism to monitor their progress to this end. The chill winds of the Cold War blew the Commission delegates this way and that, finally splitting along ideological lines over the relative importance of civil and political rights on one hand (favoured by western European and American states) and economic and social rights on the other (which were preferred by communist countries). With what seemed like the wisdom of Solomon, the Commission agreed to prepare a separate covenant for each set of rights, but these were not tabled in the UN until 1966. The General Assembly then expressed the pious hope that the twin Covenants would be 'signed and ratified without delay and come into force at an early date'. That date was set for the time when a mere thirty-five states would ratify them, but this did not happen for an entire decade. Even when they commenced in 1976, they had little superpower support – the US refused to put its money where Jimmy Carter's mouth was (it did not ratify the Civil Rights Covenant until 1992) and states which still, as of 2000, refuse to sign up include Singapore, Saudi Arabia, Malaysia, Bangladesh, Indonesia, Cuba, Burma, Pakistan and Turkey. Far fewer have signed the all-important 'Optional Protocol' to the Civil Rights Covenant, which provides a means by which individual victims of human rights violations may complain to an international body, the Human Rights Committee – established by the Covenant and situated in Geneva. The Economic and Social Covenant provides no such complaints mechanism: member states are supposed to submit five-yearly reports on their 'progress' in guaranteeing second generation rights to a subcommittee of the Economic and Social Council, but by 1996, 143 countries' reports were overdue and the subcommittee had no power to do anything about these defaults.

That these twin Covenants staggered into being at all, thirty years after they were envisaged as the machinery for enforcing the Universal Declaration, owed something to the atrocious brutality of events during those inglorious years: by 1976, most of the ratifying governments were sensitive enough to see that the world could not go on in this fashion, and that one way forward might be to recapture the idealism which had briefly surfaced after the war. National Socialism was aped, in a less extreme but generally vicious form, by apartheid – the one systemic violation of human rights which by this time had united almost every state in public condemnation. Its 'master race' ideology (the black majority were to be treated like children who would never grow up) was harnessed to pervasive discrimination enforced by brutal policing and controlled by a white Afrikaner minority with elders who had, during the war, supported the Nazis. But there was a good deal of hypocrisy about these attacks on South Africa: the Soviet Union was first to sponsor an international Convention on the Suppression and Punishment of the Crime of Apartheid, despite all the dissidents still in its gulags and its own suppression of majorities in satellite states. Black African countries, mired in corruption and brutal 'big man' tyranny, joined in hypocritical condemnation of court systems in South Africa and Rhodesia much fairer than their own. Notwithstanding such double standards, agreement between East and West that apartheid constituted a violation of human rights meant that a consensus could be reached on establishing some institutions to protect them. Hence, in 1969, the Convention on the Elimination of All Forms of Racial Discrimination (proposed, like the twin Covenants, in 1966 but entering into force much more speedily) established a Committee on the Elimination of Racial Discrimination which could, with the consent of a state, receive complaints by individuals. Hence too the eventual ratification of the Civil Covenant, and of the Optional Protocol and its Human Rights Committee. What the evils of fascism inspired in the post-war settlement, it took the evils of apartheid to put back on the global agenda.

The Human Rights Committee (HRC for short) was established under Article 28 of the International Covenant on Civil and Political Rights. Its role is two-fold: (1) to 'study' reports submitted at five-year intervals by state parties and to relay 'general comments' to those states about their performance in promoting human rights; (2) to serve as the body to which individuals or groups may complain against their state if it has signed the Optional Protocol to the Convention – a distinct treaty by which some states indicate their willingness to allow their nationals access to the HRC but not necessarily (as we shall see) to co-operate with the Committee or to implement its adjudications. Although the eighteen members of the HRC serve in theory in their personal capacities rather than as representatives of states, they are, like the members of the Human Rights Commission, none the less nominated by governments which usually make sure that their nominees are 'one of us' – i.e. are fully alive to the importance of state sovereignty and the need to avoid criticism of their nominator and its allies. The HRC should operate, at least when considering individual complaints under the Optional Protocol, as a body composed of experts independent of all countries, but the UN election system does not produce a lot of HRC members in this category. Many are ambassadors, or lawyers serving in government departments, who carry their diplomatic baggage to Geneva and New York for a few weeks of HRC meetings each year.

The Human Rights Committee and the Committee on the Elimination of Racial Discrimination (CERD) were doomed to impotence from their inception, because they had to work within the United Nations system. They are, self-evidently, 'committees' as distinct from courts (which have adversary proceedings ending with judgments in some manner binding on parties). Their operations are circumscribed by diplomatic politesse: they do not receive 'applications' or 'petitions' or 'complaints', they merely get *written communications*. These are not 'analysed' or 'investigated', they *receive consideration*. The government concerned has the allegation *brought to its attention* and must, within a leisurely six months, submit a statement which *clarifies* the matter. The committees do not hold any hearings, in public or indeed at all: they *examine communications* in a closed meeting and in due course, instead of delivering a judgment or decision, they *forward their views* to the government and to the communicant. These excruciating euphemisms need not have prevented the HRC from developing into a powerful, quasi-curial body, delivering well-reasoned and intellectually respectable decisions. But throughout its 20-year history it has become submerged within the UN culture: starved of funds, with eighteen part-time members of variable quality and integrity and a handful of overworked staff, its 'views' tend to be brief, poorly argued opinions on the facts, excessively deferential to states and quick to take refuge in technicalities as a way to avoid adverse decisions. No one who has visited its offices in a nondescript UN building in Geneva (until 1994 it did not even have a fax machine) could possibly think of it as an enforcer of any universal bill of rights.

Such significance as the Committee's decisions (sorry, 'views') may have is due to factors outside its control. For example, the time it takes to form 'views' on 'communications' from Caribbean death rows may save a communicant's life – but that is thanks to the Privy Council ruling in *Pratt and Morgan* v. *Jamaica* to the effect that undue appellate delay prevents imposition of the death penalty (see pp. 137–40). Ironically, the HRC has itself refused to adopt this principle, which has saved hundreds of lives in the British Commonwealth – an example of how street-ignorant HRC members are about lives on death row and the expedients necessary to preserve them. Judges on the European Court and the Privy Council hold (and psychiatrists agree) that leaving men on death row more than five years amounts to inhumane treatment, but the HRC finds no inhumanity in keeping men there for eleven years – or even longer, should a state so choose.[7] Judgments like this show that the majority of members of the Human Rights Committee are out of touch with human rights.

The HRC has served a useful purpose in a few cases where federal governments make use of its 'views' as a basis for taking action against their own regressive provincial legislatures, as when the HRC held that freedom of expression of English-speaking Quebecois was violated when that province passed a law forcing them to advertise in the French language.[8] Similarly, in the *Toonen Case*,[9] the federal government of Australia was able to abolish the criminalization of homosexual conduct in its least enlightened state, Tasmania, by reference to the 'view' of the HRC that this was an unreasonable measure not excused by its pretended object of curbing the spread of AIDS/HIV. The Committee did act in this case like a court, delivering an important and well-argued decision that the covenant right not to be discriminated against on grounds of sex included sexual orientation. This provides a rare example of how the HRC might, if cut loose from the diplomatic apron strings of the UN, function genuinely to advance the cause of human rights. But it provides that example only because the decision against Australia was actually encouraged and supported by Australia itself, embarrassed by the homophobic Tasmanians. Had Toonen been a Malaysian or a Cuban, the decision would have been different (in fact, since those states have not accepted the Optional Protocol, there would have been no decision at all).

The HRC, CERD and several other obscurely acronymed UN organs have another familiar function: to 'monitor progress' by receiving reports at regular intervals – every five years or so – from state parties. This at least provides a public occasion at which state representatives – often minor diplomatic functionaries rather than government ministers – are politely questioned about their reports which claim, usually falsely, that great progress is being made in protecting or extending the covenanted rights. There is no grilling, or any form of cross-examination: questions are very often parried by the delegate promising to find out the answer in order to reply later in writing. But the occasion does provide non-government organizations like Amnesty and Human Rights Watch with the opportunity to brief sympathetic committee members (under the UN election system, not all members of the Human Rights Committee have been sympathetic to human rights) and to focus public attention on a country's real failings.[10] This slight value is diminished by two aspects of the UN's own culture. In the first place, the HRC strives to avoid any criticism in its reports of the states whose records it has considered: Article 40 of the Covenant permits it only to make 'such general comments as it may consider appropriate', which it generally takes to mean uncritical and unspecific comments couched in weasel words (the most appalling violations are noted with 'regret' or 'disappointment' or an 'expression of deep concern'). Since 1992 it has become slightly more effective by calling for additional 'emergency' reports and by adopting 'conclusions' about country reports, although these are stated only where there is consensus on the committee.[11] There is a worrying trend within the UN bureaucracy to 'coach' diplomats of states which have bad human rights records on how to dress them up for public consumption at HRC meetings. Recently, a 'human rights reporting manual' made its appearance – ostensibly to encourage more states to accept the Optional Protocol, but doing so by seeking to persuade them that it holds no real terrors provided their human rights 'problems' are expressed in UN-appropriate language.

The glaring weakness of the UN committee system of state reports and individual communications is that many states which violate the human rights of their citizens are not parties to the Covenant or have not ratified the Optional Protocol permitting individuals to communicate with the Committee. Among Optional Protocol refuseniks are superpowers America and China, and even Britain, which boasts of its 'ethical' foreign policy. Many states which are party to the Optional Protocol simply ignore the Committee: in recent cases, Libya, Peru and the Central African Republic have not bothered to reply to its letters. Equatorial Guinea told the HRC in effect to get lost when it asked why an opposition MP was abducted and tortured by security forces over a period of eighteen months: this very inquiry, apparently, constituted an 'interference into domestic affairs of Equatorial Guinea'.[12] It is the old story: countries like Canada and Australia, which on the whole value human rights and co-operate with UN organs, can utilize the HRC, elevating its 'views' into decisions which strengthen their hand against provincial legislatures if they pass laws which discriminate against minorities. But countries which care nothing for human rights can quite brazenly ignore the HRC, or simply remain outside the voluntary covenant system. There is no 'universality' about this human rights system, even among its own signatories. The extent of the HRC's failure is starkly illustrated by the paucity of its customers: only 160 communications were registered in the three years 1986–9; 143 between 1989 and 1992; and a miserable total of 131 between 1992 and 1995. The HRC, like the European and the Inter-American commissions, requires individuals to exhaust any local remedies before writing to it, but the receipt of the grand total of 645 letters (more than half of which were later withdrawn or declared inadmissible) over a period of nine years shows how little the HRC really does to help victims. In most cases, it cannot help: over this same period, the Committee expressed 154 'views' which were opposed to state practice: a follow-up study showed that in only 15 per cent of cases did the defaulting state implement the HRC's views or offer any remedy to the applicant.[13] The Covenant assumes that complaints will be made by one state against another, but dog does not eat dog at the UN: not a single inter-state complaint has been made since the system came into operation in 1979.

The deficiencies in the UN committee system are due to the endemic failure of that organization to allow for criticisms of its own members.

If the 'views' of the HRC are ever to be accorded respect, the following structural problems will have to be overcome:

(1) The HRC is meant to be comprised of eighteen 'experts', but UN election procedures ensure that many are government mouthpieces (some being actually *in* government service, as cabinet ministers or ambassadors) or else owe their 'expertise' to *defending* governments. Some members are reasonably independent academics or judges, but few, if any, have acted for victims. As one long-serving member writes (delicately), appointment depends on 'the lobbying effectiveness of the nominee's country's representatives at the UN, bloc voting and general diplomatic bargaining . . . as a result, a high premium is not always placed on those individual qualities which are most important, such as competence'.[14]

(2) The HRC only meets three times a year, and CERD twice, for three-week sessions. The idea that nine weeks a year is a satisfactory commitment to monitoring and problem-solving under the Covenant is risible.

(3) The HRC holds no 'hearings' and makes no provision for oral applications or adversary proceedings. Everything is done on paper, very slowly, without the benefit of live witness testimony or cross-examination.

(4) The HRC is entirely dependent on the UN Secretariat in terms of structure, budget and status. It is not a quasi-judicial body, much less a court: most accurately, it is a UN 'organ' which goes out of its way to avoid criticizing UN members.

(5) The Civil Rights Convenant concerns the duties of states towards individuals, not the rights of individuals against states. The HRC cannot compel or even pressure states to do these duties – most violators stay outside it, or refuse to sign the Optional Protocol or (if they do) refuse none the less to co-operate with the HRC.

(6) The HRC and other UN committees lack any independent fact-finding capacity. Not only do they have no investigative powers, resources or personnel, but they cannot even make visits to alleged crime scenes or call for relevant documents or cross-examine witnesses and experts. This is a crippling weakness for the HRC, which makes its monitoring role ineffective (unless assisted by

NGOs) and leaves it to find facts on the basis of written communications, which in many cases is not possible. It has access, of course, to fact-finding reports by the Human Rights Commission, but these (as we have seen) are limited and inadequate.

(7) The HRC work goes largely unreported and all but 650-odd victims of human rights violations around the world (1986–95) have apparently never heard of it. That is partly because its proceedings are closed and its files remain confidential and its 'views', when published, are often not worth reading, in the sense that they usually lack detailed reasoning.

(8) It has no power to enforce its 'views', which states frequently ignore. Indeed, sometimes death row prisoners are targeted for execution precisely because they have written to the HRC – they, and their letters, are dead on arrival.

These problems of the HRC are endemic to CERD and all other UN bodies established to 'monitor compliance' with human rights conventions. Those oversight committees have no power to call to account states which neglect or refuse to submit reports. Non-compliance is endemic – in 1995, CERD complained that no less than 358 reports, due over the years from its 122 members, had never been received.[15] The Convention on the Elimination of All Forms of Discrimination against Women (1981) has a committee which is permitted to meet only for two weeks a year to discuss state reports; the Economic and Social Covenant also has a 'committee of experts' which is permitted a third week each year in which to discuss state compliance. These periods are ridiculously short, and inevitably much of the consideration is superficial. The Convention Against Torture, which came into force in 1987, adopts the same processes as the HRC (i.e. state reports every five years and receipt of 'communications' from individuals), although the committee established under it does, anomalously but invaluably, have power to investigate on its own initiative in cases where it receives 'reliable information which appears to it to contain well-founded indications that torture is being systematically practised in the territory of a State party'. This is, of course, an optional provision in an optional treaty: states which systematically deploy torture (seventy-three, at the last count) do not sign the Convention or, if they do, refuse to subject themselves to investigation. The UN system cannot, by its very nature, offer satisfactory methods of enforcing human rights, because it cannot compel violating states to join its protocols. Should they do so, the UN's methods for 'monitoring' performance give little confidence that this would expose violations or lead to greater obedience to the rules of international human rights law.

SOME ENFORCEMENT AT LAST: THE EUROPEAN CONVENTION, AND OTHER REGIONS

Although the United Nations dropped the human rights baton soon after the Universal Declaration, it was picked up by the Council of Europe, a body which co-ordinated the dozen democracies in that region which were determined to resist the spread of communism. In 1950 it promulgated the European Convention on Human Rights, which combined the civil liberties articles in the Universal Declaration with fair trial principles drawn from English common law. Its preamble describes the Convention as one of 'the first steps for the collective enforcement of certain rights stated in the Universal Declaration', although it turned out, for many years, to be the only step. It was real progress, none the less, and a marked improvement on the Declaration in terms of a clearer definition of the rights of suspects, habeas corpus and the requirements for fair trial, although the rights to freedom of speech and assembly and privacy were hedged by numerous exceptions and qualifications. It established a commission which could refer cases for final decision to a court, sitting in Strasbourg: state signatories to the Convention had a duty, in the event of any adverse judgment, to change their law to bring it into conformity with the Convention. This was revolutionary enough – the first time in history that states were prepared to give an external court a treaty power to *require* changes in their domestic legislation – but there was a provision more revolutionary still. Under Article 25 of the European Convention, 'any person, non-governmental organization or group' could petition the Commission alleging a violation of their rights, and if the Commission agreed with them it could bring their case before the European Court. States which accepted this 'right of individual petition' would in effect be giving their citizens the opportunity to bring them – or their own law and their own court decisions – before the bar of international justice.

The European Convention was something of a marvel at the time – 1953 – when it entered into force as a legal bulwark against the resurgence of fascism and as an articulation of the civil rights which were being threatened by communist regimes in eastern Europe. However, it took several decades before the European Court made its presence felt, largely because governments delayed in accepting Article 25 and refused to complain about each other (the only exceptions were cases brought by Ireland against the UK over 'in-depth interrogation', by several Scandinavian countries against Greece under the Colonels, and over torture in Turkey and UK dominion over Cyprus). After the mid-1970s, however, the court at Strasbourg grew in business and in reputation, so much so that it was besieged after 1989 by newly liberated eastern European states clamouring to be admitted as members. It now lays down quite sophisticated human rights standards for forty-one nations, from Iceland to Turkey and from Latvia to Malta, through well-reasoned decisions which have made governments change domestic laws in all these countries. Governments can formally 'derogate' from the Convention rather than accept an adverse decision; however, compliance is normal and the quality of the human rights law emerging from the Court's new Richard Rogers-designed building in Strasbourg is relatively high. Crucially, if negatively, its success may be due to the fact that it has no connection whatsoever with the United Nations.

What has made the European Court stand head and shoulders above any UN or other regional arrangement is the simple fact that adverse decisions are implemented, under supervision. State parties comply (albeit sometimes not quickly enough) with its rulings, even though they generally require legislation or some restructuring of the domestic legal system. It has now become a constitutional court for the whole continent. That does not, of course, mean that its decisions have always been correct or its approach beyond reproach. Under a coward's cloak called 'the margin of appreciation', this court has often dodged controversial issues by leaving them to the discretion allowed to states to protect their own values and traditions. This tendency has been particularly marked in questions of morality, where a pronounced Catholic bias in the appointed judges has led to several poorly reasoned rulings that censorship of anti-Catholic plays and films are within state 'margins of appreciation'. The Court has wrongly refused to strike down blasphemy laws in the UK and Austria, although such laws are the cause of serious human rights violations in Iran (the Salman Rushdie fatwah) and Bangladesh.[16] However, it has been prepared to extend a degree of tolerance to homosexuals, at least in countries where there is no 'large body of opinion hostile or intolerant towards homosexual acts committed in private between consenting adults'[17] – an unsatisfactory rationale which would allow sodomy to remain a crime in Malaysia or Iran or the southern states of the USA. The whole point of human rights law is to protect innocent minorities against malevolent prejudice, and the 'margin of appreciation' doctrine, appropriate for cases where there are harmless cultural differences, should not be erected into a shield for majority oppression. Outside the area of morals, however, the doctrine has been given a narrower application, and the Court has been much more rigorous in protecting the rights of suspects – even of terrorist suspects.

The European Court of Human Rights has become the model human rights court, proof positive that international law can work to enforce fundamental freedoms across a swathe of countries with some differences in culture and tradition. This court's decisions have seeped into the domestic jurisdictions of all its client countries, as every one of its original member governments has made changes in its laws for the benefit of groups such as immigrants, transvestites, prisoners and mental patients – reforms which would not have been sufficiently vote-winning in the absence of a decision from Strasbourg. Despite periods of unpopularity with particular governments, the Court has won substantial respect and support, and in 1998 the Council of Europe re-established it on an expanded and improved basis. It now has a permanent and properly salaried judiciary, unlike any of the UN commissions and committees. The 'filter' device of the European Commission has been replaced by a two-tier system in which cases are heard first by a chamber of seven judges and then –

if the legal point is important – may go on appeal to a 'grand chamber'. It is hoped that this will redress a problem largely caused by the Court's success – namely the delay (up to six years) in receiving its final judgment.

A more far-sighted reform would have been for each state to acknowledge and establish the European Court as the court of final appeal within its own judicial system. This, however, was much too dramatic a ceding of sovereignty for even the most tolerant European governments to contemplate, although it is a logical step to be taken in the future. Unfortunately, the 1998 Council of Europe reforms retain one irritating feature of international justice which is simply not just. This is the practice of having a judge from the 'defendant' state sit on every hearing and appeal as a full voting member of the court. This is a blatant breach of the rule against bias since justice cannot be seen to be done by a judge who is there to look after the defendant's interests. It provides a much clearer case of bias than appeared in *Ex parte Pinochet (No. 2)*, where a judge's connection with Amnesty International was held to disqualify him from sitting in a case where Amnesty was presenting argument.[18] The official reason for the practice was to reassure nervous governments that the court would have at least one sympathetic member who would know about the domestic legal system, but this is no longer a necessary political expedient. There have been some abject examples of the 'state party judge' defending his indefensible state (when the UK was held in breach for permitting the caning of juvenile delinquents, for example, the English judge dissented on the grounds that his own beatings at Eton had done him a power of good). By adopting this uncalled-for deference to state sovereignty (which is also to be found at the International Court of Justice) the European Court is in every case in presumptive breach of the European Convention's own guarantee of an 'independent and impartial court'. Even more objectionable is the rule that when a grand chamber is convened for what is in effect an appeal from a first chamber of seven, both the president of the first chamber *and* the national judge will sit on the grand chamber. This is an unprincipled measure – how can a judge sit on an appeal from himself? – and can only detract from the standing of the Court.

*

There are other regional arrangements outside the United Nations which purport to offer a measure of legal protection of human rights for subscribing countries within their geographical area. There is an Inter-American system, with a convention (1969), a commission (in Washington DC) and a court (sited in Costa Rica), which covers many Latin American and Caribbean members of the Organization of American States (OAS). There is also an African Charter on Human and Peoples' Rights (1981), with a commission to monitor and to receive complaints about its breach which is headquartered in Banjul in the Gambia and is financed and supervised by the Organization of African Unity. There have been occasional human rights initiatives by the forty-eight states comprising the British Commonwealth – sixteen of which accept the jurisdiction of the Privy Council, which comprises judges from the supreme UK court, the House of Lords. There is no external or regional system for Arab countries, however, or for countries in any part of Asia, and the old 'regionalism versus globalism' debate now seems particularly arid: since there is no effective global system, regional arrangements are much to be encouraged if they work. The European Court and the Privy Council do work, because their judgments have power to bind governments. The Inter-American system is patchy, but better than nothing, while the African Commission is pathetic. This varied performance has little to do with the core documents: the Inter-American Convention is, if anything, a slight improvement on the text of the European Convention, and both concentrate on the civil liberties protected by the overlapping UN Convention on Civil and Political Rights. The African Charter is worthy of note because it includes 'third generation' rights (e.g. to development) and counterbalances individual rights with 'people's duties' to African society and culture, and to its often corrupt and authoritarian governments. The dangers inherent in this charter can be exaggerated, however, because nobody, including the Organization of African Unity, seems interested in enforcing it, although the establishment of an African human rights court is now in progress.

The Inter-American system, however, has had some signal successes. Its commission, operating from Washington (the US is a signatory to the treaty although hypocritically it does not accept the jurisdiction of the Commission or the Court), conducted a number of expert on-site investigations into disappearances and atrocities in the military dictatorships of Latin America in the late 1970s and 1980s. To some extent its work was more political than legal, providing authoritative fact-finding reports which did something to galvanize international opinion against the worst offenders. It had a relatively small and cohesive composition of seven members, with staff well funded by the Carter administration. (There were cut-backs under Reagan, whose support for right-wing regimes in the region was undermined by the Commission's work.) It has been criticized for ignoring individual petitions, but at the time its role as a hemispheric accusatory agency, collecting and publicizing evidence against military dictators or their corrupt judges, was more valuable.[19] When Latin American countries began their transition to democracy, the Commission concentrated on finding legal ways of invalidating or sidestepping the amnesties and immunities which the Generals exacted for themselves and their henchmen as the price of giving up power. Much of its work is now directed to delaying executions of petitioners on death row in those Caribbean countries which adhere to the Inter-American Convention.

The Commission also serves as a filter for the Inter-American Court, which has (like its European equivalent in Strasbourg) treaty powers to require state parties to change their laws. Individuals have no direct right of access, but their cases may be taken up by the Commission which appears as a party on their behalf, although curiously a political rivalry between the two bodies has disinclined the Commission to make many referrals. This is regrettable, since the seven-person court has boasted some fine jurists, like the American Thomas Buergenthal and the Costa Rican Sonia Sotela, and the comparatively few judgments it has given have signally contributed to the development of human rights law. One of the first, in 1985, was a decision that requiring journalists to join a government-controlled association as a condition of practising their craft was an infringement of freedom of expression – a ruling which demolished a misguided UNESCO initiative to encourage government 'licensing' of journalists.[20] Then came the notable *Velasquez Rodriguez Case*, breaking new ground by ordering a government to pay reparations to the family of a young man 'disappeared' by the military in Honduras (see pp. 251–3). Needless to say, the Court would gain enormously in workload and prestige were the United States to ratify the Inter-American Convention and accept its jurisdiction – an unlikely event, given both the Senate's traditional refusal to bow to international judgment and America's fondness for the death penalty, which is not shared by the Court.

The African Charter deserves a final word, if only to explain why it has become a sad joke for a continent where some of the world's worst atrocities have been committed since the Charter came into force promising 'third generation' rights to peace, development and a satisfactory environment. The first draft, by a distinguished Senegalese judge, Kéba Mbaye, was no doubt a worthy attempt to fuse statements of individual liberty with cultural duties believed to be distinctly African (such as the duty 'to respect parents at all times, to maintain them in case of need'). However, the Charter became the creature of the Organization of African Unity, a rabidly political organization which has been dominated by some of the worst violators of human rights, such as Mengistu, Barre, Mobutu and Idi Amin (whose barbaric rule in Uganda no member state except Tanzania had the decency even to criticize). The OAU, ironically for all its commitment to anti-colonialism, has as its central concern the maintenance of Africa's old colonial borders, drawn haphazardly in the nineteenth century, and has mindlessly opposed any form of intervention in the internal affairs of states ruled by one party, or one man. Thus, the preamble to the Charter promises the elimination of 'neo-colonialism' and 'Zionism', while the duties of the African are 'to serve his national community by placing his physical and intellectual abilities at its service . . . not to compromise the security of the state whose national or resident he is . . . to preserve and strengthen social and national solidarity . . . and the territorial integrity of his country'. These are all euphemisms for the duty to follow the leader, whose 'law' circumscribes all the individual 'rights' and 'freedoms' which are sonorously declared. Thus, under Article 10 (1), 'Every individual shall have the right to free association provided that he abides by the law' – and if the law bans all but one political party, that's too bad for freedom of association. Similarly, Article 9 (2) reads, 'Every individual shall have the right to express and disseminate his opinions within the law' – and if the law prohibits any criticism of the ruler, that's perfectly all right according to the African Charter on Human and Peoples' Rights, which might more honestly have been entitled the African Charter for Keeping Rulers in Power.

The African Commission, with eleven members nominated by the OAU, has the task of promoting and applying the Charter through devices familiar from the HRC: receiving and discussing state reports, and expressing opinions on individual communications. It has no enforcement power, and no court to take on its cases: its reports go in secret to the OAU, because its complaints process is confidential. Its members are not independent of their governments – several have been serving attorneys-general. Its meetings – for a week or so twice or thrice a year – are always disorganized and often verge on the absurd. At one session in 1994, for example, three state reports were to be examined, but two of the states forgot to send a delegation and the third sent a junior official who was not authorized to answer any questions. At the 1996 sessions, half the states due to be examined about their reports did not bother to turn up, while those that did found that their reports had not been translated, so some members could not understand them. A delegate from Mozambique arrived to present a seven-page report written four years before: he could not comprehend questions in English, and no one understood his Portuguese. 'We requested translation but none was available, and so he attempted to proceed in French, a language with which the delegates were not familiar.'[21] At this slapstick session, it emerged that none of the missions which had been planned – to human rights 'black spots' like Nigeria, Sudan, Rwanda, Zaire and Mauritania – had ever taken place, and the Special Reporter on Extra-Judicial Executions (who doubled as the Tunisian ambassador) had done nothing for two years. But he could not be criticized to his face, since he had not bothered to attend.

The Commission is such a farce largely because it is under the thumb of a political organization even more jealous of state sovereignty than the UN. The OAU keeps the Commission starved of funds; its work is unknown in Africa and if it were known would be greeted with derision. By the end of 1998, it had a backlog of 200 state reports which were overdue: eighteen of its members had never bothered to submit even their first country report. It does issue brief opinions on 'communications' received from individuals and organizations, but usually years later when condemnation of state behaviour can be safely expressed because the misbehaving government has fallen. This is a motive for its delay in some cases, but the reason for delay in almost all is that governments are not bound to respond to its inquiries within any time period, and tardiness is endemic. Thus, in June 1989, serious complaints were made about indefinite detention, torture and unfair trials in Zaire. Nine months later the Commission got around to asking Zaire to reply, but for the next three and a half years it failed to respond, despite repeated requests. In September 1993, Zaire finally bothered to send a letter to the Commission's office in Banjul, claiming it had received none of the previous communications. Six months later (March 1994), the Commission wrote again, this time even sending its letter by registered post, but no response was forthcoming. More than one year later, in March 1995, the Commission declared the communication 'admissible' and in October – six years after it had been received – it 'drew to the attention' of the OAU heads of state its solemn conclusion that *if* the facts alleged by the complainants were true then they would constitute serious violations of the Charter.[22] It is difficult to know which body – Zaire or the Commission – is more at fault for the six-year delay, but cases like this show the African system up in its true light, as the hollowest of pretences. In 1999, the OAU decided to establish an African Court of Human Rights, but its failure to revise the Charter or to vouchsafe the new court any real power and independence means that it is likely to become as empty a gesture as the African Commission.

REALPOLITIK RULES OK

Notwithstanding the UN's failure to develop effective systems for the protection of human rights following the Universal Declaration of 1948, and the hypocrisy that attended diplomatic conferences and convenants on the subject throughout the 1970s, the cause has been advanced by victims throughout the world (in particular in Russia and eastern Europe), emboldened by such events as the Carter initiative, the Helsinki process and the Civil Covenant. Amnesty International, founded as recently as 1961, began to gather members in large numbers who reached out to victims through letter-writing campaigns aimed at their oppressors. Human rights was on the news agenda, and it is impossible to underestimate the importance of CNN, which in 1980 began satellite transmission across most state borders of atrocity pictures which do so much to arouse feelings of anger or solidarity. The struggle for human rights began to succeed in the 1980s, not because its rules were enforced, but because they existed and were better known and it was widely accepted that they *should* be enforced. Charter 77 and Solidarity and the refuseniks in Russia could not appeal to a court, but they could and did appeal to the new inter-state agreements which pretended to lay down international law; they turned them into a petard with which to hoist violator state signatories.

The world was still full of atrocities. In Africa, the CIA supported Holden Roberto in Angola, who armed small children with AK-47s, while the KGB backed Colonel Mengistu in Ethiopia, a tyrant even bloodier than Idi Amin (who, helped to power by MI6, was responsible for 75,000 deaths in Uganda). It seemed that their crimes against humanity would go unpunished, as part of the latitude allowed to sovereign states to go to hell in their own way, or at least in a way condoned by their superpower protectors. Something could be done, however, if a state was exceptionally small and its behaviour very bizarre. That was the case with Grenada in 1983, when government politicians on the tiny island (population 60,000) went berserk and killed their leader, Maurice Bishop, his pregnant partner and some of their supporters. America invaded, arrested the killers and in due course restored democracy. It did the right thing for the wrong reason, however: in the twisted thinking of the time, the US justified its action not as humanitarian intervention but as action against a communist threat (which Grenada did not constitute) and to save a 'campus' of pampered US medical students, whose lives were not at risk. It was typical that the US was almost universally condemned – even by Mrs Thatcher, Reagan's most uncritical supporter – for daring to invade the sovereignty of a state, despite the fact that the state in question was smaller than most city suburbs and temporarily governed by crazy political killers. Human rights still had nothing to say to governments, even those which devoured their own members.

That this attitude started to change in the 1980s was one consequence of the communications revolution, which showed to citizens in the West, and increasingly in the East, pictures which moved them to pity, and then to anger, about the inability of politicians to stop state-sponsored killings. It helped, too, that human rights had become the rallying cry of dissidents like Sakharov and Havel, oppressed under the dying dogmas of communism. Some were put on trial, at which they exuded a dignified defiance (so different from the old show trial confessions), after which they were jailed for a few years, since even Stalinist states no longer dared provoke an international outcry by executing them. Maybe it is a mistake to characterize the revolutions in eastern Europe in 1989 as a triumph for human rights rather than a result of the demand for higher living standards through free market reforms, but the heady rhetoric of freedom from censorship and secret policing and rigged justice certainly provided some of the inspiration for the movement that rolled up the Iron Curtain and brought down the Berlin Wall. It had been censorship, after all, which had kept even the politburos in ignorance of their financial as well as their moral bankruptcy, and it was in recognition of their economic helplessness, rather than any shame over their civil rights violations, that old communists voluntarily left the stage. Yet the bitterness of the break-up of the Soviet Union was not explained by communism's economic failure or a resurgence of ethnic pride – it was a legacy of hatred towards Moscow caused by all those decades of Stalinist repression. The revolt against Russia by the Baltic states and Central Asia illustrates one feature of crimes against humanity, namely their historical tendency to return to haunt and destroy the state that perpetrates them.

The progress towards making human rights the political slogan of our time – an apotheosis of the New World Order scheduled for celebration at the UN's Vienna Conference in 1993 – was not without its ironies. For example, one early target of the human rights movement had been the Shah of Iran, a corrupt and despotic ruler whose secret police (SAVAK) was renowned for its sophisticated torture techniques. Satisfaction at the Shah's popular overthrow in 1979 turned quickly to horror at the barbarities committed in the name of religion by his successor, the Ayatollah Khomeini, who fanned the fanatical flames of Muslim extremism which pose the greatest contemporary threat to human rights. Muslim extremism was much assisted by the Reagan administration, not only by its arms sales through Irangate but by the massive logistical and financial support it gave to the Mujahidin in Afghanistan, transmogrifying in due course into the Taliban and Osmara Bin Laden.

Members of the vicious military juntas in Latin America took their ill-gotten gains into retirement along with their amnesties against prosecution for murder and torture, but democracy in Nicaragua, after the Sandinista movement overthrew the Somoza dictatorship, was something Washington refused to abide. Not only did it train and supply the Contra rebels, but it showed contempt for international law by having the US navy lay mines outside Nicaraguan ports and assist attacks on harbours, oil installations and naval bases. When Nicaragua brought the US before the International Court of Justice, the US argued at first that the Court had no jurisdiction. When that argument was lost, it ungraciously walked out, announcing that it would not be bound by any decision that did not suit the interests of America. Then it withdrew its agreement under the Optional Clause, so that it could not be forced before the Court again. This arrogant attitude did not seem to matter to Cold War allies at the time, but when it resurfaced in 1997 at Ottawa (where America refused to sign the convention banning anti-personnel land mines), and at Rome in 1998 (where the US voted against the creation of an International Criminal Court), they were sorely displeased. The nation with the most to offer the human rights movement in the twenty-first century will, it appears, do so only on the strict condition that other countries are the targets.

That will be one major problem for the future. Then there is China, which chose to begin the last year of the twentieth century by jailing for the next decade its leading pro-democracy protesters, only a matter of months after it had thrilled human rights bureaucrats at the UN by ratifying the Civil Covenant. It had shown its true colours by joining with the US as the other superpower at Rome to veto the idea of an international tribunal to bring perpetrators of crimes against humanity to justice. That, no doubt, was because the category would surely include Premier Li Peng and his military commanders who in

June 1989 gave tank commanders the orders to shoot unarmed student protesters massing in Tiananmen Square. Hundreds were killed, and the media brought the wrenching horror of the massacre into homes around the world. Not so much as a squeak of protest was heard from the UN Human Rights Commission, but so strong was international revulsion that smaller states and their militias began to realize that they could no longer behave in the same way. In the squares of eastern Europe a few months later, demonstrators were spared deadly attack. After, and as a result of, Tiananmen Square, the British Parliament hastily vouchsafed Hong Kong a bill of rights, before the hand-over to China.

There were no television cameras in the streets of Halabja in the same year, when Saddam Hussein's troops gassed the Kurdish population, killing 8,000 with an improved derivative of Zyklon-B, the gas used in Nazi concentration camps and now, by obscene irony, supplied to Iraq by German chemical companies. The rush to do business with Iraq's megalomanic dictator brought trade ministers from the governments of Britain, France, Germany and Italy at the head of commercial delegations out to make a killing: they supplied him with arms and arms-making equipment in such abandon that he was genuinely surprised when they objected to his using them for the invasion of Kuwait. However, this was a crime against state sovereignty, and the Security Council, for the first time since Korea, decided upon armed intervention against a country which had lost all superpower support. Western public opinion, which was not much moved by the sight of corrupt Kuwaiti princes forced into five-star hotels, had to be galvanized by human rights images, especially a vivid (and completely false) story, propagated by the Hill & Knowlton advertising agency, of Iraqi troops throwing babies out of incubators in the maternity wing of a Kuwaiti hospital. 'Operation Desert Storm' carried all before it, until President Bush, out of kneejerk respect for state sovereignty (even Iraq's), halted General Schwarzkopf's yomp towards Baghdad. A great deal of pain and provocation would have been avoided had the allies taken the city, captured Saddam and put him on trial. There were ample precedents – the war crimes and 'crimes against humanity' defined at Nuremberg, not to mention common Article 3 of the 1949 Geneva Convention. But there was no international court to try Saddam Hussein, and no sensible thought was given to setting up an *ad hoc* tribunal for this purpose. It was over the next nine years that Saddam would make his great contribution to international justice, by providing evidence through his own recalcitrant behaviour of the need for a world criminal court.

In America, there was euphoria at the triumph of 'Desert Storm': the television picture of the first helicopter to land on the roof of the American embassy in Kuwait was the reverse image of that shameful footage of the last helicopter scuttling from the roof of the American embassy in Saigon. Another New World Order was announced by President Bush, in which human rights would be accorded a central place. The United Nations planned a jamboree in Vienna for June 1993, at which all states would celebrate alongside representatives from the 800 non-government organizations by now active in the human rights cause.

But 1993 was not, as it turned out, a good year for human rights. The new belief that 'something must be done' had already persuaded the UN to intervene in Somalia, at the insistence of President Bush, once American public feeling had been aroused by shocking television pictures of the atrocities committed by its feudal warlords during a famine of biblical proportions. At first, the 25,000 UN peacekeepers of 'Operation Restore Hope' were welcomed as saviours, but soon they were perceived as the enemy when they made the mistake of taking sides in the civil war – in this case, against the Mogadishu warlord General Aidid. His followers were responsible for ambushing a UN contingent and killing two dozen Pakistani soldiers, after which the UN forces became more concerned with capturing and punishing Aidid than with stopping the civil war or the famine.

Meanwhile, at the UN World Conference in Vienna, the lipservice paid to human rights began to curl. From the strong men of Asia and the old men of Africa came a new and unsettling refrain: 'human rights' was an invention of Western liberalism which had little to offer countries whose values derived from tribal wisdom or other communal traditions, or which were poor and politically vulnerable. Led by China, Malaysia, Indonesia and Singapore, Asian countries caucused and then came to Vienna with their own declaration: that 'universal' human rights must evolve to accommodate 'the significance of national and regional peculiarities and various historical, cultural and religious backgrounds'. To this demand the UN diplomats in Vienna surrendered – such talk-fests must be seen to end happily, however deep the cracks which the final declaration has to paper over. That declaration, at the insistence of the Asian bloc, made no reference at all to the Civil Covenant, or to individual rights such as freedom of speech and freedom of assembly (ironically, the very rights that the people of Indonesia and Malaysia exercised five years later to bring down Suharto and protest against Mahathir). The Vienna 'Declaration of Principles' was on its surface a solemn reaffirmation of the universality of human rights, but nobody was fooled: the anodyne 'action programme' showed very clearly that state sovereignty would go into the New World Order undented. The conference itself veered between shambles and sham: the governments of the world for ten days conducted an unrealistic and abstract discussion, in which under UN rules no state (apart from former Yugoslavia) was allowed to be mentioned by name as a place of human rights violations. Beneath the conference hall, some 9,000 representatives of the 800 NGOs which attended bickered among themselves and protested their virtual exclusion from the conference agenda. The true tone of the event was set when China insisted that the Dalai Lama, invited by the host state (Austria) to address the conference, should be barred from entering the hall.

There was worse to come. 'Operation Restore Hope' became 'Operation Abandon Hope' when, on 3 October 1993, a mission to capture Aidid went disastrously wrong, leaving US casualties – 18 dead and 84 wounded – and abiding images of the dismembered and dishonoured body of a young American helicopter pilot dragged by celebrating savages through dusty streets. President Clinton ordered the troops home – more pictures of the last helicopters leaving, once again, a country abandoned in an even greater mess than it was in when they touched down. This was symbolism that no US administration could risk again: the voting public could not stand the sight of bodybags. The 'Mogadishu factor' entered American calculations at every level thereafter, and explains why the Clinton administration withheld US forces from Bosnia for the next two years and ordered that Serbia and Kosovo be bombed from a height that ensured both the safety of US pilots and the deaths of hundreds of innocents below them.

As 'ethnic cleansing' re-emerged in Europe, the Security Council reached for a dramatic and almost desperate alternative: it used its Chapter VII powers to create an International Criminal Court in 1993 to punish crimes against humanity committed in the territory formerly known as Yugoslavia. The threat of international justice, rather than international armed intervention, deterred the Bosnian Serb commanders only for a few months. The fighting claimed up to a quarter of a million lives before the first trial – of Bosnian Serb torturer Duško Tadić – began in 1996. For the Security Council, paralysed by the Mogadishu factor, the invocation of international criminal law was a last resort. But the gambit seemed to work, at least in convincing a sceptical world that the UN was prepared to do something about genocide. This was a false impression, as its next disaster, Rwanda, demonstrated. There, a long history of fighting between the Hutu majority (85 per cent of the population) and the Tutsi minority culminated in a ceasefire agreement in August 1993, overseen by troops (mainly Belgian) from UNAMIR (United Nations Assistance Mission for Rwanda). A particular concern, so the Commission on Human Rights was told that month by its Special Rapporteur, was the danger of genocidal attacks against Tutsis by extremist Hutu elements in the army and the presidential guard, who were being organized into a new military force (the Interhamwe – 'those who attack together'). Despite more reports implicating the French-backed Hutu government in plans for genocide, the General Assembly proceeded to elect it to a seat on the Security Council. Armscour of South Africa supplied it with weapons, as did the French, whose diplomats must have known of the genocide preparations. In January 1994, the UN commanders on the spot received reliable information (from mercenaries training the Interhamwe) that the object of the training was to assassinate leading Tutsis and moderate Hutu politicians and judges, and commence a systematic slaughter of Tutsis. The Canadian generals heading UNAMIR sent details to the peacekeeper-in-chief at the UN, Kofi Annan, who refused their urgent request for permission to intervene.[23]

Three months later, the cue for the genocide to begin came when the Hutu extremists shot down the presidential plane: gangs armed with machine guns, machetes and nail-sprouting clubs roamed the capital killing Tutsis at random. The UN in New York was notified of the genocide while the numbers of dead were still in five figures: it did nothing. The Security Council, on which the genocidal government was represented, went repeatedly into secret session over the next twelve weeks, cowering over the Mogadishu factor which prevented action as the death toll mounted to more than 800,000. The behaviour of the major states – all signatories to the Genocide Convention – over these three months was quite extraordinary. The Clinton administration, supported to the hilt by the British Foreign Office (under John Major's government), insisted that this was 'black on black' violence in which the West should not intervene. Their diplomats refused to describe the killings as genocide: they were merely 'tribal hatred' and 'a breakdown of the ceasefire agreement'. An independent commission headed by Bengt Carlsson later condemned UN officials for failing to act despite knowledge of the impending holocaust, and accused Britain and the US of refusing to acknowledge the killings as genocide in order to avoid their obligations under the Genocide Convention. (The only members of the Security Council who cared were New Zealand and the Czech Republic; the rest voted with America to pretend that the genocide was not happening.)[24] The Belgian government had a fit of cowardice after ten of its peacekeepers were killed: against the wisdom of its own commanders on the ground, it ordered the withdrawal of all its troops, despite the fact that they alone were guarding 'safe havens' for Tutsi refugees. Thousands of refugees were massacred when their UN 'protectors' fled. The French, with the finest of racist sensibilities, landed in force but only to save their white expatriates, with their dogs and other household pets: their household Tutsi servants were left behind to be slaughtered. A few weeks into the slaughter, just as it was escalating, the UN Security Council decided to pull out almost all its troops. The ensuing blood-bath in April and May 1994 left churches and rivers full of corpses:

If we consider that probably around 800,000 people were slaughtered during that short period . . . the daily killing rate was at least five times that of the Nazi death camps.[25]

After such knowledge, what forgiveness? President Clinton visited Rwanda in 1998 to apologize for turning his back on genocide, but the case against the diplomats (the representatives of the major powers in the Security Council, the government of Belgium and the UN Secretary-General and his peacekeeping officers) was negligence at best, and at worst complicity in the most barbaric genocide since Cambodia. By July 1994, the expatriate Tutsi army (the Rwandan Patriotic Front) had invaded and was in control of most of the country but was competing with a UN-sanctioned French expedition ('Operation Turquoise') which operated to protect French interests and save many Hutu génocidaires from retribution. Hutus – most of them very willing executioners of Tutsis – fled to mass camps in Zaire, to the delight of President Mobutu who siphoned a large proportion of the international aid into his Swiss bank accounts. These camps, supported by the UN and private charities, became breeding grounds for 'Hutu power': they were run by the Interhamwe, who used them as a base for attacks on genocide survivors who might testify – an exercise they called 'killing the evidence'.[26]

Rwanda marked an all-time low for the UN, and at every level. Not only had the Security Council turned a blind eye to genocide, but its troops on the ground had been morally responsible for some of the murders – many leading Tutsis declined to flee, relying on a UNAMIR promise of protection which (in the case of the Belgian troops) had been broken in the most cowardly circumstances. The most appalling incident involved the Rwandan Chief Justice, Joseph Kovaruganda, who was being guarded by a UNAMIR detachment from Ghana. These soldiers physically handed him over to a Hutu death squad from the presidential guard, then stood laughing and drinking with his killers while they assaulted his wife and two young daughters. This incident was confirmed by the Carlsson inquiry, which reported in December 1999 on how 'the United Nations failed the people of Rwanda'. The failure was so abject that, at least in the cases of the Belgian and Ghanaian detachments, it amounted to assisting with genocide. The UN itself can hardly remain immune from legal action when it becomes complicit in a crime against humanity, and the Chief Justice's relatives are bringing an action against it for compensation.

The UN needed a figleaf for its failure. The idea of a war crimes tribunal, which had received good publicity the year before and quietened the UN's human rights critics, had returned to the agenda.

In November, six months after the killings stopped, the Security Council decided once again to invoke its Chapter VII powers to establish an international court to punish the authors of the Rwandan genocide: it would be an offshoot of the Hague Tribunal, sitting principally in Arusha (in Tanzania) but sharing the prosecutor and the appeals chamber being established in The Hague. This time China abstained, and one non-permanent member of the Security Council voted against the proposal. This state was Rwanda itself, now Tutsi-governed. Its objection was that the tribunal would not have power to execute the Hutu extremists it convicted. Some who were caught by the Rwandan Patriotic Front were summarily tried and then shot by firing squads in public, before the first proceedings in the UN court in Arusha got under way. Its prosecutors, in the course of their investigations of the genocide, came across confidential communications between the UNAMIR generals and UN headquarters in New York which suggested that many of the 800,000 lost lives could have been saved had UN officials and the Security Council acted at the outset as if the Genocide Convention meant what it said.

THE SREBRENICA QUESTION

Once it was the bombing of Guernica, captured in all its barbarism and terror in Picasso's painting, that epitomized a crime against humanity. This has been superseded by the fall of Srebrenica, in July 1995, when 7,000 Muslim men and boys were executed by General Mladić's Bosnian Serb army and 23,000 elderly men, women and children were transported. This particular exercise in 'ethnic cleansing' needs no artist for its *frisson*: that is provided by the astonishing fact that this rankest of crimes was committed under the noses of the UN's 'Blue Helmets', and in some respects with their complicity. NATO commanders deliberately decided not to save this 'safe haven' by deploying aerial bombardment, although Security Council Resolution 819 charged them with taking 'the necessary measures, including the use of force' to protect it from attack. The fall of Srebrenica exemplifies the dangers of a fashionable human rights policy when it is decreed by states unwilling to lose a single life in its enforcement. The men of Srebrenica were caught in a human rights death trap, sacrificed to the good intentions of cowardly countries.

To state this does not detract from the prime responsibility of the Bosnian Serb commanders, who planned the massacre down to the last truck needed to transport the men – civilians and soldiers – to their mass graves. Their attack on the town was in aggressive defiance of international law. By executing prisoners-of-war, they committed a war crime in breach of the Geneva Convention. By executing civilians, the crime was against humanity as well as the Geneva Convention. As the siege intensified, General Mladić was pictured on the hill overlooking Srebrenica. He turned to his tame Serb TV crews, and emoted: 'Remember that tomorrow is the anniversary of our uprising against the Turks. The time has now come to take revenge on the Muslims.'[27] His deliberate destruction of a community on ethnic and religious grounds counted palpably as genocide. It matters not how Srebrenica is characterized, because it was the worst war crime committed in Europe since the fall of Hitler – and it was committed several years *after* the United Nations had established the Hague Tribunal as a means of deterring exactly such offences.

Did Srebrenica, then, signal the futility of expecting the prospect of punishment to deter those hellbent on committing crimes against humanity?

This is an important question, but it must be remembered that by the time of the massacre – July 1995 – the Hague Tribunal was still very much a paper tiger. The intercept evidence which proves that the idea actually frightened the Bosnian Serb leaders when the tribunal was first mooted in August 1992 (and this fear seems to have contributed to a lull in the fighting) shows that insouciance quickly returned to their headquarters as the tribunal stumbled and delayed and failed to get itself off the ground. By July 1995, it had only one prisoner, a footsoldier named Duško Tadić, whom it had yet to put on trial. Its very impotence may have convinced Mladić that he could breach international criminal law so blatantly and barbarically, and avoid punishment.

In the racially jumbled geography of Bosnia, Srebrenica was a

Muslim city surrounded by predominantly Serbian countryside. It might have made sense to surrender it to Serbia with guarantees (that was the Vance–Owen plan) or even – since guarantees were often dishonoured – to transport its entire population to safety, but by 1993 this would have been an unconscionable reward to the Serbs for their brutality. Instead, at the suggestion of the Red Cross, the city was one of those declared a 'safe area' by Security Council Resolution 819, passed in April 1993 – a promise to its people that international law and, 'if necessary', international forces would protect them. To fulfil this promise, the UN correctly assessed the need for 34,000 soldiers on the ground, but none of its members stepped forward to offer troops. Eventually, some 7,400 were mustered for six enclaves (sarcastically referred to as 'safe areas lite'). Srebrenica was vouchsafed a Dutch battalion, the Netherlands being one of the few countries idealistic enough to send troops to patrol the safe areas, and naive enough not to recognize the absurdity of sending a 'peacekeeping' force to a place where there was no peace to keep.

The Dutch troops' task was doomed from the start, but it is instructive to ask why simple defeat was allowed to become a disgrace. The insufficiency of numbers, of course, meant that they simply cowered when the Serb attack came, and watched apologetically during the subsequent preparations for 'ethnic cleansing' by evacuation and massacre.[28] But their very presence prevented the UN from taking the one action which would have saved the town and honoured the promise of Resolution 819: ordering NATO air strikes to halt the Serb advance. The fear that Dutch soldiers would become hostages and that the battalion might suffer casualties caused the Dutch government (and the UN representative on the ground) to veto the essential air strikes. Unhindered, Mladić's army took the town and put into operation a carefully planned exercise in which males of arms-bearing age were separated from their families and, within sight of the Dutch 'peacekeepers', taken away ostensibly to be 'screened' for complicity in war crimes but in fact to be carted off to fields where they were killed, then buried in mass graves which have now yielded corpses with hands tied behind backs, shot from behind. The scenario is common in ethnic war: what made this massacre so horrific is that the international community stood back and allowed it to happen, as the price for protecting the peacekeepers who were there protecting the victims. The Dutch troops received heroes' welcomes on their return to the Netherlands a week after the massacre, a celebration of the fact that they were 'safe' which appeared grotesque precisely because those to whom they had promised safety had been left behind, in mass graves. The politicians who had sent these soldiers and the generals who had commanded them imposed a rule of silence which served to cover up not only their acquiescence in the genocide, but (for some months) the fact of the genocide itself. As one history of this appalling incident concluded, 'in hindsight, the Dutch failure to speak out after they left the enclave was worse than their conduct during the Serb offensive'.[29]

Srebrenica was allowed to happen because of the Mogadishu factor: states intervening from humanitarian motives refused to risk the lives of their own soldiers to make that intervention effective. The case can be put more bluntly: Western European governments preferred to dishonour promises and to allow Muslims to die in their thousands rather than to suffer one more Dutch casualty. (The loss of a Blue Helmet at the outset of the Serb attack triggered a chain reaction of national funk.) The same reaction had happened in Belgium the previous year, when its army was 'peacekeeping' in Rwanda: it failed to take action which might have prevented massacre (e.g. by closing down the radio stations which were inciting the Hutus to genocidal attacks on the Tutsi and by sending tanks against the killers on the streets). This would have been to 'take sides', stepping down from the fence on which UN peacekeeping missions can get impaled. Like the Dutch battalion in Srebrenica, the Belgians watched the massacre, and then withdrew as soon as they began to suffer casualties.

Both the Dutch and the Belgians were morally guilty for making a fashionable gesture of sending soldiers under the impossible condition that they should not be required to fight. But the problem was more fundamental: it stemmed from the diplomatic mindset that assumed peace could be secured without justice. If the UN is to protect a city or a people, it must have a clear idea of who it is protecting them from, and treat these aggressors as the enemy. Soldiers must be sent to fight, and politicians at home must be prepared for soldiers to die, in the cause of protecting the innocent (or at least the people promised protection) from attack. There is little doubt that General Mladić, a cunning calculator of odds, would have retreated under aerial bombardment and would not (at least for long) have provoked the international community by holding Blue Helmets hostage. But he knew his enemy's weaknesses: a Dutch public desperately opposed to sacrifice and a United Nations which wanted and needed him to talk about peace. The UN diplomat responsible, along with the Dutch defence minister, for vetoing air strikes was UN Special Representative for Bosnia, Yasushi Akashi: he defended his conduct on the grounds that 'the man you bomb today is the same man whose co-operation you may require tomorrow for the passage of a humanitarian convoy'.[30] This is a very good reason for leaving humanitarian assistance to the Red Cross while the UN decides which men are in the wrong and have to be bombed. The writer Michael Ignatieff confronted the UN Secretary-General as Srebrenica was falling: 'Why,' he asked, 'insist on being neutral in the face of a clear aggressor and a clear victim, when that neutrality daily undermines the UN's moral credit?' Boutros Boutros-Ghali could only reply: 'We are not able to intervene on one side. The mandate does not allow it.'[31] Until mandates to keep the peace are interpreted by the UN as mandates to fight aggressor factions, if this is the only way the peace can be kept and genocide prevented, there will be many more Srebrenicas, and (much worse) more Rwandas. Or else there will be more unilateral humanitarian enforcement action, such as NATO's intervention in Serbia over Kosovo.

Five years on, the cries from the mass graves still being excavated around Srebrenica are more haunting than ever, as war crimes prosecutors gather further evidence to incriminate the Serb commanders and to shame the Dutch army and the UN. The most moving scenes were recorded on private camcorders, the grainy images of Muslim men and boys huddled in fields, surrounded by soldiers who wait impatiently to shoot them come nightfall. The most incriminating footage comes from Serbian television: it shows Mladić toying with the lives of his terrified hostages, and blowing lies and cigarette smoke into the face of the pathetic Dutch commander, Colonel Karremans. This soldier is seen disgracing his country and his calling by accepting drink and gifts from Mladić – in return for handing over thousands of Muslims who had sought refuge in their UN compound. This was the moral nadir reached by UN peacekeeping, rivalling the behaviour of the Belgian and Ghanaian 'peacekeepers' in Rwanda who handed over the Tutsis they were meant to be guarding to Interhamwe hit squads. It was this complicity in the slaughter which provoked a bleak joke about UN peacekeeping: 'If the UN had been around in 1939, we would all be speaking German.'

3

The Rights of Humankind

The last quarter of the twentieth century witnessed a struggle between the human rights movement and its enemies (especially the diplomats) over whether the great promises made in the Universal Declaration should be recognized as having the force of international law. The battle was joined in 1976, when the twin Covenants became operational, one guaranteeing the 'liberty rights' the Universal Declaration promised to individuals *vis-à-vis* the State, the other proclaiming communal or 'fraternity' rights which were generally perceived as unenforceable aspirations, i.e. policy goals to be encouraged but not imposed on a sovereign state by any external court of the kind which might adjudicate infringements of liberty. This easy distinction is untenable, but the Civil Covenant has helped to delineate certain 'liberty rights' which can be said to have crystallized into rules of international law. A human rights principle which achieves this status has a real force in most municipal courts and before international tribunals: in the case of the most fundamental 'physical safety' rights, their widespread and systematic breach further counts as a crime against humanity. Human rights principles which have not become part of 'customary' (i.e. binding) international law (even though they are found in treaties and are accepted by some municipal courts) remain ethically attractive, but states are under no legal obligation to honour them.

'Law', in common parlance, means a rule which (unlike a rule of ethics) is actually capable of enforcement through institutions created for that purpose. But 'law' in the phrase 'international law' does not automatically have this quality: it has no police force or bailiffs, and its courts lack the capacity to punish for contempt or for disobedience to their orders. If a rule attains the status of customary international law it will be enforced by national courts (if it is not contrary to the constitution or to local statutes). At its mundane level, international law comprises treaties between two or more sovereign states which operate more in the observance than the breach because states generally find it convenient to keep the promises they exchange with other states. Treaties which facilitate trade and commerce are usually adhered to, whether between two states or 120, and when disputes arise then the decisions of an agreed arbitrator are honoured, so international law relating to the air or the sea or the Antarctic can be stated with some confidence. But the international law of human rights is grounded on treaties like the twin Covenants, by which states solemnly undertake to treat their own nationals according to certain civilized standards. If they break the undertaking, very little can be done by other states: this would interfere with 'sovereignty', which is the most essential quality of a 'state' in international law. As we shall see, this throws up an acute paradox. A human rights rule may be crystal clear from a treaty signed by the great majority of states, but whether it counts as customary international law depends largely on whether states believe it should normally be honoured in practice. If the rule against torture, or in favour of free speech, is regularly flouted by many states, can that rule be meaningfully described as 'law'? That must depend on whether the possibility exists (however rarely it may be taken) of calling the government which disobeys it to account.

The purpose of this chapter is to enumerate the 'liberty rights' of the Universal Declaration as they are reflected and extended by the International Covenant on Civil and Political Rights (the Civil Covenant) and to identify those which have become so generally accepted as to have international legal force when asserted by or on behalf of individuals. It is first necessary to explain how an interplay of factors can turn a 'right' declared in a treaty into a 'law' which is binding internationally, and not just on states which are party to the treaty. Given the uncertainties of the crystallization process, this exercise is something of an act of faith. Many overoptimistic international lawyers argue that everything in the Universal Declaration is by now part of international law, but this is the sort of wishful thinking that has made international human rights law such a fatuous academic exercise. If human rights are to have the force of law in the twenty-first century, we must abandon these norms of the imagination (which guarantee sophisticated rights to hundreds of millions of women and children who have no hope of possessing them) and concentrate on consolidating, and above all enforcing, the elemental rules which have already ripened into rules of international law.

MAKING HUMAN RIGHTS RULE: THE INTERNATIONAL LAW PARADOX

There are dozens of overlapping human rights treaties, signed and ratified by most countries. The Universal Declaration is now truly universal, in the sense that almost every country is a member of its declaratory body, the UN. Its offshoots, the twin Covenants, have (as of March 2000) been ratified by over 140 countries in the world. Treaties such as the twin Covenants do not become part of municipal law when the state *signs* them – this is an act which has no real legal significance. What matters is the subsequent act of *ratification*, the formal act by its executive government by which the state agrees to be bound. The position in some countries (including France and Spain and their former colonies in Africa and Latin America) is that ratification *automatically* incorporates the treaty as part of the national law. It is, for these so-called 'monist' nations, a very serious act with an immediate legal consequence. In Britain (and Commonwealth 'dualist' countries), however, ratification is an executive decision which has no effect unless the elected parliament subsequently passes legislation to *incorporate* the treaty into its body of local law. The position in America is more complicated: the executive (i.e. the President) may sign a treaty, but ratification – his act, which gives effect to it – must first be approved by a two-thirds majority in the Senate. The President may then 'proclaim' the treaty, which will thereafter override any inconsistent state or federal laws, although not the US constitution itself. This to some extent explains the poor US record on ratification of human rights treaties: the requirement of a two-thirds Senate majority means that any party political division will kill it. The position in both (and most) countries is that, save for 'self-executing' treaties which are framed to take effect directly upon ratification (usually by granting specific rights to a class of persons, such as aliens, or those deprived of property by another state party), the rules of international law, whether derived from treaty or custom or state practice, depend for their implementation upon national law, i.e. local implementing legislation and court decisions. Once this action has been taken, the US courts, like those in Britain, will be bound (by their own case law, or particular statutes) to apply 'the law of nations', and will have to decide whether a particular human rights principle has entered customary international law.

The point at which a human right becomes part of customary international law depends upon creative interplay between a number of factors. Everyone agrees upon the identification of those factors: they are authoritatively enumerated in Article 38 (1) of the Statute of the International Court of Justice, which enjoins that court to apply, in deciding inter-state disputes,

(a) international conventions, whether general or particular, establishing rules expressly recognized by the contesting States;

(b) international custom, as evidence of a general practice accepted as law;

(c) the general principles of law recognized by civilized nations;

(d) subsidiary means for determining rules of law, judicial decisions and the teachings of the most highly qualified publicists of the various nations.

The classic example of the interplay of these factors is the decision of the US Supreme Court in 1900 to award compensation to Cuban fishermen whose boat flying the Spanish flag, the *Paquete Habana*, had been destroyed by the US navy in the course of its war with Spain. The exemption of fishing vessels from capture as a prize of war was described as 'an ancient usage among civilized nations, beginning centuries ago, and *gradually ripening into* [my italics] a (settled) rule of international law'.[1] This 'ripening' process was assisted by a consistent exemption the court detected over the centuries – in treaties between leading nations, in decisions of prize courts in other countries and in the opinions of distinguished textbook writers. But what mattered most was that the exemption appeared to have been made by most states (originally as a matter of mercy or courtesy rather than law) and was now the invariable practice of *civilized* states. The natural law origins of this 'right reason' approach are manifest: at a time when war could still be regarded as a gentlemanly affair, a rule could 'ripen' into law if it was soundly based in both decency (the court referred to 'considerations of humanity to a poor and industrious order of men') and expedience (the next reference was to 'the mutual convenience of fishing vessels'). It is a nice case, which resulted in the poor but industrious Cubans being compensated by the US navy, but there was a vigorous dissent from a minority of judges who thought the exemption no more than a common act of mercy from which no legal right (and certainly not one against the US government) could mature. What happens if a principle recognized by *civilized* nations is not generally or customarily accepted as law by states which are, or wish to retain the option to be, uncivilized?

This is always the problem in reposing much faith in the so-called 'norms' of international law as a means of puncturing state sovereignty. No matter how persuasively 'right reason' calls for abolition or restriction of the death penalty, or prohibition of anti-personnel land mines, or an end to discrimination against women, it comes up against determined state practice: thousands of executions in countries around the world; a refusal by the United States to sign the Ottawa Agreement; the dictates of Sharia law in Islamic nations. It is not, however, a futile exercise to discover how many human rights rules have 'ripened' into rules of international law: this accords them a status which domestic courts must respect (and in some cases, apply) and it makes their breach a matter of international moment, possibly even engaging the Chapter VII enforcement powers of the Security Council. For this reason, a closer look at the four crystallizing factors is required.

INTERNATIONAL CONVENTIONS AND TREATIES

If a rule is contained in a treaty, the strength of the presumption that it is part of customary international law will vary with the number of states which are party to that treaty. There are 185 states within the UN system, and all subscribe to the Charter, the 'constitution' of world government. The Universal Declaration of Human Rights is not a treaty, but the Civil Covenant has 144 parties signatories – making its rules *prima facie* candidates for the 'universal' status of international law. Treaties which are accepted by less than half the nations of the world, such as the Optional Protocol on the Abolition of the Death Penalty (a mere thirty-six parties), cannot for that very reason be considered as serious candidates for the status. The test, incidentally, is not whether a state has signed a treaty, but whether it has agreed to be bound by it through the process known as ratification. A further complication comes from the fact that states are permitted to make reservations to their acceptance of a treaty, and subsequently to derogate from some aspect of it: these qualifications, if widely shared, will undermine the claim of the qualified rule to be part of international law. The strength of claims to customary status which can be made by the major human rights treaties, as of March 2000, may be gauged from the table of ratifications set out in appendix C.

CUSTOM AND STATE PRACTICE

The existence of an obligation in a human rights convention is not definitive: since many states in practice ignore the duties they pledge themselves to respect, an international law rule must show a high level of compliance – as evidenced by government statements, diplomatic correspondence, support for UN resolutions and, most importantly of all, actual behaviour. Given the stark difference between what governments say and what governments do, this is a particularly slippery balance: how can there be an international law against torture when all too many governments allow armies and police forces to inflict it upon prisoners? As so often in the chimerical world of international law, this problem is overcome with the help of Latin phrases. 'Custom' in customary international law is made up of state practice (what governments have done and intend to keep on doing) on the one hand, and on the other what is termed the *opinio juris*, i.e. what governments feel they are obliged to do (even if, in practice, they do the opposite). This is the way international lawyers solve the paradox of having a rule against torture in a world where many states permit it: these states lie and hide it and pretend it doesn't exist *because they know it's wrong,* so it's contrary to the received wisdom, the *opinio juris.* And if their moral (or, more probably, psychological) sense of obligation is strong enough to amount to an imperative, then it forms part of the *jus cogens,* i.e. one of the rules defined by Article 53 of the Vienna Convention on the Law of Treaties as 'accepted and recognized by the international community of States as a whole from which no derogation is permitted'. In other words – other Latin words – it gives rise to an *erga omnes* duty, owed to the whole international community. In a much-celebrated definition offered (in passing) by the International Court of Justice in the *Barcelona Traction Case,*

such *erga omnes* obligations derive, for example, in contemporary international law, from the outlawing of acts of aggression, and of genocide, as also from the principles and rules concerning the basic rights of the human person, including protection from slavery and racial discrimination.[2]

An *opinio juris* which becomes accepted as part of the *jus cogens* has a dynamite quality which invalidates any conflicting treaty: it becomes in international law-speak 'a peremptory norm from which no derogation is permitted'. This is all very well but, as a leading textbook remarks, 'more authority exists for the category of *"jus cogens"* than exists for its particular content'.[3] The ICJ in the *Barcelona Traction Case* did not condescend to define 'the basic rights of the human person' that can be included, other than the right to be free from genocide, race discrimination and slavery. This is a start, but not much of a start: the point about most human rights rules is not that governments believe them to be legally binding, it is that governments honestly believe they are not *legally* binding but that breaches are so prone to outrage world opinion that they should be hidden or, if exposed, defended on legal technicalities. But in so far as it has become common for accused states to deny human rights violations with legalistic arguments (e.g. 'psychological pressure' is not torture) without objecting to the human rights principle *per se* (that torture is always wrong), it might be said that they acquiesce in a rule of customary international law that prohibits torture. Thus the law against widespread and systematic torture belongs to this elusive body of especially powerful human rights rules, the breach of which within a state elevates its conduct from an 'internal affair' to an affront to global conscience which the world may intervene to prevent or even to punish.

PRINCIPLES OF LAW RECOGNIZED BY CIVILIZED NATIONS

Principles of law which are recognized and unanimously applied in efficient legal systems are strong candidates for international law status. The importance of providing criminal suspects with a fair trial, for example, is now universally recognized, although civilized nations may differ on whether 'fairness' requires a judge or a jury, or an adversarial or inquisitorial proceeding. There is a tendency in the ICJ to reach for this source of law only when treaties and custom are silent, or simply to confirm instinctive general principles such as the overriding importance of 'good faith', but it need not be a subsidiary source or a last resort. It was used creatively by the Permanent Court of International Justice between the wars to establish in international law the rule against expropriation of private property without compensation (see the *Chorzów Factory Case*, p. 120) and the duty of a new sovereign to honour private rights acquired under the old (the *German Settlers in Poland Case*). The very fact that most constitutions of civilized states now incorporate bills of rights which recognize many of the civil liberties in the Universal Declaration provides a powerful argument that these liberties have 'ripened' into international law. The work of identifying these principles is being done by the International Law Commission, an offshoot of the Human Rights Commission: it operates on the basis that *jus cogens* rules (i.e. those accepted by the international community as a whole) do not require universal agreement, but rather the agreement of a preponderant and sufficiently representative body of states.[4]

JUDICIAL DECISIONS AND TEXTBOOKS

These are recognized as 'subsidiary' sources, and for good reason: they are myriad, confusing and sometimes conflicting. A clear ICJ decision, although binding only on parties to the dispute, will have some force, as will decisions of the European Court of Human Rights and the Inter-American Court, and judgments by the Privy Council and respected national supreme courts. These decisions may influence international law under three conditions:

(1) if they exhibit a striking unanimity of approach to the same question, or
(2) if a particular decision has won widespread respect, either for its epic quality (e.g. the Nuremberg judgment) or for its statement of a new and subsequently accepted principle (e.g. that of compensating victims of crimes against humanity, in the *Velasquez Rodriguez Case*) or
(3) because of the power and persuasiveness of the actual opinion, even if the result is not widely accepted (e.g. the US Supreme Court ruling in *New York Times* v. *Sullivan*).

Textbook writers (the term used is 'publicists') come with caveats: those most venerated, from Grotius in the seventeenth century to Sir Hersch Lauterpacht immediately after the Second World War, have contributed to the theory of an international legal order at times when it barely existed or was rudimentary by comparison with the present day. Their opinions sometimes foreshadow a shift from diplomacy to law, but their optimism can do little to effect it: during the twentieth century, the writer who most accurately described state practice throughout its course remained Machiavelli.

State practice has been the most potent, and has become the most problematic, source of international law. It may be gleaned not only from national legislation and domestic court decisions, but also from such politicized examples of government conduct as diplomatic exchanges, policy statements, executive decisions, prime ministerial outbursts and press releases on foreign affairs. This 'practice' reflects the interests of the particular state – often, the interests of its ruling party – rather than the interests of international justice. Drawing 'law' from the conglomeration of such usages will not necessarily produce rules which are fair and just. The problem is exacerbated by the fact that the other major source of international law – treaties – is in effect state practice writ large, since treaties require ratification by governments. So international law's development has been crucially dependent upon the consent of states, as evidenced by their practice and their treaty commitments, with little contribution from court decisions or juristic writings, or even the generally acknowledged principles of justice and equity. Indeed, Article 38(2) of the ICJ Charter specifically restricts the right of the world court to decide *ex aequo et bono* (i.e. by reference to its own determination of what is just and right) to cases in which all parties have agreed to this course. Thus does the shibboleth of state consent haunt every stage in international law-creation, except where pariah states object to a rule agreed by a great and representative majority of other states (thus apartheid violated an emerging norm of international law, notwithstanding South Africa's objections). The problem is that states rarely consent, genuinely and voluntarily, to external limits on their power over their own people. So the paradox of international law, from a human rights perspective, is that it remains under the thumb of the very entities it seeks to control: state conduct determines its creation, and states effectively monopolize appointments of their representatives to its adjudicative bodies. Even the International Law Commission, charged with drafting international legal rules, has most of its thirty-four members drawn from diplomats or state government legal departments, rather than appointed on merit as distinguished academic or practising lawyers. Human rights must challenge international law to move in a less state-oriented direction, which means that the commissions and courts which develop and apply international human rights rules must henceforth do so by reference to what is right and good, rather than to what states have done in the past in their selfish national interests.

Customary international law is in the human rights field anachronistic, to the extent that it is an emanation of agreements between sovereign states. It has only recently been applied to individuals, and it has yet to bind transnational corporations, some of which are wealthier and more powerful than many sovereign states. One of its primary modern sources is found in the responses of millions of ordinary men and women, and of the non-government organizations which many of them support, to the human rights abuses they see on the television screen in their living rooms. These people do not talk about *jus cogens* and *erga omnes*: they believe in the simple language of the Universal Declaration, and they are not bound by Article 2(7) of the UN Charter to avert their eyes from repression in foreign countries. The sight affects them, in a literal sense: it makes them sad and angry, it makes them shield the eyes of their children and it makes them feel diminished to be a member of a race that can act so barbarously. These citizens, of global society rather than nation state, cannot understand why human rights rules should not rule because they are just and right, irrespective of state practice.

But, for the present, international law comes courtesy of nation states if it comes at all. There is no parliament to pass it, since the General Assembly is hopelessly unrepresentative – one vote for Antigua (population 60,000) and one vote for India (population 936 million) – and the Security Council is often poleaxed by the superpower veto. The International Court of Justice, at its gothic building in The Hague, is not permitted to become a Supreme Court for Humankind: it can only decide a case between states, and then only when a defendant state agrees to accept its jurisdiction; even so, it has no power to require compliance with its judgments. State parties to its statute number an impressive 187, but only sixty have agreed to accept its compulsory jurisdiction. Superpowers often treat it with contempt: in 1974 France disdained to appear to answer a case brought by Australia over nuclear testing in the Pacific and in 1984 the United States walked out of the case brought against it by Nicaragua, announcing that it would not comply with any ICJ decision unless it suited US interests. Both France and the US, after these discomfits, revoked their automatic consent to be made a party to any case in the world court. China and Russia have never given that consent, so Britain is left as the only permanent member of the Security Council with sufficient faith in international law to accept automatically the ICJ jurisdiction. This truculence explains why the Court's impact has not been much felt in the human rights area: less powerful states have been reluctant, on the 'dog does not eat dog' principle, to accuse other governments of violations. Unless it is empowered, by an amendment to the UN Charter, to hear cases brought by NGOs or an independent Human Rights Commissioner, the ICJ will remain of marginal significance, notwithstanding its potential. To realize it, the four superpowers will have to be brought within its jurisdiction since their refusal to submit to the court process (unless it suits their interests) fatally weakens the whole system.

In sum, international law 'reflects first and foremost the basic state-oriented character of world politics',[5] because it is a system created and controlled by sovereign states, for their convenience. It still talks, illogically, of violation of 'state rights', when it is *human* rights that are being violated. Some of its classic doctrines – sovereign and diplomatic immunity, non-intervention in internal affairs, non-compulsory submission to the ICJ, equality of voting in the General Assembly – continue to damage the human rights cause. Nevertheless, the incantations of *jus cogens* and *opinio juris* may turn out in time to be abracadabras which open, if only a crack, the doors of state sovereignty. For example, although resolutions of the General Assembly (which now strongly favour human rights) are not binding or even acknowledged as sources of customary international law, recent ICJ decisions have admitted them as evidence of *opinio juris*. By such devices, progressive claims – such as the rights of women and children – may be advanced more forcefully. The importance of customary international law is that it filters through into national law: most municipal systems have procedural and interpretative rules which permit notice to be taken in their courts of international law when it is not in direct conflict with local law. Some common law systems, including the British and American, accept customary international law as part of that common law, although treaties must be incorporated by specific legislation before they can have any direct legal effect. Even here, however, they can have an indirect effect on statutory construction: in democracies, courts must favour that interpretation of a statute which accords with an international treaty, because of the presumption that 'Parliament does not intend to act in breach of international law, including therein specific treaty obligations'.[6]

At the beginning of the twenty-first century, international law remains subordinate and subservient to state power, which tends to favour economic, political or military interests whenever they conflict with those of justice. That said, *realpolitiking* these days must take human rights into account, if only because CNN viewers cast votes and NGOs in the area attract considerable funding and popular appeal. Machiavelli's Prince is no longer Kissinger's Nixon: he must be seen to worship occasionally at the human rights altar, to say 'sorry' for past violations and to justify any present violations by reference to the exceptions and defences provided by international law. Abusive exercising of state power is becoming harder to hide and easier to condemn and the legal theory that human rights can be subjugated to 'state rights' is being recognized as a dangerous fiction. For these reasons, it is important to enumerate those rights of human-kind which can, at the turn of the twenty-first century, tentatively be said to have emerged from the Universal Declaration into the pantheon of customary international law.

THE STATUTE OF LIBERTY

The rights of humankind now accepted as universal have to do with individual freedoms from a) wanton state infliction of death and torture; b) arbitrary arrest and unfair trial; and c) unreasonable interference with choice of religion, opinion and associates. These liberties may be classified in different ways, but on any view they are designed to keep the State at a distance, to ring-fence every adult from interference with his body or his mind, until a defined point at which social dangerousness justifies intervention. These liberties are expressed negatively, as justiciable rights against the State, i.e. the government and all its agencies. Normally it will be the State itself that is the violator, through police or army or security services, but the State may also be obliged to exercise its power to stop violations by third parties – whether they be vigilante groups, death squads or potent private organizations like media groups or trade unions. It follows that the pivotal technical right, which must be implemented as a precondition of the enjoyment of basic liberties, is the right to an effective remedy. This is promised, in general terms, by Article 8 of the Universal Declaration:

Everyone has the right to an effective remedy by the competent national tribunals for acts violating the fundamental rights granted him by the consti-tution or by law.

This curiously inadequate formulation – 'law' must include 'international law', since some nations have constitutions and domestic laws which do not grant fundamental rights – is rectified by Article 2(3) of the Civil Covenant, which requires state parties to guarantee the human rights 'as recognized herein', and to ensure that when remedies for their breach are granted by national tribunals, 'the competent authorities shall enforce [them]'. In other words (and the point is surely obvious), only enforceable remedies are 'effective'.

The other pivotal principle of international human rights law is that of non-discrimination. Rights must not be vouchsafed or denied by reference to distinctions

of any kind such as race, colour, sex, language, religion, political or other opinion, national or social origin, property, birth or other status.

This organizing principle is found in Article 2 of the Universal Declaration, and it is repeated in the promise of Article 7 that

[a]ll are equal before the law and are entitled without any discrimination to equal protection of the law.

The principle is endorsed in the Covenant (Article 3 of which binds state parties 'to ensure the equal right of men and women' to the enjoyment of all its civil and political rights). But, most importantly, it is to be found entrenched in the UN Charter, the third purpose of the organization being defined to include

promoting and encouraging respect for human rights and fundamental freedoms for all without distinction as to race, sex, language, or religion.

It follows that international law is breached whenever rights of universal application are denied through racism or sexism or on religious or any other 'status' grounds. Since the UN Charter binds every state, this rule cannot be vitiated by common state practice to the contrary. But does it amount to more than a way of *testing* whether the rights are breached, or is it a freestanding right not to suffer discrimination, enforceable on behalf of individuals? If the discrimination is so widespread and severe as to amount to either apartheid or genocide, this would certainly be the case, as the conventions on these two international crimes make clear. The position would be the same if the distinct status was treated by national law as criminal or as entailing quasi-criminal consequences: hence municipal laws penalizing Jews or gypsies or homosexuals must be in breach of this international rule, notwithstanding the number of countries which still make homosexuality, for example, a crime. The rule against discrimination may also come into play to determine whether other, entrenched rights have been breached – as it did to characterize as 'degrading' the racially discriminatory treatment of Asians holding British passports who were denied entry to Britain when they exodused from Kenya and Uganda in 1973.[7] (Race discrimination is more clearly condemned than that on grounds of gender – the United Nations itself and all its principal organs are overwhelmingly dominated by men, notwithstanding Article 8 of the Charter which requires appointments to be made 'on conditions of equality'.) Incredibly, no woman has ever been appointed to the UN's 34-man International Law Commission, and only one (Rosalyn Higgins) to a permanent position on the ICJ. The Convention on the Elimination of All Forms of Discrimination against Women entered into force in 1981 and has been ratified by most states, but with reservations which preserve for Muslim countries the indelibly sexist legal regime of Sharia law, and for the United States the power to deny any woman either an abortion or paid maternity leave. This must be compared to the equivalent Convention on the Elimination of All Forms of Racial Discrimination which has been almost universally and unreservedly ratified, thereby establishing an international law against systemic racism. So it is idle to pretend that at this point in time equal treatment for women is a rule of international law. It should be, of course, and the UN made the issue a central theme of the conferences in Vienna in 1993 and Beijing in 1995, but so long as discrimination remains a basic tenet of many national legal systems, the *opinio juris* necessary to make international law is lacking, other than where violations of womanhood are so systematic and gross that the State fails in its internationally recognized duty to protect victims, if it does not possess or does not enforce laws against their violators.

Even at this elemental level, international law has been slow to recognize rape for the war crime it invariably constitutes when inflicted with impunity by victorious armies. Although prohibited in terms by

Geneva Convention IV and as a form of torture by all human rights conventions, 'spoils of war' rapes were not taken seriously until they featured in war crimes indictments handed down by the Hague International Criminal Tribunal for the Former Yugoslavia (see p. 306). States are in consequence under the clearest international law duty to ensure that military commanders take all reasonable steps to prevent and punish sexual abuse of civilians, and the commanders themselves as well as their soldiers will be criminally liable for any failure. Recent studies have shown that many governments turn a blind eye to rape in women's prisons: in Pakistan, for example, 70 per cent of inmates are sexually abused, and the problem is endemic in prisons throughout the United States, amounting to a breach by that country of its positive duty to take appropriate steps to prevent torture and inhumane treatment.[8] It is not sufficient for a state to point to a domestic legal prohibition, if in practice its police force does little to implement the law—a commonplace throughout the world in cases of wife-beating and domestic violence. This duty is difficult to enforce, unless police or prosecution inaction is caused by procedures which the State can alter. (Examples include the bizarre evidence rule in Pakistan that rape convictions require four witnesses who must all be male and Muslim, and the macho 'honour' defence in parts of Latin America which in practice produces acquittals for husbands who kill adulterous wives.) States are, for historic reasons, under a clearer duty in international law to protect foreign workers from physical abuse – hence the scandal of the 'Asian maids' routinely tortured and maltreated by the Kuwaiti princes (and, more often, princesses) for whom they work as servants. The peculiar viciousness of the Kuwaiti upper classes results in over 2,000 of their domestic servants seeking asylum each year: the government refused to act until an international outcry in 1998 over the death sentence imposed on one Filipina maid who killed her tormentor.

There are special international law duties imposed on a state in respect to persons under eighteen. Children are a very recent subject of human rights law, omitted from the eighteenth-century declarations because they were then regarded as the property of their parents. The League of Nations, moved by the numbers orphaned in war, issued a declaration in 1924 about the duty of governments to provide food, shelter and medical attention for poor children, but although the

Universal Declaration stands up for bastards (by insisting that illegitimates should not suffer discrimination) it says no more than 'Motherhood and childhood are entitled to special care and assistance' (Article 25). The Civil Covenant, too, is vague, giving protection to children only as part of a family and affording them just one right – to acquire a nationality. Eventually, in 1989, came the Convention on the Rights of the Child: its importance is demonstrated by the fact that it has been ratified by every nation except Somalia and the US. Article 3 imposes a pivotal duty:

In all actions concerning children, whether undertaken by public or private social welfare institutions, courts of law, administrative authorities or legislative bodies, the best interests of the child shall be a primary consideration.

This principle is now part of international law and is reflected in the custody laws of most states, although in tandem with Article 9 (which imposes a duty to avoid separating a child from its parents) it often comes into conflict with penal decisions – e.g. to jail a child or to deport a parent. It was in the latter situation that the High Court of Australia in the *Teoh Case* invoked the Convention as a means of reviewing a decision made without considering the interests of the deportee's children. (This was a groundbreaking decision for international law generally, because a local court found a way of holding the State to the principles of a treaty it had signed but not incorporated.)

The Convention requires states to respect the family unit as the most desirable environment for a child's upbringing, and emphasizes that the child should have 'the right to know and be cared for by his or her parents'. It recognizes the child as an independent being entitled to freedoms of thought and speech, and to have an opportunity for its opinion on any decision about its welfare to be heard and 'given due weight in accordance with age and maturity'. States must take effective steps to protect children from economic or sexual exploitation and abolish 'traditional practices prejudicial to the health of children' – a firm rejection of the 'cultural relativism' arguments which attempt to justify tribal maiming. Significantly, Article 23 endows mentally or physically disabled children with a special right to claim such assistance from the State as may be necessary to develop into full and useful members of society. Children must not be executed or jailed for life;

they must not suffer imprisonment with adult offenders and states must establish a minimum age for criminal liability (many do, but since the range is between seven and sixteen this rule is of scant assistance). These provisions may draw additional *opinio juris* support from general human rights provisions: thus under the 'inhumane treatment' prohibition in the European Convention, the European Court has held that the birching of juvenile offenders, even those convicted of acts of violence, was degrading treatment, a form of 'institutionalized violence' constituting an assault on the individual's dignity and physical integrity. School canings too were unlawful, the court later ruled, if suffered by children contrary to their parents' wishes and beliefs about how they should be educated.[9] In its controversial but correct *Bulger Case* decision in 1999, this court ruled that children charged with heinous crimes must be tried with a fairness which reflects their tender age.[10] The 10-year-olds who had sadistically murdered a small boy were put on trial in the dock of an adult court packed with prying journalists and old men in pantomime wigs and gowns quoting Latin. The youths were traumatized by proceedings they had not understood. The decision requires states to provide special treatment for children appearing in court as witnesses or as defendants.

SAFETY OF THE PERSON

The most basic right of all is that to life – guaranteed by Article 8 of the Universal Declaration. At its highest, namely when the State takes life pursuant to a policy of genocide, this right is so forcefully protected by international law (it carries every Latin tag from *jus gentium* and *jus cogens* to *opinio juris* and *erga omnes*) that it justifies armed intervention by other states, whether pursuant to Chapter VII or by way of a unilateral humanitarian mission, and the ICJ may order 'provisional measures' against a government under the Genocide Convention. Article 5 is also fundamental:

No one shall be subjected to torture or to cruel, inhuman or degrading treatment or punishment.

There can be no doubt that the rule against torture has evolved into a *jus cogens* prohibition which every state has a duty owed to the international community to outlaw and to punish. This follows from a multitude of sources, most notably the 1984 Convention on Torture, ratified by 113 states, which requires torture suspects to be put on trial or else extradited to a country which *will* put them on trial. The force of the prohibition was described by the Hague Tribunal in *Prosecutor* v. *Anton Furundžija* as 'designed to produce a deterrent effect, in that it signals to all members of the international community and the individuals over whom they wield authority that the prohibition of torture is an absolute value from which nobody must deviate'.[11] The *Furundžija Case* was specifically approved by the House of Lords in *Ex parte Pinochet (No. 3)*.[12] Torture is defined by the Convention as the intentional infliction of *severe* pain or suffering, whether physical or mental, by or with the consent of a public official, although it specifically excludes suffering attendant upon the imposition of lawful punishments (see pp. 230–4). Whether there is a binding international law against 'degrading treatment' must be open to doubt, given its breach in prisons and interrogation centres in many countries. The distinction most commonly quoted comes from a case brought in the European Court by the Republic of Ireland against the UK over the 'in-depth interrogation' to which internees in Belfast in 1970 were subjected by the British army: they were hooded and ordered to stand for several hours spreadeagled against a wall, while questioning was interspersed with disorienting effects like sleep deprivation and high-pitched noises. This was held to be degrading treatment but not torture, which the court defined as 'deliberate inhuman treatment causing very severe suffering'.[13] In cases brought against the fascist military junta in Greece, the court had no hesitation in finding that electric shocks, *bastinado* (beating of feet so as to produce pain and swelling), genital assault, burning with cigarettes and sticking pins under nails would all cause pain of sufficient cruelty and intensity to satisfy this definition of torture.[14] The Civil Covenant, with a nod to victims of the Auschwitz doctors, spells out that, when in the hands of the State, subjection to medical or scientific experimentation without consent is also a form of torture.

It is instructive to note how countries which have not signed the

Covenant or the Convention against Torture are none the less anxious to deny that their harsh treatment of prisoners satisfies the definition. In 1988, Singapore made this claim in respect of its policy of applying 'psychological pressure' to political detainees (young Catholic lawyers and playwrights who had dared to criticize Lee Kuan Yew). They were denied sleep for up to seventy hours at a time, and kept standing directly under the blast of a freezing air-conditioner. During the interrogation period they were repeatedly slapped on the face and doused with cold water, warned that their friends and relatives would be arrested and that they would be detained indefinitely, unless they confessed. This 'psychological pressure' was cunningly devised to leave no permanent physical mark: it was that very cunning, and the fact that its object was to elicit a false confession (which they were required to repeat on state television), that justified its characterization as torture.

The right to life and to be spared torture are connected with the rights under Article 4:

No one shall be held in slavery or servitude; slavery and the slave trade shall be prohibited in all their forms.

Freedom from slavery was the first human right to crystallize as international law: the Covenant expressly prohibiting it dates from 1926 and has been ratified by a majority of nations. Like the right to life and to humane treatment, it is made non-derogable by the Civil Covenant, which means that it cannot be curtailed or derogated from in a public emergency. (This let-out is provided by Article 4 of the Civil Covenant, although 'derogable' civil liberties, such as freedom of speech, may be suspended only while the emergency lasts.) The right to avoid 'forced or compulsory labour' is not made non-derogable, so this lesser freedom cannot be regarded as entrenched in international law: it is subject to numerous exceptions, such as 'hard labour' during imprisonment, conscription and 'any work or service which forms part of normal civil obligations'.

An associated non-derogable provision, Article 6 of the Universal Declaration, occurs in identical terms in the Civil Covenant:

Everyone has the right to recognition everywhere as a person before the law.

This overlaps with the prohibition on slavery, a crime which denies legal status to its victims in the sense that it treats them as property rather than as persons. It may also be relevant in attacking the most fundamental form of discrimination, which denies civic rights to persons defined in human categories, as women or homosexuals or Jews. Religious laws in many countries breach Article 6 by treating such groups not as 'non-persons' but as 'lesser persons', e.g. women and non-Muslims in Sharia law, and through the caste system which still operates in some parts of India. Article 6 is certainly incompatible with laws of the kind found in the constitution of Australia until 1968, which excluded Aborigines from being counted in the national census as part of the country's population.

A crucial physical safety right for individuals is to leave a state where their lives are in danger, and to be permitted entry to the first country they come to where they need have no fear of persecution. Sadly, the millions of refugees in the world and the reluctance of safe countries to admit them has made this a right honoured much more in the breach than in the observance. It is of historical interest to note that it appears in fairly expansive terms in the Universal Declaration, to shame the states which turned away many Jewish refugees from Nazism:

Everyone has the right to seek and to enjoy in other countries asylum from persecution.

This was a precious but increasingly inconvenient right, jettisoned by the Civil Covenant. Fortunately, the world was still idealistic enough in 1951 to agree to the International Convention on Refugees, albeit in a much narrower formulation. That covenant, which has now been ratified by 133 countries, provides international law protection in the negative sense that no country can deport a refugee to a state

to which he is unwilling to go owing to a well-founded fear of being persecuted for reasons of race, religion, nationality, membership of a particular social group or political opinion.

Governments are currently concerned to whittle this down further by insisting that the fear be objectively well founded, i.e. where persecution back home is both a near-certainty and likely to lead to loss of liberty if not of life. Europe has been particularly concerned to turn itself into a

'fortress' against the 'onslaught' of refugees, while some Asian countries, when faced with Vietnamese boat people, ignore the Convention
and allow the boats to be pushed out to sea and set upon by pirates.
Cases involving mass movements of refugees are dealt with by expedient
rather than legal measures, through the Office of the UN High Commissioner for Refugees. The refugee crisis, however, gives point to the
emerging principle of international criminal law that the forcible displacement of a settled population amounts to a crime against humanity
if conducted as an act of state policy and may, if undertaken ferociously
and on a large scale, justify armed intervention by other states on the
grounds of humanitarian necessity. On this basis NATO countries
justified the bombing of Serbia in 1999 (see chapter 11).

The Universal Declaration aimed to make everyone a citizen of the
world. Article 13 provides

(1) Everyone has the right to freedom of movement and residence within
the borders of each state.
(2) Everyone has the right to leave any country, including his own, and to
return to his country.

This is one of many articles stated in absolute terms, subject to the
all-purpose caveat of Article 29 (2) that they may be made the subject
of legal restriction to secure the rights of others or to meet 'the just
requirements of morality, public order and the general welfare in a
democratic society'. All states have gone well beyond these exceptions
in exercising emigration and immigration powers. Political restrictions
have been imposed which have no conceivable justification in terms
of public order or public morals: the apartheid pass laws; the Jewish
refuseniks prevented from leaving the Soviet Union; the entry visas
and exit visas granted or denied, by every country, by reference to
political beliefs, especially during the Cold War. This clause of the
Universal Declaration batters against a door too often closed by
custom and state practice. What it does give rise to is an international
'due process' rule requiring some prospect of opening that door
through legal action. East German border guards who shot on sight
anyone attempting to exercise an Article 13(2) right to leave their
country have recently been convicted of crimes against humanity. It
must be possible to test the necessity of the restriction through action

under municipal law, as in the notable case of *Kent* v. *Dulles*, where the US Supreme Court refused to allow the State Department to withhold passports from citizens merely because they were communists.[15]

The passport is not a legal document, although it provides *prima facie* evidence of nationality and identification and its convenience makes it indispensable for the modern traveller. It serves as the symbol of nationality, the possession of which is a separate right under Article 15 of the Universal Declaration, together with the right to change nationality. This supports an international law rule against state-lessness, under which nationals are absolutely entitled to return to their own country. Many states jealously retain petty regulations which discriminate in favour of those born within their borders, or against them when they take up another nationality, and laws like these unnecessarily hinder the working and family lives of many peripatetics. If the right to change nationality were to include a right to *dual* nationality (which some states accept) many of these problems would disappear.

Magna Carta was first to proclaim the right of every free man to leave the realm at his pleasure in time of peace. The Universal Declaration reasserts this, although subject of course to the Article 29 (2) public order exceptions (used to justify travel restrictions on British football hooligans) but also to Article 29 (3):

These rights and freedoms may in no case be exercised contrary to the purposes and principles of the United Nations.

Governments could by reference to Article 29(3) justify keeping both sanctions-busting sportsmen and would-be foreign mercenaries at home. A state is entitled – indeed, obliged – to stop anyone within its borders from leaving to fight for forces which are committing war crimes (see pp. 199–202).

INDIVIDUAL FREEDOMS

A cluster of rights in the Universal Declaration serve communal ends as well as personal development. The right to marry, and to give full and free consent to that marriage, and to found a family protected by the State *as a family* all derive from Article 16. These principles are often asserted in municipal law to challenge immigration decisions which have the effect of breaking up families, e.g. by deporting one member or refusing entry to another. Article 16 does not strike in terms at 'arranged' or proxy marriages, such as are common on the Indian subcontinent, but it does require that each partner approve of the arrangement (if not of each other). It specifically entitles them to equal rights 'during marriage and at its dissolution', thus conflicting with patriarchal systems where the father is designated head of the household, and with divorce laws which expressly favour custody for the wife or automatically penalize a 'guilty' party.

Further protection to the individual as part of a family is provided by Article 12, which prohibits 'arbitrary interference with . . . privacy, family, home or correspondence'. A few sophisticated legal systems provide their citizens with a right to privacy (generally by permitting the recovery of damages for deliberate violation) but it cannot be said that international law requires states to go that far: the right can only be universalized as one to challenge by legal process any form of bugging or burglary of the home by a state agency. In other words, as the European Court has repeatedly held, each state must put in place a system of prior authorization (normally, by way of warrants obtained on application to a judge after production of evidence of 'reasonable suspicion') before its police may enter and search a home, or intercept private mail or telephone conversations. This rule has proved useful for curbing the 'Big Brother' tendency of the State; it has not served to protect individuals from media intrusion, or in many parts of the world from having no privacy at all, thanks to poverty, homelessness and tenement living.

Privacy is a value which calls for protection because of the individual's psychological need to preserve an intrusion-free zone of personality and family. For that reason, it appears in all the main human rights treaties, although they speak in the same breath of the 'right' to freedom of expression. These two rights are often perceived to conflict and, influenced by the media's self-interest, the West has become much more concerned about free speech violations than privacy violations. The former attract the undivided attention of human rights organizations (some formed solely for this purpose) while the latter are rarely condemned. For the media, lack of privacy is perceived merely as a *quid pro quo* for being rich and famous, forgetting (as Orwell never did) that communism deprived *all* citizens of any right to privacy from the State. What matters is that municipal law should enforce respect for a few fundamental decencies, so that privacy and freedom of expression are recognized as values which are universal and complementary. Public figures, whether crowned or elected or created by happenstance, might then enjoy reputations based on truthful appreciation of all significant aspects of their lives *except* that part they live behind a door marked 'Do Not Disturb'. This cannot be dictated by international law: it needs to be located culturally, according to local conceptions of dignity and decency, and may legitimately deny the media (and other intruders) access to private places like the bedroom, the bathroom, the hospital and the grave.

That said, freedom of expression should be regarded, like the right to a remedy, as a pivotal right in international law. That is because, quite simply, international attention and action against human rights abuses cannot be aroused without it. Richard Dimbleby's broadcast from Belsen, the sound of gunfire in Tiananmen Square, the television pictures of Omarska prison camp and the agonies of the Kosovar Albanians – reports of atrocities incite people throughout the world to put pressure on governments to do something about them. There was certainly a time – during the Second World War and for many years afterwards – when the extent of human rights abuses in farflung countries was known only to the intelligence services of major powers. Gradually, NGOs like Amnesty were able to build their own intelligence networks, drawing on low-key missions and on sources promised confidentiality, and they filtered the information into the public domain through annual and special reports. Today, thanks to global television coverage, reports of large-scale violations of human rights cannot be censored (except by networks whose proprietors seek commercial benefits from the violators). Although many countries have some degree of news and opinion censorship, most information of importance to human rights can be placed on the libel-free environment of the Internet. What is needed, therefore, is a rule framed in terms which enables the media to *extract* information from governments, as well as provide freedom to disseminate it when extracted.

Article 19 provides:

Everyone has the right to freedom of opinion and expression; this right includes freedom to hold opinions without interference and to seek, receive and impart information and ideas through any media and regardless of frontiers.

Article 19 of the Universal Declaration is helpfully reproduced as Article 19 of the Civil Covenant. The latter spells out the standard qualifications, which allow the right to be overridden by considerations of reputation, national security, public order or morals. But it makes clear, like the European and American Conventions, that these exceptions are to be narrowly construed and applied only when truly necessary to protect the excepted values. They are, moreover, exceptions that can never apply to thought, which remains the one natural right – or at least capacity – that can never be shackled. Attempts to scramble or punish thought, by 'brainwashing' or psychiatric treatment or laws which permit detention of persons suspected of harbouring disloyal imaginations, are in fundamental breach of the most elemental guarantee of freedom. Article 20 of the Covenant goes on to make two controversial provisos:

(1) Any propaganda for war shall be prohibited by law.
(2) Any advocacy of national, racial or religious hatred that constitutes incitement to discrimination, hostility or violence shall be prohibited by law.

These prohibitions on hate speech were formulated in memory of Hitler's ranting rallies and the obscene racism of *Der Stürmer* magazine (whose editor, Julius Streicher, was convicted and hanged at Nuremberg). Article 20 (1) has been universally ignored, especially by the superpowers and other states involved in Korea, Vietnam and Afghanistan, wars which were trumpeted among their own people and to the world as 'just'. Many countries have implemented Article 20 (2) by enacting race hate legislation, which the European Court has consistently held to correspond to that 'pressing social need' which overrides free speech in a democracy. America, however, regards its constitutional right to free speech as virtually absolute (other than to stop people shouting 'Fire!' in crowded theatres) and has entered a reservation to Article 20. The position was famously epitomized in the 1977 action of the American Civil Liberties Union, supporting the right of a group of fascists to march through the predominantly Jewish town of Skokie, Illinois. The organization's stand on principle – that the free speech guarantee of the First Amendment was absolute – cost it thousands of members and brought it close to bankruptcy, although its stand in support of hate speech was upheld by the court and confirmed by the Supreme Court in 1992 when it struck down as unconstitutional a ban on racist symbols like swastikas and Ku-Klux-Klan crosses.[16] But the ACLU gesture was on behalf of a handful of racist malcontents of no political importance, attempting to provoke safe, prosperous and peaceful citizens. This was a world away from the teeming hamlets of Rwanda and Burundi, where in 1994 terrified Tutsis huddled to hear their own slaughter being urged from Hutu-controlled radio stations: 'The grave is only half full. Who will help us fill it?' A barbaric genocide followed which cost 800,000 human lives: its scale can partly be attributed to these ferocious broadcasts. (In former Yugoslavia as well, 'ethnic cleansing' came in the wake of race hate incitements on both Serb and Croat radio and television.) None the less, Article 20 cannot be said to resonate in international law: at most, it requires states to prohibit propaganda for *aggressive* or *genocidal* wars, and to pass laws prohibiting incitements to violence on racial, religious or ethnic grounds in circumstances where violence of this kind is likely to follow.

The most significant feature of common Article 19 for international law is that it is designed to protect the free flow of information and ideas 'through any media and regardless of frontiers'. This precludes jamming of signals (a favourite totalitarian tactic, but as yet incapable of blocking the Internet or the fax machine) as well as the easier option of impounding international newspapers at the border or raiding their printers. Throughout the 1990s, states went to extraordinary lengths to impose political censorship, especially on outside criticism of their leaders: the Seychelles banned all fax machines and Burma refused to permit satellite television, while in Malawi Dr Banda made it a crime to own a television set or to tune a radio to any but his own one-party station. Singapore even contrived a ridiculous law to ban foreign publications while pretending not to ban them: papers like the *Asian Wall Street Journal* and the *Far Eastern Economic Review* were adjudged to have 'interfered in local politics' (i.e. they accurately reported opposition to Lee Kuan Yew), whereupon their circulation was cut by ministerial order from 10,000 copies to a few hundred, distributed to government departments and tourist hotels. Lee Kuan Yew made the risible claim that by this means the international press was not banned, but merely 'restricted' for its temerity in reporting what his opponents were saying. In reality, of course, he was using the device to stop his own people from reading in the 'foreign' press the kind of news which the government-controlled Singapore press refused to print. Many states are at present trying to restrict access to the Internet, either by criminal laws which prohibit it entirely (in Libya, Iraq, North Korea, Burma and Syria) or by controlling a sole service provider (in Saudi Arabia, all traffic goes through a ministry which disallows access to sites offering 'information contrary to Islamic values'). A similar 'fire wall' has been erected by China, not only to stop information coming in other than through the official gateway, but to stop 'official secrets' (i.e. criticisms of the regime) being e-mailed abroad. China's surf wars are fascinating to watch, given popular expertise with the technology: the Falun Gong cult was banned more for its ability to organize demonstrations by e-mail than for its meditation techniques.[17]

International law provides a presumption in favour of free speech, but this protection is not (as in the First Amendment) absolute in the absence of malice. Depending on the degree of public interest in the information which it is desired to communicate, the value may be overborne by other considerations. That most commonly invoked by governments is 'national security' – often a bogus reason, especially after the end of the Cold War. The European Court has made clear, in its *Spycatcher* judgment, that suppression orders and injunctions which impose 'prior restraint' are to be avoided if possible.[18] An exception which is more formidable, both because it protects the citizen rather than the government and because Article 12 of the Universal Declaration promises protection against 'attacks upon honour and reputation', is that newspapers which publish defamations or damaging falsehoods about individuals and organizations should be obliged to correct them. On the assumption that there is a reasonable system available for adjudicating where the truth lies this is unobjectionable: in some states, however, plaintiff-friendly legal systems can cause media defendants to suffer heavy financial penalties. This is particularly so in Commonwealth countries like Malaysia and Singapore, where government ministers and their business cronies obtain massive libel awards from pliant judges to bankrupt political opponents and disrespectful journalists. Such awards constitute an improper restraint (a 'chilling effect') on freedom to communicate, so held the European Court in *Tolstoy* v. *UK* (in which the author of a book imputing war crimes to a former British general had been ordered to pay £1.5 million in damages).[19] An unattractive consequence of wide variations in press laws across the globe is that wealthy and powerful 'public figures' seek out the forum which has the most plaintiff-friendly law for their actions against newspapers, books and magazines which are distributed for worldwide sale, as well as against satellite television and the Internet. (The favourite forum at present is the UK, which places a heavy burden on the media to prove the truth of the stories and permits libel actions if only a few copies of the offending publication are circulated within the country.) This ability to forum-shop for the jurisdiction which is least tolerant to free speech should be curtailed: in a global village it makes no sense for the new breed of 'international' public figures to enjoy different reputations in different parts of town.

Common Article 19 bestows a right to 'seek' information as well as to receive and impart it. This must imply more than a right to ask questions, and may be used to support three implications of the Article 19 right: (1) to impose duties on governments to divulge information; (2) to protect whistleblowers who breach secrecy laws and employment contracts in order to speak out, in conscience, from within a government agency; and (3) to permit journalists to refuse to divulge their confidential sources for stories, no matter how much the identity may be of interest to police or security services, or to government or big business. In this last respect, in 1996 the European Court held in *Goodwin* v. *UK* that the right to freedom of information carries the implication that journalists must be permitted to protect their sources, otherwise there would be no information to be free with – sources of news would 'dry up'.[20] It has yet to consider the case of the whistleblower (who might enjoy additional support from the 'freedom of conscience' guarantee in Article 18). Although freedom of information legislation is common enough in advanced political systems, where it is seen as a part of the definition of democratic culture, no court has yet drawn it as an inference from common Article 19. Such a step might be bolstered by reference to the 'democracy rights' in Article 21, including the right to participate in government and to have 'equal access' to the public service.

Linked to freedom of speech is the freedom of belief guaranteed by Article 18:

Everyone has the right to freedom of thought, conscience and religion; this right includes freedom to change his religion or belief, and freedom, either alone or in community with others and in public or private, to manifest his religion or belief in teaching, practice, worship and observance.

This right is made non-derogable by common Article 18 of the Covenant, more perhaps as a measure of its symbolism for a world with a history scarred by religious wars than for its contemporary relevance to conflicts produced by ethnic and political hatreds, although religious differences still fuel these fires in places like Bosnia, Afghanistan and Northern Ireland. International law condemns discrimination on all grounds, and the right to one's religion is in effect a right not to suffer unfairly for practising it. Its non-derogable status does not give a dominant religion any special claim to override minority rights or to have its doctrines – themselves often cruel and prejudicial to women and adherents of other religions – specially exempted from the ground rules set out in Articles 29 and 30 for respecting the rights and freedoms of others. Thus, the inequities of Sharia law are not excused by its claim to be based on Islam (its penalties for apostasy are grotesquely incompatible with the right to change religion) any more than the right to practise Catholicism gives a state comprised mainly of Catholics the right to prevent women from choosing birth control or abortions. The *fatwah* on Salman Rushdie and his translators and publishers was not an exercise of common Article 18, but an act of international terrorism.

This article, like the others, is principally concerned to protect individuals against state tyranny, including attempts to impose religious orthodoxy, and so it must be read as a right to choose atheism, or Rastafarianism, as well as any 'recognized' religion. This follows, in any event, from the promise of freedom of thought and conscience. Religion has been objectively defined as having two criteria, 'first, belief in a supernatural Being, Thing or Principal and second, acceptance of canons of conduct in order to give effect to that belief'.[21] This means that it includes nonsense like scientology, and that in theory 'cults' enjoy the same international law protection as the great faiths, subject always to the State's duty to curtail such of their activities as may damage the general welfare. The State is not prohibited from making one creed its own 'national' religion, although it may not place severe restraints on free speech in protecting adherents from insult. Blasphemy laws which cover a number of faiths can probably be upheld if they protect adherents from obscenity or offensive abuse, but not from criticism or contempt. The right to practise religion is a right to go to heaven in your own way, while tolerating others who choose different paths or none at all.

Another overlapping right is that of association. Article 20 provides:

(1) Everyone has the right to freedom of peaceful assembly and association.
(2) No one may be compelled to belong to an association.

International law thus recognizes the right of peaceful protest, which, notwithstanding its tendency to clog the traffic, remains a potent method for demanding and obtaining change. It was the crowds who stayed for weeks in the streets which brought about the 'Velvet Revolution' in Prague in 1989, and the fall of the Suharto regime in Indonesia in 1998. The crowds in Tiananmen Square might have had a similar impact, had they not been dispersed by real, rather than rubber, bullets. The right of peaceful assembly is constrained by the need for public order; however, there is a correlative duty upon the State to disperse peaceful assemblies by peaceful means. That these may include tear gas, rubber bullets and water cannon is regrettable, but most demonstrators would rather be gassed and splashed than shot. International law accepts a proportionality test, condemning the use of excessive force in crowd dispersal. Breaches of this rule can have international criminal consequences: commanders who order their soldiers to fire upon peaceful demonstrators will be liable to trial under the Rome Statute for a crime against humanity. (This may be one reason why China voted against the creation of the International Criminal Court.)

Article 20(2) moves on to a different dimension, where it protects associations as well as assemblers. This has been of great importance to oppositionists battling against one-party states in eastern Europe and Africa, since the article is incompatible with bans on membership of non-violent political parties. Thus Paul Muite, the courageous president of the Kenyan Law Society, argued that a constitutional right in identical terms permitted his countrymen to form and belong to parties opposed to that of Daniel Arap Moi, even though local law prohibited them from contesting elections. The members of the Czech Jazz Society – the cultural front for Charter 77 in its battle against the State – kept making music and mischief together by invoking their constitutional entitlement to this right through the society's membership of UNESCO. It did not prevent their prosecution, but it forced the regime to frame them on fraud charges because it could find no legitimate basis for jailing them for belonging to a peaceful organization. Other bodies are more opaque – Sinn Fein's commitment to peace was doubtful until 1998 because it was avowedly the 'political wing' of the IRA. The right does not admit 'semi-peaceful' organizations to its protection: only if an organization is demonstrably non-violent need the State tolerate it on an equal footing with others.

Article 20 (2) is commonly taken to prohibit the 'closed shop', i.e. the use of trade union muscle to force members to join the union or else be sacked. It cannot be argued that a choice to be unemployed is any choice at all, and the European Court in *Young James and Webster v. UK* said as much in upholding the rights of railway workers to remain in employment notwithstanding their refusal to join a union with political commitments they did not share. This is a good example of a state being required to introduce laws to prevent the violation of individual rights by powerful private organizations, in this case the trade union which had effectively blackmailed the employer into sacking the complainants. The same argument is used against the one-party state, which in practice forces those who wish to become active in politics to join the only organization lawfully capable of conducting such activity.

THE RIGHT TO FAIRNESS

Legality is essentially a promise of fairness: that in the criminal and (where appropriate) civil systems, there will be no arbitrary arrests, biased judges and oppressive procedures. Derogation from these rights is permitted at times of 'emergency' – when there is an insurrection or civil war – but not disproportionately to the exigencies of the situation and never for the purpose of racial, religious or sexual discrimination. The one principle which permits of no derogation is the rule against retroactivity: no person may be convicted for an act which was not a crime at the time it was committed (Universal Declaration, Article 11(2)). Importantly for prosecutions of war criminals and perpetrators of crimes against humanity, this rule means that the act must have been punishable under either national or international law. The Nuremberg defendants could not argue (although they tried) that it was a breach of the rule to try them for offences which had no equivalent in the law of Nazi Germany, when the offence existed in *international* law. The Covenant (Article 15(2)) makes plain that nothing in the rule against *ex post facto* laws shall prejudice trial or punishment for any act which was, at the time of its commission, 'criminal according to the general principles of law recognized by the community of nations'.

The Universal Declaration does not detail the rights which must be afforded a defendant at the time of arrest and detention, and then at time of trial. The major powers had commonly interned 'fifth columnists' on the flimsiest suspicion, and they routinely detained colonial leaders under internal security laws. So the only detention right which can be spelled out, and with some difficulty (by coupling Article 9, below, with the right to an effective remedy), is that of habeas corpus:

9. No one shall be subjected to arbitrary arrest, detention or exile.

The Covenant elucidates this right: detention must be in accordance with a settled procedure, and the detainee has to be (1) informed of the grounds for his arrest, (2) brought promptly before a judge, (3) then given the opportunity to test the lawfulness of the detention and (4) entitled to ask for bail. An important new right was added which had no resonance in state practice at the time, but which is now gaining acceptance: the wrongly detained victim 'shall have an enforceable right to compensation'. The Covenant also adds some basic humanitarian rules about jails – for example, requiring remand prisoners to be segregated from convicts and juveniles from adults. Its drafters had read Charles Dickens on the evils of the debtors' prison: they made it a non-derogable duty to ensure that 'No one shall be imprisoned merely on the ground of inability to pay a debt'.

Articles 10 and 11 of the Universal Declaration identify, in the briefest terms, the rights to fair trial:

10. Everyone is entitled in full equality to a fair and public hearing by an independent and impartial tribunal, in the determination of his rights and obligations and of any criminal charge against him.
11(1). Everyone charged with a penal offence has the right to be presumed innocent until proved guilty according to law in a public trial at which he has had all the guarantees necessary for his defence.

To identify the necessary guarantees, turn again to the Covenant. In Article 14 they include the defendant's right to:

(i)   be informed promptly of the nature of the charges;
(ii)   adequate time and facilities to prepare the defence;
(iii)   trial without undue delay;
(iv)   be present at the trial, and to be defended by counsel of his own choosing, or (if indigent) to have legal aid for counsel where the interests of justice require it;
(v)   cross-examine hostile witnesses and to require the attendance of witnesses who can give evidence for the defence;
(vi)   have an interpreter where there are language difficulties;
(vii)   not to be compelled to testify against himself or to confess guilt;
(viii) if convicted, to have the right of appeal;

(ix)   have a remedy in the event a miscarriage of justice can be demonstrated, and to receive compensation for wrongful conviction;

(x)   never be placed in double jeopardy, i.e. not to be retried after a final acquittal or conviction.

These fair trial rights have been recently entrenched in the international tribunals set up in The Hague and Arusha to conduct trials relating respectively to former Yugoslavia and Rwanda, and they are reflected (or, in some cases, such as the right to silence, extended) in the Rome Statute of the International Criminal Court. They show some bias towards the Anglo-American system of adversarial trial, although they are not inconsistent with inquisitorial systems – the latter placing more emphasis upon the judge as investigator and determiner of truth than on the creative play of a defence team. Most of the guarantees can never be cast iron: the trial may need to go into closed session to protect child witnesses or rape victims; a defendant may be excluded from his own trial if he tries to disrupt it; 'counsel of choice' is always a counsel of perfection in the case of lawyers who are heavily booked or unavailable at the price offered by legal aid. The double jeopardy rule, when applied inflexibly (as in English law), can produce shocking results – as when persons acquitted of serious crimes through lack of evidence subsequently confess to guilt or have it conclusively established by advances in forensic science like DNA tests, but cannot be reprosecuted. It is difficult to accept that every specific guarantee has ripened into international law, although this certainly is the case with the more general requirement that these rules be sufficiently respected to produce a trial which is fair.

Four guarantees do seem to possess that 'normative' quality which makes them part of customary international law. First and foremost is the presumption of innocence, described as the 'golden thread' of common law.[22] It appears in every human rights treaty and in Rule 21 of the Hague Tribunal and as Article 66 of the Rome Statute of the International Criminal Court. This presumption has two effects: the prosecution must always bear the burden of proof, and must shoulder this responsibility in criminal cases to a high standard, proving the case beyond reasonable doubt. Although some latitude is allowed in requiring defendants to prove matters of which they should have a special knowledge (such as the possession of a licence to do an otherwise unlawful act), the general burden at the end of the day must fall on the prosecution. International case law is remarkably unanimous on this point.[23]

Secondly, serious criminal trials must be open to the public. Publicity, as Jeremy Bentham put it, 'is the very soul of justice. It keeps the judge, while trying, under trial.' The 'secret court' is a kangaroo or Kafka-esque court, associated over many centuries with gross abuses of power. The public nature of the trial remains the greatest safeguard against the unfair use of criminal proceedings.

The third great safeguard is the 'independence and impartiality' of the judges, as individuals with sufficient confidence and backbone to stand up to governments and other power-wielders in the society (not excluding the power of terror and intimidation wielded by criminal gangs). Impartiality is provided for by a rule disqualifying judges for bias, on the principle that 'justice must be seen to be done'. It has been rigidly applied by the European Court, ordering the disqualification of judges if they have come from offices connected with the prosecution or, in *Hauschildt* v. *Denmark*, have made any prior decision in the case as a result of which bias as to its outcome might reasonably be inferred.[24] The rule was most notably applied by the House of Lords in 1998 when it bent over backwards to do justice to General Pinochet by annulling its initial 3–2 decision against him because one of the majority judges had served (unpaid) on a charity connected with Amnesty International, which had intervened to argue that the ex-head of state was not immune from prosecution. This tenuous non-financial link was sufficient to disqualify the judge: although justice had undoubtedly been done, it had not been seen to be done.[25]

The most serious problem with many Third World judiciaries is corruption, because judges are paid so little that they become prey to temptation from richer litigants. In Indonesia until recently, for example, corruption was institutionalized as a means of paying the judiciary. Judges indicated their needs – a car, a refrigerator or whatever – and on receiving a gift from each party tried to mediate a mutually acceptable solution to their dispute. In many countries, corruption comes through political connections: since judges are appointed and promoted by governments, lickspittles are common. Infuriatingly, they are frequently appointed by the states they serve, or by the bloc-biased UN appointment system, to international tribunals, where their contribution is skewed in favour of state power. The only real guarantee against partiality would be to set up an independent and expert appointments committee. Some judges actually take orders from government (this was common in the Soviet Union and eastern Europe until the fall of communism) while others (in Singapore, for example) reflect a culture where the government is always right. But, for all the examples of judicial corruption, there are heartening (indeed, heartrending) cases from Italy and Colombia of judges prepared to do their duty according to law, notwithstanding the danger to their lives.[26]

The fourth guarantee which may have achieved international law status, although it is not to be found in the Universal Declaration, is the defendant's right 'not to be compelled to testify against himself or to confess guilt'. Article 14 of the Covenant begs the question of what amounts to compulsion: a gun to the head, clearly, and brutal interrogation and threats to family of the kind made to elicit the public confessions at Stalin's show trials. But the somewhat mundane promises and inducements ('You can have bail if you spill the beans') which can serve to exclude confessions in Anglo-American law are not compelling. The right against self-incrimination has been taken so far as to require in the Rome Statute of the International Criminal Court a rule against the drawing of inferences of guilt from a defendant's refusal to testify. This is illogical and Britain, which pioneered this 'right to silence', has recently abandoned it. Such an extensive defence right seems incompatible with the rights of victims of crimes against humanity to have the truth about them told – the most important reparation of all. Where evidence establishes a *prima facie* case of genocide or torture, the defendant surely has a moral duty to respond: common sense would infer guilt from a defendant's refusal to explain the blood that the evidence plainly shows to be on his hands.

Both the Universal Declaration and the Covenant are silent on one important consequence of the right to liberty: the principle that the State should neither spy on law-abiding citizens nor incite them to commit crimes. But there is a general rule in the Hague and Rome statutes entitling these international criminal tribunals to exclude unfairly obtained evidence, and it is through this back door – an aspect of the duty of fair trial – that the use of state *agents provocateurs* may be attacked. The principle is of importance, given the history of states fomenting crimes as an excuse for aggression, the blackmailing of diplomats and the use of stool pigeons to frame dissidents. There is also concern at the clandestine operations of intelligence and security agencies, especially when they are directed to entrapment.[27] State agencies which routinely or randomly test the virtues of citizens they have no reason to believe are engaging in crime put liberty at risk in a manner which was classically condemned by Justice Felix Frankfurter in *Sherman* v. *US*:

The power of Government is abused and directed to an end for which it was not constituted when employed to promote rather than to detect crime and to bring about the downfall of those who, left to themselves, might well have obeyed the law. Human nature is weak enough and sufficiently beset by temptations without Government adding to them and generating crime.[28]

There can be no objection to the use of undercover agents to trick and trap persons reasonably suspected of engaging in crime, so long as their involvement is limited to providing such persons with an opportunity to commit an offence, and does not go further and actually induce an offence by persons who would otherwise never have contemplated it. The line is not always easy to draw, but most legal systems strive to avoid the spectacle of trial and punishment of those who would never have broken the law without the urgings of state agents.[29] An international law rule against state instigation of criminal offences has yet to crystallize, although what does emerge consistently in human rights jurisprudence is a duty on the State to draw up strict protocols governing undercover investigations and to monitor their observance effectively. The European Commission on Human Rights says that citizens should have 'an adequate indication of the circumstances in which and the conditions on which public authorities are empowered to assent to secret and potentially danger-ous interference with the right to respect for private life'.[30] This is a general principle which applies to all measures of state surveillance:

the European Court held in *Ludi* v. *Switzerland* that domestic law must limit undercover police work to the penetration of existing conspiracies to be compatible with the right to privacy; citizens necessarily forfeit that right if they engage in crime.[31] In 1998, the Court confirmed that instigation of an offence by a police agent was a breach of the fair trial guarantee, and ordered the government of Portugal to compensate a man jailed for a drug offence he had been incited to commit.[32]

The United States Supreme Court was first to fashion an 'entrapment defence' out of the constitutional rule against self-incrimination. In the most recent case it held that 'when the Government's quest for conviction leads to the apprehension of an otherwise law-abiding citizen who, if left to his own devices, likely would never have run foul of the law, the courts should intervene'.[33] International criminal courts should similarly decline to lend authority and approval to improper and unlawful conduct by investigators and prosecutors. This is the approach taken by the High Court of Australia,[34] the Courts of Appeal of New Zealand and England[35] and the Supreme Court of Canada.[36]

The most that international human rights law can require, given the prevalence of international terrorism, drugs trafficking and money laundering crimes which require undercover methods to detect, is that states provide sufficient safeguards within their domestic justice systems for defendants to challenge the legitimacy of the police conduct to which they have been subjected – an aspect of the guarantee of fair trial – and to avoid punishment if they can prove that the criminal offence with which they stand charged was in substance the creation of government agents. The freedom to assemble and to speak openly will be infringed by secret police infiltration of political parties or pressure groups if done with the objective of turning organizations committed to lawful change into seditious and treasonable conspiracies. All secret surveillance undertaken by the State should be conducted according to clear rules and procedures, with the additional safeguard that the risk of unreliability should be guarded against by monitoring the behaviour of those agents with a motive – be it money or political spite or a wish to win immunity – to incriminate those they are sent to spy on. States which cannot produce legal rules for limiting undercover operations cannot claim that their citizens enjoy the right to liberty.

PEACEFUL ENJOYMENT OF PROPERTY

International law classically protected aliens from seizure of their land or goods on arbitrary or discriminatory grounds and additionally required expropriating states to pay appropriate compensation to foreigners deprived of their possessions. The right of nationals, too, to enjoy property was a central preoccupation of the American and French Revolutions and their Declarations. But subsequently, Marxist philosophy and practice favoured nationalization of industry and confiscation and redistribution of land, while independence movements, on attaining government, wished to extirpate foreign corporations regarded as agents of imperialism: they had stolen natural resources from the people, so they did not deserve compensation. Since this was the outlook of many states by the 1960s, little progress was made in putting further flesh on Article 17 of the Universal Declaration, which, at the insistence of President Truman, provided:

(1) Everyone has the right to own property alone as well as in association with others.
(2) No one shall be arbitrarily deprived of his property.

By the time the International Covenant on Political and Civil Rights had come to be drafted in 1966, there was rabid disagreement over whether private property was a human right or any sort of right at all. Article 17 of the Declaration was but palely reflected in a rule against arbitrary deprivation of *privacy*, which would cover intimate personal possessions and, at most, the family home. One regrettable result was that this omission in the Covenant would, over the next quarter century, be cited by Jesse Helms and other isolationists in the US Senate as grounds for refusing its ratification. But as the Cold War ideological debates over property rights have receded, so Article 17 has crystallized into a rule of international law: there would at present be a broad consensus in its favour. The principle is embodied in

Article 1 of the First Protocol to the European Convention on Human Rights, viz.:

Every natural or legal person is entitled to the peaceful enjoyment of his possessions. No one shall be deprived of his possessions except in the public interest and subject to conditions provided for by law and by the general principles of international law.

In this formulation, state acquisition of private property is viewed as arbitrary where it is not in the public interest, although Article 1 goes on to allow governments a considerable margin of appreciation to control property in 'the general interest' by pursuing radical measures of economic reform or redistributive social justice. The European Court has held that governments do not breach Article 1 by acquiring ancestral estates or nationalizing private industry, so long as they provide appropriate compensation.[37] 'Arbitrary deprivation' in contravention of international law would have to be evidenced by personal malice or favouritism, such as the confiscation of the property of a dissident in order that it can be given to a party official, or depriving one ethnic or racial group more readily or severely than others. In the absence of discrimination, however, any form of 'public interest' will suffice, however economically or politically controversial: governments may acquire private land to return it to indigenous inhabitants or 'lock it up' to protect environmental values. They may redistribute land to peasants, or take land away from peasants to build dams or railways. The State's sovereign power to act in the general interest trumps the individual's right to enjoy private property, subject always to such duty as it has under international or national law to provide an appropriate measure of compensation.

The nature and extent of the obligation to compensate is a subject of a debate which is still tinged with ideological differences. In customary international law there is a duty to compensate aliens whenever their property is lawfully expropriated: this was settled by the Permanent Court of Justice in 1928 in the *Chorzów Factory Case*.[38] Historically, aliens were owed special protection by their host state, and were more vulnerable to confiscations motivated by racism or jingoism. But it would be anomalous if the rule did not apply to nationals,[39] because it stems from a general principle of justice and equity ('Thou shalt not steal') and in modern times it is nationals who are most vulnerable to having their property confiscated arbitrarily. The 'right to own property' which Article 17 enunciates must carry as a corollary a right to compensation in the event of arbitrary deprivation: as the European Court has pointed out in respect of the First Protocol, 'the protection of the right to property . . . would be largely illusory and ineffective in the absence of a duty to provide compensation'.[40]

When a foreigner's property is expropriated, what measure of compensation must the State pay to its former owner? The words of US Secretary of State Cordell Hull, deployed by way of demand to the Mexican government when it confiscated the holdings of American landowners, provides the formula preferred by Western governments: compensation must be 'prompt, adequate, and effective', reflecting the full market value of the property which has been lost. It was described in the *Chorzów Factory Case* as 'the value of the undertaking at the moment of dispossession, plus interest to the day of payment'.[41]

These 'full compensation' principles are all very well when applied by claims tribunals assessing compensation due to multinational oil companies whose operations have been taken over as a going concern by oil-rich governments. But where inherited estates or areas of national heritage or precious ecology are taken into public ownership, a lesser standard – that of 'appropriate compensation' – may be deployed to give the former owner a reasonable sum, albeit one which falls considerably below market value. This standard was adopted by the UN in 1962 in its Declaration on Permanent Sovereignty over National Resources,[42] and again in 1974 in its Charter of Economic Rights and Duties of States.[43] These declarations were devised as justifications for developing nations who wished to 'buy back the farm' from colonial corporations at less than the market value, but in such cases a discount is fair only if the object of the acquisition is to right historical wrongs or to deprive former owners of windfall profits as the result of artificial inflation of property values prior to state acquisition. The European Court has consistently held that 'legitimate objectives of public interest, such as pursued in measures of economic reform or measures designed to achieve greater social justice, may call for less than reimbursement of the full market value'.[44]

So far as individuals are concerned, it may be said that international law recognizes in principle everyone's right to own private property, as declared in Article 17. It requires that right to be protected by states in the case of non-nationals, who must not have their property confiscated unless for a purpose which serves the general interest, and for compensation, if offered, to be given on just terms. There is an emerging international law rule requiring nationals to be compensated on the same basis. They certainly have international law rights if state action invades their privacy, which it would do by taking an individual's 'living space' – a family home, personal possessions and private goods with some element of sentimental value, and what are quaintly termed in bankruptcy law 'tools of trade'. Should the State trespass on this protected area, it can only do so in the public interest and by offering just compensation.

There is another right which is in the process of ripening rather quickly, as a result of international law's especial abhorrence of crimes against humanity. Any victim who has lost property in the course of such a heinous crime – the Jews who had their assets, their houses and their works of art confiscated in the course of the Nazi genocide, for example – have a right to its return, in specie, which trumps all local laws capable of creating difficulties (such as time bars). This is not just a right against the immediate Nazi beneficiaries, or those who acquired the property from them with knowledge of its origin. Such is the tenderness shown by international law towards victims of these crimes that their right can be asserted against third parties who purchased the property in ignorance of its origins. This right is now receiving a grudging recognition, even from Swiss banks, which have (after a lot of international pressure) offered compensation to relatives for allowing Nazi withdrawals from the bank accounts of genocide victims. What began as a class action in US courts brought by Holocaust survivors ended in a US $1.25 billion pay-out by a Swiss banking and political establishment terrified that exposure of their complicity with the Nazis would provoke US boycotts and the long justified withdrawal from Geneva of the international human rights industry.[45]

The fact that the case was arguable in law meant that the morally guilty Swiss could not bear it to be argued: nor could Germany and its best-known companies when similarly sued by victims and relatives of victims of their wartime slave labour programmes. In frenzied pre-millennium negotiations, half a million claimants were bought off with a massive US $6 billion – half contributed by the German government. Had this case been fought, the courts might well have decided that inter-state arrangements (e.g. made between Germany and the Allies in 1951 to draw a line under the Holocaust) cannot bind individuals by stopping them from suing private companies which had once tried to work them to death. Establishing that this international right of the individual cannot be overridden by the sovereignty of states, and exposing the appalling history of the manu-facturers of celebrated cars and cameras and clothing, might have been more valuable to the plaintiffs (and to everyone else) than obtaining an estimated US $5000 per head in a settlement which made hundreds of millions of dollars for their contingency-fee'd lawyers.

The right to full compensation for victims of crimes against human-ity has relevance to the plight of the Kosovo refugees whose goods and property – in most cases, all their worldly possessions – were confiscated by Serb forces during Operation Horseshoe, the brutal ethnic cleansing that took place both before and after the NATO bombing in March 1999. This appropriation was part of a crime against humanity (as defined by Article 7 of the Rome Statute – see Appendix D) because it amounted to a widespread and systematic attack on a civilian population for the purpose of persecuting and forcibly uprooting an ethnic group. Any long-term settlement with Serbia should call for the restitution of land and goods confiscated from Kosovars and compensation for their upheaval. This important detail was overlooked by the cease-bombing agreement between NATO and Yugoslavia in June 1999: this produced a restoration of Kosovar homes and land, but without any provision for compensating victims for destruction of their property or for the deaths of loved ones. In years to come, precedents used to obtain massive settlements from the German government may be redeployed to attack Yugo-slavian state assets throughout the world on behalf of Albanian victims: if immunity cannot protect states against legal action over their crimes against humanity, the consequences of Milošević's ethnic cleansing in 1999 will be felt by his country for decades after his death.

4

Twenty-first Century Blues

'From this day forward, I no longer shall tinker with the machinery of death. For more than twenty years I have endeavoured . . . along with the majority of this court, to develop procedural and substantive rules that would lend more than the mere appearance of fairness to the death penalty endeavour. Rather than continue to coddle the court's delusion that the desired level of fairness has been achieved . . . I feel mentally and intellectually obligated simply to concede that the death penalty experiment has failed.'
US Justice Harry Blackmun, from his judgment
in *Callins* v. *Collins* (1994)

Human rights standards are becoming rules of international law because a campaigning mass movement is putting pressure on democratic governments to practise what they preach when they ratify treaties which embody these standards. National courts, too, are finding ways to hold governments to these same standards. The results can be surprising and unsettling for politicians and diplomats, emerging from a world in which sovereign promises need never be kept to a future where breaches can have inconvenient legal consequences. Just how inconvenient was demonstrated dramatically in 1998, when General Pinochet tripped in his travels over the rule that crystallized from Nuremberg and the Convention Against Torture, that ex-heads of state have no sovereign immunity when accused of crimes against humanity. This serves as an example of how human rights can go on the offensive, threatening future punishment for those who deny the 'liberty' rights of the Universal Declaration and the Civil Covenant. But what on earth has happened to the 'lost rights' to social and economic development which were thought non-justiciable and sloughed off into a separate covenant?

This chapter considers their claim for a comeback, after dealing with the two most difficult problems for the human rights movement. The first is the death penalty. Colossal strides have been made in combating this popular form of state violence since it was inflicted without opposition on most of the Nuremberg defendants, and it will never again be a punishment option for an international tribunal, even for crimes against humanity. But abolition remains far from being an international law prescription, particularly as a result of the resurgence of capital punishment in the United States. The other impasse is over the rights of minorities – among the first to be identified by international law, but among the last to progress. The importance of making legal provision for ethnic minorities and indigenous peoples is underlined by the ethnic cleansing in the Balkans and Rwanda, and the potential of other melting-pot states to boil over. Can international human rights law do anything to ameliorate or mediate the blood feuds, or will nothing succeed like secession – the most fundamental of all attacks on the sovereignty of the State? More optimistically, it will be suggested that the direction in which the nations of the world are moving indicates that democracy – a political system which actually had a minority of adherents in the United Nations in 1948 – will eventually become a generally accepted form of government, and that Article 21 of the Universal Declaration will be freshly interpreted to make free electoral choice (between parties as well as candidates) an international law right in the course of the twenty-first century.

FREEDOM FROM EXECUTION

Executioners no longer burn the bowels of their victims before their very eyes or pluck out their hearts and hold their severed heads aloft, although the practice of stoning to death, still followed in some Islamic states, is of equivalent barbarity when inflicted for the 'crimes' of adultery or sodomy. Most retentionist states adopt more discreet modes of killing criminals, but no method is free from 'execution glitches'. Electrocutioners often miscalculate voltage or use faulty electrodes – the third-degree burns on the head and leg usually suppurate before the dead prisoner is unstrapped from the electric chair and his cooked flesh falls from the bone. In gas chambers in America, as in Auschwitz, prisoners fight in panic against the cyanide, 'eyes popping, tongue hanging thick and swollen from a drooling mouth'.[1] Hanging requires macabre preparation, weighing the prisoner and greasing the trap, and the strangulation (occasionally, decapitation) is traumatic: disposal of the stinking body with its elongated neck and diarrhoea-filled underwear is also a problem. The axe and the guillotine, much favoured historically for English and French aristocrats, are swift but too bloody and mutilating for Western liking, although several Middle Eastern countries still behead felons with a sword. Lethal injection is the latest American mode of despatch, although it leads to unseemly last-minute struggles to find a workable vein in some prisoners' drug-abused bodies. Missouri allows executees to invite friends to join the audience for their lethal injection: the first of such victims was seen to mouth 'I love you' to his wife before choking over his last breath. This is a more romantic ending than the offer of poison (now unfashionable, since few prisoners are prepared to co-operate like Socrates), although it does not quite reach the operatic pitch of death by firing squad, where the ritual demands that the victim has a target pinned to his chest before being offered a last cigarette, and that one of the firing squad must, for the sake of its collective conscience, shoot a blank.

All these methods of execution cause intense physical pain, of varying duration, after the mental agonies during the preparation period of maybe several days. It was Stalin, ironically, who devised the demise least painful physically and mentally for political prisoners – a bullet fired at point-blank range into the back of the head when the victim was least expecting it, usually while being escorted down a dark corridor. This method is reliable, painful for the splittest of nanoseconds, and avoids the mental anguish of brooding over the appointed time and place of death. However, it offends both the legal requirement of due process and the religious rule that life must not be taken unless and until the prisoner has had an opportunity to prepare himself for its loss. It is a method used today mainly in China.

The cold-blooded killing of a healthy human being, other than in war or in order to save other lives, is an act universally condemned as evil. It does not entirely lose that quality when committed by the State, no matter what incantations of law or religion are used to absolve the officials obliged (albeit by their own choice) to carry out executions in one of the ways described above. The law against murder, which purposes to promote reverence for human life, cannot achieve that aim when the State itself takes life in the name of its people. There is no system which can be devised for inflicting the death penalty without cruelty or degradation, or for selecting condemned persons other than arbitrarily or without lurking doubts as to their guilt. Luck can play a preposterous part: Eduardo Agbayani, condemned to die when capital punishment was restored in the Philippines, was being led to his place of execution when President Estrada granted him a last-minute reprieve. Unfortunately, the prison telephone was engaged and news of the presidential pardon arrived seconds after his death. No research has confirmed the retentionist credo that the death penalty deters crime, other than in disappearing a criminal who would be neutered as effectively by an alternative sentence of life imprisonment. The US executed ninety-eight murderers in 1999, but it still has the highest murder rate in the industrialized world, especially high in those states (Texas and Florida) which conduct the most executions.

In 1995 these arguments persuaded South Africa's Constitutional Court to strike down, unanimously, the punishment which had so often served the apartheid regime. 'Death is different,' declared Ismail Mahomed, the nation's first black Chief Justice. 'The dignity of all of us, in a caring civilization, must be compromised by the act of repeating, systematically and deliberately, albeit for a wholly different objective, what we find to be so repugnant in the conduct of the offender in the first place.'[2] The Court concluded that the death penalty was an infringement both of the right to life and of the right to avoid 'cruel, inhuman or degrading treatment', because these rights were unqualified in the new post-apartheid constitution. Although it acknowledged that capital punishment was not yet contrary to international law, the force of its decision helps to inch international law slowly in that direction. Just how slowly is demonstrated by the

Tanzanian Supreme Court, which decided in the same month that the mandatory death penalty, while cruel and degrading, was none the less constitutional because it was a 'reasonable and necessary measure to protect the "right to life" of law abiding citizens'.[3]

There is no issue more politically polarized, or more heavily litigated, in human rights law than the sentence of death and its modes and rituals of execution. Most national constitutions reflect international human rights instruments in avowing respect for the 'right to life' and in prohibiting 'cruel or unusual' or 'inhumane or degrading' punishments and treatments – descriptions which were not thought, at the time of their adoption, to apply to the sentences of death regularly passed on persons convicted of serious crimes like murder or treason. No nation of any significance had abolished the death penalty by the time it was imposed on Nazi war criminals at Nuremberg in 1946, but the half century which elapsed before the next trial of an ethnic cleanser saw abolition – by law or in practice – in most of the 191 countries of the world, leaving eighty-three retentionist states. The courts established by the UN to deal with war crimes in former Yugoslavia and Rwanda and the International Criminal Court are prohibited by their statutes from imposing death sentences. It follows that, despite the clear modern trend in state practice towards abolition, there is still not a sufficient consensus for executions to be prohibited as a matter of customary international law.

The most signal failure of human rights law, at this stage of its development, is that it does not condemn the formal extinction of the lives of those human beings convicted of crime. Although Article 6 of the Civil Covenant is worded in a way which has led the Human Rights Committee to believe that it 'strongly suggests' the desirability of abolition, which represents 'progress in the enjoyment of the right to life',[4] the second Optional Protocol to the Civil Covenant – the treaty by which states can solemnly pledge themselves to abolish capital punishment as a step towards human progress – has not attracted many signatories at all.[5] In Europe, however, there is a consensus for abolition, reflected in the fact that all the Council of Europe members (twenty-four) which have ratified the Sixth Protocol of the European Convention on Human Rights have forsworn the imposition of the death penalty as a punishment in peacetime. But in 1999 there were 1,625 executions recorded in thirty-seven countries (1,000 in China alone) and many more which went unrecorded – especially liquidations of state enemies in places like North Korea and Burma, while Iraq boasted eighty-seven public beheadings and an indeterminate number of prisoners strangled in their cells. But the lead in the death penalty stakes was taken by the US, with over 3,500 men and women on death row, engaged in see-sawing legal battles to avoid the electric chair and the lethal injection. Eighty-five death row inmates have stayed alive for long enough to prove their innocence and walk free – a sobering comment on the fallibility of human justice. America's reservation to Article 6 of the Covenant is chilling:

The United States reserves the right, subject to its Constitutional restraints, to impose capital punishment on any person (other than a pregnant woman) duly convicted under existing or future laws permitting the imposition of capital punishment, including such punishment for crimes committed by persons below eighteen years of age.

'Everyone,' says Article 3 of the Universal Declaration, 'has the right to life.' Article 6(1) of the Civil Covenant insists that 'No one shall be arbitrarily deprived of his life'; however, 'arbitrarily' may mean no more than 'without trial', in which case it merely requires a finding of guilt duly rendered by a court competent under national law. There was no consensus as to the meaning of 'arbitrarily' at the time the Covenant was drafted and it is apt to cover not only secret police or death squad killings and other executions which take place in defiance of the due process of law but those which are inflicted within legal systems which do not measure up to international human rights standards.[6] Yet even with due process, those selected for capital punishment will generally be poor and will have been poorly defended. The question of commutation may depend upon the subjective view of jurors (in the US, prospective jurors antipathetic to the death penalty are removed from the panel) or of judges, or of the governor or committee of worthies endowed with the power of mercy. Political expediency will demand human sacrifices shortly before elections, to convince the public of the 'law and order' credentials of the governing party. As one justice remarked in *Furman* v. *Georgia*, the 1972 Supreme

Court case that *almost* abolished capital punishment, 'Death sentences are cruel and unusual in the same way that being struck by lightning is cruel and unusual.' It is in this sense that every prisoner who is actually executed may be said to have been 'arbitrarily' deprived of his life, simply because others who may be equally, or more, 'deserving' of death have avoided the same fate.

A constitution which avows respect for life should not permit the State cold-bloodedly and purposefully to take it.[7] But many constitutions expressly preserve the death penalty, so international human rights instruments need to be realistic. The Civil Covenant, in Article 6(2), seeks to limit rather than abolish capital punishment:

In countries which have not abolished the death penalty, sentence of death may be imposed only for the most severe crimes in accordance with the law in force at the time of commission of the crime and not contrary to the provisions of the present Covenant . . . This penalty can only be carried out pursuant to a final judgment rendered by a competent court.

Although Article 6(6) pleads that 'nothing in this article [i.e. subparagraph (2), above] should be invoked to delay or to prevent the abolition of capital punishment by any State Party', Article 6(2) is in fact routinely invoked by retentionist states to prove that executions after due process do comply with international law. But the very next article of the Covenant, Article 7, provides that 'no one shall be subjected to torture or to cruel, inhuman or degrading treatment or punishment', and since executions undoubtedly fit that description it is logically impossible to execute anyone in a manner 'not contrary to the provisions of the present Covenant'. This is a circle which cannot be squared, and the intellectually disreputable attempts of the Human Rights Committee to do so (for example, in holding that execution in a gas chamber is cruel but killing by lethal injection is not) should be abandoned.

DEATH PENALTY SAFEGUARDS

Judges in most countries fight shy of striking down the death penalty *per se*, but what national and international courts are increasingly prepared to do is to make executions as difficult as possible, by applying human rights principles so as to limit the classes of offenders who may undergo it, or the ways in which it may be carried out. Some, for example, have insisted that execution must be done *swiftly* following conviction, yet only *after* rights of appeal have been fully explored: when expedition and due process conflict, the sentence must be commuted. Other courts have applied familiar legal principles to save mentally ill and juvenile prisoners, and women (at least if they are pregnant), and to hold that it is a disproportionate punishment for offences other than murder or treason. The more that courts are prepared to apply human rights standards to treatment of condemned prisoners, the more difficult it becomes for the State to impose the supreme punishment. The role of international law, at this stage of its development, is to play Portia: the State may have its pound of flesh, on the condition that it sheds no drop of blood. A set of safeguards has developed which limit the applicability of the death penalty in retentionist countries.

The international law status of these safeguards follows from a reference to them in common Article 3 of the 1949 Geneva Conventions, which prohibits executions 'without previous judgment pronounced by a regularly constituted court, affording all the judicial guarantees which are recognized as indispensable by civilized people'. Common Article 3 has been recognized by the International Court of Justice (in *Nicaragua* v. *US*) as expressing customary international law applicable in times of war and insurgency, so it follows that the rule must apply with all the more force in peacetime. The 'indispensable judicial guarantees' are laid down in Articles 6 and 14 of the Covenant, and most are collected in Safeguards Guaranteeing Protection of the Rights of Those Facing the Death Penalty, adopted by the Economic and Social Council and endorsed by the UN General Assembly in 1984 (the ECOSOC safeguards). They draw support from treaties on other subjects (such as the rights of children and the mentally handicapped) which make passing reference to the death penalty or are applications of other general international law rules, such as the guarantee of fair trial and the prohibition on torture and cruel and inhumane treatment. The following eight limitations on the application of the death penalty are required at this juncture by international human rights law:

THE NATURE OF THE OFFENCE

Death, the most severe punishment, 'may be imposed only for the most serious crimes' (Covenant, Article 6(2)). This rule, states the Human Rights Committee, 'must be read restrictively to mean that the death penalty should be a quite exceptional measure'.[8] Murder is the crime for which it is most commonly and most appropriately (in the retributive sense) inflicted, although murders vary so much in heinousness (from euthanasia and domestic crimes of passion to contract killings and hostage executions) that any *automatic* infliction of the death sentence on murderers would infringe this rule (and the general rule against arbitrariness). There must either be a limited definition of 'capital murder' in domestic law, or a post-conviction commutation procedure which makes these necessary distinctions. The only other serious crimes for which the death penalty can be justified are those assumed to involve indirect taking of life, e.g., by peddling heroin or by serving an enemy. However, the latter offence, generally termed espionage or treason, cannot today be regarded as requiring the ultimate punishment.[9] Article 6(2) of the Covenant requires that a capital crime must not be 'contrary to the provisions of the present Covenant', which protect the freedoms of conscience and speech and association which are often involved in treason or sedition. The frequent condemnation by the UN General Assembly of 'politically motivated executions' adds weight to the view that imposition of the death sentence for political offences short of murder is contrary to international human rights law, certainly if the offence has been motivated by ideology rather than greed or revenge.

THE FAIRNESS OF THE TRIAL

It follows from the irrevocability of the sentence that it should not be carried out unless trial procedures have been scrupulously fair. The 'equality of arms' principle, whereby defendants are entitled to sufficient legal resources to assert their innocence realistically against the State, has a particular force in this context. Those sentenced to death are predominantly poor and illiterate, and the spectacle of them being tried and sentenced without legal representation, or by newly admitted advocates of questionable competence acting without fee, is one which no nation, however impoverished, should permit. The cost of inflicting the death penalty in conformity with international law includes the cost of providing potential victims with access to advice and assistance at every stage in the proceedings. In *Robinson* v. *Jamaica*,[10] the HRC considered it 'axiomatic' that legal assistance should be provided in capital cases. In *Mbenge* v. *Zaire*, it ruled that violation of any due process rights in Article 14 of the Covenant in a capital case is a breach of Article 6(2), because this would mean the sentence would be imposed 'contrary to the provisions of the Covenant'. The State was then under a duty to vacate a death sentence passed *in absentia* and to compensate Mbenge – probably for shock, since he first heard of his trial and conviction when he read about it in a newspaper.[11]

Another aspect of fundamental fairness is that the death penalty must not be applied retrospectively, i.e. as punishment for a crime which did not carry that penalty at the time it was committed.[12] This is emphasized by the Geneva Conventions, which protect prisoners-of-war.[13] It is sometimes argued that states which have abolished the death penalty cannot lawfully reintroduce it, but such a rule (found only in the American Convention on Human Rights) would impinge too dramatically on national sovereignty. What is emerging, however, is a rule that executions should not take place in any period during which there is a real political prospect that the death penalty will be abolished. Thus death sentences were commuted in Britain in 1948 during a period when Parliament was divided over abolition, and executions were suspended in Jamaica between 1977 and 1981 while a Royal Commission studied the issue.

RIGHTS OF APPEAL

One of the abiding arguments against the death penalty is the fallibility of human justice, and the consequent prospect that it will sometimes be imposed on the innocent. The ghosts of Sacco and Vanzetti haunt the death cells of America; the wrongful convictions of the Birmingham Six, the Guildford Four and the Maguire Seven ensure that the gallows will not return to Britain; in Jamaica, the Royal Commission reported in 1981 that up to 20 per cent of the hundreds on death row were likely to be innocent (mainly dreadlocked Rastafarians convicted on unreliable eyewitness evidence). The UN safeguards for capital convictions require 'clear and convincing evidence leaving no room for an alternative explanation of the facts' and there must be a right to appeal to a higher court. These rules require that each capital case is carefully scrutinized by domestic courts for the possibility of error. If, in the course of the appellate process, there is a judgment which dissents from the majority decision to uphold the conviction, the death sentence should in principle be commuted because any judicial disagreement will leave a question mark over guilt, or at least over the propriety of the procedures used in establishing guilt.

PETITIONING FOR MERCY

The condemned prisoner must always be accorded the right, under Article 6(4) of the Covenant, to seek a pardon or commutation of sentence after appeals to the courts have been exhausted.[14] It is essential to provide an extra-legal forum in which the issue of whether the prisoner really deserves to die may be resolved as a matter of common humanity. There may be a residual uncertainty about guilt (despite the rejection of all appeals); there may be evidence that the prisoner is of unsound mind; there may be mitigating features which make execution a punishment disproportionate to his moral culpability. The ultimate question of whether the public interest demands death is usually left to the judgement of the head of state or a senior government minister, often advised by a specially appointed 'mercy' committee. International law requires that the condemned person be given facilities to petition the appropriate body. Little attention has been paid, however, to the procedure for clemency petitions: the executive, charged with making what is literally a life or death decision, should on principle be bound to act fairly and consistently.

STAYS OF EXECUTION PENDING APPELLATE AND
CLEMENCY PROCEDURES

The rule that executions must not be carried out while appeals or clemency petitions are pending is of increasing importance to legal struggles against the death penalty. Derived from the principle of legality and the prohibition on 'arbitrary' deprivation of life, it has the backing of General Assembly resolutions and the American Convention (Article 4(6)), and is spelled out in Article 8 of the Economic and Social Covenant safeguards. Unhappily, governments capable of inflicting death penalties often resort to dishonest and devious ways of carrying them out. Trinidad, for example, hanged Black Power leader Michael X a few hours after serving the execution warrant late at night, when the court registry was closed and his lawyers were asleep. In 1994 it deliberately executed a prisoner named Glen Ashby while the court was considering his application for a stay, and after its attorney-general had given an undertaking to the Privy Council the previous day that the execution would not proceed. Ashby had been on death row for almost five years, and the government feared that, unless he were killed quickly and secretly, he would not be killed at all.[15] When apparently civilized states resort to behaviour exhibiting this degree of dishonesty, it is crucial that they be called to account by international law.

Many lives have been saved by the rule that no execution should take place while an appeal is still under consideration, even if it is to an external body like the HRC or the Inter-American Court, which has no direct power to order commutation. (These procedures are lengthy and the delay will often take the case over the five-year threshold for commutation decreed in *Pratt and Morgan* (see p. 138). The ICJ has held, unanimously, that a stay of execution should be granted pending determination of a point of international law. In *Paraguay* v. *US* (1998) it issued an order for 'interim measures' against the US to stop the state of Virginia from lethally injecting a Paraguayan national who in breach of the Vienna Convention had not been told, on his arrest, of his right to consular advice. The US, required by this convention to appear at the Court, apologized to Paraguay for the police oversight but still went ahead and executed its national, in breach of the ICJ order. This provides another example of America's blatant contempt for the international legal system, although it is right to note that the Clinton administration did ask the governor of Virginia and the Supreme Court to stay the execution in compliance with the ICJ request. Both refused (the court by 6 votes to 3) and that major human stumbling block to human rights, Senator Jesse Helms, condemned the President's request as 'surrendering US sovereignty'.

EXEMPTED PERSONS

International law firmly forbids the execution of pregnant women – a rule found in all conventions and in domestic laws of most retentionist states, only one of which, Iran, is reported still to engage in this practice. Anglo-American tradition required a special jury to decide whether a woman prisoner was 'quick with child', in which case execution was stayed until after the baby's delivery. The rationale of allowing an innocent life to be born should extend to its interests in being suckled and mothered, yet only the additional Geneva Protocols forbid execution of women with dependent infants: state practice variously allows execution after delivery (United Arab Emirates, Turkey, South Korea), forty days after birth (Indonesia), two months after birth (Egypt and Libya), or later – Yemen allows a full two years for lactation to finish before orphaning the child.[16] A pregnancy planned to delay execution is a ploy familiar to female felons in such countries, although there are a few sexist governments, such as Jamaica, which always commute death sentences on women no matter how heinous their murders.

There is also a clear rule of international law which forbids the execution of children who are under eighteen at the time of the commission of the offence (rather than at the date of passing the sentence).[17] The US Supreme Court has been prepared to declare unconstitutional the execution of children aged fifteen when their offence was committed, but has (by a 5–4 majority) permitted the killing of juveniles who offended at ages of sixteen and seventeen.[18] In 1986, the Inter-American Commission ruled that this violated an 'emerging norm' prohibiting the execution of persons who committed capital crimes before the age of eighteen.[19] This norm may be considered as having 'emerged' in 1989, when it was embodied in Article 37 of the Convention on the Rights of the Child, which all countries (the US and Somalia excepted) have ratified. The Inter-American Convention also prohibits the execution of persons over seventy, although this respect for old age has not found much support: is the taking of a life which has almost run its course logically any less distasteful than cutting one off in its prime?

Most domestic legal systems jib at carrying out death sentences on mentally handicapped offenders. Even in an age of the most savage punishments, English judges who had no compunction in burning witches drew the line at hanging village idiots. As Chief Justice Coke explained, four centuries ago:

The execution of an offender is for example, but it is not when a madman is executed; that should be a miserable spectacle, both against law, and of extreme inhumanity and cruelty, and can be no example to others.

This blunt reasoning applies to render the execution of insane persons a form of cruel and inhuman treatment which is plainly contrary to international law. Even the US Supreme Court, in its recent phase of reluctance to disturb death sentences, has ruled that execution of the mentally incompetent is unconstitutional, and that procedures must be available for testing the prisoner's sanity prior to carrying out the sentence.[20] It should make no difference whether mental incapacity was present at the time of the crime or supervened subsequently, except that in the latter case a state could theoretically be entitled (subject to the rule against delay) to execute a prisoner who in due course recovered.

DELAYED EXECUTIONS

Two important international courts – the Privy Council and the European Court of Human Rights – have accepted that it is unlawful to execute a prisoner who has been held for a substantial period of time under death row conditions, because there has to come a point at which he is deemed to have suffered cruel, inhuman and degrading treatment. Subjection to such treatment is outlawed by the Universal

Declaration (Article 5) and by all human rights conventions, in terms which derive from the prohibition on 'cruel and unusual punishments' in the 1688 English Bill of Rights. This phrase originally referred to unreasonably severe or disproportionate penalties: in human rights law (where the adjectives 'inhuman and degrading' are often used instead), it refers to premeditated ill-treatment of such severity that it produces mental or physical anguish beyond that which is inevitable in the infliction of a legitimate form of punishment.[21] The brooding horror of contemplating one's own death, alternating between hope and despair over a period of years, in a specially sterile environment and in the company of other men who are also liable to be taken out and executed, creates what the European Court describes as a 'death row phenomenon' – a trauma which exceeds the severity threshold imposed by human rights law. The Privy Council put it more simply:

There is an instinctive revulsion against the prospect of hanging a man after he has been held under sentence of death for many years. What gives rise to this instinctive revulsion? The answer can only be our humanity; we regard it as an inhuman act to keep a man facing the agony of execution over a long extended period of time.[22]

In that case – *Pratt and Morgan* v. *Attorney-General of Jamaica* – the senior court of the Commonwealth decided that no executions can take place within its jurisdiction (which embraces sixteen independent nations and all British colonies) of prisoners still alive more than five years after sentence was passed, and that any prisoner is entitled to argue that his execution would be unlawful if he has been kept on death row for more than two years as a result of state inaction or delay. This ruling in 1993 led to the immediate commutation of sentences of death on 160 prisoners in Trinidad and Jamaica and has required many more commutations since in retentionist countries of the Commonwealth. It was preceded, in 1989, by a European Court ruling that the United Kingdom could not extradite a man named Soering to the US to face trial for murder in Virginia, where conviction for a capital offence entails an average wait of between five and seven years before execution.[23]

These judgments focus on the peculiar nature of an institution – death row – which is common to prisons in most retentionist states.

Its special regime seems to have originated in England in 1752, when 'an Act for better preventing the horrid crime of murder' attempted to do so by providing that executions should take place two days after sentence, and that until that time the condemned person should be kept in a special place within the jail, isolated from all other prisoners. In due course rituals developed in this place of dread, where no productive work or education was permitted: the execution warrant was formally read; the prisoner was weighed for the trapdoor and measured for the noose; a 'last supper' was permitted, and so on. The institution and its special regime was exported to many other countries through British conquest and colonialism, and some of its features have remained post-independence, despite the fact that men may spend years there before the government decides to hang them. Common to all such institutions is the alternating hope and despair provoked by legal actions and mercy petitions; the traumatic awareness of the execution of fellow prisoners; the inability to engage in productive work; the reading of warrants and the preparations for death. All these become part of the mounting anguish of awaiting execution. If permitted to continue for years, this will exceed the 'severity threshold' set by the prohibition on cruel and inhuman behaviour. To the objection that condemned prisoners welcome delay and most of them try to cause it by filing appeals and petitions, the Privy Council points out that 'it is no answer to say that the man will struggle to stay alive. In truth, it is this ineradicable human desire which makes prolongation inhuman and degrading.'

The practical issues which arise from this determination are: firstly, how long must a prisoner wait on death row before the severity threshold is exceeded? and secondly, should any adjustment be made for delays induced by the prisoner's own actions in taking legal proceedings which stave off the evil day? There is a general consensus in the cases that five years' delay gives rise to an irrefutable presumption that the threshold has been exceeded, no matter how relaxed the physical conditions on the particular death row may be. The period to be measured is that between the passing of the death sentence and the date of the proposed execution, although account may be taken of any inordinate delay in bringing the prisoner to trial after his arrest. Obviously, any period of time during which the prisoner is at liberty as a result of escape must be discounted, as should periods attributable to legal proceedings which are unarguable and vexatious. But delay caused by exercise of rights of appeal, motions based on tenable (albeit not upheld) arguments, petitions for mercy and complaints to international human rights bodies cannot be overlooked merely because they are self-induced by the prisoner. As the Privy Council ruled in *Pratt and Morgan*: 'It is part of the human condition that a condemned man will take every opportunity to save his life through use of the appellate procedure.'

Where the severity threshold has been exceeded, the proper remedy is to commute the sentence to life imprisonment.

CRUEL AND INHUMAN EXECUTIONS AND PRELIMINARIES

The rule against cruel and inhuman treatment prohibits modes of execution which inflict torture and degradation, such as burning at the stake, or drawing and quartering, or the Chinese procedures which have reportedly been designed to keep the prisoner alive while organs (mainly kidneys and corneas) are removed for subsequent transplant to worthier citizens. Public executions are regarded as degrading in some countries and as essential for deterrent purposes in others, and there is a serious legal issue being litigated in America as to the right of television to transmit death scenes live to what would probably be massive audiences. Public execution cannot, therefore, be considered cruel and inhuman, at least by the standards of countries which permit executions at all. It may well be that televised hangings, gassings and injectings (and the reaction to them) would provide the proof necessary to establish their inhumanity *per se* as punishments: the film taken in Spandau prison in 1944 of Adolf Hitler gloating while the bodies of his would-be assassins danced on piano wire (an example of the conduct Montaigne envisaged as the ultimate in cruelty) helped to convince many European statesmen to abolish the death penalty. Stays of execution have been ordered in American courts where there is reason to suspect that the lethal apparatus will malfunction, and either botch the job or kill slowly and with unnecessary pain; the rule might also be invoked where conditions on death row are particularly gruesome (e.g. where inmates watch their fellows being put to death) or in the case of prisoners who have had a number of death-defying last-minute reprieves.

Prisoners facing execution in circumstances which infringe the international law rules described above may be able to seek relief in their national courts, failing which they can complain to the United Nations Human Rights Committee (if their country has signed the Optional Protocol) or to a regional human rights court, if there is one available. The prisoner's execution should be postponed while the claim is investigated and, if held admissible, while it is being adjudicated. Failing such recourse, there is the possibility of attracting the attention of the UN Special Rapporteur on 'summary and arbitrary' executions, at least if there has been a demonstrable failure by the State to comply with the safeguards referred to in the Covenant. The Rapporteur is entitled to then send a formal 'urgent message' to the defaulting government, followed by intervention from the Secretary-General pursuant to his 'best endeavours' mandate. As an absolute last resort, the Pope may intercede. None of these expedients have moved governors in the thirty-eight retentionist states of the United States when they wish to send a 'tough on crime' signal to voters or on the ruling cliques in China (which has the most executions), Pakistan, Nigeria, Malaysia, Saudi Arabia, Iran and Iraq.

Human rights law has had a dramatic effect on the death penalty: it has saved thousands of lives, by enabling appellate judges throughout the world to find good legal reasons for staying executions. Judges are hamstrung by domestic law, but are increasingly willing to adopt principles reflected in the UN safeguards. In 1958, Chief Justice Warren briefly fashioned the US constitution into an instrument for striking down the death penalty by reference to 'the evolving standards of decency that mark the progress of a maturing society'.[24] Thirty years later, Justice Scalia joked that 'the risk of assessing evolving standards is that it is all too easy to believe that evolution has culminated in one's own view'.[25] Cynics deride liberal judges, insulated by high salaries and burglar alarms from suffering the fear and grief of people who vote for capital punishment. Their votes are not informed by evidence or argument, however, but by terrors of the night which can best be calmed by effective policing, rather than by lynching a scapegoat.

MINORITY RIGHTS

From the sixteenth century onwards, treaties were haphazardly entered into by European rulers which guaranteed to minorities within their domain the enjoyment of their 'traditional religious liberties'. The most influential – the Treaty of Westphalia of 1648, the first pact to recognize sovereignty in nation states – granted religious freedom to German Protestants on the same terms as Roman Catholics. Centuries later, the League of Nations at its inception took this idea a step further by promoting 'minorities treaties' by which Allied powers required states with minorities problems to guarantee civil and political rights and religious and cultural toleration. These treaties were enforceable at the instance of a state signatory, through the compulsory jurisdiction of the Permanent Court of International Justice, and were also supervised by the League Council, which could be addressed by a petition from an individual or association. In the case of other states with poor records in minorities treatment – Albania, Latvia and Iraq, for example – admission to the League was made conditional upon their acceptance of an equivalent obligation to safeguard the rights of minorities within their borders.

So between the wars the international community was alive to the significance of minority rights and the attention given to the subject recognized its importance as a precondition for peace in Europe. The Permanent Court of International Justice began to develop a jurisprudence which addressed the problem of reconciling, on the one hand, demands for equality and non-discrimination with, on the other, the special need to preserve the characteristics and culture of minority groups. Thus its advisory opinion on *Minority Schools in Albania* (1935) condemned that government's decision to close private schools serving the Greek minority, on the grounds that 'there would be no true equality between a majority and a minority if the latter were deprived of its own institutions'. The Court held that peaceful co-existence required two legally enforceable objectives:

The first is to ensure that nationals belonging to racial, religious or linguistic minorities shall be placed in every respect on a footing of perfect equality with the other nationals of the State. The second is to ensure for the minority element suitable means for the preservation of their racial peculiarities, their traditions and their national characteristics.[26]

The Court adopted these principles to support German settlers in Poland and Polish nationals in Danzig, but these promising beginnings came to a sudden end in 1939, when the League's Minorities Section was disbanded and its subjects thrown to the werewolves of the Second World War. What emerged from that darkness – in which minorities suffered horrifically – was a new way of thinking about human rights which ironically denied them any special protection. It was the notion, which seemed blindingly obvious to Eleanor Roosevelt and the brahmins of warfree Washington as they planned a New World Order, that all relevant human rights belonged to individuals: take care of the rights of persons, and the rights of peoples would as a matter of logic take care of themselves. As Sumner Wells, US Secretary of State, concluded in 1943, 'in the kind of world for which we fight, there must cease to exist any need for that accursed term "racial or religious minority"'. So it came to pass that neither the Charter of the United Nations in 1945 nor the Universal Declaration of Human Rights in 1948 made any mention of minority rights. The UN adopted the position that everyone would be protected by guarantees of rights for individuals and adherence to the principles of equality and non-discrimination.

The unreality of this position should have been evident from the beginning: the Nuremberg trials, after all, concerned the rights of Jews and gypsies to survive not merely as individuals, but as ethnic groups. The 1948 Convention on the Prevention and Punishment of Genocide outlawed serious crime committed 'with an intention to destroy in whole or in part a national, ethnic, racial or religious group'. In 1951, the International Court of Justice declared genocide a crime under customary international law, confirming that such groups had at least a right to exist, maintainable against states which sought to splinter or extinguish them by physical force. The definition of the crime did not, however, cover state actions designed to subvert or eliminate minorities indirectly, such as the destruction of an environment which sustains them or abolishing their schools, and so preventing them from thriving. Remarkably, it was not until the advent of Article 27 of the Civil Covenant that even this modicum of protection was extended by international treaty. As early as 1946, the UN had set up a subcommittee on the Prevention of Discrimination and the Protection of Minorities, which must rank as one of its laziest and least effective organs, having done nothing for minorities in fifty years except to define them. Even this was the work not of the subcommittee but of Francesco Caportini, the UN's Special Rapporteur, whose report in 1977 provided a definition of a minority as a 'group numerically inferior to the rest of the population of the State, in a non-dominant position, whose members – being nationals of the State – possess ethnic, religious or linguistic characteristics differing from those of the rest of the population and show, if only implicitly, a sense of solidarity, directed towards preserving their culture, traditions, religion or language'.[27]

THE RIGHT TO EXIST

For all the currently fashionable talk at the UN about 'minority rights', it is only possible to say that minorities have two rights: to exist, and to be different in their existence from the majority of people in their state. The right to exist derives from the Genocide Convention, and is enforceable according to the post-Nuremberg theory of a universal jurisdiction to try 'crimes against humanity'. This right has been boosted by the establishment of tribunals to punish genocide in Rwanda and former Yugoslavia, although it remains a protection only against *deliberate* steps taken by the State to 'destroy in whole or in part' a national, ethnic, racial or religious group. It does not protect such peoples against wanton destruction of the environment or culture which sustains them, or against acts intended to prevent them from thriving or developing; nor does it provide redress against a state which 'accidentally' extinguishes a group by neglect or by creating conditions which conduce to the dissolution of the group by death or departure from it. The 'right to exist' is a basic but bare right, which protects against ethnic cleansing by threatening prosecution of perpetrators – if they can be captured – and by inviting the intervention of other states, on the 'humanitarian necessity' principle of Kosovo, if breached on a large scale. Such breaches should – at a point yet to be defined by international law – give rise to a right of secession (see chapter 11).

THE RIGHT TO BE DIFFERENT

The right to be different has now crystallized into a rule of international law, to the extent that it is expressed in Article 27 of the International Covenant on Civil and Political Rights:

> In those states in which ethnic, religious or linguistic minorities exist, persons belonging to such minorities shall not be denied the right, in community with other members of their group, to enjoy their own culture, to profess and practise their own religion, or to use their own language.

'Persons', be it noted, rather than the minorities to which they belong, are the subject of Article 27. Its language hovers uneasily between treating minority rights merely as individual rights writ large, the sum total of the rights to religious or cultural tolerance enjoyed by individual 'persons' or individual 'members' of the group, and a genuinely collective right exercisable on behalf of all members either by the group leader, or by any one member as representative of the others. It is a negative right which has supported very few complaints to the Human Rights Committee, and those which have succeeded might have done so because individual rights were also breached. The classic case is that of Sandra Lovelace, a Canadian Indian who left her tribal reserve to marry a non-Indian, thereby losing her status under the Canadian Indian Act and hence being refused permission to return to the reserve after her divorce. The regulations under which she was excluded plainly discriminated against her as an individual woman, and additionally infringed her right to freedom of association, although the HRC made great play of condemning the regulations as contrary to Article 27.[28] It would be interesting to know whether the result would have differed had the legislation (which Canada changed in consequence of the HRC decision) reflected an inflexible tribal rule, or indeed had her expulsion been ordered by the tribal council.

The HRC has so far dodged this sensitive question of what happens when minority rights under Article 27 conflict with individual rights. The answer must be that the minority right gives way: cultural traditions which infringe basic human rights cannot be supported. Decisions will doubtless depend on findings of fact and degree: some level of sex discrimination may be acceptable in harmless tribal or religious rituals, but if it amounts to inhuman or degrading treatment (e.g. clitorodectomies on young girls) or threatens the right to life (the practice of *sati*, which requires newly widowed women to commit suicide) it is nonsensical to accord such barbarism the description of a minority 'right'. Minorities are as capable of breaching human rights as majorities, and it is absurd to elevate Article 27 into a general licence for them to maintain cruel or discriminatory practices. On the other hand, Article 27 should mean more than just a general right to be tolerated, although that has often been its interpretation. Unhappily, it does not grant *locus standi* for domestic public law purposes to minorities, or even give them the standing to petition international bodies like the HRC. It does not carry the crucial right to representation in government, nor to manage their own communal affairs within the structure of the State. It does not include any right to communicate with minorities or majorities of the same ethnic origin in other states, or even to enjoy affirmative action programmes. Beyond existing guarantees to individuals (and hence to groups of individuals) of equality, non-discrimination, freedom of worship and freedom to assemble, Article 27 has added little in practice except the right to use the minority language in courtrooms and in schoolrooms. Even this is qualified by reference to the reasonable needs of the State to 'strike a fair balance' in its allocation of resources: affirmative action is not a duty, even if it is the only effective way to maintain minority culture.[29]

Politicians find it difficult to admit to the existence of minorities, for fear that any such concession will encourage separatist claims. The states of Latin America have been particularly critical of 'collective rights', while Turkey could not until recently bring itself officially to acknowledge the existence of the millions of Kurds within its borders: they were always described by its diplomats at international gatherings as 'mountain Turks'. No state has, however, gone quite so far as France to deny any meaning to Article 27: that nation arrogantly refuses to be bound by it, on the grounds that 'Article 27 is not applicable so far as the Republic is concerned' because there *are* no minorities in Greater France. The peoples of Papeete, who rioted in 1995 in protest against the pollution of their culture and environment by the French nuclear tests at Mururoa Atoll, are not entitled to complain to the HRC under Article 27 because France has entered this reservation. The Tahitians are irredeemably French, so far as France is concerned, as are the peoples of New Caledonia, Guadelonia, Martinique and any minorities inhabiting the suburbs of Paris. The French state claims the right to annihilate their culture, language and religion if it chooses, on the grounds that 'minorities' can be constitutionally defined out of existence. This claim to immunity is such a sleight of hand that the HRC might have been expected to reject it outright. Regrettably, in a series of cases brought against France by its Breton minority seeking protection against the defilement of their language, the HRC upheld the French reservation to Article 27.[30] To add insult to injury, it obliged the complainants to use the French language to challenge the domestic laws which required them to use French at the expense of their mother tongue! These cases were wrongly decided: Article 27 enjoys the status of international law, and cannot be overridden by a specious guarantee of equality in the French constitution.

INDIGENOUS PEOPLES

Article 27 has more resonance when applied to indigenous peoples than to other minorities. This may be appreciated from the HRC decision in the case of the Lubicon Lake Band, a Canadian Indian tribe whose traditional land had in the distant past been seized by the province of Alberta, and whose very existence was precarious as a result of industrial development of that land's oil and gas deposits. The tribal chief claimed that the State was engaged in a process of non-deliberate genocide by permitting the degradation of the environment to such an extent that it was now impossible for the tribe to survive as a people. The Committee ruled that 'historical inequities (conceded by Canada) and certain more recent developments threaten the way of life and culture of the Lubicon Lake Band, and constitute a violation of Article 27 as long as they continue'.[31] The Canadian government was obliged to pay $45 million compensation, to set aside a reserve for the tribe and to sustain its separate existence with special community services.

Indigenous peoples have been regarded as an emerging object of international law, although it may be more logical to regard them as one class of minority group which has a particularly strong claim for fair treatment from a nation state with a majority of settler descendants. The strength of indigenous peoples' claims derives not only from sentiment: their forebears will usually have been massacred or enslaved by settlers, or at very least cheated out of their land, to which they will often retain a quasi-spiritual attachment. Western feelings of guilt and shame at colonial treatment of conquered tribes reached such a pitch that the UN proclaimed 1993 as the 'International Year of the World's Indigenous Peoples'. Reckoned to comprise 300 million people from 5,000 groups, and defined as 'descendants of the original inhabitants of conquered territories preserving a minority culture and recognizing themselves as such',[32] indigenous peoples have a particularly strong claim under Article 27 to maintaining their cultural traditions. Much is fashionably made of their 'right to development', although more often their claim is to a right *not* to develop in ways which their state of residence wishes. Their claim is 'promoted' at UN level by its Working Group on Indigenous Populations, which is driven by the statist strategy of avoiding demands for secession by offering indigenous leaders lesser alternatives, described in buzzwords like 'self-management' and 'cultural integrity' or 'cultural independence'.

The rights of minorities – and indeed of majorities – to enjoy culture has spawned endless UNESCO debates and one convention in 1970 which required states to return the 'cultural property' of other states, although only if stolen from public museums or monuments in the country of origin. This restriction protects European museums from losing the Third World plunder donated by nineteenth-century explorers and archaeologists. The ICJ ruled in 1962 that cultural relics taken by Thai authorities should be returned to Cambodia, but the decision turned on locating the temple from which they were taken in that country, rather than on the cultural significance of the relics.[33]

There is as yet no international law rule requiring the return of cultural treasures, and attempts to develop one have bogged down in the sterile debate over whether such artefacts are part of 'the common heritage of mankind' or the particular heritage of the peoples who venerate them. If Article 27 is to develop as a genuine collective international law right to cultural enjoyment then it must provide minorities with the standing to go to court to stop sales of their cultural treasures and to obtain their return. But the legal helplessness of minorities, even when supported by their state, in the face of the shameless international trade in such artefacts, is demonstrated by *Attorney-General of New Zealand* v. *Ortiz*, where the House of Lords refused to stop the sale at Sotheby's of Maori relics unlawfully exported from New Zealand, on the technical ground that the New Zealand government did not have title in the property.[34]

In the case of indigenous peoples, Article 27 has been used to help clear away two stumbling blocks to independence: the traditional doctrines that conquest extinguishes native land claims, and that treaties signed after surrender have continuing validity. The pernicious common law theory of *terra nullius* – which in countries 'discovered' by European explorers allowed native inhabitants to be treated as if they were part of the flora and fauna – was condemned by the Australian High Court in 1992, in the course of allowing Aborigines to claim historic title to land still in state (although not private) ownership.[35] In other countries, treaties signed centuries before with tribal chiefs terrified by guns or bribed by trinkets have been renegotiated to provide descendants with some compensation in cash or kind or status. These developments have been essentially domestic, although they have in common the recognition that indigenous minorities have a special relationship with the land and a claim to benefit from its wealth, of which their forebears had been wrongfully dispossessed. It is a matter for individual states as to how they should right their historic wrongs and give meaning to the cultural and spiritual traditions of their particular indigenes: Article 27 is too easily satisfied by avoidance of discriminatory laws and practices. What states have never countenanced is any right of an ethnic minority to share sovereignty, even when history and anthropology establish that an indigenous people, now a minority among the descendants of its invaders, governed themselves and their territory, prior to the invasion, through tribal or other communal structures.

SELF-DETERMINATION

At first blush, independence for ethnic minorities – whether indigenous or not – appears to be promised by Article 1 of the Civil Covenant, which announces that 'All Peoples have the right of self-determination'. But this blunt language is deceptive, because minorities are not peoples. 'Peoples' refers to *all* inhabitants of *each* existing state, and the guarantee denotes little more than the right of the population of every sovereign state to determine their own form of government without interference from other states. This is made clear by Article 1(2) of the UN Charter, which declares the UN's purpose, *inter alia*, 'to develop friendly relations among nations based on respect for the principle of equal rights and *self-determination of peoples* . . .' – the collective noun again defining the sovereign nation which is to be protected from unfriendly interference by other nations. 'Self-determination' does not entail the right to be independent, or even to vote for independence: as Rosalyn Higgins succinctly puts it, 'International law provides no right of secession in the name of self-determination.'[36] At best, the people's right to self-determination connotes the right of all citizens to participate in the political process, but this gives power to majorities and not minorities.

However much a minority may be oppressed by a majority, and however geographically obvious and politically convenient secession may be (for a province with a majority for secession either to become a self-governing state or to join another state with which it has ethnic congruence), the UN Charter sets its face against any change to the territorial integrity or political independence of its member states, other than by peaceful agreement. When the Grand Captain of the Mikmaq tribe complained that the Canadian government was denying his members their Article 1 right to self-determination (they wanted to form an independent state), rather than reject his argument, the HRC refused to hear it, on the ground that this right belongs not to individuals as a group, but to 'peoples'.[37] But even when 'peoples' properly so called are truly claiming a right to self-determination against an aggressor state, international law speaks with a forked tongue. Throughout the decolonization period, the right of peoples to reject imperial rule, by free vote for independence at a UN-monitored plebiscite, was such an article of faith that the ICJ described it as having an '*erga omnes*' character (see chapter 11). But now that decolonization has been deemed complete, the application of the self-determination principle comes up against the brick wall of state sovereignty. In 1995, the ICJ pusillanimously refused to adjudicate the clearest possible case of a breach of the right – Indonesia's invasion of East Timor – and there has been a marked nervousness in applying the doctrine to other cases, for example to the five million Palestinian Arabs or even to those (about half this number) who live in the Golan Heights and the West Bank, annexed by Israel through military conquest in 1967.

Since the UN Charter, the right of self-determination has implied the right of peoples of a territory to decide the status of their homeland (by a free and genuine vote) for independent statehood, integration with another state, or through some form of political association with another state (such as autonomy within it).[38] However, an irrational but apparently insurmountable qualification to self-determination has been the '*uti possidetis*' rule that its exercise must not involve changes to existing frontiers, other than by agreement between the states concerned. Since states rarely concede territory, *uti possidetis* has prevented the early and sensible resolution of disputes which later flare into ethnic violence. The rule was applied by the Arbitration Commission set up by the EC conference on Yugoslavia in the early 1990s to decide, according to the principles of self-determination, the fate of that dissolving state. Instead of attempting to carve a Bosnian Serb republic out of the Serb-dominated areas of Bosnia-Hercegovina and Croatia, and recommending independence for Kosovo, the Commission decided that the wishes of the minorities must be denied because they would require border changes opposed by Croatia and Serbia. Fatuously, it emphasized instead the international law duties of a state towards its minorities.[39] As the Serbs in the Krajina soon discovered, followed by the Muslims in Kosovo, this was akin to leaving the fox in charge of the hen house with a reminder of its duties towards the chickens. As with so many international law rules fashioned to perpetuate the territorial status quo, *uti possidetis* can be a potent recipe for that which it claimed to prevent, namely fratricide and oppression. And, as Diane Orentlicher points out, coupling the right of self-determination with the restraint of *uti possidetis* drains the right of its point for minorities who are in a majority in a province or part of a state: 'Through this legal alchemy, international law could claim to preserve a principle that had acquired a potent symbolic power while simultaneously depriving that principle of its power to threaten established states' "territorial boundaries".'[40]

International law advances not so much by justice as by state practice: since 'territorial integrity' is in the self-interest of each state, boundaries have become shibboleths. In Africa, where many boundaries were drawn arbitrarily and artificially by colonial powers in the nineteenth century (at places, for example, where the English explorer met the German missionary) and today make no ethnic or economic sense, the first principle of the Organization of African Unity is to maintain and protect the colonial carve-up of the continent at the Berlin Conference on Africa in 1885. The African Charter on Human and Peoples' Rights actually imposes duties on individuals to preserve and strengthen 'national solidarity' and 'territorial integrity' – in other words, to forget about minority rights and follow the national leader, who has the all-purpose excuse for infringement of civil liberties, namely that he is 'building the nation'. African political leaders claim that any alternative would lead to chaos: a more cynical view is that any alternative would in fact reduce bloodshed, but would also reduce the power of African political leaders. This subversive thought is not permitted to intrude at the UN General Assembly, or even in the ICJ – where judges might be expected to give 'self-determination' some meaning. When the opportunity arose, in 1986, in the case of *Burkina Faso* v. *Republic of Mali*, they sacrificed it to the principle of territorial integrity, with a gratuitous compliment to some violent and corrupt African leaders:

[A]t first sight this principle [of territorial integrity] conflicts outright with another one, the right of peoples to self-determination. In fact, however, the maintenance of the territorial status quo in Africa is often seen as the wisest course ... The essential requirement of stability in order to survive, to develop and gradually to consolidate their independence in all fields, has induced African States judiciously to consent to the respecting of colonial frontiers, and to take account of it in the interpretation of the principle of self-determination of peoples.[41]

The right of self-determination is, therefore, an illusion so far as UN diplomats and 'politically correct' ICJ judges are concerned. It is rendered meaningless by the Machiavellian fiction that 'peoples' and their government ('the State') are conceptually interchangeable. Although the right has been deployed, historically, to justify the overthrow of colonialism and the attainment of independence, it has thereafter been hypocritically disallowed to ethnic minorities living within the independent state, however reasonable their claims to autonomy. It has also – and even more irrationally – been withheld from peoples (such as the inhabitants of islands in the Pacific and Caribbean colonized by the French) when their colonizers have adopted the device of making them citizens of the 'mother country'. The UN General Assembly, in its Declaration on Granting of Independence to Colonial Countries and Peoples in 1960, made clear that self-determination had gone far enough: 'Any attempt aimed at the partial or total disruption of the national unity and the territorial integrity of a country is incompatible with the UN Charter.' The General Assembly's Declaration of Principle of International Law Concerning Friendly Relations among States attempts to square the circle:

Nothing in the foregoing paragraphs [of the Declaration] shall be construed as authorizing or encouraging any action which would dismember or impair, totally or in part, the territorial integrity or political unity of sovereign and independent states conducting themselves in compliance with the principle of equal rights and self-determination of peoples – and thus [sic] possessed of a government representing the whole people belonging to the territory without distinction as to race, creed or colour.

The conclusion does not follow, and the pretence that it does is dishonest. The International Labour Organization, in its 1957 Convention on Indigenous and Tribal Populations, is more upfront, rejecting self-determination for indigenous peoples in favour of 'their progress-ive integration into the life of their respective countries'. This 'assimi-lation' doctrine, so popular in the 1950s, led to the degradation and destruction of peoples perceived as 'primitive' in an effort to have them accept 'superior' white values, laced with alcohol. It should not be forgotten that the UN's insistence on reconciling minorities to their fate within a larger polity (throwing to them the scant consolation of Article 27) reflects the interests of the old USSR (struggling to suppress the nationalities which became sovereign states on its collapse in 1991), France (justifying its colonial retentions), India (afraid of its own fragmentation) and the bullyboy leaders of some African and South American nations, who insist that the penalty for promoting irredentism must be death. These are the bad reasons why there is no support in UN instruments for construing 'self-determination of peoples' in a manner helpful to minorities or indigenous populations within a state, or to transfrontier minorities like the Kurds, whose homelands cross national borders and who can expect 'safe havens' from the UN only when they are threatened with extinction by Saddam Hussein.

It is open to future courts, with judges independent of states and their trade union (the General Assembly), to give the right of peoples to self-determination some meaning beyond the historic process of decolonization (a process now artificially deemed to have ended). Pressure from African countries has allowed the right to include 'liberation from racist domination' (revolution was always acceptable against minority white governments in South Africa and Rhodesia); Arab countries have wanted it to include liberation from some forms of foreign domination (i.e., from Israel occupying Palestinian terri-tories). In due course the Charter principle of self-determination of peoples came quite illogically to denote some right of governments to avoid interference from other states.[42] But now that the main progenitor of this doctrine, the USSR, has collapsed under the weight of its own ethnic minorities, while South Africa and Zimbabwe have conceded majority rule and Israel is slowly removing itself from Arab territories, there must be some hope that the right of peoples to self-determination can revert to something akin to its true meaning, namely a right conferred on peoples against their own governments.[43]

The reason why international law has made so little contribution to the reduction of ethnic strife is because of its positivist composition: it constructs its rules as a synthesis of what states in fact do, rather than by reference to what they *should* do according to principles of fairness and justice. This approach has denied to minorities all but the bare rights to exist and to maintain innocuous cultural differences. In 1966, the ICJ had an opportunity to give self-determination some meaning in terms of justice when it adjudicated upon Namibia's right to independence, but the craven majority of its judges insisted that secession – however morally, politically or socially necessary – was beyond the cognizance of international law.[44] By ruling the very subject non-justiciable, they withheld from the world the one tried and tested means of resolving grievances short of conflict and strife, namely the submission of the question to impartial arbitration.

The ICJ and a host of *ad hoc* arbitral tribunals have developed principles and precedents for dealing with land ownership disputes between states: it is not an impossible step to adjudicate claims by ethnic minorities to statehood or to increased political recognition. Teams of lawyers are less expensive than armies, and do not slaughter each other. Millions of lives have been lost through secessionist movements, and while it may be idealistic to hope that all sides will respect an international court decision, at least that reasoned adjudication would provide some guide as to whether and on what side other states or the Security Council should intervene to stop the conflict. Imbroglios in places like former Yugoslavia and Somalia, where politicians and diplomats could not agree on which ethnic claims were justified, might well have been better handled had UN action been preceded and guided by an international court decision as to the sovereign rights of competing groups. It may be over-idealistic to imagine that blood feuds can be diverted to courtrooms, or staunched by the redrawing of boundaries, but the massive loss of life occasioned by secessionist movements surely warrants an attempt. However, as international law now stands, it offers no means of relieving ethnic strife: only states are entitled to be parties to cases before the ICJ. 'As a result, indigenous peoples cannot under any likely set of circumstances have their claims of abuse resolved under international law as assessed by the International Court, or even by some special tribunal with any authority to assess claims put forward on behalf of indigenous people.'[45]

Preservation of minority culture is not achievable by Article 27's recognition of the group's right to exist alongside the majority and to receive equality of treatment: those who are members of ethnic minorities are also entitled to special protection by law to secure that same enjoyment of their language, religion and lifestyle which the majority (at least in democracies) may take for granted. Thus, Article 27, and the domestic law which reflects it, should not only work to allow members of minorities a level playing field when competing with other citizens for jobs and services, but must also give them a communal right to enjoy a culture from which those other citizens are excluded. It is necessary to recognize these 'communal rights' (the portmanteau phrase 'minority rights' is misleading) as genuinely belonging to groups, rather than to individuals who happen to be members of groups, and to allow them to be asserted by group representatives in domestic or international tribunals seized of their grievances. In an ideal world, such tribunals would have power to decide at what point minorities deserve representation in government or some measure of self-management or territorial autonomy within the framework of the wider state, or even when they should be permitted to secede.

The value of this approach over the individual rights focus would be to give minorities as such the opportunity to submit their disputes with states – in effect, with the majority in their state – to arbitration rather than to the sword, by seeking a peaceful resolution before embarking upon terrorist or guerrilla action. While some blood feuds are much too bitter to be amenable to law, the prospect of adjudicative settlement must be worth exploring by an international community whose diplomacy and politicking has failed for too many years in the Balkans and Africa, and most recently in Indonesia. The simple procedural way forward is to give minorities the standing to bring cases before the ICJ: exclusion from the Court of all potential litigants except states has prevented it from picking up the pioneering pieces of PCIJ jurisprudence on the minorities treaties. This solution would have to be accompanied by an extension of the ICJ's jurisdiction beyond the consent-based optional covenant which only sixty-two states at present accept.

ECONOMIC AND SOCIAL RIGHTS

Civil and political rights may be fundamental, but they cannot be enjoyed on an empty stomach. Talk to Holocaust survivors, and they will tell you that racial discrimination, slavery and loss of liberty were not their immediate concern in the concentration camps, but rather an aching and all-enveloping hunger. Of course, starvation was inflicted as a consequence of an inhumane racist policy, but it endangered their 'right to life' more directly than depriving them of civil liberties. The Universal Declaration recognizes that the duty of states to protect the 'inherent dignity' of humankind goes much further than clothing individuals with legal powers: they must be clothed with clothing. They must be fed and housed and educated; given access to medical and social services when needed; able to find work paid sufficiently to make leisure time – spent with family and in the cultural life of the community – a fulfilling experience. States' duties to afford a basic standard of living for their peoples are expressed in Articles 22–7 of the Universal Declaration as 'rights' which are 'indispensable for dignity and the free development of personality'. But the highly politicized Human Rights Commission of the UN decided that these 'socialist' ideals were qualitatively different from liberty rights, both in theory (they must depend on government policies, not court decisions) and in practice (they need a great deal more money to implement). So when they were consigned to a separate treaty, the International Covenant on Economic, Social and Cultural Rights, it was decided that this covenant should have no adjudicatory body like the Human Rights Committee. It would instead be overseen by an Economic and Social Committee, which would receive and study reports provided by states on their progress towards realizing the treaty goals. It was noised abroad that these 'second generation' rights were not *real* rights but merely aspirations, ideals for states to achieve under their own steam or with charitable assistance from the international community, and they would never reverberate in international law because living standards were within the sovereign domain of the nation state for which it could never be called to account.

This approach has had a baleful influence, withdrawing from the scope and hope of international enforcement the set of Economic Covenant rights which are not only justiciable, but essential to human dignity. While it is true that no one can insist on the right to work (let alone in chosen employment with paid holidays) in a country where there are no jobs on offer, that does not preclude a legal right to such modicum of care and subsistence as is necessary to sustain life. And if that provision is beyond the resources of the particular state, then there should arise an international law duty upon other states to assist, on terms which may properly entail some breach of sovereignty. A government which abjectly fails in its duty to feed and clothe its citizens should be liable to international intervention, all the more so because in practice its failures will often be caused by the corruption of the ruling élite or a preference for spending the national wealth on armaments.

State sovereignty has been a crumbling stumbling block in the advance of *civil* rights, but it has proved a complete impasse to securing economic and social rights for citizens of many, if not most, countries in the world. The state sovereignty principle affords protection to rulers who loot or otherwise misappropriate vast sums of public money, generally transmitted to Swiss bank accounts which by Swiss law remain secret. The careers of Marcos and Suharto testify to the brazenness with which some rulers enrich themselves and their families, and most 'developing' countries have high-level insti-tutionalized corruption which hinders their development. (For example, it has been estimated that up to 30 per cent of World Bank loans to Indonesia went into the pockets of Suharto and his cronies.) IMF studies have shown that endemic official bribery, usually laun-dered through the device of 'commission' payments to intermediaries, operates as a tax on foreign investment, and works to reduce growth and to divert resource allocation from essential services like education and health (where bribery potential is low) to grandiose projects and expenditure in areas riddled with massive bribes (such as armaments and acquisitions for national airlines).[46] The chief villains are rapacious rulers and politicians, but equally responsible are the multinational corporations which queue up to pay the 'commissions'. To combat this, the US has taken the lead, firstly with its Foreign Corrupt Practises Act (which prohibits American companies from bribing foreign officials) and then (because the Act put American business at a competitive disadvantage) by promoting an OECD convention, which became effective in 1999, under which the major trading states pledge to pass similar laws.

The United Nations system of 'state reporting', which obsessively avoids hurtful criticism, has been inadequate other than in helping to pinpoint priorities for the UN's aid agencies, which cannot be seen to take issue with the political policies of member states which are assisted. More has been achieved through the muscle of the main donor countries, which in the last decade have sometimes imposed conditions on aid grants – such as transition to democracy. The World Bank and the International Monetary Fund also have the power to make client states change their policies, although the price they exact will often be to the detriment of economic and social rights (usually, it will involve an insistence on free market reforms, and often a dismantling of social security arrangements). The international community has failed to establish any system by which collective claims to economic and social rights can be heard and determined, and which directs the aid necessary to satisfy them to states on conditions that address their failings, e.g., requiring them to reduce their military budgets or to take steps to combat political corruption.

Contemporary statistics show that hundreds of millions of people live in utter poverty, without access to basic health care. Two million children die annually from preventable diseases, and several hundred thousand women lose their lives in childbirth. Over a hundred million children receive no schooling and adult illiteracy is massive. These statistics arise primarily from Africa, but the problem is not confined to that disastrous continent: one fifth of the world's population is affected. The failure of governments, either regionally or in political blocs or through the UN, to establish any framework for allocating resources to cope with a fight against immunizable disease and illiteracy is tragic: Western aid is subject to the 'compassion fatigue' which affects both foreign policy and NGO funding. Equally striking is the failure of governments to provide legal mechanisms for people (or 'peoples') whose economic or social rights have been violated. This is evidenced by their inability to make progress towards an Optional Protocol to the Economic Covenant, which would permit individual complaints to a committee equivalent to the HRC. The United States, which has been particularly opposed to this step, is inclined to forget that President Roosevelt nominated 'freedom from want' as one of his four basic freedoms in the speech in 1941 which launched the modern human rights movement.

What is certain is that many of the economic and social rights listed in the Universal Declaration are appropriate for enforcement by individuals, or better still by groups, in national courts. Examples are the right to receive equal pay for equal work, to access a social security system, to join trade unions, for children to have free education at primary level, and to have the overarching right of non-discrimination which can be asserted in respect of every welfare service. States with advanced legal systems have experienced no difficulty in having their courts and administrative tribunals deliver 'distributive justice' in respect of both individual and group entitlements to housing and social services. There is no reason in principle why decisions as to whether states are in breach of their obligations under the Universal Declaration and the Economic Covenant could not be made by an international body of experts sitting as the equivalent of the Human Rights Committee, or even by the Human Rights Committee itself (suitably enlarged and resourced). This must be the way forward for promoting fair entitlements for individuals to whatever welfare services a state in fact makes available, although any enforcement action would collide with the sovereignty barrier. What the world community must be entitled to do, in minimum recognition of Articles 22–7, is to create a quasi-legal system for

(1) ensuring that a reasonable amount of resources actually available to the State are spent on providing for basic rights of health and education and social security, as distinct from being spent (for example) on armaments and monuments and the servicing of debts rather than people, and

(2) identifying those states where available resources, although reasonably allocated, are simply insufficient to satisfy basic rights, a situation which attracts the duty which falls on other states to provide aid and assistance.

Poor states never jib at (2) because they will always accept (and often demand) hand-outs from the West (to be geographically more accurate, the North). But they cannot accept the logical consequence that such hand-outs should be predicated upon the exercise described at (1), which would entail not only independent external evaluation of domestic policy but the ultimate insult to a state's sovereignty by subjecting it to an international body with power to *dictate* how policy must change, or at least to *force* that change by, for example, making aid conditional upon it. Although some direction is suffered, usually with ill grace, when loans and debt-reschedulings are held out as carrots by the IMF, these preconditions usually relate to management of the economy, free market reforms and greater financial stringency: the IMF and the World Bank are not in the business of setting human rights targets as priorities. Ultimately, some international adjudicatory body must be empowered to do so, if the great pledge of Article 28 of the Universal Declaration is to be honoured, namely:

Everyone is entitled to a social and international order in which the rights and freedoms set forth in this Declaration can be fully realized.

Under Article 2 of the Economic Covenant, each state party (and there were at last count 141 of them)

undertakes to take steps, individually and through international assistance and co-operation, especially economic and technical, to the maximum of its available resources, with a view to achieving progressively the full realization [of the Covenanted rights].

This can be construed as imposing on wealthier states a 'Good Samaritan' duty to help neighbours in distress, at least when they are in the grip of famine or poverty or natural disaster. But this duty does not bestow a correlative human right on the distressed state to demand an allocation of resources – indeed, it is nonsensical (and dangerous) to endow states with 'human' rights. The duty can only be owed to suffering individuals or groups within the distressed state, not to its government and not to its people as a whole (since there are always élites who insulate themselves from poverty). The collective right of victims to press the international community for a relief allocation cannot be formally asserted at the bar of any adjudicative body, not because it would be incapable of adjudication but because no such body exists. Should one be established, it would need the power to make the state of which its suppliants are nationals a party to the action, in order that its government could be given directions on how to change its present policies so as better to satisfy the basic needs of its citizens. Whether this would be hailed as a sensible step in global governance or as human rights imperialism is beside the point, since it would empower those most affected by poverty, transforming them from passive recipients of aid into plaintiffs who had obtained their due by asserting before the international community their human right to a remedy for the hopelessness of their collective life.

The same procedure, if established to enforce the 'lost rights' of Articles 22–7 of the Declaration, could be used as a means of securing other collective rights which have come to be recognized in recent years as fundamental. The most important of these relate to the environment: they range from the right to enjoy the natural wonders of the world (which requires states to preserve natural heritage areas falling within their territorial domains) to the right to breathe clean air, now and in the future. These 'prospective rights' could be exerted on behalf of future generations, much as parents and guardians may litigate on behalf of children in most domestic legal systems. International conferences on such subjects as greenhouse gases and CFCs occur regularly, of course, and occasionally sovereign governments manage to agree upon co-ordinated action. Their failures are more notable than their successes, and if real progress is to be made in respect of any treaty or agreement it will turn on states' willingness to accept the decision of an international arbiter as to whether and when they are in breach and the nature of any penalty.

The 'right to development' has been solemnly identified by the General Assembly as a new 'inalienable human right', declared as such in 1986, although its content is defined as 'a comprehensive economic, social, cultural and political process' – whatever such an elusive formula may mean. 'Development', in the sense of an increase in a country's GNP, is welcome, but has nothing to do with inalienable human rights – indeed, it is sometimes achieved at their expense (see Mussolini's achievements in making Italian trains run on time). The 1986 Declaration was one of the first indications of how fashionable human rights were becoming: governments which had bridled at their very mention suddenly rallied to a concept which seemed to offer something to *them*, in the name of the human beings within their borders who – thanks largely to governmental incompetence and corruption – were not 'developing'. Fraternal obligations on rich states to help the poor are much to be encouraged, but not by a process which devalues *human* rights by trusting governments with them. When the fleshy rhetoric is stripped away to reveal the bare legal bones, the hidden agenda behind this 'right' becomes clear: 'the most important and comprehensive aspect of [the right to development] is the right of each people freely to choose its economic and social system without outside interference or constraint of any kind, and to determine, with equal freedom, its own model of development'.[47] In other words, more power to one-party government (disguised as 'people') to shore up state sovereignty – the traditional enemy of the human rights movement. Beware this 'right to development', which asserts the right of underdeveloped states to receive money without strings attached, because its promoters fear strings which will require government ministers to reduce their military budgets or their Swiss bank accounts or the monuments they build to perpetuate their memory.

A RIGHT TO DEMOCRACY?

Customary international law has been profoundly apolitical, in the sense that its rules have been carefully tailored to suit sovereign states irrespective of whether that sovereignty inheres in a monarch or a military dictator or a popularly elected president. Treaties are ratified by whomsoever holds executive power, and the rule of non-intervention applies no matter how unpopular the head of state may be. 'Sovereign immunity' is often claimed by, and always accorded to, rulers and their diplomats whose own people, if given the vote, would emphatically cast them from power. But the most remarkable feature of the last two decades of the twentieth century is the triumph of democracy as the central organizing principle for the nation state: many of those in Latin America have made the transition from military dictatorship; one-party rule is diminishing in Africa and in Asia; the USSR has splintered into a dozen crypto-democratic pieces. More countries within the Muslim tradition were turning to democratic elections – most notably Indonesia, but also (although without female suffrage) Iran, Oman and Kuwait. By 1999, eighty-eight states were accounted fully democratic, compared with fifty that were not and fifty-three that seemed to be moving in a democratic direction. It would be wishful to think that dictators are a dying breed, but they are certainly in a defensive minority. So is a rule of international law, requiring democratic elections, in the process of developing?

The problem is 'state practice', because states have always condemned – loudly, and in the UN – any other state which has acted by armed invasion to restore democracy. This is invariably described as a 'blatant breach' of international law and Article 2(7) of the Charter. This was the fate of Tanzania, when it courageously sent its troops to overthrow Idi Amin, the bloody tyrant of Uganda, and of the US for ridding Grenada of the fratricidal maniacs who murdered their elected prime minister. Among sensible observers, these 'unlawful' interventions are followed by universal sighs of relief. Of course, they antagonize diplomats, but they are morally justified by the Security Council's failure to act in cases which demand humanitarian intervention. Attempts are made at the UN, however, to justify them on spurious grounds such as threats to the life of American students, and not on the basis of vindicating any international law right to participate in democratic government.

Such a right *is* ripening, however, in favour of what Winston Churchill described as 'the worst system of government except for all the others'. Its seed is Article 21 (1) and (3) of the Universal Declaration:

(1) Everyone has the right to take part in the government of his country, directly or through freely chosen representatives.
(3) The will of the people shall be the basis of the authority of government; this will shall be expressed in periodic and genuine elections which shall be by universal and equal suffrage and shall be held by secret vote or by equivalent free voting procedures.

This is the language of democracy, but it is broad enough to include systems which grant the right to vote only if it is a vote for candidates approved by a single political party. Rousseau's 'general will' is identified as the source of state power, and its mode of expression must be through the ballot box, although beyond this the Article (and its counterpart in Article 25 of the Covenant) does not go. But the argument for a right to democracy is given additional force by the Charter and Covenant principle of 'self-determination of peoples'. Although this originally meant no more than the right of the whole populace to select its form of government – democratic, communist or whatever – it is now being hailed, post the Cold War, as a right to participate in democratic government, or at very least a right to a referendum on any alternative system.[48]

On any sensible reading, Article 21 of the Universal Declaration and the Charter principle of 'the self-determination of peoples' invalidate all remaining military regimes run by savage soldiers in places like Burma, where the patient courage of Aung San Suu Kyi, an elected leader detained by military despots, has elicited much sympathy but not much action (democracy only gets restored in small countries without powerful allies). The United Nations is by definition undemocratic: the superpowers rule the Security Council, and in the General Assembly the vote of a country with 10,000 inhabitants is worth exactly the same as the vote of a country with a population of 900 million. Although history shows that democracies are less inclined to go to war against each other, and have better track records on human rights than alternative systems, they score just as badly on corruption levels (especially in the small islands which make up many UN votes) and 'the will of the people' often urges capital punishment and discrimination against minorities.

None the less, international law is nudging domestic and international courts towards decisions which favour the democratic process,[49] and it is likely that the Article 21 guarantee of 'genuine' elections will eventually be interpreted to mean 'democratic' elections. The monitoring of elections by observers from the UN or the Council of Europe, to decide whether they are truly democratic, has become a feature of 'transitional' states, which increasingly need a clean bill of health as a condition both for recognition by the world community and for loans from the World Bank. The problem in achieving customary international law status for a right to democracy is not the number of surviving military regimes or absolute monarchies, but China – the superpower and Security Council member which signed the Civil Covenant in 1998 and the following year imposed long prison sentences on its main pro-democracy campaigners. It may therefore be said at the turn of the twenty-first century that although the loss of democracy through a military coup or suchlike is a matter which concerns the law of nations, and restoration of democracy may therefore be a Chapter VII objective, there is as yet no right to democracy in countries which have not enjoyed that system of government in the recent past.

5

War Law

'The road to hell is paved with good Conventions.'[1]

There has been no diplomatic exercise so persistent, yet so unfulfilled, as the twentieth-century search for a law to preserve the peace of the world. A century of arms control efforts, commencing in 1899 with a peace conference in The Hague at which twenty-six nations debated whether to use dum-dum bullets, ends with 50 million Kalashnikov rifles in circulation and without an international rule preventing the use – let alone the development – of nuclear weapons. Innumerable treaties, conventions and conferences, and the charters of the League of Nations and the United Nations, have made all the provision for world peace that language can describe, but the failure to establish authoritative bodies to interpret and to enforce that language has turned the laws against war into a graveyard of good words. There is, as always, no shortage of rules: endless, overlapping, repetitive formulae devised by delegates in the expensive comfort of Geneva hotels, later to be signed and ratified by states secure in the knowledge that should any question arise about their meaning or application, they will be judges in their own cause. They need never construe their aggression as a threat to peace, or if such construction is unavoidable they may deem it the exercise of an inherent right of individual or collective self-defence. Thus the century ended much as it began, in a world of small wars and occasional genocides combated by great powers if it suited their national interest.

International law has sought to regulate wars in two ways: initially, by restricting the justifications for waging them, and (when that failed) by prescribing rules for conducting them humanely. But the notion of a 'humane war' is a contradiction in terms, while wars always seem 'just' to those prepared, on whichever side, to die fighting them. Today, states which are civilized enough to abide by the letter of the Geneva Conventions on the Treatment of Prisoners-of-War and Non-Combatants in Occupied Territories do not, on the whole, start wars or occupy territories, and the states which do are unlikely to treat prisoners and civilians with any degree of decency. None the less, the detailed conventions on these subjects serve to set standards, any obvious breach of which will result in a propaganda windfall for the enemy. The importance of the Hague and Geneva Conventions is that a party ignores them at its peril precisely because its behaviour is now transmitted by satellite television to an international public whose outrage (especially from the American section of that public) pressures politicians to 'do something' by way of armed intervention. The laws of war may not be directly enforceable, but they do function to help viewers know a war crime when they see it on CNN. It is the collective anger produced by that knowledge and its application to the conduct of one side in a foreign war which serves both to tilt international opinion towards intervention on behalf of the opposing side and (more importantly) to overcome the Mogadishu factor – that low tolerance of casualties which militates in America against any intervention at all.[2] In this way, rules of war remain important, as providing a basis for UN intervention, or even for humanitarian intervention without specific UN approval, if they are regularly or dramatically flouted in the course of a conflict.

Most of the rules discussed in this chapter were formulated or consolidated after the Second World War, and hence were designed for a drawn-out conflict between Great Power opponents which would ebb and flow across land borders and open sea. What they did not cater for was the low-intensity civil war or internecine struggle in which one state seeks to suppress rebel militias or armed dissidents. The idealists who drafted the UN Charter and the 1949 Geneva Conventions could not have foreseen the eruptions of nationalist and racist blood feuds in the Middle East, on the Indian–Pakistan border, in an eastern Europe ultimately liberated from communism, or between African tribes corralled in artificial colonial borders. The rules for POWs drafted so painstakingly to perpetuate memories of the RAF

officers' mess at Colditz would hardly serve for wars in which combatants took no prisoners or, if they did, where the diet prescribed for
them at Geneva was beyond the wildest dreams of their ill-fed captors.
The traditional etiquette of European war, with its prohibition of
poisons and dirty tricks, makes no sense to liberation front guerrillas
fighting for their lives and their lands against states which deploy
tanks and ballistic missiles. Nor does it chime with the dilemmas of
'virtual war', of the kind waged by NATO against Serbia. What
entitles a combatant to value the lives of its pilots so highly that all
bombs are dropped from a height at which the pilots are safe and
civilians are certain to die? The availability of 'smart' weaponry
capable of distinguishing between a barracks and the hospital next
door carries a moral obligation to use these weapons to make such
distinctions. As advances in military technology lift the 'fog of war'
and facilitate surgical strikes, the law of war may come to resemble
the law of tort, with combatants liable to be sued for negligence if
they miss their approved military target.

The other fundamental flaw in customary law is that it accepts war
as a legitimate and inevitable instrument of national policy, which
can be made more bearable for both soldiers and non-combatants if
armies follow rules. The task of law for the future is to change that
assumption: war is unnecessary and starting war is criminal, hence
those who make it as well as those who conduct it with exceptional
viciousness must be punished. There has to be a defined point, a
trigger test, for the international community to intervene forcibly to
restore the peace and round up those who can be held criminally
responsible for its breach. Planning or waging a war of aggression is
a crime against humanity, which the statute of the International
Criminal Court recognizes in its terms but declines to punish because
governments cannot yet agree on the definition of 'aggression'.

There have, however, been modest advances as a result of the
Second World War. The UN framework has established the Security
Council as the body empowered, if the 'Big Five' permanent members
agree, to marshal international forces and to wage a war the justice
of which is widely recognized. Although its first such excursion, to
Korea in 1950, was owed to happenstance (the USSR was absent from
the Council when the vote was taken), forty years on there was

sufficient unanimity among its permanent members to invade Iraq because of its annexation of Kuwait. That too owed much to expediency: Iraq in 1991 had no powerful allies, and the punishment of Saddam Hussein's breach of international law coincided with the economic interests of most states prepared to hazard their armed forces in the venture. This was not a motive for the subsequent military action to create 'safe havens' for Iraq's Kurdish people, which was taken by the US, UK and France for reasons of urgent humanitarian necessity, and retrospectively received the unanimous blessing of the UN Security Council. Since the approval of that wayward and politicized body cannot be counted upon in cases where a grave emergency is caused by a state with one friend among the 'Big Five', can the right to breach sovereignty as a matter of humanitarian necessity be claimed in the absence of Security Council approval?

This was the legal issue raised by NATO's aerial bombardment of Serbia in 1999. It was plainly a breach of Article 2(7) of the Charter (non-intervention against a sovereign state) because it was not taken pursuant to a Security Council resolution under Chapter VII. Although the Council had adopted various resolutions to the effect that the situation in Kosovo constituted a threat to international peace, these did not authorize military action, which Russia and China would certainly have vetoed. But in the three months before the air strikes, evidence emerged of massacres of ethnic Albanians by Serb troops, directed from Belgrade, going far beyond what could ever be justified as reprisals for some terrorist killings committed by an insurgent Albanian group, the Kosovo Liberation Army. Evidence mounted that Serbia was engaged in a plan to terrorize the ethnic majority in the province, to 'ethnically cleanse' it not by genocide (comparisons between Hitler and Milosevic are false) but by persecuting the Albanian majority so severely that most would flee, creating a refugee crisis for neighbouring states. This would amount to a crime against humanity under Article 7 of the Rome Statute (see p. 498). The legal justification for NATO's attack, absent Security Council approval, was that (a) the Serbian state was engaged in an ongoing conspiracy to commit a crime against humanity; (b) this conspiracy was producing a humanitarian emergency which threatened international peace; and (c) military intervention in the form of air strikes was a proportionate deterrent offering a reasonable prospect of avoiding the tragedy, or at least of punishing its perpetrators. The satisfaction of conditions such as these could provide a legal basis for humanitarian intervention, certainly by a united and regional bloc like NATO, when the Chapter VII mechanism is blocked by superpower politics (see chapter 11). This must sorely disappoint those who have placed their faith in the United Nations, but it is a result of that organization's systemic failure to commit to justice as a necessary precondition for peace, and to the illogical rules of its executive council, by which any one of five governments may outvote the rest of the world.

IN SEARCH OF THE JUST WAR

DR LIEBER'S CODE

All civilizations have fought wars according to rules designed to make them marginally less bloody. Humanitarian concerns may sometimes be detected in the customs of Greek and Roman armies, through the chivalrous Christian tradition of St Augustine which forbade attacks on women and the wounded, and the heraldic influences on medieval city states. But the main purpose of war law was to cut the losses and distribute the gains of the potentates and princes who joined battle in the first place. Scholars like Grotius and Vattel who rationalized war law in the seventeenth and eighteenth centuries were at pains to identify 'just' wars and to protect non-combatants, but always subject to military exigency and to the policy requirements of rulers for whom wars, like marriages, were necessary diplomatic activities. The first set of war rules to show any genuine concern for the enemy was compiled by Dr Franz Lieber in 1863 at the direction of Abraham Lincoln, anxious that fellow Americans who followed the Confederate flag should not be permanently disaffected by brutalities committed by his government army. While it was no doubt true that 'what could be got away with in wars against Red Indians and Mexicans would not wash in a contest with Southern gentlemen',[3] the Lieber code – *Instructions for the Government of Armies of the United States in the Field* – remains the first source of modern military law. It was the model for military codes in many other countries (ironically, for the Serbian army in 1879) and its principles are even now being applied by the Hague Tribunal to help ascertain customary international law.

The military manual has been supplemented by innumerable treaties and conventions and by the principles distilled from the Nuremberg and Tokyo Tribunals. The modern rules governing the conduct of hostilities are now collected in the four Geneva Conventions of 1949 (which the vast majority of states have ratified). The earlier treaties remain of some importance, however, in tracing the extent to which various rules have entered customary international law – a body of principles which draws upon treaty law as a source, but exists independently of it. This is recognized in the treaties themselves, through a sweeping-up provision (called the 'Martens Clause') which acknowledges the duty of all belligerents, quite apart from the treaty, to obey the rules of customary international law 'as they result from the usages established between civilized nations, from the laws of humanity and the requirements of the public conscience'.[4]

THE HAGUE CONVENTIONS

The origins of the modern 'humanitarian' law of war lies less in concern for humankind than for the coffers of the warring states. This was the motive for holding the first international conferences, at St Petersburg (1868) and The Hague (1899), to limit the development of expensive armaments, notably poison gases and the newly invented explosive bullet. The 1868 conference dressed up this desire to save money in the language of humanity: projectiles weighing less than 400 grams which were explosive or inflammable were denounced because they 'uselessly aggravate the sufferings of disabled men'. So the conference fixed 'the technical limits at which the necessities of war ought to yield to the requirements of humanity', and promised to maintain this balance 'in view of future improvements which science may effect in the armament of troops'. The 1899 conference ended with a convention which followed Dr Lieber in codifying the rules of land warfare. It issued special declarations against the use of dum-dum bullets and 'projectiles the sole object of which is the diffusion of asphyxiating or deleterious gases'. The first Hague Convention, notwithstanding its financial motivation, may be seen as an application of a traditional principle (reflected in the ancient codes prohibiting poison and in the Lateran Council's 1139 edict against the 'unchristian' crossbow):

That the right of belligerents to injure the enemy is limited by their duty to avoid doing so by methods which cause unnecessary suffering, and which are either novel or generally perceived as dishonourable.

At the second Hague Peace Conference in 1907, forty-four states reached general accord on the basic rules of war, but signally failed to put in place any mechanism for limiting armaments. They repeated the fundamental principle that 'the right of belligerents to adopt means of injuring the enemy is not unlimited' – a principle objectionable today not so much for the questions it begs as for the notion that states have any right to be belligerent in the first place. It forbade the use of poison and poisonous weapons, attacks on surrendered soldiers, the killing or wounding of the enemy 'treacherously' or by weapons 'calculated to cause unnecessary suffering'. Attacks on undefended towns were prohibited, and belligerents were required to spare hospitals, churches, universities and historic buildings 'provided they are not being used at the time for military purposes'. There was a duty placed on all belligerents to treat prisoners-of-war humanely, to allow them to keep their personal belongings and to practise their religion, and to exempt officers from work and spare their men from tasks connected with the war. A further convention dealt with duties owed to peaceful shipping by belligerents which laid mines; it prohibited bombardment by naval forces of undefended ports and asserted the immunity of hospital ships, fishing boats (see the *Paquete Habana Case*, p. 83) and neutral shipping.

THE WORLD WARS

All of these rules were broken, sometimes systematically, by all the belligerents in the First World War. War criminals – even among the defeated Germans – escaped punishment (see p. 211), although in 1921 one German court set an important precedent in the case of *The Llandovery Castle* by convicting machine-gunners who massacred defenceless sailors as they took to the lifeboats after their ship was sunk. The defence of superior orders was rejected because the order in question was 'universally known to be against the law'.[5]

After the war, and as a result of its horrors, the futile movement to humanize conflict was superseded by the idealistic goal of preventing it altogether. The Covenant of the League of Nations pledged renunciation of 'resort to war', and provided a resort instead to settlements brokered by the League Council or adjudicated by the Permanent Court of International Justice. To this end in 1928 was directed the Paris General Treaty for the Renunciation of War (the Kellogg–Briand Pact) by which the signatories (including the US, which never joined the League) renounced war as an instrument of national policy and agreed to settle disputes by 'pacific means'. With these fine, unreal words the nations of the world hastened towards the Second World War, pausing only to clarify the rules relating to their new weaponry.

Aerial warfare had been on the agenda at The Hague in 1923: bombing was only legitimate 'when directed at a military objective', and not when used 'for the purpose of terrorizing the civilian population', although causing civilian terror is, as both the Luftwaffe and the RAF were to prove twenty years later, a modern military objective *par excellence*. In NATO's 'espresso machine war' on Belgrade, too, the enemy appeared to weaken only when bombing of power plants and water supplies deprived its middle classes of their morning coffee. The problem – encountered acutely in the war over Kosovo (see pp. 416–17) – is that many installations have dual civilian/military uses. A television station, for example, may provide news and entertainment to the public while also being used to send military signals: it will usually have a propaganda function and may be used (like radio in Rwanda) to incite crimes against humanity. At what point does targeting such a station become legitimate because it is a 'military objective'?

In 1925 came a Geneva Protocol prohibiting the use of poisonous gases, immediately ratified by Italy (which then gassed the Ethiopians) and Japan (which used gas in its war on China). This protocol had some relevance when both Britain and Germany seriously considered using chemical weapons at various stages of the Second World War. Their decisions against doing so, however, were taken not to comply with the protocol but out of fear that the other side's chemical weaponry, unleashed in reprisal, might do more damage. Finally, as late as 1936, there was an agreement in London on the rules of submarine warfare, somewhat impractically requiring submarines to surface and to save the crew of any merchant vessel it had just torpedoed. Unrestricted submarine warfare was soon conducted in breach of these rules by all major belligerents in the Second World War: Admiral Dönitz had to be acquitted at Nuremberg for ordering his U-boats to attack merchant convoys crossing the Atlantic, after US Admiral Chester Nimitz confessed to issuing similar orders to his submarines in the Pacific.

It was in the Nuremberg Charter and judgment, and in the war crimes trials which followed in Germany and Japan, that the rules of war first took on the true meaning of law, namely a rule for the breach of which there is some prospect of punishment. The Charter empowered the Tribunal to punish not only war crimes, as they could readily be described from the earlier conventions, but crimes against peace (i.e. waging a war of aggression, in violation of international treaties) and a new category of 'crimes against humanity'. This was to prove highly significant in the development of international justice, even though this category was initially limited to heinous large-scale persecution of civilians in pursuance of a war. (This particular consequence of the Nuremberg Charter forms the subject of chapter 6; the examination of war law here focuses on the 'good conventions' which followed.)

THE GENEVA CONVENTIONS

THE 1949 CONVENTIONS

There was one final achievement of humanitarian law before the Cold War set in to ferment conflicts of a kind which the post-war peacemakers failed to envisage. The four Geneva Conventions of 1949 state the principles of international law as they had by then emerged in relation to the treatment of: sick and wounded combatants on land (I) and at sea (II), prisoners-of-war (III) and civilians (IV).

The 1949 Geneva Conventions provide:

I 'For humane care of sick and wounded combatants on land', irrespective of their race, religion or politics; immunity for hospitals and medical personnel and army chaplains; special recognition of the role of the Red Cross and Red Crescent organizations.

II Similar provisions applied to those 'wounded, sick or shipwrecked at sea', with detailed rules for the immunity of hospital ships.

III 'Rules for securing the humane treatment of prisoners-of-war', protecting them from being used for military labour or in medical experiments or as objects of public insult or curiosity. Use of POWs as hostages in combat zones (i.e. to deter enemy fire) is absolutely forbidden, as is torture or any form of coercion designed to extract information. The prisoner must give his name, rank, regimental number and date of birth: on thus achieving POW status he is entitled to 'be quartered under conditions as favourable as those for the forces of the detaining power' and to have nutritious food, warm clothing and bedding, and permission to pray and to smoke. POWs are to receive monthly pay (75 Swiss francs for generals, 8 Swiss francs for privates) and must be allowed to receive food parcels and send and receive mail. They must be permitted to organize discipline in their own camps, and to make formal complaints about their treatment.

IV 'For the Protection of Civilian Persons in Time of War'. This Convention secures humane treatment for persons in occupied territories and those who have been interned on suspicion of involvement in resistance movements. The former class of 'protected persons' are entitled to respect for their family and customs and religion, and women are guaranteed protection from rape and forced prostitution. Civilians must not be used for reprisals or as hostages, or as forced labourers or subjects of mass deportations. The occupying power cannot punish civilians for activities prior to the occupation, and is entitled to execute them only for acts of spying, sabotage or murder.

These Conventions begin, most importantly, with three articles which are common to each of them. The first (common Article 1) pledges respect for the Convention 'in all circumstances', thereby excluding any excuse of national necessity or self-defence. Common Article 2 applies the Convention rules not only to declared wars but to 'any other armed conflict' arising among the parties, and requires signatories to abide by the rules even if other states do not (thus excluding a familiar reservation to previous treaties entered by states only prepared to stick to the rules as long as their enemies did). The point at which 'armed conflict' begins, thereby attracting the Geneva regime, is not defined. It would require hostile acts by an army rather than a police force, and would seem to exclude occasional border skirmishes and destabilizing tactics which did not involve the use of force.

It is important to note that the Geneva Convention scheme which state parties promise to enforce by tracking down individuals suspected of 'grave breaches' and putting them on trial applies only to crimes committed in the course of international armed conflict. Although common Article 3 promises a minimum of humane treatment in 'armed conflict not of an international character' to all civilians and non-combatants, this promise comes without an enforcement mechanism for breaches, however grave. This is because in 1949 no state was prepared to allow international law to intrude upon its sovereignty when it came to putting down insurgencies and armed revolt. Genocide apart, states were not ready to concede to the international community a jurisdiction as of treaty right to punish their officials for torture or other brutalities inflicted upon citizens within their own borders. It was the achievement of international human rights law, by the time of the *Tadić Case* in 1996, to render academic this distinction between 'international' and 'internal' atrocities (see pp. 308–15). Common Article 3 none the less contributed to that achievement. It extends the promise of a minimum standard of humanity to wars that are not declared, and to violent insurgencies, internecine struggles and armed resistance to state power (although not to riots, criminal disorder or sporadic outbreaks of civil disturbance). There has been some dispute over the level of internal violence needed to invoke common Article 3: there would have to be fighting between two armed forces with the rebels having a sufficiently organized command structure to impose Convention discipline.

Common Article 3 is apt to protect all non-combatants who are caught in the crossfire of a civil war. It specifically prohibits murder, torture, hostage-taking, 'outrages upon personal dignity' and extra-judicial executions, and covers any military, police or guerrilla action which has the deliberate result of killing or maiming civilians or prisoners. It applies to the 'High Contracting Parties to the Conventions', which means virtually every state, and must also as a matter of customary law apply by analogy to the leaders of organized guerrilla forces, since those who seek forcibly to control the state take on the basic humanitarian duties of the government they wish to supplant.

Common Article 3 helps to integrate human rights with the law of war. It was no mean achievement to persuade colonial powers that their right to put down rebellions should be limited by some basic humanitarian duties to citizens and to injured rebels. Nuremberg idealism played some part (as, more craftily, did the Soviet Union's desire for a legal stick with which to beat Western states opposed to the rebellions it was fomenting in their colonies). Asian countries, led by Burma, opposed the article on the ground that it was bound to 'incite and encourage insurgency', apparently by protecting rebels from summary execution and by giving their causes some form of legitimacy by making *them* subject to international legal obligations. At a sensible level, common Article 3 does no more than record the obligation undertaken by all state parties to observe basic human rights in times of conflict, thereby imparting to conflicts within a state an obligation recognized in wars between states.[6] The position has been confused, however, by a 1977 protocol relating to the Protection of Victims of Non-International Armed Conflicts (Protocol II) which covers similar ground to common Article 3. Here the diplomats who did the drafting were much more careful, and clearly wished to take a step backwards. Their definition of armed conflict is much narrower (the rebel force must possess troops and control territory), yet forty-three nations (including the US, Israel, France and the UK) have still declined to ratify it.

Each state has a duty, under articles common to the four Conventions which deal with 'repression of abuses and infractions', to search out suspects alleged to have committed 'grave breaches' of the Conventions and to put them on trial, regardless of their nationality. 'Grave breaches' are crimes so serious that in 1949 states were prepared, by ratifying the Conventions, to undertake to put the suspect on trial themselves or to extradite him to a country prepared to do so. They do *not* encompass crimes against common Article 3, committed in civil war, but include the following crimes if committed in *international* conflict:

wilful killing, torture or inhuman treatment, including biological experiments, wilfully causing great suffering or serious injury to body or health, and extensive destruction of property, not justified by military necessity and carried out unlawfully and wantonly.[7]

This is, inevitably, a 'catch as catch can' approach, in which few in practice are caught. Occasionally, ratifying states have acted to bring their own officers to justice – Lieutenant Calley for the My Lai massacre in Vietnam, for example. In Calley's case, however, politics (in the form of President Richard Nixon) intervened to ensure that justice was not done. Calley was properly convicted of complicity in the deaths of seventy innocent Vietnamese villagers by ordering his troops to 'waste them': he personally shot a 2-year-old child. He was sentenced to life imprisonment, which Nixon ordered to be reduced to three years. Calley served only three days in prison, spending his sentence at his home on a military base, replete with live-in lover.

Convention III (treatment of prisoners-of-war) and Convention IV (treatment of civilians) adopt an enforcement mechanism through the agency of 'protecting powers' – one nominated by each combatant – tasked with visiting prisons and war zones and generally monitoring the treatment of persons caught up in the conflict. This was always an unworkable idea (adopted from the role played by 'seconds' at a duel) and has generally been ignored: in only four conflicts have 'protecting powers' been appointed, and their role has been limited to exchanges of diplomatic niceties. More helpful work on the ground has been done by the International Committee of the Red Cross (ICRC), whose role is written into the Conventions (common Article 3 gives it a right to enter into battlefields and war zones). However, the Red Cross, to justify this privilege, makes a fetish of its commitment to confidentiality, both in observations within war zones and in its dealings with governments and militias. Its present ethics of humanitarian intervention (which are not shared by other aid agencies) require its workers to turn a blind eye to human rights violations, in the belief that their silence is the price of being invited back, or into the next war zone. It has declined for this reason to give evidence to the Hague and Arusha Tribunals, depriving them of valuable first-hand accounts of atrocities and reliable evidence against those responsible. The problem is important, since Red Cross officials always acquaint commanders with evidence of atrocities being committed by their troops, and if they take no action then these commanders will be guilty of command responsibility for any war crimes those troops subsequently commit. Their conviction, however, may depend on whether evidence of their knowledge is forthcoming from the Red Cross, in breach of its self-imposed duty of confidentiality.

THE 1977 PROTOCOLS

The Geneva Convention system comprised a fine set of rules for the protection of the victims of war, but said nothing sensible about enforcement. In 1974, the Swiss government (which a cynic might think to have profited from these Conventions rather more than the victims of war) issued invitations to a diplomatic talk-fest which lasted on and off for three years and resulted in even more rules and even less prospect of enforcing them. As a drafting exercise, Protocols I and II serve to update the language of the 1949 Conventions and to elaborate, in particular, the duties owed to civilian populations by military commanders. Protocol I summarizes, in Article 35, the three basic rules of war:

(1) In any armed conflict, the right of the parties to the conflict to choose methods or means of warfare is not unlimited.
(2) It is prohibited to employ weapons, projectiles and material and methods of warfare of a nature to cause superfluous injury or unnecessary suffering.
(3) It is prohibited to employ methods or means of warfare which are intended, or may be expected, to cause widespread, long-term and severe damage to the natural environment.

Rule 3 is elaborated in some detail, confining bombardment to military targets in the hope of minimizing civilian casualties and avoiding damage to churches, historic monuments or other cultural property. Special provision is made for the treatment of spies and mercenaries (the latter making their first appearance in these treaties) and henceforth warring parties must take care not to cause serious damage to the natural environment. Specially defined protection is given to refugees, women and children, and even to journalists, who on the production of an identity card from their government are to be accorded civilian status so long as they take no action inconsistent with that status (a reference, presumably, to shooting for one side, not to the common journalistic practice of propagating one side's disinformation).

Swelling the ranks of 'diplomats' in Geneva to produce these protocols were, for the first time, representatives of national liberation fronts, and care was taken to apply Protocol I to 'armed conflicts in which peoples are fighting against colonial domination and alien occupation and against racist regimes in the exercise of their right to self-determination' (Article 4). This definition extends a full-blooded humanitarian regime (rather than just the 'elemental decency' guarantee of common Article 3) to many civil wars. An international element must be proved, however, to attract the full Protocol I regime, and will generally be found in countries where the belligerent parties are supported by foreign powers. This is not necessarily the case with 'racist regimes' (the protocol drafters had South Africa and Rhodesia in mind) unless the international element is located in the moral and financial support given by other states to liberation groups or in the economic sanctions applied in support of their rights to self-determination.

Protocol II applies extensive humane treatment principles (taken from the Civil Covenant) to victims of government or anti-government forces in *non*-international armed conflicts, so long, at least, as the dissident forces are armed, under responsible command and 'exercise such control over a part of its territory as to enable them to carry out sustained and concerted military operations and to implement the Protocol'.[8] This formulation gives rise to definitional difficulties. It is not even clear that it would apply to organizations like the ANC in South Africa in the period when it had no 'territories' of its own but operated from bases provided or suffered by other countries, and it would not seem to apply to an armed underground resistance, however disciplined and justified in its cause.

But definitions do not much matter, because neither protocol has teeth. Protocol II, indeed, lacks gums: its Article 3 ('non-intervention') provides:

(1) Nothing in this Protocol shall be invoked for the purpose of affecting the sovereignty of a State or the responsibility of government, by all legitimate means, to maintain or re-establish law and order in the State or to defend the national unity and territorial integrity of the State.

(2) Nothing in this Protocol shall be invoked as a justification for intervening, directly or indirectly, for any reason whatever, in the armed conflict or in the internal or external affairs of the High Contracting Party in the territory of which that conflict occurs.

So what is the point? There being no enforcement provision attached, even as a pretence, to Protocol II, the result of this clause is to negate the other protocol promises of humane treatment. A state party might openly order genocide, rape, pillage and torture of any civilians and POWs, and bomb all Red Cross hospitals: however barbarically its own rules are broken, Protocol II refuses to contemplate even indirect intervention by other states. It does, indeed, provide a possible argument against the legality of NATO's attack on Serbia in 1999: Milosevic could claim that his army was 'maintaining law and order' in Kosovo against an insurrectionary force, by cleansing the province of all potential support for the Kosovo Liberation Army.

The enforcement provisions of Protocol I (applying in situations of international armed conflict) appear at first blush to be an improvement on the 1949 Conventions which merely called on states to investigate and punish 'grave breaches' (presumably identified by the 'protecting powers' who would hover like referees over the contest). There are provisions introduced in 1977 to emphasize command responsibility, requiring military commanders to ensure their troops were aware of their obligations and making them 'responsible' (but to whom?) for violations. There are pious duties imposed on states to assist other states in respect of criminal proceedings and extradition involving war crimes (subject always to the terms of extradition treaties) and there is an impressive provision that states whose armies violate the Geneva Conventions or the Protocol shall 'if the case demands, be liable to pay compensation'. But there is no court or tribunal nominated or given the power to assess any such payment, let alone order it to be made.

Most fantastical of all is Article 90, which provides that serious violations of the 1949 Conventions or of Protocol I should trigger the establishment, in conjunction with the United Nations, of an international fact-finding commission, comprising fifteen members 'of high moral standing and acknowledged impartiality' who shall inquire into 'grave breach' allegations by seeking out evidence and visiting the *locus in quo*. The commission must send its report to all parties, but *'shall not report its finding publicly* [my italics], unless all the parties to the conflict have requested the Commission to do so'.[9] No international fact-finding commission has ever been set up, notwithstanding repeated violations of the Conventions and the Protocol since 1977. The procedure is so cumbersome and so carefully designed to ensure secrecy (because no state would agree to publication of an adverse report) that it was obvious to all delegates that it would never be invoked. There is evidence from some of the diplomats who enjoyed themselves conferencing for three years in Geneva that these protocols were never really intended to be more than a comforting pretence that their member states (many of whom subsequently refused to ratify them) were active in the cause of peace. In one respect, as we shall see in chapter 7, Protocol II has seriously damaged the development of international human rights law, by an irresponsibly drafted subsection (Article 6(5)) which invites authorities in power at the end of hostilities to 'endeavour to grant the broadest possible amnesty to persons who have participated in the armed conflict' – a passage which has been seized upon by courts anxious to uphold pardons extracted by tyrants and torturers and death squads against future prosecution for committing crimes against humanity (see page 262). Although the 1949 Geneva exercise was informed by a genuine optimism that it would work, and is properly regarded as the modern bedrock of international humanitarian law, the 1977 Protocols are badly drafted exercises in cynical diplomacy and have failed to achieve normative status.

GOOD CONVENTIONS: CHEMICAL, NUCLEAR AND CONVENTIONAL WEAPONS AND LAND MINES

The result of these exercises is a set of overlapping rules spanning hundreds of pages, supplemented by hundreds of thousands of pages of minutes and conference transcripts and '*travaux préparatoires*'. These war laws are, on paper, exquisitely humane. It is difficult indeed for most Third World readers of Geneva Convention III not to yearn for the pleasures of POW status, given the three-star treatment they mandate, at least for the officer class. Convention IV accords rights to civilians in occupied territories which many impoverished peoples in unoccupied territories do not possess. As one delegate put it, 'The cure for all China's problems would be to persuade some other power to occupy the entire country.'

The fact that these rules are unreal has undoubtedly contributed to the extent to which in real life they have been flouted or (worse) rejected out of hand, the 'elemental decency' provisions having been jettisoned along with the luxury articles. Thus the Vietcong and North Vietnam refused to recognize the 'bourgeois' POW convention: Senator John McCain's experience is a reminder that the prisoners they took could have done without an officers' mess or regular wages in Swiss francs, if only they had been accorded a 'bread and water' prison existence monitored by the Red Cross. It is ironic to have to condemn humanitarian law for being *too* humane, but that fact has undoubtedly contributed to its uselessness. The United Nations should have put in place a simple system which delivered on basic rights to prisoners-of-war, internees and citizens of occupied territories. Instead, we have complicated rules, sophisticated to the point of unreality, and a delivery system which depends on what the International Committee of the Red Cross is able to make of it. In some cases (notably Israel and Palestine), it has been able to negotiate entry to prisons. In others, it has signally failed to obtain access to government torture chambers or to the makeshift jails of guerrilla groups.

The test of international law is not, however, whether it is regularly flouted but whether it is occasionally enforced – a prospect which is apt to diminish the number of future floutings. The enforcement machinery does not need to involve criminal responsibility: in the case of obnoxious weaponry, for example, what matters most is a proper verification system. And as a last resort there must be a rule requiring the international community to take preventive action to demolish weapons of mass destruction before they destroy masses. On this most anxious score, how does international humanitarian law rate? Regrettably, even when conventions, conferences, treaties and the pronouncements of the UN's General Assembly all lead logically to one result under customary international law, it is more customary to ignore that result if it interferes with military thinking.

Take, for example, the practice of carpet-bombing an area of both military significance and high population density. This is directly contrary to the Hague Rules of Aerial Warfare, which require all bombing to have a military objective. Aerial bombardment which 'terrorizes the civilian population' is prohibited. Nothing could be plainer than this rule against indiscriminate bombing; yet Allied embarrassment over the RAF's use of 'area bombardment' against Dresden and other German cities means that this war crime does not feature in the 1949 Geneva Conventions (a point unpersuasively made in defence of Nixon and Kissinger when they ordered the bombing of Cambodia). Saturation bombing of a city is a crime, and the failure of the plenipotentiaries in Geneva to acknowledge it either in 1949 or 1977 means Picasso painted *Guernica* in vain.

CHEMICAL WEAPONS

There has been rather more agreement, at least on paper, over atrocious weaponry which the military is either prepared to give up or regards as incapable of further development. The use, or at any event the first use, of chemical weapons has been contrary to international law since 1925, when a surprisingly large number of states ratified the Protocol for the Prohibition of the Use in War of Asphyxiating, Poisonous and Other Gases and of Bacteriological Methods of Warfare. These signatories did not raise so much as an eyebrow to stop Italy using poison gas a few years later in its Abyssinian campaign. Although chemical weapons have been routinely condemned at the UN Conference on Disarmament held (in Geneva, of course) every year since 1972, most states looked the other way when Iraq and Iran mustard-gassed each other's troops during the Iran–Iraq War. In March 1989 Iraq used gas to kill 8,000 Kurds at Halabja, thanks to German companies shipping stocks of Zyklon-B gas, of the kind once used to exterminate Jews in the concentration camps. This produced a certain amount of embarrassment when it was exposed as part of 'Iraqgate'. However, the UN conference caravanserai moved on to finalize the Convention on the Prohibition of the Development, Production, Stock-piling and Use of Chemical Weapons and on Their Destruction.

In due course, 121 states, including (ironically and ominously) Iraq itself, pledged to forswear the manufacture or use of chemical weaponry, and were this time prepared to permit their good intentions to be checked by an organization headquartered in The Hague, which has certain powers to require on-site inspection of chemical facilities. States wishing to keep chemical weapons up their sleeves will not ratify the treaty, and those which do are not *bound* to come to the assistance of fellow parties who are attacked by such weapons. (They can withdraw from the Convention – on ninety days' notice – if they wish to obtain supplies of toxic gas for their own use against the enemy.) Although the Chemical Weapons Convention was very much the pride of the human rights movement when it came into force in 1993, its ratification by major powers was more the result of signals from their military that chemical weapons did not now matter very much (and, if they did, they could be put together very quickly from civilian stocks) than from any newfound humanitarian zeal. Meanwhile, Iraq has been free of inspections since its break with UNSCOM after 'Operation Desert Fox' in December 1998, and is reliably reported to be stockpiling VX nerve gas, a single drop of which can kill within the hour, together with vats of the virus for camel pox, an unpleasant disease which Saddam has fantasies of inflicting on a Western world which lacks experience of camels.[10]

NUCLEAR WEAPONRY

Chemical weapons pale by comparison with nuclear arms, and it is in respect of this terrifying force that international humanitarian law has failed. The letter of the law is not to blame. If the Geneva principles have any meaning, then:

(1) if the right to choose methods of warfare is not unlimited, the very first limit must be upon use of nuclear weapons;

(2) if it is prohibited to employ weapons which cause superfluous injury, then *a fortiori* nuclear weapons are prohibited;

(3) if it is prohibited to use means of warfare which will cause severe damage to the natural environment, then it follows that nuclear weapons are prohibited.

So it is as clear as the noiseless flash which blinded Hiroshima's citizens on 5 August 1945 and killed 100,000 of them, that 'the threat or use of nuclear weapons would generally be contrary to the rules of international law applicable in armed conflicts, and in particular the principles and rules of humanitarian law'. This was the conclusion in 1996 of the International Court of Justice, although it was carefully limited to times of war (and hence has no impact on acquisition or testing of nuclear weaponry in peacetime) and was undermined by this astonishing proviso:

The Court cannot conclude definitively whether the threat or use of nuclear weapons would be lawful or unlawful in the extreme circumstance of self-defence, in which the very survival of a state would be at stake.[11]

The nuclear bomb has been unlawful ever since its drop in 1945 proved massively, indiscriminately and environmentally damaging. That first use on Hiroshima, and even the second, on Nagasaki, might have been justifiable – not as a reprisal (the consequences of 'Fatboy' were out of all proportion to Japanese bombing attacks) but under the defence of military necessity, by bringing the war to a speedier end with less overall loss of life than would otherwise have been the case. The argument for dropping the bomb elsewhere than on a civilian city, however, seems overwhelming. At first, the bomb remained in

Allied (in effect, US) possession, and there was a remarkable moment in 1946 when President Truman, encouraged by Clement Attlee and advised by Henry Stimson and Dean Acheson, actually offered to put all atomic weapons (at the time there were only three) under UN control.[12] That would have required a renunciation of nuclear development by every other nation and careful control of uranium through an environmental agency, but the plan could have worked. It did not: the Soviet Union, at first tempted, exploded its own bomb three years later and the nuclear race began, joined enthusiastically by France, Britain and (in 1964) by China.

These 'Big Five', having established their own nuclear arsenals, were mainly concerned to prevent other states from joining them, and brokered a series of non-proliferation treaties under the aegis of the UN which created the International Atomic Energy Agency in order to inspect signatory countries and verify compliance. There are test ban treaties and regional nuclear-free zone treaties and treaties by which even the Big Five powers promise to keep their nuclear bombs away from the Antarctic, the sea bed, the moon and other celestial bodies and outer space. These faintly absurd pacts, solemnly ratified by governments prepared to use nuclear weapons in places where human life *does* exist, were undermined when the 'Star Wars' programme was approved for development in 1983, heedless of the Outer Space Treaty of 1967 which obliges states 'not to place in orbit around the Earth any objects carrying nuclear weapons'. 'Star Wars' would also have breached the principles of the Strategic Arms Limitation Talks (SALT I and SALT II), which had made some progress in reducing ballistic missile systems. Fortified by American and French contempt for international treaties, some middle-rank nations developed a secret nuclear agenda of their own. Israel has stockpiled nuclear bombs since the 1970s and, in 1998, first India then Pakistan broke cover with nuclear tests. By that time, there were more than 40,000 nuclear warheads in existence with a total destructive capacity about a million times greater than 'Fatboy'. The prospect raised by Bertrand Russell and Albert Einstein in their 1955 manifesto, that 'a war with H-bombs might possibly put an end to the human race', was now in sight.

Such comfort on this score as presently exists hinges on the Non-

Proliferation Treaty regime, under which in 1995 the Big Five powers gave solemn promises not to use nuclear weapons against those states which had promised to abjure nuclear ambitions by becoming parties to the NPT. This is all very well, but it does not affect pariah states such as Libya, Iraq, Iran and North Korea, or states like Israel, Pakistan and Ukraine which deliberately avoid the NPT regime in order to cling to their nuclear programmes. Even full accession to the NPT has not stopped wealthy states equipping themselves with the technology and material to produce nuclear weapons within a few months (or, in the case of Japan, within a few weeks) of any decision so to do – about twenty such countries possess or are on the point of possessing the technology to make nuclear missiles speedily available. Even Sweden was at one point making a Scandinavian nuclear bomb.[13] A general scepticism about the NPT is demonstrated by the fact that although 152 states felt obliged to sign it, a mere thirty-three of these have been prepared to ratify.

The scepticism deepened in October 1999, when the US Senate voted much on party lines against ratifying the progeny of the NPT, the Comprehensive Test Ban Treaty which the Clinton administration had negotiated and signed in 1996. It would have had the effect of 'freezing' positions (with America far in the lead) and making it difficult for new nuclear powers to emerge. The plan was for it to come into effect once ratified by forty-four nuclear-capable nations and twenty-six of these had done so: the leaders of Britain, France and Germany pleaded with the Senate to ratify, in order to pressurize refuseniks like India, Pakistan, Israel and North Korea, and gather in cynics like Russia and China, whose attitude to ratification was 'We will if you will'. Notwithstanding the hopes of all US allies, Republican senators (led, as in most initiatives damaging to human rights, by Foreign Affairs Committee chairman Jesse Helms) refused to contemplate a world in which America could not experiment with bigger and better bombs. It was their 'Fortress America' obsession with building nuclear missile muscle (testing tells whether new weapons work) and a certain irresponsible pleasure at humiliating President Clinton (who had hailed his signature on the CTBT as one of the most important acts of his presidency) which produced a 48–51 vote falling far short of the two-thirds majority required for ratification.[14] The stalling of the CTBT and the insufficiency of the NPT gives little hope of development of any treaty law which would allow the destruction of new nuclear arsenals in states prone to aggression.

The NPT has served as a useful brake on nuclear development, but it does not answer the question which arises once it has occurred: What steps may lawfully be taken to destroy the nuclear arsenal of a state which has a potential for aggression? In 1981, the Israelis bombed Iraq's nuclear facility at Osiraq, to general condemnation – and general relief. Saddam's nuclear programme was delayed but, as the UN nuclear inspectors who visited Iraq after Operation Desert Storm revealed, it had continued at multiple sites thereafter. In December 1998 chief UN weapons inspector Richard Butler reported that Saddam Hussein remained determined to pick up his nuclear pieces and put them together, a report which the US and the UK used to justify air attacks on Iraqi military targets (Operation Desert Fox), to the fury of Russia. China, France and Kofi Annan have led the appeasement of Iraq, with the result that there have been no weapons inspections since. What makes Iraq's recalcitrance so alarming is that, unlike other middle-rank countries which persist in developing nuclear weapons, Iraq signs all the non-proliferation treaties and then goes right ahead with a nuclear programme, delighting in hiding evidence and making a mockery of the NPT verification system.[15] The weakness of the NPT as an international safeguard against nuclear war is that it contains no provision for preventative action against a non-party which has obtained nuclear weapons, and no provision for preventative action against *any* state which tests or even uses them. If Iran and North Korea are bent on acquiring nuclear bombs, what can the rest of the world do to stop them?

On these matters, so crucial to the survival of humankind, international human rights law should speak very clearly. After all, it has rules prohibiting the use of dum-dum bullets and setting the size of blankets in POW cells; it must have rules for a weapon which, if exploded over a city, could kill a million people and maim and poison millions more for generations to come. This, perhaps the ultimate test for international law, has been collectively failed by the International Court of Justice, which has, in two important cases, found nuclear bombs too hot to be handled by the law of nations.

The ICJ exists to declare international law based 'on certain general and well-recognized principles, namely: elemental considerations of humanity, even more exacting in peace than in war, and every state's obligation not to allow knowingly its territory to be used for acts contrary to the rights of other states'.[16] This simple approach was first adopted in the *Corfu Channel Case* of 1949, where Albania was ordered to pay compensation for failing in its elemental humanitarian duty to notify foreign shipping of a minefield it had secretly laid in international waters. This finding of state responsibility for creating a hazard to human life was relied upon by Australia in its attempt to stop France from conducting atmospheric tests in the Pacific. The question was eminently justiciable, but nine of the ICJ's fifteen judges in the *Nuclear Tests Case* found an excuse not to decide it: since France announced that its 1974 series of atmospheric tests was the last it would hold, 'the claim of Australia no longer has any object' and thus did not need to be adjudicated.[17] This reasoning was dishonest: the case was of crucial and continuing importance, since atmospheric testing by other countries continued, and France was soon to dishonour the spirit of its undertaking by further testing in the Pacific, albeit underground rather than in the atmosphere.

The ICJ displayed the same jurisprudential funk in the face of nuclear *realpolitik* two decades later when called upon by the World Health Organization to decide the case of the *Legality of the Threat or Use of Nuclear Weapons in Armed Conflict*. As a UN body, the World Health Organization (WHO) has the standing to request an advisory opinion on any question which arises 'within the scope of its activities'. In a piece of breathtakingly specious reasoning, the ICJ decided that since 'whether nuclear weapons are used legally or illegally their effects on health would be the same',[18] the issue was *outside* the scope of the WHO's activities! As one of three dissenting judges observed, noting the evidence of the health and environmental devastation wrought by the bombing of Hiroshima and Nagasaki, 'to hold as the court has done that these matters do not lie within the competence or scope of activities of the WHO borders on the unreal and smacks of cynicism, and the law is not cynical'.[19]

However, an advisory opinion on the *Legality of the Threat or Use of Nuclear Weapons* had been requested by the UN's General

Assembly under Article 96(1) of the Charter. The ICJ could not refuse, although the Western superpowers curiously claimed that any decision that nuclear weapons were illegal would be bad for disarmament.[20] They may have succeeded in rattling the judges by intimating that they would ignore any decision which did not suit their military plans. The majority opinion (adopted only by the casting vote of the president) notes: 'The destructive power of nuclear weapons cannot be contained in either space or time. They have the potential to destroy all civilization and the entire ecosystem of the planet.'[21] The principles of humanitarian law, from St Petersburg in 1868 onwards, certainly apply to nuclear weapons: 'States must never make civilians the object of attack and must consequently never use weapons that are incapable of distinguishing between civilian and military targets . . .'[22] However, nuclear weapons are not unlawful *per se*, and all states individually and collectively have a right to self-defence under Article 51 of the UN Charter, although as the Court ruled in *Nicaragua* v. *US*, 'self-defence would warrant only measures which are proportional to the armed attack and necessary to respond to it'.[23] It follows that any threat to use nuclear weapons which is disproportionate or unnecessary would be unlawful under the Charter, but there is no specific prohibition against recourse to nuclear attack in any of the treaties concerned with weapons of mass destruction. The NPT and other 'nuclear-free' conventions can be seen as 'foreshadowing a future general prohibition on the use of such weapons, but they do not constitute such a prohibition by themselves'.

In other words, the bomb is not banned by law. States can make it, and even use it according to the rules of self-defence, the occasion for which they alone are judge. The UK, for example, envisaged 'the use of a low-yield nuclear weapon against warships on the high seas or troops in sparsely populated areas', a prospect which, however likely to lead to escalation into a full-scale nuclear imbroglio, gave the Court the key to switch itself off: 'The Court considers it does not have sufficient elements of fact to enable it to *conclude with certainty* that the use of nuclear weapons would *necessarily* be at variance with the principles and rules of law in armed conflict *in any circumstance*.' These are weasel words, although the judges nervously venture the thought that, given the characteristics of nuclear weapons and the requirements of international humanitarian law, 'the use of such weapons in fact seems scarcely reconcilable with respect for such requirements'. Such use is not reconcilable at all, as a matter of the meaning of language, or of common sense, but this passing comment is the furthest they are prepared to go, because 'the Court cannot lose sight of the fundamental right of every state to survival and thus its right to resort to self-defence, in accordance with Article 51 of the Charter, where its survival is at stake'. For this reason, 'in view of the present state of international law viewed as a whole, as examined above by the Court, and of the elements of fact at its disposal, the Court is led to observe that it cannot reach a definitive conclusion as to the legality or illegality of the use of nuclear weapons by a state in an extreme circumstance of self-defence in which its very survival would be at stake'.[24]

But no state – i.e. government – which retaliates with nuclear weapons, whether against nuclear or conventional attack, can possibly ensure its own survival. The ICJ is talking MAD – mutually assured destruction – or upholding some ultimate 'right' in a state to commit suicide, taking millions of human beings with it. What the ICJ opinion means is that states are not acting unlawfully by stockpiling nuclear weaponry or by acquiring the technology to build the bomb or by testing that technology. It means that states do not act unlawfully by threatening to use the bomb, or indeed by using it, so long as their leaders genuinely believe that their survival is at stake – an excuse for states outside the NPT, like India and Pakistan, to have a nuclear weapons programme. The notion of a state securing its survival by actions which threaten to exterminate all human life is risible, as is the British 'low-yield' scenario in which combatants politely nuke each other's ships on the high seas or aim their nuclear missiles only at military targets located in deserts. What the Court is saying (by reference to 'inadequate elements of fact at its disposal') is that international law contains no general prohibition against nuclear weapons, but must judge each use according to the actual 'elements of fact' surrounding it. By the time those 'elements' can be presented, as evidence of what caused nuclear war, we may all be dead. Some future form of life may stumble upon these 300 pages of juridical cowardice, carefully paragraphed both in English and French, and wonder how international law in 1996 could circumlocute itself to death.

There are an equal number of dissenting judgments, but they do not speak with the same voice. There are judges who confidently declare nuclear weapons illegal, and judges – like the American Steven Schwebel – who declare their own country's possession of them to be the best guarantee of world peace. The majority is accused (reasonably enough) of evasiveness and indecisiveness, to which accusation some of its number respond by pointing out that international law is a 'defective legal system' – which it will remain, if the ICJ continues to render judgments like this one. The decision entirely fails to elucidate the question of whether and *when* the Security Council can forcibly override state sovereignty to remove nuclear weaponry from nations which are not party to the NPT, and it fails to explain whether the Israeli bombing of Osiraq was a crime or a legitimate prophylactic. The *Legality of the Threat or Use of Nuclear Weapons Case* stands for not much more than the rule that a state must not stockpile nuclear weapons in numbers far beyond the reasonable needs of deterrence or self-defence.

CONVENTIONAL WEAPONS

The urgency of controlling the weapons of mass destruction – nuclear, ballistic and chemical – has obscured the problems of policing the traffic in the ordinary guns and bombs which cause 80–90 per cent of casualties in modern wars. This has been left, unsatisfactorily, to domestic laws and to the policies of individual states, except in relation to conflicts condemned by UN imposition of arms sanctions. There is unanimity in favour of maintaining effective controls over the sales of conventional weapons and supervision over their transhipment to ensure that they do not fall into the hands of terrorists and criminals, but the frequency with which they do is indicative of the failure to police such controls at an international level.

The international law rule was first stated in the 1937 Convention for the Prosecution and Punishment of Terrorism, which required states to avoid assisting wilful acts causing death to public officials or endangering the lives of members of the public. Under this, states were obliged to prohibit within their borders the manufacture, possession or supply of arms, ammunition, explosives or harmful substances with a view to assisting unlawful terrorist organizations in other countries. Although this convention never entered into force, these provisions were embodied in the Friendly Relations Resolution passed by the General Assembly in 1970 and are echoed in a number of international and regional conventions agreed since then, all endorsing an international duty on states to prohibit the supply of lethal weapons to unlawful organizations in other countries.

Where there is probably a consensus in state practice as well as in principle is in forbidding military assistance to criminal organizations which have no political agenda. Thus, Israel and Antigua were condemned in 1990 when it emerged that negligence in the former's defence department, and corruption in the latter's government and army, had combined to permit a large order of machine guns, rifles and ammunition to reach the forces of the Medellin drugs cartel, who used them in the assassinations of judges and political leaders.[25] This was one of the rare occasions on which illegal arms traffic was exposed: usually it thrives under the system of 'end-user certification', by which arms-dealing nations purport to comply with their international law obligations. In fact, the EUC system is farcical: compliance is achieved merely by asking the purchaser to make a statement to the effect that the weapons will be kept and used in a particular country for a legitimate purpose. This is not worth the paper it is written (or, increasingly, faxed) on: it is not legally binding in the country of import, and is required only to protect the exporting state from criticism when its weapons are found in the wrong hands or in the wrong place. The commission which exposed the scandalous way in which Israel and Antigua armed the Colombian drug cartels recommended that an international register of end-user certificates should be established under the auspices of the United Nations, so that at least arms exports by member governments would be identified and monitored.[26] This necessary step is resisted by most arms-exporting states fearing for the 'commercial confidentiality' of their arms merchants and, in some cases, for exposure of their own links with unsavoury regimes or guerrilla forces.

In the aftermath of international action against Iraq over its invasion of Kuwait, more attention was focused on the need to regulate the traffic in conventional weapons. Most arms-exporting nations were complicit in Saddam Hussein's massive military build-up in the years before the invasion, notwithstanding his record of brutal internal repression, his use of chemical weapons and the appalling casualty figures of the drawn-out war between Iraq and Iran. Assistance was not merely afforded by export of lethal weapons, but by providing pilot training and fighter planes for his air force (France); by building him a navy (Italy); and by supplying chemicals for poison gas (Germany). Companies from Britain (notably Matrix-Churchill, helped by the government to evade its own sanctions) made machine tools programmed to provide Iraq with the indigenous capacity to produce bombs and rockets. Sanctions were circumvented by accepting false end-user certificates from Jordan for arms obviously intended for Iraq. Considerations such as maintaining employment at home and enhancing military or diplomatic leverage abroad disincline arms-exporting states to reduce their trade with governments prone to use those arms for repression or for unnecessary enhancement of their military strength.

If international law is to have an impact on the trade in arms, it must impose incremental duties requiring states to prohibit exports to:

(1) criminal gangs and cartels;
(2) political groups which engage in terrorism;
(3) governments or armies which are subject to UN arms embargoes;
(4) states which are engaging in, or are likely to initiate, hostilities with other states in breach of the UN Charter;
(5) states which intend to use the arms for domestic repression in breach of human rights law; and
(6) governments of developing countries whose arms budget exceeds to an unacceptable degree their spending on public welfare.

At present, (1) reflects an established rule of international law, while (6) remains wishful thinking from a few NGOs. There is some movement towards (2), subject to the inevitable dispute over whether militant resistance movements are 'terrorists' or 'freedom fighters', and towards (3): state practice is to talk as if UN arms sanctions are binding, although non-compliance by nationals is infrequently the subject of prosecution. There will be little progress without a compulsory UN register of end-user certificates and the establishment of an international monitoring body with powers to investigate and prosecute unlawful arms deals and to apply to an international court for injunctions against states which permit the export of arms to prohibited destinations. The situation at (4) and (5) above will sometimes call forth UN sanctions, or embargoes imposed by individual states with particular foreign policies: there must, however, be an international law obligation to prevent export to forces which are committing war crimes or crimes against humanity.

There is a further definitional problem which must be addressed, namely the nature of the goods that are to be embargoed. States which are prepared to impose sanctions on warring parties do so by imposing export restrictions on lethal weaponry and various descriptions of arms-related equipment. The Iraqgate scandal exposed how easily these regulations could be circumvented by the export of 'dual use' machinery such as machine tools, not specifically designed to make arms but when *in situ* in Iraq easily programmed to produce bombs and rockets. Another area of unprohibited export was the provisioning of the Iraqi army with 'non-lethal' material, such as communications equipment, radar and mine-detection devices – all helping to locate and kill the enemy in greater numbers. The problem is acute for aid programmes: since armies march on their stomachs, it can clearly be contemplated that a proportion of the food charitably distributed to refugee camps will be passed over the wire to feed the soldiers fighting in genocidal conflicts. In Africa, it is estimated that up to 20 per cent of food aid provided by tender-hearted donors in the West is diverted to 'the boys in the bush' to fuel the genocide which has produced the refugee problem in the first place. Governments frequently make absurd 'humanitarian' distinctions: Britain refused to supply Iraq with guns and fuselages for 'lethal' fighter planes, but happily trained fighter pilots and provided them with ejector seats so that they could live to fight (and kill) another day. It boasted of its 'humanitarian' decision to provide the Iraqi army with a million AIDS-testing kits, without a thought for the grim disciplinary fate in store for any Iraqi soldier who tested HIV-positive.

The one conventional weapon which the international community has made recent progress towards outlawing is the anti-personnel land mine. These objects, each sold for about £2.00, are designed to blast off the foot which steps on them and to project metal upwards into the stomach and chest. There are about 70 million of them lurking beneath the surface of former and present conflict zones, and as many in stockpiles in countries like Singapore, Chile, India, Israel, the USA and even Sweden. In 1997, some 26,000 people – many of them children – were killed or maimed by the weapons (that's seventy victims a day, or one every fifteen minutes). These statistics (and a glamorous campaign featuring Princess Diana) brought forth in that year a convention signed in Ottawa by 129 nations, on the Prohibition of the Use, Stockpiling, Production and Transfer of Anti-Personnel Mines and on Their Destruction. It was ratified in double-quick time by over seventy states, and came into force in March 1999. This shows what governments can do if they try, and if their politicians are made to recognize (like Canadian foreign minister Lloyd Axworthy) the political mileage in promoting a popular human rights initiative. It also shows the limits of what states – i.e. politicians and diplomats – are prepared to do, even for such a cause, because, for all the hideousness of the anti-personnel mine:

(1) Nobody was prepared to ban the real killer, i.e. the anti-tank mine. This blows up trucks and passenger cars as well as tanks, and has caused far more casualties among UN peacekeepers and aid workers. Indeed, the only reason why the anti-personnel mine was developed was to stop 'the enemy' defusing these much larger anti-tank mines. If the latter were banned, there would be little demand for the anti-personnel mine.

(2) The most significant mine-producing nations have refused to sign the Convention: China, India, Pakistan, Iran and Cuba (to name but a few of the 'usual suspects') and Russia and the United States, the latter because it wants to continue to lay them on the north–south border in Korea.

(3) The Convention's compliance provisions, in Article 8, are excruciatingly weak. As usual, in deference to state sovereignty only a 'state party' may complain that another state party is in breach – there is no provision for NGO complaints, or for an independent enforcement agency. A

complaint is euphemistically called 'a request for clarification' and is submitted through the Secretary-General to the suspected violator. If the answer is unsatisfactory, a majority of state parties 'may' (not 'must') hold a meeting and in that unlikely event might just order a 'fact-finding mission' which can stay no longer than fourteen days in the suspect state; if its report concludes that there has been a violation, then the government might be 'requested', ever so politely, to comply with the Convention in the future, if, and only if, such a 'request' is first approved by more than two-thirds of the state parties.

The Land Mines Convention is instructive, because it demonstrates the difficulty for even the most fashionable and acceptable human rights cause to intrude on state sovereignty so as in any way to curtail the military might of the major powers. At the very time the Convention was receiving its ratifications, anti-personnel mines were being laid with abandon by Serbian forces along the borders between Kosovo and Albania, by India and Pakistan, Ethiopia and Eritrea, and by Savimbi's troops in Angola – if the US, Russia and China can do it, they said, why can't we? The cost of the Ottawa Conference might have been better spent on developing mine-detection equipment.

THE DOGS OF WAR

The international community has been slow to act against ex-soldiers, often dishonourably discharged from élite national forces, who make themselves available for hire to fight in internecine wars raging in countries which are not their own. Although most nations have domestic laws prohibiting preparations made within their borders for levying war against friendly foreign governments, few deign to stop their 'soldiers of fortune', in that over-romantic phrase, from travelling abroad to kill and maim the innocent victims of conflicts with which they have no patriotic connection. In Britain, memories of the 'soldiers of conscience' who fought against Franco stays sentimentally alive in the literary works of Orwell and Hemingway, updated by the disgusting record of British mercenaries in Angola in 1976 who killed civilians indiscriminately and then turned their guns on each other.[27] During the Reagan administration, the CIA aided the recruitment of mercenaries to fight with the Contra forces against the government of Nicaragua, while 'dogs of war' from Belgium and France served national interests brutally but unaccountably in the Congo and in other parts of Africa and Asia. These are the Western nations that have tried most vociferously and most successfully to stop attempts made by the majority at the United Nations to develop international law rules against the recruitment and deployment of mercenaries.

In 1989, the General Assembly condemned states which permit the recruitment or training of mercenary soldiers,[28] although its denunciation was based on their use for aggression against established governments and (note the contradiction) 'for fighting against national liberation movements of peoples struggling for the exercise of their right to self-determination' (in which case they were fighting for established governments). The armed forces of most states voting for the motion were in receipt of weapons and training and logistical support from Russia or America, but since they had themselves emerged as a result of armed struggle against colonialism, they took care to note that the legitimate struggles of peoples for independence 'can in no way be considered as or equated to mercenary activity', even when assisted by foreign powers, or, presumably, mercenaries! Notwithstanding these confusions, the UN went on to establish an International Convention against the Recruitment, Use, Financing and Training of Mercenaries which has attracted few signatories (twenty-seven) and a derisory number of ratifications (seventeen). The states from which mercenaries are normally recruited remain adamantly opposed to any general prohibition, citing the rights of their citizens to risk their lives in a cause in which they believe, and the practical difficulties of deciding which wars are so unjust that joining the wrong side should be condemned by prosecution and the withdrawal of passports. If, however, a particular conflict has been made a subject of UN sanctions, it seems entirely reasonable for international law to place a duty upon states to prohibit mercenaries from departing to fight in it, certainly if that would mean fighting against UN forces or in a war of aggression which the Security Council has condemned.

In one significant respect, the convention against mercenary activity is acquiring the status of an international law rule, namely in its concern 'at the new unlawful international activities linking drug traffickers and mercenaries in the perpetration of violent actions which undermine the constitutional order of States'. There is a fundamental difference between allowing mercenaries to travel abroad to fight for one side – even a despised side – in a civil war, and allowing them to travel to help a gang of criminals. The Convention was established in the year in which it was revealed that Israeli and British mercenaries had run camps in Colombia teaching commando techniques to the forces of the Medellin drug cartel, turning untrained killers into trained killers who used those techniques to commit crimes against humanity, namely systematic assassinations of judges, journalists and elected politicians. Cartel money was behind an audacious plot to bribe the Antiguan government to permit the establishment of a permanent training school for narco-terrorists and to order lethal weapons from Israel for transhipment to cartel forces in Colombia.[29] In Jerusalem the leader of the mercenaries, Colonel Yair Klein, was mildly fined for 'exporting warlike equipment and military knowledge' from Israel, and in Antigua one minister identified with the corruption was relieved of his office, but because he was the Prime Minister's son he remained an MP. This was meagre retribution for an international conspiracy to aid a criminal organization to murder the defenders of Colombian democracy.[30]

The 1989 Convention may be limited to prohibiting the recruitment of mercenaries to commit crimes against humanity, whether for criminal gangs or sovereign governments. At present, most states will only contemplate a ban if required by UN sanctions: few have laws which prevent enlistment, outside the jurisdiction, in foreign forces of states which are not current enemies.[31] In America, the First Amendment prohibits the suppression of *Soldier of Fortune* magazine, which remains the house journal of the modern mercenary.

There is, however, one bizarre development which is turning some dogs of war into angels of mercy. Western commitment to privatization coupled with the reluctance of governments to risk the lives of their own soldiers – the Mogadishu factor – has tempted them to risk instead the lives of employees of private corporations like Sandline, directed and staffed by recruits from senior or seasoned positions in the British and South African armies. They are prepared, for increased payment, to do exactly what they would have done in government service, namely to wage and win small wars. The prospect of democratic governments hiring 'legitimate' mercenaries to do dirty work that might decimate or divide their own troops began controversially when in 1997 New Guinea hired Sandline to put down a secessionist movement on Bougainville island. Sierra Leone's own army revolted, but Sandline was hired to help restore a democratically elected prime minister and British diplomats argued that the end (of restoring democracy) justified the means (of hiring mercenaries to do so). There is now serious talk of hiring 'corporate security services' to conduct dangerous peacekeeping operations for which countries like the US would be prepared to pay – in money, if not in the lives of their own soldiers. South Africa has been the first government to make a virtue of necessity and to 'license' its private security firms to conduct particular overseas operations, and now Britain is contemplating the same course. So the mercenary may make a comeback – not as a soldier of fortune but as a well-insured employee of a multinational corporation, directed by decorated officers who have taken early retirement from a national army in order to do some real fighting.

A final despairing word should be said about 'the pups of war' – the 300,000 serving soldiers aged under eighteen who are presently fighting – often as conscripts – in armed conflicts around the world, especially in west Africa.[32] (The CIA-backed Holden Roberto was first to recognize how much it demoralizes an enemy village to have its chief executed by a child.) There is much hand-wringing by UNICEF over these statistics, but its proposal to amend the 1989 Convention on the Rights of the Child to ban under-age combatants was vigorously opposed by both the UK and the US, whose armies wish to keep on recruiting 16- and 17-year-olds. Conscription is a more serious violation of human rights than the acceptance of under-age volunteers, and this should really be the focus of UNICEF's campaign: posed photographs of small boys toting AK-47s have become the stuff of NGO fundraising, but the real problem is how to take the war out of the boy, not the boy out of the war.

6

An End to Impunity?

'When someone kills a man, he is put in prison. When someone kills twenty people, he is declared mentally insane. But when someone kills 200,000 people, he is invited to Geneva for peace negotiations.'   Sarajevo joke, circa 1994

THE NUREMBERG LEGACY

It is trite, and therefore true, to say that there are no 'rights' without remedies: equally, there are no human rights without remedies for human wrongs, in the sense of arrangements for punishing those guilty of crimes against humanity. These were defined, broadly but clearly, by the Nuremberg Charter provision (Article 6(c)) under which a number of Nazi leaders were convicted on 30 September 1946:

murder, extermination, enslavement, deportation, and other inhumane acts committed against any civilian population, before or during the war, or persecutions on political, racial or religious grounds in execution of or in connection with any crime, within the jurisdiction of the tribunal, whether or not in violation of the domestic law of the country where perpetrated. Leaders, organizers, instigators and accomplices participating in the formulation or execution of a common plan or conspiracy to commit any of the foregoing crimes are responsible for all acts performed by any person in the execution of such plans.

Responsible they may be, morally and legally, but in the half-century which followed the judgment leaders were rarely made responsible, precisely because their political power gave them the ability to negotiate their exit from the bloodstained stage, secret Swiss bank accounts intact, to discreet retirement in places like Panama and the south of France. The legion of crimes against humanity committed since the masters of war stood in the Nuremberg dock have been brought home to very few of those responsible for committing them. *'Impunity'* – leaving retribution for such crimes to history or to God – began immediately, with the American decision not merely to exempt Emperor Hirohito from trial but to keep him on the throne of Japan, relieving him from the prosecution he deserved for approving a war of aggression and smoothing away any sense of national shame or guilt over the atrocities committed by Japanese forces: the generals executed by military tribunals were regarded as patriotic heroes and in due course their ashes were placed in the holiest of Shinto shrines at Yasukuni (the imperial equivalent of the Kremlin wall). Blame for the war was erased from the national consciousness, as school textbooks omitted all mention of Japanese atrocities and explained their nation's aggression as a justifiable response to economic encirclement. Reparations to enslaved and tortured prisoners-of-war were fixed at a risible amount in 1951, and the country has steadfastly refused to increase them. Barbaric leaders of more recent times, even when overthrown, live happily ever after, protected by amoral governments like that in Brazil, which welcomes Paraguay's Nazi-loving Alfredo Stroessner, or Panama, a retirement home for the mass-murdering military of Latin America. African states are all happy to forgive and forget: Hissène Habré, who killed 40,000 and tortured 200,000 during his rule in Chad, fled with $12 million looted from his country's treasury to Senegal in 1990 and lived there in luxury for a decade until he became the first tyrant to be prosecuted under the Pinochet precedent. All the perfumes of Arabia may not wash away the crimes of Idi Amin, but those of Saudi Arabia sweeten his retirement in Jeddah. He killed 73,000 people – fewer than the maniacal Marxist of Ethiopia, Colonel Mengistu, who lives happily ever after his monstrous crimes against humanity under the personal protection of Robert Mugabe in Zimbabwe. The late Pol Pot went into hospital in Thailand periodically for haemorrhoid treatment, protected by the UN's need to keep the Khmer Rouge from upsetting its peace plans in Cambodia, and its former Secretary-General, Boutros Boutros-Ghali, warmly embraced the bloodiest Khmer leaders when they emerged from hiding in 1998. In 1994, the Haitian generals provided a copybook example of how to ransom their crimes against humanity: they were prepared to stop committing them in the future in return for being allowed to keep the profits from those they had committed in the past.

This was all the doing of international diplomacy, which until the Bosnian crisis simply pretended that Nuremberg had never happened. The diplomats who represented national leaders were instructed not to countenance the prosecution of other national leaders: tyranny was a matter for negotiated climbdowns, never for justice. This approach has been reflected at a national level by the choice of amnesties and 'Truth Commissions' over trials for the crimes committed by former regimes. Thus, the middle-ranking military officers of the Argentinian junta who waged the 'dirty war' against dissidents by torturing and then causing them to disappear – often by having them pushed out of aeroplanes over the Atlantic – received a blanket amnesty in 1987. Leaders of the death squads in El Salvador received an amnesty in 1994, which embraced those responsible for killing over a hundred children in the El Mozote massacre. Go to South Africa today, and for the price of a few drinks you can listen to loquacious ex-majors tell how they tortured and killed the opponents of apartheid: the Truth and Reconciliation Commission forced them to talk, but did not reconcile them with many relatives of their victims. Those who order atrocities believe at the time that their power will always enable them to bargain with any new government to let bygones be bygones, and history since Nuremberg has tended to prove them correct. The main resolve to punish crimes against humanity has been to prosecute in national courts a handful of very old Nazis suspected of war crimes. Some of these trials (hinging on identification evidence, hopelessly unreliable after fifty years) have collapsed: with war crimes, as with other crimes, justice long delayed can be justice denied.

This is why it has been the great achievement of international law, by the dawn of the twenty-first century, to lift the veil of sovereign statehood far enough to make individuals responsible for the crimes against humanity committed by the states they formerly commanded, while at the same time developing a rule that those states have a continuing duty to prosecute and punish them, failing which another state or the international community may bring them to justice. This chapter places that achievement in historical perspective, focusing on the epochal judgment at Nuremberg. Chapter 7 examines the duty to prosecute and the temptations of amnesties and Truth Commissions, while chapters 8–10 will explain how the world community is working, with difficulty, towards a universal jurisdiction to try crimes against humanity, and with even greater difficulty (see chapter 11) towards a system which will stop them being perpetrated in the first place.

Nuremberg was a precedent that the United Nations ignored until the ethnic cleansing policy of the Bosnian Serbs turned its New World Order into a joke. The International Criminal Tribunal for the Former Yugoslavia was established by the Security Council on 27 May 1993 as if to stop the world laughing at its impotence, as a substitute for effective military action to stop the war. After catching one criminal in two years (and a footsoldier at that) the Tribunal finally lifted a formal finger against the Bosnian Serb leadership on 15 May 1995, by taking over the investigation into their culpability from the courts of Bosnia and Hercegovina. This step seemed insignificant at the time (the Bosnian Serb leaders were not under arrest, but on the contrary were in a position to authorize the arrest of UN peacekeepers, which they did a few weeks later). It marked, nevertheless, the first time since Nuremberg that an international court had assumed jurisdiction over the masters of war crimes, towards the close of a century in which 160 million human beings were slaughtered in war.

At this level, it was a deeply symbolic occasion. Richard Goldstone, the South African judge appointed as the Tribunal prosecutor, assisted by two Australian barristers, stood before a court in The Hague comprising a judge of the Supreme Court of Nigeria, a female judge who was formerly the Minister of Justice for Costa Rica, and a judge who had been Procurator-General of the Court of Appeal for Paris. He sought leave to proceed with an investigation into crimes against humanity allegedly committed by Radovan Karadžić, president of the Bosnian Serb administration and architect of its ethnic policies; Ratko Mladić, commander of its army; and Miko Stanišić, the Home Affairs minister who unleashed police terror against the non-Serbian population.[1] Goldstone reminded the court of the Nuremberg ruling that 'a plea of head of state immunity will not constitute a defence, nor will it mitigate punishment' and of the salutary 'command responsibility' rule for political and military leaders adopted at the Tokyo trial of General Yamashita and approved by the US Supreme Court:

a person in a position of superior authority should be held individually responsible for giving the unlawful order to commit a crime, and he should also be held responsible for failure to deter the unlawful behaviour of subordinates if he knew they had committed or were about to commit crimes yet failed to take the necessary and reasonable steps to prevent their commission or to punish those who had committed them.[2]

Thus far had we come, in the fifty years since Nuremberg and the 860 years since the Second Lateran Council of 1139 forbade the use of crossbows in wars between Christians, thereby imposing the first international law rule against inhumane conduct. It was not very far: an empty dock, and cells holding at the time only one Serbian defendant, Duško Tadić. He was not even a soldier, just a freelance torturer – but here he was, the sole representative of those who had instigated or committed the millions of crimes against humanity perpetrated since the end of the Second World War. None the less, history may view it as a deeply symbolic moment: the first sign of a seismic shift, from diplomacy to legality, in the conduct of world affairs. Or history may view it as a false start. That seemed likely for several years, until NATO forces began to arrest some army and concentration camp commanders and send them for trial, and some convictions were obtained against authors of genocide in Rwanda. With some ground-clearing judgments behind it and twenty-seven of its seventy-five indictees in custody, the Hague Tribunal looked good enough to justify the core belief of the 120 nations at the Rome Conference in July 1998, that an International Criminal Court could actually work. Just three months later there came the arrest of one of the most wicked men left in the world. Senator Augusto Pinochet, former torturer, tyrant and state terrorist, was placed under guard at a private clinic in London while judges and politicians and people throughout the world argued about whether and where he should stand trial for crimes against humanity. Irrespective of his eventual fate, the very fact that prosecutors had the power to arrest Pinochet, that judges (a majority of them) could find arguments to approve the arrest (at least for some of his crimes) and that politicians had the gumption initially to ignore the advice of diplomats to free him, all suggested that the age of impunity may be drawing to a close.

INTERNATIONAL CRIMINALS: PIRATES, SLAVERS AND KAISERS

International law is binding on states, not on persons. To this classic doctrine an exception has now been made in the case of individuals who commit crimes which – whether at a time of war between sovereign states or not – are of such ideologically motivated heinousness as to permit classification as crimes against humanity. Crimes of that class are distinguished from acts which may have the same result – murder, torture and the like – by virtue of the fact that they are perpetrated by state officials or agents, systematically and in furtherance of an unlawful policy of denying to political or racial groups the right to life or physical integrity. They are also distinguished, in practical terms, by the perpetrator's impunity from domestic law-enforcement measures: he is punished, if at all, only after a change of government or in a foreign or international court. As one Nazi war crimes tribunal explained, 'crimes against humanity . . . can only come within the purview of this basic code of humanity because the State involved, owing to indifference, impotency or complicity, has been unable or has refused to halt the crimes and punish the criminals'.[3]

The first individuals to be brought within the reach of international criminal law were pirates or 'sea brigands'. They were fair game for any state to capture and punish, irrespective of their nationality or whether their depredations on the high seas involved the murder or robbery of its subjects. Piracy may be regarded as the very first 'crime against humanity', its peculiarly barbaric quality derived from the taking of lives which were especially vulnerable while outside the protective realm of any nation. It took much longer for states happy to hang pirates as if they were highwaymen to conceive a similar fate for slave traders, whose contribution to their economies was generally welcomed until the nineteenth century brought in its course a series of international treaties prohibiting the practice as 'contrary to justice and humanity'. These mark the gradual recognition of a crime against humanity so repulsive that all states are assumed to have a legal interest in its suppression: they become bound by what the International Court of Justice later termed 'an obligation *erga omnes*'[4] once treaties on the subject and the decisions of important courts are virtually unanimous. Principles of morality or dictates of humanity are a necessary but not sufficient condition for the emergence of an international law rule: as explained in chapter 3, there must be evidence of widespread 'state practice'. Thus, as late as 1825, the US Chief Justice was able to demonstrate in the *Antelope Case* that slave-trading was lawful, notwithstanding international condemnation of its immorality, because it was then 'sanctioned by the laws of all nations who possess distant colonies'.[5]

The precise point at which slavery became prohibited by inter-national law is impossible to fix: there was no defining moment like the Nuremberg judgment, but rather an accumulation of treaties throughout the nineteenth century and a gradual abandonment by the Great Powers of their toleration of the practice, marked in turn by military offensives against traders (such as British naval action to liberate victims of Arab slavers along the east coast of Africa) and by domestic court declarations that freed any slave brought within the jurisdiction. The point came somewhere between 1885 (the Treaty of Berlin forbidding slave-trading) and 1926, when the Slavery Conven-tion confirmed that states had jurisdiction to punish slavers wherever they were apprehended. That Convention defined the crime as reducing an individual to the status of a person over whom powers of ownership are exercised, but gave no reason why this was wrong: a supplementary convention in 1956 explained that the basis for the prohibition was the freedom, dignity and worth of the human person. To this end it added 'practices similar to slavery', such as serfdom and debt bondage, and the purchase from their families of women as wives or children as labourers. Parties are not permitted to make reservations to this Convention because *erga omnes* obligations admit by definition no qualifications.

The other class of individuals to be brought within the purview of international law at its pre-Nuremberg stage were soldiers, as explained in chapter 5. There was the customary right of belligerents to punish captured enemy soldiers who could be proved individually to have violated the laws of war, but heads of state and senior military commanders were traditionally immune from any trial, on the theory that as the embodiment of the State they were entitled to sovereign immunity. This illogical proposition was perceived as a diplomatic necessity: leaders would be less willing to settle or surrender if there was any likelihood that they would lose their necks. It was a doctrine congenial to all leaders, who could never be sure that in future conflicts they would be always on the winning side.

The first major challenge to this principle of head of state immunity came at the Versailles peace conference after the First World War. A commission appointed by the Allies to examine the responsibility of the 'authors of the war' rejected the sovereign immunity of high officials, on the basis that this would give credence to a claim by lesser ranks that they were merely obeying the orders of immune superiors. It recommended that 'all persons belonging to enemy countries, however high their position may have been, without distinction of rank, including Chiefs of State, who have been guilty of offences against the laws and customs of war or the laws of humanity, are liable to prosecution'. This recommendation was vehemently and successfully opposed at Versailles, especially by America, whose secretary of state (Lansing) believed that any trial would jeopardize his plans to restore good relations with Germany. He put two arguments for non-justiciability, which were to prevail until Nuremberg: that 'war was and is by its very nature inhuman', so acts inconsistent with the laws and customs of war were inevitable, and should be punished by God rather than by man; in any event, 'there is no fixed and universal standard of humanity', and hence no hope of an objective and unbiased judge.[6]

Although Article 227 of the Versailles Treaty formally proposed the establishment of a special international tribunal to try Kaiser Wilhelm II 'for a supreme offence against international morality and the sanctity of treaties', it was designed as an empty gesture to Allied public opinion – Lloyd George's slogan, 'Hang the Kaiser', required token acknowledgement. The Kaiser remained in Holland, unhung, as a guest of the Dutch government, until his death in 1941. Articles 228 and 229 provided that Germany should try its own war criminals:

evidence against 901 of its nationals was handed over, and they were duly arraigned in Leipzig. There, 'loser's justice' proved farcical: 888 were acquitted, and of the thirteen convicted several were allowed to escape by prison officers who were publicly congratulated for assisting them. The Leipzig trials of 1922 were a complete flop: they produced no sense of shame for inhumane actions in wartime, since the verdicts emphasized with shoulder-shrugging resignation that 'the fog of war' remained an effective defence. So it seemed that the only way to stop war crimes was to stop war – a solution embraced in 1928 with the Kellogg–Briand Pact, by which state signatories falsely promised to renounce war as an instrument of national policy. The League of Nations, concerned by random assassinations of politicians and diplomats, managed by 1937 to draft a convention for the creation of an International Criminal Court with jurisdiction to try terrorist offences, but it failed to attract many signatories before most of its members slid into another world war.[7]

THE NAZI LEADERS: SUMMARY EXECUTION?

That the course of international law was changed so dramatically by the Nuremberg Charter, trial and judgment, is attributable to a curious mixture of American idealism and Stalinist opportunism, overcoming British insistence on summary execution for the Nazi leaders. As early as 1941, punishment for war crimes was declared by Churchill to be a principal war aim, and by 1943 the Allies were sufficiently confident of victory to set up a commission to gather evidence. But Nazi crimes against humanity did not figure expressly in this thinking (the Allies themselves did not, for instance, bomb the railway lines to Auschwitz) and the idea of any trial process was the last thing that British leaders had in mind. Churchill simply wanted a political decision made as to whom to kill – a list of fifty prominent Nazis was proffered, to be executed without trial as and when they were captured. Eden, his foreign secretary, observed that 'the guilt of such individuals as Himmler is so black that they fall outside and go beyond the scope of any judicial process'.[8] Lord Chancellor Simon adopted Lansing's second argument at Versailles and insisted that judges were not up to the task. 'The question of the fate of the Nazi leaders,' he wrote in a Cabinet memorandum, 'is a political, not a judicial, question. It would not rest with judges, however eminent or learned, to decide finally a matter like this, which is of the widest and most vital public policy.' The Foreign Office pointed to the lack of precedent for a trial, and the danger that any charges formulated might breach the *nulla poena sine lege* rule against retroactivity. More persuasively, it warned of delays and procedural problems and (even more persuasively) of the risk of defendants propagating their policies from the dock and pointing an accusing finger at Allied war crimes. The UK maintained its position 'that execution without trial is the preferable course' until mid-1945, citing these 'dangers and difficulties' of attempting to do justice to international arch-criminals.[9] At first, its view won American support: when the question was first discussed – at the Moscow conference of foreign ministers in November 1943 – US Secretary of State Cordell Hull declared, 'If I had my way I would take Hitler and Mussolini and Tojo and their accomplices and bring them before a drumhead court martial, and at sunrise the following morning there would occur an historic incident.'[10]

That Hull did not have his way was due to the fact that it repelled Henry Stimson, the secretary for war. He wrote to Roosevelt the following year, 'The very punishment of these men in a dignified manner consistent with the advance of civilization will have the greater effect on posterity . . . I am disposed to believe that, at least as to the chief Nazi officials, we should participate in an international tribunal constituted to try them.' Hull was eventually persuaded, and joined with Stimson to urge that 'a condemnation after such a proceeding will meet the judgement of history so that the Germans will not be able to claim, as they have been claiming with regard to the Versailles Treaty, that an admission of war guilt was exacted under duress'. Roosevelt wavered, but his successor, Harry S Truman, had utter contempt for the British solution of summary execution, which was anathema to his idealistic belief in the 'beneficent power of law and the wisdom of judges'.[11] He appointed Supreme Court Justice Robert Jackson to report on the feasibility of a trial, and approved his conclusion:

To free them without a trial would mock the dead and make cynics of the living. On the other hand, we could execute or otherwise punish them without a hearing. But undiscriminating executions or punishments without definite findings of guilt, fairly arrived at, would violate pledges repeatedly given, and would not sit easily on the American conscience or be remembered by our children with pride. The only other course is to determine the innocence or guilt of the accused after a hearing as dispassionate as the times and horrors we deal with will permit and upon a record that will leave our reasons and motives clear.[12]

So Truman wanted an international tribunal to try the Nazi leaders – for good reason. Joseph Stalin wanted one, too, but for reasons which were bad. He wanted show trials, of the kind that his UN ambassador, the vicious ex-prosecutor Andrei Vyshinsky, had rigged for him in the 1930s: proceedings in which guilt was predetermined, confessions unravelled according to a rehearsed script and, most important of all, each significant defendant would be convicted and shot. It was precisely this danger which makes the British position in some respects defensible in retrospect, but in terms of Allied power politics it meant one Russian vote for American idealism. De Gaulle cast the French vote the same way, and the British reluctantly fell into line, consoling themselves that the suicides of Hitler, Himmler and Goebbels had diminished the danger that the trial would become a soapbox for Nazi self-justification. Supreme Court Justice Robert Jackson was nominated by Truman as chief prosecutor, and the tribunal at Nuremberg took shape with eight judges (two from each of the four Allied powers) presided over by English Lord Justice Geoffrey Lawrence. International law would never be the same again.

THE TRIAL

The dispute between the Allies over whether Nuremberg should have happened at all is important in any analysis of its achievement. The bleak alternative – summary execution of the German political and military leaders – would have left their crimes against humanity to be revealed by posthumous propaganda rather than in an open forum where only those facts which were incontestable were not subjected to examination. Nuremberg was a show trial, but one in which the victors' sense of fairness was as much on show as the vicissitudes of the vanquished. The odds were stacked, of course: all prosecutors and judges were nationals of the Allied powers, and all defendants and, more regrettably, all their lawyers were German. (It was a measure of the contemporary collapse of adversarial ethics that the General Council of the English Bar refused to allow an English barrister to defend the Krupp family, while several provincial Bar associations in Germany later took reprisals against members who had defended Nazis 'too vigorously' at Nuremberg.) The German defence lawyers, floundering in the alien Anglo-American environment of the adversary trial, were given limited facilities to prepare their cases and little notice of prosecution evidence.

The counts in the indictment prosecuted by the Americans (conspiracy to wage aggressive war) and the British (crimes against peace) were overblown and hypocritical: as E. L. Woodward, the Foreign Office historical adviser, noted on the eve of the trial, 'up to September 1st 1939, His Majesty's Government was prepared to condone everything Germany had done to secure her position in Europe'.[13] The Russian prosecution team had the easiest task of proving war crimes, but did so with the most repellent dishonesty, insisting on laying Soviet guilt for the Katyn Forest massacre of Polish officers on the Wehrmacht. And if anyone was guilty of being an accessory to the crime of aggression it was Stalin, who approved the Molotov–Ribbentrop Pact of August 1939 with its secret promise of a slice of *Lebensraum* for Russia as a reward for acquiescing in Nazi conquest. Convictions for the war crime of 'wanton destruction' came ironically from judges whose nations had bombed Dresden and Hiroshima, and that strand of the Nazi conspiracy alleged to consist in 'subverting the League of Nations' was positively comic, given that the US had never joined it and the USSR had been expelled from it for attacking Finland.

These elements of humbug in the first three counts were not exposed in the court; the defence of '*tu quoque*' ('I did it, but you did it too', or 'You did it first') was ruled irrelevant with such a predetermined speed and emphasis that it was obvious that the judges were bent on silencing any allegations about Allied war crimes. As a matter both of law and of morality, they were plainly wrong: *tu quoque* evidence is highly relevant to any assessment of whether a particular mode of warfare is justified by military necessity, or is sufficiently beyond the common pale to count as a war crime. So far as the counts alleging the conspiracy to wage aggressive war and the commission of crimes against the peace were concerned, the *tu quoque* argument was most pertinent: the Germans were charged *inter alia* with violating the rearmament provisions of the Versailles Treaty which the French had ignored and the British had joined the Germans in circumventing. As Jackson confessed to Truman, the Allies had 'done or are doing some of the very things we are prosecuting Germans for. The French are violating the Geneva Convention in their treatment of prisoners of war ... we are prosecuting the Germans for plunder and our allies are practising it ... we say aggressive war is a crime and one of our allies asserts sovereignty over the Baltic States based on no title except conquest.'[14] This double standard pervaded the trial, until counsel for Admiral Dönitz persuaded the Americans and the French that evidence from Admiral Chester Nimitz, commander of the Pacific fleet, should be admitted to show that American submarine practices had been the same as those his client was standing accused for ordering.[15] Dönitz was in consequence acquitted of this charge. Otherwise, the *tu quoque* objection continued to be taken and upheld throughout the trial, depriving the court of the opportunity to make any meaningful comment on the irregular commando practices of both sides, the criminality of carpet-bombing, or on the distinction, if any, between the deportations and the forced labour which the Germans were accused of ordering, and the deportations and forced labour to which the Soviets were enthusiastically subjecting the people they now had at their mercy.

For all these failings, Nuremberg stands as a colossus in the development of international human rights law, precisely because its Charter defined crimes against humanity and its procedures proved by acceptable and credible evidence that such crimes had been instigated by some of the defendants. The spontaneous drama of the courtroom provided the defining moment of de-Nazification on the afternoon when the prosecutor showed newsreels of Auschwitz and Belsen and the defendants, spotlit for security in the dock, averted their eyes in horror from the ghastly screen images of the emaciated inmates of their concentration camps. Some sobbed, others sweated, or put their heads in their hands; they sat in stunned silence until the court rose, their individual and collective guilt and shame brought home to them for ever and beyond reasonable doubt.[16] This was the moment – or at least, the afternoon – of truth, but it came after painstaking months of meticulously translated documentary evidence, showing the defendants' signatures on 'night and fog' decrees, on orders for the extermination of 'useless eaters' and 'lives unworthy of living', a record the judgment accurately described as one of 'consistent and systematic inhumanity on the greatest scale'. It was that record, emerging in a largely truthful evidential shape, which can be credited with effectively destroying any future for Nazism. It prevented – as summary executions of the Nazi leaders could not – myths and fantasies about the Second World War developing in Germany in the way they did about the First in the 1920s. For that reason alone, international justice worked.

In retrospect, the most astonishing feature of Nuremberg was how the adversary dynamics of the Anglo-American trial sucked in the defendants, who played an earnest and polite, at times desperate, part in making it work. Their leader, Göring, had initially advised them to confine their evidence to three words, 'Lick my arse' – the defiant catchcry of one of Goethe's warrior heroes.[17] But as months passed they became flattered by the fairness (at least, fairishness) of the procedures and rose to the bait of making their excuses to posterity. So they played the justice game – none more effectively than Goering himself. His defence (that the resurgence of Germany after the failure of both democracy and communism was only achievable by total support of Nazi ideology) drove Jackson, his American cross-examiner, to petulant rage. At this level, Goering was able to rebut the absurd conspiracy charge, which sought to try Germany alone for its pre-war political manoeuvrings. To his French accuser, who unemotionally put the case for his involvement in crimes against humanity, he had no answer.

What mattered above all else was that justice was seen to be done: the accused were accorded the right to defence counsel (but only from

Germany), to a trial translated into their own language, to a detailed indictment and copies of all documents relied on by the prosecution, to the right both to give evidence on oath and to make unchallenged final summations. The only serious departures from Anglo-American trial procedures were standard features of Continental systems, namely the absence of any jury and the admissibility of hearsay evidence. Neither were disadvantages: the post-war populace of Nuremberg had lost its love for the Nazi politicians who had led them to ruin (to such an extent that they demonstrated in their thousands against the acquittals of three defendants) and the hearsay rule is a shibboleth which can handicap the defence as much as the prosecution. In both these respects, Nuremberg set a precedent followed by the Hague Tribunal and by the International Criminal Court statute. Guilt on charges of crimes against humanity should be based on logical reasoning by experienced judges and not on the inscrutable verdict of a jury potentially prejudiced by media attacks on the defendant. And all relevant evidence should be available to a court where the discovery of truth is more important than in the ordinary adversary process: the weight of hearsay evidence (because it cannot be cross-examined) may be less than direct testimony, but it should not be discarded whenever it raises doubts or confirms suspicions.

JUDGMENT DAY

Nuremberg changed and clarified international law in many ways. The Charter itself was the outcome of the four-power agreement signed in London on 8 August 1945, which provided for 'an international military tribunal for the trial of war criminals whose offences have no particular geographical location'. This was, in form, no more than the exercise by belligerents of an established customary right to try captured enemies who had infringed the laws of war as defined by the early Hague Conventions. The definition of crimes against humanity in Article 6(c) of the Charter, however, was not found in these earlier conventions, and was applicable to tyrannous behaviour within a state as much as to wartime conflict between states. Article 7 expressly rejected the 'sovereign immunity' principle which the

Americans had at Versailles insisted must protect military and political leaders:

The official position of defendants, whether as Heads of State or responsible officials in Government Departments, shall not be considered as freeing them from responsibility or mitigating punishment.

It was on this basis that Jackson blew away the dust of sovereignty in his prosecution opening, rejecting the notion that individual leaders could escape responsibility by arguing that they were merely agents of an immune state:

The idea that a state, any more than a corporation, commits crimes, is a fiction. Crimes always are committed only by persons . . . It is quite intolerable to let such a legalism become the basis of personal immunity.

The charter recognizes that one who has committed criminal acts may not take refuge in superior orders nor in the doctrine that his crimes were acts of state. These twin principles working together have hitherto resulted in immunity for practically everyone concerned in the really great crimes against peace and mankind. Those in lower ranks were protected because their orders were called acts of state. Modern civilization puts unlimited weapons of destruction in the hands of men. It cannot tolerate so vast an area of legal irresponsibility.

These defendants were men of a station and rank which does not soil its own hands with blood. They were men who knew how to use lesser folk as tools. We want to reach the planners and designers, the inciters and leaders . . .

The Tribunal, in its judgment, anchored its Charter in 'an exercise of sovereign legislative power by the countries to which the German Reich had unconditionally surrendered'. It was 'an expression of international law existing at the time of its creation; and to that extent is itself a contribution to international law'. It rejected the argument that international law is concerned only with the actions of states, and therefore cannot punish individuals, or (alternatively) cannot punish them for carrying out the orders of a sovereign state: 'the very essence of the Charter is that individuals have international duties which transcend the national obligations of obedience imposed by the individual state . . . if the state in authorizing action moves outside its competence in international law'.

The significance of this ruling is that it provides an authoritative basis for holding individuals at all levels, whether footsoldiers or leaders, liable for crimes against humanity. The torturers cannot rely on the defence of superior orders, any more than the commanders can rely on the privileges and immunities of the state they serve. Article 8 of the Charter provides:

The fact that the defendant acted pursuant to the order of his Government or of a superior shall not free him from responsibility, but may be considered in mitigation of punishment . . .

The true test, the Nuremberg judgment decided, was 'whether moral choice is in fact possible' for a soldier or official ordered to kill or torture in defiance of international law.[18] This leaves the proven perpetrator of a crime against humanity only two avenues of exculpation if the action was taken under orders: either that he did not appreciate its unlawfulness, or that he acted under a duress so threatening to himself or his family that it left him no reasonable option but to comply. The Nazi leaders tried at Nuremberg were superiors who gave the orders. In the follow-up trials, duress usually failed as a defence for bankers and doctors, industrialists and bureaucrats, who were personally or politically disposed in any event to carry out Nazi orders,[19] or for officers and soldiers who feared disciplinary sanctions or minor punishment in no way comparable to the gravity of the harm they inflicted by choosing to obey the order.[20] But it was crucial to the perceived fairness of these trials that 'duress' was available and availed of as a defence, however rarely it succeeded (a point which was overlooked by Amnesty International when in 1998 it demanded abolition of duress as a defence to war crimes (see p. 343)).

Criticisms of Nuremberg are justified, but only up to a point: it was not the model of an unbiased international tribunal (that would have required judges from countries which had remained neutral); counts one and two (conspiracy to wage aggressive war and crimes against peace) were novel and infringed the rule against retrospectivity; the fairness of the trial on count three (war crimes) was affected by the ruling against *tu quoque* evidence. But the great achievement of Nuremberg was count four: the crime against humanity – in effect, an ordinary crime committed on a scale of barbarism unimaginable until the Holocaust. This was the crime recognizable even to its architects when they saw the concentration camp films: the words of the Charter – 'extermination, enslavement, deportation and other inhumane acts . . . persecution on political, racial or religious grounds in connection with any crime' – hardly convey the unspeakable horror. These were not war crimes against enemy soldiers, but against German civilians – Jews, gypsies, homosexuals, the handicapped – who were regarded as pseudo-humans. They were not committed because of the exigencies of war, but because of the vicious racism of Nazi leaders. Unlike the crimes of pirates and slave traders, the traditional targets of individual responsibility in international law, they did not need any international or transborder element to attract jurisdiction: these were crimes that the world could not suffer to take place anywhere, at any time, because they shamed everyone. They were not, for that crucial reason, crimes against Germans (which therefore only Germans should punish); they were crimes against humanity, because the very fact that a fellow human could conceive and commit them diminishes every member of the human race. For this precedent alone, with its potential to destroy sovereign immunity, the Nuremberg judgment was one large legal step forward for humankind.

VICTOR'S JUSTICE?

That humankind did not progress much beyond the Nuremberg verdicts for the next fifty years was due to many factors, only one of which can be laid at the door of the Tribunal. In its end lay the negation of its beginning: it created crimes against humanity and then punished them inhumanely. Twelve defendants were sentenced to death by hanging, after which – by some grisly irony appealing to the Allied high command – the bodies were cremated in the ovens at Dachau. The ashes were consigned to an unidentified fast-flowing river so no grave would ever serve as a place of neo-Nazi pilgrimage. Goering eluded this act of vengeance by taking a capsule of poison on the night before the executions, choosing to die privately in brief convulsive agony rather than in a macabre ritual laid on for the Allied press. The worst feature of the executions was that they had been preordained, at least by the Russians. As early as the Tehran Conference, Stalin had proposed that the trial dispense 'the justice of the firing squad'. Very early in the trial he had it visited by Andrei Vyshinsky, choreographer of his own show trials. It was an excruciating occasion, as the Allied judges and prosecutors hosted a dinner in honour of a man who had been complicit in more crimes against humanity than those they were trying. True to form, Vyshinsky raised his glass and proposed a toast 'to the speedy conviction and execution of the defendants'. The judges drank it, to their subsequent mortification. The British Attorney-General Hartley Shawcross clamoured for death sentences, in breach of an ethical rule of the English Bar that prosecutors must not urge a particular punishment. He argued, perversely, that upon executing these defendants depended 'the ways of truth and righteousness between the nations of the world'.[21] Since he also accepted that they were broken and discredited men, 'the ways of truth and righteousness' were hardly paved by killing them.

But victor's justice required executions. The Russian judges followed their orders from Stalin and insisted on the death penalty for everyone, while only one of the French judges, De Vares, was in principle opposed to hanging. That three of the twenty-two defendants were acquitted, and seven spared the death penalty, gave the Tribunal's decision that element of weighing and balancing which is necessary to any 'judgment', but its punishments subsequently provided a precedent used to excuse the politically motivated execution of other fallen leaders (like Pakistan's Zulfikar Ali Bhutto) whose guilt was much less clearly proven. Something of this stain was removed in the 1990s, when the death penalty was abjured as an option for the international tribunals for former Yugoslavia and Rwanda, and then as a penalty available to the International Criminal Court. It remains historically the most regrettable aspect of the Allied war crimes trials that a process which commenced with Henry Stimson's call to punish 'in a dignified manner consistent with the advance of civilization' should end at Hamelin prison with the English hangman Albert Pierrepoint slavering over Irma Griese ('as bonny a blonde as one could ever hope to meet') as he measured her for the drop.[22]

Once the Nazi leaders had been tried, interest in prosecuting underlings and accomplices waned. A few industrialists – notably Alfred Krupp – received jail sentences, but the corporations which had profited by deliberately working Jews to death, such as Siemens, Volkswagen and I. G. Farben, were not forced to compensate their surviving relatives. By the end of 1947 the Allies ran out of both money and motivation for war crimes trials. The lawyers who had insisted on reasonable standards of fairness no longer called the shots: prosecutions fell to army officers, who were untrained for the task and uninterested in carrying it out. Most debilitating of all was the onset of the Cold War: Nazi scientists and businessmen who might be of use in the forthcoming battle between communism and capitalism were given immunity, by East and West alike. Justice became a mockery of power politics: while the palpably insane Rudolf Hess remained incarcerated at Soviet insistence for the rest of his life, the US released Krupp in 1951, before half his sentence had expired. This caused Jackson (who had returned to the US Supreme Court) to write despairingly to Shawcross that, 'This country is so heated up about communism at the present moment that the public temper identifies as a friend of the United States any person who is a foe of Stalin.'[23]

It had been fear of 'communism and chaos' which determined the fateful decision of General MacArthur's administration in occupied Japan to exempt from trial – indeed, from all retribution – the worst surviving war criminal of all, the Emperor Hirohito, who had personally approved all his country's barbaric military ventures and had held out against surrender until the radio-active dust cleared from Hiroshima. It was this crucial decision which made the Tokyo trials a mockery of justice, with their death sentences on politicians and generals who had served as the Emperor's accomplices. The French judge, Henri Bernard, said that the failure to prosecute the Emperor vitiated the entire proceedings, while the presiding Australian judge, Sir William Webb, argued that because 'the leader of the crime, though available for trial, had been granted immunity', his accomplices should have their death sentences commuted to life imprisonment. This was the tragic flaw in a trial which should have been as significant as Nuremberg and was in some ways an improvement on it – for example, the defendants were provided with American lawyers, who were permitted to challenge the jurisdictional basis of the Tribunal on the grounds that it was 'victor's justice' imposing '*ex post facto* criminality'. The proceedings dragged on, from May 1946 to November 1948, because most of this time was occupied with the defence case (George Kennan commented caustically that 'at no time in history have conquerors conferred upon the vanquished such elaborate opportunities for public defence and for vindication of their military acts').[24] The Tokyo prosecution served the historical purpose of collecting hard documentary evidence of systematic atrocities which in their elemental bestiality were beyond even Nazi contemplation: this imperial army impaled women on stakes, after raping them and cutting their children in half. It dropped bubonic plague germs on Chinese citizens, and boasted of its contempt for the laws of war by executing Allied airmen alongside their parachutes and by sending surviving prisoners, at war's end, on death marches. The sadism that flourished with official approval in the prisoner-of-war camps cost 27 per cent of the Anglo-American prisoners their lives (compared with 4 per cent who died in German or Italian captivity). While Nuremberg had confined the concept of the crime against humanity to the wartime genocide of civilian Jews in concentration camps, the Tokyo trial extended the description to peculiarly barbaric acts of murder, generally of prisoners-of-war, in circumstances which amounted in isolation to war crimes, but which were given the extra dimension of guilt because they were proved to be widespread and systematic emanations of a policy approved (or at least tolerated) by Japan's military and political leadership.[25] The Tokyo trial's contribution to humanitarian jurisprudence was the concept of criminal liability for permitting, as distinct from intending, atrocities: this was the 'command responsibility' theory, approved by the US Supreme Court in General Yamashita's appeal, which half a century later would become the basis for the Hague Tribunal indictment of Karadžić and Mladić (see p. 207).

The absence of Hirohito, the supreme commander, undermined the trial both as a precedent and as a method of guilt acknowledgement. The Emperor, who had previously been psychologically incapable of contemplating surrender, did so on 14 August 1945, only because the atom bomb had been dropped on Hiroshima eight days before. His 'surrender' broadcast to his people was a monument of evasion ('the war situation has developed not necessarily to Japan's advantage, while the general trends of the world have all turned against her interests') and he should have occupied Goering's place in the Tokyo dock. But MacArthur and his right-wing advisers decided that the imperative of avoiding 'communism and chaos' required the Emperor to remain in place, as an American puppet, even though this meant rigging the Tokyo trial to pretend that he was innocent. The proceedings were very much an American affair: the International Military Tribunal of the Far East was established by MacArthur's declaration, rather than by any international agreement, and he appointed the judges (eleven, which proved too many). His chief counsel, Joseph Heenan, edited Hirohito out of the prosecution evidence and encouraged the twenty-five defendants to make no mention of him (they happily colluded, 'for the future of the Japanese race'). When Tojo accidentally testified that it was inconceivable for a high Japanese official to take any action against the wishes of the Emperor, Heenan stage-managed a bogus retraction. Other indefensible decisions were taken by the American prosecutors: they exempted Japan's warmongering industrialists and its violent (but violently anti-communist) nationalist leaders; they overlooked the enslavement of Koreans and Formosans and hundreds of thousands of 'comfort women' forced to slake the lust of the imperial army. They made a Faustian bargain with the wicked scientists of Unit 731 in Manchuria (where thousands of human guinea pigs were killed in the course of Mengele-type experiments), giving them immunity in return for disclosing the results of their 'research' to the US rather than the USSR.[26] Although there can be little quarrel with the actual verdicts of the Far East military tribunals, which tried some 6,000 war criminals (imposing 900 death sentences but acquitting about one fifth of all defendants), these inadequacies diminish the main Tokyo trial as a historical example of international justice. Bizarrely, the Americans decided not to publish an official transcript of the judgments: in consequence, the best known is a querulous dissent by Justice Pal, privately published by the author in 1952 and distributed in Japan under the title *On Japan being Not Guilty*. Pal (who did not bother to attend many trial sessions) declared everyone innocent. He made the correct criticism that criminal liability for 'crimes against the peace' could not be derived retrospectively from the Kellogg–Briand Pact, but irresponsibly he chose to turn a blind eye to the amply proved charges of war crimes, and unforgivably he tried to justify the summary murder of captured Allied airmen ('the conscience of mankind revolts not so much against the punishment meted out to the ruthless bomber as against his ruthless form of bombing').[27]

Pal's dissent provides an example of how a judge's nationality and politics (he was a bitter Indian anti-colonialist) can override his duty to do justice, but it proved influential – especially through its denunciation of the US bombing of Hiroshima. The absence of the Emperor from the dock meant that the US lost for all time the opportunity of proving in court that Truman's first use of the A-bomb did indeed, as he predicted, save hundreds of thousands of Allied and Japanese lives, since it was the only way to force this implacable man to surrender. More significantly, of course, the Emperor's immunity sent the indelible message that the nation itself was guiltless: subsequent generations felt no shame in having an executed war criminal in the family, and the Japanese government even today refuses to contemplate compensation for the victims of its atrocities, unlike the German government, which in 1999 stumped up over £1 billion in the settlement with wartime slave labourers. The received wisdom in the US supreme command was that Japanese crimes against humanity were more readily forgivable than German, because the latter race were so much more civilized and hence deserved more punishment because they 'knew better'. This thinking, articulated by MacArthur in evidence to a US Senate inquiry, was ignorant as well as paternalistic. Imperial Japan was in fact more thorough-goingly racist than Nazi Germany, its innate superiority lauded over other Asian races as well as over 'decadent' Europeans. Japanese generals, diplomats and government lawyers knew all about the pre-war Hague and Geneva Conventions, and boasted of flouting them. The arrogant amorality with which Japanese soldier and general alike would hack or march to death inconvenient prisoners was arguably as wicked as the perverted ideology which could justify the destruction (by working them to death) of Jews, gypsies and homosexuals. The Nuremberg trial saw off the racist perversion of Nazism; but the Tokyo trial did nothing to deter the bestial military blood-vengeance that has been the hallmark of modern crimes against humanity, from Rwanda and Bosnia to East Timor. Emperor Hirohito stayed on his throne until his death in 1989,

masquerading as a meek marine biologist, touring in 1971 to meet
Queen Elizabeth II and in 1975 to meet Mickey Mouse and Dr
Kissinger: in that era when crimes against humanity were so regularly
overlooked, few bothered to demonstrate against him. For all the
promise of Nuremberg, the equivalent trial in Tokyo served more to
underline a traditional Japanese song:

> There is a law of nations, it is true,
> But when the moment comes, remember,
> The strong eat up the weak.

Meanwhile, in Cold War Europe, the Nuremberg precedent was
being ignored (although in West Germany, once the country had
recovered, it was commendably applied in over 6,000 cases of Nazi war
crimes). Once the Allies lost interest, nobody bothered to investigate
thousands of crimes against humanity whose perpetrators quietly
shipped themselves off to begin new lives in Allied countries which
accepted them as refugees and did not wake up to their past until the
1990s, by which time most were too old to be satisfactorily tried.
Some Nazi criminals found refuge in nations which needed them or
sympathized with their crimes. In Perón's Argentina, they organized
the army and much of industry; in East Germany, they occupied
political positions as administrators and propagandists.[28] President
Stroessner of Paraguay personally protected the Auschwitz doctor
Josef Mengele, while successive Syrian rulers have not only extended
hospitality to Alois Brunner, Eichmann's exterminator-general, but
have employed him in anti-Israeli work and rejected every request for
his extradition.[29]

More positively, however, the United Nations General Assembly
in December 1946 unanimously confirmed that the Nuremberg Charter
and reasoning of the Tribunal reflected the principles of international
law.[30] As the House of Lords was to recognize in the *Pinochet Case*,
this set the seal on Article 6 of the Charter, which proclaims that there
shall be 'individual responsibility' (notwithstanding that individual's
exercise of state power or obedience to superior orders) for

(a) Crimes against peace (waging or initiating a war of aggression or a war
  in violation of international treaties);

(b) War crimes (violations of the law or customs of war); and

(c) Crimes against humanity.

Questions remained, however, about the latter category, which the Nuremberg judgment itself had treated as if they were particularly heinous examples of war crimes rather than as a separate category of crime which could be committed irrespective of the existence of any inter-state conflict. On this approach, one significant distinction between a war crime and a crime against humanity would be that the latter could be committed by a government against its own nationals (e.g. the Nazis against German Jews), while war crimes could be perpetrated only upon enemies or foreigners. Article 6(c) of the Charter defines crimes against humanity as 'murder, extermination, enslavement, deportation and other inhumane acts committed against any civilian population *before or during* [my italics] the war', and is therefore apt to cover barbarities committed within a state against its own nationals, irrespective of the onset of war. Although the Charter may not have been intended to render individuals responsible in international law for the crimes against humanity they committed in time of peace, the question is now academic since 6(c) designated a class of crime which later treaties and precedents – culminating in the appeal judgment in the *Tadić Case* (see p. 293) – have recognized as capable of punishment, whenever and wherever committed.

It should be noticed, however, that an ingredient of the crimes defined as 'against humanity' in Article 6(c) was that they are committed 'in execution of or in connection with any crime within the jurisdiction of the Tribunal'. This suggested (ambiguously, since the absence of a prefatory comma could indicate that this was a requirement only for charges of 'persecution on political, racial or religious grounds') that any prosecution would have to prove a nexus with other crimes over which the Tribunal had jurisdiction, namely war crimes or the crime of aggression. The Tribunal itself adopted this approach, declining to convict any defendant for persecution of German Jews before the outbreak of war, and the Allies in the Tokyo and post-Nuremberg trials confined their crimes against humanity charges to conduct clearly linked with armed conflict. A requirement to prove such linkage can therefore be said to have been an ingredient of the offence at the time it was established by the Nuremberg Charter and judgment: however, it was to disappear as a customary international law requirement over the following decades as treaties (beginning with the Genocide Convention) and the draft criminal codes promulgated by the International Law Commission contained no such limitation. The statutes for the Rwanda Tribunal and the International Criminal Court exclude this artificial linkage requirement, and after the *Tadić* decision it can be confidently stated to have withered away as an element of the offence.[31] Crimes against humanity may therefore be committed in peacetime, and irrespective of any internal conflict (although the requirement for widespread and systematic oppression will normally mean that such crimes will be committed at times of civil unrest). An element that does remain is the linkage of the conduct charged as a crime against humanity with an exercise of the power of the State, or state-like power asserted by a political organization. The Nuremberg Charter provided authority to punish persons 'acting in the interests of the European Axis countries', but decisions of the Hague and Rwanda Tribunals establish that the act need not be carried out on behalf of a recognized state. However, there must be some connection with an 'official' body, which governs *de facto* or which aspires to govern through organized terror.

TOWARDS UNIVERSAL JURISDICTION (GENOCIDE, TORTURE, APARTHEID)

THE GENOCIDE CONVENTION

The first liberation of crimes against humanity from any temporal connection with a declared war came while the Nuremberg judgment still reverberated, in the form of the 1948 Convention on the Prevention and Punishment of Genocide. Article 1 simply states that 'genocide, whether committed in time of peace or time of war, is a crime under international law'. This treaty has been ratified by such a large majority of states that it can now be considered a rule of modern customary international law, binding on all states (whether they have ratified the Convention or not) and *requiring* them to prosecute acts of genocide.

As the ICJ explained in its decision in the *Reservations to the Convention on Genocide Case*, 'The origins of the Convention show that it was the intention of the UN to condemn and punish genocide as "a crime under international law" . . . involving a denial of the right of existence of entire human groups, a denial which shocks the conscience of mankind and results in great losses to humanity, and which is contrary to moral law and to the spirit and aims of the UN.'[32]

The Convention defines genocide as the committing, with the intention to destroy in whole or in part a national, ethnic, racial or religious group, of any one of the following five acts:

(a) killing members of the group;
(b) causing serious bodily harm or mental harm to members of the group;
(c) deliberately inflicting on the group conditions of life calculated to bring about its physical destruction in whole or in part;
(d) imposing measures intended to prevent births within that group;
(e) forcibly transferring children of the group to another group.

This definition reflects contemporary preoccupation with genocidal Nazi policy towards the Jews as revealed at Nuremberg: it is wide enough to cover ethnic cleansing and religious pogroms, but it does not address Stalin's extermination of a particular economic class (the kulaks) or the millions he liquidated for suspected dissidence or disloyalty. It would cover gypsies and Rastafarians, but not homosexuals or members of a political or social organization unless membership was confined to a particular tribe, race or nationality. On this basis the British government declined to credit the Spanish prosecutor's allegation of genocide against General Pinochet: it could not by definition cover his attempts to exterminate left-wingers. Attempts to liquidate a political group could, however, be prosecuted as a crime against humanity consisting of 'persecution on political grounds': on this basis the French Court de cassation held that Klaus Barbie could be prosecuted for eliminating members of the French Resistance.[33] It is, moreover, limited to *material* destruction of a group, either by physical or biological means, rather than the destruction of the national, linguistic, religious, cultural or other identity of that group.[34] The concept of 'cultural genocide' – by prohibiting the use of a group's language, rewriting or obliterating its history or destroying its icons

– did not appeal to members of the UN in 1948, many of whom were engaged in doing just that to troublesome minorities within their own borders. In *Prosecutor* v. *Akayeru*,[35] the Rwandu Tribunal stressed that genocide required a specific intent to destroy a group as such, and on this basis Australian courts have held that degradation of Aboriginal people through confiscation of traditional lands cannot justify a charge of genocide against the government ministers responsible.[36]

The procedural provisions of the Convention are of some significance. Parties must: legislate to punish the crime effectively; make it extraditable irrespective of any political motivation; and have it tried 'by such international penal tribunal as may have jurisdiction' – an indication in 1948 that recurrence of this crime against humanity should in the future call forth an international criminal court. Article VIII permits any signatory to call upon the UN Security Council to act under the UN Charter to suppress genocide or incitements to commit it. Although the Genocide Convention places a primary duty to prosecute on the state where the genocide occurs, it expressly contemplates that other courts – including international tribunals – will have jurisdiction. That there is universal jurisdiction to punish this offence has been confirmed by courts in Israel (the *Eichmann Case*) and America (the *Demjanjuk Case*)[37] and by the House of Lords in the *Pinochet Case*.

THE TORTURE CONVENTION

Torture is the other, and much more common, crime to be recognized post-Nuremberg as involving individual responsibility under international law. For many centuries, torture was regarded as a legitimate, and indeed necessary, method of obtaining information and confession: its use by the Star Chamber and the Spanish Inquisition was ordered and regulated by judicial authorities. Evidence of torture's unreliability as a means of eliciting truth has been as much a reason for its official abandonment as revulsion at its inhumanity, but it is still widely practised by police and military forces around the world. Reaction to Stalin's deployment of 'medieval methods' led to the proscription of torture in Article 5 of the Universal Declaration of

Human Rights, which has been followed by the rule against to
or other inhuman and degrading punishment found in every con
hensive human rights treaty and in many national constitution
bills of rights. It was not until the brutal overthrow of Dr Allende's
democratic government in Chile, however, accompanied by widespread torture of his supporters by the Pinochet military junta, that
the General Assembly was moved to do anything to make these
guarantees effective. The first step was to have them crystallize as a
rule of international law.

This process began in 1975, drawing upon the obligation of states
under the UN Charter to take 'effective measures' to prevent torture
and to provide redress for its victims. This Declaration Against Torture
asserted that no exceptional circumstances – war, instability or public
emergency – could justify torture, defined as

any act by which severe pain or suffering, whether physical or mental, is
intentionally inflicted by or at the instigation of a public official on a person
for such purposes as obtaining from him or a third person information or
confession, punishing him for an act he has committed or is suspected of
having committed, or intimidating him or other persons.

Declarations of this kind assist the emergence of international law
rules, but do nothing to enforce them. It took the death under torture
of Steve Biko to provoke the General Assembly into drafting and
accepting the 1984 Convention against Torture and Other Cruel,
Inhuman and Degrading Treatment or Punishment, which requires
state parties to take jurisdiction to punish torture committed within
their territory either by or against their nationals. The definition of
torture was taken from the Declaration, which requires the pain to
be inflicted by or with the consent of a 'public official', but excludes
suffering 'arising only from, inherent in, or incidental to, lawful
sanctions'. Significantly, the Convention requires states to arrest and
bring proceedings 'where the alleged offender is present in any territory
under its jurisdiction' and has not been subject to a request for
extradition.

The 1984 Convention establishes a Committee Against Torture,
which can receive complaints (including complaints from individuals)
and conduct investigations with the co-operation of signatory states.

(This has not proved very effective, since offending states do not ratify the Convention or else do not co-operate with the committee.) A more worthwhile deterrent within its region is the European Convention for the Prevention of Torture or Inhuman and Degrading Treatment or Punishment, which has established a committee empowered to visit prisons and police cells in signatory countries and to publish reports and recommendations following its visits. This non-judicial exercise has served to monitor and improve prison conditions in a number of European countries, but the committee is unable to sheet home responsibility for torture to particular individuals by commencing prosecutorial action against them.

For all this array of international condemnation, torture remains a malignant reality throughout the world, routinely exposed by human rights organizations but rarely punished by the states – seventy-three at the last count – who connive in its use by their functionaries. The UN has appointed a Special Rapporteur on the subject (who counts the states who torture) and the Human Rights Committee has found some complaints proved, but the most concrete form of assistance, the Voluntary Fund for Victims of Torture, set up by the General Assembly to finance medical and psychological support schemes for victims, is a *de facto* recognition that preventative measures have failed. The most that can be said is that the treaties evidence a state practice that torture is contrary to international law, with the corollary that individuals accused of inciting or directing it must be detained wherever they are found and either brought before a court in that country or extradited to a state prepared to exercise what is now generally regarded as a universal jurisdiction over them.

The most significant recognition of criminal liability in international law for torture was in the *Pinochet Case*, where the House of Lords confirmed that

ever since 1945, torture on a large scale has featured as one of the crimes against humanity . . . [which] . . . has the character of *jus cogens* . . . [which] justifies states in taking universal jurisdiction over torture wherever committed. International law provides that offences *jus cogens* may be punished by any state because the offenders are 'common enemies of mankind and all nations have an equal interest in their apprehension and prosecution . . .'

What was needed therefore was an international system which could punish those who were guilty of torture and which did not permit the evasion of punishment by the torturer moving from one state to another. The Torture Convention was agreed not in order to create an international crime which had not previously existed but to provide an international system under which the international criminal – the torturer – would find no safe haven.[38]

The most remarkable feature of the Torture Convention is that it applies the universal jurisdiction principle – either you extradite or you punish – to any person suspected of committing a single act of official torture. In this respect it is wider than the crime against humanity constituted by the official use of torture, which must be part of a widespread or systematic attack directed against civilians as a measure of state policy. The *Pinochet Case* galvanized compliance with the Torture Convention: in 1999 a 17-judge Grand Chamber of the European Court of Human Rights unanimously condemned France for sustained truncheon assaults by its gendarmes on an arrested drugs suspect. This decision established that repeated beatings during interrogation, causing severe pain over a period of time, amount to 'torture' rather than inhumane treatment. In the same year, the Israeli Supreme Court, notoriously reluctant to rein in the nation's security service (Shin Bet), at last decided that the extraction of information from terrorist suspects did not justify the continual 'violent shaking' which had become a trademark torture technique of Israeli secret agents.

In 1981 the New York Court of Appeals paved the way for the Pinochet decision by approving a civil action brought under the US Alien Tort Statute by the Filártiga family, whose young son had been kidnapped and tortured to death by a Paraguayan police chief subsequently resident in the United States. The statutory claim for damages hinged upon whether the action, committed abroad, had been 'in violation of the law of nations', and the court had little hesitation in ruling that 'deliberate torture perpetrated under colour of official authority violates universally accepted norms of the international law of human rights, regardless of the nationality of the parties . . . among the rights universally proclaimed by all nations is the right to be free of physical torture. Indeed, for the purposes of civil liability, the torturer has become – like the pirate and slave trader before him – *hostis humanis generis*, an enemy of all mankind.'[39]

PIRACY AND SLAVERY

These were the first crimes against humanity. So far as piracy is concerned, the old definitions[40] have been updated by Article 15 of the Convention on the High Seas, which provides that piracy shall consist of any illegal act of violence, detention or depredation, committed for private ends by the crew or passengers of a private ship or aircraft, and directed (on the high seas or in space) against persons or property aboard another ship or aircraft. This definition represents modern international law, and justifies any state in assuming jurisdiction to try attackers of ships or aircraft who are acting for private gain and not on behalf of governments. One of the least attractive human rights failures has been the refusal of states to deploy these traditional powers so as to protect refugees in south-east Asian waters: here, the pirates come from fishing communities on the coasts of countries hostile to the boat people, while the states best equipped to provide naval protection (Indonesia, America and Australia) fear that by doing so they will incur responsibility for guaranteeing refugee status. So all the relatively stable, prosperous and powerful countries of the region have suffered boatloads of Vietnamese they labelled 'economic immigrants' to be robbed, raped and murdered in the unspoken hope that this would deter other Vietnamese from making the voyage. With this exception, pirates and slave traders no longer serve the interests of sovereign states, and their international outlawry is uncontroversial: their atrocities are no longer formally regarded as crimes against humanity since they have no linkage with governments. However, there is some overlap with crimes against humanity in the 1979 Convention against the Taking of Hostages, which can apply to hijacking by terrorist groups or hostage-taking by death squads linked to military juntas. It provides an example of what is termed compulsory universal jurisdiction, in that states are required either to prosecute suspects or to extradite them to a country which will prosecute.

The only discomfiture which modern governments may feel from the prohibition on slavery derives from treaties which condemn compulsory labour practices akin to it. The first Forced Labour Convention was agreed by the General Conference of the International Labour Organization in 1930: it justified the conviction at Nuremberg of Albert Speer and other architects of Nazi deportation and forced labour schemes, which were devised quite literally to work Jews to death. In 1957 it was valuably supplemented by the Abolition of Forced Labour Convention extending the prohibition to the punitive 'political re-education camps' which were becoming such a common feature of post-revolutionary communist states. Although there have been no end of examples of gross violations by governments of the right not to be subjected to forced labour – on the killing fields of Cambodia or in the re-education camps of Chairman Mao's Cultural Revolution – this is a right too difficult to enforce directly. The 'good offices' of the Director-General of the International Labour Organization may have some effect, at least if labour policies antagonize international trade union bodies, but the victims most in need of assistance do not belong to trade unions. In any event, these conventions are silent on the most objectionable and obsolete form of compulsory forced labour, conscription for military service. Indeed, they exempt 'any work or service which forms part of the normal civic obligations of the citizens of a fully self-governing country'. They do not prohibit governments from forcing nationals to fight against their will or compelling citizens to do 'civic duty' in labour camps or on national service.

APARTHEID

As a doctrine which asserts the genetic inferiority of non white races, apartheid constitutes a breach of the anti-discrimination clause of every human rights convention, and it was the determination of a growing number of states to attack the architects of apartheid which contributed most to the development of enforcement measures such as economic sanctions (see p. 40). By 1973, when the Soviet Union (busily engaged in jailing its own dissidents) sponsored the International Convention on the Suppression and Punishment of the Crime of Apartheid, South Africa had become a pariah state and its policy of separate development could be condemned as a violation of international law. In so far as apartheid involved genocide, torture or slavery, it already amounted to a crime against humanity, albeit one which was not native to South Africa. There was a propagandist flavour to this loosely drafted convention, and the nations which refused to sign – the USA, UK and many other Western states – have denied it any practical significance, other than as further recognition of the fact that crimes against humanity could be committed in peace as well as in war, and by a single sovereign state within its own territory.

The consequence that individuals should be held responsible for committing apartheid was spelled out in Article 3:

International criminal responsibility shall apply, irrespective of the motive involved, to individuals, members of organizations and institutions and representatives of the State, whether residing in the territory of the State in which the acts are perpetrated or in some other State, whenever they commit, participate in, directly incite or conspire . . . (or) . . . directly abet, encourage or co-operate in the commission of the crime of apartheid.

This absurdly broad definition would incriminate most of the white population of South Africa for 'co-operating' with their own government by obeying its laws – as if they were the equivalent of SS officers obeying orders to execute innocent Jews. The Apartheid Convention remained propaganda rather than law, and the fact that it was propaganda in a good cause does not excuse its sponsors for exploiting the concept of a crime against humanity. Although 101 nations have signalled their good intentions by signing this convention, Nelson Mandela's new South Africa has ironically but sensibly declined to join. It must clearly be understood that in order to fix individual responsibility for a crime against humanity in international law, the act committed must be a politically motivated command or conduct which results in a pattern of serious crimes (torture or murder, for example). The millions who obeyed the apartheid laws without personal responsibility for its acts of violence may be condemned for apathy and acquiescence, but it is absurd to require, as does the Convention on Apartheid, that they be tried and punished wherever they are found. Needless to say, none were, and not a single prosecution anywhere in the world for the 'crime' of apartheid was recorded before the policy was progressively dismantled by South Africa under the impetus of economic sanctions. Apartheid reappears in the 1998 Rome Statute of the International Criminal Court, but the lesson has been learnt: the crime against humanity constituted by apartheid is confined to systematic murder, enslavement and torture committed with the intention of maintaining the hegemony of the dominant racial group.

UNIVERSAL JURISDICTION

Crimes against humanity will only be deterred when their would-be perpetrators – be they political leaders, field commanders or soldiers and policemen – are given pause by the prospect that they will henceforth have no hiding place: that legal nemesis may some day, somewhere, overtake them. That prospect is only realistic if there exists an international criminal court cognizant of their offence, or, in its absence, a rule permitting their punishment by courts of countries into whose jurisdiction they may come or perchance be brought. It is this practical consideration which makes universal jurisdiction the most important attribute of a crime against humanity: it is an offence so serious that any court anywhere is empowered by international law to try it and to punish it, irrespective of its place of commission or the nationality of the offender or the victims. Jurisdiction arises, in other words, wherever an offender is found, and it arises because he is alleged to have offended in a particularly outrageous way.

There is no doubt that universal jurisdiction is recognized in customary international law as the basis for proceedings in domestic courts against pirates and slave traders. Equally, universal jurisdiction over aircraft hijackers, hostage-takers and other types of international terrorists has been partially achieved through the modern machinery of an international treaty requiring signatories to punish offenders found within their borders or else to extradite them to countries which will put them on trial. But these are all crimes which occur across borders, or on the open seas, or in air space of questionable ownership: universal jurisdiction arises not because they are crimes against humanity, but because they are crimes *simpliciter*, under any domestic law, which might otherwise go unpunished. As the Permanent Court of

International Justice explained universal jurisdiction against pirates in the *Lotus Case*:

It is an offence against the law of nations; and as the scene of the pirate's operations is the high seas, which it is not the right or duty of any nation to police, he is denied the protection of the flag which he may carry and is treated as an outlaw – as the enemy of mankind – *hostis humanis generis* – whom any nation may in the interest of all capture and punish.[41]

In fact, pirates – and the modern criminals such as hostage-takers, terrorists and international drug-traffickers, against whom universal jurisdiction is developing through treaties– are not usually implicated in crimes against humanity. The terrorist under one treaty may be a freedom fighter under another; the drug dealer is a common criminal, heedless of the harm he puts in others' way, but it is an exaggeration to regard his offence as the equivalent of politically motivated mass murder. It follows that those courts and writers who have argued that universal jurisdiction for crimes against humanity arises on the same basis as universal jurisdiction over piracy are advancing a fundamentally flawed argument. Piracy occurs in a place, the high seas, which requires universal jurisdiction, as the alternative to there being no jurisdiction at all. The crime against humanity normally occurs in a country where there is jurisdiction, albeit one which (because of the power of the state-backed perpetrator) will not be exercised, and the issue arises years, perhaps decades, later, when the perpetrator is found (or brought) within the jurisdiction of a nation with the exceptional resolve to bring a prosecution.

One case which stands as an authority for the right of universal punishment of crimes against humanity is in some respects an unhappy precedent. Adolf Eichmann was without doubt guilty of directing much of the Holocaust: he would inevitably have been convicted at Nuremberg had he not escaped to Argentina, where he was kidnapped by Israeli agents and subsequently brought to trial in Jerusalem under a local law condemning to death anyone who had participated in Nazi atrocities. Eichmann's challenge to the law was rejected on the principle that jurisdiction to try crimes against humanity was universal. Both the Israeli District Court and Appeal Court relied on precedents from piracy and slavery, which do not go far enough to establish the principle in relation to state persecution of its own people within its own territory.[42] A much better — because it was more honest — explanation was given by the French Court of Appeal in brushing aside a challenge to Klaus Barbie's arrest by French officials in Guyana: the crimes against humanity of this SS officer, who sent thousands of Jews to their deaths from Lyon, 'do not simply fall within the scope of French municipal law but are subject to an international criminal order to which the notions of frontiers and extradition rules arising therefrom are completely foreign'.[43]

This is the best, because it is the simplest, statement of the Nuremberg legacy. Article 6(c) of the Charter defined a class of crime of which sixteen Nazi leaders were convicted, which is so peculiarly horrific that the very fact that educated, rational and otherwise respected rulers of men were capable of conceiving and committing it must diminish whatever value there is in being human. The judgment at Nuremberg and the Conventions which followed gave this particular crime a special status in international law, as imposing an *erga omnes* obligation on every state to assist in its trial and punishment. This power to bring alleged perpetrators to justice is described by the phrase 'universal jurisdiction': states have the power, individually or collectively, to conduct a trial even if they have no link with the place where the crime was committed, or with its perpetrator or its victims. Jurisdiction over ordinary crime depends on a link, usually territorial, between the state of trial and the crime itself, but in the case of crimes against humanity that link may be found in the simple fact that we are all human beings. So an international tribunal, a court without a country, may be empowered to punish, as may (if no such tribunal exists) the courts of any other country which gets its hands on an accused. Of course, universal jurisdiction in any state will normally proceed under a local statute empowering a court to exercise it, and any international tribunal will require a charter or statute subscribed to by the states which bring it into existence, either collectively through the UN (as a subsidiary organ of the Security Council) or individually through a treaty like the Nuremberg Charter or the Rome Statute of the International Criminal Court. The concept of universal jurisdiction for crimes against humanity is the solution that international law offers to the spectacle of impunity for tyrants and torturers who cover themselves with domestic immunities and amnesties and pardons. They can still hide, but in a world where jurisdiction over their crimes is universal, they cannot run.

Court rulings upholding the principle of universal jurisdiction before the *Pinochet Case* were confined to cases involving old Nazis extradited to jurisdictions anxious to try them. This in itself poses a problem which cannot be brushed under the carpet: the danger of a show trial. There has never been any doubt about the indelible guilt of Eichmann and Barbie, or of the fairness of most of the recent trials of old Nazis, like Sarwonick in Britain, Priebke in Italy and Maurice Papon in France (see p. 278). But the case of John Demjanjuk, extradited from the US and sentenced to death in Israel on the false finding that he was Treblinka concentration camp guard Ivan the Terrible, demonstrates the potential for injustice in a country bent on revenge. The Demjanjuk proceedings were a disgrace. The televised trial was held in a theatre, as an avowed exercise in 'Holocaust education'; the audience was permitted to display its emotions as elderly survivors came on stage to misidentify the defendant as their tormentor half a century before. The judges permitted the most hysterical and prejudicial media publicity, ignored the clearest evidence that the crucial documents were forgeries, and even ended the reasons for their decision by emotionally dedicating their judgment 'to the souls that have been lost'.[44] Demjanjuk stayed on death row for some years until an appeal court grudgingly accepted that fresh evidence, forthcoming from Poland, proved his innocence. The trial stands not only as another warning of the unreliability of eyewitness evidence and of the risk of justice miscarrying when it is too long delayed, but more importantly of the danger that some states will exploit universal jurisdiction for political ends. Israel wanted so badly to convict Demjanjuk that three experienced judges ignored exculpatory evidence and presided over an outrageously unfair show trial.

The episode is not an argument against universal jurisdiction, but rather in favour of it being exercised in many cases by an international criminal court, free from municipal pressures, whether political or psychological. It was indeed the prospect of malicious or partisan prosecution which caused the lone dissent in the *Pinochet Case* and which has been the basis for hostility to that decision from those arch-exponents of *realpolitik*, Dr Kissinger, George Bush, Jesse Helms and the Vatican (see p. 400). However, the principle of universal jurisdiction is the only way to ensure that there will be no safe haven for suspects: either you extradite or you punish. If a state demeans this principle by using it as a pretext to bring sham prosecutions or to stage show trials, these issues will need to be addressed forcefully by the international community. But it is notable that those who are most voluble about the danger, like Senator Helms, are also the most emphatically opposed to its solution, i.e. the advent of an International Criminal Court. That is because they are opposed to international justice, both as a general proposition and as a potential stumbling block for American hegemony. They represent some of the forces against which the human rights movement must continue to struggle well into the twenty-first century.

The reason why crimes against humanity, unlike ordinary crimes, in the absence of treaties attract universal jurisdiction is not found in the seriousness of the actual offence – the psychopathic serial killer may do more harm than the casual police torturer. Nor is it found by any literal analogy with the pirate or slave trader – unattractive criminals certainly, but ones who are rarely acting on government service. What sets a crime against humanity apart, both in wickedness and in the need for special measures of deterrence, is the simple fact that it is a crime of unforgivable brutality ordained by a government – or at least by an organization exercising political power. It is not the mind of the individual torturer, but the fact that this individual is part of the apparatus of a state, which makes the crime so horrific and locates it in a different dimension from ordinary criminality. This factor also explains why individual responsibility and universal jurisdiction are necessary responses if any deterrence is to be achieved. There is a reasonable chance that torture and murder will not be committed by secret police, or ordered by generals or ministers, if they believe they may one day, under a different regime, or in another country, be called to account for their participation in criminal acts of state. Crimes against humanity are committed confidently, by officials who believe that their regime will continue in power – that, after all, is often the purpose of committing the crime. In the unlikely event of its collapse, a negotiated withdrawal is possible: at best, you keep the Swiss bank account; at worst you appear before a truth commission. The doctrine of universal jurisdiction over crimes against humanity is justified because it may make some torturer pause at the prospect that some time somewhere some prosecutor may feel strongly enough about his crime to put him on trial.

7

Slouching Towards Nemesis

The idea of insecurity became increasingly entrenched in society: the dark fear that anybody, no matter how innocent, could fall victim to that infinite witch hunt. Some were absorbed by overwhelming fear, while others were controlled by the conscious or unconscious proclivity to justify horror: 'There is something she must have done' was the whisper, looking at the children or parents of the disappeared as if they were pest ridden. These sentiments were vacillating, because it was known that so many had been swallowed up by that abyss without bottom without being guilty of anything: because the struggle against the 'subversive', with the drift that characterizes the hunting of witches and the possessed, had turned into a demented generalized repression. Because the epithet 'subversive' had such a vast and unpredictable reach.

Ernesto Sábato

Prologue to *Nunca Más*[1]

The most notable improvements in human rights have come as the result of the toppling of tyrannous regimes: the military juntas in South America in the early 1980s, followed at the end of that decade by the party machines of eastern Europe and eventually of the Soviet Union, and then the disintegration of apartheid and the onset of democracy in South Africa. These governments were all characterized by systemic violations of the rights of their citizens through the brutal secret policing which kept them in power: at worst, by torture and murder committed by death squads, and at best by harassment and detention of dissidents through the apparatus of state spies and informers. The political changes had in common both a suddenness and a comparative lack of violence: old and discredited regimes gave up the struggle against civilian rule, or took little by way of pushing. Although the Ceauşescus had to be executed in Romania to prevent counter-attack by their secret police, the Securitate, other communist dictators slunk from the stage after token resistance, while the generals and juntas in South America negotiated well-pensioned retirement. Dr Hastings Banda even presided over his own electoral demise in Malawi, in the misapprehension that the fear he had instilled in his people over thirty years would follow them into the polling booths. In all these countries, transition to democratic rule begged one crucial question: whether the new government had a duty to investigate and to punish the unforgivable crimes of its predecessors.

That the answer differed from country to country should not obscure either the importance of the question or the significance of the fact that in every case some investigation was initially ordered, before the pressure for pardons, amnesties and 'national reconciliation' set in. Ironically, this pressure proved successful in respect of the perpetrators of the most atrocious human rights abuses, generally because these had been sanctioned by senior policemen or military officers who still commanded some power – or at least, loyalty – within their old organizations. In some countries, impunity was the price exacted by the military for giving up its pretensions to govern; in others, it was a realistic way of avoiding a counter-coup. The organizers of these atrocities are therefore safe for the moment, unless, like General Pinochet, they over-confidently travel abroad. But their names are known, and there are increasing doubts about whether their amnesties are valid. There is a resurgence of interest in the 'universal jurisdiction' to prosecute the perpetrators of crimes against humanity: a few nations have exhumed old Nazis for trial fifty years after they thought that nemesis had been indefinitely postponed, while in 1998 no less than 120 nations supported the Rome Statute for an International Criminal Court. That statute, to appease present leaders, denied the logic of universal jurisdiction by excluding all crimes committed before it comes into force some time in the future, so the torturers of South America will be safe from its clutches. They might, however, be brought to trial in civil or criminal suits at some point, should courts in their country of residence accept the view that there can be no amnesty for crimes against humanity.

INTO THIS BLACKNESS

Of all such crimes, the most evil and most poignant of modern examples is causing a 'disappearance' – a process by which a citizen suspected of harbouring subversive sentiments is kidnapped, detained and tortured for some time before being finally killed, all within a secret police or military operation which is utterly unlawful but none the less agreed in outline by the government. As a method of disposing of suspected dissidents without the inconvenience of proving guilt at delayed trials, and as a means of terrorizing others, the device is useful to a lawless government, which can pretend it has no responsibility because it knows nothing about any specific crime. For the victims, and for their society, disappearance at the hands of police or military forces amounts to the most complete abnegation of human rights imaginable: arbitrary arrest, detention without trial, inhumane and degrading treatment and torture, followed by murder and secret disposal of the body. For friends and relations, the continuing horror of not knowing any details of the victim's fate adds a special layer of cruelty, driving them either to despair or to the courage displayed by the Mothers of the Plaza del Mayo, whose weekly demonstrations on behalf of their lost children did more than anything else to expose the wickedness of the Argentinian junta.

The rise of the death squad is a recent phenomenon, and ironically an offshoot of international concern about human rights violations. In the past, tyrannies publicly detained and executed opponents, as a lesson to other would-be dissidents. In the 1970s, many did it clandestinely and deniably, in an attempt to avoid international con- demnation. As a means of destroying dissent without answerability, the disappearance seems to have begun on a widespread scale in Guatemala in the 1960s (when the word *desaparecidos* was first used for victims);[2] it was adopted by Pinochet in Chile in 1973 and then at his urging in Operation Condor by other military governments in South America – Uruguay, El Salvador and, most barbarously, by Argentina. The technique has also featured in Uganda and South Africa, Sri Lanka and the Philippines. Typically, disappearances are planned by a central agency within the military (such as the notorious

DINA – Directorate of Intelligence – in Chile) and distance from government is often sought by using retired or off-duty soldiers or policemen, albeit under overall military command.

The science of physical terror was taught by Pinochet's torturers to the military junta which ruled Argentina between 1976 and 1983. The grill (*parilla*) was inflicted upon more than 10,000 'suspects', the great majority of whom the military took care to 'disappear' (by dropping them from planes or burying them in mass graves) so they would not live to tell the tale, like many of Pinochet's victims who had been released in order that they should spread fear. *Nunca Más* records the testimony of one Argentinian survivor:

'I was taken straight to the *parilla*. That is, I was tied to the metal frame of a bed, electrodes were attached to my hands and feet, and they ran an electric prod all over me, with particular savagery and intensity on the genitals . . . When on the "grill" one jumps, twists, moves about, and tries to avoid contact with the burning, cutting iron bars. The electric prod was handled like a scalpel and the "specialist" would be guided by a doctor who would tell him if I could take any more . . . The worst was having electrodes on your teeth – it felt as if a thunderbolt was blowing your head to pieces.'[3]

The complicity of the medical profession – hooded doctors were normally present, to advise on the voltage that would maximize suffering without causing unconsciousness or premature death – gives the grill a peculiar clinical horror. To this was frequently added the excruciatingly inhuman dimension of the presence of a partner or family member, to suffer vicariously the agonies of a loved one prior to their own. Jacobo Timerman, another rare Argentinian survivor, notes that 'of all the dramatic situations I witnessed in prison, none can compare with those family groups who were tortured, often together, sometimes separately but in view of one another . . . the entire world of affection, constructed over the years with the utmost difficulty, collapses with a kick in the father's genitals . . . or the sexual violation of a daughter'.[4]

Some retribution came in 1985, when five of the junta leaders were sent to prison after a five-month trial which featured the testimony of the torture survivors and the striking debut of a new breed of prosecution expert – part forensic scientist, part archaeologist – whose skill was to put names to skulls, matching dental, medical and DNA records of the 'disappeared' with skeletal remains excavated from mass graves. Liliana Pereyra was a 21-year-old pregnant law student at the time she was abducted by the military in 1977 and taken to a special section of the Navy Mechanics School in Buenos Aires, where she was permitted to give birth (so the child would be adopted by a loyal naval family) before she was murdered. It was her picture, and photographs of remains from a mass grave, which produced the most dramatic moment at the trial. There were X-ray pictures of her skull, with a single gunshot hole to the head; of a ribcage, identified as hers with the help of a chest X-ray from her childhood; then the close-up of the telltale shallow trench in front of the sacroiliac joint which meant she had just given birth.[5] The defence of Generals Videla and Galtieri – that the battle against terrorism necessitated 'unconventional methods' – could never begin to excuse the inhuman treatment of Liliana Pereyra.

Can crimes of this blackness be forgiven, or at least allowed to go unprosecuted? In El Salvador, death squads sometimes massacred dozens of people at a time, including children, while in Argentina the treatment of women like Liliana Pereyra became a speciality: pregnant women were deliberately kidnapped and, when they had given birth, their children were fostered to military families loyal to the junta. If the phrase 'human rights' has any meaning, the perpetrators of such crimes must be punished, more surely than the old Nazis who are occasionally dragged to trial a half century or so after their offences. Indeed, it is precisely because the death squad organizers are part of a modern militia, fully aware of the requirements of law and morality in a way that many brainwashed Nazi stormtroopers were not, that their crimes are more serious. Prosecution is the only real means of retribution, and certainly the only process which offers any hope of deterring such crimes in the future. The alternative, for a new government or for the international community, is to admit that political torturers and murderers have – and may continue to have – impunity.

The stark fact, however, is that today almost all of these commanders or killers are free men, although many have had their names and their offences exposed by official inquiries after the transition to civilian governments. Invariably, these men have received amnesties or pardons, because the incoming regime finds it too inconvenient or too dangerous to proceed against them, and the United Nations is powerless to help. In 1980, the UN set up a Working Group on Disappearances, over the objections of Uruguay and Argentina: on receiving complaints from relatives, it wrote polite letters to the government concerned, asking it 'to look into the matter and to inform the Group of its results'. In its first decade of operation, the Group 'investigated' 28,000 disappearances by writing letters to governments; in this way it 'clarified' 7 per cent of them, by which it means 'the Group has established beyond reasonable doubt *where* the missing person is, whether alive or dead'.[6] This pathetic effort was the best the UN could do at a time when governments taking over from military juntas needed – but did not obtain – its support to mount prosecutions.

THE DUTY TO PROSECUTE

If crimes like this engage the world's conscience sufficiently to attract universal jurisdiction, it must follow that the state where they have been committed has the primary duty to investigate and prosecute them. This will in theory always be the most convenient and most fitting forum, in terms of witness availability, local knowledge and language, and the desirability of confronting and understanding the past. Although it cannot be said that the Nuremberg judgment establishes an *obligation* to punish crimes against humanity, it served to delineate those offences which, by virtue of their level of atrocity, attract universal jurisdiction – which must in turn entail an obligation to punish. The work of the lesser Nuremberg tribunals was useful in making this distinction: expropriation of Jewish property and other acts of callous but not life-threatening discrimination did not produce sufficiently harsh consequences to amount to crimes against humanity.[7] This latter class of offence attracted international jurisdiction, so some military tribunals reasoned, precisely because 'the State involved, owing to indifference, impotency or complicity, has been unable or has refused to halt the crimes and punish the criminals'.[8] The corollary is that such involved states do have a duty to act, at least when conditions become propitious. Thus, when West Germany recovered its confidence and independence, it accepted responsibility for prosecuting Nazis: its courts convicted 6,000 of them between 1959 and 1981.

The duty to bring perpetrators to justice may also be deduced from international human rights treaties. By Article 2(3) of the Civil Covenant, state parties undertake to ensure that victims of rights violations 'shall have an effective remedy, notwithstanding that the violation has been committed by persons acting in an official capacity'. This imposes on states the obligation to permit civil actions for damages, although in case of violations as grave as crimes against humanity, no remedy short of prosecution and imprisonment could be considered 'effective'. The HRC has repeatedly held that Article 2 (3) does not provide a right in individuals to force a state to prosecute, but does impose a duty on the state to investigate, and thereafter to prosecute any suspects who have been convincingly identified. Thus, in 1995, it ordered Colombia to compensate the family of Nydia Batista, a suspected M19 sympathizer abducted and killed by Brigadier-General Velandia Hurtando.[9] Since the government had promoted and honoured this officer after the evidence of his guilt had emerged, it also directed the government to pay for protection of Nydia's family against military reprisals.

The Torture Convention is explicit in requiring each state party to 'establish its jurisdiction' over offences committed in its territory either by or against its nationals (Article 5) and to 'submit the case to its competent authorities for the purpose of prosecution' (Article 7). Each state must ensure that its appropriate authorities promptly and impartially investigate torture allegations (Article 12) and 'ensure in its legal system that the victim of an act of torture obtains redress and has an enforceable right to fair and adequate compensation' (Article 14). Governments which refuse to prosecute persons reasonably suspected of causing 'disappearances', or which grant them amnesties, are plainly in breach of these 'no safe haven' provisions. Similarly, the Genocide Convention imposes an obligation to punish, irrespective of whether perpetrators are 'constitutionally responsible rulers, public officials or private individuals' (Article 4), after trial either by 'a competent tribunal' of the state where the act occurred or by an international penal tribunal (Article 6). The 1949 Geneva Convention provides that states have an obligation to search for war criminals, and to bring them (irrespective of their nationality) before their own courts or else extradite them for trial in another jurisdiction. Although the main human rights treaties – the Civil Covenant and the European and Inter-American Conventions – have no comparable provisions, they all affirmatively require that rights (notably the right to life) be respected and protected by law and that victims shall have an effective remedy: objectives which presuppose deployment of the legal process against perpetrators.

The duty is supported by implication from other international instruments. In 1967, the UN adopted a resolution urging states not to grant asylum to anyone seriously suspected of committing crimes against humanity, because such suspects should be returned to face trial in their own countries.[10] The following year it opened for signature the Convention on the Non-Applicability of Statutory Limitations to War Crimes and Crimes against Humanity, a self-explanatory treaty which assumes both that there is a duty to punish such offences and that this duty cannot be attenuated by the passage of time. (It is a measure of the political reluctance to accept the principle that only forty-three states have ratified this convention.) In 1973, the General Assembly adopted a set of Principles of International Co-operation in the Detection, Arrest, Extradition, and Punishment of Persons Guilty of War Crimes and Crimes against Humanity, Principle 1 of which is that 'crimes against humanity, wherever they are committed, shall be subject to investigation and the persons against whom there is evidence that they have committed such crimes shall be subject to tracing, arrest, trial and, if found guilty, to punishment'. In recent years, as the reality of death squads in South America and elsewhere became recognized at the UN, the General Assembly has been prolific in its calls to governments to investigate and to 'prosecute or extradite' suspects. There are other declarations and statements of principle, and a section of the 1993 Vienna Declaration, to the same effect.[11] All this goes to show that there is in international law a duty on states to punish crimes against humanity, but there is in international practice a failure to do any such thing.

In classical international law, a state has always had a duty to investigate and punish serious crimes committed against innocent foreigners ('aliens') resident within its borders. The clearest precedents were set by the US–Mexican General Claims Commission, a tribunal established in 1926 to decide, according to rules of international law, on claims by US citizens for damages arising from the Mexican Revolution. In the *Janes Case*, the court awarded damages to relations of an American killed by a Mexican who had been allowed to escape by the local authorities: Mexico was 'liable for not having measured up to its duty of diligently prosecuting and properly punishing the offender'.[12] Damages were not merely compensatory: in this context, they were increased because of both the insult to the family and the fear and instability caused by the Mexican government's behaviour. This principle was applied to the same government's decision to grant an amnesty to rebels who killed an American oil company employee: the legal formality of the grant was not allowed to disguise the fact that it amounted to a state refusal to bring the killers to justice, as much as if prison officials had deliberately permitted them to escape.[13] This precedent (the *West Case*) is important for the proposition that the granting of a lawful amnesty in order to save lives or bring a civil war to an end does not affect a state's international obligations, or the right of any state which has not granted an amnesty to prosecute and punish the beneficiaries of amnesties granted elsewhere.

That this international law duty imposed on states in their treatment of foreign residents is now being extended to their treatment of their own citizens is clear from the important 1988 decision of the Inter-American Court in the *Velasquez Rodriguez Case*. Velasquez was a student activist who disappeared after being abducted by the Honduran military, which subsequently carried out an investigation and declared itself innocent of his kidnap and murder. The Court had no difficult in deciding, from the evidence of a pattern of disappearances of radicals in Honduras at the hands of the military, that the snatching of Velasquez was part of the pattern. It condemned the Honduran government for its failure to 'ensure' the civil rights of its citizens, holding that this language in the Inter-American Convention implied an affirmative obligation on the state to organize the governmental apparatus and, in general, all the structures through which public power is exercised, so that they are capable of juridici-ally ensuring the free and full enjoyment of human rights. As a consequence of this obligation, the state must prevent, investigate and punish any violation of the rights recognized by the Convention . . . The state has a legal duty to take reasonable steps to prevent human rights violations and to use the means at its disposal to carry out a serious investigation of violations committed within its jurisdiction, to identify those responsible, impose the appropriate punishment and ensure the victims adequate compensation . . . If the state apparatus acts in such a way that the violation goes unpunished and the victim's full enjoyment of such rights is not restored as soon as possible, the state has failed to comply with its duty to guarantee the free and full exercise of those rights to the persons within its jurisdiction.[14]

This decision is a logical consequence of the language of the IAC and other conventions. What else can be meant by a state undertaking to 'respect the rights and freedoms recognized herein and to ensure to all persons subject to their jurisdiction the free and full exercise of those rights and freedoms' (IAC, Article 1)? Similar language is found in Article 2 of the Civil Covenant, and the HRC has repeatedly asserted a duty upon states to investigate, to prosecute suspects (and punish them in the event of their conviction) and to provide compensation for victims and relatives.[15] These Conventions promise an 'effective remedy' for violations – but what remedy can be effective in the case of persons who have disappeared? Habeas corpus – a demand to produce the body, dead or alive – will be met with an official pretence of ignorance and, too often, with judicial handwashing. (Velasquez's relatives brought three habeas corpus petitions against Honduran officials, who ignored them because intimidated judges refused to convene hearings.) Com-pensation may be a sufficient remedy if state authorities are in no way complicit in the disappearance – if it really is a result of factionalism in which military and police have not taken sides. But where the State is implicated, either directly or through failing to establish a system to prevent disappearances, then the remedy must include some public examination (preferably through the trial process) and accountability of those officials whose negligence or malfeasance has permitted the violation.[16] There must be a truthful accounting, a naming of the names of all those involved in the kidnap, torture and death. Preferably, they should be prosecuted or at very least stripped of rank – in appropriate cases the State should be required to disband that section of its security forces which has organized the disappearances.

Velasquez was followed in 1993 by *Aloeboetal* v. *Suriname*,[17] a case which arose from an incident where Suriname government soldiers had arrested and tortured a group of innocent Indian fishermen, ordering them to dig their own graves before shooting them. The Inter-American Commission gathered sufficient evidence to prove Suriname's responsibility for the crime: the court ordered that it pay some half million US dollars for the benefit of the victims' children and relatives. These reparations were made up of *actual damage* (compensation for the trauma of having a close relative viciously assassinated) and *moral damage* (compensation for the terror suffered by the victims in the hours before their deaths, the right to which becomes enforceable by their heirs). This latter head of damages is particularly appropriate in the familiar case where the right to life is extinguished after torture and terror. The court sensibly ordered the government to establish a trust fund and arrange for the award to be distributed through a foundation, and further (and imaginatively) directed it to establish a school and a clinic in the village where the massacre had taken place. The court declined, however, to order that Suriname prosecute the soldiers, perhaps reasoning that the amount of the reparations would be a more effective deterrent.

If perpetrators of crimes against humanity cannot be prosecuted or even sued for damages in their home state – because they remain in power or have been granted amnesties – then a secondary duty may devolve upon another state to bring or permit proceedings should they come within its jurisdiction, on the principle that 'crimes against international law may be punished by any state which obtains custody of persons suspected of responsibility'.[18] It follows that civil actions can be brought as well, certainly where the damage flowed from an act of genocide or torture or other breach of a *jus cogens* rule (i.e. a rule defined by Article 53 of the Vienna Convention on the Law of Treaties as one 'accepted and recognized by the international community of States as a whole from which no derogation is permitted'). Since the infringement of such a compelling law – even by a state itself – involves the breach of an *erga omnes* obligation to the international community of all states, there is no reason why one of those states should not make its courts available for a victim to sue any torturer who wanders within its jurisdiction. This is the express result of the 'try or extradite' duty on all 113 state parties to the Torture Convention, and the implicit result of Article 2(3) of the Civil Covenant, which calls upon state parties to provide an effective remedy for victims of human rights abuses – a duty which must devolve on these parties if, because of an amnesty or a lack of prosecutorial will, no effective remedy is available in the country where the abuse took place. This duty is fulfilled in the US by statutory provision: the 1789 Alien Tort Claims Act permits suit for any tort 'committed in violation of the law of nations' and the 1992 Torture Victim Protection Act extends the right to US victims or relatives in respect of acts of torture and summary execution committed by officials in foreign countries where there is no remedy. In Britain, a 1988 provision gives criminal courts extraterritorial jurisdiction to try any suspected torturer whatever his or his victim's nationality and irrespective of where the torture took place. There is, however, no equivalent to the US statutes which permit civil actions.

The efficacy of civil remedies is limited by the doctrine of state immunity, which will preclude the State itself from being made a defendant, even in respect of acts of torture and extrajudicial killing which it has authorized. This means that a human defendant will have to be found, in the form of an individual who ordered or carried out the atrocity. It will not be often that such persons will reside beyond the protection of their own state, and if served with a writ it is even less likely that they will stick around to contest the case. Civil actions, therefore, are only feasible in respect of torturers who are exiled or 'on the run' from their own country, and have assets within the foreign jurisdiction which can be frozen or otherwise used to satisfy damages awards. That was the case with Ferdinand Marcos: despairing of the cowardice of the Filipino government and the corruption of its courts, victims of torture and relatives of those who 'disappeared' under the Marcos regime brought a class action against him in Hawaii, where he was living in exile. Their evidence established that he had taken personal charge of the state security apparatus and must have personally approved the atrocities which were the subject of the suit – such as the kidnap, torture and murder of student Decleimedes Trajano, whose only crime had been to ask embarrassing questions of Marcos's daughter when she was head of the national youth organization. Marcos pleaded that, as president at the time, he was immune under the 'Act of State' doctrine, but in *Trajano* v. *Marcos* the Federal Appeals Court held that this doctrine did not apply to acts of torture, kidnap and murder. For the same reason, he could not invoke the claim of sovereign immunity.[19] Marcos died while the litigation was in progress, and damages of US $150 million were awarded against his estate. Eventually, in 1999, this sum was split between 10,000 plaintiffs in the class action, the money having been recovered from the dictator's Swiss bank accounts. This happy happenstance, however, is uncommon: most foreign defendants to Alien Tort Statute claims do not stay for the verdict. In the leading case, *Filártiga* v. *Peña-Irala* (1980), the relatives of a Paraguayan victim were awarded $1,000,000 damages against his torturer who evaded payment by fleeing the US.[20]

It may be doubted whether civil proceedings bring much satisfaction other than to the individual plaintiff. A criminal conviction, for relatives of the deceased in domestic murder cases, has a cathartic effect: it enables them to end their grieving and get on with their lives. An award of damages for the loss of a loved one through abuse of state power can be demeaning unless it comes with an acknowledgement of guilt. Civil actions are therefore second best, although they may have advantages in circumventing obstacles inherent in a criminal prosecution such as a higher burden of proof, time bars, stricter exclusion of hearsay evidence and the right of criminal defendants to remain silent. Civil proceedings may also be a means of circumventing the reluctance of Western governments to prosecute dictators and generals who have come within the jurisdiction to retire or to benefit from advanced medical treatment: old allegiances die hard (as right-wing British politicians showed by supporting General Pinochet) and where politicians control the prosecution process there will be a natural reluctance to cause diplomatic uproar. In such cases, civil proceedings will be better than no proceedings at all. Under the ruling in *Pinochet (No. 3)*, however, it will be much easier to prosecute under the Torture Convention, which extinguishes sovereign immunity, than to sue for damages and face an immunity defence (see chapter 10).

THE LIMITS OF AMNESTY

Every state has power – normally but not necessarily defined by its constitution – to pardon those who offend against its laws. A pardon offered or proclaimed to a whole class of offender is described as an amnesty, a word bearing favourable connotations in the human rights lexicon through its association with Amnesty International. Pardons and amnesties have been used from time immemorial, benevolently (as a measure of forgiveness to those who have already suffered some punishment for their crimes), politically (to bring to an end civil wars and insurrections), legally (to absolve convicts who later appear innocent), and even festively (to celebrate a ruler's birthday). Domestic law will provide the rules for determining the validity of a particular pardon and its legal consequences. There is much learning on the subject in Anglo-American law, establishing, for example, that pardons are invalidated by fraud or non-disclosure in their procuration, but that otherwise they operate 'to clear the person from all infamy . . . it makes him, as it were, a new man', although it does not create the legal fiction that the beneficiary never committed the crime in the first place.[21] None the less, amnesties are good things historically and get favourable treatment in American law, as a result of the litigation from the amnesty proclamations by President Abraham Lincoln to encourage defection in Confederate ranks during the Civil War. Lincoln had insisted, against heavy congressional criticism, that former enemies should be forgiven and former enmity forgotten once the oath of allegiance (the condition of obtaining an amnesty) had been taken. In his State of the Nation message to Congress in 1863, he declared that any reneging on an amnesty would be 'a cruel and astounding breach of faith'. The Supreme Court agreed, ordering the return of property seized from 'amnestied' ex-Confederates and striking down all congressional laws discriminating against them.[22]

Pardon is unexceptional when it is used like this, as a military option that can save many lives by ending a war or revolution. Indeed, the wide presidential pardoning power in the US constitution was put there precisely because, as founding father Alexander Hamilton explained, 'In seasons of insurrection or rebellion, there are often critical moments, when a well-timed offer of pardon to the insurgents or rebels may restore the tranquillity of the Commonwealth; and which, if suffered to pass unimproved, it may never be possible afterwards to recall.'[23] Hamilton could hardly have had in mind the occasion almost 200 years later on which his words were used to justify the pardon granted by President Gerald Ford to his crooked predecessor, Richard Nixon, saving him from the impeachment proceedings commenced by Congress. Ford acted, so he claimed, in the public interest 'to end the divisions caused by Watergate', an unravelling scandal which had already seen criminal convictions imposed on sixty-six senior officials of the Nixon government (including his vice-president and three cabinet ministers) for 'high crimes and misdemeanours'. Ford's pardon was upheld on the ground that the pardoning power was, under the constitution, unlimited and thus could extend to offenders prior to their conviction: the court found that Nixon, in Hamilton's terms, was 'conducting a covert assault on American liberty and an insurrection and rebellion against Constitutional government itself and so his successor was entitled to restore the tranquillity of the Commonwealth'.[24]

The Nixon pardon, widely condemned as a political interference with the legal process, had great appeal to corrupt politicians throughout the world, conscious of their own vulnerability once they left or were excluded from office. The government in Trinidad, for example, immediately pushed through a constitutional change enabling the island's president to grant pardons for any offence prior to conviction. Ironically, the first beneficiaries were a group of deranged Muslim terrorists who broke into Parliament House and held hostage the country's prime minister and cabinet. Eventually these MPs were released after an amnesty was granted to the terrorists by the president, but the government then proceeded to dishonour it by detaining and prosecuting them on capital charges of treason and murder. The ensuing legal proceedings, in the Privy Council, illuminate the moral difficulties in the modern concept of amnesty, a device which can be used by the State to save lives in the short term, at the expense of injustice to the victims of those pardoned. In this case the Muslims had killed eight policemen, injured dozens of citizens and caused millions of dollars of damage, yet after obtaining habeas corpus on the strength of their amnesty, they ungratefully turned around and sued the State for damages for wrongfully detaining them! The decision of the Privy Council in *Attorney-General of Trinidad and Tobago* v. *Lennox Phillip* establishes that while an amnesty may expunge past offences, it cannot be used to dispense with future lawbreaking: 'The State cannot be allowed to use a power to pardon to enable the law to be set aside by permitting it to be contravened with impunity.'[25] The significance of this ruling for invalidating amnesty laws purporting to pardon death squads is that kidnapping is a continuing offence until the body is found – and no statute can forgive a crime which is still afoot.

The Trinidad case demonstrates how 'amnesty' – that word associated with peace and compassion and forgiveness – can be exploited by the perpetrators of appalling crimes. So an increasingly important issue in human rights law is whether states can be bound by amnesties extracted under duress – for example, by a threat on the part of the army to revolt unless its officers are given amnesties for crimes against humanity. Clearly, no pardon signed under threat of direct physical violence – a gun at the head of the president – can be valid: it is not the deliberate act of a head of state.[26] But pressure, even to the point of threatening calamitous loss of life, cannot invalidate through duress the presidential act of granting an amnesty if the president is physically free and makes a deliberate decision that amnesty is in the public interest as the lesser of two evils. Thus, in the Trinidad case, the Privy Council declined to invalidate the amnesty on the ground that it was extracted from the president by threats to kill the prime minister and cabinet ministers who were all being held as hostages. The court invalidated it, instead, because the Muslims did not immediately accept its condition – that they surrender their hostages unharmed – but continued to hold them for several days while negotiating an eventual surrender. With Solomnic wisdom, the court thus denied murderous fanatics any damages for wrongful arrest, but at the same time stopped the State from proceeding to hang them by ruling that it would be an abuse of process to continue prosecution because they had surrendered in the belief (induced by the government) that they were entitled to a pardon once they did eventually comply with the condition. The repugnant prospect that terrorists who killed and caused vast damage to the country might actually be awarded millions of dollars of compensation for false imprisonment (they had been detained for two years while the validity of the amnesty was considered by the courts) was a Gilbertian conclusion to be avoided at all costs, and the Privy Council avoided it by ruling that the insurgents had not surrendered quickly enough. But governments which do deals with terrorists and common criminals may be legally obliged to keep them, and in such situations 'amnesty' is really no more than a formal means of promising immunity from prosecution in return for surrender. The crimes in respect of which it may legitimately operate, although heinous, lack the crucial element of a crime against humanity attracting international consequences, namely that they are perpetrated by, or with the approbation of, the government itself.

For this reason, domestic rules upholding the validity of amnesties do not answer the question of whether in international law it is ever possible to grant a valid pre-conviction pardon in respect of a crime against humanity. There may be no objection to a state remitting the sentence, in whole or in part, on persons convicted of such crimes, as an act of humanity or even of politics (e.g. where it is believed that insufficient weight was given to obedience to superior orders as a mitigating factor). What cannot be countenanced is either the ludicrous spectacle of the State forgiving itself its own wrongs, or the increasing phenomenon of new governments giving amnesties at the insistence of one continuing branch of the old — usually the military or the police. The State, in other words, is entitled to grant amnesty to individuals who break its laws, but not when they do so on behalf of the State itself. The State as victim may forgive, but when complicit with the perpetrator, it cannot be forgiven.

It is well established that new governments inherit the legal responsibilities of their predecessors. The principle of the continuity of the State in international law means that state responsibility exists independently of change of government and continuously from the time of the act for which the State is responsible to the time when the act is declared illegal. The State cannot therefore obliterate its own crimes, or those of its agents, committed against its subjects. This is the case whether the government granting the amnesty is the government at fault or the successor to that government. Just as genocide and torture are repugnant to international law to such an extent that no circumstances can justify them (hence these convention obligations are non-derogable), so amnesties given to perpetrators of such deeds by frightened or blackmailed governments cannot be upheld by international law.

In other words, states which pardon torturers before trials have taken place are in breach of their international obligations to bring perpetrators of crimes against humanity to justice. The amnesty may be valid under domestic law, and the action justified in international law either under Article 4 of the Civil Covenant (a derogation taken 'in time of public emergency which threatens the life of the nation') or under the accepted customary law notion of necessity: obligations may be ignored to save a state from grave and imminent peril. Governments which fail in their duty to prosecute the military sometimes do have reason to believe that to do so would amount to 'political suicide' by provoking another takeover. But such amnesties are not binding on other states, which may take universal jurisdiction to try a torturer who comes within their borders, or on the future International Criminal Court, as established under the Rome Statute (see chapter 9). And since a grant of amnesty can under most constitutional arrangements be revoked by whichever body has plenary power in the State, a duty to do so may retrospectively arise under international law once the danger of reprisals has passed. This is the position taken by the HRC in respect of the covenant obligation to provide an effective remedy against official violation of guaranteed rights. Amnesties granted for acts of torture, it has ruled, 'are generally incompatible with the duty of states to investigate such acts; to guarantee prosecution of such acts within their jurisdiction; and to ensure that they do not occur in the future. States may not deprive individuals of the right to an effective remedy, including compensation and such full rehabilitation as may be possible.'[27]

This is the position favoured by the Inter-American Commission, which has had to cope with the recent rash of amnesty laws in Argentina, Brazil, Chile, Uruguay, Guatemala, El Salvador, Nicaragua and Suriname. Most of them have been passed under pressure from the military, although in Uruguay's case the measure was approved at a referendum. This cut no ice, however: the excuse that it showed 'the express will of the Uruguayan people to close a painful chapter in their history' was condemned by the IAC as contrary to the obligation to investigate and punish human rights violations and hence a violation of the rights of relatives of the disappeared.[28] All too typical of the cases it has had to adjudicate was that of the 1983 Los Hojas massacre, in which seventy-four civilians, most with no known subversive connections, were shot in the head by members of the Salvadorian security forces and their bodies dumped along the banks of a river. The prosecution brought charges against thirteen soldiers, including the captain and major who led the death squad and Colonel Araujo, who directed its operations. After several frightened low-level judges had refused to hear the case, the Appeal Court directed that the trial go ahead, whereupon the Legislative Assembly passed an amnesty decree specifically providing impunity for all who participated in politically motivated massacres (or, lest the large number of non-subversives left dead at Los Hojas put political motivation in question, 'common crimes in which the number of persons involved is no less than twenty'). The Inter-American Commission ruled that 'the present amnesty law, as applied in these cases, by foreclosing the possibility of judicial relief in cases of murder, inhumane treatment and absence of judicial guarantees, denies the fundamental nature of most basic human rights. It eliminates perhaps the single most effective means of enforcing such rights, the trial and punishment of offenders.'[29] The government responsible for the massacre was, by whitewashing it, breaching the victims' rights to life (Article 4), personal security and integrity (Article 5), due process (Article 8), and judicial protection (Article 25), and had failed to comply with its Article 1 obligation to guarantee human rights to all its citizens. El Salvador was ordered not only to pay compensation to the massacre victims, but to prosecute the perpetrators irrespective of the amnesty. Instead, its government passed an even broader amnesty law, which its constitutional court ruled to be valid.

Domestic courts in Latin America, mainly staffed by judges complicit in human rights violations under previous military dictatorships, have been reluctant to uphold arguments invalidating amnesty statutes – because, for example, the offence of abduction continues after the period covered by the amnesty or because torture and summary execution are committed during periods of internal armed conflict, so the Geneva Conventions apply as a treaty obligation to trump local time limitation and amnesty statutes. Occasionally, local courts have had the courage to apply the Geneva Conventions and the Convention against Torture and the Civil Covenant: the Santiago Court of Appeal ruled in 1992 that 'the authorities of a State Party may not prescribe internal laws which contravene the fulfilment in good faith of the international conventions and treaties under consideration [the 1949 Geneva Conventions] as from their entry into force. Hence, crimes which constitute serious infractions of the Conventions are not subject to any statute of limitations and not subject to amnesty.'[30] This was a correct application of Article 27 of the 1969 Vienna Convention on the Law of Treaties, which forbids the use of domestic laws to override international obligations. However, on appeal the pro-Pinochet judges on Chile's Supreme Court upheld the amnesty by ruling that there was no armed conflict in 1974 so Geneva Convention IV did not apply – despite the fact that the army had formally declared a state of war.[31] This may be a tenable argument, of course, where a 'conflict' essentially takes the form of the army liquidating without opposition those it suspects of harbouring subversive thoughts.

Judges who strive to uphold amnesties for crimes against humanity granted by military governments which approved of the killing will usually talk about the need for courts to defer to the legislature on matters of national security, or (since these amnesties will be in conflict with constitutional guarantees of the rule of law) will pretend there is an overriding rule of interpretation which permits impunity 'to preserve the higher value of safeguarding the constitution's own survival'. That is how the Argentinian justice Carlos Fayt explained his decision to uphold a 1987 law which pardoned all soldiers for obeying obviously illegal orders to torture and murder suspects.[32] A more worrying trend is for courts to uphold amnesties on the strength of Article 6(5) of the 1977 Protocol II to the Geneva Conventions. The wholly unsatisfactory state of this protocol has been described earlier (see p. 183), and the large number of significant states which have refused to sign it deprives its provisions of any force as international law. None the less, it is being mistakenly cited, even by the South African Constitutional Court, as a basis for validating amnesties.[33] Article 6(5) provides:

At the end of hostilities, the authorities in power shall endeavour to grant the broadest possible amnesty to persons who have participated in the armed conflict, or those deprived of their liberty for reasons related to the armed conflict, whether they are interned or detained.

The drafting of this article is irresponsibly loose, but it is plain from the context (section 6 provides minimum standards for war crimes prosecutions) that it is not intended to encourage amnesties which would infringe international law, such as unilateral pardons for war crimes and crimes against humanity which the State is under a duty to prosecute. The drafting history of the subsection shows that it contemplates an Abraham Lincoln-style amnesty ('to restore the tranquillity of the commonwealth') for combatants who have fought on opposite sides according to the laws of war, 'a sort of release at the end of hostilities for those detained or punished for the mere fact of having participated in hostilities. It does not aim at an amnesty for those having violated international law.'[34]

The real purpose of an amnesty statute is not to promote 'national reconciliation' or to diminish in a new democratic society the debilitating desire for revenge, it is to enable government officials, and military and police officers, to escape responsibility for the crimes against humanity which they ordered or committed. The new government may be acting under direct threat: General Pinochet warned Chile's elected president, as he handed over power in 1990, 'No one is going to touch my people. The day they do, the state of law will come to an end.'[35] It took five years before a democratic government dared to put Pinochet's vilest henchman, Mañuel Contreras, the head of DINA, on trial – and only because the US insisted on his prosecution for organizing the Letelier bombing in Washington. Contreras was sentenced only to seven years' imprisonment. Argentina's elected President Alfonsín, who subsequently abrogated the amnesty law passed by the military junta in order to put that junta's leaders on trial, was then forced to abandon consequent proceedings against more junior officers as a result of army rebellions. His achievement, however, was to have military leaders fairly tried and five of them convicted for overseeing crimes against humanity, after persuading his congress to declare null and void the amnesty which they had granted themselves, on the grounds that it was imposed by an authoritarian government and did not emanate from the democratic process.[36] Alfonsín's Perónist successor, Carlos Menem, undid his work by pardoning the convicted generals. Menem was elected (as in most democracies) on the strength of economic and social policies, although by a populace who did not widely protest the pardons: six years after the fall of the junta, retribution was low on the agenda. Yet Alfonsín's first years do show what can be achieved, even against a military that had been discredited but not disbanded.

This highlights the failure of other transitional governments in Latin America and elsewhere to bring torturers to justice. In the Philippines, Cory Aquino's refusal at the outset of her term of office to call the military to account cannot be put down to necessity or public emergency: to nervousness, certainly, and her desire to be supported by the military to the same extent as it had supported her predecessor Ferdinand Marcos. Her most notable failure, however, lay in her inability to reform the notoriously corrupt Filipino judiciary, from whom no 'justice' of any kind could be expected. In consequence, of the thousands of cases brought by human rights bodies, only six resulted in convictions, allowing the subsequent Ramos government to introduce a total amnesty for crimes against humanity committed under Marcos, as part of a package deal promising immunity to leftist guerrillas.[37] More sinister uses of amnesty powers have occurred in Zimbabwe, for the benefit of members of the security forces accused of participating in massacres in Matabeleland in the 1980s, years after the Lancaster House Agreement which gave amnesties to all participants in the civil war. This had been reasonable enough, on the precedent set by Lincoln, but it hardly behoves the State to deploy the same power long after the war had ended to exempt its soldiers from liability for violating the human rights of the citizens they are meant to protect.[38] (Robert Mugabe, who personally protects Colonel Mengistu, the mass murderer of Ethiopia, clearly has no conception of his human rights duties under international law: in 1999 he threatened

Zimbabwe's judges with dismissal for ordering the release of journalists who were being beaten up in military custody.) These failures, however, are to be set against the comparative success of the Karamanlis government, which re-established civilian rule in Greece while permitting prosecutions of senior officers for torture and murder. This produced dissension in the armed forces, but they were weakened and dishonoured by their failure to stop the Turkish invasion of Cyprus, and thus unable to destabilize the democratic government which insisted upon prosecution.

In summary, international law now imposes an *erga omnes* obligation on states to investigate and prosecute crimes against humanity, even if this means annulling amnesty laws and taking some risk of counter-revolution. If the risk is significant, the State may rely on necessity or emergency to postpone its obligation, which can be reasserted years later, when the danger has passed. In the meantime, the rules of universal jurisdiction mean that political torturers and murderers later found in other states may be tried there, although the appetite for punishing offences committed in other times and other countries is severely limited. The cost is invariably high, since most of the evidence must be brought from abroad, and this factor will generally make the proceedings hinge on some co-operation from the state which has original jurisdiction, i.e. the country where the crimes were committed. Outside the traditional concern about Nazi war criminals, this co-operation has been achieved in relation to drug trafficking (notably Panama's support of the prosecution in the US of its former ruler General Noriega) and fraud – the Aquino government supported the prosecution commenced against Marcos in the US for corruption and refused to protect him by claiming sovereign immunity for his actions when they became the subject of claims by torture victims. Neither state had the confidence in itself to pursue the charges of crimes against humanity which should have been levelled at their former leaders. This is the clinching argument for the existence of an international criminal court with power to prosecute those former rulers whom transitional governments lack the resolve or the political power to indict.

TRUTH COMMISSIONS AND TRANSITIONAL JUSTICE

The starkness of the dilemma – whether to pardon or to punish gross violations of human rights by former government and military officials – has been temporarily resolved in many South American and African countries by the intermediate device of the truth commission. This is a portentous name for the inquiries set up by reforming – generally democratic – governments which have just taken over from brutal military rulers or dictators. Established in the first flush of popular freedom, their reports should be a prelude to the trial of the old regime's murderers and torturers, although they are more often used as alternatives to justice. That is because truth commissions have reported enough of the truth to discomfort the perpetrators of crimes against humanity who still hold rank in the military and the police: their continued influence frightens politicians, who in consequence invoke the 'interests of national reconciliation' as an excuse for granting them amnesties and pardons, despite emerging evidence of their guilt.

Fact-finding followed by forgiveness may be a plausible exercise in reconciling the political divisions in a particular society, but it is hardly consistent with the view that crimes against humanity attract an *erga omnes* obligation to prosecute and punish. The Salvadorian captains who led death squads to massacre dozens of suspects at a time and the Argentinian commanders who directed the secret torture and murder of many thousands of the disappeared are more culpable, on any league table of evil, than the octogenarian Nazis still occasionally paraded for trial in the West. The blood on their hands is fresher, for a start, and they cannot claim the pressure of war or of racist brainwashing by Dr Goebbels' propaganda machine. A truth commission can serve a valuable purpose if it is independent of the new government and collects evidence for subsequent prosecutions, but incoming politicians are rarely confident enough to entrust a commission with this task. The record of the truth commissions in South American countries, which have witnessed some of the worst human rights violations of recent times, is telling:[39]

BOLIVIA

A National Commission of Inquiry into Disappearances was set up within days of the restoration of democracy in 1982. It produced no report and inspired no prosecutions, to the palpable relief of a government which had starved it of funds. In 1986 a more satisfactory course was taken: prosecutions commenced against the country's former military leader, General García Meza, and some of his henchmen: they were not completed until 1993, by which time the General had gone into hiding to avoid his thirty-year sentence for directing torture and murder. This court decision, despite its belatedness, is notable for rejecting the propriety of pardons for those convicted of crimes against humanity.[40]

URUGUAY

In 1985, at the end of twelve years of brutal military rule, the new government deliberately excluded any inquiry into the systematic use of torture by the military during its period in power. Instead, in 1986, President Sanguinetti issued a pardon to all soldiers and policemen involved in murder, torture and rape – whether they had given, or acted upon, superior orders. In so doing, the government excluded the victims from their rights to civil compensation. Sanguinetti justified his action as 'the safest path' but admitted 'it was a political, not a moral, decision'. Uruguay's torturers remain in high office within its police and military.

CHILE

After the overthrow of democracy in 1973, Chileans suffered widespread torture, and about 4,000 'disappearances', at the hands of General Pinochet's militia (see chapter 10). Pinochet granted himself and his death squads an amnesty in 1978. After the restoration of democracy in 1990, a Commission for Truth and Reconciliation was established under Senator Rettig. It was not permitted to name individuals responsible for the crimes or to recommend sanctions. Its report analysed several thousand disappearances, but the new government dared not lift a finger against assassins who remained in high position in (or in honourable retirement from) the armed forces. President Alywin was being disingenuous when he claimed, in his 1992 State of the Nation address, that 'we could have chosen to avenge offences . . . we chose however to tread the path of understanding and reconciliation': in truth, Pinochet and the army gave him no alternative. Pinochet personally described the Truth Commission report as 'unpardonable' and announced that, 'The army certainly sees no reason to ask pardon for having fulfilled its patriotic duty.' Pinochet's supporters loudly claimed that his arrest in the UK in 1998 would destabilize Chile and endanger its fragile democracy. On the contrary, his absence from Chile throughout 1999 served to give courage to the country's judiciary: army officers who had led the 'Caravan of Death' (a travelling band of torturers who killed Allende supporters) were at last placed under arrest, on the basis that disappearances could be defined as kidnapping, an offence which continued, in the absence of a body, *after* the amnesty.[41] The whirligig of time saw a socialist elected peacefully as president and a brain-damaged Pinochet return to a country which was healthier and happier than when he had left sixteen months previously.

EL SALVADOR

The Commission on the Truth for El Salvador was established in 1991, headed by three respected international jurists, and was staffed and financed by the United Nations. It managed to investigate fully only thirty-three disappearances (22,000 more were brought to its attention). However, it did identify forty individuals connected to the armed forces who had been involved in committing crimes against humanity, and its forensic scientists confounded the lies of the Reagan administration by proving that a massacre of almost a thousand villagers, including hundreds of children, had taken place at El Mozote.[42] The Commission found so much corruption, complacency and bias in the judges of the Supreme Court that it called on them all to retire (an invitation to which the Court responded by declaring the

Commission 'subversive of the Constitution').[43] It named René Ponce as the general who ordered an élite military unit to kill six Jesuit priests (one the rector of the Central American University, another the head of its Human Rights Institute). But Ponce had played a vital part in negotiating a peace settlement between the military and the FMLN: his retirement (there was never any prospect of his prosecution) was only achieved by the new Clinton administration threatening to withhold $11 million in aid after he had been exposed. The Truth Commission Report was rejected by the Salvadorean president because it 'did not respond to the wishes of the majority of Salvadoreans who seek to forgive and forget everything having to do with that very sorrowful past'. The government immediately granted a comprehensive amnesty for all political crimes, including El Mozote and the Jesuit murders. In 1995, the corrupt Supreme Court judges declared this blanket amnesty to be valid.

HAITI

The psychopathic cruelty and greed of 'Papa Doc' and 'Baby Doc' and their Tontons Macoutes made Haiti a human rights blackspot from 1957 until 1986, when the US airlifted Jean-Claude Duvalier ('Baby Doc') to luxurious retirement in the south of France. Over this period, 40,000 citizens were senselessly killed. After an army interregnum, Jean-Bertrand Aristide was elected president in 1990: he was ousted by General Raoul Cedras, whose soldiers tortured many civilians; hundreds were also killed by a paramilitary group, Fraph, funded in part by the CIA. After frantic lobbying by the UN and ultimately a show of force by the US, the military returned power to Aristide in October 1994 as part of a deal which provided them with a blanket amnesty for all murders, rapes and political killings. Aristide himself was reluctant to return at this price: the amnesty provisions were forced upon him by the US. Once again, Aristide established a National Commission for Truth and Justice, which reported in February 1996, urging that those responsible for crimes against humanity should be prosecuted before an international tribunal. There is no tribunal and there have been no prosecutions: the US has refused to extradite the leader of Fraph, Emmanuel Constant, because of his service to the CIA, and Panama has declined to extradite Cedras, who lives there in great luxury.[44] At least 'Baby Doc' has fallen on hard times: after a ruinous divorce his Swiss bank accounts have been frozen, and he had to offer himself for work as a house painter.

ARGENTINA

This nation has made the most determined effort to hold its military commanders accountable for their crimes. When the military skulked in shame from government after defeat in the Falklands War in 1983, new civilian President Raoul Alfonsín had no hesitation in annulling the ludicrous amnesty they had bestowed on themselves. He set up a Commission on the Disappeared, and its report, *Nunca Más* (*Never Again*), became a national bestseller. This commission – the most successful of its kind in Latin America – amassed evidence which led to prosecutions and prison sentences against the five most senior members of the military junta. But when the prosecutors indicted some middle-ranking soldiers and police who had manned the 'Dirty War' detention centres and participated in the killing of at least 9,000 of the disappeared, this triggered an army revolt. In 1987, its junior officers staged a series of rebellions against the government, which Alfonsín could only dissipate by agreeing to end the trials. He refused to give any permanent pardons – that was the craven act of his Perónist successor, Carlos Menem, who pardoned ex-President Videla and the other convicted leaders on the familiar ground of 'national reconciliation'. The Supreme Court, by a majority, declared the amnesty constitutional. Notwithstanding this pliable court, Argentina is at last making some efforts to confront its past by prosecuting men like Jorge Acosta, head of the Navy Mechanics School in Buenos Aires where some 300 mothers were murdered after the births of their children, subsequently stolen for adoption by loyal families.

What emerges from recent South American legal and political history is that the process of transition from military dictatorship to popular rule is not a time to punish crimes against humanity: transitional justice is a contradiction in terms. Democracy may be a necessary, but certainly not a sufficient, condition for retribution. In Argentina, for example, the colonel who led the rebellion against the Alfonsín government because it was threatening to put military torturers on trial formed a political party which had striking electoral success, and one general responsible for the murder of many prisoners enjoyed widespread support as a political candidate (he was narrowly beaten by a Perónist pop singer).[45] There is always some popular support for human rights violations: they are measures taken against persons suspected of subversion, and as Sábato reminds us in his prologue to *Nunca Más*, even innocent suspects 'must have been up to something' in the eyes of the public. Hitler's willing executioners, although not so many as Goldhagen would have us believe, were still legion. In Latin America the military remained powerful, if not in power: many of the worst offenders were, precisely for that reason, crucial to peace agreements and democratic transition. They were unrepentant, and still capable of staging a coup if provoked.

But what the history of 'transitional justice' – or the lack of it – in Latin America demonstrates in the longer term is that the emergence of any measure of truth is not a basis for reconciliation. Quite the contrary, since revelation of the details of official depravity only makes the demands for retribution by victims and their sympathizers more compelling. Time wounds all heels: democratic governments become more confident, prosecutors more daring, the public more inclined to do something about old men whose behaviour in uniform has brought their country international contempt. Thus it has proved in Argentina, after a retired navy officer, Adolfo Scilingo, confessed in 1995 to his junta days of throwing political prisoners out of aeroplanes over the Atlantic. General Martin Balza, the new army chief, refuting all the 'national reconciliation' rhetoric of frightened presidents, announced that he was in favour of 'initiating a painful dialogue about the past that was never sustained and that acts like a ghost within the collective consciousness of the country, always returning from the shadows where it occasionally hides'.[46] It was then discovered that the amnesty did not cover the crime of child-stealing, so prosecutors began preparing cases against the generals involved in disappearing pregnant women like Liliana Peyrera, whose babies were handed over to military families. The former dictator, Jorge Videla, pardoned by Menem in 1990, was re-arrested for this crime (which had not been included in the previous amnesty) in 1998. And in the same year, the notorious torturer Captain Alfredo Astíz, whom Britain refused during the Falklands War to hand over to France, was detained for several months after he boasted of his role in killing politicians and journalists. Some of this *schadenfreude* was due to the activities of Spanish judge Balthasar Garzón, who issued an international arrest warrant against Leopold Galtieri and obtained orders freezing the foreign assets of junta members. In Honduras, under the pressure of the *Velasquez Rodriguez* decision, an ombudsman rather than a truth commission was empowered to investigate disappearances, and recommended prosecutions rather than amnesties for the perpetrators. But Guatemala, the country with the most recent peace settlement (December 1996), has limited its amnesty so as to exclude disappearances, torture and genocide; it has learnt that the balm applied by truth commissioners is short-lived: reconciliation cannot happen without some measure of justice.

In principle, of course, forgiveness is the prerogative of the victims, not of the majority of members of the society in which they happen to live, let alone of any government. As crimes against humanity leave few victims living, it may be said that forgiveness is the prerogative of humanity, which generally extends it only by way of lighter sentence after a confession, the sincerity of which is supported by a willingness to give evidence in court against accomplices.

This is to some extent consonant with the approach of the Commission of Truth and Reconciliation established in 1995 in South Africa, which offered immunity from prosecution only to political criminals prepared to earn it by testifying fully and frankly, and if necessary testifying as prosecution witnesses at subsequent trials. This is not so much an amnesty as a form of plea-bargaining, familiar for centuries in most common law countries: conspirators may turn informers, acknowledge their guilt and earn their pardon by convicting their associates. It is not a perfect system, because it provides informers with an incentive to make false allegations. None the less, it has proved an essential weapon in ordinary law enforcement and the South African Supreme Court defended truth commission immunities for witnesses on the pragmatic basis that survivors would prefer to grieve over the truth than over prosecutions which failed for lack of evidence. In the *Azanian People's Organization Case* it upheld constitutionality on the basis that it was not a Pinochet-style immunity given by the State to cover up its own crimes, but was more a Lincoln-style pardon to restore the tranquillity of a state which had been at war with itself.[47] Bishop Tutu, while waxing overlyrically about the virtues of forgiveness, has portrayed his South African exercise as a negotiated part of a peace settlement and has been anxious to distinguish it from the kind of amnesties insisted upon by juntas in Latin America as a condition of giving up power, or granted by dictators to themselves.[48]

In the case of crimes against humanity, however, it sticks in the craw to allow torturers and assassins to walk entirely free as a reward for talking to a truth commission. Bishop Tutu's pleas for forgiveness sounded hollow to Steve Biko's widow, and ridiculous to Marius Schoon, an anti-apartheid activist whose wife and 6-year-old daughter were blown apart by a letter bomb sent on the direction of notorious double agent Craig Williamson. As Schoon put it:

There can be no indemnity, no forgiveness, without remorse. We see no signs of Craig being sorry. I mean, are we going to have a situation where people can qualify for indemnity just by saying, as if they were reeling off a grocery list, 'I killed this one and poisoned that one and beat the shit out of the third one'. It seems untenable to me, morally and philosophically.[49]

It is unacceptable that state torturers and assassins should go scot free: confessions, followed by pleas of guilty and evidence against colleagues and superiors, may earn pardons or light sentences but it is absurd to believe that such crimes will be forgiven or that reconciliation with the families of victims is possible. Amnesty is always excused as an exercise in *realpolitik*, a crude accommodation which avowedly subordinates justice to political expediency. What cannot be countenanced is any attempt to dress up expediency *as* justice, which is one mistake Bishop Tutu's truth commission made, by adopting 'principles' drawn up by Professor Nørgaard to determine whether an act of violence is 'political' (and hence indemnifiable). These so-called 'principles' were largely derived from the criteria once used in extradition law, and so are hardly relevant to the question of whether a particular criminal deserves amnesty. What makes the Nørgaard–Tutu criteria particularly unattractive is that they pardon crimes against humanity on grounds that should never amount to a defence, e.g. because they were committed under superior orders or for a political master. It angered the white and Afrikaan communities when judges on the Commission's amnesty committee granted blanket pardons to thirty-seven ANC leaders (including Thabo Mbeki) without requiring disclosure and then amnestied necklace killers and the bombers who had massacred a church congregation at prayer. The black community was similarly outraged by amnesties granted to Dirk Coetzee, commander of the Vlakplaas secret killing unit, and other senior police torturers. Gillian Slovo, daughter of the ANC's Joe Slovo, probably spoke for most victims' relatives after hearing Craig Williamson testify that 'it made absolutely no difference to me' that the letter bomb he sent to her father killed instead her mother, the academic Ruth First. 'I thought that coming here would give me some sense of closure. But I have been shaken in that belief . . . I cannot believe that my mother, not even in their terms, was a legitimate target.' Bishop Tutu had no warrant for imputing his own brand of forgiveness to those entitled not to forgive.

None the less, the South African commission succeeded where the South American commissions failed, in identifying criminals and either shaming them (if they testified) or recommending their prosecution (if they did not apply for amnesty or did not receive it or failed to tell the truth). Its report, published in October 1998, did expose the most shocking crimes against humanity (including the unrepentant Dr Basson's scientific experiments to create bacteria that would kill only blacks and a vaccine to make black women sterile) and demonstrated the complicity of P. W. Botha and some ministers in approving the bombings of cinemas and the headquarters of the Council of Churches. It also obtained evidence of Winnie Mandela's vicious penchant for murder and torture. That it produced a lot of truth but not much reconciliation is shown by the numerous legal actions it has attracted, including writs from the ANC (which tried to injunct the report), Chief Buthelezi, F. W. de Klerk and Steve Biko's widow.

Bishop Tutu's truth commission sat in public, 'named names' and had its conclusions fully reported. The 1985 commission of inquiry into the Matabeleland atrocities in Zimbabwe has still not been published, because the government claims it will 'open old wounds'. The point, of course, is that wounds of this kind – army killings of several thousand people – do not close without the application of some balm of retribution, or at least compensation. At Prime Minister Mugabe's hands, the families have received nothing, the main army murderers have been promoted, and the report which fastens guilt upon them remains suppressed. A more satisfactory approach was taken by the democratic government of Malawi which in 1991 succeeded the tyrant Hastings Banda. It established a commission of inquiry into the deaths of four cabinet ministers, which he had attributed to a road accident. The commission reported that they had been murdered at Banda's instigation, and at subsequent trials some of the Special Branch killers confessed their crimes and offered testimonies against their accomplices in return for short prison sentences. Banda was then accorded the fair trial that he had denied so many of his own citizens – so fair, in fact, that the case was heard by a jury of his own tribespeople, who acquitted him on evidence that pointed compellingly to his guilt. But overall justice was done, in that historical truth was told and Banda was, at the age of ninety-six, finally disgraced and prosecuted.

The experience of Latin American and African countries in the hard-won transition from dictatorship to democracy is very different from that of eastern Europe, where repressive communist regimes collapsed rapidly at the end of the 1980s. Communism subjected its citizens to the scrutiny of secret policemen and their networks of informants, to political trials and oppressive prison sentences: dissidents were denied many of the freedoms guaranteed by human rights conventions. There was a massive institutional invasion of privacy: in East Germany, the Stasi kept files on six million – one in three – citizens. In general, however, these systematic human rights violations were committed under cover of law and did not often extend to genocide, torture, disappearances, or other measures extreme enough to warrant the description of crimes against humanity. So 'settling accounts with communism' cannot be compared with settling accounts with torturers in uniform: the former must, in Václav Havel's phrase, be settled in the pages of history books; the latter, eventually, in the criminal courts. In eastern Europe, commissions have had a different truth to tell: not of massacre, but of friends and relations who turned informants; of dissidents who betrayed their colleagues and apparatchik judges and prosecutors who decided cases according to political commands. The purging process (inappropriately known in Czechoslovakia as 'lustration') has undoubtedly removed dishonest timeservers from political and public life, at the expense of some unfair accusations based on unreliable records made by secret policemen prone to exaggerate or even fictionalize their dealings with 'informants' in order to claim credit or expenses.

There are, however, several significant post-communist precedents. In 1993, the Hungarian Constitutional Court paved the way to prosecuting the persons responsible for mass shootings of innocent civilians during the 1956 uprising, on the basis that this was a crime against humanity under international law (pursuant to the Nuremberg Charter and common Article 3 of the Geneva Conventions) and so statutes of limitation could apply no time bars. Domestic law, the court ruled, must secure the enforcement of 'universally accepted rules of international law'.[50] In 1999, the trials finally began in Budapest of elderly ex-army officers accused of firing into unarmed crowds protesting against the Soviet invasion. In former East Germany, appellate courts have used international human rights law to justify the conviction and sentencing of soldiers and senior politicians responsible for the slaying of unarmed civilians as they endeavoured to flee across the Berlin Wall. These homicides (there were over 200 killings at the border between 1961 and 1989) inexcusably breached the right to life and the right to leave a country (Articles 6(1) and 12(2) of the Civil Covenant). It followed that orders to shoot to kill unarmed fugitives were unlawful, as even indoctrinated and 'intellectually simpleminded' border guards must have realized. Several have been convicted and imprisoned, as have members of the National Defence Council which formulated the policy and directed its implementation: most notably the last GDR leader, Egon Krenz, jailed in 1999 for six and a half years.[51] His defiant claim of 'victors' justice' (his Leipzig appeal judges were from West Germany) fell on deaf ears. This is an important contribution to the *Yamashita* line of precedents for prosecuting commanders and political decision-makers: their liability as accessories to manslaughter was fixed by their knowledge that the orders violated internationally protected rights and by proof that they intended that those unlawful orders should be routinely carried out. The proceedings against Erich Honecker, the former East German leader, were abandoned, however, because of his terminal illness.

No such mercy was extended in Romania to President Ceauşescu and his wife Elena, who were executed immediately after a short and farcical trial in which their appointed defence lawyer declared them guilty of genocide. Their summary execution could have been justified on grounds of necessity, since some units of the Securitate (their secret police) would otherwise have rallied against the popular revolution, causing extensive loss of life. The mistake was to hold a mock trial, which breached every principle of fairness and demeaned all who participated (the judge, who could not live with his conscience, committed suicide soon afterwards). Some of Ceauşescu's henchmen were rushed into televised show trials, appearing with heads shaven and in striped prison pyjamas to confess to complicity in genocide – the whole proceedings smacked of an update of the Moscow trials. Meanwhile, in Moscow the victims of those trials were all 'rehabilitated' in the course of *Glasnost*, and Russia's transition to democracy was marked more by desecration of statues of old Bolsheviks than by trials of Stalin's willing executioners. Stalin, in his embalmed self, the perpetrator of more crimes against humanity than anyone else in this or any other century, has been removed from public display beside the body of Lenin. But he is not dishonoured in death: his remains were cremated and sealed respectfully in the Kremlin Wall, close by the ashes of Andrei Vyshinsky, the producer of his show trials who had called upon the Nuremberg judges to drink a toast to the death of the defendants they were trying. Stalin's victims, shot without warning in the back of the head and buried in unmarked or mass graves, may have been posthumously rehabilitated and remembered, but they have not been avenged.

THE CASE FOR RETRIBUTION

There is now little dispute in Europe about the need to bring Nazi war criminals and their collaborators to justice: their crimes, ironically, seem to gain in magnitude as they recede in time. This is a *fin de siécle* phenomenon, however: it is hard to credit all the high-minded hostility in Britain as recently as 1990 to the War Crimes Act, which was rejected at one point by the House of Lords on the over-scrupulous ground that promises had been made to end these prosecutions back in 1951. In 1999, not a single voice was raised to protest the conviction under that Act of 83-year-old Anthony Sarwonick, who had shot Jews as if they were wild geese in the swamps of Latvia, before working happily for a half century as a guard on British Rail. Unlike the Demjanjuk trial, his Old Bailey proceedings were demonstrably fair (judge and jury even flew to visit the scene of his crimes) and the evidence, despite the passage of time, was overwhelming. More difficult, but much more significant, have been the war crimes trials which have forced countries to confront their Nazi past. Croatia bowed to pressure from the European Union over the commandant of its worst concentration camp. In 1999, at the age of seventy-eight, he was sentenced to twenty years for killing 2,000 Jews and Serbs, some of whom he personally bludgeoned to death with sledge-hammers.[52] In France Maurice Papon, at eighty-nine, received a ten-year sentence for complicity in crimes against humanity – he had arranged the arrest and transportation to death camps of many Jews while he was an official of the Vichy regime. The reckoning had been stalled for many years by his friends in high places, but although France has a time limit of twenty years for the prosecution of murder, it makes an exception for crimes against humanity. The documentary evidence against Papon was devastating, although the gravity and fairness of the trial was jeopardized by the loud posturing of lawyers for victims' families who were permitted to appear as 'civil parties'.

None the less, the proceedings served as a long-overdue reminder that pushers of pens can be as guilty of crimes against humanity as pushers of people into gas ovens. Papon was a functionary who signed deportation orders: his guilt was fixed by the fact that he knew that he was implementing a state policy of racial persecution, even though he had no ideological commitment to that policy. Papon was jailed for what the prosecution described as an 'office crime', because 'genocide could be abetted by the routine obedience of functionaries'.[53] His claim to have been a scapegoat was true enough, but irrelevant: he was guilty, along with many other Vichy officials who happened to evade justice. It was a sign of the time (October 1999) that when he absconded to Switzerland just before the rejection of his appeal, the Swiss government was so horrified at this reminder of its pro-Nazi collaborative past that it bent its own laws in order to hand him back immediately. France aims to close its Vichy casebook in the year 2000 by trying *in absentia* the last living Nazi war criminal, Alöis Brunner, the well-bred secretary to Eichmann who ensured the deaths of hundreds of Jewish children in the last days of the Second World War. Syria has long protected him, and he is believed to be still living in Damascus. The decision to put him on trial was applauded by Serge Klarsfeld and other Nazi hunters, but is really deserving of ridicule.[54] Any trial *in absentia* is by definition unfair: the cause of human rights is not advanced by procedures which are rigged in their assumed favour.

The worst atrocity since the Holocaust was played out on the killing fields of Cambodia, as 1.7 million lives were sacrificed to the perverse dream of a return to a pure primitive agrarian society which had struck the young Pol Pot when he was waiting on tables in Paris. Many years later, he and his principal lieutenants – Ieng Sary, Khieu Samphan, Nuon Chea and Hun Sen – conspired to inflict their orgy of genocide and slave labour upon an unwilling population, ironically driven into their crazed arms by the US carpet-bombing of Cambodia. Hun Sen was the first to defect – to the Vietnamese – and became in due course the prime minister who pardoned and welcomed back into the orthodox communist fold first Ieng Sary (in 1996) and at Christmas 1998, after Pol Pot's death in April of that year, Khieu Samphan and Nuon Chea. Hun Sen invited the press to join their 'family celebration' at Phnom Penh's most luxurious hotel, where he announced that instead of putting his former comrades on trial for their command responsibility for killing 1.7 million human beings, 'we must dig a hole and bury the past' – presumably in a mass grave. These men of manic viciousness have never apologized or admitted to a single mistake: Khieu Samphan, on the contrary, congratulated himself for agreeing to forget the past so 'we can begin to rebuild this country'. That rebuilding, necessitated by the deliberate destruction by the Khmer Rouge of Cambodia's infrastructure and culture and morality, has already cost the international community billions of pounds in aid and the loss of dozens of peacekeeper lives, quite aside from the tidal wave of familial anguish at 1.7 million deaths. Whether as pardoned citizens or as potentates of 'Democratic Kampuchea', the continued freedom of these men mocks humankind. By early 2000 they were still at liberty, as the Hun Sen government continued to resist UN demands to put them on trial before an international tribunal.

Crimes against humanity are, by definition, unforgivable, even if the worst in Latin America were committed by devoted members of a Roman Catholic faith which offers forgiveness in return for a secret confession. Any church which can in this way become complicit in the crimes of René Ponce, who ordered the gunning-down of the Jesuit priests, or of Jorge Videla, who directed the theft of the babies of 300 murdered women, cannot expect others to believe its promise of hellfire and damnation for sinners in some afterlife. Nor can nervous politicians be credited in their claim that amnesties will 'secure the stability of democracy' or 'promote national reconciliation'. This is just an excuse for cowardice or inaction: as Hannah Arendt noted, 'men are unable to forgive what they cannot punish'. International law is entitled to ignore the special pleading of the prelates and the politicians, who speculatively invite us to leave these crimes respectively to God or to history, and insist that they be left to prosecutors, as soon as it is safe to arrest the suspects. That is the position taken by the 1968 Convention on the Non-Applicability of Statutory Limitations to War Crimes and Crimes against Humanity, which has been said (by the French courts in the *Barbie Case*) to reflect customary international law in requiring some retribution for these classes of crime, no matter how long it may take. The duty, it is suggested, is not actually to punish, but only to prosecute: the outcome of a fair trial, no matter how compelling the evidence, can never be pre-ordained. A serious prosecution discharges the duty to victims, forces the perpetrator to explain or expiate, and allows some truth to be told in public proceedings. Prosecution is not revenge, because it does not necessarily entail punishment: fair trials often acquit the guilty. It is justice by the very due process that torturers and death squads deny to their victims.

The duty to prosecute the perpetrators of crimes against humanity will also serve the right in their victims' families to truth and to compensation. As the Inter-American Commission put it, surveying the closed ranks of army death squads throughout Latin America, 'every society has the inalienable right to know the truth about past events, as well as the motives and circumstances in which aberrant crimes came to be committed, in order to prevent repetition of such acts in the future';[55] more simply, families have the right to know the fate of their members. Torture victims or, in the event of their death under torture, their dependants deserve some recompense for pain and suffering, and anyone who has been the victim of unlawful arrest and detention must be accorded an enforceable right to compensation, under Civil Covenant Article 9(5). Reports by truth commissions cannot order compensation, although they generally recommend psychiatric assistance to victims of torture. (The Rettig Committee in Chile went so far as to propose psychological care for the torturers themselves.) Where prosecution is a political impossibility, commissions of inquiry can bring benefits if they recommend for violators the alternatives of disqualification from public office or dishonourable discharge from police or army.

Does the duty to prosecute extend to trying *in absentia* defendants who are in hiding or beyond the jurisdiction? If their escape is made prior to the commencement of proceedings, there is nothing (short of extradition requests) which can properly be done – see the 1979 trial *in absentia* of Pol Pot and Ieng Sary by the Vietnamese-backed government of the People's Republic of Kampuchea, which presented overwhelming evidence of genocide, but so lacked due process (the defendants were safely across the border in Thailand) that it had little impact. The absurd sentence of death *in absentia* (why not execution *in absentia*, as well?) made the proceedings a mockery. An independent international inquiry, establishing facts rather than purporting to punish, would have had much more credibility. The position is different if defendants absent themselves in the course of proceedings, or formally request to be excused. The Bolivian Supreme Court was right to uphold the conviction of General García Meza, who went into hiding only after his initial testimony to the court and who had his case presented by lawyers appointed by the government to do their best for him. Similarly, the trial *in absentia* of Malawi's Dr Hastings Banda cannot be criticized on this score, since his absence was at his own request: he informed the court that he 'would rather die than face cross-examination' and was permitted to remain at home, a few miles away, while his imported QC challenged the evidence against him. There can be no objection to a trial *in absentia* when the defendant deliberately waives his right to be present.

Undoubtedly the greatest obstacle to fair trial, whether in a society transiting from dictatorship to democracy or one in which the old repressive order has suddenly collapsed, is corruption in the judiciary and weakness of the local legal profession. One depressingly familiar feature of states in which crimes against humanity are regularly permitted is how judges connive at them by declining to investigate or hear habeas corpus petitions. This behaviour is criminal, too, in perverting justice, but it is noteworthy that professional bodies like the International Bar Association, active in complaining about attacks on lawyers, have never attacked those of their members implicated in covering up crimes against humanity. It is difficult enough for transitional governments to reform the police and the army: invariably, they inherit judges with a vested interest in protecting the regime by which they were appointed. The failure of civil rights prosecutions in the Philippines after the fall of Marcos was largely the responsibility of that country's corrupt and incompetent judiciary. In El Salvador, the UN-appointed truth commission explained that the reason it hesitated to recommend prosecutions was because the country's judiciary lacked integrity and had perverted justice in order to protect the death squads. The commission particularly condemned the president of the Supreme Court, Gutierrez Castro, for his attempts to stop cases arising from the El Mozote massacre: the government responded by appointing him to sit on important international judicial committees.

The duty to prosecute perpetrators of crimes against humanity has not had very much appeal at the UN. Its officials – themselves often culled from national diplomatic corps – are instinctively averse to any settlement of an international dispute which does not include an amnesty clause. They urged the US to foist an amnesty for Cedras and his army of killers upon President Aristide, against his will, as an essential condition of support for his return to Haiti. The UN Secretary-General and his representatives recommended uncon-ditional amnesty in their mediations over democratic change in South Africa, and insisted upon protecting the genocidal Khmer Rouge – even assuring them posts in the new government – when it came to brokering a settlement in Cambodia. (One of the most astonishing, and disgusting, sights of recent times was Boutros Boutros-Ghali, the retired UN Secretary-General, embracing 'an old friend', the genocidal killer Khieu Samphan, when the latter emerged from hiding at the end of 1998.) From his fall in 1979 to his death in 1997, Pol Pot was protected by diplomats at every turn: no country was prepared to invoke Article 9 of the Genocide Convention (which permits the ICJ to rule on state responsibility for failures to punish genocide) and the US and China both vetoed proposals in 1989 to establish an international criminal court to try such members of the Khmer Rouge as could be apprehended. All five permanent members of the Security Council vetoed a provision in the final peace settlement which would have permitted prosecutions under the Genocide Con-vention. Their subsequent decision to establish an international court to try crimes against humanity in former Yugoslavia was a face-saving device, after the media revealed ethnic cleansing on a horrific scale in Bosnian Serb prison camps. Even so, the two Security Council members which had most to lose from any advance in human rights – China and Brazil – were initially opposed and, to comfort them, the resolution emphasizes that the court is an 'ad hoc measure' and not a precedent.

Such ad hoc measures for former Yugoslavia and then Rwanda leave many well-documented crimes against humanity impervious to punishment, as a result of local amnesty statutes passed in contra-vention of international humanitarian law. If these particular crimes are the most heinous of all, because they touch not only the families of victims but decent people throughout the world, then some retribution at international level is required. It is difficult to understand why certain states should still vigorously pursue aged Nazis, while ignoring the question of punishing identifiable persons clearly responsible for massacres in Latin America, Africa and Asia. For them awaits no avenging Israel, no assiduous Simon Wiesenthal to track them to the grave: they remain, many still in positions of continuing power, sheltered by unlawful pardons given under duress or by the collective guilt of societies which silently condoned crimes too monstrous for the world to forgive. Death has robbed us of the satisfaction of seeing Pol Pot and Hirohito behind bars and brain damage has rescued Pinochet, but as ways are worked out which have put Videla and Habré in the dock, can Ponce, Cedras, Khieu Samphan, Milošević, Mengistu, Amin, Botha, Stroessner, Saddam, Karadžić, Wiranto, Astíz, Mladić, Guterres and the others all expect to go unpunished to their graves?

8

The Balkan Trials

An international tribunal shall be established for the prosecution of persons responsible for serious violations of international humanitarian law committed in the territory of the former Yugoslavia since 1991.　　　　Security Council Resolution 808

February 1993

By the simple device of invoking its mandatory powers to preserve the peace, endowed by Chapter VII of the UN Charter, the Security Council unanimously established by its Resolutions 808 and 827 the first truly 'international' criminal court. Nuremberg, after all, had been a tribunal set up by four victorious nations, while the Hague Tribunal was a subsidiary organ of the Security Council with which all countries were required to co-operate. But the comparison soon pales. The Nuremberg defendants were speedily arrested in a country under Allied occupation and most of them were convicted on overwhelming documentary evidence within the space of twelve months. But the tribunal in The Hague, far away from a continuing and ferocious war, was infuriatingly slow: its first defendant, Duško Tadić, did not arrive until April 1995 and his trial did not commence until 7 May 1996. Much blood flowed under the bridges of the Drina in the meantime: the worst of the Bosnian Serb crimes against humanity, namely the killing of 7,000 Muslim men and boys from Srebrenica, took place in July 1995 while lawyers in The Hague were still arguing their preliminary motions. The decision convicting Tadić of eleven separate crimes against humanity was not handed down until 7 May 1997; incredibly, his appeal did not even begin until April 1999! So Tadić's fate (he was given twenty years' imprisonment) and that of several Bosnian Serb soldiers who followed him into the dock did not deter the atrocities committed in Kosovo in the years which followed his arraignment. The real problem has been that for all the obligations to co-operate with the Hague Tribunal which were written into the Dayton Peace Accords after Srebrenica, *realpolitik* was the message of a NATO spokesman widely quoted in the summer of 1996: 'Arresting Karadžić is not worth the blood of one NATO soldier.' The mandate of the 60,000-strong I-For force was 'to detain those indicted persons whom they come across in the course of their duties', so NATO commanders ensured that their duties would make such encounters unlikely.[1] This is not so much a case of dereliction of duty as of correctly divining the real purpose of the Hague Tribunal in the minds of the Security Council representatives who set it up, which was never to put major criminals like Karadžić and Mladić behind bars, but to pretend to an anxious and appalled world that something was being done.

That this pretence was felt to be necessary in respect of Yugoslavia in 1993, rather than in any previous conflict, was due to a combination of factors. Most important were the television atrocity pictures, given added force by the shelling of historical holiday places like the Dalmatian coast and Dubrovnik, which showed the spectre of ethnic cleansing returning to Europe. American television audiences were bewildered that this should be part of the New World Order promised after the defeat of Iraq. There was, too, the futility of the diplomatic soft shoe shuffle, as Vance and Owen solemnly worked out how richly the aggressor factions should be rewarded, only to produce a plan that failed to assuage their greed. There had been a disastrous failure of sanctions – most ironically of the blanket arms ban, which left Muslims defenceless against the already well-equipped Serbian armies. Then, more television pictures, this time of 'an elegant, cosmopolitan European city, Sarajevo, being systematically pulverized from a safe distance by cigarette-smoking, Šljivovica-drinking gun and mortar crews while they and the snipers leisurely targeted school children, bread queues, housewives doing their shopping, funeral ceremonies and the like'.[2] The United Nations could not be taken seriously unless something was done: the utter failure of diplomacy and sanctions, and the refusal to risk the lives of allied soldiers by armed intervention, made a war crimes tribunal the only face-saving device left. So it was set up fortuitously, but upon its success (everyone started to say) the prospects for an international criminal court, first foreshadowed by the Genocide Convention in 1948, would depend.

What, however, is meant by 'success'? Nuremberg 'succeeded' as a trial process because it proved beyond doubt the guilt of most of the Nazi leaders, and acquitted those whose guilt could not be proved. That success derived from the efforts of a thousand investigators and lawyers, with defendants already under arrest, who had complete access to archives and witnesses within the control of an Allied army of occupation. It was 'victor's justice', not in a cynical sense, but because victory brought the power to do justice to some of those who deserved it. But there has been no 'victory' in Bosnia, other than for Croatian forces, some of whose commanders were guilty of crimes as wicked as those of their Bosnian Serb counterparts. With calculated contempt for the Hague Tribunal, President Tudjman announced the promotion of an indicted Croatian commander, Tihomir Blaskić, on the very day that diplomats in Dayton were hammering out its clause requiring the Bosnian Serbs to surrender their suspects (but see p. 320).[3] The Hague Tribunal spent much of 1996 and 1997 concerned with the trial of Duško Tadić, a sadistic freelance thug permitted to torture prisoners at Omarska camp, while the commanders and 'intellectual authors' of the genocide remained impervious to its warrants for arrest. Most impervious of all was Slobodan Milošević, who bears a guilt of Göring-esque proportions for the entire tragedy, but whose position as head of state and as broker of any possible peace gave him an effective immunity that the Hague prosecutors could not challenge until 1999, when NATO finally divulged intercept evidence they had been requesting for years. Until it has suspects of real significance to put on trial (and by March 2000, it had only three senior officers in custody), the Hague court cannot be accounted a success, no matter how many footsoldiers it manages to convict for following orders.

By 'success', of course, most supporters of the Hague Tribunal mean convictions. True success, however, will only attend a tribunal with judges sufficiently robust to acquit wherever there is reasonable doubt. The Trial Chamber's Tadić decision, which by acquitting on many counts displeased the prosecution, was a good start. The Tribunal's rules of procedure and evidence recognize that the requirements of 'fairness to the defence' have become stricter since Nuremberg. But most of the judges are old men (the average age is sixty-six, and the Chinese judge, Haopei Li, died in office at ninety, to be replaced by the sprightly Beijing jurist Tieya Wang, a mere eighty-five). They are mainly academics or long-serving appellate judges: none has had any recent hands-on experience in criminal defence work and the current president, Claude Jorda, is a long-serving Paris prosecutor. There is a real problem about getting public evaluation of their work, because human rights lobbyists (scenting the beginnings of a human rights industry) have been uncritically supportive. There have been few independent legal observers at The Hague, and fewer still in Arusha, monitoring these cases of foreign prisoners pitted against multistate power. Organizations like Amnesty have in the past been concerned at the treatment of political prisoners irrespective of the colour of their politics, but the fate of defendants accused of crimes against humanity has not attracted much interest, notwithstanding one suicide in the Hague cells and several serious attempts. This double standard is unfortunate, because any court derives its legitimacy from the justice that it does. What the Hague Tribunal is establishing is its capacity to get at the truth while sitting far from the scene of the crime, and notwithstanding media prejudice against the defendants and the difficulties their lawyers have in obtaining witnesses and procuring documents (especially security-sensitive material in the hands of the prosecutor).

Many politicians, generals and diplomats view the exponential growth of international humanitarian law with distaste. They have, behind the scenes, accused the Hague Tribunal president and prosecutor of irresponsibility for demanding that Dayton include a surrender clause for indicted suspects, and have actually blamed the human rights lobby for causing thousands of deaths by opposing the Vance–Owen compromises with Serbian aggression.[4] This is the voice from the Pentagon, brayed most loudly by Senator Jesse Helms, who in 1998 threatened to block US ratification of any international criminal court if it had power to indict a single American soldier (even were his name Lieutenant Calley). What Richard Goldstone and his successors Louise Arbour and Carla del Ponte have demonstrated, by their willingness to speak out against all attempts made to marginalize the Tribunal, is the optimistic fact that enterprises of this sort have a tendency to develop a momentum of their own, independent of the concerns of those who create them. The diplomats fear that an international criminal court, once established, would be a power in the world, prone to upset the bargains they make with unjust regimes. The Hague Tribunal will succeed once it teaches them to live with the idea that justice, in respect of crimes against humanity, is non-negotiable.

LEGAL BASIS OF THE HAGUE TRIBUNAL

Civil war in Yugoslavia began in earnest in 1991, with the Serb army bombardments of Vukovar and Dubrovnik; by May of 1992, when the Security Council imposed mandatory economic sanctions on Serbia, the atrocities had reached a level Europe had not experienced since the Second World War. Arms embargoes had little impact (imposed on all parties, they had actually tilted the balance towards the well-prepared Serbian army) and in the autumn the United States proposed a war crimes tribunal. There is some tantalizing intercept evidence to suggest that this proposal actually gave pause to the Serbian military commanders – until they realized that any such tribunal would take years to establish.[5] The Security Council began by appointing a commission of experts, eventually headed by Professor Cherif Bassiouni, to investigate violations of international humanitarian law. With commendable speed he issued an interim report on 26 January 1993, describing ethnic cleansing, mass murder, torture, rape, pillage and destruction of cultural, religious and private property. That led, on 22 February, to Security Council Resolution 808, determining that the situation constituted a threat to international peace and security, and deciding to establish an international tribunal to contribute to the realization of peace by putting an end to war crimes and punishing their perpetrators. Resolution 827, in May, adopted a report by the Secretary-General which set out the legal and procedural basis for the new institution.[6]

This report serves as the Tribunal's mandate. It commences defensively, describing Resolution 808 as 'circumscribed in scope and purpose . . . the decision does not relate to the establishment of an international criminal jurisdiction in general nor to the creation of an international criminal court . . .' It accepts that the normal method of establishing a prosecution agency and a court would be for state parties, either through the General Assembly or after special conferences, to draw up a treaty which would then be open for signature and ratification. But that would take years. The need for urgency permitted action under Chapter VII of the United Nations Charter, given that the Security Council had already determined the existence of a threat to the peace. The Tribunal would derive its legitimacy from the fact that it constituted 'a measure to maintain or restore international peace and security'. It would be a 'subsidiary organ' of the Council, albeit a judicial one which would in the performance of those judicial functions be independent of the Council or of any political considerations, although (as another sop to the state sovereignty brigade) its lifespan as an *ad hoc* court would be limited to the restoration of peace in former Yugoslavia.

In setting up the Hague Tribunal, the Security Council acted within its powers under the UN Charter. By Article 24(1), all members 'confer on the Security Council primary responsibility for the maintenance of international peace and security, and agree that in carrying out its duties under this responsibility the Security Council acts on their behalf'.

Article 39 provides:

The Security Council shall determine the existence of any threat to peace or act of aggression and shall make recommendations, or decide what measures shall be taken in accordance with Articles 41 and 42, to maintain or restore international peace and security.

The Security Council had, of course, determined that other local conflicts constituted a threat to international peace: Haiti and Somalia in 1993, Iraq in 1991, the Iran–Iraq War, insurgencies in Lebanon, South Africa and Southern Rhodesia. But in none of those conflicts did it create a court to punish responsible parties. The legality of the Hague Tribunal depended on the scope of Article 41:

The Security Council may decide what measures not involving the use of armed force are to be employed to give effect to its decisions, and may call upon the members of the United Nations to apply such measures. These may include complete or partial interruption of economic relations and of rail, sea, air, postal, telegraphic, radio and other means of communication, and the severance of diplomatic relations.

It is fair to say that the drafters of Article 41 did not have an international criminal court in mind: it is hardly *sui generis* with the examples they chose to give of economic and diplomatic sanctions. But the power is a wide one, and does not *exclude* the imposition of criminal responsibility on persons whose capacity for acts of aggression can only be deterred by the prospect of punishment. Through Resolutions 731 and 748, the Council had already imposed sanctions on Libya as a means of forcing Colonel Gaddafi to surrender for trial two of its nationals accused of the Lockerbie bombing; now it was imposing criminal sanctions on individuals more directly. The power of the United Nations to establish courts and tribunals to render binding civil judgments had been upheld by the ICJ;[7] now it was establishing a court with the power to imprison rather than merely to award compensation. So far as the familiar bogey of state sovereignty was concerned, there was a crucial let-out. Article 2(7), which forbids the United Nations to 'intervene in matters which are essentially within the jurisdiction of any State', expressly commands that 'this principle shall not prejudice the application of enforcement measures under Chapter VII'.

The first, and most significant, decision by the Hague Tribunal was to rule itself lawfully constituted by the Security Council. Duško Tadić's preliminary objection that it had no power to put him on trial was rejected by both the Trial and the Appeals Chamber.[8] The Trial Chamber did so on the unsatisfactory basis that the Hague Tribunal itself had no power to review acts of the Security Council, because this would be to enter a forbidden political territory which was 'non-justiciable'. This is a conservative position, much favoured by appeal judges like Chinese judge Li, who believe courts should be subservient to political masters. He denounced the very idea of judicial review of the Security Council as 'imprudent and worthless' because his colleagues were 'trained only in law' and had 'little or no experience in international political affairs'. The appellate majority, however, treated these arguments about 'political questions' and 'non-justiciable issues' with the contempt they deserve, as part of the old no-go areas of national honour and state sovereignty. It ruled that legal questions of whether the Security Council had charter power to act as it did, and whether its action was taken rationally and in good faith, invited legal answers which the judges were qualified and entitled to give, 'particularly in cases where there might be manifest contradiction with the Principles and Purposes of the Charter'.

The first precedent set by the Hague Tribunal was therefore to assert the primacy of the rule of law. The Security Council itself could, within a narrow scope, be judicially reviewed, i.e. corrected if it plainly misinterpreted its charter or invented a 'threat to the peace' which demonstrably did not exist. What is heartening about the Appeals Chamber majority is that it was prepared to analyse its own legitimacy by passing judgment on the action of the Security Council, rather than automatically accepting that action as a loyal UN instrumentality. This is an important assertion of independence: international judges are entitled to disbelieve governments, even when they are powerful and unanimous, and it is to be hoped that the approach in the *Tadić Case* will be followed in time by the ICJ.

The Hague Tribunal set another important precedent in its preliminary ruling, namely that international jurisdiction to punish both war crimes and crimes against humanity did not require proof of an *international* armed conflict – an internecine conflict was enough. The reasoning behind this decision settles an arid scholastic debate, and establishes beyond doubt the competence of the international community, should it wish, to punish rulers who brutally oppress their own people, irrespective of whether their plight directly attracts foreign intervention.

Article 1 of the Hague Tribunal statute empowers it to 'prosecute persons responsible for serious violations of international humanitarian law committed in the territory of the former Yugoslavia since 1991' – a formula which, unbeknowns to the UN at the time, would empower the prosecutor years later to investigate allegations about NATO war crimes during the bombing of Serbia. (This had the beneficial result that more attention was paid to the Geneva Conventions than in any previous war: see p. 416). The standard was chosen to avoid any argument about retrospective punishment: the offences would be those clearly established by the time of the outbreak of the

Balkan conflict in 1991. By that time the laws and customs of war had been well established, as had the class of 'crimes against humanity' defined at Nuremberg. This precedent, however, related to crimes committed during a period of international armed conflict: the Nuremberg judges, notwithstanding the language of Article 6(c) of the Charter, declined to convict the Nazis in relation to crimes committed against Jews prior to the outbreak of the Second World War (see p. 222). (The first exception to be established was genocide, which under both the 1948 Genocide Convention and customary international law may be committed in peace as well as war.) Article 2 of its own statute empowers the Hague Tribunal to punish 'grave breaches' of the 1949 Geneva Convention (i.e. wilful killing or torture of civilians, wanton destruction of property and ill-treatment of prisoners-of-war and civilians in the course of international armed conflict). Article 3 empowers the Tribunal to punish violations of the laws and customs of war as defined by the 1907 Hague Convention (i.e. use of poisonous weapons, wanton destruction of cities, bombardment of undefended towns, destruction of churches, hospitals or cultural property in the course of armed conflict, whether international or internal). Article 4 empowers it to punish genocide, i.e. attempts to destroy persons because they are members of a national or ethnic or religious group. And Article 5 gives it the jurisdiction to punish crimes against humanity.

It was argued on behalf of Tadić that the Tribunal's jurisdiction was confined under Article 3 of its statute to war crimes committed during international armed conflict, and that the Balkan imbroglio was purely internal. This issue is of import for the future ability to punish human rights violations committed in the course of civil strife, and the Tribunal's broad definition of 'armed conflict' extends customary law to cover the treatment of rebels, at least when they are both 'armed' and 'organized'. The Appeals Chamber found that

an armed conflict exists whenever there is resort to armed force between States or protracted armed violence between governmental authorities and organized armed groups or between such groups within a State. International humanitarian law applies from the initiation of such armed conflicts and extends beyond the duration of hostilities until a general conclusion of peace is reached; or, in the case of internal conflicts, a peaceful settlement is achieved. Until that moment, international humanitarian law continues to apply in the whole territory of the warring States or, in the case of internal conflicts, the whole territory under the control of a party, whether or not actual conflict takes place there.[9]

The Appeals Chamber accepted, with some reluctance, that Article 2 (covering 'grave breaches' of the Geneva Convention) could only apply within the framework of international armed conflicts, since the Geneva Conventions themselves were so limited in 1949 when customary law had not advanced far enough to permit the world to put on trial the rulers of a country who chose to put down armed insurrection with inhumane violence (see p. 177). As if to underline the anachronism, the Appeals Chamber went on to hold that Article 3 (violation of the law or customs of war) *did* apply to internal armed conflict, because those who conducted it, whether on behalf of the State or on behalf of insurrectionists, were bound by international law to respect 'elementary considerations of humanity' – a conclusion reached by the ICJ in its 1986 decision in *Nicaragua* v. *US*.[10] Since there is a considerable degree of overlap between the conduct condemned by the Geneva Conventions (Hague Statute, Article 2) and by customary war law (Hague Statute, Article 3), the distinction drawn by customary law – requiring an international conflict in order to exert jurisdiction over one but not the other – is no longer sustainable. Historically, as the Appeals Chamber points out, there was a 'stark dichotomy' between belligerency – an armed conflict between sovereign states – and insurgency within the territory of a sovereign state. The former was regulated in detail by international law, which turned a blind eye to civil strife so as to avoid encroachment on the sovereignty of a state, i.e. its power to put down its rebels and traitors as it pleased. It was time the dichotomy was abandoned, because

a State-sovereignty-oriented approach has been gradually supplanted by a human-being-oriented approach. Gradually the maxim of Roman law *hominum causa omne jus constitutum* (all law is created for the benefit of human beings) has gained a firm foothold in the international community as well. It follows that in the area of armed conflict the distinction between interstate wars and civil wars is losing its value so far as human beings are concerned. Why protect civilians from belligerent violence, or ban rape, torture or the wanton destruction of hospitals, churches, museums or private property, as well as proscribe weapons causing unnecessary suffering when two sovereign states are engaged in war, and yet refrain from enacting the same bans or providing the same protection when armed violence has erupted 'only' within the territory of a sovereign State?[11]

This logic is impeccable, and made irresistible by the overlap between 'war crimes' on the one hand and 'genocide' and 'crimes against humanity' on the other, which are not limited to times of international conflict. This latter category, jurisdiction over which was granted by Article 5, covers inhuman acts directed against a civilian population 'in armed conflict, whether international or internal in character'. The specific examples, ranging from murder, torture, exter-mination and rape to the lesser offences of deportation, imprisonment and persecution on political grounds, cover most of the crimes pun-ished (but only when committed in international conflict) under the 'grave breaches' regime of the Geneva Conventions. By ruling that it was 'a settled rule of customary international law that crimes against humanity do not require a connection to international armed conflict' or perhaps to any conflict at all,[12] the court effectively side-stepped the limitation of the 1949 Geneva Conventions. State parties had obviously been reluctant in the Cold War era to give foreign states the right (indeed, under the Convention, the duty) to punish any of their nationals for acts of internal oppression and hence the Geneva limitation to 'international' conflicts: now the *Tadić* precedent rids the law of this anachronistic distinction and permits its full force to be concentrated on the State as internal oppressor as well as external aggressor.

The end result of the Hague Tribunal's exhaustive analysis of customary and conventional international humanitarian law as it had developed by the time of the break-up of Yugoslavia may be summarized as follows:

1. Crimes against humanity are inhumane acts of a very serious nature committed as part of a widespread or systematic attack against a civilian population on political, ethnic or religious grounds. They may be committed in times of peace or of war.

2. 'War crimes' (i.e. violations of the laws and customs of war, otherwise described as international humanitarian law) cover unlawful methods of warfare deployed against the enemy or civilians in armed conflict, whether international or internal.
3. 'Grave breaches' of the Geneva Convention are committed by unlawful treatment of certain categories of combatants (the sick and wounded, prisoners-of-war, etc.) and of civilians, but only in time of international armed conflict.
4. Genocide, under both customary and conventional law, is punishable whether it is attempted or committed in peace or in civil war or international war.

It was not on the cards that the judges of a tribunal upon which so many humanitarian hopes were riding would abolish themselves at the request of the very first defendant, or be persuaded to limit their own jurisdiction over him. None the less, these appellate judgments were an intellectually impressive beginning, all the more important for emanating from the first truly international criminal court. By defining 'armed conflict' and its temporal and spatial connotations, by severing so forcefully the category of crimes against humanity from any requirement of a connection to international wars, or indeed to any state of conflict, the judgments marked a significant advance in international law. Although the crimes committed in former Yugoslavia were obviously part of an armed conflict, the law which is emerging from The Hague is equally tailored to states where there is no conflict at all – sometimes because potential subversives have been liquidated by death squads.

In November 1994 the Security Council established, as an appendage of the Hague Tribunal, a further court sitting in Arusha to hear cases arising from the genocide in Rwanda earlier that year (see p. 71). The Hague prosecutor serves as prosecutor for the Rwanda Tribunal, although most investigative and legal staff are separately based in Arusha and Kigali, and new judges have been appointed to fill three Rwanda Trial Chambers. The Appeals Chamber for both courts is the same body, based in The Hague, thus assuring consistency in the law applied by both tribunals. The Rwanda Tribunal statute does advance international criminal law in one important respect, by imposing individual responsibility for breach of common Article 3 of the 1949 Geneva Conventions. It will be recalled that the 'grave breaches' regime of these conventions imposes criminal liability only for war crimes committed in the course of international armed conflict, and the atrocities in Rwanda were plainly not of that description. The tribal killings had no relation to any interstate conflict and the only international element in the country – the UN 'peacekeepers' looking on in horror – could not get out of Rwanda quickly enough. The Rwanda Tribunal statute provides jurisdiction to punish genocide and crimes against humanity, and additionally contraventions by individuals of common Article 3 of the Geneva Conventions. It is this last addition which provides an argument from 'state practice' that common Article 3, devised in 1949 as merely a minimum human rights standard for states to honour during internal armed conflict, has crystallized as an international criminal law for the breach of which individuals can properly be punished by international courts.

The Rwanda Tribunal began even less satisfactorily than its big brother in The Hague. There was admitted incompetence and sloth, and some corruption, in its early years, and in Arusha in Tanzania this was out of sight and for too long out of mind. However, in the *Kanyabashi Case* (1997), its Trial Chamber rejected a jurisdictional challenge to the Security Council's exercise of Chapter VII powers in setting it up, ruling that the conflict in Rwanda did indeed pose threats to international peace and security because it unleashed 'a massive wave of refugees, many of whom were armed, into the neighbouring countries which by itself entailed a considerable risk of serious destabilization of the local areas in the host countries where the refugees had settled'. The danger of the conflict spreading to neighbouring states was ample justification for the Security Council's exercise of power.[13] The Rwanda Tribunal has commenced a programme of trials of very significant 'authors' of the genocide, including a number of leading politicians and civil servants ('*bourgmestres*' or district prefects alleged to have planned and organized some of the massacres) and senior executives of the radio station Libre des Mille Collines which broadcast specific incitements to kill more Tutsis (and gave details of their hiding places) during the time of the genocide. It has been easier to net these 'big fish' because they have no state in which to hide, and some have been content to co-operate with the Arusha prosecutors and accept a long prison sentence rather than face the alternative of a summary trial followed by firing-squad execution in Rwanda under the new Tutsi-dominated government.[14] The Tribunal holds thirty-two of its forty-five indictees in custody. In September 1998 came a real breakthrough when the former Rwandan prime minister Jean Kambanda pleaded guilty to genocide. He is the highest ranking political leader to have been convicted by an international court thus far.

HOW THE TRIBUNAL OPERATES

We have seen that Articles 2–5 give the Hague Tribunal jurisdiction over crimes which in 1991 were accepted in customary international law as attracting individual responsibility, so no defendant could be heard to argue that he had been charged with an offence which did not exist at the time he was alleged to have committed it. Article 6 limits the range of defendants to 'natural persons' (i.e. individuals, excluding organizations or associations) and Article 7 sheets home responsibility to all who 'planned, instigated, ordered, committed or otherwise aided and abetted' the offences. The Nuremberg precedents are repeated: there is no sovereign immunity for heads of state or government agents; commanders are liable for acts of subordinates if they knew of them or failed to take reasonable measures to prevent them; 'superior orders' constitute mitigation but not a defence. The rule against double jeopardy, or being tried twice for the same offence ('*non bis in idem*'), is upheld by giving the Hague Tribunal concurrent jurisdiction with national courts, but a primacy over them which it may take by way of a formal request to any national court to defer proceedings in respect of a suspect and hand him over for trial at The Hague. In this important respect, its primary power is much more effective than the 'complementarity' for the ICC (see p. 349).

The organization of the Hague Tribunal is more problematic. The judges – there are three trial courts (of three judges apiece) and a five-judge appeal court – are elected by the General Assembly of the UN, 'taking due account of the adequate representation of the principal legal systems of the world' and 'of the experience of the judges in criminal law, international law and human rights law'. The eleven originally selected had a reasonable range of international law experience, but their human rights experience, if any, was obtained in the service of governments accused of human rights abuses, rather than any voluntary service for organizations like Amnesty. More worrying was the almost total lack of any relevant or recent experience of defending accused persons, which might be thought the most important qualification for a trial role as judge and juror, deciding factual issues based on identification evidence and witness credibility. The statute says nothing about the age of judges: had it been set at seventy, several would have been disqualified.

The prosecutor is an appointee of the Security Council, and Article 16(2) requires that he or she 'shall act independently as a separate organ of the International Tribunal [and] not seek or receive instructions from any Government or any other source'. The Security Council's first choice, Venezuelan Attorney-General Ramón Escobar-Salom, proved a disaster: he delayed taking up the job for five months, then decided to accept a better offer. His irresponsible behaviour put the whole enterprise in peril: it was only saved by the Australian government making available an experienced deputy, Graeme Blewitt, and then by President Mandela persuading Richard Goldstone to forgo his seat on the South African Constitutional Court to provide distinguished leadership. None the less, the Tribunal was excruciatingly slow in getting under way: by the summer of 1995, when the Srebrenica massacre took place, it had not commenced a single trial. Judgment in its first case, *Tadić*, was not delivered until May 1997, with the appeal taking a further two years (it was not decided until July 1999) and subsequent appeals over sentence strung it out until January 2000. Delays of this magnitude may be understandable for a first case, but they are continuing to undermine the confidence in the Tribunal which began to return slowly in 1998, when NATO forces began arresting some important defendants, including General Krstić, charged with ordering some of the butchery at Srebrenica, and later General Galić, charged with directing the murderous mortar fire into Sarajevo. A welcome breach in diplomatic niceties came when Austrian security police arrested the chief-of-staff of the Bosnian Serb army, who had been invited to Vienna as a conference delegate. He was immediately diverted to The Hague, for trial on charges of ordering massacres of Muslims and Croats in northern Bosnia in 1992. Of course there were ambassadorial protests, but the episode served to emphasize the post-Pinochet principle that there must be no hiding place for perpetrators of crimes against humanity.

The Tribunal's main organizational problem stems from Article 11(c), which provides that its registry shall serve both the judges and the prosecutor. Fairness to the defence, and the requirement that justice must be seen to be done, demands a complete separation of the prosecutorial from the judicial function. At The Hague, there is a very real impression that judges and prosecutors are on the same side: they are housed under the same roof and 'serviced' by the same administration and public relations departments, equally committed to the 'success' of the exercise. This was a problem at Nuremberg, where judges and prosecutors fraternized to the exclusion of the German defence lawyers; regrettably, this history has been allowed to repeat itself to some extent at The Hague.

The true measure of the Hague Tribunal's 'success' will not be the number of convictions it records – or even the number of high-ranking defendants it is able to try (trials *in absentia* being excluded by Article 14 of the Covenant). It will be judged, at the end of what will be a very long day, by the standards of fairness it is able to demonstrate – by the extent to which it can avoid the dangers of a 'show trial' epitomized by the *Demjanjuk Case* (see p. 240). The primary reason why Nuremberg commands retrospective respect is that its judges (against the wishes of their Russian brethren) acquitted on many counts and found three defendants to be innocent of all charges on the evidence presented. The presiding judge, Lord Justice Geoffrey Lawrence, was not a great lawyer, but he kept an open mind and gave a scrupulously fair hearing. The first Hague Tribunal president, Antonio Cassese, an Italian professor of international law, was a man of outstanding intellectual breadth (as his Appeals Chamber judgments attest) but had difficulties appreciating the need for judicial impartiality. In February 1995, his impatience caused him to issue a press release demanding the prosecutors issue a 'programme of indictments' to 'meet the expectations of the Security Council and of the world community at large' – hardly appropriate language for a judge whose duty it is to stand above the prosecution and to do justice, irrespective of the world's expectations, let alone the Security Council's. One commentator attributed Cassesse's behaviour to his 'civil law roots, where the prosecutor and the judges are often more or less on the same side, as well perhaps as the *hubris* and inexperience of a law professor turned judge'.[15] The following year, he appeared at an international conference on the Dayton Accords to urge that Serbia be prevented from participation in the Olympic Games in Atlanta, unless it helped to arrest the 'war criminals' Karadžić and Mladić.[16] The question of whether these men were in fact war criminals was for his tribunal to decide, under a statute which presumed them innocent until proven guilty (Article 21(3)). His presumption of their guilt, and agitation for their arrest, would have disqualified him for bias in many domestic legal systems. Frustrating as it was for the judges to wait for suspects to fall into a net that NATO was not prepared to cast (at the time, only eight out of fifty-seven indictees were in the Tribunal's clutches) it was inappropriate for the president to demand their arrest in language which suggested he had made up his mind about their guilt.

The charges against the Serbian and Croatian defendants at The Hague do not infringe the rule against retrospectivity, since they refer to conduct which was at the time contrary to international law and (for the most part) Yugoslavian law as well – the latter generally prescribing the punishment of death, which the Hague Tribunal is not empowered to impose. The rule does not prevent trial by courts or under procedures which did not exist at the time, so the Security Council (in framing the Tribunal statute) and the judges (in drawing up its rules of procedure and evidence) had a free hand, guided by the basic rules for fair trials reflected in human rights conventions. The Anglo-American adversary system of trial (as opposed to the Continental inquisitorial system) was selected as the model, so the statute and rules generally accord 'equality of arms' to the defence, including the right to free legal representation both at trial and during any pre-trial questioning.[17] The accused is 'not to be compelled to testify against himself or to confess' at the investigation or the trial stage, and the prosecutor may only question suspects in the presence of an interpreter after they have been provided with (or at least offered) legal assistance.

They have the right to remain silent, being cautioned that 'any statement you make shall be recorded and may be used in evidence'. Before any trial can take place the prosecutor must submit the indictment to a judge of the Trial Chamber, who can dismiss it if satisfied that no *prima facie* case has been made out.

The rules of procedure and evidence, drafted by the judges, provide a model of 'due process' in criminal courts. The prosecutor has a duty to disclose all evidence upon which he relies to defendants once they have appeared for trial: this obligation, reasonably enough, does not apply in respect of those who remain in hiding. (Radovan Karadžić's counsel was therefore refused access to the evidence used to obtain a warrant for his arrest.) Rule 66(c) permits the prosecutor to approach the Trial Chamber in secret to relieve him from his disclosure duties in respect of information which might prejudice ongoing investigations or 'may be contrary to the public interest or affect security interests of any State' – a formula appropriate for intercept material and the like. It is regrettable that such information must be disclosed to the Trial Chamber in the course of the application, since it may have the effect of prejudicing the judges against the accused. If the prosecution wishes to use it at the trial, it must be disclosed to the defence. In one case, the prosecution was permitted to call, in closed and highly confidential session, a serving diplomat to repeat information clandestinely obtained by his embassy. His government was extremely nervous about him appearing in the witness box, with the defendant and his lawyers present, but so far (except to this extent) there has been no leak. There is no rule against hearsay evidence: sensibly, since the trial is by experts rather than by lay jurors, the court 'may admit any relevant evidence which it deems to have probative value',[18] including evidence of 'any consistent pattern of conduct'.[19]

There is one important limit on what is described as 'evidence obtained by means contrary to internationally protected human rights', namely Rule 95, which is couched in these terms:

No evidence shall be admissible if obtained by methods which cast substantial doubt on its reliability or if its admission is antithetical to, and would seriously damage, the integrity of proceedings.

This ambiguously drafted rule gives the court a wide discretion:

'methods [which] cast substantial doubt on ... reliability' might include confessions extracted by force or threats by soldiers or police, or from witnesses who had been paid by the media for telling their story, or elicited by investigators acting as *agents provocateurs* (see pp. 117–19). Notwithstanding the *prima facie* admissibility of hearsay, one Tribunal judge has already invoked the rule to reject second-hand evidence about what eyewitnesses to a crime said to others.[20] The rule would certainly cover identification evidence obtained by methods which have often proved unreliable (confrontations rather than line-ups, for example), or given by witnesses who had only a fleeting glance.[21] However, it may not include evidence obtained by surreptitious or unlawful means or by invasion of home or privacy – bugging, telephone-tapping, mail-opening, trespass, kidnapping and burglary are not methods prone to produce unreliable evidence, but rather evidence which is all too reliable. Would the admission of such unfairly or unlawfully obtained evidence seriously damage the integrity of the proceedings? On one level it might be argued that any court of law is compromised if it accepts evidence obtained by violence or other illegality, and on the other that clear evidence of the commission of a crime against humanity should always be admissible, even if obtained as a result of a payment, beating or an illegal bugging. The court will have to elucidate the meaning of the rule on a case-by-case basis.

One form of surreptitiously obtained surveillance evidence to which no objection should be taken comprises the satellite photographs and electronic intercepts obtained and analysed by intelligence agencies. This evidence can be devastatingly reliable – as the then US Ambassador to the United Nations, Madeleine Albright, revealed in August 1995 by showing photographs of mass graves taken by a U-2 spy plane after the fall of Srebrenica. The real problem faced by the prosecutors has been to extract such evidence – and it is believed to include satellite pictures of mass killings and telephone intercepts of unlawful commands to commit crimes against humanity – from secretive intelligence agencies which wish to avoid publicizing their methods.[22] The arguments used by the CIA, MI6 and similar agencies to deny the court timely evidence of atrocities are specious, because there is no secret about the role of electronic surveillance: it has replaced the human spy as the mainstay of modern intelligence-gathering. The court's request for access to relevant intercepts by Western intelligence was blocked by Britain, which had a major stake through the operation of GCHQ. It was not until April 1999, after the British prime minister had made the indictment of Slobodan Milošević for crimes against humanity a NATO 'war aim' that his foreign secretary personally handed to the Tribunal prosecutor evidence against the Serb leader gathered by GCHQ through signals intelligence.

The most important question to be asked about the Hague Tribunal is whether it can be fair to defendants like Karadžić, Mladić and Milošević after massive media publicity presuming, and indeed trumpeting, their guilt. This inevitably produces expectations at every level and throughout the world that they will be found guilty, thereby placing a heavy burden on the judges to live up to those expectations by their verdicts. This burden becomes more onerous when some Tribunal judges are required to make a preliminary but public finding of guilt – which is the regrettable consequence of the Rule 61 'procedure in case of failure to execute a warrant'. In cases where an indicted defendant has not been arrested or has not turned up voluntarily for trial, the judge who confirms the indictment should order the prosecutor to submit it to the Trial Chamber:

Upon obtaining such an order the Prosecutor shall submit the indictment to the Trial Chamber in open court, together with all the evidence [and] . . . may also call before the Trial Chamber and examine any witness . . . If the Trial Chamber is satisfied on that evidence, together with such additional evidence as the Prosecutor may tender, that there are reasonable grounds for believing that the accused has committed all or any of the crimes charged in the indictment, it shall so determine [and] . . . shall also issue an international arrest warrant.

What is this, other than a public trial *in absentia*, of suspects who may in due course be arrested and put properly on trial, but by a court which has already found 'reasonable grounds for believing' in their guilt? This finding, of course, reverses the presumption of innocence promised by Article 21(3) of the Statute. Rule 61 was proposed by President Cassese at a time of great frustration, when his court had no defendants to try, and was referred to as the equivalent of US Grand Jury proceedings. However, these remain secret: Rule

61 proceedings must be in open court, so that an indicted suspect will be publicly prejudged prior to his trial, by three judges of the court and by the media. Rule 61 offends the rule against bias, both by requiring a prejudgment of likely guilt and by putting the prosecution evidence, unchallenged, in the public domain. The Tribunal claims that 'Rule 61 is not a trial *in absentia* [because] there is no finding of guilt',[23] which overlooks the fact that there is a determination of likely guilt, by way of a finding of reasonable grounds for judicial belief 'that the accused has committed' a crime for which he has been indicted. Any court which eventually hears the case must be influenced by the judicial identification of the accused as a war criminal. Rule 61 is indefensible – one judge has described it as 'basically an apology for this tribunal's helplessness' – and the Rome Statute rightly eschews it for the International Criminal Court. International arrest warrants, and requests to freeze assets, should be issued as soon as the prosecution can show a *prima facie* case and no finding of 'likely guilt' should be made unless the suspect has eluded justice for several years and there is no reasonable expectation of an arrest. The Rule 61 hearing regarding Karadžić and Mladić lacked the appearance of justice: their lawyers were ordered to sit in the public gallery while prejudicial evidence against their clients was unveiled without challenge, then a ruling that they were presumptively guilty of crimes against humanity was delivered without hearing any argument for the defence, by judges of the very court which then demanded their surrender for an 'unbiased' trial.

At Nuremberg, there was no system for appeal. The Hague Tribunal reflects another development in human rights law by providing a right of appeal against errors of law and fact to a five-judge Appeals Chamber, exercisable by either defence or prosecution. The right of a prosecutor to appeal on questions of fact, however, is unnecessary and oppressive: if two or three experienced judges in the Trial Chamber have delivered a reasoned written judgment in support of a 'not guilty' verdict, it must follow that a 'reasonable doubt' exists. The same mistake was made in drafting the Rome Statute for the International Criminal Court (see p. 363). The Tribunal's second contested trial, over murders of prisoners by Bosnian Croats, resulted in a 500-page judgment which unanimously acquitted one defendant, Zejnil Delalić, but the prosecution – a bad loser – immediately announced an appeal. This kept him in prison, when a reasonable doubt obviously existed about his guilt. The Hague Tribunal is a court supreme unto itself, in the sense that a complaint about its procedures cannot be made to any other curial body. The UN's Human Rights Committee is excluded, because the Optional Protocol to the Convention does not apply to proceedings before international tribunals.[24] Although geographically located in Europe, the Tribunal falls outside the catchment area of the European Court of Human Rights, because its decisions are not the responsibility of any individual state. Given the inevitable closeness between judges and prosecutors and between judges of the Trial and Appeals Chambers, it is regrettable that some form of judicial review proceedings is not available. As an organ of the Security Council it may be that court decisions, at least on jurisdiction, could be tested in the ICJ, but only at the instance of a state and not a defendant.

One of the most notable achievements of the Hague Tribunal for the Former Yugoslavia has been to identify and to stigmatize rape as a war crime rather than a spoil of war. It did not feature in any of the indictments of Nazi war criminals – understandably, because the worst example of tolerated and systematic rape was during the Russian army advance on Germany through eastern Europe, during which an estimated two million women were sexually abused with Stalin's blessing that 'the boys are entitled to their fun'. The rape of civilians was formally outlawed by Article 27 of Geneva Convention IV, but was signally omitted from the 'grave breaches' regime in Article 147. The systemic rape of an estimated 200,000 Bengali women by Pakistani soldiers in 1971 went entirely unpunished, and although the crime was widely committed by the military and by Fraph in Haiti under Cedras it was readily amnestied by UN negotiators in 1995. The Hague Tribunal has restored it as a war crime, and as a crime against humanity too, when committed on a widespread scale with a preplanned tactical purpose. In the case of some Serb battalions, gang rapes of Muslim women took place in public in order to terrorize and demoralize the local population by threatening 'to make Chetnik babies'.[25] By indicting Serb police who participated in and oversaw the abuse of Muslim women prisoners in a 'rape camp' at Foca, the Tribunal established the offence as a war crime. In December 1998, the Tribunal delivered an important judgment in the *Anto Furundžija* ['Jokers Wild'] *Case*, where the commander of a Croatian paramilitary force, 'The Jokers', was held liable as a 'co-perpetrator' of torture for permitting a soldier to rape a woman during an interrogation session at which he presided.

It should be emphasized, however (and this point has been obscured in some Tribunal judgments), that what justifies international condemnation is not an opportunistic act of violation of individual women, but the deployment of rape as a tool of ethnic cleansing. Bosnian Serb militiamen were permitted to rape publicly, so as to humiliate Muslim women in front of witnesses – their village neighbours and fellow camp inmates – in the knowledge that the victims would thereafter carry a cultural stigma. Rape becomes a crime against humanity not because of the act itself, but when it is permitted or committed for political ends – in the Bosnian episodes in 1992, as obscene public exhibitions of the scattering of Serbian seed. The Hague Tribunal has been criticized for giving too much fashionable attention to rape (which as war crimes go is not as serious for women as the massacre of their husbands and children),[26] and in some cases it has failed to insist on proper proof of a racist or other political motive. In the *Celebići Case*, for example, a trial chamber seemed to argue that every rape of a woman (although not, curiously, of a man) was by definition torture, irrespective of motive.[27] This is to blur an important distinction: an act which is wicked in itself becomes especially wicked (that is, a crime against humanity) when deployed systematically and for political ends. Two judges in the *Tadić Case* even ruled at one point that a man could be convicted of rape on the word of an anonymous accuser – a fundamental breach of the right to a fair trial.[28] These mistakes should in due course be corrected, and it does appear that the Tribunal's rape indictments may have had some deterrent effect: the mass rapes which were a phenomenon of the early stages of the Bosnian conflict have not recurred, although this may equally be due to a command perception that the international disgust these atrocities attracted outweighed their domestic value as a measure of ethnic terror.

THE TADIĆ CASE

Duško Tadić was forty when he stood in the Hague dock, the first accused to face a truly international criminal court. Born to a prominent Serb family in a small town in Bosnia-Hercegovina, he had excelled at school in karate and made a living teaching it before opening a popular café: the town, and his customers, were mainly Muslims, with whom he had excellent relations until ancient blood hatreds were stirred up in 1990. The nation – Yugoslavia – was fracturing along ethnic lines, as manipulative politicians like Milošević commandeered the media to urge revenge for historic wrongs. There were plenty of those, suppressed for the previous forty-five years by Marshal Tito: the bloody battles with the Turks (i.e. Muslims) over the centuries; the massacre of 250,000 Serbs by the Nazi-supporting Ustashi (i.e. the Croats) in 1941, avenged in turn by the murder of 100,000 Croatians by Tito's partisans (Serbian communists) in 1945. Now the initiative was taken by heirs to the Chetniks – the Serbian nationalist fighters who got it (and gave it) in the neck from all sides during the Second World War. Tadić's father had been one of them, and his mother was a survivor of Ustashi concentration camps.

As ethnic tensions rose, fanned by rabid Serb politicians on radio and television stations which broadcast anti-Muslim and anti-Croat propaganda, Tadić became a typical recruit for Serbian nationalism. His café began to attract like-minded Chetniks from far around: they dressed in paramilitary outfits, gave nationalist salutes, and generally behaved with the puerility and crudity which racist causes throughout the world seem to attract. They supported Serb paramilitaries called 'The Wolves' and 'The Tigers' (fascist killers always seem to identify with ravening animals) and their song, 'We are going to kill all of the *balijas* [an offensive word for Muslims], fuck the *balija*'s mother', was all too prophetic. Tadić began to hero-worship Milošević, to the point of announcing that his next son would be named Slobodan after him. He became at the same time a devout orthodox Christian (the better to hate his former Muslim friends) and went into local politics. By the summer of 1992, he was leader of the nationalist clique which had taken over the town, and was in charge of 'population resettlement' – a euphemism for getting rid of its Muslim majority.

The above facts were found by the court, and it is a regrettable oversight that its statute gives it no power to order psychiatric reports after a conviction: the mental pathology of Bosnian Serb war criminals is more interesting than their crimes. There can be no doubt about Tadić's guilt: he was well-known locally, and the evidence of witnesses who recognized him from Omarska concentration camp rang true. He took an active part in ethnic cleansing, by detaining Muslim civilians, separating the men and boys from the women and old men, and beating the former then assisting the deportation of the latter. Although he was not a regular soldier (he worked part-time, as a traffic policeman), he was allowed the run of Omarska, the nearby concentration camp for Muslim men and boys, where he delighted in arranging severe beatings and grotesque forms of torture (on one occasion, forcing an inmate to chew off another prisoner's testicles and discharging a fire extinguisher into another prisoner's mouth). He was involved in similar brutalities (including rape) at Trnopolje, a prison for Muslim women. In all probability he was a member of the 'shooting parties' which executed Muslims in this period, although the Tribunal, lacking evidence, acquitted him on these charges. Tadić was a licensed thug, a freelance torturer, an enthusiastic participant in the persecution and degradation of hundreds of civilians on account of their religion and their race. His defence to the numerous charges, all alleging instances of brutality and torture, was one of alibi: 'I was not there at the time.' He claimed, for example, never to have visited Omarska, even though the evidence against him was overwhelming. It came from dozens of people who knew him well (some had been to school with him, others he had taught karate) and recognized him at the scene of his crimes: they had no motive to lie about him.

But Duško Tadić was no Hermann Göring. He was a coward – a bullyboy who enjoyed strutting the camps torturing defenceless prisoners in the Serb dominated summer of 1992, but when in the following year the war became more bloody, he could not face enlistment. He was called up for military service so he fled to Germany, where he lived in Munich at a club run by his brother. Here Tadić was identified in the street by one of his victims, arrested by the

German police and in due course transferred to become the first defendant in the Hague Tribunal's cells. His lawyers – an experienced Dutch firm, and some English barristers (who insisted, somewhat comically, on wearing wigs) – were given every opportunity, first to challenge the jurisdiction of the court, and then to cross-examine prosecution witnesses and call evidence to support the defence. The Serbian Republic was reluctant to co-operate with the prosecution, which meant that most of its witnesses were refugees living in the West and had to be brought to The Hague, although later in the trial the court was permitted to take evidence (mainly from defence witnesses) by video link from Banja Luka. On 7 May 1997, the Tribunal found Tadić guilty on eleven counts of crimes against humanity; it dismissed eleven further counts of Geneva Convention 'grave breaches' on the technical ground that they had not been proved to have been committed in international conflict and it rejected nine counts – the most serious alleging participation in mass killings – on the ground of insufficient evidence.

This vile man will go down in history as the person whose case settled the principles and scope of international criminal law at the end of the twentieth century. The most interesting question must be whether he was worth it: an ordinary Serb turned into a vicious torturer by two or three years of racist propaganda, but hardly a person with any command authority or ability to influence events. In so far as a virtue may be made of his very ordinariness – he represents a large class of Bosnian Serbs outside the army who 'did their bit' to help with the torture, murder or deportation of Muslims – then he takes on a symbolic capacity, a scapegoat almost, for the community of which he was part. His punishment is less an example of individual responsibility than of collective guilt. This central problem did trouble the Appeals Chamber, when it finally pronounced Tadić's punishment on 26 January 2000. Despite his heinous behaviour, it had to concede that 'his level in the command structure, when compared to that of his superiors, or the very architects of the strategy of ethnic cleansing, was low'. He was given a maximum sentence of twenty years, with a minimum incarceration period of ten. (The 'very architects', presumably, will receive life imprisonments that really mean life.)

The trial itself was reassuring, in that it showed that international criminal justice can operate acceptably and effectively (so long as the delays can be reduced in the future). The Trial Chamber's three judges were Gabrielle Kirk MacDonald, a no-nonsense American trial judge who later took over from Cassesse as Tribunal president; Sir Ninian Stephen, an outstanding intellect and former High Court judge from Australia; and Lal Chand Vorah, one of Malaysia's dwindling band of competent jurists. They were working from a shared common law tradition which required objective findings of fact and evidential rulings which maintained the 'equality of arms' principle of adversary trial. Their 300-page final judgment was a measured and impartial finding of historical fact: the *Tadić Case* decision stands as the most authoritative analysis so far of evidence about the factors which brought such a barbaric war to the Balkans, and about the role of Belgrade in orchestrating the slide into such a war with mindless racism. War crimes tribunals must avoid the show trial danger of propagating one version of history for 'educational' purposes (see the *Demjanjuk Case*, p. 240), but also try to lay bare so much of the truth about the origins and nature of the conflict as to destroy myths which might arise among future generations. As Nuremberg demonstrates, this is the most valuable byproduct of an adjudication process which sifts evidence and produces an objective account of what really happened, and the court's judgment in *Tadić* fulfils this important purpose.

The court's principal achievement, however, was to produce a verdict which was demonstrably fair. Tadić was guilty, on overwhelming evidence, of the eleven Geneva 'grave breaches' counts which the court dismissed on the technical legal ground that they had not been proved to have connection with an 'international' conflict (its decision on this point was reversed on appeal). He was probably – although not certainly – guilty of several of the nine counts it rejected for lack of sufficient evidence. Those verdicts displeased the prosecutors as much as the convictions dissatisfied the defence, and both sides appealed. Yet the very care with which the verdicts were reached, and the court's refusal to bend the law against an obnoxious defendant, gave its judgment credibility and impartiality.

In one respect, however, the Tribunal allowed its natural sympathy for victims to override its fundamental duty of fairness to the defendant. It rightly rejected a defence argument that 'one witness is no witness', i.e. that all charges, and especially charges of a sexual assault, require corroboration. However, it wrongly permitted certain prosecution witnesses to remain anonymous, their names and personal details known to the court but not to the defendant or his lawyer. The matter arose because some witnesses who claimed to have suffered assaults were reluctant to testify in public for fear of reprisals. The statute empowers the court to 'order appropriate measures for the privacy and the protection of witnesses, provided that the measures are consistent with the rights of the accused'.[29] To this end, the court could order that their evidence be heard behind closed doors, or by closed circuit television (so that the witness would not be in the same room as the accused) or through technical devices which would distort voices and facial features. This could effectively conceal their identity from all except the defendant and his counsel, whose right to know an accuser's identity is fundamental to the fairness of the trial, as the European Court of Human Rights has repeatedly held.[30] Article 20 of the Hague Statute requires that trials be conducted 'with full respect for the rights of the accused': plainly, justice is neither done nor seen to be done to an accused who is not permitted to know the identity of crucial prosecution witnesses – a point carefully and unanswerably made by the dissenting judge, Sir Ninian Stephen.

Judges MacDonald and Vorah made a fundamental error in their ruling that Tadić was not allowed to know the names (or even the nicknames) of certain crucial witnesses. They claimed to be entitled to ignore the European Court rulings, for no better reason than that 'the International Tribunal is adjudicating crimes which are considered so horrific as to warrant universal jurisdiction. The International Tribunal is, in certain respects, comparable to a military tribunal, which often has limited rights of due process.' But the Hague Tribunal is not comparable to a court martial and, even if it were, fundamental defence rights should not be sacrificed. If the crimes are regarded as 'so horrific', then all the more reason for extending basic rights to defendants. The majority judgment calls throughout for 'a balance' between the right to a fair trial and the need to protect witnesses. But the fair trial right is, most certainly for 'horrific' crimes, absolute and uncompromisable. The judges speak of the Tribunal's 'unique legal framework' as if this excuses unfairness to defendants, but its uniqueness obviously demands more, not less, attention to due process, since it is standard-setting for criminal courts throughout the world. It drew on several *amicus* briefs from women's organizations, apparently explaining how 'non-disclosure to the accused can be made compatible with the right to a fair trial and is justified by policy considerations in sexual assault cases'. But this is nonsense: no trial can be fair if the defendant is not allowed to know his accuser. No 'policy consideration' can justify an unfair trial: the majority shrugs and offers the lame excuse that 'even criminal justice is not perfect', ignoring its duty to strive to make it so. Its lamentable decision was rejected by a Trial Chamber of three different judges in the *Blaskić Case*, who expressly agreed with Judge Stephen's dissent in *Tadić*: it is to be hoped that this will prevail in all future cases.[31] If accusers cannot face giving evidence in a closed court or even on closed circuit television, or being cross-examined in the limited manner permitted by the Statute (Rule 9 excludes questions as to prior sexual conduct), then the charge cannot proceed: no court set up to serve human rights can achieve that goal by permitting a fundamental breach of the right of fair trial.

The danger of granting anonymity, especially to witnesses whose testimony might be motivated by malice, was dramatically illustrated in the *Tadić* trial itself by the perjury of 'Witness L'. This man – real name Dragan Opacić – had been made available to the prosecutors by the Muslim authorities in Bosnia-Hercegovina, where he had been convicted of serious crime. Entirely on the strength of his proffered evidence, Tadić was accused of executing thirty male prisoners in an orchard adjacent to Trnopolje camp, and with raping twelve of the camp's female detainees. He became the prosecutor's star witness: the court granted him special protection and allowed him to testify to it in secret for three days. The prosecutors were sure he was telling the truth – he had even taken them to where some of the bodies were buried. And Opacić swore he had been present when Tadić killed his father – a sight he would obviously never forget. 'But isn't your father still alive?' the defence asked on day three. Opacić insisted that he had watched him die. 'But this man is your father,' said the cross-examiner, calling to court an old man who rushed to embrace the witness. At this point the prosecution called for an adjournment, then sheepishly returned to ask the court to disregard all that 'Witness L' had said. Denying on oath any knowledge of the father who is embracing you deserves an entry in the Guinness Book of Perjurors. This episode damaged the Tribunal, although not as seriously as it would have had his perjury been uncovered after its judgment. It should serve as a warning to future international courts: no matter how importunate the prosecutor in requesting witness anonymity or secret hearings, publicity is the greatest protection against perjury and should not be discarded, save with the agreement of the defence or in respect of persons who have no conceivable motive to bear false witness against the accused.

Jurisprudentially, the *Tadić Case* is important for defining the preconditions for international humanitarian law. There must in the first place be an 'armed conflict', i.e. an intense conflict between organized parties as distinct from 'banditry, unorganized or short-lived insurrections or terrorist activities'. Secondly, there must be a sufficient link established by the prosecution between the conduct charged as a crime against humanity and the armed conflict. Thirdly, where the charge relates to a war crime under the Geneva Conventions, it must additionally be proven that the armed conflict is international in character and the victims were persons protected by the Conventions. The test to be applied under this third element is whether a party to the conflict (in *Tadić*, the Bosnian Serb forces) were co-ordinating and co-operating with a foreign power (Milošević's Serbia) to such an extent that international force was being used against the other party (the Muslim force of Bosnia and Hercegovina). The Trial Chamber had acquitted Tadić because Milošević was not in 'command and control' of the Bosnian Serbs, but that was too strict a test: a sufficient link, the Appeals Chamber ruled, was provided by the fact that Milošević trained, equipped and maintained his Bosnian Serb allies. This sufficed to make the conflict 'international' so as to attract the 'grave breaches' regime of Geneva.

Most of Tadić's crimes were contrary to the 'laws and customs of war' which apply to all armed conflicts, whether international or not. These cover all acts in times of civil war which outrage 'elementary considerations of humanity' when inflicted upon civilians, or even soldiers who are placed *hors de combat* by detention or hospitalization. Thus war crimes can be characterized as crimes against humanity whenever committed 'on a widespread and systematic basis, and in pursuance of a policy'. The thrust of this requirement is to exclude from the class of crimes against humanity random atrocities which are not part of a plan or a campaign against the civilian population. However, the *Tadić* court approved the *Vukovar Hospital Decision* that a single act could qualify as a crime against humanity as long as there is a link with the widespread or systematic attack on a civilian population.[32]

The court identifies the rationale for crimes against humanity: they 'so shock the conscience of mankind and warrant intervention by the international community . . . because they are not isolated, random acts of individuals but rather result from a deliberate attempt to target a civilian population'.[33] This presumes there must be a *policy* – to terrorize or discriminate against classes of civilian – and that it will generally emanate, as in Nazi Germany, from the State itself. The policy which makes crimes carried out in its name inhuman need not emanate from *de jure* government: it may be that of 'forces which, although not those of the legitimate government, have *de facto* control over, or are able to move freely within, defined territory'. It follows that, under international law, crimes against humanity *can* be committed 'by a terrorist group or organization' if it is large and powerful, effectively controlling territory without permanently occupying it. The court approves the view of the International Law Commission, whose draft code on crimes against humanity recognizes 'the possibility that private individuals with *de facto* power or organized in criminal groups might also commit the kind of systematic or mass violations of human rights'.[34] This would include the atrocities committed by terrorists gangs if they are systematic and widespread. The bombings of airliners or of civilian shopping precincts by the IRA or the Medellin cartel or the forces of Osmara Bin Laden may on this view be accounted crimes against humanity, even though they lack one element hitherto thought essential, namely the abuse of sovereign power.

INDIVIDUAL RESPONSIBILITY

The accused, to be convicted, must be proved to have some knowledge of, and sympathy for, the inhumane policy, so as to give him a mental element more culpable than that of the ordinary criminal. This was readily proved against Tadić, from evidence of his racist leanings and his activity in nationalist politics. On this point, however, the Tribunal judgment is unacceptably fuzzy – it seems prepared to convict a defendant who is merely *aware* that his crime is also being committed by others on a widespread basis. Surely 'awareness' must include some *approval* of the policy? Otherwise, the crucial distinction between ordinary and extraordinary criminals becomes blurred, and the point of individual responsibility is lost if the mental element for the crime is satisfied merely by proof of collective awareness.

The court turned for legal precedents to the Allied Zone trials which followed Nuremberg, although these were conducted by military tribunals overanxious to convict Nazis and collaborators regarded as 'collectively responsible'. A modern international court needs to be more careful about principles of criminal responsibility than the US military tribunal in the *Mauthausen Case*,[35] which found every single worker in a concentration camp culpable for the gassing of Jews, whether they had any part in it or not; or the French Permanent Military Tribunal, which sentenced to death persons who had informed on members of the Resistance, without having any part in their subsequent torture by Nazi interrogators.[36] The *Tadić* tribunal erroneously approved these decisions, which are really examples of 'victor's justice' (i.e. revenge) imposed without proper consideration of the limits of criminal responsibility. It was on safer ground in approving the approach of the *Zyklon-B Case*, where a British military tribunal ruled that manufacturers of a poison gas commonly used to kill rats were guilty of a war crime if they supplied the gas to the concentration camps with actual knowledge that it would be used to kill humans and not vermin.[37] They became a party to the Holocaust by making and selling the gas for this inhuman purpose, and bore a culpability different in kind, rather than degree, from the concentration camp gardener or cook. These military precedents must be handled with care, although the *Zyklon-B Case* was worth disinterring, as a warning to the modern German businessmen who may again be tempted (as they were before the Gulf War) to supply large quantities of a Zyklon-B derivative to Saddam Hussein.

Duško Tadić was not employed at Omarska concentration camp; he was a local thug allowed to enter occasionally to torture prisoners. He was implicated, however, in the ethnic cleansing of his village, by 'calling out' Muslim civilians from homes, forcibly separating the women and children and elderly from the men and boys, and dispatching these two groups to their different camps. These acts took place during an armed conflict as part of a widespread and systematic attack on civilians in furtherance of a political policy of racial discrimination with which Tadić sympathized and to which he attached himself as an individual. The court held that this behaviour amounted to a crime against humanity compendiously described as 'persecution', namely repeated inhuman acts of harassment, torment, oppression and discrimination intended to cause suffering and inflicted because the victims belonged to a different ethnic group from their persecutors. There are ample precedents from Nuremberg and the Allied military tribunals for such an offence, although there it tended to be charged against officials of much higher status. The Nazi judges, for example, were convicted of it for systematically bending the law against Jews and Poles and implementing it in an arbitrary and brutal fashion to further Nazi policy.[38] At Nuremberg the rabid anti-Semitic propagandist Julius Streicher was held to have committed a crime against humanity by inciting the murder and extermination of Jews: he was deemed to have persecuted them through his editorship of official and quasi-official publications. Judges and editors are at one end of the spectrum, exercising a power to persuade which footsoldiers like Tadić, at the other end, actually put into practice. All are guilty: their responsibility as individuals may differ in degree, but not in kind.

Tadić's responsibility, however, was at the lower end: he deserved punishment just enough (given the hundreds who deserved it more) to be made an example. But Tadić must be seen as a baseline, a person with a level of culpability below which universal jurisdiction should not be attracted, otherwise the Tribunal will itself be open to the charge of discrimination: it pulls in an occasional piranha while all the sharks swim free. Mladić and Karadžić remained in safe retirement in the ski resorts to which few skiers now resort in the Serbian Republic; the tribunal's recitation of the factual background to Tadić's crimes lists a number of army commanders and prison commandants who were far more culpable. This makes the judgment on Tadić an unsatisfactory beginning. It is the tale of a café in Kozara which changed over eighteen months from a happy multiethnic meeting place to a den resounding to the racist obscenities of nationalist thugs. Who was responsible for that sea change? Tadić as an individual bears enough responsibility to go to prison, but the men who polluted and changed his mind – the 'intellectual authors' of the genocide in former Yugoslavia – remained outside the reach of the enforcers of international law, until Operation Horseshoe in Kosovo in 1999.

The first Tribunal president, Antonio Cassesse, argued that criminalization of individuals was necessary to prevent the 'primitive and archaic concept of collective responsibility' gaining hold among future generations. Collective responsibility is not an archaic concept, however, because it is relevant to non-combatants who complicitly or unquestioningly support a government which directs atrocities. This may be unfortunate if it works to perpetuate group hatreds, but it is a consequence of genocide that only time, and not a tribunal, can erase. Indeed, the Hague Tribunal, by prosecuting insignificant camp followers like Tadić, only gives more credence to this 'primitive' notion. Tadić is not in himself important; perhaps what really justifies his pursuit and punishment is that he is a representative example of a people the majority of whom actively supported ethnic cleansing. The rationale for establishing the Hague Tribunal was that it would assist the peace process by punishing at least some of those guilty of atrocities. The argument is that by so doing, feelings of hatred and resentment can be satisfied to an extent which may make them less likely to erupt in the future. As Cassesse said in his first report to the UN General Assembly in 1994:

How could one hope to restore the rule of law and the development of stable, constructive and healthy relations among ethnic groups, within or between independent states, if the culprits are allowed to go unpunished? Those who have suffered, directly or indirectly, from their crimes are unlikely to forgive or set aside their deep resentment. How could a woman who had been raped by servicemen from a different ethnic group or a civilian whose parents or children had been killed in cold blood quell their desire for vengeance if they knew that the authors of these crimes were left unpunished and allowed to move around freely, possibly in the same town where their appalling actions had been perpetrated? The only civilized alternative to this desire for revenge is to render justice . . .[39]

Many diplomats – especially from France and Britain – feared that the behaviour of an independent tribunal, under its own impetus and uncontrolled by diplomats, might hinder timely peace initiatives by threatening some would-be peacemakers with jail. The evidence does not bear this out: the creation of the Tribunal and its slow progress towards its first trials does not seem to have had any damaging effect on the peace process. The indictments of Karadžić and Mladić led to their gradual loss of power and position, and their absence from Dayton did not hamper the peace agreement. The Dayton Accords, which required all parties to co-operate in the arrest and surrender of persons indicted by the Tribunal, were negotiated without this condition becoming a sticking point. Gradually, NATO began to net some big fish – police chiefs, concentration camp commandants, men charged with genocide for giving orders to kill hundreds of Muslims. With their transfer to the Hague cells in 1998–9, joining a group of indicted Bosnian Croats surrendered by Croatia in 1997 after Western economic pressure, the Tribunal started to look like an equal-handed and significant player in the peace process. Whether it will have much of a positive effect is difficult, and too early, to say, although one reason that has been advanced for the relative absence of reprisals against Bosnian Serbs is the sight of justice being done, slowly but on television, from The Hague. Had an International Criminal Court been already in place, with powers to arrest political and military leaders (beginning with Milošević) after the war crimes of 1992, it may be that the massacre in Srebrenica and ethnic cleansing in Kosovo would not have happened. For want of proof to the contrary, the official position that the Hague Tribunal is a proper instrument to restore peace and security, under Chapter VII of the UN Charter, is justified.

That it has not worked as well as it could, and should, after its inception in 1993 cannot entirely be blamed on the UN's incompetent bureaucracy and inadequate funding, or on NATO's quite deliberate failures to arrest Karadžić and Mladić or to make Milošević's surrender a condition of the Kosovo peace. The delays, acceptable at the outset, have become intolerable, and some responsibility must be laid at the door of the prosecutor. For this reason, the Appeals Chamber was right in 1999 to apply the common law principle of abuse of process to order the release of Jean-Boso Barayagwiza for 'cumulative breaches of the accused's rights': he had been held in detention for almost four years and still no Arusha trial in sight. What made this a hard case to bear was the fact that the defendant was highly placed in the Hutu genocide machine and the evidence against him was so strong that it had already persuaded a court in New York to award massive damages in a civil action brought by relatives of his victims. The Rwanda tribunal managed to try only six defendants in its first five years, although those convicted (and others who have pleaded guilty) are at least commanders rather than footsoldiers. Its real test will come with the trial of Colonel Theoneste Bagosora, allegedly the chief planner of the genocide.

The tribunal for ex-Yugoslavia completed eight contested trials by March 2000. The most significant crime it punished was the My Lai-like destruction of the village of Ahmici and its Muslim community (116 inhabitants, including thirty-three women and children) by a squad of Bosnian Croat soldiers known as 'The Jokers'. Their unit commander was jailed for twenty-five years, but Antonio Cassesse, presiding over the Trial Chamber, regretted that the 'major culprits' were not before the court.[40]

The first 'major culprit' to be convicted – ironically, on the very day that General Pinochet returned to Chile – was General Tihomir Blaskić, put away for forty-five years for his command responsibility for massacres in 1993 of Muslim families in Ahmici and other villages in the Lašva valley (about thirty kilometres north-west of Sarajevo). Blaskić feigned ignorance of the barbarous behaviour of his troops, blaming poor communications and maverick units like 'The Jokers', but the Tribunal found he was imbued with Tudjman's 'eternal dream' of a Croatia expanded by conquest and had given orders to attack undefended villages, mosques and targets of no military interest. His guilt of crimes against humanity and 'grave breaches' of the Geneva Conventions came from the use of terror against Muslims: women, old men and children were purposefully shot down as they fled, or burned alive as they cowered in their houses. Blaskić's hand-wringing defence was undermined by the fact that, when told about them, he did nothing to investigate these outrages, using propaganda instead to blame them on the Serbs. As generals go, Blaskić was a junior and his crimes, though black, pale by comparison with those of Mladić or Milošević. Since forty-five years' imprisonment is about the highest specific penalty that can sensibly be given, leaders higher than Blaskić in a command chain can expect life sentences.

The Hague Tribunal has established some significant benchmarks and persuaded most impartial observers that international criminal justice is here to stay as a measurable contribution to global security. The court's prosecutors and judges have shown a capacity to get at the truth through the fog of war in complicated and distant countries, and to deal fairly with unprepossessing defendants. Its moderation and professionalism belie the fears about an International Criminal Court which were whispered by diplomats and then bellowed obsessively by the Pentagon before the Rome Conference (see chapter 11). The UN, which initially starved it of funds, now views the Hague Tribunal as one of the few feathers in its cap. The Tribunal's most serious problem has been NATO's failure to bring in the 'major culprits' it has indicted, and there are real dangers lurking in its dependence on the Security Council. Some indication of trouble in store was the behaviour of China and Russia after Louise Arbour's resignation: they truculently refused to accept any chief prosecutor who was a national of a NATO country. Carla del Ponte, a Swiss prosecutor mainly of Italian Mafia members, emerged as a compromise. Like her predecessors, she has great difficulty in extracting from Western security services the intercept and intelligence material needed to incriminate 'major culprits'. (Many suspect a French connection in leaks of the Tribunal's work to the Serbs, and claim it is no coincidence that most of its absent indictees live undisturbed in the French-patrolled areas of the Serbian republic.)

By the year 2000 the Tribunal had three operational trial chambers in The Hague, conducting twelve trials, and a further three in Arusha; it had a surfeit of cells awaiting prisoners in Italy, Finland and Norway. The Hague Tribunal was about to start the trials of Bosnian Serb generals who attacked Srebrenica and Sarajevo. It had issued its first citation for contempt, fining one of Tadić's lawyers, Milan Vujin, US $10,000 for fabricating evidence. Although its existence has not stopped atrocities, there are signs that it is beginning to exert a certain fear: Serb killers in Kosovo took greater care than previously to hide the evidence (by burning corpses and even burying them in graves) and in East Timor the militias carried victims hundreds of miles to mass graves over the border, for fear that war crimes investigators would catch up with them. It may be a back-handed compliment, but at least the Hague Tribunal is making killers aware of the potential reach of international justice.

Slobodan Milošević is widely held to bear heavy personal responsibility for a war that raged for more than seven years and cost a quarter of a million lives. His command responsibility in this period may seem no more criminal than that of Croatia's president, Tudjman, who died in December 1999 unindicted for the massacres and extirpations his troops perpetrated on the Serbs in the Krajina and elsewhere. Yet one theme of the dawning 'age of enforcement' for human rights is its 'catch as catch can' quality; Tudjman got away, and Milošević remains to be caught. There is substantial evidence requiring judicial assessment that he actually directed his Bosnian Serb surrogates, and that he personally approved the infamous killing of 200 patients and staff at Vukovar hospital at the outset of hostilities. But when his indictment was finally approved at The Hague in May 1999, these crimes did not feature. He was accused of bearing command responsibility for the Kosovo atrocities and of using the start of the bombing campaign as an excuse for unleashing mass murder (almost 10,000 victims) and mass extirpation (1.4 million refugees). Milošević, in the dock, could not claim sovereign immunity, since it is expressly excluded by Article 7(2) of the Hague Tribunal Statute. No doubt his answer to the charges of responsibility for the massacres would be that he knew nothing about them. He would have to argue that the mass expulsion of ethnic Albanians was a justifiable act of self-defence (the removal of a potential fifth column) in response to an unlawful attack by NATO upon Serbian sovereignty. It is this argument which might require the Hague Tribunal to rule on NATO's assertion (discussed in chapter 11) that it was lawful to breach Serbia's sovereignty in a humanitarian emergency in order to prevent (or to punish) an ongoing crime against humanity.

The trial of Milošević may well test the Hague Tribunal as much as it would test the defendant. 'Victor's justice' is not what it used to be, at Nuremberg and Tokyo: for a start, Milošević could object to being tried by any judge from a NATO country and the court would be quite capable of questioning the legality of NATO's bombing and demanding proof beyond reasonable doubt that Operation Horseshoe was under way, with Milošević's approval, before it started. The court is independent enough to have this capacity to embarrass governments, which is why so many of them are very uneasy about the consequences of international justice. For this reason, NATO did not make it a war aim to bomb Milošević into the dock – only back to the conference table. It will take a Milošević trial to put fledgling international criminal law to a test it still needs to pass, by sloughing off the rebuke of 'victor's justice' and delivering verdicts which depend on evidence rather than the national allegiances of judges.

9

The International Criminal Court

On 17 July 1998 in Rome, 120 nations voted to adopt a statute creating an International Criminal Court – the culmination of a fractious five-week diplomatic conference. Twenty-one nations abstained, but only seven were opposed – although these included the United States, China, Israel and India, representing a massive concentration of people and of power. The Rome Statute is a long and detailed document containing 128 articles: it will not come into effect until ratified by sixty states – a lengthy procedure unlikely to eventuate for several years (by March 2000 it had gathered ninety-three signatures but only seven ratifying state parties). It was meant to be the millennium moment for a human rights movement which had become fashionable since the Gulf War: the UN worked at breakneck speed to produce an agreed treaty in only twenty-seven months. Pre-millennium tension played its part, as this Diplomatic Conference of Plenipotentiaries (with hundreds of NGOs cheering them on) made feverish compromises in the days and even hours before the deadline, creating a lowest common denominator court in time for the photo opportunity finish scheduled for 17 July. It should have marked the triumph of international law over superpower expediency, but in fact it demonstrated how far the human rights movement had yet to go before reality would catch up with its rhetoric.

The idea of a world criminal court received its first concrete shape in 1937, when a draft statute for a court to try international terrorists was produced by the League of Nations. After the Nuremberg and Tokyo tribunals, the UN made a passing reference to an 'international penal tribunal' in the 1948 Genocide Convention and draft statutes were produced over the next few years by the International Law

Commission. But the project soon went into the deep freeze of the Cold War, and was not brought out again until the 1980s, when Gorbachev suggested it as a measure against terrorism and Trinidad urged it as a means of combating drug trafficking. The General Assembly asked the ILC to resume work, hurrying it along in 1993 after the favourable public response to its creation of a War Crimes Tribunal for the Former Yugoslavia. The ILC draft was delivered in 1994, and the following year the General Assembly set up a 'preparatory committee' to canvass agreement on a text which could be submitted to a treaty conference in 1998. The committee met for five gruelling sessions prior to the Rome Conference, over a period when many governments, under pressure from NGOs active in the human rights arena, came to support the creation of an International Criminal Court.

What kind of court should be created, however, was a matter of wide disagreement, reflected in the 1,700 'alternative choices' within the draft submitted to state representatives in Rome. At the commencement of the conference, the delegations fell into three main categories. The 'like-minded' group of forty-two nations, led by Canada and Germany (and joined, since the advent of the Blair government, by the previously hostile UK), wanted a powerful prosecutor and a court genuinely independent of the Security Council, endowed with universal jurisdiction over war crime suspects anywhere in the world. They wanted, in other words, a court that would work. The United States initially wanted a court, but one that would never work against the interests of the United States. The model preferred by the US, joined by China and France, was a court controlled by the Security Council, where they could use their superpower veto to stop any embarrassing prosecutions. The third group – all the usual suspects, like Iraq, Iran, Libya and Indonesia – did not want a court at all. This group had, surprisingly, been led at preparatory committee sessions by India, its motives becoming apparent shortly before the Rome Conference when it test-exploded a nuclear weapon.

The Rome Conference was remarkable for the intensity and detail of the lobbying campaigns mounted by NGOs, led by Amnesty and Human Rights Watch. Some 175 of these organizations had representatives in Rome, while by the end 800 bodies in all were involved in pressurizing governments. For human rights campaigners, of course, the creation of a court to punish human rights violations is a consummation devoutly to be wished, but what was truly ironic was their zeal for a court so tough that it would actually violate the basic human rights of its defendants. Thus Amnesty International, in its main briefing paper, argued for an all-powerful prosecutor because 'State practice demonstrates that prosecutors are unlikely to bring cases where the evidence is extremely weak'.[1] Such complacent assertions – the kind that, when made in the past by governments, Amnesty would devote itself to refuting – were accompanied by a call to do away with traditional defences. Amnesty argued that the Rome Statute should abolish the defence of duress, the defence of necessity, even the defence of self-defence, at least unless the defendant could prove (the burden being on him) that he had 'retreated to the utmost'. Insouciance about the danger of miscarriages of justice was common among NGOs like Amnesty, which should have been the first to recognize that the danger of wrongful conviction is greatest when the crime charged is most horrible and unnatural, when the defendants have for years been tried and convicted in the media and when prosecutors and perhaps judges are trying to carve out careers in a growth industry like international human rights. The Rome Conference was no time to worry about how to prevent defendants from being acquitted: all energies should have been directed to ensuring that at least a few were likely to be put on trial in the first place.

On paper, the Rome Statute is impressive and serves in its definitional sections to consolidate many of the conceptual advances in international human rights law which have been traced in earlier chapters of this book. Crimes against humanity are established as offences which may be committed at times of comparative peace as well as internal or international war, while war crimes, for their part, may be committed during internal conflict: common Article 3 of the 1949 Geneva Conventions becomes the basis for individual criminal liability rather than remaining an unenforceable promise that states will not devastate their own people. Sexual violence is indelibly identified as a crime, command responsibility is clearly established as a basis for liability, and (notwithstanding pressure from human rights 'poachers turned gamekeepers') full and indeed generous provision is made for the rights of defendants. The basic achievement – and perhaps it may not go further than this – is to turn the Hague Tribunal into a permanent institution, shorn of its '*ad hoc*' connection with the Balkans and Rwanda, and with some improvements in its procedures and personnel, which will be available for the UN to invoke instantly in respect of future genocidal conflicts.

The five-week conference in Rome was not a great success, despite its photo-call finish. Concessions were made throughout in an effort to keep the United States – today's only true superpower – on side, and those flaws remained embedded in the Statute at the end after the US had denounced it. Through their naivety, the well-intentioned 'like-minded' group allowed America to weaken fatally a court which, by a policy backflip towards the end of the conference, it decided to oppose. Although the Clinton administration had previously advocated a world criminal court and Clinton himself called for it in his 1998 visit to Rwanda, his personal authority was eroded at the crucial time by the Lewinsky affair, and he capitulated to the Pentagon, which had for some months been briefing the military attachés of its allies that the Court was a danger to soldiers of the Western alliance.[2] Jesse Helms, chairman of the Senate Foreign Relations Committee, announced that the Rome Treaty would be 'dead on arrival' in Congress if there was any prospect of the indictment of a single American soldier.

Given the traditional Washington stance that the US is above international law, it should have been obvious to diplomats from the 'like-minded' group that America would not ratify the treaty for years, until the Court was operating to its satisfaction. But they tried desperately to placate Senator Helms (with his demand for '100 per cent protection' of America GIs), going so far as to require a state's consent before one of its nationals could be prosecuted. (Imagine Cambodia, ruled by Pol Pot, surrendering Pol Pot or any of his henchmen for trial.) Even this obeisance to state sovereignty was not enough, in the end, to win the American vote, which was lost when the Conference insisted that the Court should have jurisdiction over UN peacekeepers (which could include American soldiers). Although in principle Blue Helmets should be amenable, this hardly counts as a priority: it was petty insistence on this particular principle, when so many others had been surrendered, which inflamed American paranoia and allowed the Pentagon to get the better of President Clinton. The US delegation rejected the principle of universal jurisdiction over war crimes and crimes against humanity so vehemently that the US defence secretary William Cohen threatened Germany and South Korea with a US troop pull-out if they persisted in their support for its endorsement in the Statute.[3]

In the end, the Rome Statute gives the Court jurisdiction either by remit from the Security Council acting under Chapter VII of the UN Charter, or by consent of the state of which the defendant is a national or in which the crime was committed. These state consent provisions mean that nobody occupying a position of *current* political or military power in any state (even one which has ratified the Treaty) is likely to be put on trial unless they invade another state and commit war crimes on its territory. Any retired war criminal who (like Pinochet in Chile) retains a power base in his state of nationality will in practice be safe, since in retirement they do not constitute a Chapter VII threat to international peace, and their home state will lack the resolve to surrender them to world justice. The class of criminal most likely to be arraigned at The Hague comprises persons who commit barbaric crimes in a cause which has utterly failed, in a country which decides to surrender them because it lacks the facilities to try them itself. Otherwise, the ICC will become a kind of 'permanent *ad hoc*' tribunal, dependent on references from the Security Council to investigate countries like Rwanda and former Yugoslavia, where none of the combatants has superpower support.

The Rome Conference was hardly an advertisement for wise global governance. The Vatican (why should this religious enclave count as a state?) took up valuable time by trying to include drug trafficking as a crime against humanity (hardly apt for a court in The Hague surrounded by cannabis-vending coffee bars) and by fears that a definition which made 'forced pregnancy' a crime might justify abortion. India, having led the opposition to the creation of a court at the preparatory sessions, now demanded an extension of the Court's jurisdiction to punish the users of nuclear weapons. This was a hypocritical attempt to deflect criticism over its nuclear test the previous month, and the proposal's defeat provided India with a pretext for condemning the whole enterprise as an exercise in 'European neo-colonialism'. These puerile posturings (from delegates of India's governing Bharatiya Janata Party) were irresponsible enough, but the gold medal for hypocrisy was won by Israel, a state founded by victims of the worst crime against humanity, in whose memory (and, perhaps, for whose future benefit) the movement to create the Court had been inspired. The Netanyahu government voted against it, as a petulant protest after the Conference agreed to make forced settlement of occupied territory a war crime. Israel had settled Jews in the West Bank and the Gaza Strip after the 1967 Six-day War, but since the Statute is not retrospective, Israel's fears that its leaders might be put on trial were nonsense. Forced population transfers can be a potent means of ethnic cleansing, as Serb actions in Kosovo in early 1999 showed, and Israel's decision to vote against the Court merely because its Statute included this as a potential crime was a betrayal of the memory of the Holocaust.

None the less, the Rome Statute was an achievement of sorts: the best deal the human rights movement could do with the *realpolitik* of state power as the twentieth century drew to a close. It would have been sensible to opt for one of the two competing models – either the independent court system preferred by the 'like-minded' nations but operating initially without US support, or else the court controlled by the Security Council which the United States and China would support because they could veto prosecutions of their nationals or allies. This latter model was obviously wrong in principle, because it offered impunity to suspects protected by superpowers, but in its limited area of operation it would have the funding and logistical support necessary to make its decisions stick. Each model offered, in its own way and within its different limits, a coherent and workable international court which might in time and by the force of its perform-ance have overcome its deficiencies. The mistake made in Rome was to erect a compromise with which America would not compromise, and then quite stupidly (and undiplomatically) to close the door on renegotiation by a clause banning amendments until seven years after the Statute enters into force.[4]

ROME 1998: THE STATUTE

The Preamble to this first stab at global justice is introduced with these mixed metaphors:

Conscious that all peoples are united by common bonds, their cultures pieced together in a shared heritage, and concerned that this delicate mosaic may be shattered at any time . . .

This dire attempt at literary inspiration moves in meaningless progression from bonds to cultural jigsaws to breakable mosaics, images irrelevant to crimes against humanity, which are generally committed in the name of preserving some culture perceived as incapable of coexistence with others. The Preamble continues more prosaically by recalling the 'unimaginable atrocities' (although they are by now all too imaginable) of the twentieth century and then asserting that grave crimes 'threaten the peace, security and well-being of the world' – the factual formula necessary to attract UN intervention under Chapter VII of the Charter. Significantly, the Preamble declares it a 'must' – a moral imperative – that 'the most serious crimes of concern to the international community as a whole must not go unpunished', and announces a determination 'to put an end to impunity' by exercising criminal jurisdiction over perpetrators, initially at a national level. The ICC is established as a permanent court with 'complementary' back-up jurisdiction.

This language (care is taken not to say so in terms) is apt to reflect a universal jurisdiction over crimes against humanity, although the Preamble hurriedly genuflects to state sovereignty by 'emphasizing that nothing in this Statute shall be taken as authorizing any State Party to interfere in an armed conflict in the internal affairs of any State', thereby reassuring governments that it is not encouraging humanitarian intervention or cross-border raiding parties bent on snatching indicted suspects and delivering them to The Hague. The Preamble confines the Court to jurisdiction over 'the most serious crimes of concern to the international community as a whole' and establishes its back-stop role where national justice systems have failed or broken down. The rationale for the Court's creation is found in the belief that crimes 'that deeply shock the conscience of humanity' threaten world peace, or at least 'the well-being of the world' – this is true, in the sense that our psychological well-being suffers from the sight of atrocities by fellow humans. The Court itself is described as an 'independent permanent international criminal court *in relationship with* the United Nations system' – coy phraseology which avoids spelling out the nature of the 'relationship'. Read on, and it emerges that the Security Council is in control: the Court will mainly have jurisdiction over such political leaders as may be thrown its way following intervention by the Council under Chapter VII of the Charter. With this exception, state sovereignty remains sacrosanct, even when that state is riven by civil war: there is no power in the Court or in other states to arrest super-criminals safe behind state lines.

The Court is established by Article 1 as a permanent institution with jurisdiction to try persons its prosecutor accuses of the most serious crimes of international concern. It is endowed with international legal personality, which means that it has the capacity to enter into contracts and commitments necessary for its purposes. However, it may only exercise its statutory functions and powers 'on the territory of any State Party and, by special agreement, on the territory of any other State'. In reality, of course, states which are civilized enough to ratify the Treaty are unlikely to be run by, or to harbour, persons who have committed crimes against humanity – they will generally live or lurk in states which have not signed up for justice. Such states are unlikely to allow the Court and its prosecutor to operate 'by special agreement' on their territory, at least without intense pressure from the World Bank, the IMF and the United States (which combined in 1997 to threaten Croatia with economic collapse unless it surrendered its indicted suspects to the Hague Tribunal).

Article 3 locates the seat of the Court at The Hague – the Netherlands was the only country to volunteer, and was perceived as the natural choice, because it already hosts the International Court of Justice (in a gloomy mock-Gothic mansion) and the Hague International Criminal Tribunal for the Former Yugoslavia (in a nondescript plaza named after Churchill, who was all for shooting, not trying, the Nazi leaders). It is predicted that the ICC will occupy the Hague Tribunal building when its trials are completed – a cost-effective move, although the site (formerly an insurance office) lacks majesty and has no aesthetic qualities to compare with London's Old Bailey or the US Supreme Court or the European Court building in Strasbourg designed by Richard Rogers. Architecture has both symbolic and practical significance: countries where justice is valued have distinct and imposing court buildings, while those where it is preordained or seen as an administrative adjunct of the state generally have courtrooms which are indistinguishable from government offices. The idea that The Hague is symbolically suitable because it is 'the capital of international law' sends exactly the wrong message: this obscure and boring place is where international law failed to thrive, or to make much of a difference, in the twentieth century.

The International Criminal Court should have been located in a historic or else a specially designed building, home to the judges and the registry, but not to the prosecution. The mistake of Nuremberg (where the prosecutors socialized regularly with the judges to the exclusion of the defence lawyers) and of the Hague Tribunal (where both organs are housed under the same roof and are served by the same registry) should not have been repeated. Regrettably, the Rome Statue structures the Court so that it comprises both the judicial and the prosecutorial arm which are not at length from each other. The court president 'co-ordinates' with the prosecutor (Article 38 (4)); the registrar, the president and the prosecutor jointly decide upon staffing matters (Article 44); the prosecutor and registrar must be consulted on court rules and procedures (Article 52); the registry will operate as a press office for both the prosecutor and the judges. Worst of all, the registrar's duties, under Article 43, include the partisan role of running the Victims and Witnesses Unit, which in conjunction with the prosecutor's office arranges counselling and protection for victims who are witnesses – usually for the prosecution. In this clumsy way, court administration is harnessed to help the prosecutor. These arrangements are much too intimate and interconnected: the principle of impartiality requires a complete procedural and physical separation between prosecutors and judges. The demands of even-handed justice are met neither organizationally nor architecturally.

INTERNATIONAL CRIMES

The Court's jurisdiction extends to four offences: genocide, crimes against humanity, war crimes and the crime of 'aggression'. There will, however, be no prosecutions for 'aggression' until states agree on a definition, which will be an item on the agenda of their Review Conference, seven years after the Statute comes into force. These four categories are described as 'the most serious crimes of concern to the international community as a whole' and it is to be hoped that the test of 'seriousness' will be applied in deciding whether to prosecute in actual cases (which may not be serious examples of the crime in question). The Court will hardly fulfil its purpose if its targets are confined to footsoldiers like Duško Tadić, whose offences (while vicious enough) are comparatively minor beside those of the people who instigate or order the crimes defined in the Statute. The crimes within the jurisdiction of the ICC endlessly overlap: genocide, for example, is a crime in its own right as well as a crime against humanity and a war crime, and the latter category includes behaviour which in peace time would be classed as a crime against humanity. As the Appeals Chamber in the *Tadić Case* pointed out, there is now no good reason why the behaviour of nations at war should be judged by rules different from those for internecine conflicts: these legalistic distinctions have occupied the Hague Tribunal for much too long, and the same hairsplitting exercises are likely to be visited upon the ICC. It is difficult to understand why this court should not simply have jurisdiction over crimes against humanity, whether committed in war, in times of internecine struggle, in periods of riot and unrest, or at times of utter and seemingly blissful peace. The individuals responsible for any widespread pattern of barbarity, imposed or supported by the State (through its politicians or police or military) or by armed organizations fighting to attain some (or more) power, should be indictable and the charges against them should not depend on technical legal characterization of the nature of the background conflict.

GENOCIDE

This is the crime which was first to attract universal jurisdiction. Article 6 defines it in terms identical to the 1948 Genocide Convention (see p. 228). The essential element which must be proved is an 'intent to destroy in whole or part a national, ethnical, racial or religious group as such'. Acts of destruction other than by killing or maiming specifically include infliction of conditions of life causative of death and 'forcibly transferring children of the group to another group'. 'Group' does not include 'social' or 'political' groupings, so General Videla – who infamously ordered babies to be stolen from Argentina's disappeared left-wing mothers and farmed them out to loyal army families – could not be indicted for genocide. The Australian policy of taking babies and small children from their Aboriginal mothers and fostering them with white families has been alleged to be genocidal, but this would depend on whether force (rather than persuasion) was used and whether the purpose of the policy ('assimilation') was to destroy the group 'as such', as distinct from altering its culture. At the insistence of the Vatican, genocidal acts are defined to include 'imposing measures intended to prevent births within the group'. Birth control, even when imposed by law, is hardly a crime equivalent to mass murder – it can only count as genocide if it is imposed by discriminatory measures motivated not for health or population control, but as a means of extinguishing a racial group. Genocide is not an appropriate term to describe the behaviour of a sovereign state which goes to war with the purpose of annihilating the enemy nation, although this behaviour should be expressly included when the UN manages to define the crime of 'aggression'. When Yugoslavia activated the Genocide Convention in 1999 with its claim that NATO bombing amounted to genocide against Serbs, the ICJ pointed out that 'the threat or use of force against a State cannot in itself constitute an act of genocide'.[5] The intention must be to destroy human beings on account of their race – not to discipline, partition or even destroy the state which is persecuting them.

CRIMES AGAINST HUMANITY

Article 7 of the Rome Statute is set out in Appendix D: it contains what will become the authoritative definition of crimes against humanity. The acts themselves are for the most part crimes which cause great and unnecessary suffering – murder, torture, rape and other forms of sexual violence, enslavement, false imprisonment and unlawful persecution or deportation. What gives them their abhorrent quality is that they are committed deliberately 'as part of a widespread or systematic attack [a course of conduct involving multiple acts] directed against any civilian population . . . pursuant to or in furtherance of State or organizational policy to commit such an attack'.[6]

This definition has been criticized as too narrow by NGOs, which preferred the broad sweep suggested by the International Law Commission ('any inhumane acts instigated or directed by Governments or by any organization or group'). The delegates in Rome were right to resist their pressure for such a dragnet definition, which would have tempted the world court to investigate the crimes of minions and footsoldiers. The definition at least ensures that the ICC should confine itself to the most heinous offences, carried out systematically rather than on the spur of the moment, and pursuant to a policy conceived either by a state instrumentality (such as the police or the army) or by an organized entity as distinct from a criminal gang. The Article 7(1) definition makes clear that a prosecution may be brought in respect of a single act ('*any* of the following acts . . .') so long as it is known by the defendant to be part of a course of conduct involving multiple atrocities against civilians.

Just how 'organized' the perpetrating entity has to be in order for its members to be subjected to arrest is not, however, clear: there is no requirement that it should be invested with state power, so a structured opposition force, such as the IRA or the ANC in its freedom-fighting days, would seem to qualify. So would terrorist groups if organized on the scale of that led by Osmara Bin Laden, which trains thousands of adherents and was in 1998 responsible for the bombings at US embassies in Kenya and Tanzania which took hundreds of civilian lives. These multiple acts of murder were part of a systematic attack against a civilian population pursuant to an organizational policy to commit such attacks: in common parlance, the bombings were 'crimes against humanity'. Although the Rome Conference rejected jurisdiction over a specific crime of terrorism, there seems no legal reason why the prosecutor cannot investigate terrorist groups which consistently carry out atrocities causing loss of civilian lives, or an organized criminal enterprise with a political agenda like the Medellin drugs cartel in the days when it systematically killed judges and journalists and politicians and destroyed airliners. Complementarity provisions permit states to opt to exercise jurisdiction over any arrested nationals, although the past experience of Colombia (where at some points justice could not operate against Pablo Escobar and other cartel leaders because of their intimidation of the local judiciary) provides an example of cases appropriate for transfer to the International Court.

Included among the acts which may, if carried out systematically, amount to a crime against humanity is the 'enforced disappearance of persons' – defined to mean the detention or abduction of people by or with the acquiescence of 'a State or a political organization', followed by a refusal to acknowledge their whereabouts or fate, with 'the intention of removing them from the protection of the law for a prolonged period of time'. This clumsy wording (most disappearances remove people for ever, by secret execution) was intended to describe the behaviour of a number of South American governments which have allowed death squads to operate in conjunction with the military, and have made no attempt to trace victims. The definition would incriminate those in the squads, or ministers and officials who covered up their activities. Apartheid is re-categorized as a crime against humanity, but is much more carefully defined than in the Apartheid Convention (criticized on pp. 235–7). Henceforth, this crime will require commission of an inhumane offence with the purpose of maintaining the hegemony of a regime of systematic racial oppression.

There are a number of crimes against humanity, as defined in Article 7, which are appropriately charged against political or military leaders, because soldiers and civil servants may implement them without inhumane intent. 'Deportation or forcible transfer of population' is one example, where the object of the policymakers (but not necessarily of those ordered to carry out the policy on the ground) is to breach international law. The crime of 'persecution', defined as 'the intentional and severe deprivation of fundamental rights contrary to international law' committed against an identifiable group by reason of its politics, race or culture, can be deployed against those leaders whose 'ethnic cleansing' falls short of genocide. It will also be appropriate against those who help out – the drivers of the Ford Falcons used by death squads in Argentina; the doctors on hand to regulate the torture of 'subversives' at the Pinochet centres, the judges who take political instruction to refuse habeas corpus applications, and so on. It is an essential element of the crime of persecution that the act charged is known by the defendant to have a connection with a crime within the court's jurisdiction (such as genocide or torture or another crime against humanity). After this knowledge, there can be no forgiveness for the 'willing executioner' who prostitutes his or her profession in the service of barbarism. This crime of persecution (defined, confusingly, by overlapping sections 7 (1) (h) and 7 (2) (g)) will be an important new weapon in the prosecutor's armoury, for use against the lawyers, bankers, propagandists and parasites who use their professional diplomas to wipe the blood of client regimes off their own hands.

The Hague International Criminal Tribunal for the Former Yugoslavia was the first court to recognize rape as a crime capable of political direction, at which point it can become a crime against humanity. The Rome Statute incorporates this advance – Article 7 duly lists rape, along with sexual slavery, forced pregnancy and enforced prostitution and sterilization, as capable of constituting a crime against humanity if carried out systematically. The idea of raping Muslim women in order that they produce 'Chetnik babies' was not a policy of the Serbian state, but a perverse notion which infected soldiers and their senior officers in a number of Serb battalions – and would therefore still count as an 'organizational policy' sufficient to fall within Article 7. The inclusion of 'sexual slavery' and 'enforced prostitution' provides a belated recognition that the Japanese army's enslavement of 'comfort women' from Taiwan and Korea to service its soldiers during the Second World War constituted a crime against humanity – one that the Allies did not dream of punishing in 1946 and which Japan did not think necessary even to apologize for until

1996. 'Forced pregnancy' means rape followed by 'unlawful confine-ment' for the purpose of 'affecting ethnic composition'. The Vatican was alarmed that making such monstrous pregnancies the subject of a crime against humanity might justify their termination by abortion, and insisted on the rider that 'this definition shall not in any way be interpreted as affecting national laws relating to pregnancy'. This religious enclave, wrongly elevated to statehood by an unthinking international community, was responsible for including as Article 7 (3) the most ridiculous clause in any international treaty ever devised. 'Persecution' had been defined in Article 7 (1) (h) to include persecution on grounds of gender. The Vatican, and other homophobic Catholic and Islamic states, insisted on appending clause 7 (3):

For the purpose of this Statute, it is understood that the term 'gender' refers to the two sexes, male and female, within the context of society. The term 'gender' does not indicate any meaning different from the above.

This means, presumably, that you can do what you like to transex-uals. Persecution is a crime if directed against men as men, or women because they are female, but homosexuals and lesbians may still suffer the thumbscrew and the rack, the 'intentional and severe deprivation of fundamental rights' when this is 'within the context of society', i.e. approved by a gay-bashing government or culture. The inclusion of Article 7 (3) is a distasteful but realistic reminder that a majority of states in 1998 favoured the withdrawal of human rights on grounds of sexual orientation.

Article 7, otherwise, must be hailed as the high point of the Rome Statute. It crystallizes the concept of a crime against humanity which nations of the world are obliged to punish, and distinguishes it from other crimes by reference to its genesis in the policy of a state or political organization. It is not defined by the gravity of the offence: the lone serial killer may do more widespread damage than the routine police torturer. What sets a crime against humanity apart both in wickedness and in the need for special measures of deterrence is the simple fact that it is an act of real brutality ordained by government – or at least by an organization exercising or asserting political power. It is not the mind of the torturer, but the fact that this individual is part of the apparatus of a state, which makes the crime so horrific and locates it in a different dimension from ordinary criminality. This is why individual responsibility and universal jurisdiction are necessary responses if any deterrence is to be achieved. Just as the eighteenth-century pirate and the slave trader used to be legally untouchable – because being on the high seas they were subject to no state's jurisdiction – so the twentieth-century politician and general were invulnerable while they exercised the sovereignty of the State. Now universal jurisdiction will attach to their crimes against humanity: Article 27 abolishes all immunities for heads of state and members of governments and parliaments. This will apply to states that are party to the ICC Treaty, but it will also have the effect of moving customary international law beyond the position it reached in the case of General Pinochet (see chapter 10).

WAR CRIMES

Article 8 of the Rome Statute contains a lengthy definition of the war crimes over which the ICC shall have jurisdiction, 'in particular when committed as part of a plan or policy or as part of a large-scale commission of such crimes'. These war crimes are defined in four categories, reflecting the historical evolution of the subject by distinguishing between crimes capable of commission at times of international conflict and at times of internal armed conflict. There is a substantial overlap and the distinction is otiose, although apparently too embedded in the minds of international lawyers (where it gives rise to endless technical arguments) to be extirpated in the interests of simplicity and comprehensibility.

The first category – Article 8 (2) (a) – includes all 'grave breaches' of the 1949 Geneva Conventions (see pp. 177 and 294). The second category – Article 8 (2) (b) – covers 'other serious violations of the laws and customs applicable in international armed conflict within the established framework of international law'. Twenty-six such violations are spelled out, in a subsection which serves to update the limited horizons of 1949. Thus it now includes attacks on peacekeepers or others providing humanitarian assistance under UN auspices (sub-paragraph (ii)); attacks launched in the knowledge that they will cause disproportionate loss of civilian life or 'widespread long-term and severe damage to the national environment' excessive in relation to any military objective (iv); intentional attacks on non-military targets such as churches, schools, museums, hospitals and places of historical or cultural significance (ix); and the use of asphyxiating or poisonous gases (xviii). The behaviour of Bosnian Serbs in deploying captured UN peacekeepers as hostages against NATO aerial bombardment provides the rationale for a new war crime of 'utilizing the presence of civilians or other protected persons to render certain points, areas or military forces immune from military operations' (xxiii). There is another new offence of 'conscripting children under the age of fifteen years' to participate actively in hostilities – an indictment of the recruiters of the 'child armies' of Africa (xxvi). The Hague Tribunal's emphatic condemnation of systematic rape and sexual slavery is repeated: under Article 7 they constitute crimes against humanity; during international hostilities they amount as well to war crimes under Article 8, whether committed as part of a policy or simply to demoralize the populace.

The delegates in Rome deliberately fudged the lawfulness of land mines and nuclear weapons as weapons of international law. The treaty banning anti-personnel mines, concluded in 1997, had been opposed by the United States and China (see p. 198). The International Court of Justice had delivered an abjectly confused decision over the legality of nuclear weaponry (see p. 187). So the ban in subparagraph (xx) on weapons and methods of warfare 'which are of a nature to cause superfluous injury or unnecessary suffering or which are inherently indiscriminate' (all of which description applies to nuclear bombs and to anti-personnel mines) is expressed 'within the framework of international law' – which does not currently regard them as illegal *per se*. The ban will only apply to them – or to ballistic missiles or other weapons of mass destruction – if they subsequently become subject to a 'comprehensive prohibition' which is then incorporated in the Statute at its seven-year review. If, before that time, some deranged dictator launches a nuclear strike on a military target, the non-retrospectivity rule means he could not be prosecuted at the ICC.

Article 8 goes on, rather gingerly, to provide jurisdiction over two classes of war crime if committed in 'armed conflict not of an international character'. This class of conflict is clearly distinguished from 'situations of internal disturbances and tensions' such as riots or unrest characterized by 'isolated and sporadic acts of violence'. Crimes committed in the latter period are not 'war crimes' under Article 8, so they must qualify as genocide or crimes against humanity if the ICC is to have any power to punish them. As a concession to states beset with internal security problems, the Statute provides that in respect to 'common Article 3 crimes' involving attacks on civilians, 'nothing shall affect the responsibility to maintain or establish law and order in the State or to defend the unity and territorial integrity of the State by all legitimate means'. This provides a wide, albeit question-begging, exculpation for governments fighting secessionist movements and other politically motivated armed groups. If 'legitimate' means simply 'justified under domestic law', then no government leaders who impose internment or detention without trial can subsequently be prosecuted at the ICC.

Article 8(2)(c) extends jurisdiction over internecine armed conflicts in respect of all *serious* violations of common Article 3 of the 1949 Geneva Conventions, i.e. inhumane attacks on civilians or sick or surrendered soldiers (including putting them on trials which lack the basic attributes of fairness). To these 'core' crimes Article 8(2)(e) adds a selection of some twelve of the war crimes listed in Article 8(2)(b) as arising in international conflict, notably the use of children as soldiers, or engaging in systematic sexual violence, or attacking UN peacekeepers or historic, cultural and humanitarian targets. These twelve crimes reflect customary international law as it has developed for internal conflicts, which are specially defined as 'armed conflicts that take place in the territory of a State where there is protracted armed conflict between governmental authorities and organized armed groups or between such groups'. This makes it crystal clear that even if terrorist forces or liberation armies fall outside common Article 3 of the Geneva Conventions, their leaders can be dragged before the ICC for specific atrocities against civilians. The aimless banditry of a murderous organization like Renamo in Mozambique (before an amnesty gave it a political status to which it had never previously aspired) would henceforth be caught, while the leaders of 'Shining Path' in Peru may yet have their moment in the international dock, where their indelibly vicious crimes against women (they have assassinated twelve leading feminists and encouraged wide-spread rape) would receive a fairer trial than from any court in Peru.

For all the ingenuity displayed in the drafting of Article 8, the central irony remains its assumption that state leaders commit no crime at all in declaring and waging aggressive wars in which millions of combatants and civilians may be killed. Warlike acts of aggrandize-ment, like Saddam's occupation of Kuwait and Galtieri's invasion of the Falklands, should count as the gravest of crimes, given the multiplicity of international mechanisms available to prevent them through negotiation or arbitration. 'Just wars' in the future will mainly be fought by the side which intervenes to oppose them, or which goes to war out of humanitarian necessity as the only way to stop a state committing crimes against humanity. The inability to agree on the definition of the crime of aggression – most commonly the prelude to international conflict – was a serious failure, given that this was addressed at Nuremberg and that drafts have been debated by the Human Rights Commission and the International Law Commission since 1948. The failure is only exacerbated by the device of pretending to include it, but postponing its operation until a definition is agreed at the seven-year review stage (i.e. circa the year 2010). What was most required was the definition of a war crime which would have put leaders like Saddam Hussein and General Galtieri in jail for life. Sadly, the nations assembled at Rome missed the opportunity finally to outlaw war as an instrument of national policy.

CRIMINAL LAW PRINCIPLES

Part 3 of the Statute adopts basic principles found in most advanced legal systems. The prosecution must prove that the criminal acts are committed with *mens rea* (that is, intentionally, and with knowledge of the likely consequences). Defendants will be liable for crimes committed jointly or with a common purpose, for acts of assistance and for ordering, soliciting and inducing crimes and for attempting to commit a crime by taking a substantial step towards its completion. The Statute applies to heads of state, elected representatives and all others who have acted in an official capacity: the plea of 'act of state' will be heeded no longer. The criminal responsibility provisions

(Article 25) spell out that guilt of genocide includes the public incitement of others to commit it – a recognition of the role of radio in encouraging the massacres in Rwanda, and an override of any free speech arguments in respect of this crime.

Jurisdiction is confined to natural persons – men and women, to the exclusion of governments or corporations or political parties. This was a mistake (as we shall see) because reparations cannot be ordered against parties which are not criminally responsible. Why should a multinational chemical corporation not be prosecuted (as well as its directors) for supplying poison gas in the knowledge that it will be used for a crime against humanity? Why should that company, if convicted, not be ordered to pay massive reparations to survivors and to victims' families? Another questionable exception (in Article 26) is for any person aged under eighteen at the time of the crime. Some appalling atrocities have been committed by 'boy soldiers'. Article 8 makes it a war crime to enlist persons under fifteen for an active part in hostilities, so why should those of sixteen or seventeen, old enough to participate fully in war, be immune from prosecution for war crimes?

The Rome delegates sensibly resisted the demands by Amnesty and other NGOs that they should deny to persons suspected of crimes against humanity some of the defences which these organizations had, in the past, urged should be available to political prisoners. Self-defence, duress, mistake which negates *mens rea*, insanity and even intoxication will exclude liability in a proper case. 'Command responsibility' is defined precisely in Article 38: military commanders will be responsible for atrocities committed by their forces if they knew, or should in the prevailing circumstances have known, of the unlawful behaviour of subordinates but failed to take reasonable measures to stop or to punish them. This is an endorsement of the *Yamashita* principle, upon which the Hague Tribunal indicted Karadžić and Mladić (see p. 207).

However, the Rome Statute does attenuate one great principle to emerge from Nuremberg, namely that 'superior orders' may mitigate punishment but can never amount to a defence. Article 33 provides that any order – by a military, police, governmental or civil authority – may indeed provide a defence to persons who were under a 'legal obligation' to obey orders (which soldiers and police invariably are) and who did not know the order was unlawful, where the order in question was not 'manifestly unlawful'. Although orders to commit genocide or crimes against humanity are deemed to be 'manifestly unlawful' this will not be the case in respect of military operations amounting to war crimes. Indeed, a bomber crew ordered to drop a nuclear weapon would be under a legal obligation to obey an order that (thanks to the ICJ decision analysed in chapter 5) is not 'manifestly unlawful'. Under Article 33, 'superior orders' may thus constitute a defence – another victory for the Pentagon lobby concerned that soldiers should not be emboldened to disobey military edicts of dubious legality.

Article 29 provides that the Court's jurisdiction must not be affected by any time bar or statute of limitations. This will ensure that complementarity cannot be invoked on behalf of persons suspected of crimes which fall outside time limits for prosecutions imposed by national legal systems. (Many Francophone countries, for example, bar prosecutions after a lapse of fifteen years, even for murder.) Crimes against humanity are of such seriousness that they should be amenable to prosecution for as long as their perpetrators remain alive. However, many national legal systems do provide their courts with power to abort long-delayed prosecutions, at least where the defendant has not been responsible for the delay by evading capture. The ICC has no equivalent power to rule a case inadmissible if there has been unconscionable and prejudicial delay by the prosecuting authorities in preparing it. In national systems, this has proved a salutary power to avoid injustice to defendants where prosecutions are incompetent, oppressive or unfair. It may be that the Trial Division can, however, dismiss the case in such circumstances: Article 64(2) mandates it to 'ensure that a trial is fair and expeditious and is conducted with full respect for the rights of the accused', one of which is, under Article 67(c), 'to be tried without undue delay'. Where the delay is both unjustified and prejudicial and has arisen from prosecutorial incompetence or other factors outside the defendant's control, the only way that a trial division could give effect to these principles will be to dismiss the prosecution and free the defendant, as the Hague Appeals Chamber ordered in *Barayagwiza* (see p. 320).

Article 66 enshrines the fundamental presumption of innocence, and places the burden on the prosecution to prove guilt beyond reasonable doubt. Article 67(1) guarantees that the onus of proof or even an 'onus of rebuttal' shall not be imposed on a defendant, although many of the defences adumbrated elsewhere in the Statute (such as 'superior orders' and duress) place precisely such burdens – and reasonably enough – on the defendant. Questions of burden and standard of proof can be crucial in jury trials, although they tend to be academic when verdicts take the form of a reasoned judicial decision: in practice, once the prosecution proves beyond reasonable doubt complicity in a crime against humanity, the onerous task of establishing exculpatory circumstances such as duress or intoxication or mistake will shift to the defendant.

THE COURT

JURISDICTION

The most direct mechanism for triggering the power to investigate and try international crimes is provided under Article 13 (b), whereby a 'situation' is referred to the prosecutor by the Security Council acting pursuant to Chapter VII of the UN Charter. This is the method, it will be recalled, under which the Hague and Arusha Tribunals were established, by resolutions which asserted that the 'situations' in former Yugoslavia and in Rwanda constituted a threat to world peace (see p. 289). No longer need the UN establish *ad hoc* tribunals: when there is superpower agreement on the need to punish crimes against humanity, committed in peace or war, by or on the territory of any state (whether it is a party to the Treaty or not) then the Security Council may simply resolve to refer the matter to the ICC prosecutor. That action automatically attracts the jurisdiction of the Court over those the prosecutor chooses to indict.

In the event of Security Council disagreement or inaction, the position is more complicated. The Court cannot acquire jurisdiction without a Security Council resolution unless, for a start, the conduct in question occurred on the territory of a state which is party to the

Statute, or else the suspect is a national of a state which is party to the Statute. Neither of these preconditions is likely to be fulfilled in the case of political and military leaders engaging in vicious repression of dissident civilians or ethnic groups, because it is inherently unrealistic to expect that states run by such persons would ratify the Statute.

This impasse results from a serious split at the Rome Conference. The US, it will be recalled, came to Rome wanting an ICC, but one which had a cast-iron guarantee that no American would ever be indicted. That could best be achieved by a court with jurisdiction triggered *only* by the Security Council, where the US would have a veto, although the US was prepared in addition to let state parties to the Statute have the option of allowing their nationals to be tried (since the US could always decline to agree). Its European allies, led on this issue by Germany, took the 'universal human rights' position: the ICC should have universal jurisdiction, over everyone everywhere, irrespective of their nationality or the state in which the crimes were committed. This position would make the Court a true instrument of international justice, insulated from the superpower politics of the Security Council. South Korea, in an attempt to placate the US, suggested that the Court might at least sidestep the Security Council in respect of crimes committed on the territory of a state which was party to the Treaty (so Kuwait, if such a party, could ask it to indict Saddam Hussein over some future invasion). Then it added a second possibility – jurisdiction if a state party happened to capture a suspect who was a national of another state – and that was when the American delegation threatened both Germany and South Korea with a reduction in US forces unless they withdrew these proposals. The US, said delegation leader David Sheffer, would 'actively oppose' the Court, even if its jurisdiction was based only on the South Korean compromise. The conference was thus bullied into dropping the German proposal for true universal jurisdiction, as well as the second Korean proposal, but it retained a measure of self-respect by insisting the Court have jurisdiction over crimes committed on state party territory. It was partly over this act of defiance that the US, with a show of petulance, voted against the entire Statute. It is difficult to disagree with Kenneth Roth, director of Human Rights Watch, that 'in weakening the Korean proposal, the Rome delegates apparently felt the need to make concessions to Washington in the naive hope that the Clinton administration would at least tolerate the Court. Instead, they got the worst of both worlds: the Court has been considerably weakened and the US Government is still determined to destroy a historically important new institution.'[7]

In the result, the Statute theoretically permits jurisdiction against the will of the Security Council where the suspect is a national of a state party or the crime was committed on its territory. But even here there are obstacles, because the Court's theoretical power must be triggered in one of two ways. The state party itself may refer the matter to the prosecutor, providing evidence and requesting a formal investigation which may lead directly to arrests and trials. But states, as we have seen from the total absence of state complaints at the HRC and their rarity at the European Court, are reluctant to point the finger at other states, and it follows that they will be extremely reluctant to do so when the result is to trigger a jurisdiction the Security Council does not wish the ICC to have. Alternatively, the prosecutor may initiate investigations *'proprio motu'* (i.e. on his or her own initiative) and seek evidence from states, UN agencies and other 'reliable sources'. But in this case there remains a legal hurdle in the prosecutorial path: a pre-trial division of the Court must examine the evidence, hear any jurisdictional objection, and decide whether to authorize 'the commencement of the investigation'. This clumsy procedure confines the prosecutor's initial investigation to public or volunteered sources: his special investigative powers cannot be engaged unless or until the pre-trial division rules that there is a *prima facie* case, 'a reasonable basis to proceed'.

In short, the politicians and diplomats of the superpowers remain in the driving seat. These provisions were heavily influenced, at Rome, by the desperate need to keep the US onside. The last thing the Clinton administration wanted was a 'superprosecutor' empowered to investigate incidents that they might wish to cover up – in July 1998, they had an example of that close to home, as Kenneth Starr announced an examination of Monica Lewinsky's blue dress for traces of presidential semen. So the 'like-minded' group, against its will, shackled the prosecutor by subjecting him to control by the Court on a matter over which judges should have no say at all, namely who should be investigated as a candidate for prosecution. Although *proprio motu* investigations will be the only way to 'do something' about appalling human rights violations in and by countries which have superpower support:

(1) They will only get under way if it happens to involve the territory or nationals of a ratifying state – and the chances of pariah regimes ratifying the Statute are minimal.

(2) Even if this does actually happen, the prosecutor cannot 'commence the investigation' unless – from readily available sources and helpful governments – he or she can lay hands immediately on evidence sufficient to satisfy the Court of a 'reasonable case'.

But there was worse to come. The 'like-minded' group had to mollify not only the US, but France and China, which also wanted a court which would be dependent upon the Security Council. So they offered another, fatal concession, which appears as Article 16:

No investigation or prosecution may be commenced . . . for a period of twelve months after the Security Council, in a resolution adopted under Chapter VII of the UN Charter, has requested the Court to that effect; that request may be renewed by the Council under the same conditions.

The word 'request' is used dishonestly: the Security Council resolution is mandatory – it stops an investigation or trial dead in its tracks. The order will operate initially for one year, but may be renewed on an annual basis until the evidence is dissipated, the crime forgotten or the prosecutor loses interest. The effect of Article 16 is to give the Security Council ultimate control over the Court, which operates either by a reference from the Council or (in the event of a reference by a state party or on investigation *proprio motu*) subject to the Council's power to freeze any proceedings it does not like by passing an Article 16 resolution.

Does the Court have any discretion to reject an Article 16 'request'? The resolution must be adopted under Chapter VII of the Charter, which empowers the Security Council to deploy extraordinary measures 'to maintain or restore international peace and security' once it determines 'the existence of any threat to the peace, breach of the peace or act of aggression . . .' An order to *stop* proceedings against reasonably suspected war criminals cannot logically help to restore peace or security, unless the suspects are so powerful that peace negotiations depend on their continuing freedom from arrest. In the *Tadić Case* the Hague Tribunal Appeals Chamber was prepared to scrutinize Security Council resolutions to ensure that they were a rational compliance with the powers granted by the UN Charter, so on this precedent the Court might reject an Article 16 resolution if it cannot sensibly have been directed to restoring peace. This would certainly be the case were a deferral resolution motivated by a desire on the part of embarrassed Council members to cover up the evidence of their own involvement in a crime, or to protect politicians or peacekeepers from justice. Otherwise – if the Security Council is incapable of judicial review – its power over the Court will be final.

The Preamble to the Rome Statute emphasizes that the ICC jurisdiction shall be 'complementary' to that of nation states, although the provisions of the Statute itself suggest that 'subordinate' would be a more accurate description of the legal relationship. Article 20 states the fundamental double jeopardy rule, that no person shall be tried twice for the same offence ('*ne bis in idem*') so that there can be no proceeding brought against a suspect in the ICC for conduct in respect of which he has been convicted or acquitted in a national court. This rule is made subject to the reasonable qualification that it does not apply when the national court case was a sham, either because it was brought in order to shield the subject from further action, or because it was not conducted with any real intent to establish criminal responsibility. Article 17 applies the same test to the investigation stage: if a suspect is already being dealt with under national law, in a manner which appears genuine and effective, then the ICC must stay its hand, even when local authorities conclude that persons suspected by its prosecutor have in fact no case to answer. This last exculpation is much too broad, although there are safeguards: the ICC itself will decide whether it was reasonable for the domestic prosecutor to drop the charges, and may none the less pick up the case if satisfied that the decision was made to shield the suspect or because of a breakdown in local law enforcement.

These double jeopardy provisions impose much stricter limits on the power of the ICC than the equivalent sections of the Hague

Tribunal Statute. That court has a broad power to intervene at any stage of proceedings in a national court, requesting it to 'defer to the competence of the Tribunal', i.e. stop its proceedings and send the defendant for trial at The Hague. Such a deferral request, which states are obliged to grant, may be made not only when the Hague prosecutor thinks that the local court is biased in the defendant's favour or the local prosecution lacks diligence, but whenever the case is relevant to the Hague Tribunal's own work or is appropriate for an international prosecution. This primacy power is necessary to make sense of international criminal justice, and so that defendants like Pinochet (who could never be convicted in Chile) and Demjanjuk (who would be convicted, but unfairly, in Israel) find a forum where they can be properly tried. But Article 17 of the Rome Statute kow-tows to state sovereignty: the ICC will not be permitted to put anyone on trial who has been 'under investigation' by a national prosecutor and has had charges dropped or the investigation stopped. The only exception will be where the ICC prosecutor can convince the court that national authorities have been 'unwilling or unable' to carry out a genuine investigation – a difficult allegation to prove, especially if ICC judges are deferential to nation states' sensitivities about their justice system. So it will be easy for states to deny the ICC jurisdiction over their nationals by pretending to put them on trial, and the legal chauvinism recently displayed by Chile, the US (through Jesse Helms) and Indonesia, insiting that *their* courts alone must have jurisdiction over *their* soldiers, foreshadows how often ICC prosecutors will be robbed of their prey. In the guise of double jeopardy, the diplomats in Rome threw a lifeline to every mass-murderer whose home state, out of fear or bribery or misguided national pride, will be prepared to save them from the indignity of international trial by the simple device of putting them in sham jeopardy by subjecting them to an 'investigation' which will block the ICC prosecutor for ever.

These complementarity provisions determine the 'admissibility' of any particular case. In references by Security Council resolution it will be for defendants to raise any double jeopardy issue at the outset of their trial. But there are special provisions for state references or *proprio motu* investigations: the prosecutor is obliged to notify *all* state parties, together with other, non-party states which could exercise jurisdiction. The notification may be confidential, but when made to a state anxious to protect suspects (who may, indeed, lead the government of that state) it will serve to tip off criminals and permit destruction of evidence and intimidation of witnesses. States which are hostile to a prosecution may also (whether or not they have signed the Treaty) have the investigation suspended by challenging the Court's jurisdiction over, or the admissibility of, the case – at first in pre-trial chambers, and then by way of appeal. These provisions in Articles 18 and 19 mean that pariah states will have numerous legal opportunities to derail a prosecution, or to delay it for years through appellate manoeuvres, especially in cases which are not referred by the Security Council.

COMPOSITION

The viability of the ICC will ultimately depend more on the calibre and experience of its judges and prosecutors than on the fine print of its statute. International appointments systems are prone to throw up mediocrities trusted to toe the line of their nominating government: usually they are appointed from within government departments or are in other ways beholden to the State. Often missing are persons of real independence with first-class minds and imagination. Yet one of the main reasons why Nuremberg worked was that the English, French and American judges had experience as criminal *defenders* and not merely as prosecutors; from that experience developed a sense of fairness that infused the proceedings. So what the ICC needed was an appointments system independent of governments, and a set of statutory qualifications which gave weight to those with careers characterized by some criminal defence work. In this respect, the statutory arrangements for appointing the Court's eighteen full-time judges leave much to be desired. They are to be elected by an assembly of the state parties – a recipe for political caucusing – and nominated by respective governments with an eye to such matters as 'equitable geographical representation' and 'a fair representation of female and male judges'. At least half the judges must have 'relevant' criminal law experience, although this may be entirely prosecutorial. Defence experience is not specifically mentioned as a qualification, although

351

nominating states must take into account 'legal expertise on violence against women and children' – a qualification calling, quite irrationally, for judges who were formerly prosecutors of rapists and child molesters.

Article 40 requires the judges to be 'independent in the performance of their functions' (their salaries may for this reason not be reduced during their nine-year tenure of office) and there are appropriate provisions for disqualification (by decision of all the other judges) in the event of reasonably apprehended bias. This issue is given a certain piquancy by the problems encountered by the House of Lords in the *Pinochet Case* after discovering that one judge was director of an Amnesty charity. (Interestingly enough, none of the Pinochet judges had the sort of criminal law or human rights experience required to qualify for the ICC.) On principle, ICC judges should not be disqualified by virtue of connections with human rights organizations unless they are actually parties to the case. The ICC Statute makes no provision for '*amicus*' briefs or third party submissions, although the Hague Tribunal has found these helpful and the Court should accept that it has inherent power to accept legal submissions, in writing at least, from other interested parties. All the judges – and, more importantly, the senior prosecutors – shall be accorded full diplomatic immunity by state parties, which can only be waived by a decision of the majority of judges of the court. The judges shall themselves elect a president, who will chair the five-judge Appeals Division and be responsible for the administration of the Court. The other judges will be divided between trial divisions, which will comprise three judges, and pre-trial divisions, which may be constituted by a single judge. The prosecutor and deputy prosecutors (also elected by the Assembly of State Parties) shall be elected for a nine-year term, and must have extensive practical experience of criminal trials.

THE TRIAL

PROSECUTION POWERS

Much of the debate prior to the Rome Treaty concerned the power of the prosecutor. As already noted, the US (its president caught at the time in the coils of Kenneth Starr) feared a 'superprosecutor' who might choose to flex legal muscles or play to the non-aligned gallery by investigating as crimes against humanity American attacks on its enemies (such as its cruise missile onslaught being planned at the time on the bases of Osmara Bin Laden in Sudan and Afghanistan). The NGO lobby and the 'like-minded' nations foresaw the need for a prosecutor with a plenitude of powers, at arms length from the Security Council. The compromise was to establish a prosecutor whose initiatives would be closely monitored by the judges. Instead of fashioning a true adversary system, with an entirely independent judiciary deciding between a prosecutor with whom they have no close connection and the defence, they gave to the judges sitting in the Pre-trial Division excessive powers to interfere with a prosecution, either by reigning it in or unleashing it.

The prosecutor may begin an investigation on his own initiative, or as the result of a referral by the Security Council or a state party (see above). If there is insufficient evidence, then obviously no prosecution will ensue. Even where there is 'a case' there may be good public interest reasons not to proceed: victims may be too traumatized to give evidence; the defendant may have a terminal illness; and so forth. The prosecutor's decision not to proceed in such cases will only be effective if it is approved by a three-judge Pre-trial Division which can, by withdrawing approval, force the prosecutor to bring what he regards as unfair or oppressive proceedings.[8] The judges are required to encroach on the routine investigative work of the prosecutor's office in other ways. Under Article 56 (3), for example, the prosecutor must apply to them for permission to take a 'unique investigative opportunity' (such as a statement from a potential witness who is about to die) and the judges may even take such measures on their own initiative, against the prosecutor's wishes. These provisions are misguided because they invite the judiciary to take over the job of prosecuting, in the inquisitorial role (familiar in Continental systems) which is incompatible with the Anglo-American adversarial model upon which the Court is principally based.

In one important respect, the Rome Statute corrects an unfair and prejudicial provision in Rule 61 of the Hague International Criminal Tribunal for the Former Yugoslavia, criticized at pp. 304–5. The ICC will have a Pre-trial Division which issues arrest warrants and in due course holds a committal hearing (at which defendants and lawyers are present) to determine whether there is sufficient evidence to justify the defendant being put on trial. If defendants flee or evade arrest, however, there is no 'Rule 61 hearing': under Article 61, the Court simply confirms that the prosecutor has sufficient evidence to justify his charges, and at this hearing the Court may permit the absentee to be represented by counsel (who will not, therefore, be exiled to the public gallery, like the counsel for Karadžić and Mladić).

State parties are bound to co-operate with the prosecutor, although the very fact that a state has ratified the Treaty means that it is unlikely to harbour many war criminals, so the Court will have to try to make *ad hoc* agreements with non-party states. Requests to state parties must be made by the Court (presumably by the registrar, as directed by a Pre-trial Division) and made through 'diplomatic channels'. This is cumbersome and lacking in confidentiality. It would be better for the prosecutor's office to be represented in the law enforcement apparatus of every state party, and be permitted to make co-operation arrangements directly, rather than by application to ICC judges who then pass the request on through the registrar to diplomats at The Hague. State parties are obliged to ensure that their local law procedures permit effective co-operation: by arranging for the execution of ICC warrants; by requiring suspects and witnesses to attend for questioning; by permitting ICC prosecutors to inspect sites and execute searches and seize records and documents and freeze assets. A state party may attach a condition of confidentiality to the security-sensitive information it provides: in such cases the prosecutor cannot turn the information over to the defence, so may use it only as a *lead* to gathering additional evidence, rather than as evidence to be placed secretly before the Court.

The ICC can issue a warrant for arrest if the prosecutor demonstrates 'reasonable grounds to believe' complicity in crime. Suspects who are apprehended in co-operating countries must be transported to The Hague and surrendered into the custody of the Court. Their basic rights throughout the investigation stage are protected under Article 55: they must be informed, prior to questioning, of their rights to remain silent and to have legal assistance free of charge and a competent interpreter if necessary. Article 101 contains the rule of speciality, familiar from extradition law, whereby a person who has been arrested and surrendered to the ICC cannot be proceeded against for conduct other than that referred to in the arrest warrant. In its strict form the rule would tie the prosecutor's hands in the common situation where further and more compelling evidence of involvement in other crimes comes to light after the arrest. For this reason the rule is watered down by a provision which encourages state parties to waive it, at the request of the Court, once notified of the additional evidence. The ordinary costs of co-operating with court requests for evidence gathering and surrender of suspects are to be borne by the state party, although the Court must fund all expenses related to its own personnel and witnesses. There is no provision for prosecution costs to be awarded against convicted defendants, although such a rule would not be unreasonable in the case of wealthy defendants who have profited from their crimes, such as tyrants and high officials who have maintained their positions through oppression. It would be just and appropriate in some cases to order the states in whose name they have committed their crimes to pay for their prosecution.

THE HEARING

The trial will take place at The Hague, although Article 3 gives the Court power to sit elsewhere if this is desirable. There can be no trials *in absentia*: the accused must be present, although if disruptive may be removed to a cell video-linked to the courtroom. The trial shall be in public, although Article 68 empowers the Court to move into camera if such a measure is not inconsistent with the fair trial rights of the accused and is necessary 'to protect the safety, physical and psychological well-being, dignity and privacy of victims and witnesses'.

There is no reference in the Statute to televising the trials – a commonplace in America and Europe which is stoutly resisted in the British Commonwealth. The principle that justice must be seen to be done, and the educative force of the medium, argues in favour. In the case of war crimes, the argument is exceptionally strong. There is a special need for truth-telling, for the sake of victims and to combat sanitizing myths gaining credence among the vanquished and to rebut charges of 'victor's justice'. The Hague Tribunal allows most of its proceedings to be televised without damage to their fairness, and the coverage has been watched with great interest in parts of former Yugoslavia. It offers victims some satisfaction in seeing at least a few representative perpetrators brought to justice. In fact, such coverage is essential to give the truth an airing in places like *Republica Srpska*, where, as Lawrence Wechsler has commented, the media remains controlled by 'the same parties and mafias whose hyper-nationalist exhortations back in the early nineties had set the stage for war in the first place'.[9] Although George Soros's Open Society Institute beamed in full satellite coverage of the Tadić trial, few could afford the necessary satellite dish and so the transmissions did little to confound local propaganda lies about the trial and indeed about the war.[10] Another problem is that hearings in this class of case are not often dramatic – the proceedings are lengthy, slowed down by simultaneous translation and plodding advocacy that has no jury to impress. (The American cable channel Court TV planned to show in its entirety the Tadić trial – advertised as 'the real trial of the century' – but it hardly compared to O. J. Simpson and viewers soon lost interest.) The ICC should certainly use its inherent powers to permit broadcasting (except for the evidence of witnesses who reasonably object to reliving their experiences of degradation before an international audience), but further thought should be given to producing comprehensible edited versions and requiring them to be broadcast through media outlets in the defendant's country.

Article 67 enshrines the basic rights of the accused, drawn from the 'fair trial' provisions common to all human rights treaties. The accused must have all proceedings translated into a language he understands and speaks, and is entitled to have lawyers of his choice (assigned by the court if he is indigent) and to communicate with them confidentially.[11] He has a right to trial 'without undue delay', but must also have adequate time and facilities to prepare his defence and to cross-examine all witnesses against him and to obtain the attendance of witnesses capable of giving relevant evidence on his behalf. He has a right to remain silent, without having this refusal to explain the evidence against him taken as an indication of guilt. It is remarkable how the 'right to silence' is being entrenched in human rights law at the very time it is being rejected by some advanced legal systems, where the view is taken, not unreasonably, that a person confronted with substantial evidence of serious crime has a basic human duty to explain himself, and that failure to do so in these circumstances at trial (as distinct from at the time of arrest) permits a rebuttable inference of guilt. It is always wrong to *compel* defendants to answer questions, although the gravity of the charge of a crime against humanity, and above all the interests of victims and relatives to know the truth, would surely justify an incentive to tell it once the prosecution evidence is held sufficient to require an answer. However, the Rome Statute entrenches the right to silence in absolute terms, and goes even further by permitting an accused who declines to testify and undergo cross-examination 'to make an unsworn oral or written statement in his or her defence'. This is a relic of the 'dock statement' permitted to defendants in England in the nineteenth century, when they were not allowed to enter the witness box. It has been abolished in England and in some Commonwealth jurisdictions, and has no rational justification, other than to permit a defendant to provide an explanation when he is afraid to go into the witness box for fear of cross-examination. At any event, the Trial Division will have three judges with experience of criminal trials: an accused's failure to explain away convincingly a compelling case will in practice indicate guilt, however many legal rules say that it must not.

The Rome Statute's provisions on evidence fudge the problem that split the court in the *Tadić Case*, namely the extent to which prosecution witnesses who have been victims of sexual violence may remain anonymous (see pp. 311–13). The ICC is directed by Article 68 to take 'appropriate measures to protect the safety, physical and psychological well-being, dignity and privacy of victims and witnesses' who are given the valuable right of separate legal representation to allow their own views to be canvassed. If there is 'grave danger' apprehended to a witness or his or her family, the prosecutor may withhold details of identification or evidence at any pre-trial stage. However, come the trial itself, any measures to withhold identification 'shall not be prejudicial to or inconsistent with the rights of the accused' (Article 69 (2)). Although the matter will doubtless be further litigated, this formula should ensure that the correct dissenting opinion of Sir Ninian Stephen in the *Tadić Case* is adopted by the ICC, so that we will never have the spectacle of a defendant convicted of a monstrous crime on the word of an accuser whose identity he is not permitted to know.

The defendant is entitled to examine all the evidence upon which the prosecution relies, but this it will have selected from a large body of material collected in the course of the investigation, some of which may point the other way or be helpful to the defence team in its own investigations. The right to disclosure of such material follows from the overriding guarantee of fair trial, and the European Court of Human Rights has ruled that the 'equality of arms' principle requires full defence access.[12] There can be limited exceptions – for example, to protect the names of police informers – but if the information is likely to be relevant to the defence, then refusal to disclose means, in European law, that the trial cannot be fair and must be abandoned. The Statute addresses these difficulties in Article 67 (2) by imposing a limited duty on the prosecutor to disclose evidence which 'he or she believes shows or tends to show the innocence of the accused, or to mitigate the guilt of the accused, or which may affect the credibility of prosecution evidence'.[13] This approach is unsatisfactory. Disclosure should not hinge on the 'belief' of an adversary party, which will inevitably be coloured by its commitment to prove guilt. Only the defence can judge what will be helpful to the defence, and for that reason it deserves full access to prosecution files, subject to the removal or redaction of documents which are judged (by the court, and not the prosecutor) to be both sensitive and of no significance for the resolution of the charges. Where material which the prosecution cannot or will not disclose is relevant to the defence, then the charge should be withdrawn rather than expose the accused to a trial which carries a real prospect of unfairness.

The prosecutor will, it must be hoped, have access to material collected by states through secretive diplomatic channels, and by surveillance and intercept systems which in the interests of their national security they may not wish the prosecutor to divulge to defenders linked with enemy forces. The availability of such material will in any event be known to the prosecutor, who may seek it (as may the defence) under the provisions for state party co-operation. The prosecutor may request evidence from an intelligence officer or security chief of a state which refuses the request on grounds of national security. All such cases can be brought to the Court for resolution, if possible, under Article 72 which provides for every kind of compromise on disclosure. If co-operation fails, the Court *must* order disclosure if the material is relevant and necessary to establish guilt or innocence, and a state party which defies the order will be reported to the Security Council. In the meantime, however, the trial will still continue and the Court 'may make such inference in the trial of the accused as to the existence or non-existence of a fact, as may be appropriate in the circumstances'. This is a curiously permissive power: since vital evidence is being withheld, the trial should either be stopped or the Court precluded from drawing any inference adverse to the defence about a fact which hinges on the missing evidence.

Article 69(7) attempts to grapple with a problem litigated more than any other in adversary systems of criminal trial, namely whether and to what extent evidence obtained by unlawful or unfair means should be admitted and used to prove guilt. This is the 'fruit of the poisoned tree' doctrine which relates (for example) to evidence elicited by *agents provocateurs* and confessions obtained by threats or tricks or torture: methods which are objectionable both because such confessions are prone to be unreliable, and because a court's approval of evidence of this sort would only serve to countenance or encourage the ugly behaviour which produced it. The Statute frames the exclusory rule as follows:

Evidence obtained by means of a violation of this Statute or internationally recognized human rights shall not be admissible if:
(a) The violation casts substantial doubt on the reliability of the evidence; or

(b) The admission of the evidence would be antithetical to and would seriously damage the integrity of the proceedings.

This paragraph is taken, almost verbatim, from Rule 95 of the Hague Tribunal, and its decisions will provide precedents for the ICC (see p. 302). The formulation is less favourable to the defendant than in some domestic laws: it means that minor breaches of defendants' rights will not lead to exclusion of evidence, and even serious breaches (a confession obtained at gunpoint) may be countenanced unless there is 'substantial doubt' about its reliability, e.g. if part of it can be proved untrue. The curious phrasing of the alternative part of the rule will call for a value judgement on whether the Court's integrity is likely to be publicly affected by the spectacle of a defendant being convicted on evidence collected in breach of his fundamental rights. If the crime would not have been committed but for the activities of *agents provocateurs*, or the evidence comprised a confession obtained by torture, this would certainly be the case.

PUNISHMENTS

Article 70 gives the Court a special power to punish, by imprisonment for up to five years, witnesses and defendants who deliberately perjure themselves or forge documents for presentation in evidence. State parties must extend their domestic perjury laws to include attempts to pervert justice at the ICC. This provision is necessary: there are notable examples of attempts to frame defendants charged with crimes against humanity. Armand Hammer advanced his commercial interests by presenting Israel with forged documents to secure the wrongful conviction of Ivan Demjanjuk (see p. 240) and perjury was committed against Duško Tadić (it is a wise witness who knows his own father – see p. 313).

The gravest crimes call for the gravest penalties compatible with human rights treaties: Article 77 provides that for the worst offences a term of life imprisonment which means life is appropriate. In other cases sentences may have a length of up to thirty years, and sentences imposed consecutively for multiple crimes may not exceed this maximum. Convicts may additionally be fined, and have property or assets which represent profits from their crimes forfeited. Article 109 requires state parties to co-operate in freezing and seizing assets within their jurisdiction, so whether these financial penalties have any purpose will very much depend on whether Switzerland, Liechtenstein and other havens for 'dirty money' become parties to the treaty.

The most notable achievement of the penalty provisions is to eschew the death sentence, following the UN's lead with the Hague and Arusha Tribunals. The provisions of the Rome Statute provide further evidence of the movement of international law towards the abolition of capital punishment. States which cling resolutely to it, however, insisted on the insertion of a clause to ensure that the absence of the death penalty from the Rome Statute would not commit them to halting executions of persons convicted of equivalent offences under their national laws.[14] This will have the ironic effect that perpetrators with no place to hide will do their utmost to be tried by the ICC, rather than face execution in their home state. Such a phenomenon has already been witnessed by the Arusha Tribunal, as Hutu leaders are prepared to plead guilty to genocide and suffer lengthy imprisonment rather than face the prospect of trial for the same crime at a kangaroo court in Rwanda, swiftly followed by public execution.

There are provisions for ordering reparations to victims of crimes, following the lead in this respect of the Inter-American Court. After any conviction, the Trial Division may hear representations on behalf of victims and their families, and make an order against the convict requiring compensation or restitution of stolen property. Where the convict has no assets, the award will be made out of a trust fund set up by the state parties for this purpose. This is welcome, especially if the trust fund attracts wealthy private individual benefactors, for the prospects of making convicts like Tadić 'pay' for their crimes against humanity are remote. The Court may in time deal with a few fallen dictators with millions salted away in Swiss bank accounts, but its focus on individual rather than state responsibility means that the countries and the peoples for whose benefit and in whose service most crimes against humanity are committed will be spared all financial consequences. The Treaty makes no provision for reparations from countries where international crimes have popular support. Were another Hitler to be convicted of genocide, his six million victims would look forlornly for compensation from his personal assets, despite the fact that the collective (or at least governmental) responsibility for the Holocaust would justify reparations. Germany, indeed, has paid out US $60 billion over the last half-century to Holocaust victims, and in February 1999 Chancellor Schröder announced a further US $6 billion in compensation for surviving slave labourers. The scandalous failure of the Japanese government and its courts in 1998 to provide reparations to English and Australian prisoners-of-war treated barbarically in its camps provided a topical example for diplomats in Rome: it was precisely because they feared the ICC could embarrass states suffering from human rights amnesia that they declined to allow the Court to order reparations against governments. This omission reflects one of the key weaknesses in the current philosophy behind the international justice movement, which denies the existence of collective responsibility in order to fasten upon the blameworthy individual. Where crimes against humanity are concerned, the two are not mutually exclusive.

APPEALS

The right of a convicted defendant to have both the verdict and the sentence reviewed on appeal – a right notably denied at Nuremberg – is vouchsafed by Article 81, and will take the form of a hearing by a five-judge Appeals Division. Commendably, there is also provision for a prisoner or (after his death) his relatives to make a later application to review the conviction on the ground that fresh evidence, unavailable at the time of trial through no fault of the defence, has been uncovered which might have resulted in an acquittal if it had been presented at the trial. Victims of a miscarriage of justice may be compensated by the Court, and anyone who has been unlawfully arrested or detained under its process shall have an enforceable right to compensation. The necessity for such provision was demonstrated in 1998 by the case of two Bosnian Serb brothers who were forcibly snatched by NATO forces and immediately transported to prison in the Netherlands, where it turned out, to everyone's embarrassment, that they were not the individuals referred to in the arrest warrant.

Unnecessarily, and indeed oppressively, the prosecution is also given a right of appeal against an acquittal, and the defendant may even be imprisoned pending such an appeal. If the burden of proof 'beyond reasonable doubt' has any meaning, then an acquittal by all or a majority of the experienced judges in the Trial Division, who have had the benefit of seeing and hearing all the witnesses, means as a matter of logic that reasonable doubt *must* exist, whatever the Appeals Division may say (see p. 305). This right of the prosecution to appeal against an acquittal on the facts is a feature of inquisitorial systems, where the trial judge will often have been involved in the investigation and justice may require that an appeal tribunal take a fresh and impartial look at the facts. But the delegations which insisted upon prosecutorial appeal failed to understand the adversary system, and the logical consequence of having a standard of proof 'beyond reasonable doubt'.

When the Treaty is eventually ratified by at least sixty states, the Court will be set up by an assembly of these state parties. By March 2000 it had attracted ninety-three signatures, but only seven ratifications – an indication that it will not commence until several years into the millennium. Thereafter, the assembly will meet annually to review the Court's progress and ensure its funding, which will come from contributions the state parties levy upon themselves, funds provided by the UN and voluntary contributions from anyone else (Ted Turner's lavish contribution to the UN has given encouragement to the soliciting of private benefaction, and the ICC offers a unique opportunity for arms corporation conscience money). Any disputes between state parties over interpretation of the Rome Statute may, under Article 119, be referred to the International Court of Justice. A conference to review the Statute and consider amendments to it shall be convened by the UN Secretary-General seven years after it enters into force. Regrettably, there can be no amendment to any substantive provision until the Review Conference, which (given several years' delay in obtaining necessary ratifications) will not be held until the end of the first decade of the twenty-first century.

There are two last concessions to state sovereignty. There are no reservations allowed to this Treaty, but Article 124 permits a state party to ratify, but in doing so to make a declaration which exempts it for seven years from the Court's jurisdiction over war crimes committed by its citizens or on its territory. It follows that any state party contemplating an aggressive war in the near future would be well advised to make an Article 124 declaration. (It is a measure of America's hostility to international justice that it wanted the opt-out to include crimes against humanity as well, and to last for ten years.) A state which has thus exempted its leaders from responsibility for war crimes may still be concerned about their prosecution for genocide: in this event it should exercise its right to withdraw, under Article 127, a year or more before the genocide is scheduled to begin. Such action – by a letter to the UN Secretary-General – will pull the jurisdictional rug from under the Court in respect to any investigation commenced more than a year after he receives the letter.

THE FUTURE

Much of the support for an International Criminal Court was governed by the wish to see the great villains of the late twentieth century behind bars. Pol Pot was alive and well through most of the preparatory sessions, with 1.7 million deaths to his discredit. Idi Amin had retired to Saudi Arabia and 'Baby Doc' Duvalier to the south of France; the torturers and death squad leaders of Latin America clung to the amnesties they had extracted and General Pinochet was preparing to fly first-class to take tea with Mrs Thatcher and have his spinal problems attended by top surgeons in Harley Street. Newspaper articles about the Rome Conference were illustrated by their mug shots – unpaid endorsements of the ideal of international justice. But as the diplomats well knew (even if the journalists did not) these malefactors would all be allowed to escape: the governments of the world would never countenance a court with the power to reach back into history, or even to feel the collars of leaders who were currently in power. The UN insisted from the outset that the Court was a futuristic project, for a 'future generation' of criminals. So obsessed were the diplomats with the need to cast a veil over the past, and indeed the present, that *two* articles of the Rome Statute say so, in terms. Their headings both lapse into Latin, as if trying to cloak their embarrassment. Article 11 (headed 'Jurisdiction *ratione temporis*') emphasizes that 'The Court has jurisdiction only with respect to crimes committed after the entry into force of this Statute.' Article 24 (headed 'Non-retroactivity *ratione personae*') repeats that 'No person shall be criminally responsible under this Statute for conduct prior to the entry into force of the Statute.' The Statute, be it remembered, enters into force sixty days after it has been ratified by sixty nations – an event not likely to occur until well after the year 2000. On 17 July 1998, the torturers of the twentieth century must have thought they were safe for ever from international justice.

This global cop-out is dressed up dishonestly as an application of the well-recognized rule against retrospective criminal prosecutions. It is nothing of the kind: genocide, war crimes and crimes against humanity were established in customary international law long before 1998, and if there *were* any question as to whether a charge brought at the ICC over atrocities in the 1970s had by that time crystallized as an international offence, then the defendants could be given the benefit of the doubt. In principle, the ICC should have been as little bothered by the rule against retroactivity as the courts which tried Eichmann or Barbie or any of the more recently captured Nazis. Why should Nazis be treated as a special case, when people like Mengistu and Amin and Khieu Samphan and Pinochet are actually *more* culpable because their crimes were not committed in a world war and they were well aware of the Nuremberg judgment and the Conventions which made their actions criminal at the time they were committed? By the dishonest devices of Articles 11 and 24, the UN was insisting they should live happily ever after.

This support for impunity was another victory for diplomacy over law, for state sovereignty over human rights. The nations of the world were not prepared to surrender their most wicked residents to international justice: the petty notion of sovereignty still requires them to be tried locally or not at all. Article 11(2) goes further: it even provides that, after the Statute has come into force, if it is then ratified by state A the ICC can still have no jurisdiction over crimes occurring in state A or perpetrated by its nationals before the date of ratification. This means that if the Statute came into force (after sixty ratifications) in 2003, without being ratified by Indonesia, and a genocidal massacre of local Chinese by the Indonesian army took place in 2005, Indonesia's ratification of the Treaty in 2006 would still not serve to bring the massacre within the Court's jurisdiction. In the absence of a reference from the Security Council under Chapter VII, nation states will retain the right to harbour suspects from international justice.

There were, however, some positive aspects of the Rome Conference. Most notable was the solid support for the idea of global justice demonstrated by hundreds of non-government organizations and professional associations, demonstrating the extent to which this mass movement has come to influence 'like-minded' democracies. The new political importance of satisfying this constituency had been apparent at the 1997 Ottawa Conference on Land Mines, and then in the worldwide campaign to stop the use of child soldiers. But for all the lobbying skills and co-ordinated pressure of the NGO coalition, it has so far failed to break the stranglehold of the Pentagon over American foreign policy. The US military will not abandon anti-personnel mines, or the recruitment of 17-year-olds, or its obsessive determination to save its soldiers from international justice. The NGO movement, which does not lack for Americans or American funding, must for the immediate future concentrate on bringing the US military out of its bunker: an international court without US support makes it impossible to credit the triumphalist nonsense emanating at the conclusion of the Rome Conference from the NGO coalition. Under the banner headline 'We Won', its convenor declared, 'the establishment of the ICC will prevent the senseless murder and torture of millions of persons in the next century . . . I think what was accomplished in Rome was a kind of miracle . . .' The kind of miracle, it might be suggested, that relies upon smoke and mirrors, not to mention deluded propagandists.

The concept of an International Criminal Court, with independent prosecutors putting tyrants and torturers in the dock before independent judges, has been a great post-war dream. The Rome Statute demonstrates how much of a dream it remains, even after the pre-millennium pressure exerted by all the NGOs in the world (over 800 of them joined the lobby by the end) to bring it to fulfilment. They got their court all right, but it ended up being a court of a curious sort, where superpowers pull the strings (through the Security Council) yet at the same time (in the case of the US and China) refuse to support it. This ICC will not, however, dispense 'victor's justice' and it may, if blessed initially with prosecutors and judges of skill and integrity, gather the confidence and credibility to overcome the distrust and suspicion manifested by the US delegation in Rome. The US obsession about protecting its soldiers from international criminal justice is illogical, firstly because the model for it – the Hague tribunal – is painstakingly fair to the defence (rather more so than many US army courts martial) and secondly because the 'complementarity' provisions mean that the ICC will have no jurisdiction over a national who is proceeded against in America. That country shows no recent reluctance to prosecute its soldier-criminals; quite the contrary: in early 2000 it appointed a high-powered inquiry into allegations which had just surfaced of mass murder by its troops at the South Korean hamlet of No Gun Ri in 1950. There could be no better example of a proper response to war crimes accusations, and the same spirit should inform a willingness – at least in principle – to submit to international judicial scrutiny. In this event, and granted the continuing momentum of the human rights movement, its seven-year review conference may be the occasion for making universal jurisdiction over crimes against humanity truly universal.

IO

The Case of General Pinochet

Compatriots, I take leave of you. The air force is bombing the radio towers, but I will not resign. Placed in this historical timewarp, I will pay with my life for my people's loyalty, telling you that conscience will not be blindfolded for ever. They have the power, and they will dominate us, but social progress cannot be halted by criminal force. History is ours, determined by you the people. Defend but do not sacrifice yourselves. Do not let yourselves be humiliated, do not for my sake let yourselves be crushed or murdered. I have faith in the destiny of Chile, to rise above this grey and bitter moment when treason prevails. Sooner rather than later free men and women will walk our avenues full of trees to construct a better society. These are my last words. I die knowing that there will come a moral law to punish the felony and the cowardice and the treason.

Thus did Dr Salvador Allende, the elected head of the state of Chile, bid a broadcast farewell to his people on 11 September 1973 as war planes circled to bomb the presidential palace. That day's putsch was joined by General Pinochet in his role as commander-in-chief of the armed forces: he unlawfully commanded his forces to overthrow the democratic government and to murder its most prominent supporters, whether they resisted or not. The conspiracy, soon led by Pinochet, envisaged not only these extrajudicial executions but the capture of thousands of potential opponents and their vicious suffering at centres which were already designated and equipped with electrodes and iron beds (for 'the grill') and other torture paraphernalia. About 4,000 people were disappeared over the next few years, and tens of thousands were processed through the torture centres as part of a preconceived plan to break the spirit of opposition to military rule and to spread

terror among potential dissidents. The torture always involved infliction of physical pain by electric shocks, and in many cases it included
degradation of the human personality through rape and bestiality, and
ritual humiliation in front of family and friends. Pinochet appointed
himself president of a military junta, and in due course styled himself
'Supreme Chief of the Nation' and then 'President of the Republic'.
He ruled in this capacity, as self-appointed head of state, until 1990.

What sets Pinochet's behaviour so high on any scale of wickedness
was his systematic and institutionalized use of torture as a device
to keep himself in power by terrifying and demoralizing potential
opposition from unarmed and unorganized civilians. The rituals of
the torture centres were intended to send horrific whispers throughout
the populace: this was the punishment for thinking and speaking ill
of the regime. For this reason, many were eventually released, broken
in body and spirit, to tell of the disappearance of those who had
been killed and secretly buried. What fixes Pinochet with personal
responsibility is that he set up an organization – DINA – within the
military to supervise the operations of the torture centres under the
directorship of Colonel Mañuel Contreras, who reported daily and
directly to him.[1] Pinochet extended the torture conspiracy to Chilean
subversives abroad, targeting potential victims in Spain and Italy,
and approved the assassination in Washington of Orlando Letelier,
Allende's popular ambassador to the US, who was killed in 1976 by
a car bomb which also took the life of his driver, a US citizen. Pinochet
exported his revolution through Operation Condor – a grandiose plan
to rid Latin America of left-wingers, which involved co-operation
with other military juntas, most enthusiastically that of Argentina.
But since Pinochet's strategy necessarily involved the release of some
victims to spread alarm, the evidence quickly mounted and in 1975
became the subject of debates and resolutions in the UN General
Assembly. There, Chile's diplomats dishonestly denied that torture
had taken place, but significantly they voted for one resolution
(No. 3452) which recognized the practice as an international crime.

In 1978, Pinochet granted an amnesty to 'all persons who as
authors, accomplices, or accessories committed . . . criminal offences
during the period of the State of Siege between 11 September 1973
and 10 March 1978', excluding only (at the insistence of the Carter

administration) the Letelier car bombing. This ludicrous self-amnesty was upheld in every case by the country's pro-Pinochet judiciary (two days after the coup, its Supreme Court expressed its 'most intimate pleasure' at the new military regime) despite two rulings by the Inter-American Commission that it violates the American Convention's guarantee of an effective remedy for human rights violations.[2] After seventeen years, Pinochet made Hastings Banda's mistake of holding a referendum in the belief the people loved him or else feared him too much to vote against him: they voted instead for democracy, which he had to grant, although on terms which allowed him to appoint some senators and remain as commander-in-chief of the armed forces. On retirement from that position in 1998 Pinochet was made senator-for-life, which carries under Chilean law yet further immunity from prosecution. Although cases have been brought against him in Santiago, the judge before whom they have been consolidated publicly recognized that the immunity left him powerless to arrest the senator-for-life. (Were it ever lifted, any case against Pinochet would automatically be transferred to the jurisdiction of the military courts, where his conviction would be inconceivable.)[3] It was from this impregnable position in 'the Fatherland' that he sallied forth in October 1998, to have his bad back attended to by doctors in Harley Street, London W1.

AN ARREST IN HARLEY STREET

That Augusto Pinochet felt free to travel the world in 1998 was a measure of the impunity which had to this point been enjoyed in practice by tyrants, notwithstanding the accumulation of treaties under which their crimes were declared contrary to international law. Never before had a former head of state, visiting another friendly country, been held legally amenable to its criminal process. Little attention was paid when 'The Association of Progressive Prosecutors of Spain' began a private action in 1996 against Pinochet and members of the Argentinean junta, or when their action was taken over by Madrid investigating magistrate Balthasar Garzón (whose previous investigation into the Spanish state involvement in 'death squads' in the Basque country had helped to bring down the Gonzalez government).

Garzón's case against Pinochet over 'Operation Condor' and DINA torture and killings of Spanish nationals gelled when Manuel Contreras testified that DINA had followed the dictator's personal orders.[4] But Garzón was in Spain, the evidence was in Chile, and Pinochet was careful to travel only to Britain, where he was a frequent and frequently honoured visitor. He had always received red-carpet treatment: as commander-in-chief of the Chilean army he was fêted by the Ministry of Defence in the hope he would purchase British arms. These previous visits had been open and uneventful, even when he dined at the gastronomic hub of London's liberal intelligentsia, the River Café: its proprietress, Ms Ruthie Rogers (wife of the architect who designed the European Court of Human Rights), was so stomach-churned at the sight of his name on the gold card print-out that she donated the cost of his meal to Amnesty International. In October 1998 he did not even bother to take the elementary precaution of obtaining a diplomatic visa: he was, so he thought, clad in the impregnable armour of state sovereignty, which had for centuries shielded every tyrant against legal attack. On arrival at Heathrow Airport, Senator and Mrs Pinochet were duly met by representatives of the UK's ethical Foreign Office, who ushered them to the Hounslow Suite, a VIP room hired for their comfort while FO lackeys went to collect their bags and have their passports stamped. The ageing mass murderer later took tea (I am reliably informed it was whisky) with his good friend Lady Thatcher and then went into the private clinic.

It was then that the *Guardian* reported Pinochet's presence in London. Under the headline 'A Murderer among Us', the paper's Latin-American veteran Hugh O'Shaughnessy tongue-in-cheekily reported, 'there is a foreign terrorist in our midst who is hiding somewhere in London . . . If you are a patient in the London Clinic, be particulary alert. Some people say General Augusto Pinochet Ugarte is holed up there for treatment'.[5] This tipped off magistrate Garzón, who through the Spanish Embassy made a request for Pinochet's arrest under the European Convention on Extradition by which almost all Continental countries agree to surrender persons wanted for serious criminal offences. The post-operative Pinochet became nervous and prepared to flee on the next plane, scheduled to depart at 7 a.m. on Saturday, 17 October. On 16 October, Garzón obtained a warrant in

Spain for Pinochet's arrest: it was rushed to London where late that evening Scotland Yard anti-terrorist officers moved in to surround the clinic and its recumbent torturer, just a few hours before his flight. This arrest, one of Scotland Yard's finest operations, was greeted at first with astonishment and even outrage: Lady Thatcher condemned the inhumanity of the police, disturbing the rest of a 'sick and frail old man'. The Chief Justice refused the Spanish government (represented by the Crown Prosecution Service) an adjournment to prepare its case, and after a two-day hearing pronounced it plain that an ex-head of state had sovereign immunity for every crime he committed in exercising the functions of office, no matter how heinous. The argument that this immunity did not cover torture and other crimes which are contrary to international law had 'some attraction', said the Chief Justice, but 'where is one to draw the line?' Crimes against humanity were committed by heads of state pursuant to their official functions, said another judge, because 'history shows that it has indeed on occasions been state policy to exterminate or oppress particular groups'.[6] General Pinochet was granted habeas corpus, but was ordered to stay in the clinic to recuperate from his operation and his law suit pending a prosecution appeal.

The *Pinochet Case* proceeded directly to Britain's highest court, the House of Lords. Amnesty International and Humans Rights Watch, concerned that developments in international law had not been appreciated in the lower court, were given leave to intervene in the action in support of the prosecution. After hearing argument for six days and deliberating for two weeks, the panel split 3–2 in favour of extradition, on the basis that sovereign immunity applied only to sovereigns who were exercising *legitimate* state functions and by no stretch of the imagination could widespread torture be regarded as legitimate conduct by anyone, let alone a head of state. It followed that the doctrine of sovereign immunity did not bar Pinochet's extradition to stand trial in Spain, if the Home Secretary decided in the exercise of his discretion that to do so would be neither unjust nor oppressive. The spotlight swung from the legal to the political arena as Home Secretary Jack Straw was showered with demands that he should show 'compassion' for an old man and respect for the state sovereignty of Chile by sending its former ruler back where he belonged, where his impunity was said to be part of the deal for 'national reconciliation'. The Chilean government made loud diplomatic noises that refusal to return the Senator would be to insult its sovereign dignity. In the end Jack Straw played a scrupulously straight bat, finding no reason not to let the law take its course. So it came to pass that on 11 December 1998, fifty years almost to the day after the Universal Declaration, a man who had done much to destroy its promises finally stood in the dock of a top security court in London.

A few days later, however, another panel of law lords was persuaded that one of their brethren, Lord Hoffmann, who had joined in the 3–2 majority decision, should not have sat because he had helped to fundraise for Amnesty International. On the grounds, therefore, that justice had not been seen to be done, Pinochet was entitled to a fresh hearing before a court comprising seven judges who had never manifested support for human rights by connections with Amnesty.[7] Their 6–1 judgment on 24 March 1999 proved historic: they held that an international law prohibition which had achieved *jus cogens* status, such as the rule against torture committed systematically for policy reasons (i.e. a crime against humanity) dissolved the sovereign immunity which customary law granted to former officials and heads of state. However, a quirk of statutory extradition law – the 'double criminality' principle that Britain could not extradite for a crime it could not itself punish at the time it was committed – meant that Pinochet could be sent to Spain only for crimes committed since 1988, when Britain introduced extra-territorial torture as an offence in its own law. Since his conspiracy to use torture to maintain power lasted until 1990, Pinochet could not hide behind the shield of Chile's immunity in respect of his last two years as dictator. In due course, the indefatigable Garzón uncovered thirty more cases of torture in 1988–9 for which Pinochet could be held responsible, and on 8 October 1999 the Bow Street magistrate ordered his extradition to Spain. Terrified of facing trial, Pinochet launched an appeal, but shortly before it was due to be heard, medical experts pronounced him unfit for trial due to brain damage caused by a stroke, whereupon the Home Secretary extended to Pinochet a compassion notably denied to victims of his own secret police, and he fled back to Chile.

The *Pinochet Case* came to crystallize the legal and political problems of accountability for crimes against humanity. It was the potency, in international law, of that concept which finally found the Achilles heel in the armour of state sovereignty, the organizing principle of international affairs which is based on the fiction of the State as an entity that can do no wrong. Governments may come and go, with more or less barbarity, led by kings or by generals or by demagogues, but the shell of statehood remains impregnable: there must be no intervention in the internal affairs of 'the State', so the theory goes, even if it is run by Idi Amin or Adolf Hitler. Its ambassadors and diplomats must carry with them the shield of immunity from prosecution, whether for non-payment of parking fines or for mass murder. The *Pinochet Case* was momentous because – for the first time – sovereign immunity was not allowed to become sovereign impunity. The great play of sovereignty, with all its pomp and panoply, can now be seen for what it hides: a posturing troupe of human actors, who when off-stage are sometimes prone to rape the chorus.

The line that the Chief Justice could not at first locate turned out on closer examination to be plainly drawn by the concept of a crime against humanity: a crime so black it does not admit of human forgiveness. Pinochet's crimes in this class were no more Chile's business than they were Britain's business or Spain's business: they were committed against humanity in general because the very fact that a person can order them diminishes the human race. That such crimes override sovereignty was a doctrine first propounded by Robert Jackson at the Nuremberg trial, and remained for decades a talking point in university common rooms and post-graduate theses; however, until the Serb and Croat bloodfeuding it had no practical application other than as a legal lasso for old Nazis like Eichmann and Barbie. Convicting war criminals in Yugoslavia and Rwanda was no great jump: these were states in the process of dissolution, their armour of sovereignty cracked in the course of their disintegration. Apparently helpful precedents forged in the United States in respect to General Noriega and the ex-Philippines president, Ferdinand Marcos, were not true exceptions to the sovereignty rule, because the Philippines government waived its immunity over Marcos, while Noriega, never formally Panama's head of state, was prosecuted not for abusing state power but for his private criminal enterprise in running drugs. So the

Pinochet Case became the first and paradigm test of international human rights law, because Pinochet travelled to Britain with the sovereignty of Chile wrapped as tightly around him as the felt-collared military cloak which featured in most of his posed photographs. For that collar to be felt by Scotland Yard required twelve law lords to leap over the fiction upon which modern nation states have always based their conduct towards one other.

THE STATE IN INTERNATIONAL LAW

A state, for the purposes of international law, is an entity which possesses a defined territory, occupied by a permanent and governed population, and has a recognized capacity to enter into relations with other states.[8] Frontiers may be uncertain or disputed, but there must at least be a community occupying some territory which is subject to a nominally independent political authority, however organized. Size does not matter, hence statehood is accorded to tiny islands like Nassau and Tuvalu, each occupying some ten square miles with only 10,000 inhabitants, and to the sleazy casino land of Monaco (0.4 square miles and 32,000 people) and the tax havens of San Marino and Liechtenstein (twenty-four and sixty-two square miles respectively) with some 30,000 occupants, mainly accountants. These are states with equal sovereign rights and the same voting powers in the UN General Assembly as China (1.2 billion people) and India (935 million). Statehood is, quite wrongly, usually accorded to the Holy See, although the Vatican City is 0.2 square miles and is occupied only by 1,000 Catholic bureaucrats. It is no more than an Italian city which has, through historical anomalies and lack of principle, been accorded the status of a 'party' to many international treaties.[9] The behaviour of its diplomats ('papal nuncios') has often damaged the cause of human rights – as with their obsessions about abortion (they even attempted to stop NATO supplying 'morning-after' pills to victims of Serb rapes) and their secret urgings of the British government to return Pinochet to Chile.

'Recognition' of statehood has been a matter of *realpolitik* rather than law, and 'puppet' or 'client' states of major powers have usually passed muster. However, an important principle was established by the world's refusal to recognize the bantustans granted nominal independence by South Africa: they were no more dependent than some Soviet puppets, but the difference was that they were emanations of apartheid, an illegal policy amounting (when imposed by violence) to a crime against humanity.[10] Although this was not the reason advanced for denying recognition to Transkei, Ciskei, Venda and 'Bop', it may be seen in retrospect as the rationale. It was certainly the UN's rationale for depriving South Africa of its longstanding mandate over Namibia (South-west Africa) and the ICJ eventually confirmed that introducing apartheid was a breach of its trust obligations.[11] There was a principle here, beginning to chip away at sovereignty, but it was not yet identified as having that effect.

The high-water mark of sovereign independence is the 'non-intervention in internal affairs' rule, contained in Article 2(7) of the UN Charter and most expansively in the General Assembly's 1970 'Friendly Relations' resolution:

No State or group of States has the right to intervene, directly or indirectly, for any reason whatever, in the internal or external affairs of any other State. Consequently, armed intervention and all other forms of interference or attempted threats against the personality of the State or against its political, economic or cultural elements, are in violation of international law.

This resolution doubtless encouraged Pinochet and Pol Pot and Mengistu and the Duvaliers and all the other rulers subsequently guilty of crimes against humanity to believe in their impregnability. It begs so many questions (what amounts to 'indirect intervention' or a threat to a state's 'cultural elements'?) and was so immediately and routinely ignored by superpowers, busy destabilizing each other's spheres of influence, that it cannot be given much force beyond a rule against unilateral attack, and even that is undermined by state practice. In March 1999, NATO, without Security Council approval, launched air attacks on Serbia, heedless of its sovereignty, in an effort to halt its brutal persecution of the Albanian majority in Kosovo. Pariah states have been warned: they now put their sovereignty at risk by committing crimes against their own people's humanity, because this can no longer be accounted an 'internal affair'.

One important attribute of sovereignty is jurisdiction – in other words, power – to try criminal offences and to adjudicate civil disputes. The State, through its legal system, exercises power over acts which take place on its territory or disputes which are brought there by agreement. A state's power to try an offence which has taken place abroad must be exercised with respect to international law – and, apart from treaties which make up that law, it may not exercise jurisdiction over actions by non-nationals taken outside its boundaries unless these impact adversely on its own people. When an alleged offender is found in a foreign country, it must make a formal, state-to-state request for his extradition. What will halt any of these legal processes in their tracks is a claim to 'state' (or 'sovereign') immunity asserted on behalf of a defendant, whether that defendant is the State itself (sought to be made liable in a civil action for damages) or a present or past official or diplomat on whose behalf the immunity attaching to the State itself may be asserted to stop any proceedings, be they civil or criminal. Immunities are of two kinds, and are (naturally) expressed in Latin. Absolute immunity (*ratione personae*) is bestowed upon those who embody or represent the State (i.e. on heads of state and heads of diplomatic missions) but it lasts only during their tenure of office. Ex-heads, along with agents such as generals and police chiefs and ministers, enjoy only restrictive immunity (*ratione materiae*), which covers all acts performed officially but does not include actions taken for private gratification. Whether such people can be sued or prosecuted in a foreign court depends first on the nature of their immunity, if any, and then on whether the case is barred by the 'Act of State' doctrine – a self-denying ordinance by which municipal courts refuse to sit in judgment on politically fraught questions about how foreign sovereigns have behaved within their own territory. These issues are said to be 'non-justiciable' because the court finds them too hot to handle. These doctrines are different – sovereign immunity is a limit on the court's power imposed by international law and 'Act of State' derives from the court's own nervousness about its competence to decide a foreign political issue – but both tend to be raised whenever and wherever litigation seeks to make a foreign state and its officials responsible for human rights violations.

SOVEREIGN IMMUNITY

Sovereign immunity followed in the first place from the divine right of kings: you could not put an infallible ruler on trial since, if you did, the verdict must always go in his favour. Machiavelli's princes were attracted by its convenience in the city states of Renaissance Europe: it reduced the need for poison and gave them some protection while travelling. It was viewed as a logical development from old heraldic principles which allowed emissaries to pass unmolested through the battlelines. Later, American courts followed the English 'divine right' authorities, although quite why a country which had fought to free itself from this very tyranny should adopt its organizing principle that the King could do no wrong is 'one of the mysteries of legal evolution'.[12] The answer is probably found in the nineteenth-century preference for positivism, reflected in the acceptance of the doctrine that international law could bind states only when they consented to be bound, and not (as the natural lawyers asserted) whenever an objective morality required some limit on their power. This latter position had been commonly accepted in the sixteenth century by natural lawyers as a necessary precondition for peaceful coexistence:[13] they never doubted a head of state's liability for war crimes.[14] Positivism denied such liability, as inconsistent with political convenience and reality. It followed – and this was positivism's second disastrous legacy – that only states could be subject (and only if they agreed) to international law, which could afford no rights of any kind to individuals. These nineteenth-century positivist doctrines fashioned the wide state immunity rule, which prevailed until Nuremberg gave back to international law a principle of external moral restraints on sovereign action and a precedent for incriminating individuals.

A country's deference to 'sovereigns' – its own, and those who visit – fluctuated between according them complete exemption from the law and a 'restricted immunity', which covered them only in their public capacity and not for 'private' acts which had nothing to do with their leadership of the State. The choice between the two theories –

immunity 'absolute' or 'restrictive' – became of increasing commercial importance as the twentieth century progressed, because sovereign immunity was state immunity, and states (especially those run by communist and socialist governments) began to engage in commerce through nationalized industries and wholly owned trading corporations which were legal emanations of the State. If these state traders were to enter the market on a fair and rational basis, it was obvious that 'absolute' immunity would have to be abandoned, because it did not permit them to be sued for debt or breach of contract or anything else. But for many years the English judiciary resisted any change to the absolute immunity principle suggested in 1880 by the case of the *Parlement Belge*, namely that the courts of every state must decline to exercise jurisdiction over 'the person of any sovereign or ambassador of any other State, or over the public property of any state . . . though such sovereign, ambassador or property be within its jurisdiction'.[15] Consequently, later courts refused to impound a ship owned by the Portuguese government which failed to pay up on contracts in Liverpool, even though it was engaged in non-government trading operations; and they refused to allow the Tass news agency to be sued for libel because it was a propaganda organ of the USSR.[16] In 1977, in the *Trendtex Trading Case*, the Court of Appeal at last looked at the reality: a Nigerian government bank trading in Britain was not entitled to immunity, because it was not part of the apparatus of the State.[17] Executive government has no need to set up a bank to trade abroad; if it decides to do so, the bank must pay its debts or else be sued on them, like any other company.

This was the position which had been reached by the courts of a number of other European countries, on the basis that state commercial activity had made the absolute immunity theory an anachronism. The US State Department had been wont to formally restrict state (or sovereign) immunity, but in practice restricted it to those states and sovereigns which supported the US. The government claimed the right to 'suggest' to courts by formal letter whether immunity requests by foreign states were valid, and its determinations were made not upon objective criteria but upon current considerations of diplomacy and US interests.[18] Immunity was for friends, not foes. In 1976, Congress enacted the Foreign Sovereign Immunities Act (FSIA), which set out clear tests, hinging on the commercial nature of the activity, for deciding whether sovereign immunity was lost, and a State Immunity Act to similar effect was adopted in Britain in 1978. These two statutes were passed in the interests of certainty and of trade, but they gave sovereign immunity an inflexible, once-and-for-all meaning which drained the law of its dynamism and capacity to evolve. At that stage of its development, the doctrine was moving from an absolute jurisdictional bar to a position where interference would be permitted in respect of a state's trading activities or its ex-head's private transactions. The distinction which emerged in this period, expressed as usual in Latin, was between governmental actions (*jure imperii*), which remained immune, and acts of a private or commercial nature (*jure gestionis*), which were amenable to justice in foreign courts. The distinction was never very satisfactory in practice, and local courts attempting to apply it came to different decisions on similar subjects, such as the purchase of military equipment and the promotional activities of government tourist agencies.[19] The House of Lords split 3–2 over whether an action for breach of contract could proceed when a ship operated by an agency of the Cuban state was prohibited by that government from delivering its contracted cargo to Chile, as a political protest against the Pinochet coup.[20] It is hardly surprising that a doctrine productive of such confusion in commercial cases should prove even less satisfactory when invoked by torture victims attempting to sue their tormentors.

It is only necessary to revisit the rationale of state immunity to recognize its irrelevant and ceremonial basis where crimes against humanity are concerned. The classic statement is that of Marshall CJ in the 1812 US Supreme Court case of *The Schooner Exchange* v. *McFaddon*:

One sovereign being in no respect amenable to another, and being bound by obligations of the highest character not to degrade the dignity of his nation, by placing himself or its sovereign rights within the jurisdiction of another, can be supposed to enter a foreign territory only under an express licence, or in the confidence that the immunities belonging to his independent sovereign station, though not expressly stipulated, are reserved by implication, and will be extended to him.[21]

But this imputes dignity to a state which has none, whenever the shell of statehood covers a government which engages in torture and murder. It was based as well on the classic fiction that all states are equal, although in the real world some states are more equal than others, especially in their level of respect for international human rights law.

Whether or not one state has immunity from civil suit in another state will therefore depend on whether the action which causes the damage is characterized as 'sovereign' or 'non-sovereign', but this distinction is entirely unhelpful for victims of human rights abuses who seek to sue the states where they have been falsely imprisoned or tortured. First they have to squeeze their case within statutory exceptions to the immunity rule (which usually relate to a commercial context), and then they must confront the characterization problem that police or military action will be classified as 'governmental' rather than 'private'. Scott Nelson, a US citizen recruited through an American company to do engineering work in Saudi Arabia, fell at both hurdles when he tried to sue that state for the wrongful imprisonment and torture he suffered as a reprisal for publicizing the safety hazards at his work place. Although he entered Saudi Arabia pursuant to a contract for his services, the Supreme Court ruled that he was not within the FSIA's 'commercial activities' exception (hurdle one) because his action arose from the tortious conduct of the Saudi police. He fell at hurdle two (characterization) because the conduct alleged 'boils down to abuse of the power of its police by the Saudi Government, and however monstrous such abuse undoubtedly may be, a foreign State's exercise of the power of its police has long been understood for purposes of the restrictive theory as peculiarly sovereign in nature'.[22] The solution to this problem was duly provided by another American case, namely that 'international law does not recognize an act that violates *jus cogens* as a sovereign act. A State's violation of the *jus cogens* norm prohibiting official torture therefore would not be entitled to the immunity afforded by international law.'[23] However, victims like Nelson would still fall at hurdle one: the impossibility of bringing torture within the commercial exception to the FSIA would deny them the right to sue the foreign state.

A similar result was reached in Britain under the 1978 State Immunity

Act, which expressly permits actions against foreign states in relation to loans, contracts and other commercial transactions, but which is silent about human rights violations. The Court of Appeal in *Al-Adsani v. Government of Kuwait* said the scheme of the 1978 Act was to give full force to sovereign immunity subject to limited statutory exceptions, and since torture and human rights abuses were not listed as exceptions, Parliament must have intended to leave them out.[24] This case, decided in 1996, illustrates the damage that was done by freezing the law of sovereign immunity in 1978 legislation. These period immunity statutes permit civil actions against governments where agents are responsible for negligent loss of cargo or failure to pay debts, but not if they engage in kidnap or torture or murder. *Nelson* and *Al-Adsani* were relied upon to give Pinochet total immunity, until the House of Lords pointed out that they turn on distinctions made by statutes which apply only to civil actions, and not to crime or to extradition (which is a criminal process).

The one exception is where agents of a foreign state engage in torture or murder or other tortious acts within the territory of the forum (i.e. the state in whose courts the action is brought). It is this territorial connection which permits jurisdiction over another 'sovereign'. In 1976 General Pinochet and his henchman Mañuel Contreras ordered the assassination in Washington of Chile's former ambassador Orlando Letelier: agents killed him with a car bomb which also took the life of his driver. Their relatives sued the Chilean government in the American courts, and its claim to sovereign immunity was rejected on the ground that the lawless act which caused the death took place in the US.[25] The relatives were awarded $5 million in damages, although the Pinochet government, lawless as ever, at first refused to pay a cent. Anomalously, sovereign immunity reasserts itself with absolute force in respect of execution of judgment orders against diplomatic property, so the relatives could not levy execution against the Chilean government's property in the US.[26]

While the 'territorial tort' exception to sovereign immunity is welcome, it remains a logical curiosity: why should the liability of a state for an international crime depend on the happenstance of where the outrage eventually took place? The assassination of Letelier was plotted in Santiago and might have been perpetrated outside the US, in which case his relatives would have had no access to the American courts. And when the territorial connection suspended the immunity and they obtained a judgment in their favour, it sprang back to life to deny them any right to recover their damages from property and bank accounts owned in the US by the sovereign but murderous State.

The change made to sovereign immunity by statute for civil actions was necessitated by the needs of global commerce. It is now time to make a similar settlement in a compromise with global human rights, to reflect the changes in international law over the past half-century. It has been recognized that punishment for crimes against humanity is vital to the well-being of peoples, whether they suffer from them directly or suffer by seeing them on CNN. So these offences are contrary to *jus cogens* – the peremptory rules of international law, which no state or state official can ever claim a licence to breach. State practice forswears genocide and torture and extra-judicial execution, and consequently gives such international crimes the status of *jus cogens*, which in turn means that each state has an *erga omnes* obligation to the international community of states, not merely to refrain from committing such crimes but to co-operate in ensuring their investigation and punishment. Sovereign immunity, based on little more than respect for the dignity of foreign governments, must give way to a legal obligation owed to every member of the international community either to put on trial or to extradite for trial elsewhere any person reasonably accused of violating *jus cogens* by perpetrating a crime against humanity.[27] This is the principle confirmed in the Preamble of the Statute of the International Criminal Court ('it is the duty of every State to exercise its criminal jurisdiction over those responsible for international crimes') and by the 1993 Vienna Declaration and Programme of Action, which called for states to 'abrogate impunity legislation for those responsible for grave violations of human rights such as torture and prosecute such violations, thereby providing a firm basis for the rule of law'.[28] Most powerfully, of course, it was the judgment at Nuremberg which heralded the removal of the shield of state sovereignty for crimes against humanity:

Crimes against international law are committed by men, not by abstract entities, and only by punishing individuals who commit such crimes can the provisions of international law be enforced . . . It was submitted that . . . where the act in question is an act of state, those who carry it out are not personally responsible, but are protected by the doctrine of the sovereignty of the State. In the opinion of the Tribunal [this contention] must be rejected . . . The principle of international law, which under certain circumstances protects the representative of a state, cannot be applied to acts which are condemned as criminal by international law. The authors of these acts cannot shelter themselves behind their official position in order to be freed from punishment in appropriate proceedings.

And that, in a nutshell, is what did for Augusto Pinochet.

BRING ON THE DIPLOMATS

The concept of state sovereignty produces another class of immunity, namely the inviolability accorded to diplomats and to their embassy premises, and even their diplomatic bags. This privilege, recognized through almost universal subscription to the 1961 Vienna Convention on Diplomatic Relations, is based both on the function of the diplomat in representing his state (which cloaks him in its sovereignty) and on the practical convenience and international public interest of keeping open lines of communication between unfriendly states. There is a dated ring to this rationale in an age of e-mail and video conferencing, but the ICJ insists that diplomacy remains 'of cardinal importance for the maintenance of good relations between States in the interdependent world of today'.[29] This was said in 1980, when condemning the Iranian government for permitting student militants to invade the US embassy in Tehran, where they discovered evidence of spying operations which also breached the Vienna Convention. But there was nothing quite so comical during the Cold War as this convention, in so far as it established by law 'inviolable' premises which were invariably bugged in every conceivable way by the host state, and were the control centres for spies run by the sending state.

But the Vienna Convention was drafted by thirty-four government lawyers, who were under orders to puff their diplomats up with as much sovereignty as possible: hence they bestowed it *ratione personae,* to cover absolutely every crime and misdemeanour perpetrated during foreign service, whether or not in the course of duty. This may have been appropriate at a time when diplomats were often blackmailed and honey-trapped: without total immunity they could have been framed for serious crime. But it produced the converse result that diplomats could fearlessly engage in serious crime, using their inviolable premises and diplomatic baggage for drug and gun running, or to assist terrorists with whom their state was in political sympathy. The most notorious abuse was by the Libyan embassy – or rather 'People's Bureau' – in St James's Square, London, which had a firing range in its basement and at least one 'diplomat' who deliberately aimed and fired at PC Yvonne Fletcher, because it was thought she was not doing enough to stop an anti-Gaddafi demonstration outside. To the chagrin of the murdered policewoman's colleagues, they were required to escort to the airport the Libyan killers, who carried the murder weapon inside one of their untouchable diplomatic bags. Each had been declared a *persona non grata*, which is the worst – indeed the only – thing that can happen to an ambassador, unless his sending state waives the immunity so as to permit his prosecution. The problem, of course, is caused by an immunity which is much wider than is necessary to protect the essential functions of a mission. At street level, abuse is reflected in the host city's unpaid parking tickets and unprosecutable offences of shoplifting: in the 1980s, London police reckoned that 40 per cent of these crimes were committed by the vehicles or wives of diplomats. (The US, plagued by more diplomats than other countries, has adopted a novel approach to unpaid parking fines: it tallies the penalties incurred by every embassy and deducts the total from that country's foreign aid.)

The Vienna Convention gives ambassadors total immunity, even in time of war, from arrest (Article 29) and from civil and criminal jurisdiction (Article 31). This lasts from the moment they take up their posts to the moment they leave the country. Thereafter, however, they shed that total immunity and wear its undergarment: immunity *ratione materiae*, covering only their actions done in the course of official duties. They may at last be sued for gambling debts and prosecuted for rape committed during their time of duty, if they can be found. This rule for ex-ambassadors has consequences for ex-heads of state – their functions are quite different, but for various reasons they tend to be assimilated in customary international law and in the relevant local statutes. (In Britain, for example, the State Immunity Act applies the incorporated Vienna Convention to 'a Sovereign or other head of State . . . as it applies to a head of a diplomatic mission'). It follows that a head or acting head of state is totally immune from legal slings and arrows, but an ex-head, whether of state or of mission, is immune only on the restrictive basis, *ratione materiae*, for acts characterized as official functions.

There is, of course, a measure of artificiality about the very concept of 'head' of state, because different political arrangements can allocate this title to ceremonial personages like monarchs, or bestow it upon the actual heads of government. (Thus, Hitler had total immunity when he became Reich chancellor; Tojo remained but partly immune because he was 'under' a hereditary emperor.) None the less, the consequences of shedding absolute immunity can be dramatic, as King Farouk of Egypt discovered to his cost after he blithely ordered eleven expensive dresses for his queen from the Paris salon of Christian Dior. Shortly afterwards he was deposed and all his property confiscated (including the dresses). When the bill arrived he refused to pay, and when sued for the debt relied upon sovereign immunity. But in *Ex-King Farouk* v. *Dior* the Paris Court of Appeal made him pay for his private purchases: for the purposes of trade, there is nothing so ex as an ex-king.

So where does this leave ex-dictators?

American cases on head of state immunity are confused, thanks to the survival of the procedure by which the US State Department may issue a 'suggestion of immunity', which courts accept as binding, whenever attempts are made to sue the former head of a friendly state. This has been used to stop a nuisance writ against Prince Charles (an incipient head of state) while he was visiting the US,[30] and was similarly used to 'suggest' that ex-President Aristide had absolute immunity, during his exile in the US, from an action alleging his responsibility for an unlawful killing in Haiti. Rather than yield its jurisdiction up to the State Department, the court should instead have considered, on the basis that he had only restricted immunity, whether the allegation involved his official conduct during his time as president.[31]

When the Marcos family fled to Hawaii in 1986, America finally had a dictator in residence for whom nobody – except the Marcos family – wanted to suggest immunity. Ferdinand Marcos had for fifteen years in the Philippines personally directed disappearances and what was euphemistically termed 'tactical interrogation' – which meant, for some 10,000 citizens, being asked questions while they were tortured. Victims and their relatives issued an avalanche of writs, and the new Aquino government declined to claim immunity either for Marcos or for his daughter, who was additionally sued for ordering the kidnapping and killing of Decleimedes Trajano, the student who had dared to ask her an embarrassing question (see p. 255). In 1992, the Federal Appeals Court held that neither Marcos nor his daughter could claim any sort of immunity: torture and arbitrary killing were contrary to international law, and were not within the legitimate scope of an official's duty.[32] This was confirmed in the class action brought by victims, on the basis that since systematic torture breached a *jus cogens* rule of international law, it could not be considered a legitimate act of state even when authorized by the head of state: 'a lawsuit against a foreign official acting outside the scope of his authority does not implicate any of the foreign diplomatic concerns involved in bringing suit against another government in the US Courts'. This is not always true, of course, but it meant that the ruling was not directly based on the waiver of immunity by the Philippines. It decided in principle that a ruler loses immunity for unlawful actions breaching *jus cogens*, because they cannot be sovereign acts.[33] Marcos died mid litigation, and finally in February 1999 his estate was ordered to pay $150 million to his victims out of loot totalling $500 million which had been recovered from his Swiss bank account.[34] The happy ending was undoubtedly conditioned by the fact that neither the friendly Philippines government nor the US felt any diplomatic embarrassment over the litigation, although the case serves as a legal precedent because the court rejected immunity on the grounds that torture could not be an official act.[35]

THE LAW TAKES ITS COURSE

Had Augusto Pinochet chosen to fly to New York rather than London, to take tea with Henry Kissinger instead of Margaret Thatcher, his fate would have been determined by politics rather than law. A 'suggestion of immunity' would surely have issued from the State Department, both to placate the friendly state of Chile and to avoid embarrassing details about US complicity in his coup. But the General came to Britain, where his dogged pursuer, magistrate Garzón, sought his extradition to Spain, to the fury of the state of Chile. In most countries, this issue would have been decided quickly and politically, in terms of alliances and trading ties and (in the seventy-three countries which still torture) out of fear of creating a precedent which might affect their rulers' retirement plans. But the British government did something which could not have been expected, and which deserves a considerable measure of praise: it let the law take its course. The course that it took – a magical mystery tour through the jungle of sovereign immunity and into the mire of extradition – could not have been predicted, but in the course of the ride international human rights had acquired the quality of law: it had become, in some small degree, enforceable in the courts of the world. The judges who thought it had no impact against the sovereign state dwindled, from 3–0 at the initial hearing to 2–3, and then lost the last set, 1–6. Four judges held that the allegation of a crime against humanity set up an overriding imperative for trial, while five (the final majority) allowed the Torture Convention to override claims to immunity *ratione materiae*. Thanks to the refusal of Britain's Home Secretary Jack Straw to intervene in the legal process, the *Pinochet Case* became the most important test for international law since Nuremberg itself.

The prosecutors levelled a general conspiracy charge accusing the General of using torture throughout his dictatorship as a means of engendering fear and keeping himself in power:

That you between the 1st August 1973 and the 1st January 1990 agreed with others that a course of conduct would be pursued, namely:

(a) that persons, whether living in Chile or other countries, that you knew or

suspected would be disposed to pose a threat to the lives, safety, occupations, political positions, comforts and beliefs of yourself and other members of the conspiracy, and persons in respected social positions who might be considered by members of the public to pose such a threat, would be abducted, would undergo the infliction of severe pain and suffering, causing grievous bodily harm, whether over a brief period or a period of several months or years;

(b) that some of those victims would thereafter be killed;

(c) that instruments for the purpose of inflicting such pain and suffering would be obtained and distributed in advance to military and other premises where such infliction of pain, suffering, harm and murder would be carried out;

(d) that such pain, suffering, harm and murder would be inflicted by public officials who would take instructions from and report to you;

(e) that such pain, suffering and harm would include rape, buggery and other sexual assault and humiliation;

(f) that such pain, suffering, harm and murder would be inflicted in Chile and in other countries;

(g) that the pain and suffering to be inflicted was not to be limited to such pain and suffering as would bring forward information useful to you from the victims, but would extend to such pain and suffering as would, through the medium of the accounts of survivors and rumour, terrify and subdue persons, both in Chile and in other countries, who might be disposed to criticize or oppose you or your fellow conspirators;

(h) that the victims of the torture would include children and minors;

(i) that such activities would be carried out in secret places and disavowed in public and international forums;

which course of conduct would necessarily involve the commission of the offence of torture, whether in Chile or elsewhere, by one or more public officials in the performance or purported performance of his or their duties, and pursuant to which conspiracy hundreds of thousands of persons were tortured.

Thirty other charges made specific and grisly allegations in respect of particular victims. To take some typical examples:

That you on or about 29th October 1976 being a public official, namely Commander-in-Chief of the Chilean Army, jointly with others intentionally inflicted severe pain or suffering on José Marcelino Gonzalez Malpu, by applying electric current to his genital organs, shoulders and ankles and pretending to shoot his captive naked mother in front of him, in purported performance of official duties.

That you jointly with others intentionally inflicted severe pain or suffering on Pedro Hugo Arellano Carvajal by

(a) tying him to a metal bed and forcing his hands against an electrified metal plate, throwing him across the room from the shock;

(b) electrocuting him with electric wires attached to his chest, his penis and his toes;

(c) tying him to a tree and whipping him;

(d) placing him on board a helicopter, pushing him out with ropes tied to his trousers, and dragging him through thorns;

(e) tying him to a rope and lowering him into a well, until he was nearly drowned, pulling him out, and lowering him back into the well when he failed to answer questions;

(f) subjecting him to 'Russian roulette';

(g) forcing him take all his clothes off in the presence of the captive Rodriguez family who had been arrested with their sons, forcing him to witness torture of that family as the father was made to bugger his son, as, simultaneously, that son was made to bugger his younger brother;

(h) forcing him to bugger one of those sons himself;

in purported performance of official duties.

That you jointly with others intentionally inflicted severe pain or suffering on Irma del Carmen Parada Gonzalez by:

(a) stripping her of her clothes;

(b) applying electric current to her mouth, vagina and breasts;

(c) subjecting her to rape by two men;

(d) putting her hands into chemicals and introducing them into a machine causing her to lose consciousness;

(e) forcing her to eat putrid food and the human remains of her dead fellow captives;

in purported performance of official duties.

That you on 24th June 1989 being a public official, namely Commander-in-Chief of the Chilean Army, jointly with others intentionally inflicted severe pain or suffering on Marcos Quezada Yanez, aged seventeen years old, by inflicting severe electric shocks causing his eventual death,
in purported performance of official duties.

That you in 1974 being a public official, namely Commander-in-Chief of the Chilean Army, jointly with others intentionally inflicted severe pain or suffering on others by the employment of 'Papi', a man who had visible open syphilitic sores on his body, to rape female captives and to use on them a dog trained in sexual practices with human beings,
in purported performance of official duties.

General Pinochet was not accused of participating personally in any single act of torture, but rather with directing them all through his personal command over the DINA, the secret military police who staffed the torture centres in Santiago and elsewhere. The object of his conspiracy with other soldiers and some civilians (including the hooded doctors who attended every session to advise on the level of pain the particular victim could sustain before lapsing into unconsciousness) was to seize and maintain power through terror. That these atrocities were in fact committed was confirmed in 1992 by a commission headed by Senator Rettig, although it was prohibited from 'naming names' and identifying Pinochet and his willing executioners. Prior to his arrest in 1998 the General had never denied responsibility or apologized: he had always boasted of his conduct and occasionally joked that the disappearances had saved bereaved families the cost of coffins. A massive public relations effort was belatedly mounted on his behalf during his enforced stay in Britain, seriously claiming that he had to kill Chileans in order to save them from Cuban-style communism – that they were better dead (or destroyed by torture) than red. His paid propagandists failed to deal with the central allegation, that the conspiracy to terrorize opponents, by torture if necessary, continued until 1990, seventeen years after the fall of Allende, any communist threat having ended, on his own reckoning, by 1978. That was a decade before the torture of Marcos Yancz, a 17-year-old youth who campaigned against Pinochet and was arrested by the secret police, who electrocuted him. There were some in Britain, led by former Prime Minister Thatcher, who believed Pinochet should be rewarded for help he had given during the 1982 Falklands War (by which time he had fallen out with the Argentinians over the Beagle Channel, and permitted some SAS operations from Chile). This was a political consideration: the question of principle was whether he could claim immunity from legal process on the basis that his crimes were committed while he was head of a sovereign state.

A pellucidly clear answer was given by the 3-judge majority in the first House of Lords hearing, *Pinochet (No. 1)*. The dictator enjoyed absolute immunity *(ratione personae)* at the time the crimes were committed, by virtue of his position as head of the state of Chile. Once removed from this sovereign position, his immunity metamorphosed: it no longer attached to his person, but only to his acts – and only to those acts which had been properly performed in the course of his duties as head of state. The court said, quite simply, that the Vienna Convention read with the 1978 State Immunity Act

is apt to confer immunity in respect of acts performed in the exercise of functions which international law recognizes as functions of a head of state . . . And it hardly needs saying that torture of his own subjects, or of aliens, would not be regarded by international law as a function of a head of state. All states disavow the use of torture as abhorrent, although from time to time some still resort to it . . . International law recognizes, of course, that the functions of a head of state may include activities which are wrongful, even illegal, by the law of his own state or by the laws of other states. But international law has made plain that certain types of conduct, including torture and hostage-taking, are not acceptable conduct on the part of anyone. This applies as much to heads of state, or even more so, as it does to everyone else: the contrary conclusion would make a mockery of international law.[36]

The court was fully satisfied that this was the law in 1973 when Pinochet seized power. The Nuremberg judgment, that those who commit crimes against humanity cannot invoke state immunity if that state, by authorizing their action, has moved outside its competence in international law, had been unanimously approved as a statement of international law principles in 1946 by the General Assembly.[37] Although the US Supreme Court had said in *Nelson* that acts of torture by police, army and security services are quintessentially 'official' acts, this required further analysis. They are acts by officials, certainly, but they are not legitimate actions for officials to take. Because sovereign immunity is an international law rule, the functions of the sovereign cannot sensibly include behaviour which is contrary to *jus cogens*, and which therefore every sovereign has an *erga omnes* obligation to the international community to forswear. Hitler was acting 'officially' when ordering the Final Solution, but his personal immunity could not subsequently avail him against prosecution for a crime against humanity. A head of state who kills his gardener in a fit of rage, or tortures for the pleasure of watching the death agonies of his victims (Montaigne's definition of the furthest point in cruelty) could always have been prosecuted after his overthrow for these 'private' crimes, because they are outside his retirement immunity, which is restricted to acts related to his official function. So too said the *Pinochet (No. 1)* majority: because the commission of international crimes is outside any official function, it is outside sovereign immunity.

This simple approach was eschewed by most of the seven judges in *Pinochet (No. 3)* after *Pinochet (No. 2)* had set aside the first decision because of one judge's connections with Amnesty International. Their long and laborious reasoning is a measure of the complexity and confusion of international law, but there was at least clear agreement that a head of state's personal and absolute immunity ceased, like the diplomat's, on relinquishing that position, and was replaced by a restrictive immunity that attached only to actions that had been performed as an official duty. Thus, there could be no immunity for ex-King Farouk's private shopping sprees, or for murdering gardeners in fits of rage or for enjoying Montaigne's ultimate in torture as a means of personal gratification. (Emperor Bokassa, accused of eating children, could not therefore have immunity in retirement from charges of cannibalism.) Where the law lords parted intellectual company was over whether crimes against humanity were outside the restrictive immunity because they could never be a legitimate function of a head of state, as *Pinochet (No. 1)* had held, or whether they were indeed, as the Supreme Court held in *Nelson*, paradigm official acts. If the latter, however, surprise, surprise: nobody in *Pinochet (No. 1)* had noticed that the Torture Convention, by defining 'torture' as a crime which could be committed only by a person acting in an official capacity, had (for cases of torture) abolished sovereign immunity altogether! Since the Convention defined the offence of torture as an action done by a public official, it logically excluded the possibility of a plea for immunity being based on the fact that the defendant *was* a public official, because 'no rational system of criminal justice can allow an immunity which is co-extensive with the offence'. Otherwise, there would be the self-defeating syllogism:

Only public officials can commit torture.

Public officials are immune from prosecution.

Nobody can ever be prosecuted for torture.

The judges were simply not prepared to credit the diplomatic community with the breathtaking hypocrisy of producing a Torture Convention with this result.[38]

There was general agreement with the analysis of Sir Arthur Watts, a distinguished jurist who had argued that individuals became subjects of international law when they committed crimes which 'offend against the public order of the international community':

States are artificial legal persons: they can only act through the institutions and agencies of the State, which means ultimately through its officials and other individuals acting on behalf of the State. For international conduct which is so serious as to be tainted with criminality to be regarded as attributable only to the impersonal state and not to the individuals who ordered or perpetrated it is both unrealistic and offensive to common notions of justice.[39]

Where the judges in *Pinochet (No. 3)* differed was over the way to effectuate this insight: most of them thought that lifting the veil of sovereignty required not only an allegation of criminality so serious that it breached *jus cogens*, but in addition the availability of universal jurisdiction, in the sense of a machinery that would permit prosecution in any national court. The better view (that of Lord Millet) is that this follows automatically from the *jus cogens* quality of the rule, but others more cautiously required a convention which imposed a duty on state parties to 'prosecute or extradite'. This practical machinery had been supplied by the Torture Convention, to which Britain, Spain and Chile were parties, which expressly required them to prosecute suspects found within their borders or else extradite them to a jurisdiction which was prepared to put them on trial. The Convention requires all states to outlaw torture, defined as the infliction of severe pain 'by or with the acquiescence of a public official or other person acting in an official capacity'. It follows that the most official person of all, the head of state, could not possibly escape an accountability which fell on the apparatchiks who carried out his orders.

For simplicity and conceptual neatness, the reasoning in *Pinochet (No. 1)*, that immunity is lost in respect of crimes against humanity because these are not state functions, is to be preferred. It was vaguely supported by Lord Hutton and given an interesting twist by Lord Millet, who suggested that any immunity should be confined to acts performed in the 'representative' capacity of the head of state, and not to killings and torture ordered in the capacity of a head of government or army commander or party leader. Warning of the danger of raising the concept of sovereignty to the 'status of some holy fetish',[40] this judge displayed the most accurate understanding of the post-Nuremberg development of universal jurisdiction over crimes against humanity, for which state officers of any rank have no immunity.

The trend was clear. War crimes had been replaced by crimes against humanity. The way in which a state treated its own citizens within its own borders had become a matter of legitimate concern to the international community . . . crimes attract universal jurisdiction if two criteria are satisfied: first they must be contrary to a peremptory norm of international law so as to infringe a *jus cogens*. Secondly, they must be so serious and on such a scale that they can justly be regarded as an attack on the international legal order.[41]

Pinochet (No.3) confirmed the trend. Nuremberg had established liability for crimes against humanity committed in wartime, and later developments had removed the requirement for any connection with hostilities. In the case of torture, the judges confirmed that, as with genocide, the prohibition has been elevated in the hierarchy of international rules to *jus cogens*, signalling 'to all members of the international community and the individuals over whom they wield authority that the prohibition of torture is an absolute value from which nobody must deviate'.[42] The Torture Convention established a regime under which there could be no safe haven – the duty it imposed on all states which found a torturer in their midst was either to try him or to extradite him. Pinochet had been arrested in Britain, which in December 1988 ratified the Convention by passing a local law which made it a crime for anyone to torture anyone else anywhere in the world. It followed that the General could be put on trial at the Old Bailey for tortures committed after that date, or else extradited to Spain to stand trial there.

This conclusion was a striking example of a court taking a treaty not just at its word but (in the absence of express words) at its spirit. The Torture Convention has no reference to any waiver by the parties of sovereign immunity, and there is not a single mention in the *travaux préparatoires* or the literature that any state indicated during the years of drafting that it was prepared to give up this attribute of sovereignty. Indeed, many of the signatories to the Convention are among the seventy-three states which regularly use torture, and their leaders would never have signed it if they had thought it might impact on their retirement plans. None of the lawyers on the anti-Pinochet teams (a number of them QCs or professors of international law, or both) even advanced the argument that the Torture Convention was intended to abolish sovereign immunity, because it wasn't. It was ratified as another exercise in cynical diplomacy, without any belief that it would be enforced. But what nobody could have anticipated is that the English judges would approach this treaty as if it were a contract or a parliamentary statute, without a trace of the scepticism that affects anyone who knows with what hypocrisy these conventions are drafted and ratified, by diplomats who never intend them to have any effect beyond inducing a feel-good factor and a good human rights rating to wave in front of aid donors. The Torture Convention was signed by dozens of states which still torture, by Chile while Pinochet himself was still head of state and could never have intended to provide for his own arrest, and by the government of Mrs Thatcher, the General's most effusive supporter. The General's tactics of objecting to judges who might know about human rights produced an apolitical bench who, with an almost touching naivety, took the Torture Convention to mean what it said. With uncanny, uncynical decency, they proceeded to hoist the old torturer by his own petard.

There was one anxious dissent, from a judge with some international law experience, who feared that an RUC officer on holiday in Florida might suddenly be accused of torture in Northern Ireland. This is a bad example, because a 'suggestion of immunity' would immediately issue from the State Department, just as it had for Prince Charles. But it is not difficult to think of more likely cases, and the objection must be addressed. Some of the majority judges did so, by arguing that immunity is only extinguished by an allegation of torture 'when committed as part of a widespread or systematic attack against any civilian population', i.e. when what is being alleged fits the Rome Statute definition of a crime against humanity. This solution is reasonable, because no doubt there will be politically motivated accusations against former leaders whose conduct is more debatable than Pinochet's (his role as torturer of our time is a matter of historical record). The answer is surely to confine prosecutions to crimes against humanity, and to rely upon domestic legal systems to eliminate charges based on insufficient evidence. The logical response to anxiety about malicious prosecution is not to abandon the pursuit of torture suspects, but rather to hasten the establishment of an international criminal court to try them with every guarantee of fairness.

The case of General Pinochet assumes its historic dimension because he was the first to be held potentially liable to prosecution for a crime against humanity committed in peacetime, notwithstanding a cloak of sovereign immunity which the state he headed was determined not to waive. It was symbolic that the ruling in *Pinochet (No. 3)* came on 24 March 1999, the very day that NATO countries began to bomb the sovereign state of Serbia in an effort to stop the atrocities its forces were committing against its own nationals in Kosovo. It was as if the world community had finally decided to obliterate its memory of appeasing Hitler by evolving international law to a position where it could no longer accept that the way in which a state treats its own citizens is purely an internal matter. The point at which interference with sovereignty was justified was when the repression reached such a level of severity that it disturbed world peace. No longer is this a messy and overly subjective test, because it can now be satisfied by evidence that the State, through officials of its government, is committing crimes against humanity as a matter of policy.

It does not follow from *Pinochet (No. 3)* that sovereign immunity will no longer bar *civil* actions by victims and relatives against states or their agents who have inflicted torture. Old doctrines die hard, and the basic principle behind immunity – that states are all equal and one state does not sit in judgment on the conduct of another – may still be invoked as it was against Al-Adsani and Scott Nelson, unless (as in the *Marcos* cases) the state to which the immunity belongs decides to waive it, or unless the action can be related in some way to commerce or to the 'private gratification' exception (under this heading, of course, an official who raped a prisoner, even as part of state-sanctioned torture, could be sued for damages). However, it will be open to other courts to follow the logic of *Pinochet (No. 1)* that a crime against humanity can never be part of the functions of a head of state, and so is outside the State's *ratione materiae* immunity. Otherwise, international criminal law will have moved much faster than its civil equivalent, and the right to a remedy – guaranteed in every human rights treaty – will extend only to the satisfaction of seeing the human tormentor behind bars, paying for his crimes but without compensating his victims. This gap makes it important for Britain and other common law countries to legislate an equivalent of the US Alien Tort Claims Act, so that civil claims can be brought when torturers or their assets come within the jurisdiction.

The Pinochet cases do not directly affect the absolute immunity (*ratione personae*) enjoyed by actual heads of state and serving diplomats. This is based on the fiction that the head embodies the State, and it would diminish its dignity to permit litigation to trouble him. A more practical consideration, of course, is found in the need to do business – economic or political – with rulers who still hold power, however irresponsibly they may exercise it. This will be the next bridge for international law to work out a way to cross, given the propensity of nationalism and militarism to throw up rulers like Saddam Hussein and Slobodan Milošević. Why, in principle, should nemesis wait upon their retirement or their overthrow? If crimes against humanity are so potent as to trigger action against *former* heads of state, why should the world stand by and allow more of them to be committed by existing heads of state? The absurd consequence would be to encourage tyrants to remain in place to preserve their immunity, committing more crimes against humanity in order to remain in power.

The reality is that states are not equal. There can be no 'dignity' or 'respect' when statehood is an attribute of the governments which presently rule Iraq and Cuba and Libya and North Korea and Serbia and the Sudan. The dignity of international recognition and even UN membership is vouchsafed to Somalia, a 'state' without any effective government other than through clan-based militias, and to Bhutan, a Himalayan 'state' completely controlled by India. What sort of respect is owed to the SLORC generals who supervise the heroin trail out of Burma? The head of the tribal state of Equatorial Guinea recently murdered his uncle; the head of Turkmenistan sends his opponents to mental hospitals and supervises every PhD thesis; the ex-head of Antigua almost went into partnership with the Medellin cartel. Charles Taylor, the popular president of Liberia, is said by *The Times* to gourmandize on the body parts of dissidents, who have been arrested, dissected and cooked by a special unit of cannibal police.[43] It is absurd to kowtow to people like this, who run governments which claim an 'immunity' from justice on the basis of a dignity they entirely lack. It is dangerous, too, lest rulers follow Machiavelli's advice to do not what is right but what other states do, because the best must emulate the policy of the worst in order to survive. If we could write sovereign immunity on a clean slate, we would undoubtedly confine its operation to ceremonial visits and symbolic actions of the kind expected of kings and aped by dictators, leaving the State and its agents liable, criminally and civilly, for crimes against humanity.[44] This is the way forward, but it calls for amendments to the Vienna Convention and an 'unfreezing' of all the state immunity legislation passed by countries in the 1970s. Reform then was needed for states to be able to trade freely between each other: further amendment is required in order to make them behave with a minimum of civility towards their own people.

In the meantime, General Pinochet was forced to greet the millennium under house (well, mansion) arrest in the south of England. His days were spent in the company of lawyers – a form of torture, although defying comparison with that inflicted on his victims. More evidence of his guilt came from freshly opened US National Archives, but this did not deter an international campaign for his release from predictable quarters: Jesse Helms, Dr Henry Kissinger – and even the Pope, who had interceded for Pinochet 'to repeat to the world that at no time can the sovereignty of any state, big or small, be violated, stripping the local government of the power to judge a fellow national'.[45] (The Vatican's unfitness for any role in world affairs could hardly have been better illustrated.) The most ironic call for Pinochet's freedom came from his mortal enemy, President Fidel Castro, at the Latin American leaders' summit in June 1999, where he declared Britain's compliance with international law 'an affront to national sensibilities'. This outburst – from the region's only remaining leader whose disregard for human rights may have reached criminal proportions[46] – did not help the Pinochet cause.

But on 3 March 2000, seventeen months after his arrest, Augusto Pinochet arrived back in Chile, where he is as likely to go to trial as he is to heaven. Medical experts had diagnosed irreversible brain damage from his recent strokes, causing such loss of memory and understanding as would render him incapable of being fairly tried under the European Convention guarantees. His last contribution to human rights came when the UK government was ordered by the Court of Appeal to disclose the confidential medical reports, because *any* claim to avoid charges of crimes against humanity must be decided by 'the highest standards of transparency'.[47] Pinochet's victims were angry at his escape, believing that he had gulled the doctors, but it was richly ironic that a dictator who denied human rights to thousands he killed and tortured should end his life as the pathetic beneficiary of human rights standards. The real lesson, however, is about the need to round up the other torturers while they are still in sound mind. There was consolation, on the day of Pinochet's return, to be taken from the conviction and 45-year sentence imposed on General Blaskić, and from the criminal proceedings brought on the Pinochet precedent in Senegal against the retired dictator of Chad, Hissène Habré. Augusto Pinochet had at least served one noble purpose in his life: that of helping the world to work out how to put tyrants on trial.

II

The Guernica Paradox:
Bombing for Humanity

'We are fighting for a world where dictators are no longer able
to visit horrific punishments on their own peoples in order to
stay in power ... Just as after World War II, a war crimes
tribunal will bring those responsible for ethnic cleansing to
justice.'   Tony Blair on the bombing of Belgrade,
                                                          April 1999[1]

As international lawyers scurried to the television studios of European
capitals in the early evening of 24 March 1999 to explain the Pinochet
judgment handed down that afternoon, they found themselves instead
improvising answers to a more urgent question: Is NATO's bombing
of Serbia (which had just begun) lawful? The following day George
Robertson, then Defence Secretary and now head of NATO, gave to
Parliament the considered British answer: 'We are in no doubt that
NATO is acting within international law. Our legal justification
rests upon the accepted principle that force may be used in extreme
circumstances to avert a humanitarian disaster.'[2]

The right to humanitarian intervention an *accepted* principle? As
recently as 1986, the UK Foreign Office had concluded: 'The overwhelming majority of contemporary legal opinion comes down against
the existence of a right of humanitarian intervention.'[3] It noted that
no such right was contained in the UN Charter and it questioned
whether state practice afforded any 'genuine' examples, but its real
reason was based 'on prudential grounds, that the scope for abusing
such a right argues strongly against its creation'. However, this is a
diplomat's argument: the very purpose of legal definition is to narrow

the scope for abuse, and international law would be an obscenity if it *required* the world to turn its back rather than act to save the lives of thousands of men, women and children, merely because the massacres were located in an unco-operative sovereign state. Yet it was this position, as bystander to genocide, that was cold-bloodedly adopted by NATO's legal opponents, who argued that if an attack on Serbia was not taken by the Security Council then it could not be taken at all. And it would not have been taken by the Security Council in the spring of 1999, even if 1.7 million Kosovars were in the process of being murdered, because Russia would cast its veto (for both sentimental attachment to Serbia and fear of creating a precedent for Chechnya) followed by China (tender over Tibet).

And so, on the cusp of the millennium, the Western alliance had to wrestle with what might be termed the Guernica paradox: When can it be right to unleash terror on terrorists, to bomb for human rights, to kill to stop crimes against humanity? It decided that it was right to use force in extreme circumstances to avoid a humanitarian disaster, but this simple proposition begged many questions. When are circumstances 'extreme'? Who decides the amount of force necessary – or proportionate – to deal with the disaster? These are the questions which must be asked after an intervention that was not an unqualified success, either in its conduct (bombing from 15,000 feet, a height calculated to cause civilian casualties while protecting allied pilots) or in its settlement (without providing for the surrender of Milošević or those of his commanders indicted for crimes against humanity). As with modern war of any kind, the result of NATO's bombing was tragedy and terror, the greatest anguish being that much of it was inflicted on the very people that the West had intervened to save in the name of that 'indignant pity' first identified by Theodore Roosevelt as the well-spring for humanitarian intervention. *Guernica* came once again to life, its screaming victims this time hit by accident rather than design. The bombs scattered the political aviary, as hawks urged peace while doves fought in the dovecote over whether NATO's action was too little, too late, or better late than never.

These arguments bypassed the threshold question of whether NATO's action was lawful at all. There was a specific right, under Article 51 of the UN Charter, for states to go to war in self-defence (as Britain did to recapture the Falkland Islands from their Argentinian invaders), but no NATO member was at risk from what remained of the state of Yugoslavia (Serbia, Kosovo and Montenegro). Alternatively, under Chapter VII the Security Council might determine that war on a sovereign state was necessary to restore international peace and security – the basis for the Gulf War on Iraq in 1991. But although the Security Council had passed a number of resolutions about Kosovo in the year before the bombing, none authorized the use of force. It was not asked for a mandate, for the very good reason that Russia and China made clear they would veto any such move. Since international law has the habit of pulling itself up by its own boot straps (actions by states which have no precedent in 'state practice' serve in their turn as evidence of a new 'state practice', thereby helping to create a new rule of customary international law which will justify similar state actions in the future), the legitimacy of NATO's attack on Serbia must be settled. It was, on any view, an uneasy start to the third age of human rights enforcement. Was it unlawful as well?

THE RIGHT OF HUMANITARIAN INTERVENTION

The duty to intervene in the internal affairs of a sovereign state, in order to stop 'systematic and long-extended cruelty and oppression', was forcibly articulated by Theodore Roosevelt at the turn of the twentieth century (see p. 15). He was concerned to justify a war which had curtailed Spanish barbarities in the dominions of Panama and Cuba, but had secured US interests as well. There had been sporadic interventions by European powers in the Ottoman Empire in the nineteenth century, prompted by massacres of Christians in Bosnia and Crete and Syria: these punitive expeditions were justified in the name of the God on our side, and without much anxiety about their lawfulness. When early international lawyers like Grotius and Vattel searched for definitions of a 'just' war, they routinely included the rescue of oppressed peoples: 'If tyranny becomes so unbearable as to cause the Nation to rise, any foreign power is entitled to help an oppressed people that has requested its assistance.'[4] This was, after all, a logical development of Locke's theory of government by consent: If tyrants can be overthrown when they abuse their power and destroy the people they are obliged to protect (see p. 5), then it follows that other governments may lawfully render 'humanitarian' assistance to those battling for their lives. Indeed, if the tyrant is a colonial power committing widespread atrocities and is opposed by a majority of the native people, this 'right of humanitarian assistance' is really a right in aid of self-determination. The difficulty arises in law when the victims are not in the majority in a state – when they are peoples of a province, or a race, or both. Just how bogus may be a claim made on their behalf was demonstrated by Hitler's claim of a right to invade Czechoslovakia in order to protect German minorities from alleged Czech brutality, and then to invade Poland to save German minorities there from the allegedly inhumane Poles.

Hitler gave the 'right of humanitarian intervention' a bad name, but there were better twentieth-century precedents. After the First World War, when the rights of minorities were overseen by the League of Nations, the question of secession was squarely addressed in two reports of jurists called upon by the League to determine the future of Finland's Aaland Islands. They reported in 1920 that the League would be entitled to consider the claim of a minority group to secede in the event of 'a manifest and continued abuse of sovereign power, to the detriment of a section of the population of a State'.[5] It was this 'Aaland Islands Question' which loomed over Kosovo in 1999: a historically defined province of Serbia, comprising 90 per cent Albanian Muslims who were being driven out of their homes and out of the country by Milošević's continued abuse of Serbia's sovereign power. If the Kosovars had in these circumstances a right to secede, would their cries for assistance entitle NATO to respond? This would depend, first and foremost, on whether any right of humanitarian intervention (or right to assist secession) could survive outside the binding international law regime established by the United Nations Charter, which prevails over any other international agreement (see Article 103 of the Charter) and to which indeed Article 7 of the North Atlantic Treaty genuflects by providing that membership of NATO does not affect 'the primary responsibility of the Security Council for the maintenance of international peace and security'.

The heart of the UN Charter is Article 2. Paragraph 4 provides:

(4) All members shall refrain in their international relations from the threat or use of force against the territorial integrity or political independence of any state, or in any other manner inconsistent with the purposes of the United Nations.

Article 2(7) allows the UN itself to 'intervene in matters which are essentially within the domestic jurisdiction of any State . . .', but only through application of Chapter VII enforcement measures by the Security Council, which must first 'determine the existence of any threat to the peace, breach of the peace, or act of aggression' (Article 39). It may then, if measures short of armed force are insufficient, 'take such action by air, sea or land forces as may be necessary to maintain or restore international peace or security' (Article 42).

Critics of NATO's action argue that these sections of the Charter cover the field and by implication extinguish any pre-existing customary law right of humanitarian intervention, whether by a single state or a regional group, without Security Council approval. They place additional reliance on the second sentence of Article 53 – 'no enforcement action shall be taken under regional arrangements or by regional agencies without the authorization of the Security Council' – although this in fact refers (as the opening sentence of Article 53 makes clear) only to situations where the UN has *already* utilized regional agencies. To fall within the 'just war' permitted by Chapter VII of the Charter, Security Council condemnation of the enemy for crimes against humanity is not enough: there must be a resolution to use force, passed by at least nine of the fifteen members without any of the five permanent members (US, China, Russia, France and Britain) casting a veto.

This was the case made on behalf of Yugoslavia when it took NATO countries to the International Court of Justice in May 1999 in a forlorn effort to injunct the bombing campaign.[6] Where it breaks down is in its failure to demonstrate that the Charter outlaws the use of force other than pursuant to Chapter VII. This cannot be the Charter's effect because Article 51 provides that it shall not 'impair the inherent right of individual and collective self-defence' of a state subject to armed attack, irrespective of whether or not the Security Council decides to intervene. This is one 'inherent' right which has not been abrogated by the UN Charter, and the same may be said of the customary international law right of humanitarian intervention. The only legal precedent that Yugoslavia's lawyers relied upon to dispute its existence was a comment by the ICJ in the 1986 *Nicaragua Case*, that the US Congress was entitled to criticize the Sandinista human rights record but not to seek to improve it by mining Nicaraguan harbours, destroying oil refineries and sending the Contras as surrogate soldiers.[7] The right of humanitarian intervention arises in an emergency, to stop the continuing commission of crimes against humanity: it has never been suggested that a state's poor human rights record could justify armed intervention. The ICJ in *Nicaragua* was demolishing a hypothetical 'right of ideological intervention' urged to justify destabilization of a particular political system: it was not deciding whether a regional group of states were entitled to use force to stop another state in the region mass-murdering a section of its people. Indeed, the ICJ goes on to emphasize that 'the UN Charter . . . by no means covers the whole area of the regulation of the use of force in international relations' and explains that 'customary international law continues to exist alongside treaty law [i.e. the Charter]'.[8] So NATO's critics are wrong: the UN Charter does not 'cover the field' and exclude the use of force pursuant to a rule of customary law which has crystallized independently of it.

Whether the right of humanitarian intervention did exist in customary international law was an issue ducked by the International Court of Justice, two months into the NATO bombing, when it delivered its ruling rejecting Yugoslavia's request for 'provisional measures'. It declared itself 'profoundly concerned with the use of force in Yugoslavia' (as well it might be, since it has a responsibility under the UN Charter to help maintain peace and security) and 'in the present circumstances [the bombing] raises very serious issues of international law'.[9] Fatuously, it then went on to demand that all parties act in conformity with their obligations under international law – obligations which it had declined to elucidate (other than to describe them as 'very serious').

Yugoslavia was knocked out on a technicality. It had always refused to consent to the Court's jurisdiction until, a month into the bombing, it opportunistically decided to avail itself of this international tribunal: most defendant states refuse to consent to jurisdiction in these circumstances, so the predictable result was a refusal to adjudicate, since (as Judge Higgins commented), 'the jurisdiction of the court – even if one might regret this state of affairs as we approach the twenty-first century – is based on consent'. The court did not lack jurisdiction, however, under the Genocide Convention, to which both the UK and Yugoslavia were fully fledged parties, and the latter (with breathtaking hypocrisy, given its own persecution of the Kosovars) accused NATO of genocidal intent towards the Serbs. The Court delivered a legal ruling that 'the threat or use of force against a State cannot in itself constitute an act of genocide within the meaning of Article II of the Genocide Convention', so it is not genocide to mount a lethal attack on a state which is oppressing a section of its own people. Further than this, the ICJ refused to be drawn.

It was Václav Havel who best expressed the purpose of NATO's intervention, namely to punish a nation state for committing crimes against humanity. In a speech to the Canadian parliament six weeks into the bombing, he updated the definition of the 'just war':

This war places human rights above the rights of the State . . . although it has no direct mandate from the UN, it did not happen as an act of aggression or out of disrespect for international law. It happened, on the contrary, out of respect for a law that ranks higher than the law which protects the sovereignty of states. The alliance has acted out of respect for human rights as both conscience and international legal documents dictate.

Havel was referring to what might be termed the evolving principle of humanitarian necessity, whereby force of a proportionate kind may be used to prevent a humanitarian catastrophe. This is the Good Samaritan paradigm, writ large: the obligation to stop mass murder of innocents must override the rule about not intervening in the affairs of other states. This exception to sovereignty can be developed juristically from defences familiar in most national legal systems: *necessity* (which excuses unlawful actions taken to prevent serious and imminent peril) and *distress* (which permits illegality to protect life during an emergency). The International Law Commission, dominated by state-serving lawyers, allows these defences only to states which use force to protect themselves or their national interests, rather than to save people in other states from being massacred – a backward view, blinkered by sovereignty. It is safer and simpler to build on the ICJ decision in the *Corfu Channel Case* in 1949, which condemned Albania for neglecting to warn foreign shipping that its waters were mined. This rogue state had overlooked 'elementary considerations of humanity, even more exacting in peace than war'.[10]

These elementary considerations are built into the Charter, which begins with a reaffirmation of faith in fundamental human rights and sets out as a purpose the promotion of respect for human rights and fundamental freedoms. So when Article 2(4) says that

All members shall refrain in their international relations from the threat or use of force against the territorial integrity or political independence of any state, or in any *other manner inconsistent with the purposes of the UN . . .*

it really means to prohibit any armed attacks which are inconsistent with Charter purposes, and does not necessarily exclude those which are directed to uphold those purposes (unless they are actually *contrary to* or *condemned by* a specific Security Council resolution). This interpretation might permit the use of force where it is directed not to the conquest of territory or the overthrow of a political system, but to the rescue of innocent persons at risk of extermination. This is an extension of Israel's justification for its incursion into Ugandan sovereignty, committed in order to rescue the hostages at Entebbe airport: the military action was taken to protect nationals, after evidence showed that Uganda was collaborating with the hijackers. The wider principle might retrospectively legitimize the Tanzanian invasion of Uganda which put an end to Idi Amin's reign of terror (an incursion condemned by the UN at the time but greeted with universal relief). Other instances might include the US invasion of Grenada when murderers took over the government, and India's intervention in 1971 to both stop genocide in and permit the right to self-determination of Bangladesh. Mixed motives make some of these interventions questionable, especially when the intervenor keeps territory or installs a more congenial government or political system. But if only, say, Kenya, Uganda and South Africa had invaded Rwanda in April 1994 to stop the genocide after Security Council action had been vetoed by Britain and the US (as it undoubtedly would have been), who would now complain about its illegality?

An important precedent for humanitarian intervention with Security Council acquiescence but not approval was the 'Safe Havens' operation in northern Iraq after the Gulf War. Displaced Kurds hostile to Saddam were massing there, vulnerable to his violent reprisals. The Security Council passed Resolution 688, calling for humanitarian relief efforts, but the US, Britain and France went further and invaded Iraq to establish protected enclaves. Eventually Iraq agreed to their presence and the position was regularized, but the initial intervention could only be squared with Articles 2(4) and 2(7) on the assumption that these paragraphs of the Charter did not exclude the use of multi-national forces in a humanitarian emergency, so long at least as this promoted a Security Council-approved purpose and the invading states harboured no territorial ambitions. These are reasonable limitations on a 'right' which would otherwise have too much scope for abuse. It would hardly be exorbitant for international law to allow humanitarian intervention to stop or punish state perpetration of crimes against humanity, where

(a) the violating state has been condemned by the Security Council, and action against it will further a clear Security Council purpose;
(b) the intervenors represent a regional alliance, or at least a coalition of UN members with no territorial ambitions or other prospects of national profit;
(c) the armed force is a proportionate response which has a reasonable prospect of stopping or deterring the perpetrators.

A further precedent for punishing a state for its defiance of rules made by the Security Council to achieve humanitarian purposes was set in December 1998, when Britain and the US conducted the 'Operation Desert Fox' bombing of Iraq. This operation would have attracted three vetoes, had it been put to a Security Council vote. China, Russia and France had all supported the Gulf War over Kuwait and the Council's ceasefire resolutions requiring UNSCOM inspections of Iraq's weapons of mass destruction, but were for various reasons disinclined to use force to punish Iraq's deceptions and obstruction of UNSCOM. The bombing was defended on the narrow (and shaky) legal ground that the US and UK were Gulf War coalition partners acting in order to enforce the ceasefire agreement,[11] but given the evidence of Saddam's secret stockpiles of nerve gas it might have been better justified as punishment for preparing a crime against humanity. In the event, the bombing was ineffective, indeed counterproductive (Iraq took advantage of allegations about US manipulation of UNSCOM to refuse all future inspections). It may be a precedent in state practice for use of force without a Security Council mandate, but it is not one to be followed other than by a majority of permanent members with support from most, if not all, temporary members.

The moral imperative must be to stop crimes against humanity whenever they occur, not merely when the five permanent members of the Security Council have unanimously resolved to act. A UN structured (understandably, in 1945) for collective defence against aggressor states like Nazi Germany and imperial Japan finds itself constitutionally debarred from stopping internecine violence by states which oppress their own people if those states include or are in close alliance with one of the five members entrusted with a superpower veto. Indeed, so obsessed is China with sovereignty at all costs that it has threatened to exercise its veto to prevent UN action in any state which does not welcome it, notwithstanding that state's responsibility for continuing genocidal attacks. (This was China's position when Indonesian militias were killing East Timorese after the referendum in September 1999.) Although only seven vetoes have been cast formally since the Cold War ended in 1990 (compared with 240 previously), the Security Council is pole-axed by the very threat of a veto, on matters great and small.[12] Some threats are puerile: China blackballed valuable peacekeeping operations in Macedonia and Guatemala for no better reason than that these countries had dealings with Taiwan. Others are irrational: Russia has stood firm in its protection of North Korea (despite its breaches of the Nuclear Non-Proliferation Treaty) and throughout 1999 it was joined by France in protecting Saddam Hussein against any further UN insistence on inspecting his progress towards nuclear and ballistic weapons. On 10 December, the last Human Rights Day of the century, the Security Council was still deadlocked in debate over Iraq, while CNN was showing a sick (or drunk) Boris Yeltsin grabbing the Chinese premier for support and hurling a slurred threat at the US ('Remember, we have as many nuclear weapons as you do') for criticizing the Russian army's merciless actions in Chechnya. It was hard to believe that the world had much improved since Khrushchev banged his shoe on the UN table, but all this evidence of superpower irresponsibility underlines the necessity for an international law principle permitting intervention in a humanitarian emergency, if need be without the unanimous support of permanent members of the Security Council.

WE BOMBED IN KOSOVO

'These wretched and unhappy little countries in the Balkan peninsula can, and do, have quarrels that cause world wars,' explained a once-popular guidebook for American tourists. 'Loathsome and almost obscene snarls in Balkan politics, hardly intelligible to a Western reader, are still vital to the peace of Europe, and perhaps the world.'[13] President Clinton had to play geography teacher to his people, explaining where Kosovo was before proclaiming, 'We could not stand aside and let history forget the Kosovo Albanians.' We could – and would – if Henry Kissinger had prevailed, since US national interests were not remotely involved ('We have no dog in this fight,' as James Baker crudely put it). What made it all the more remarkable that the US would go to war against Slobodan Milošević was that his crimes against humanity they had tolerated for years, and his role as powerbroker in the Balkans they had assiduously courted.

It was Milošević, an old communist boss in the process of reinventing himself as an aggressive Serb nationalist, who first lit the racist fuse in 1989 with his rhetoric against the 1.7 million Albanians in Kosovo. They constituted 90 per cent of the population of the province and had enjoyed under Tito a considerable degree of autonomy. This Milošević ended, in the name of Kosovo's historical importance to Serb nationalism: he introduced direct rule from Belgrade and oversaw pro-Serb discrimination in public offices. For the next eight years the Kosovars lived in a sullen silence within their own 'alternative state', led in passive resistance by Ibrahim Rugova.[14] In 1990 Milošević had announced the 'time for struggle', which he simultaneously positioned himself to lead, and called upon the Muslims ranged against his Bosnian Serb surrogates to 'surrender or die'. There is evidence that he personally approved the infamous killing of 200 patients and staff at Vukovar hospital at the outset of hostilities with Croatia in late 1991, and that he bears 'command responsibility' for some of the outrages unleashed against Muslims in Bosnia thereafter. But at Dayton, when he was relied upon to deliver agreement from the Bosnian Serbs, no Western diplomat wanted to complicate matters by raising the question of Serbia's southern province, whose ethnic Albanians wanted either independence or absorption into a 'greater Albania'. So, after Dayton, the Kosovo teenagers who had in previous years thrown the odd stone at Serb soldiers acquired guns and took to assassinations, calling themselves the Kosovo Liberation Army (KLA). Sporadic attacks by these terrorists-cum-freedom fighters provoked (as they intended) reprisals and further repression by Serb security forces, which in turn (as the KLA also intended) caused Albanian victims to support the KLA *en masse*.

The first massacre by Serb troops – in Kosovo's Drenica valley – came in March 1998, and caused a refugee exodus. Throughout the year Western diplomats struggled, without success, to find a solution to the increasing violence. Milošević refused to accept NATO peacekeepers in Kosovo, and the KLA, the new champions of Kosovar aspirations, refused to accept anything short of independence. In October 1998 an excessively brutal Serb military offensive against the KLA drove 400,000 Albanians from their homes: many returned, however, after a ceasefire agreement was brokered by Richard Holbrook which introduced to the province unarmed monitors from the Organization for Security and Co-operation in Europe (OSCE). But by the year's end Yugoslavia had breached this agreement by refusing to reduce its troops and police, and Serb atrocities, 'reprisals' though some of them were, were meted out with a savagery that deeply shocked the OSCE monitors, going far beyond legitimate counterterrorism. 'Police action' directed by the Yugoslav army killed defenceless old men, women and children. Forty-five bodies were left for television camera crews to pick through in the village of Racak in January 1999 and it was this atrocity more than anything else which convinced the US administration that NATO must meet force with force.[15] Its European allies agreed, after watching Milošević defiantly refuse the Hague Tribunal prosecutor, Louise Arbour, permission to enter

Kosovo in order to gather forensic evidence from these crimes against humanity, as seen on television sets around the world. In the early months of 1999 about 1,800 civilians were killed in Kosovo by the Serbs, in fighting and in deliberate massacres; after eight years of Serb atrocities in the Balkans these latest slaughters, replete with lies and defiance from Milošević, were the last straw for the Western alliance. The Security Council had adopted a number of resolutions under Chapter VII in relation to Kosovo – number 1160 (March 1998) imposed an arms embargo and called on the Serbs to reconsider the 'political status' of Kosovo, while further resolutions in September and October had demanded an end to ethnic repression and threatened 'further measures' if Milošević refused a political settlement.

In the end, what tipped NATO into an enforcement action which the Security Council itself would not take was evidence that the killings were part of Operation Horseshoe, a plan to 'ethnically cleanse' the province of its 1.7 million Albanians by persecuting them so severely that most would flee, thereby creating a refugee crisis for neighbouring states. On 23 March NATO reported to the UN (and its figures have never been doubted) that 100,000 Kosovars had been forced from their homes in the previous three months, and that the number was increasing – evidence that Operation Horseshoe was underway. Although killings were not central to it (the goal was 'depopulation, not extermination'), this purpose would none the less amount to a 'crime against humanity' as defined by Article 7 of the Rome Statute (see p. 498). It was a widespread and systematic attack directed as a matter of government policy against an ethnic group, and it took the form both of *persecution* on racial and cultural grounds and of *forcible transfer of population* (defined in Article 7 as 'forced displacement of the persons concerned by expulsion or other coercive acts from the area in which they are lawfully present').

At the peace conference at Rambouillet in March, both sides were presented with an ultimatum: a political settlement giving Kosovo autonomy and self-government within the Federal Republic of Yugoslavia, with human rights protected by a continuing NATO presence. This was reluctantly accepted by the KLA (it meant abandoning its independence for this dubiously workable 'autonomy') but rejected by Milošević, ostensibly because it came with a military clause giving

NATO troops the right to unimpeded transit through Serbia. This has been condemned by Serb apologists as an unacceptable intrusion on sovereignty (Kissinger hysterically described the clause as 'a provocation . . . an excuse to start bombing'), although it was no more sinister than a routine 'status of forces' agreement, giving peacekeepers direct access to Kosovo through a hostile country where they would need some immunity. There is evidence that the real reason Milošević refused the Rambouillet Agreement was not because of its clauses giving NATO forces free passage through Serbia, but in order to enable Operation Horseshoe to continue: NATO's very failure to arrest Karadžić and Mladić had convinced him that it would not take an action that would imperil its own force. In Priština, a week before the bombing, Serbs suddenly put signs on their houses announcing their nationality, so Milošević's men in ski masks would pass them by.

NATO had no game plan for this war, other than a naive belief that the bombs would quickly work, as they had at Dayton, to bring Serbia to its senses. Instead, war united the Serbs around Milošević, who quadrupled his troops in Kosovo and let them loose on a murderous rampage, in the course of which they massacred about 10,000 Kosovars and raped and tortured many more, unrestrained by the presence of OSCE monitors, who were pulled out (for fear they would be held hostage) just before the bombing commenced. Towns and villages were destroyed, and over a million inhabitants were put to flight. The refugee crisis destabilized Montenegro and Macedonia and created an endless stream of human misery to testify to the barbarity of Serb soldiery. Serb apologists like Lord Carrington have perversely claimed that 'the bombing caused the ethnic cleansing',[16] but it did no such thing. In the first few days, many bombing missions targeted empty buildings, but the very first attack on 24 March became an excuse for the Serbs to unleash murderous violence on the Kosovars, speeding up Operation Horseshoe to uproot the Albanian population virtually in its entirety. These inexcusable crimes against humanity were 'caused' by politically directed racial hatred, not by bombing; if anything, the barbaric behaviour of the Serb forces in the early days of the NATO campaign is an indication of what was always in store for the Kosovars, and retrospectively underlines the need that existed for the international community to come to their rescue. Even though hundreds of them were killed from the air during the campaign, this did not dampen the fervour of the Kosovar Albanians' support for NATO's action.

Where Western political leaders can certainly be faulted, both militarily and morally, was in their foolish promise at the outset that ground troops would not be committed to the battle. This was designed to take care of the Mogadishu factor for the Americans and some nervousness from Serbia's friends in NATO (notably Greece), but it persuaded Milošević that an air war could only serve to sustain him in power. The decision to bomb from 15,000 feet minimized allied casualties – incredibly, not a single NATO life was lost in the 78-day campaign – but this put at certain risk innocent civilian lives, Serb and Albanian, 500 of which were lost in what was euphemistically described as 'collateral damage'. NATO refused to strike in less than perfect weather conditions, afraid that low-level bombing might endanger its pilots. The 1999 war has been dubbed 'the first post-heroic war', conducted by one side in a safety perfect except for the certainty of civilian casualties, a 'virtual war' for airmen and citizens of NATO democracies alike, as they witnessed the spectacle on television, or through cameras mounted on gunsights.[17]

One great humanitarian purpose was achieved, however, namely the restoration of the Kosovars to their homeland. This took over two months because in the first weeks NATO indecisively targeted empty buildings; only later did it mount a massive attack on economic infrastructure, like power grids and bridges, to 'turn the lights out in Belgrade' and undermine middle-class support for the war. But this late shift to infrastructure bombing brought allegations of war crimes against NATO, a concern voiced by Mary Robinson and others who were no friends to Serbia. The strategy came perilously close to breaching the rule expressed in Article 8 of the ICC Charter, which follows the Geneva Convention by making it a war crime to direct attacks against non-military objects, or in ways likely to cause incidental civilian damage disproportionate to military advantage. NATO's 'espresso machine war' (cynically so called because it shook enemy morale when electricity failures denied the Belgrade middle classes their morning coffee) involved bombing civilian bridges, a TV station and even a water purification plant. It is questionable whether these last three examples can be justified under the rubric of 'military necessity', although NATO scrupulously took legal advice about its targets from legal teams serving the US, British and French forces, which sometimes came to different conclusions. For example, the bombing of the Serbian TV station (which killed sixteen technicians) was opposed by the French, but the Americans insisted it was a military target because it supported the war effort. (The US argument is clearly wrong: the station was not inciting war crimes or genocide, like Rwanda's radio Libre des Milles Collines.) The Americans were, however, right to stop using cluster bombs, as soon as they realized these caused an unnecessary number of civilian casualties: the British kept dropping them throughout the war, and they took about 160 of the 500 civilian lives lost in the campaign. These and other targeting decisions were taken by NATO honestly, if mistakenly: isolated misjudgements cannot amount to war crimes, but they show that it is time to tighten that over-elastic test, 'legitimate military objective'.

This unprecedented attention to obeying the laws of war was a result of the existence of the Hague Tribunal, which had jurisdiction over all 'serious violations' committed in the territory of the former Yugoslavia, including any which might be committed by NATO. In order to avoid the humiliation of a Western general being placed in the Hague dock, lawyers sat at NATO command computer screens and assessed the legality of every proposed target and air strike: the texts of the Geneva Conventions were available on-screen.[18] One consequence was that NATO refused to launch a 'cyberwar' (by bombing banks or 'offensively hacking' into their computers) to close down Serbia's financial systems.[19] This decision was overcautious: cutting off water to a population is disproportionate because civilians can die of thirst; when those civilians are as insouciant about crimes against humanity as were most Serbs, throwing their finances into disarray would have served them right and helped, psychologically, to secure the military objective of surrender. Inducing a computer virus is not the same as spreading camelpox.

But is it ethical (since it is legal, up to a point) to punish a people for the wickedness of their leaders or their soldiers? (This question has real point in Iraq, where sanctions have caused suffering and death to a populace which has had no realistic opportunity to remove

Saddam Hussein.) When the Hague Tribunal was set up, many argued that it would demonstrate how war crimes were committed only by a handful of evil individuals, thus relieving their countrymen from the stigma of 'collective responsibility' for crimes against humanity. This idealistic notion has been called into question – by historians who revealed just how many Germans were 'Hitler's willing executioners', and by Hutu power in Rwanda. Most of Serbia's eight million citizens were guilty of indifference towards atrocities in Kosovo, although their degree of moral callousness can hardly be compared to that of the Germans during the Holocaust. The only answer that can be given – and it has relevance to economic sanctions as well as bombing – is that 'punishing the people' can be justified if those people have real power to remove the rulers for whose decisions they are to be punished. That cannot be said of the Iraqi nation but is sadly true of Serbia, a country where, despite a courageous opposition, the majority of the public have supported Milošević and his commanders in the knowledge of their record for 'ethnic cleansing'.

On any view, however, NATO's action over Kosovo was an awkward beginning for the age of human rights enforcement. The unbridled ferocity of the Serb troops once the war started may have retrospectively vindicated the use of force, and NATO had to act without a Security Council mandate because any resolution to that effect would have been vetoed by Russia and China. Yet NATO's disarray in the first weeks of the war, and the disastrous 'collateral damage' done by inaccurate high-level bombing, began to dismay those who had been calling for military action against Serbia for years. One prominent sponsor, George Soros, hitherto an ardent supporter of bombing, admitted midway through the war:

I'm shocked by the consequences of our intervention. We have accomplished exactly the opposite of what we have intended. We have accelerated the ethnic cleansing we sought to interdict. We have helped to consolidate in power the Milošević regime and we have helped to create instabilities in the neighbouring countries, not to mention our relationship with China.[20]

NATO's critics were men acquainted with strange bedfellows: Dr Kissinger ('The whole business was misconceived') joined Noam Chomsky ('If you can't do no harm, then do nothing'), while in

Britain Tony Benn embraced Lord Carrington in declaring the exercise unlawful. Ordinary people thought differently: the Scottish National Party lost its hopes in the Scottish election because its leader described the bombing as 'unpardonable folly', while in America a majority remained in support for Kosovo intervention throughout, listing 'protecting innocent life' as the reason and rejecting the pollsters' alternatives of 'preserving regional stability' or 'maintaining NATO credibility'.[21] But NATO had none the less acted without serious thought for war aims or long-term objectives, and it was a few weeks into the war before Prime Minister Blair found an effective justification in terms of punishing crimes against humanity. This played well to the public – ironically, since NATO had previously gone out of its way to protect Milošević against indictment by the Hague Tribunal. Now, war required his criminalization, so the Hague prosecutor, Louise Arbour, was summoned to London to be handed by UK Foreign Secretary Robin Cook some NSA/GCHQ intercepts she had long requested. Doubtless she was grateful – this surveillance evidence was important – but she was unwise to take photo opportunities with Mr Cook and the belligerent NATO general, Wesley Clark, which cast a shadow over her impartiality. Shortly afterwards Milošević was in fact indicted, on evidence of his command responsibility for Operation Horseshoe, which had been assessed as probative by David Hunt, an Australian judge of great criminal trial experience. The allegation put about by the Russian and Greek governments – that this indictment was 'political' – was false, but it gained unfortunate credence from the Arbour photo follies.

A few weeks later, the indicted criminal surrendered his country, although not himself. By a 'peace agreement' signed on 9 June the Serbs agreed to leave Kosovo, 'bag and baggage', within the week: it was to become a completely autonomous province run by the Security Council and policed by NATO joined by a token Russian contingent. There were some facesaving clauses for Milošević (the province was to remain, illogically, within the Yugoslav federation, and by now NATO troops had no desire to transit Serbia), so these terms were marginally better than those offered at Rambouillet. But this is beside the point: Milošević had lost Kosovo for the foreseeable future, and the bomb damage inflicted on his country was estimated at US $60 billion. The West made clear that there would be no reconstruction aid, no Marshall Plan for Serbia, until Milošević had gone from its government and all the 1.4 million Alabanian refugees had returned to Kosovo. Astonishingly, the great majority of refugees chose to return, even from the beaches of Australia, to their burned-out homes – a few were actually killed by land mines in their rush to re-enter their villages. NATO could take heart from the fact that so many human beings had regained their lost political rights along with the liberty to live in their homes, free from the nationalist rampages of Serb security forces. The KLA instantly showed its gratitude for this restoration of their human rights by murdering hundreds of Kosovo Serbs – a few of them collaborators, but most just guilty of being in the wrong race at the wrong time.

Human rights initiatives cannot be judged by the lack of humanity shown by their beneficiaries, whether in Kosovo or in Kuwait (whose restored princes continue to resist democracy and keep on torturing their maids). What probably made these reprisal killings inevitable was that the surrender agreement, disastrously, made no provision for justice. Although Milošević and six of his senior commanders had already been indicted, NATO lost sight of its one proclaimed war aim – to punish the perpetrators of ethnic cleansing. Security Council Resolution 1244 of 10 June, concluding the war, asked only 'full co-operation of all concerned, including the international security presence, with the International Tribunal for the Former Yugoslavia'. This was the same feckless formula of Dayton, which five years on has yet to produce the arrest of Karadžić or Mladić. The moral purpose of the war was betrayed by NATO diplomats who failed to insist, as a condition for stopping it, on the surrender of those its object was to punish.

And so, once again, the world watched genocidal killers exit the bloodstained stage, this time in wraparound sunglasses and black bandanas. Lorry loads of Serb soldiers gestured obscenely at bereaved families and shouted defiant confessions about the number of Kosovars they had killed, as they went home to guard their indicted political leaders and high army commanders. The lack of any provision for justice was NATO's real defeat in the war. No doubt it felt pressure, as did the UN, from the pragmatic imperative of getting over a million refugees back into some kind of housing in the months before winter, but it succumbed without a thought for the consequences of leaving Milošević's crimes unrequited. Firstly, the KLA took the law into its own hands, wreaking vengeance on the remaining Serbs so unrelentingly that Kosovo will become (contrary to everything the humanitarian intervention stood for) an 'ethnically cleansed' province – cleansed of its Serb minority, that is, and of its gypsies (Roma people were blamed by the KLA for siding with the Serbs). The second consequence of peace without justice has been an absence of any guilt or shame in Serbia itself. Milošević has remained unbowed, his public sullen and self-pitying but as incapable as the post-war Japanese of sensing that their state has done anything wrong. For a people given to celebrating their defeats (beginning with the battle of Kosovo Polje in 1389) it is likely that future anniversaries of the Kosovo peace agreement will become days of national Serb rejoicing and muscle-flexing.

Meanwhile, UN occupation of Kosovo has enabled forensic scientists to begin the long and laborious task of disinterring bodies and then identifying them from dentistry records and the happenstance of old X-rays. In December 1999, Carla del Ponte, the new Hague prosecutor, told the Security Council that 2,108 bodies had so far been exhumed from 195 of an identified 529 massacre sites covering what she believed would be about 10,000 victims. She took the opportunity to denounce Serbia for its 'total defiance' of Tribunal demands to surrender accused men. But what did she expect? The UN's peace resolution sold out the Hague Tribunal because its diplomats lack any genuine commitment to international criminal justice. Of the Tribunal's ninety-one indictees, only thirty-four were in custody by March 2000.

JUST WAR

There is no court as yet to stop a state which murders and extirpates its own people: for them, if the Security Council fails to reach superpower agreement, the only salvation can come through other states exercising the right of humanitarian intervention. Thanks to Kosovo, that right has re-entered international law, but must be qualified in ways which will restrict its potential for abuse. The preconditions for a lawful humanitarian mission may be stated as follows:

(1) A target state where there is continuing commission of crimes against humanity either by the government or (if the country is ungovernable) by armies, militias or organized terrorist groups.

(2) Security Council resolutions which have identified the situation as a threat to world peace and imposed duties on the perpetrators which they have ignored.

(3) An intervention with the primary and dominant object of stopping crimes against humanity or punishing their perpetrators. Where victims are an ethnic majority within a definable territory, the overall object may be to assist their right to self-determination from a state which has by its barbaric behaviour forfeited any entitlement to rule them.

(4) An armed response, preferably through a regional organization or a 'coalition of the willing', supported by the majority of the permanent members of the Security Council. (The mission must end if, notwithstanding that support, it is subsequently condemned by a Security Council resolution.)

(5) The mission states must not stand to profit, e.g. by acquisition of territory or resources or through settlement of old scores.

(6) The method of warfare must comply with international law and be proportionate to the legitimate objectives.

(7) The intervention must be assessed, at its outset and in subsequent stages, to have a reasonable prospect of securing those objectives.

These are the seven principles by which the lawfulness of NATO's intervention over Kosovo must be judged. They were met in the following ways:

(1) Serb policy in Kosovo, namely the use of terror to drive the ethnic majority from their homes and from the country, amounted to the crime of persecution. This does not bear moral equivalence to the Holocaust, NATO rhetoric notwithstanding: Hitler exterminated, Milošević extirpated. But Serb action was none the less an ongoing crime against humanity, in pursuance of the Operation Horseshoe plan to terrorize Albanians.

(2) A number of Security Council resolutions to this effect were passed in the twelve months before the bombing. Resolution 1199 (September 1998) was pursuant to Chapter VII, and branded Serb behaviour in Kosovo as a threat to the peace.

(3) NATO's immediate objective was, transparently enough, to force Serbia to accept the Rambouillet Agreement, which would end the persecution of Kosovars and turn the province into an 'autonomous' NATO protectorate within a wider Yugoslavia. The bombing escalated in response to the Serb army's barbarity at the outset of the war and hence to the need to win it so as to enable the return of all the Kosovar refugees.

(4) NATO was the appropriate regional organization to exercise military power, and it did so throughout the war without Security Council opposition. Indeed, when Russia moved a resolution to condemn the NATO attack on Serbian sovereignty a few days after it commenced, it lost by 12 votes to 3.

(5) NATO allies had little to gain from the intervention: northern Kosovo has some mineral wealth, but there were no oilfields or other resources which could begin to offset the massive cost of bombing and then of reconstruction. Conspiracy theorists have lacked evidence for their accusations that NATO secretly determined to enhance its role and its credibility in time for its fiftieth anniversary celebrations (this would have been a reckless gamble) or was being manipulated by the US military/industrial complex which desired more armaments spending.

(6) The high-altitude bombing was of questionable morality, but it did not contravene the laws of war. The use of cluster bombs soon proved disproportionate, and some infrastructure targets (notably the TV station, water supply and several civilian bridges) were not 'legitimate military objectives', but no war crimes were committed.

(7) NATO miscalculated in its belief that bombing of strategic targets would bring about quick Serbian acceptance of Rambouillet. Continuing, and escalating, the bombing war was thought necessary in order to bring about some sort of a surrender, which it did after seventy-eight days. A ground war (even a threat of ground war) would have brought an earlier and much more satisfactory surrender, although at the expense of some NATO casualties.

On balance, then, Kosovo was a just and lawful war, and the victims of Serbia's crimes against humanity are better off as a result of it. They have been restored to their homeland, if not to their homes, and have regained the political power they lost in 1989, albeit without a sensible UN plan for independence. NATO failed to condition Yugoslavia's surrender on the handover of indicted war criminals, but this may not be a terminal setback, since Milošević and co. must skulk for the rest of their lives in Serbia (or find a bolthole in Baghdad) if they are to avoid a cell in The Hague. Sanctions may in due course lever them to justice, like the Lockerbie suspects disgorged by Colonel Gaddafi, although by the year 2000 Milošević was having no difficulty in raising loans from China and supplies from Russia. Only if the UN holds its resolve that not a penny's worth of aid or reconstruction assistance should go to Serbia until Milošević and his indicted commanders are presented for trial will there be hope that Serbian self-interest will produce a compliance with international law that nationalism and ethnic hatred have hitherto prevented. So, although the UN's peace resolution failed to deliver justice, this may come in the fullness of time if the world maintains its rage against the men who fill mass graves.

The millennium celebrations in Priština were muted, although happy enough for the ethnic majority which now enjoys a UN-protected 'autonomy'. It is a measure of NATO's failure to anchor its intervention in the bedrock of self-determination that the constitutional future of this UN protectorate is anyone's guess. The country is being run by UNMIK forces under Bernard Kouchner, a French doctor-turned-politician who founded Médecins Sans Frontières: after six months in occupation, he still had no legal system and no effective police force, and the 40,000 troops from thirty-five countries lacked the cohesion and purpose which could be expected from a permanent force (which the UN is not permitted to possess). He has an unelected 'consultative council', but neither Serb members nor moderate Albanians turn up for meetings. These are dominated by 29-year-old KLA leader Hashim Thaci, who has replaced Rugova as the country's president-in-waiting.[22] The KLA's political direction is uncertain: its members come from an Islamist culture 'steeped in the tradition of extended patriarchal families, blood vengeance and an incomprehension of women's rights'.[23] The original Rambouillet plan provided for a referendum after three years of NATO-protected autonomy: the ceasefire agreement (confirmed by Security Council Resolution 1244 of 10 June 1999) fudges this issue. It requires the UN

to provide an interim administration for Kosovo under which the people of Kosovo can enjoy substantial autonomy within the Federal Republic of Yugoslavia and which will provide transitional administration while establishing and overseeing the development of provisional self-governing institutions to ensure conditions for a peaceful and normal life for all inhabitants of Kosovo.

This is incoherent: inhabitants of Kosovo will never have a peaceful life while they are within the political grasp of Yugoslavia (i.e. of Serbia). Elsewhere, 'substantial self-government for Kosovo' is defined in the Resolution, oxymoronically, as 'taking full account both of the Rambouillet Accords and the principle of the sovereignty and territorial integrity of Yugoslavia'. Resolution 1244 has made long-term government of Kosovo impossible, as Russia and China mischievously use it to stop any step towards self-government, or even the establishment of effective customs controls.[24] Tito's genie of Yugoslavia cannot be squeezed back into its geographical bottle (its only other remaining province, alongside Serbia and Kosovo, is Montenegro, whose 650,000 citizens are demanding a return to the independence they enjoyed before the Versailles Conference in 1919). Kosovo is a state within a state, morally and legally entitled to secede from the greater state which has made its people the victims of a crime against humanity. They are as entitled to vote for their independence as, say, the people of East Timor, whose act of self-determination triggered a genocide which called forth the last humanitarian intervention of the century.

THE CASE OF EAST TIMOR

That intervention happened in Kosovo at all was due to many years of human rights education in Western democracies, where politicians were put under pressure to 'do something' about the massacres in

Drenica and Racak as seen on the television news. The leaders of the nineteen NATO countries knew that they would not lose votes so long as the 'something' they did was relatively bloodless for their own side, although from the outset Britain's Blair government was unequivocally prepared to suffer casualties in a ground war. It made the novel and interesting political calculation that voters were now so keen to see the end of barbarism that casualties would be countenanced (at least in the short term) and would serve to unify the national resolve. This was emphatically not a calculation shared by the US, where the Mogadishu factor remains potent. The case of East Timor was important because an invasion force was mustered which was prepared not only to kill but to be killed in the cause of human rights. It was 70 per cent Australian, with some Gurkhas and a sprinkling of Asian soldiers, with America providing logistical support well behind the front line. At the time the operation was mounted, it was believed that UN troops would suffer significant casualties in jungle fighting – a prospect the Australian government, like the British, was prepared to accept. The impact on a modern democracy of its soldiers dying for the cause of human rights was not tested: miraculously, once the INTERFET force landed, the cowardly militias fled across the border and stayed there. In its last humanitarian operation of the century, the UN got lucky – or lucky enough for Kofi Annan to welcome 'this developing international norm in favour of intervention to protect civilians from wholesale slaughter'.[25]

Timor was carved up, centuries ago, by colonial powers. The western part of the island was occupied by the Dutch, who yielded it up in 1949 as part of Indonesian independence, but the east remained a province of Portugal until the fall of the Caetano dictatorship in 1974. The new Portuguese government wanted to wash its hands of the encumbrance as soon as possible, and proposed self-determination after a direct parliamentary election scheduled for 1976. Fretilin, the Revolutionary Front for an Independent East Timor, was frontrunner: it was opposed by an 'anti-communist movement' backed by the US, which wanted integration with Indonesia. The brutal Cold War diplomacy of the era was epitomized by the visit Dr Kissinger and President Ford paid to Indonesia in December 1975: the moment they left, after indicating that American 'national interest' did not favour an independent East Timor under Fretilin ('another Cuba'), the Indonesian army invaded and occupied this small part of Portugal. It was a swift war of aggression and annexation: a few months later an unelected puppet assembly resolved that East Timor should become the twenty-seventh state of Indonesia. Diplomats from East and West urged recognition of this *fait accompli*, notwithstanding that it breached two rules of customary international law, namely

(1) that colonial peoples must, at the end of their colonial status, have the opportunity freely to determine their political future at a plebiscite;

(2) that peoples whose territory is occupied by a foreign power have a right to self-determination.[26]

Although the UN General Assembly endorsed Portugal's protests about the invasion, the Security Council buckled under US pressure and declined to condemn it either as aggression or as a plain breach of Article 2(4) of the Charter. Indonesia was vital to Western interests in Asia and in the wake of its Vietnam débâcle the US would do anything to prevent a socialist toehold in Timor. So Fretilin became the more broadly based Falintil and went underground to continue the struggle through the next twenty-five years of Indonesian occupation. Indonesia invested heavily in infrastructure for East Timor, previously lamentably ignored by the Portuguese, but its army put down sporadic pockets of opposition with ferocity. Tens of thousands died in these bloodbursts over the quarter century: for example, the entire village of Kravas was wiped out in 1983, and in 1991 there was a notorious massacre of protesters at Santa Cruz cemetery, followed by another massacre later the same day as soldiers dragged wounded protesters from hospital beds and executed them. Those and other atrocities were committed by the élite Kopassus force, trained in the US and Australia and commanded in some periods by Lieutenant-Colonel Prabowo. He was the son-in-law of Indonesia's massively corrupt President Suharto, who had come to power in 1965 in a military coup which led to the killing of over a million citizens, ostensibly because they were communists but essentially because most were Chinese. The UN, while it never formally recognized East Timor's annexation, turned a blind eye to all these outrages, although the Santa Cruz killings were captured on video and did much to alert human rights groups to the East Timor issue.

If the right of self-determination means anything – and its constant invocation by the General Assembly as the rationale for decolonization has made it a rule of international law – then the East Timorese were certainly entitled to it in 1975. They were ethnically, religiously and culturally distinct, forming in a discrete territory an overwhelming majority to throw out the Portuguese administrators and to vote to determine their own future – be it independence as a sovereign nation or integration or association with Indonesia. The Indonesian invasion in December was an unlawful act of aggression intended to destroy the right of self-determination just as it was coming to fruition. The occupation was condemned by the General Assembly as a blatant breach of the 1960 Declaration on the Granting of Independence to Colonial Territories and Peoples – an important stage in the elucidation of the right as requiring a free and genuine expression of the will of the peoples concerned.[27] This declaration condemns 'all armed action or repressive measures' against a dependent people aimed at preventing free and peaceful determination of political status (paragraph 4). In the short term Indonesia 'got away with it', but it follows in principle from the *erga omnes* nature of the right to self-determination that military occupation which defeats it continues to be illegitimate.

But in 1995 the ICJ failed the East Timorese by ducking this issue in a case brought on their behalf by Portugal over a treaty Australia had signed with Indonesia to carve up the oil-rich Timor Gap. Portugal, exhibiting a concern for the East Timorese which it had never shown during its colonization of the country, took Australia to the world court, claiming that the treaty had failed to respect East Timor's right to self-determination. Australia argued that 'there is no binding international legal obligation not to recognize the acquisition of territory that was acquired by force'[28] – a crude contention (that might makes right after about fifteen years of wrong) which the court should have emphatically refuted. International criminal law is a sham if its worst offenders are rehabilitated by no more than the effluxion of time. The ICJ portentously declared that 'the right of peoples to self-determination has an *erga omnes* character and is one of the essential principles of contemporary international law'.[29] But all the *erga omnes* force in the world would not move its judges to condemn Australia's behaviour, lest this 'imply an evaluation of the lawfulness of the conduct of another state which is not a party to the case'. Australia had made an 'optional clause' declaration of submission to the ICJ, while Indonesia of course had not, so in its absence the court declined to state the obvious – that Indonesia's annexation had been, and still was, unlawful.

The *East Timor Case* was a shocking cop-out, even by the standards of a court whose judges constantly disappoint those who believe that international law will bring about a better world. Indonesia was in effect rewarded, both for its continuing illegal occupation and for its cynical refusal to accept international justice, by a ruling that its non-consent operated to prevent even indirect criticism by the world court. There could be no greater inducement for states to refrain from signing the Optional Protocol (only sixty-two have thus far) than the assurance that they will be damned if they do, but not damned if they don't. Indonesia's refusal to submit to ICJ jurisdiction should have been interpreted as a waiver of its right to defend its invasion of the island – for which, incidentally, no legal justification has ever been offered. Alternatively, the court could have assumed the illegality of Indonesia's invasion (since this was admitted by Australia) and gone on to decide the vital question of whether lapse of time meant that the annexation could be treated as a lawful *fait accompli*. But the ICJ judges fear to apply the letter of the law they so confidently enunciate (i.e. self-determination has an *erga omnes* character) to any factual situation where the honest result would be to embarrass states, especially their own or those in alliance with them. So, until 1999, the 800,000 East Timorese proved inconvenient and insignificant, not only in the political arena where states wished to trade with and befriend Indonesia, the fourth largest country in the world, but at the bar of international justice as well. The judicial custodians of international law refused to apply one of its established principles – that acquisition of territory by force has no legal effect – because to advance the cause of human rights would embarrass Indonesia, notwithstanding that its army was engaging with apparent impunity in sporadic massacres of East Timorese.

International law aside, the problem of the Indonesian army in

East Timor was in microcosm the problem of Indonesia under a neo-dictatorial political system in which the army ruled 210 million people spread through eighty islands and its officers thrived on the corruption consequent upon this power. Military governors cracked down viciously on dissent, notably on democracy and human rights campaigners in Jakarta, and on the separatist movements not only in East Timor but in the Muslim province of Aceh and in Irian Jaya (the western part of Papua New Guinea annexed by Indonesia after a bogus 'Act of Free Choice' in 1969).

In 1998, President Suharto was forced to resign by mass demonstrations – initially put down by the army with lethal force, but eventually unstoppable. His short-term replacement, President Habibie, had to cope with economic ruin as he nursed the unstable nation through its transition to democracy. Like most Indonesian civilians, he viewed the East Timorese as ungrateful and disposable: in January 1999, without consulting the army, he announced a UN-sponsored referendum for the province, giving its citizens the choice of becoming either an autonomous province of Indonesia or an independent country. His decision was astonishing, and its wisdom may be questioned in terms of the suddenness of the transition it envisaged, but the UN's role in this double decolonization (a 'yes' vote would free them of both Indonesia and Portugal at the same time) delighted human rights NGOs. Those with any knowledge of the country cautioned that a UN peacekeeping presence would be necessary in the run-up to the referendum, and especially thereafter. However, Habibie insisted that the Indonesian army could keep control, and neither the UN nor the US (vital in keeping his economy afloat) demurred. But the army was furious about the referendum, because independence would mean loss of face as well as loss of power. In February, some army leaders conspired to intimidate the population before the vote, agreeing to set up and arm militia groups in each of the thirteen provinces: their object would be to threaten havoc unless the referendum was lost. The chief conspirators were intelligence chiefs in Kopassus special forces who reported to General Zacky Anwar, together with East Timor's military governor (Abilio Soares) and militia leader Eurico Guterres.[30] The collaboration between the Indonesian military and the freelance militias was obvious to all observers in the months before the ballot: they worked together quite brazenly, and bore joint responsibility for attacks on pro-independence families, such as the massacre at a Liquica church on 6 April in which sixty-seven people were shot or hacked to death. The purpose of the terror was to spread the militia's message: What is the point of voting for independence if you are going to be killed the next day? There could be no doubt about the certainty of a bloodbath after a 'Yes' vote unless the UN insisted upon having troops on the ground to prevent it.

The referendum was held on 30 August, and attracted an amazingly high turn-out of 98.6 per cent. On 4 September, in the face of expert warnings that this would trigger a militia uprising, the UN announced the result: 78.5 per cent in favour of independence. Overnight, the militias and sections of the Indonesian army began systematically to kill, loot and scorch the earth. It would be wrong to say that they ran amok: there was method in their madness. Typically, the Falintil intelligentsia and its supporters in the professions were the first to be rounded up and murdered. It is still not known how many died over the fortnight before the Australian force landed; the actual number will probably be a few thousand, very much lower than the early estimates. What is certain is that the scorched earth policy of the rampaging militias forced 500,000 East Timorese to flee into the jungle in fear of their lives, while 130,000 were forced at gunpoint across the border to West Timor. Fourteen Catholic priests and nuns were murdered in Dili, as well as the head of the protestant church. The UN mission which had supervised the referendum quickly evacuated itself to Darwin, where survivor accounts of killings were difficult to bear for the simple reason that this was all the UN's doing. By going ahead with the referendum in the absence of reliable military protection, they had in effect lured the East Timorese into a trap: their vote for independence was the cue for them to be butchered by the Indonesian army. Failure to rescue them from a graveyard of good UN intentions would be unconscionable, and everyone connected with the UN knew it.

For that reason, the UN's diplomacy was more desperate than in any other crisis: five UN ambassadors immediately rushed to Jakarta to ask the government's permission for an international force to enter

East Timor. 'Don't lecture us,' the country's foreign minister shrieked at them, in public. As hundreds were being slaughtered, Indonesia's obsession with its own sovereignty held up any rescue mission for eight days. 'We cannot stand by and allow the people of East Timor to be killed,' said Kofi Annan, described as 'visibly shaken', on day five of the massacres. 'Because we bombed in Kosovo doesn't mean we should bomb in Dili,' snapped back Sandy Berger, President Clinton's national security adviser, who talked in Kissinger-esque terms of America's national interest, to which East Timor was insignificant besides the importance of Indonesia's transition to democracy.[31] The UN Security Council simply froze for those eight shameful days, as America waited vainly for Indonesia's defence chief, General Wiranto, to restore discipline among its troops, and China made it clear it would veto *any* armed intervention under Chapter VII which did not have Indonesian approval. Meanwhile, the militias and supporting Kopassus troops took their revenge on the 'Yes' voters (some of whom had signed their death warrants by answering irresponsible Western TV journalists who asked how they had voted). The slashing and burning spree developed a momentum of its own, fuelled not only by hatred of the East Timorese but by a more general frustration at the army's loss of power and prestige after the fall of Suharto.

As the death toll mounted, Australia and New Zealand called for a 'coalition of the willing' to go in, Kosovo style, but answer came there none. Indonesia unhelpfully announced that it would not permit foreign troops to enter until November, after its new parliament met to ratify the independence vote.[32] (By then, of course, there would be very few East Timorese alive to be independent.) At last, on 12 September, President Clinton acted as he should have from the outset and threatened President Habibie with loss of billions of dollars in loans and aid unless he permitted a UN peacekeeping force to enter East Timor. Habibie yielded, and the 7,000-strong Australian-led force was gathered and prepared. By the time it came ashore a week later, East Timor lay in ruins – its buildings torched and earth scorched by the Indonesian soldiers who then exited in surly silence, while the militias slunk across the border to West Timor. It took many more weeks before the majority of the East Timorese felt enough trust in UN protection to come down from their hiding-places in the hills, most of them suffering from diseases that would spread with the onset of the rainy season. Their one joy was that the referendum result was ratified by the new Indonesian parliament and, on 25 October 1999, East Timor was formally handed over to the UN by Habibie's elected replacement, President Wahid.

The UN survived East Timor by the skin of its teeth and thanks, in the end, to the sense of President Habibie who on 12 September gave in to economic threats from the US, against the wishes of the nationalist faction in his party and his country. He signed his political death warrant by allowing the UN intervention, and his party was duly defeated in the elections two months later. Had he refused, China would have blackballed any use of force under Chapter VII of the Charter, and the world would have watched while Indonesian soldiers exterminated the East Timorese. Unless, that is, the Kosovo precedent had inspired an *ad hoc* 'coalition of the willing' to mount a humanitarian invasion, risking a conflict with the Indonesian armed forces which would have spelled disaster for Indonesia (its transition to democracy would have been hijacked by martial law and the country may even have reverted to military rule). By temporizing for two weeks the UN permitted several thousand East Timorese to be slaughtered – and some such time lag is inevitable, however appalling the genocide, until the UN is permitted (over the dead body of Jesse Helms) to have its own rapid reaction armed force.

In due course, the occupying force began to excavate mass graves and to take witness testimony after the UN Human Rights Commissioner, Mary Robinson, claimed there had been 'a well-planned and systematic policy of killings, intimidation, displacement and destruction of property'. Yet the Human Rights Commission, at an emergency meeting in Geneva, split on whether it should bother to mount an investigation: most Asian countries (including Japan, China, India and even the Philippines) were prickly and opposed to embarrassing Indonesia with further evidence of the misdeeds of its army. Although the obvious solution was for the Security Council to establish a war crimes tribunal for East Timor, under the Hague umbrella which already covered former Yugoslavia and Rwanda, China made clear that in defence of Indonesia's sovereignty it would veto any such proposal – so none was made. In order to obtain China's agreement to a resolution approving the UN's protective role in East Timor, the HRC dropped all references to a human rights inquiry. Eventually it did set up an inquiry (with no power to bring anyone to trial), but Indonesia refused to grant visas for its members to enter West Timor or Jakarta to interview witnesses.

However, in Jakarta, some heartening human rights events have happened. The majority of Indonesians were conscious of being oppressed by the leaders responsible for the atrocities: their overthrow of Suharto and transition to democracy in late 1999 brought a popular demand for human rights and an initial resolve, in the new parliament, to investigate and punish military transgressors in East Timor, as well as in other parts of Indonesia. Parliament established a civilian human rights commission which soon uncovered evidence of massacres in East Timor and of how bodies of victims were transported across the border for secret disposal in West Timor. It called in and cross-examined senior generals and uncovered the conspiracy to form and arm the militias, and to fund them from the budget of East Timor's civil administration. Its report, in January 2000, accused thirty-three leaders of crimes against humanity and demanded their prosecution: command responsibility was fixed on the former military chief, General Wiranto, five other generals and a number of senior officers, together with the militia commanders and the former civilian governor of East Timor, Abilio Soares.[33] The UN Human Rights Commission inquiry reported at the same time with broadly similar conclusions, except that it recommended an extension of the Hague Tribunal, including judges from Indonesia, to try the accused. The Indonesian government rejected this affront to its sovereignty, but renewed its promise to bring the suspects to justice – although as yet it had no court capable of managing their trials.

The battle by Indonesian generals to avoid international justice has been illuminating. They have made no secret of their fears of suffering the fate of Pinochet, or of the indignity that would attend their appearance in uniform in the Hague dock.[34] What appears to exercise them most is the humiliation of being tried in another country, under the world's gaze, rather than in their own courts. (So eager are they to co-operate with being tried at home that they have hired a team of Indonesian human rights lawyers, led by the veteran Adnan Buyung

Nasution, to present their defence.) If this fear of suffering the *indignity* of international criminal justice is widely shared in military circles, and if it infects political leaders as well, then the prospect of trial at The Hague can have a real deterrent effect. The army and the militias behaved like nervous murderers, transporting the corpses, at great inconvenience, long distances to bury them across the West Timor border. The advent of international criminal law, for all the pot luck of its enforcement, had at least made them afraid of retribution for their crimes against humanity.

The first nation to quake at the prospect of human rights law enforcement was, ironically enough, representative of the race whose history has made it necessary. Israel refused to support NATO's action against Serbia, because its right-wing government worried about Arab demands for a Kosovo-style 'autonomy' for Galilee. Shimon Peres was ashamed: 'For the first time after the Nazi Holocaust, when the world does not stand by, we do not know what to say?' But in NATO, too, Kosovo was an awkward precedent – certainly for Spain, which has used state terror against Basque separatists, and for Turkey, engaged in a war with its Kurds (which they had tactically suspended in an effort to save the life of Ocelan, their captured leader). It was precisely the fear of opening cans of ethnic worms which caused NATO's rhetoric to emphasize the humanitarian emergency and to avoid mention of Kosovo's right to self-determination, which was at the heart of the whole matter. By failing to adopt this goal as a war aim and a principle of peace, NATO and the UN face a constitutionally confusing (and very long) future in the province. In East Timor, by contrast, the future is clear and optimistic: nation-building begins apace for a people the protection of whose post-plebiscite right to self-determination was the acknowledged reason for the intervention. The KLA and Falintil were both fighting for control of a discrete patch of earth where the great majority were suffering under a brutal, militarized state, and international law was on their side. It should have been declared to be on their side – in the Dayton Accords and in the judgments of the *East Timor Case*. But the West long ago developed a kneejerk hostility to the right of self-determination, because it was asserted first by colonial rebels and later by communist-backed liberation groups. But the lessons of Kosovo and East Timor are that in an age of human rights enforcement it should no longer be necessary for peoples to fight and die for their international law rights: the world must develop an enforcement system which will do this for them. Until international law clearly confronts the problem of secession, and lays down some ground rules for its exercise – including the existence of cast-iron guarantees for dissenters and minorities in the new seceded state – liberation struggles will be endless, and some great power claims, e.g. over Chechnya, New Caledonia and (most dangerously) Taiwan, will continue to trouble the peace of the world.

Kosovo and East Timor demonstrate the rudimentary nature of the human rights enforcement system at the turn into the twenty-first century. There is a world court, full of judges determined to save states from embarrassment by refusing to rule on the legality of NATO's war in former Yugoslavia or of Indonesia's annexation of East Timor. There is a world government, its executive unable to act without the support of the five most powerful nations in 1945, only one of which has prospered greatly since. It has no 'rapid reaction' force to parachute in when genocide is underway; Senator Jesse Helms has seen to that, threatening US withdrawal whenever the idea of the UN's own army is mentioned. So the East Timorese were butchered for two weeks because one Security Council member refused to act other than by invitation of the state whose army was committing the butchery. NATO only avoided Security Council stalemate through a legal loophole of humanitarian intervention which many international lawyers did not believe to exist: the characterization of Kosovo as an emergency rather than as a long standing violation of the right to self-determination precluded any sensible constitutional settlement, with the result that it now exists in a twilight, lawless zone, permanently denied self-government while festering revenge eliminates its minorities. Human rights lessons are easy to teach, but politicians and diplomats show little inclination to learn.

Kosovo and East Timor were both depicted in the media as 'ethnic conflicts' underlain by blood hatreds between races and religions: the Catholic Serbs against the Muslim Albanians; the Catholic East Timorese against the Muslim Indonesians. This analysis is simplistic, and essentially false. As historian Noel Malcolm points out in respect to Kosovo, 'It ignored the primary role of politicians (above all, the Serbian nationalist-communist Milošević) in creating conflict at a political level . . . between low-level prejudices on the one hand and a military conflict, concentration camps, and mass murder on the other, there lies a very long road: it was the political leaders who propelled the people down that road, and not vice-versa.'[35] The East Timorese have never hated the Indonesians as a people or as Muslims: leaders like Gusmao and Ramos-Horta always talked of both peoples sharing a common enemy in the form of the corrupt parapolitical generals of the Indonesian army. What emerges starkly from both situations is the criminal responsibility of political and military leaders for preparing and permitting crimes against humanity. The actual killers were soldiers and mad-dog militias, but criminal responsibility lay indelibly with commanders who had long before built their power upon racism and nationalism, in the course of which they offered impunity to the killers they inspired. Milošević and Suharto, and their respective army commanders now in boltholes in Belgrade and Jakarta, provide the latest argument in favour of developing a system of international criminal justice which has power to humiliate and incarcerate the masterminds of crimes against humanity.

Epilogue

'There is nothing culture-bound in the great evils of human experience, re-affirmed in every age and in every written history and in every tragedy and fiction: murder, and the destruction of life, imprisonment, enslavement, starvation, poverty, physical pain and torture, homelessness, friendlessness.'

Stuart Hampshire, 'Innocence and Experience' (1989)[1]

It is against such elemental evils that the Universal Declaration of Human Rights was erected, in 1948, as a talismanic barricade, a pile of decent principles to impede the onward march of tyrants and tanks and torturers. The Declaration and its progeny, the good conventions, only serve this purpose to the extent that they offer some prospect of enforcement, the true test of progress towards the great promise of Article 28, 'Everyone is entitled to a social and international order in which the rights and freedoms set forth in this Declaration can be fully realized.' After a half-century of ineffectual treaties and diplomatic thumb-twiddling, we had a *fin de siècle* stampede to put global justice systems in place: an International Criminal Court, a 'prosecute or extradite' regime for torturers, a claim to intervene in the internal affairs of sovereign states out of humanitarian necessity. This movement may have owed something to PMT (pre-millennium tension) — a sickness at the atrocities of the twentieth century and a wish to do better in the twenty-first. Also to the NPT, in its failure to corral weapons of mass destruction, and hence the search for legal excuses to lop the trigger fingers off despots before they are lifted to press nuclear buttons. So we may be witnesses to a kind of millennial shift, from diplomacy to justice as the dominant principle of global relations, achieved through the evolving force of international human rights law, carrying *jus cogens* compulsion in municipal courts and in an increasing number of international tribunals. The pioneering discovery (law being a science in its content, an art only in its practice) has been how the crime against humanity, defined at Nuremberg, can become the key to unlocking the closed door of state sovereignty, and to holding political leaders responsible for the great evils they visit upon humankind.

The modern history of human rights, from an aspiration born of the concentration camp and the gulag to a set of powerful international law propositions to which enforcement mechanisms may be attached, has been accomplished by a movement which now has millions of members throughout the world – twelve million, for a start, who signed a petition pledging support for the Universal Declaration in its fiftieth anniversary year. Some have been inspired by the courageous examples of dissidents who have suffered in freedom's cause, and many more by a revulsion against atrocities brought into their homes through a billion television sets and twice as many radios, creating a vast audience beginning to think like global citizens. It is their reaction to human rights violations which constitutes, in Theodore Roosevelt's phrase, 'the indignant pity of the civilized world' and, when transmitted to different but democratic governments, it impels international and UN response. Horizons have widened: the old newspaper joke 'Small Earthquake in Chile: Not Many Dead' rings hollow when television pictures of corpses in Racak, Kosovo, put such obscure places on the map of everyone's mind and galvanize the West to war. That crimes against humanity occur in 'a far away country between people of whom we know nothing' – Neville Chamberlain's reason for appeasing Hitler's invasion of Czechoslovakia – is no longer an excuse. Cynics may deride the framing of foreign policy by reference to focus groups tuned to CNN, but what is happening is that modern media coverage of human rights blackspots is rekindling the potent mix of anger and compassion which produced the Universal Declaration and now produces a democratic demand not merely for something to be done, but for the laws and courts and prosecutors to do it.

The first rumblings of this New World Order were challenged, at the 1993 Vienna Conference, by the objection – from Mahathir and Kuan

Yew and Suharto – that human rights are 'culturally relative'. 'Asian values' like stability, they said, are undermined by free speech and the Universal Declaration embodies Western individualism at odds with communitarian societies. But human rights principles afford individuals such elemental protections against the State that they are likely to be sought by intelligent beings everywhere, at least so long as the State refrains from punishing them for that search. 'Cultural relativism' is the death-knell of multiculturalism: the German attempt to extinguish the Jews was 'culturally relative' (in the sense that it developed from a tradition of German anti-Semitism), but that did not make it any less of an anathema. By treating Jews as less than human, just as Serbs were later to reduce Bosnian Muslims and then Albanians to pseudo-human status, they committed crimes which cannot be excused by setting them within any national history or tradition. This is the case with all culturally ordained killing and torture inflicted for whatever reason: the footbinding of young girls in China; widow-burning (sati) in India; apostate-hunting in Iran; or the stoning to death of adulterers in Saudi Arabia. 'Cultural relativism' has recently been asserted to defend the practice of female circumcision (more accurately, female genital mutilation) inflicted upon an esti-mated 137 million women in twenty-eight countries, usually as a tribal initiation ritual before puberty.[2] Say its apologists, 'The practice serves as an affirmation of the value of women in traditional society.' The World Health Organization describes this value-affirming exercise:

Infibulation involves the amputation of the clitoris, the whole of the labia minora, and at least the interior two-thirds and often the whole of the medial part of the labia majora. The two sides of the vulva are then stitched together with silk, catgut or thorns, and a tiny sliver of weed or reed is inserted to preserve an opening for urine and menstrual blood. The girls' legs are usually bound together from ankle to knee until the wound has healed, which may take anything up to forty days.[3]

This is inflicted upon small girls with the consent of their mothers: should a culturally neutral world send surgeons and anaesthetic, or rather condemn it as torture and inhuman treatment contrary to Article 5 of the Universal Declaration? It is the torture of children, a crime against humanity when permitted on any scale. If the danger to health could be minimized by surgical procedures, the suppression of female sexuality which is an intended consequence of the ritual cannot be tolerated even in a society which rewards women for undergoing it. No doubt Western individualism would permit an independent adult woman to choose to undergo the operation, but no claim of culture can be permitted to defend torture inflicted permanently on those who cannot give consent. Culture can offer no escape clause for barbarism. The Covenant on Civil and Political Rights permits states to derogate in times of poverty or economic collapse or civil war, but no circumstances justify departure from the elemental protection from arbitrary execution or torture or slavery. It is at this level that Dr Mahathir's challenge to universality becomes as ridiculous as his suggestion that the bruises seen on Anwar Ibrahim after his arrest were self-inflicted.

Objection to the Universal Declaration from some Asian and African governments is not joined by their people. When given the choice (as Suharto in Indonesia, Banda in Malawi, Marcos in the Philippines and Ershad in Bangladesh discovered to their cost), they usually turn out to prefer the so-called Western values, rights in fact that belong to everyone, everywhere. When Asian leaders condemn them as a threat to national order and stability, they really mean a threat to their own power. Thus they fail to explain why, if they have such a harmonious society, they insist on keeping from colonial times draconian internal security laws, secret police, censorship and sedition laws, or why they need (in China, Burma and Singapore) to outlaw human rights organizations.[4] They provide some notorious examples – the Indonesian military's brutal repression in East Timor, Nigeria's execution of environmental protesters in the face of world condemnation, the SLORC generals in Burma keeping the democratic leader, Aung San Suu Kyi, under permanent arrest, separated from her dying husband – but the irony is that these 'traditional cultures' never approved such monstrous actions; their military rulers just used the argument to pull themselves up by the straps of their own jackboots.

Before the economic crisis turned the Asian tigers mangy, leaders were emerging like South Korean president Kim Dae Jung, a former human rights activist, who derided Lee Kuan Yew's Asian values argument as both unsupportable and self-serving, pointing out that the real problem was not Western liberalism but 'authoritarian rulers and their apologists'.[5] Africa, too, has a few younger statesmen prepared to criticize the Organization of African Unity's hypocrisy over human rights: the host of its 1999 conference, Dr Navin Ramgoolam (prime minister of Mauritius), eschewed diplomatic platitudes and demanded revision of the weasel clauses of the African Charter in the interests of universality. This serves to encourage those within Asian or Islamic cultures who are endeavouring to think and to nuance their way around cultural stumbling blocks. For example, Muslim reformers are finding in the Koran support for the dignity of 'humankind' which may reduce the discrimination against women in Sharia law, ordaining as it does their veils, their incompetence as witnesses, their amenability to male chastisement and their incapacity for public office. There is much more work to be done in identifying what worthily belongs to 'the cultural life of the community', the free participation in which is protected by Article 27 of the Declaration.

Cultural relativists betray their own people by obscuring the economic and social rights in the Declaration. The human rights movement, too, has been guilty of neglecting these 'lost rights' vouchsafed by Articles 22–7. It must henceforth champion the creation of international legal mechanisms to require governments to share fairly what wealth there is, and to ensure that scarce resources are not spent on arms and monuments and the servicing of debts rather than people (the Third World burden of debt repayment, currently running at about $43 billion a year, makes economic recovery an impossibility for many countries). Compliance with human rights standards, increasingly the touchstone for aid donors, has been criticized for its subjectivity, but the guarantees of the Universal Declaration do provide one yardstick for assessing the entitlement of states to international charity: a state committing crimes against humanity will forfeit any claim to assistance.

The next challenge for international law, having made individuals as well as governments its subjects, must be to encompass entities which are neither states nor persons but increasingly more powerful than either. Transnational corporations were not much in evidence when the UN was founded, but of the hundred most wealthy entities in the world today, fifty-one are corporations not countries. (Texaco, for example, has global earnings four times greater than those of

Ecuador.) In some respects, of course, they are more vulnerable to pressure and open to argument than governments concerned about retaining power rather than making profits. The bad publicity which dogged Shell for its complicity with the repressive military regime in Nigeria, and which damaged Disney for the sweatshop conditions of its toymakers in Hong Kong, has made other transnational corporations more wary of dealing with abusive regimes and more vigilant in ensuring that their Third World factories and contractors have defensible policies on child labour and working conditions. Now 'human rights auditing' is the fashion, and a new breed of accountants is busy producing ethical impact reports on behalf of multinationals wishing to persuade NGOs that their business policies in the developing world measure up to some very minimal standards. But all this is voluntary and done largely as a public relations exercise: accounting principles are not human rights principles, which are about fairness and the obligation of the world community to ensure that a reasonable amount of resources, whether available to states or to transnational corporations, is spent on providing for basic rights of health, education and social security. This obligation cannot be enforced by 'ethical auditors' at PriceWaterhouse and KPMG: it must be made an *erga omnes* duty for multinationals as much as for states.

There are dangers and confusions which follow from the very suddenness of making human rights a moral imperative in world affairs. The first books hailed as dispensing millennium wisdom – Francis Fukayama's *The End of History and the Last Man* and Paul Kennedy's *Preparing for the Twenty-first Century* – thudded on to reviewers' desks in 1993, but neither made a single reference to human rights as a factor in the futures they envisaged. Who would then have thought that before the century was out a British prime minister and a US president would proclaim a duty to go to war to protect not the national interest, but human rights. That this could happen so dramatically is a tribute to the work of human rights NGOs, building on the work of international lawyers who have returned to Nuremberg and re-examined and reinstated its great legal legacy, the notion of the crime against humanity. To sum up, this is a crime with a peculiar horror deriving from the fact that otherwise rational rulers and officials are capable of conceiving and committing it, thereby diminishing us all as fellow human beings. Such crimes are not only unforgettable; what Nuremberg established in international law is that they are unforgivable. They cannot be the subject of amnesty or of time limits on prosecution. Punishment cannot be left to history (which depends, after all, on who writes it) or to hellfire (even the Pope now doubts the availability of this sanction). There is a legal duty on all states to investigate and (if the evidence is available) to prosecute persons suspected of this class of offence, narrowly defined as the commission of widespread and systematic murder, torture, enslavement or persecution of innocent civilians pursuant to a political policy. Individuals who commit such crimes must have no hiding-place: there is a universal jurisdiction to punish them. This legal principle draws practical support from the consideration that crimes against humanity will be deterred only if would-be perpetrators – whether political and military leaders or footsoldiers and policemen – are given pause by the prospect that one day, under a different regime or in another country, they may be called to account. And irrespective of claims of sovereignty, a state which commits crimes against humanity on its own people now risks armed intervention – whether it has a Security Council protector or not.

That the commission of crimes against humanity should serve as the legal justification for international intervention in the internal affairs of sovereign states does provide one escape from the limited horizons of the UN Charter, which was designed as a mechanism for collective defence against sovereign nations, like Nazi Germany, which waged wars of aggression. Today, inter-state violence is rarely the problem and if it occurs (as with Iraq's invasion of Kuwait) the Charter can be readily invoked. The Charter's bias towards sovereign independence is anachronistic when the real evils are civil war (Rwanda, the Balkans, Chechnya, Somalia, etc.) and state-sponsored terrorism – neither of which are sensibly addressed by Charter provisions, which make enforcement measures depend upon the unanimous approval of five nations with their own diplomatic games to play (and in the case of Russia and China their own minorities to oppress). The record of the superpower veto, as threatened or exercised inconsistently and cynically in crisis after crisis, deprives the Security Council of that moral authority which is necessary for 'law' of any kind, national or international. UNanimity cannot be the *only* test of legitimacy, since Security Council mandates for intervention have so often been withheld for politically squalid reasons which have nothing to do with justice or morality. On the other hand, blank cheques should not be handed to vigilante states – which is why there must be a legal process providing an objective determination that crimes against humanity are being or are about to be committed. This is the precondition which legitimizes the use of a degree of force sufficient to carry a reasonable prospect of ending the criminal conduct. Such interventions may be justified, not through the politically unpredictable mechanism of the Security Council, but by the dimension of the evil.

President Clinton justified a bombing attack on a sovereign state which had done nothing to damage US interests on the grounds that 'We could not stand aside and let history forget the Kosovo Albanians.'[6] His rhetoric reached new heights as the millennium approached:

In Kosovo, we did the right thing, we did it the right way and we will finish the job. Because of our resolve, the twentieth century is ending not with helpless indignation, but with hopeful affirmation of human dignity and human rights for the twenty-first century.[7]

But as the smoke from all the fireworks cleared on New Year's Day, Milošević was still in power in Serbia, buoyed by Chinese loans, and 'human dignity' was not hopefully affirmed by the KLA in Kosovo whose hit squads were effortlessly outwitting NATO patrols and exterminating, at the rate of about twenty a week, the few Serbs who remained in their homes. Karadžić and Mladić were still unarrested, in the *Republica Srbska* of their own making. The first war criminals to see the dawn were the generals in Jakarta and old Khmer Rouge comrades still at liberty in Cambodia. Mengistu welcomed the new year with his patron, Mugabe, and Idi Amin watched an early sunrise in Jeddah, although Duvalier had gone into hiding in the south of France and Pinochet was under doctors' orders in the south of England. Alfredo Stroessner, the Nazi-loving ex-dictator of Paraguay, watched the carnival from his balcony in Rio. At luxurious but discreet Panama penthouses, killers in uniform from Haiti and states of South America welcomed the millennium by witnessing the US handover of the canal.

Rwanda apart, not a single key perpetrator of post-Nuremberg crimes against humanity was in prison, although at least some were in hiding or in exile or in fear. Human dignity, the assumption upon which the Universal Declaration was built, was not much in evidence in places like Colombia or the Congo, or on the outskirts of Grozny, under attack from Russian troops prepared to die in the cause of refusing Chechens their right of self-determination. There had only been six ratifications of the ICC statute, the Hague Tribunal had not fully completed its very first case (Tadić's sentence appeal) and there was as yet no court to try the known perpetrators of genocide either in East Timor or (despite constant UN pressure) in the killing fields of Cambodia. The struggle for global justice became a twenty-first century struggle, without becoming any easier.

The new century brought some grounds for optimism. The doleful soothsayers who in 1998 had predicted an army coup if Britain dared upset 'the delicate balance of Chile's reconciliation process' by holding Pinochet were confounded when in his absence Chile peacefully elected its first socialist president since Allende. In reliance on the Pinochet precedent, a court in Senegal began to hear a prosecution for crimes against humanity brought against exiled Chad dictator Hissène Habré. But human rights campaigners have a tendency to count chickens before they hatch. Michael Ignatieff worried that 'the language of human rights provides a powerful new rhetoric' which might 'lure citizens into wars that end up abusing the very rights they were supposed to defend'.[8] Not much chance of that, given the intransigence of states and the still embryonic methods for penetrating the shield of their sovereignty. Can anything be done about the Security Council other than paving emergency bypasses for the times when (as with Kosovo) threats of the superpower veto make it seize up? And is it not a confidence trick, albeit no longer inspiring of much confidence, to speak of the ICJ as 'the world court' when most states in the world exclude themselves from its jurisdiction for no better reason than that they do not choose to be judged? Its members are appointed through UN horsetrading (each of the superpowers is guaranteed its own judge) and many are still unable to deliver opinions which might inconvenience their own country, or their own country's allies. As for the world's parliament, the General Assembly will remain a global gerrymander, no more than a convenient forum for setpiece speeches in New York, until the myth of state equality is demolished and votes can be cast that are more representative of the world's six billion citizens. The UN suffered one of its most embarrassing moments on 20 January 2000, when Security Council ambassadors were obliged to fawn diplomatically upon the sworn enemy of international justice in person, Senator Jesse Helms, while he fulminated like a confederate bullyboy against their plans for a world criminal court.[9] It was an event made all the more excruciating by the fact that it was necessary: as chairman of the US Senate Foreign Relations Committee, Helms holds hostage the UN's purse strings. American dues are not paid on time, or in full, and only on strange conditions (the latest is that its dollars must not support birth control programmes). They will not be paid at all, Helms threatens, if the ICC ever indicts an American or the UN ever acquires its own military force.

Yet this is precisely the sort of capacity the UN must acquire if it is to stop genocide in places like Rwanda and East Timor, where rapid deployment of a full-time UN force would have saved so many lives. An ICC is needed to deter genocide in future by humiliating in the eyes of the world those who have perpetrated it in the past. The UN cannot cling to its 'peacekeeping mandate' of impartiality and avoidance of military action (discredited at Srebrenica) or refrain much longer from supporting the lesser of the two evils in Angola, i.e. the elected government against Jonas Savimbi, whose forces are guilty of horrific war crimes (including the deliberate shooting-down of UN planes). It has proved incapable of depoliticizing the Human Rights Commission or of turning the Human Rights Committee and similar treaty bodies into effective adjudicators and overseers. It is blind to the symbolic irony that its human rights effort is concentrated in Geneva, not just a wastefully expensive and irrelevant location but one which serves to reward, in money and in prestige, a country which knowingly profited from the Holocaust and has been ever since the trusted banker of the likes of Marcos and Mobutu and Abacha (the Nigerian junta leader who salted away £550 million in Geneva before his death). Switzerland's 'neutrality', like Vatican 'statehood', is a legal and historical fiction. The Swiss should join the UN and start paying their dues, while the Vatican should put its head back into Italy. The

UN may well be beyond any fundamental reform: its appointments procedures are irredeemably politicized and sometimes corrupt, throwing up as leaders such flawed men as Kurt Waldheim and Boutros Boutros-Ghali (he was 'Africa's turn' and the francophone bloc outmanoeuvred his anglophone rival). In 1999 Japan bought the leadership of UNESCO for its candidate, by offering aid for votes, while the UK accused the disastrous head of FAO of securing his re-election by using its own funds for his campaign. In the last weeks of the century, following official reports of how UN incompetence had permitted genocide, Kofi Annan offered three grovelling apologies: he said sorry to the people of Rwanda, Srebrenica and East Timor.

The radical possibility occurs that human rights might have a healthier future if it parted company with the United Nations, if that body were replaced or marginalized by a democratic 'coalition of the willing': an organization comprising only countries which are prepared to guarantee fundamental freedoms through representative government, independent national courts and by pledging to support an independent international justice system. This was the vision of H. G. Wells, progenitor of the modern human rights movement, when he advocated a 'new world order' confined to 'parliamentary peoples' (i.e. democracies) committed to fundamental freedoms (see p. 21). Wells sought this alternative because he despaired of the League of Nations model, a lowest common denominator organization dedicated to state sovereignty and powerless to act against outlaw regimes, even by excluding them from membership. It was, however, to this model, somewhat strengthened, that the world turned in 1945, with the result that its good conventions were drained of force as the century ran its course. Might it now be worth constituting a world government of 'parliamentary peoples' which would safeguard human rights by being premised upon them, a kind of global NATO, no longer lumbered with backward or barbaric states but having the force not only to deal with the occasional villainy of a Saddam Hussein but to deter the likes of Russia from breaking the Geneva Conventions by vacuum-bombing defenceless Chechen villages, or China from invading Taiwan?

This would, inevitably, require the involvement of the United States, as first among equals rather than as master of servants. But Senator Helms spoke in Leviathan language to the Security Council, of withdrawal unless 'the United Nations respects the sovereign rights of the American people and serves them as an effective instrument'. This caricatures human rights agreements as threats to individual liberty and assumes that international organization exists to further the national interests of the most powerful member. He complained bitterly of 'the raucous cheering of the UN delegates in Rome when US efforts to amend the ICC treaty to protect American soldiers were defeated', without understanding that the applause was for a principle – of even-handed justice – to which the US has in other contexts nobly contributed. He personifies the paradox of a nation which took the lead in promoting the idea of universal human rights – the first to make trade and diplomatic relations contingent upon compliance – but which refuses to be part of that universe in case minimum world standards, objectively determined, cause a little local difficulty. Doubtless Senator Helms needs the United Nations as much as it needs America, and the prospect of replacing the world body is far-fetched, but its systemic failures demonstrate the importance of giving the new institutions of international justice an independence which keeps them at arm's length from the Security Council.

At the close of the twentieth century, the dominant motive in world affairs was the quest – almost the thirst – for justice, replacing even the objective of regional security as the first principle of international action. That explains, at least at a jurisprudential level, the refusal to accept Chile's sovereign immunity for Pinochet or Serbian sovereignty over Kosovo, and the convoluted political arrangements made to put on trial the two Libyan intelligence officials suspected of planting the bomb which in 1988 took 259 lives above Lockerbie and eleven on the ground below. The tenacity of the Lockerbie relatives, although at first their cause seemed hopeless, drew in the UN and many world leaders, negotiating eventually – in April 1999 – a surrender of the Libyans for trial under Scottish law on an airbase in the Netherlands. In the same month the Arusha Tribunal announced the capture in the Cameroons of three former Rwandan government ministers suspected of planning the 1994 atrocities, including the foreign minister (who broadcast appeals to 'kill all Tutsis') and the ambassador who lied to the Security Council to cover up the genocide. Also in the same month, the UN finally sent a special envoy to Cambodia to demand the trial of Khmer Rouge leaders before an international tribunal.

These events should presage the end of sovereign impunity, by recognizing that political leadership (a role for which there is no shortage of candidates in any country) carries as a concomitant of wielding state power an accountability for abusing it. Cynics might point out the present and pragmatic limitation of this principle, namely that it does not apply to high officials of states with a permanent seat on the Security Council. However, if the principle means there will be no more Rwandas, at least it will mean something. And then the challenge will be to invest the international legal system with the power – or, failing that, the respect – to investigate the legitimacy of behaviour like China's in Tibet or Russia's in Chechnya or America's in firing missiles at a pharmaceutical factory in the Sudan. That challenge, as superpower opposition to the Rome Statute demonstrated, will take many years before it prevails, but the best start is to get the International Criminal Court up and running as early as possible. Justice, once there is a procedure for its delivery, is prone to have its own momentum.

This has been demonstrated, although the momentum has been slow, by the work of the Hague Tribunal in trying crimes against humanity committed in the Balkans and Rwanda. Its record gives no cause for the kind of alarm that was sounded by the US delegation in Rome in 1998: there has been no prosecutorial excess, no politically motivated indictments, no judicial over-reach. There have been errors, mostly corrected on appeal, and an unacceptable delay – sometimes due to painstaking regard for the defendant's rights. The most serious criticism – the lack of 'major culprits' – must be directed to NATO and the UN over their failure to prioritize arrests of indicted leaders. But the evidence collected in chapter 8 shows that international criminal justice is operating fairly in those two limited, 'ad hoc' spheres in which it is presently allowed. What is perhaps more important is the intellectual momentum of the Hague court, which is both synthesizing and popularizing the principle of retribution for international crimes. The English Law Lords in their Pinochet rulings drew on Hague definitions and precedents for incriminating torturers, and the Tribunal's jurisprudence – notably in the judgments of Cassesse and

Stephen – has an epic quality which is beginning to be cited in national courts around the world. It is giving lawyers good ideas, and not just for prosecuting and extraditing, but for dipping into the growing body of international human rights law to find new ways of arguing cases for victims of crimes against humanity. This may smack of lawyerly hand-rubbing, but that profession exists to satisfy popular as well as individual desire for justice: what has taken politicians as well as diplomats by surprise is the public insistence that they maintain pressure on states to punish the crimes against humanity they would rather forget. That is why the UN is right to persist in its demands for international control of a tribunal to try the Khmer Rouge leadership, notwithstanding Hun Sen's objection that this infringes Cambodia's sovereignty – it does, and must, because the country has failed in its duty to prosecute them. Indonesia, too, is on the line: although it has the popular will to put its generals on trial, there are doubts whether its legal system will cope. If it does stumble, international justice must be provided – not out of pity for the East Timorese, but to protect the international community, since its trust in Indonesian army super-vision of the referendum was so barbarically betrayed. In these differ-ent ways – through *ad hoc* tribunals, international pressure for domestic prosecutions, Pinochet precedents and eventually an inter-national criminal court, the third age of human rights – the era of enforcement – will prove less threatening than Senator Helms would have his constituency believe.

In the twenty-first century the human rights movement will struggle on, against its traditional enemies – armies, churches and states – looking increasingly to international law to provide a lever against these institutional powers. Most of the crimes related in this book were committed by professional soldiers, blessed by bishops and approved by governments. The new role of peacekeeping has muted the military brass, but not changed its tune: the Pentagon organized a global campaign to undermine the International Criminal Court, ensuring that commanders in most of its client countries lobbied governments against the idea. (What was hopeful and heartening was that it failed – in every country except the US.) Transnational religion has proved a forceful opposition to women's rights, especially since the collapse of communism. In Afghanistan under Russian puppet governance women made up half the doctors and university students and most of the teachers, but the Taliban fundamentalists refuse to allow women to work or to study, or even to venture outside the home without a male relative (who is expected to beat them if their dress does not cover every inch of their flesh). The problem is not only with Islam: a resurgence of Roman Catholicism in eastern Europe has been particularly damaging to women's rights – Lech Wałesa lost his civil liberties halo when as president of Poland he vetoed abortion reform, and the Vatican aroused widespread disgust by trying to stop supplies of 'morning-after' pills reaching refugee women raped by Serb battalions during the cleansing of Kosovo. Vatican diplomacy has blessed most of the tyrants and torturers of recent history, betraying Catholic idealists in Singapore to Lee Kuan Yew and secretly exerting pressure on the British government to free the unpenitent General Pinochet.

As for governments, *realpolitik* still rules when human rights comes up against superpower interests. Although Britain has adopted an 'ethical' foreign policy, this tends to falter if opposed to the interests of its arms manufacturers. It insisted on supplying war planes to the Indonesian military at the very moment it was running amok in East Timor. Russia's financial bankruptcy has reduced its Security Council clout, but in 2000 this remained sufficient for it to reject Mary Robinson's efforts to investigate mounting allegations of war crimes in Chechnya, and to breach the Geneva Conventions by refusing the Red Cross access to Chechen prisoners.[10] China remains deeply suspicious of any international legal development which threatens sovereignty: the mildest criticism at the Human Rights Commission it condemns as an 'interference in China's internal affairs'. It persists in treating advocacy of democracy as a crime punishable with upwards of ten years in prison, but since it boasts the world's largest army – 2.5 million soldiers – and possesses nuclear bombs and intercontinental ballistic missiles, no one is prepared to argue with it very strenuously. France blows hot and cold on human rights: it is not above committing terrorist crimes (the sinking of the *Rainbow Warrior*) and its record in francophone Africa includes arming genocidal Hutus and harbouring President Mobutu, for long the world's most corrupt ruler. In December 1998, France hosted the fiftieth birthday celebrations for the Universal Declaration at the Palais Chaillot in Paris: it refused to invite Chinese democrats or Tibetan representatives, for fear of upsetting Beijing.

Then, of course, there is the problem of America, a nation much given to spurts of world leadership followed by periods of self-regarding isolationism. Its scholars have made vast contributions to the literature of human rights, reflecting its history as the land of the free, but its refusal to qualify its own sovereignty in any way by accepting international jurisdiction reduces its influence and sets bad examples. It can speak through its president with eloquent moral fervour, but its Senate Chamber resounds to isolationist voices. As the only true superpower, America will determine the 'humanitarian necessity' for any intervention without UN approval, but haphazardly (ignoring genocide in Rwanda but not in Serbia) and without clear or objective criteria. Unless it shows greater consistency in its approach to human rights (it has been notably protective of 'friends' such as Israel and Saudi Arabia) and some eventual willingness to bind itself to the justice it prescribes for others, its emergence as the 'benign hegemon' (in Samuel Huntington's phrase) will make for partisan and inequitable human rights enforcement.[11]

Although Deputy Secretary of State Strobe Talbott asserts that American foreign policy is consciously intended to advance *universal* values, his nation is inclined to forget the wise words of Eleanor Roosevelt:

Where, after all, do universal rights begin? In small places, close to home – so close and so small they cannot be seen on any maps of the world . . . Unless these rights have meaning there, they have little meaning anywhere. Without concerned citizen action to uphold them close to home, we shall look in vain for progress in the larger world.

Unfortunately, in America human rights do not begin at home, and certainly not in jail: conditions in some state penitentiaries are barbaric, as women prisoners are routinely assaulted and both male and female convicts are made (particularly in the south) to serve on chain gangs, are 'hog-tied' with their wrists bound to their ankles, and are kept in line by guards who use chemical sprays and electric prods. The provisions for legal representation of the poor are uniformly inadequate in this richest of nations, and death penalties are inflicted with scant regard to the ECOSOC standards. The result of incompetent representation is wrongful conviction, especially in capital cases.[12] The US is a country which plans to disappear almost as many of its citizens as did Pinochet, namely the 3,500 currently condemned to die on its death rows. The year 1999 saw ninety-eight executions, thirty-three of them in Texas, where prisoners were automatically refused clemency by Governor George W. Bush. American courts breached international law by allowing states to kill juveniles (seventy current death row inmates were under eighteen when their crime was committed). Elected judges in the Supreme Court of Texas have made a mockery of judicial independence, canvassing for votes by undertaking to uphold death sentences (thus compromising their bench as an 'independent and impartial tribunal').[13] America stands alongside Somalia as the only countries which refuse to ratify the Convention on the Rights of the Child (because it wants to execute juveniles and to recruit teenage soldiers). Its bedfellows in objecting to the ICC were China, Libya, Iraq, Algeria, Sudan and Iran. For the sake of its own humanitarian missions it cannot much longer have it both ways by asserting a right to bomb states which harbour terrorists or commit genocide while vetoing any system for international human rights protection which could conceivably impinge on its own interests. In 1999 the team of pliant law professors it had sent to Rome to sabotage the ICC statute were redeployed to collect evidence of Serbian war crimes in Kosovo: the nation which refuses to be bound by international human rights law now demands the prosecution of foreigners who violate it. As the one great superpower with pretensions to police the world, its opposition to the ICC and the Land Mines Convention shows it up as a truculent opponent of the demand for *universal* human rights.

The most significant change in the human rights movement as it goes into the twenty-first century is that it will go on the offensive. The past has been a matter of pleading with tyrants, writing letters and sending missions to *beg* them not to act cruelly. That will not be necessary if there is a possibility that they can be deterred, by threats of humanitarian or UN intervention or with nemesis in the form of the International Criminal Court. Human rights discourse will in the future be less pious and less 'politically correct'. We will call a savage a savage, whether or not he or she is black. There will be less mealy-mouthedness about behaviour which cries out for condemnation, fewer attempts to suggest that hideous practices like cliterodectomies are culturally relative, or that the West should respond to them by providing doctors and anaesthetic to reduce the suffering. We'll become a little more sophisticated about humanitarian aid (remembering how the British government used this as an excuse when supplying AIDS-testing kits to the Iraqi army, never bothering to find out what happened to a soldier who tested positive). Although the twenty-first century will have its share of despots, they will be fewer and, in the absence of the Cold War, they will not have superpower support. There will no longer be any need to say, as FDR said of Grandfather Somoza, 'He may be a son of a bitch, but he's our son of a bitch.' Sons of bitches will not be tolerated, especially if their fingers are itching for nuclear triggers.

But optimism about the future must be tempered by the dreadful failures of the past, especially the failure of the UN, with its bureaucratic, politicized machinery, to implement the promises of the Universal Declaration in its first half-century (excluding refugees, it still spends less than 2 per cent of its budget on human rights). In 1999 the Security Council was incapable of intervening to stop crimes against humanity in Kosovo because Russia turned a blind eye and China's leaders could not care less about man's inhumanity to man. However, states prepared to kill were not yet prepared to sacrifice: hence the insistence on high-altitude bombing and the refusal to contemplate ground troops. This marked an uneasy and unpopular beginning for the third age of human rights enforcement, although it deserves to be remembered as the first war waged for ethical principle alone, because – as Václav Havel put it – 'no decent person can stand by and watch the systematic state-directed murder of other people'. In East Timor, decent people could stand by and watch for only a fortnight, which was two weeks too long. The commission of crimes against humanity provides an indisputable warrant for punishment of violator states. After a century in which 160 million human lives were wasted by war and genocide and torture, the world best remembers those its pledges have failed by determining that in the future, at whatever cost, it is going to make these pledges stick.

Notes

1. THE HUMAN RIGHTS STORY

1. Thomas Paine, *Dissertation on First Principles of Government* (1795).

2. John Locke, *Second Treatise of Government: Of the Beginning of Political Societies* (1690).

3. Cook's opening speech, undelivered because the King refused to plead, is printed in *The Tryal of King Charles the First, Volume II State Tryals* (1648) (Goodwin Edition), p. 521.

4. Cesare Beccaria, *Of Crimes and Punishments* (1764).

5. Quoted in J. A. Joyce, *The New Politics of Human Rights* (Macmillan, 1978), p. 7.

6. Letter of 12 January 1789, *The Papers of Thomas Jefferson*, J. Boyd (ed.), (Princeton University Press, 1958), ch. 14, p. 436.

7. Thomas Paine, *The Age of Reason* (1792). See Michael Foot and Isaac Kramnick (eds.), *The Thomas Paine Reader* (Penguin, 1987) and John Keane, *Tom Paine – A Political Life* (Bloomsbury, 1995).

8. See Simon Schama, *Citizens* (Penguin, 1989), pp. 521, 781.

9. Ibid., p. 851.

10. *Marbury* v. *Madison* (1803), 5US (1 Cranch) 137, p. 163.

11. Jeremy Bentham, *Supply without Burthen or Escheat Vice Taxation* (1794), Objection V.

12. See Jeremy Walden (ed.), *Nonsense upon Stilts – Bentham, Burke and Marx on the Rights of Man* (Methuen, 1987).

13. V. I. Lenin, *Report to the First Congress of the Third International* (1919).

14. See Oppenheim (ed.), *International Law: A Treatise* (1912), section 292.

15. Theodore Roosevelt, 'On Human Rights in Foreign Policy, State of the Union Message 1904', republished in Walter Laqueur and Barry Rubin (eds.), *The Human Rights Reader* (Penguin, 1978).

16. See Jan Burgers, 'The Road to San Francisco', *HRQ* 14 (1992), pp. 447, 455–9.

17. See Walter Laqueur, *Stalin, the Glasnost Revelations* (Macmillan, 1990), pp. 123–7.

18. Under *Glasnost*, a Politburo commission was established to investigate archival material relating to the show trials: its report in 1989 established without doubt that the confessions had been obtained by torture and that the defendants had been seduced into their public performances at first by promises of clemency and later by promises to protect family members. See Laqueur, *n.* 17 above, p. 297 ff.

19. George Katkov, *The Trial of Bukharin* (Batsford, 1969).

20. See Burgers, *n.* 16 above, pp. 459–64. One rare exception was a declaration adopted by the Institut du Droit International in New York in 1929.

21. Harry S. Truman, *Years of Decision, Memoirs* vol. 1 (Doubleday, 1955), p. 292.

22. See John P. Humphrey, 'Human Rights and the United Nations: A Great Adventure', *Transnation* 1984, pp. 29–32.

23. See generally Johannes Morsink, *The Universal Declaration of Human Rights* (University of Pennsylvania Press, 1999), pp. 14–20.

24. See Johannes Morsink, 'World War Two and the Universal Declaration', *HRQ* 15 (1993), p. 357.

25. Morsink, *n.* 23 above, p. 268.

26. Ibid., p. 274.

27. Drafting session, UN Commission on Human Rights, 1st session, 5th meeting (1947), 11 UN Doc. E/CN.4/AC.1/SR.5.

28. Cited in Stephen Marks, 'The Roots of the Universal Declaration of Human Rights in the French Revolution', *HRQ* 20 (1998), pp. 483–4.

29. Morsink, *n.* 23 above, pp. 222–6.

30. Upendra Baxi, 'Mambrino's Helmet? Human Rights for a Changing World' (Har-Anand, New Delhi, 1994).

31. Immanuel Kant, *Foundations of the Metaphysics of Morals*, L. W. Beck (trans.) (Prentice Hall, 1990), pp. 49–50.

2. THE POST-WAR WORLD

1. The evidence has been summarized by Jeremy Isaacs and Taylor Downing in *The Cold War* (Bantam, 1998), pp. 186–95, 231–2.

2. ECOSOC Resolution 1235 (XLII) of 6 June 1967.

3. Declaration on Principles of International Law Concerning Friendly

Relations and Co-operation among States in Accordance with the Charter of the United Nations, Resolutoin 2625 (XXV) (24 October 1970).

4. See William Shawcross, *Sideshow – Kissinger, Nixon and the Destruction of Cambodia* (André Deutsch, 1979).

5. Andrei Sakharov, *Memoirs* (Hutchinson, 1990), ch. 35.

6. See Philip Alston, 'The Commission on Human Rights' in Philip Alston (ed.), *The UN and Human Rights: A Critical Appraisal* (Oxford, 1992), p. 126ff.

7. See *Johnson* v. *Jamaica* (1997) 4 1HRR21.

8. *John Ballantyne & others* v. *Canada* (31 March 1993), Comm. nos. 359 and 385/1989 *HRLJ* (1993), p. 171.

9. *Nicholas Toonen* v. *Australia* (31 March 1994), Comm. no. 488/1992.

10. See, for example, Michael O'Flaherty, 'The Reporting Obligation under Article 40 of the ICCPR: Lessons to be Learned from Consideration by the Human Rights Committee of Ireland's First Report', *HRQ* 16 (1994), p. 515.

11. Ineke Boerefijn, 'Towards a Strong System of Supervision: The Human Rights Committee's Role in the Reporting Procedure under Article 40 of the ICCPR', *HRQ* 17 (1995), p. 766.

12. See Manfred Nowak, 'The Actualities of the UN HRC: 1992–1995', *HRLJ* 16, pp. 388–9.

13. See Louis Henkin *et al.*, *Human Rights* (Foundation Press, 1999), p. 501.

14. Torkel Opsahl, 'The Human Rights Committee' in Philip Alston (ed.), *The UN and Human Rights: A Critical Appraisal* (Oxford, 1992), p. 374.

15. CERD Report, GAOR, 49th Session, Supp. 18 (1995), p. 95.

16. See the decision in *Otto Preminger Institute* v. *Austria* (20 September 1994), 19 EHRR 34, followed by *Wingrove* v. *UK* (25 November 1996), 24 EHRR 1.

17. *Norris* v. *Ireland* (1989), 13 EHRR 196; *Dudgeon* v. *UK* (1982), 4 EHRR 149.

18. *Ex parte Pinochet (No. 2)* (1999), 1 All ER 577.

19. Tom Farer, 'The Rise of the Inter-American Human Rights Regime', *HRQ* 19 (1997), pp. 511–12.

20. *Compulsory Membership in an Association Prescribed by Law for the Practice of Journalism*, Advisory Opinon no. OC-5/85 of 15 November 1985, series A: Judgment and Opinions no. 5.

21. Rachel Murray, 'Report on the 1996 Sessions of the African Commission on Human and Peoples' Rights', *HRLJ* 18 (1997), p. 16.

22. African Commission on Human and Peoples' Rights, Banjul, Comm. no. 25/89, opinion delivered 4 April 1996.

23. See Philip Gourevitch, 'The Genocide Fax' in the *New Yorker* (11 May 1998), p. 42; *When Good Men Do Nothing*, BBC *Panorama* programme broadcast on 8 December 1998.

24. 'Investigations Condemn UN Chief', *Guardian* (17 December 1999).

25. Gérard Prunier, *The Rwanda Crisis 1959–94: History of a Genocide* (Hurst, 1995), p. 261.

26. See Philip Gourevitch, *We Wish to Inform You That Tomorrow We will be Killed with Our Families* (Picador, 1998), pp. 154–8, 271–81.

27. *A Cry from the Grave* (Antelope Films; Producer: Leslie Woodhead), screened BBC2 (27 November 1999).

28. The fairest instant history, before the events can be dissected in court, is provided by Jan Willem Honig and Norbert Both, *Srebrenica – Reward of a War Crime* (Penguin, 1996).

29. David Rohde, *A Safe Area* (Pocket Books, 1997), p. 336.

30. Yasushi Akashi, 'The Limits of UN Diplomacy', *Survival* vol. 37, no. 4, p. 96.

31. Michael Ignatieff, *The Warrior's Honour* (Chatto & Windus, 1998), p. 73.

3. THE RIGHTS OF HUMANKIND

1. *The Paquete Habana* (1900), 175 US 677.

2. *Barcelona Traction Case* (1970), ICJ Reports 3 at p. 32.

3. Ian Brownlie, *Principles of International Law* (5th edn) (Oxford, 1998), p. 517.

4. See Igor Lukashuk, 'The Law of the International Community' in *International Law on the Eve of the 21st Century* (UN, 1997), p. 51 at 62–3.

5. Malcolm Shaw, *International Law* (4th edn) (Cambridge, 1998), p. 37.

6. *Salomen* v. *Customs & Excise* (1967), 2 QB 116 at 143, *per* Lord Diplock.

7. *East African Asians Case*, 3 EHRR 76 (1973).

8. See *The Human Rights Watch Global Report on Women's Human Rights* (Human Rights Watch, 1995).

9. *Tyrer* v. *UK* (25 April 1978), 2 EHRR 1, *Costello-Roberts* v. *UK* (25 March 1993), 19 EHRR 112.

10. *T and V* v. *UK*, ECHR judgment of 16 December 1999.

11. *Prosecutor* v. *Anton Furundžija*, Hague Tribunal (10 December 1988) para. 153.

12. *Ex parte Pinochet (No. 3)* (1999), 2 All ER 97, pp. 108–9.

13. *Ireland* v. *UK* (1976), 2 EHRR 25.

14. *Denmark* v. *Greece* (1986), *Yearbook of the European Convention II*, p. 690.

15. *Kent* v. *Dulles* (1958), 357 US 116.

16. See Samuel Walker, *ACLU: In Defence of American Liberties* (Oxford, 1990), p. 232ff and note the Supreme Court confirmation in *RAV* v. *City of St Paul, Minnesota* (1992).

17. Ian Buruma, 'China in Cyberspace', *New York Review of Books*, 4 September 1999.

18. *Observer and Guardian* v. *UK* (1991), 14 EHRR 153.

19. *Tolstoy* v. *UK* (13 July 1995), 20 EHRR 442.

20. *Goodwin* v. *UK* (1996), 22 EHRR 123.

21. *Church of New Faith* v. *Commissioner for Payroll Tax* (1983), 57 ALJR 785 (High Court of Australia).

22. *Woolmington* v. *DPP* (1935), AC 462.

23. See the Privy Council decision, *A-G of Hong Kong* v. *Lee Kwong-Kut* (1993), AC 951, and the European Court of Human Rights in *Salabiaku* v. *France* (1988), 12 EHRR 379; also, the South African Constitutional Court in *State* v. *Mbatha* (1996), 2 LRC 208; the Canadian Supreme Court in *R.* v. *Oakes*, 26 DLR (4th) 200 and the English High Court in *R.* v. *DPP ex parte Kebilene* (Divisional Court, 30 March 1999; *The Times* Law Report, 31 March 1999).

24. *Hauschildt* v. *Denmark* (24 May 1989), 12 EHRR 266.

25. *Ex parte Pinochet (No. 2)* (1999), 1 All ER 577.

26. See Gabriel García Márquez, 'The Future of Colombia', *Granta Magazine* (1989).

27. See 'Ali Daghir and the Forty Nuclear Triggers' in Geoffrey Robertson, *The Justice Game* (Chatto & Windus, 1998), p. 285.

28. *Sherman* v. *US* (1958), 356 US 369 at p. 382.

29. See *Sorrells* v. *US* (1932), 287 US 435.

30. *Ludi* v. *Switzerland* (1992), 15 EHRR 173 at para. 73 (Commission).

31. Ibid., para. 49 (Court).

32. *Teixeira de Castro* v. *Portugal* (9 June 1998), 44/1997/888/1034.

33. *Jacobsen* v. *US* (1992), 112 S St 1535.

34. *Bunning* v. *Cross* (1978), 141 CLR 54 at pp. 74–5; *R.* v. *Hsing* (1991), 57 ACrimR 88.

35. *Police* v. *Lavelle* (1979), 1 NZLR 45; *R.* v. *Smurthwaite* (1993), 98 Cr App R 437; and see Geoffrey Robertson, 'Entrapment Evidence: Manna from Heaven, or Fruit of the Poisoned Tree?', *Criminal Law Review* (November 1994), p. 805.

36. *Amato* v. *The Queen* (1982), 69 CCC 2d 31; see also *Mack* v. *The Queen* (1988), 44 CCC 3d 513 at p. 541.

37. *Lithgow and others* v. *UK* (8 July 1986), ECHR series A 102, para. 121.

38. *Chorzów Factory Case* (1928), PCIJ series A, no. 17.

39. See *James* v. *UK* (1986), series A 1267, para. 60.

40. *Lithgow and others* v. *UK*, as *n.* 37 above, para. 121.

41. *Chorzów Factory Case*, as *n.* 38 above. See also *American International Group Inc.* v. *Iran* (1983): 'fair market value at the date of nationalization'; and *Amoco* v. *Indonesia* (1985): 'the full compensation of prejudice, by awarding to the injured party the *damnum emergens* [loss suffered] and the *lucrum cessans* [expected profits]'.

42. Resolution 1803 (XVII) (14 December 1962).

43. Resolution 3201 (S–VI) (1 May 1974).

44. See, for example, *James* v. *UK*, as *n.* 39 above at para. 54.

4. TWENTY-FIRST CENTURY BLUES

1. Stephen Trombley, *The Execution Protocol* (Century, 1993), pp. 12, 36.

2. *The State* v. *Makwanyane & Mchunur* (1995), HRLJ 16 (1995), p. 195, para. 272.

3. *Mbushuu* v. *The Republic* (30 January 1995), Tanzanian Court of Appeal.

4. See ICCPR, Article 6(2) and (6).

5. The Second Optional Protocol to the ICCPR, signifying 'an international commitment to abolish the death penalty', has been signed by only thirty-six states, although twenty-four European nations have forsworn executions other than 'in time of war or imminent threat of war' by acceding to the Sixth Protocol of the ECHR.

6. See William A. Schabas, *The Abolition of the Death Penalty in International Law* (Grotius, 1993), pp. 99–103.

7. *The State* v. *Makwanyane & Mchunur*, *n.* 2 above, p. 194, para. 269.

8. Schabas, *n.* 6 above, p. 310, excerpt from general comment on Article 6 by Human Rights Committee.

9. For example, Article 4(4) of the American Convention on Human Rights provides: 'In no case shall capital punishment be inflicted for political offences or related common crimes.'

10. HRC Doc A/44/40, notwithstanding a contrary decision by the Privy Council: *Robinson* v. *The Queen* (1985), 2 All ER 594. The dissenting judgment of Lords Scarman and Edmund-Davies, p. 604, reflects the international law rule: 'there can, save in very special circumstances such as a national emergency, be no greater public interest than that one who is accused of an offence conviction of which carries with it a sentence of death has a proper opportunity of defending himself . . . it is a serious error of law to hold that a man accused of a capital offence can be denied the option of defence by a legal representative of his own choosing'.

11. *Mbenge* v. *Zaire*, HRC Doc A/38/40.

12. This follows from Article 6(2), echoing the general rule against retrospective law embodied in Article 15 of the Covenant.

13. See Articles 99 and 100 of Geneva Convention III (1949) and Article 68 of Geneva Convention IV (1949).

14. *Safeguards Guaranteeing Protection of the Rights of Those Facing the Death Penalty*, ECOSOC res. 1984/50 (25 May 1984), endorsed by General Assembly, res. 39/118 of 14 December 1984. See Article 4, Article 6 (which goes too far by requiring mandatory appeals against conviction in death sentence cases even when defendants do not contest their guilt) and Article 8.

15. See Geoffrey Robertson, *The Justice Game* (Chatto & Windus, 1998), ch. 4. An example of a senior domestic court refusing to buckle under government pressure for an immediate execution, and insisting that execution be stayed until every possible point could be carefully and calmly considered, is provided by the High Court of Australia in *Tait* v. *R.* (1962), 108 CLR 620.

16. Roger Hood, *The Death Penalty* (Oxford, 1995), pp. 91–2.

17. Covenant, Article 6(5); American Convention, Article 4(5); ECOSOC safeguards, Article 3; Convention on the Rights of the Child, Article 37.

18. See *Thompson* v. *Oklahoma* (1988), 108 S. Ct 2687; *Stanford* v. *Kentucky*, *Wilkins* v. *Missouri* (1989), 492 US 361.

19. Res. no. 3/87, Case 9647, *Roach & Pinkerton* v. *US*, *Annual Report of the Inter-American Commission on Human Rights 1986–7, HRLJ* 8 (1987), p. 345.

20. *Ford* v. *Wainwright* (1986), 477 US 399. The common law always permitted a reprieve of a death sentence to test an allegation that the prisoner was insane; see the judgment of Judge Smith in *Tait* v. *R.*, *n.* 15 above.

21. *Tyrer* v. *UK* (1978), 2 EHRR 1, para. 80; Anthony F. Granucci, 'Nor Cruel and Unusual Punishments Inflicted: The Original Meaning', *Californian Law Review* 57 (1969), p. 839.

22. *Pratt and Morgan* v. *A-G of Jamaica* (1994), 2 AC 1.

23. *Soering* v. *UK* (1989), 11 EHRR 439.

24. *Trop* v. *Dulles* (1958), 356 US 86 at p. 101.

25. *Thompson* v. *Oklahoma* (1988), 487 US 815.

26. *Minority Schools in Albania* (1935), PCIJ Scr. A/8, no. 64, at p. 17.

27. Francesco Caportini, *Study on the Rights of Persons Belonging to Ethnic, Religious and Linguistic Minorities*, UN Doc. E/CN4 Sub 2/284.

28. *Sandra Lovelace* v. *Canada* (1981), Comm. no. 24/179, UN Doc. A/3/40, p. 166.

29. *The Belgian Linguistics Case* (1968), 11 YECHR, p. 832. This was decided by reference to family and educational rights provisions of the European

Covenant, but the same reasoning would apply under Article 27.

30. See *TK* v. *France* (1987), Comm. no. 220 (note dissent of Professor Rosalyn Higgins), UN Doc. A/45/40; and see Nigel Rodley, 'Conceptual Problems in the Protection of Minorities: International Legal Developments', *HRQ* 17 (1995), p. 48. *Guesdon* v. *France No. 2* (1990), Report of HRC, UN Doc. A/45/40.

31. *Lubicon Lake Band* v. *Canada* (1984), HRC Comm. no. 167, UN Doc. A/45/40.

32. A definition suggested by the UN Working Group on Indigenous Populations. See Corntassal and Primeau, 'Indigenous Sovereignty and International Law', *HRQ* 17 (1995), p. 343.

33. ICJ Rep. (1962), p. 6.

34. *A-G of New Zealand* v. *Ortiz* (1983), 2 All ER 93; 78 ILR 608 and 631.

35. *Mabo* v. *Queensland* (1992), 175 CLR 1.

36. R. Higgins, comment on 'Post-modern Tribalism and the Right to Secession' in Brolmand, Lefeber & Zieck (eds.), *Peoples and Minorities in International Law* (Martinus Nijhoff, 1995), p. 33.

37. *AD* v. *Canada* (1980), HRC Comm. no. 78, UN Doc. A/39/40, p. 200.

38. See the *Western Sahara Case* (1975), ICJ Reports 12, para. 57.

39. See D. J. Harris, *Cases and Materials on International Law* (Sweet & Maxwell, 1998), pp. 122–31.

40. Diane F. Orentlicher, 'Separation Anxiety: International Responses to Ethno-Separatist Claims', *Yale Journal of International Law* 23 (1998), p. 43.

41. *Frontier Dispute Case (Burkina Faso* v. *Republic of Mali)* (1986), ICJ Rep. (1986), p. 566.

42. See the analysis by Antonio Cassesse in *UN Law/Fundamental Rights: Two Topics in International Law* (Alphen aan den Rijn, 1979), pp. 154–5.

43. See James Crawford (ed.), *The Rights of Peoples* (Oxford, 1988), p. 56.

44. *South-west African Cases*, ICJ Rep. (1962), p. 319; ICJ Rep. (1966), p. 6. This is a rare example of states (Ethiopia and Liberia) invoking the jurisdiction on behalf of other non-state 'peoples'.

45. Richard Falk in Crawford, *n.* 43 above, p. 19.

46. 'A Global War against Bribery', *Economist* (6 January 1999).

47. Mohammed Bedjaoui, 'The Right to Development', cited by Henry Steiner & Philip Alston (eds.), *International Human Rights in Context* (Oxford, 1996), p. 118, para. 34.

48. Rein Müllerson, *Human Rights Diplomacy* (Routledge, 1997), p. 52.

49. Examples are found in the European Commission and Court cases upheld against the Greek Colonels, and in the Inter-American Court rulings that widespread electoral fraud is of international concern: *Mexico Elections*

Decision (cases 9768 and 9780) (1990). See James Crawford, *Democracy in International Law* (Cambridge, 1994).

5. WAR LAW

1. Bert Rölling, *The Law of War and National Jurisdiction since 1945* (Hague Academy, Recueil des Couis, 1960), p. 445.
2. See Edward Luttwak, 'A Post-Heroic Military Policy', *Foreign Affairs* (July/August 1996), p. 33.
3. Comment by Geoffrey Best, *War and Law since 1945* (Clarendon Press, 1994), p. 41.
4. Preamble to Hague Convention II (1899), repeated in 1949 Geneva Conventions (I: Article 63; II: Article 62; III: Article 142; IV: Article 158) and in 1977 Geneva Protocols.
5. *The Llandovery Castle* (1921), Annual Digest of Public International Law Cases, 1923–4, case no. 235.
6. See Best, *n.* 3 above, pp. 171–9.
7. See Geneva Convention I: Article 50; II: Article 51; III: Article 130 (including 'compelling a prisoner-of-war to serve in the forces of the hostile power, or wilfully depriving a prisoner-of-war of the rights of fair and regular trial'); and IV (including 'unlawful deportation or transfer or unlawful confinement of a protected person, compelling a protected person to serve in the forces of a hostile power . . . taking of hostages').
8. Protocol Additional to the Geneva Conventions of 12 August 1949 and Relating to the Protection of Victims of Non-International Armed Conflicts (Protocol II), Article I (material field of application).
9. Geneva Protocol I relating to the Protection of Victims of International Armed Conflicts, Article 90 (5) (c).
10. Richard Butler, 'Why Saddam is Winning the War', *Talk* magazine (September 1999), p. 197.
11. Request for Advisory Opinion on Nuclear Weapons by the World Health Organization (8 July 1996), summarized in *HRLJ* 17 (1996), p. 392.
12. See James Chace, 'Sharing the Nuclear Bomb', *Foreign Affairs* (January/February 1996), p. 129.
13. Michael Mandelbaum, 'Lessons of the Next Nuclear War', *Foreign Affairs* (March/April 1995), p. 22.
14. See Hans A. Bethe, 'The Treaty Betrayed', *New York Review of Books* (21 October 1999).
15. Richard Butler, 'Why UNSCOM Matters', *Newsweek* (23 November 1998), p. 31.

16. *The Corfu Channel Case* (1949), ICJ 4.

17. *Nuclear Tests Case (Australia v. France)* (1974), ICJ 253, para. 53.

18. *Legality of the Threat or Use of Nuclear Weapons*, ICJ advisory opinion (8 July 1996), para 22. Reported in *HRLJ* 17 (1996), p. 253ff.

19. Ibid., dissent of Judge Korona, p. 6.

20. *Legality of Threat or Use of Nuclear Weapons*, ICJ advisory opinion (8 July 1996), para. 15 (argument of US).

21. Ibid., para. 35.

22. Ibid., para. 95.

23. *Military and Paramilitary Activities in and against Nicaragua*, ICJ Rep. (1986), p. 94, para. 176.

24. Ibid., para. 97.

25. See Arms Trafficking, Mercenaries, and Drug Cartels, Hearing Before the Permanent Sub-Committee on Investigations of the US Senate (27 and 28 February 1991).

26. Louis Blom-Cooper QC, *Guns for Antigua* (Duckworth, 1990).

27. Wilfred Burchett and Derek Roebuck, *The Whores of War* (Penguin, 1977).

28. UN General Assembly Resolution 44/81, Rep. A/44/717, on the Use of Mercenaries as a Means to Violate Human Rights and to Impede the Exercise of the Right of People to Self-determination (8 December 1989).

29. Blom-Cooper, *n.* 26 above, the Report of the Commission of Inquiry into the Circumstances Surrounding the Shipment of Arms from Israel to Antigua and Transshipment to Colombia.

30. Arms Trafficking, Mercenaries and Drug Cartels, *n.* 25 above.

31. Thus, in American law there is no basis for incriminating acts of enlistment in foreign forces outside the jurisdiction: Neutrality Act: Title 18 s.959(a); *Wiborg* v. *US* (1896), 163 US 632. The UK Foreign Enlistment Act (1870) does apply to British nationals who render services to armies at war with friendly states, but its provisions have become a dead letter: Report of the Committee of Privy Counsellors Appointed to Inquire into the Recruitment of Mercenaries (1976), Cmnd. 6569. Britain is considering whether to follow the South African legislation: 'Cook to Lift Ban on Mercenaries', *Sunday Times* (3 October 1999).

32. See *War and Children's Rights* (Amnesty UK, 1999) and the *Economist* (12 December 1998) on the UNICEF campaign.

6. AN END TO IMPUNITY?

1. Deferral hearing, Bosnian Serb Leadership Investigation (15 May 1995).

2. *R. Yamashita* (1946), 327 US 1. The irony of citing this precedent is that the 'command responsibility' theory was misapplied to the facts at the trial of Yamashita (who was wrongly convicted), and rejected as a basis for criminal liability at the 1971 trial of Captain Ernest Medina over the My Lai massacre: see Ann Marie Prévost, 'Race and War Crimes: The 1945 War Crimes Trial of General Tomoyuki Yamashita', *HRQ* 14 (1992), p. 303. The question of when a commander is criminally responsible if his troops run amok requires a more careful analysis than is provided by either case.

3. *United States* v. *Ohlendorf (Case 9)* (1946–7), IV Trials of War Criminals before the Nuremberg Military Tribunals, p. 498.

4. *Barcelona Traction Case (Spain* v. *Belgium)*, ICJ Rep. (1970), para. 33.

5. *The Antelope* (1825) 23 US (10 Wheat) 64.

6. Quoted by Lyal S. Sunga, *Individual Responsibility in International Law for Serious Human Rights Violations* (Martinus Nijhoff, 1992), p. 44.

7. Proceedings of the International Conference on the Repression of Terrorism, League of Nations (1937).

8. Foreign Office Paper (18 July 1942).

9. UK Aide-memoire (May 1945). *Life Sentence – The Memoirs of Sir Hartley Shawcross* (Constable, 1995), pp. 90–1.

10. Conference minutes, quoted by Sir Hartley Shawcross, *Tribute to Justice Jackson* (New York Bar, 1969).

11. Ann and John Tusa, *The Nuremberg Trial* (Macmillan, 1983), p. 66.

12. Ibid., Report (1 June 1945) Jackson to Truman.

13. Quoted by Michael Biddiss, 'Victor's Justice?', *History Today* (May 1995), p. 40.

14. Robert E. Conot, *Justice at Nuremberg* (Weidenfeld & Nicolson, 1983), p. 68.

15. Ibid., p. 325. And see Michael Walzer, *Just and Unjust Wars* (Basic Books, 1991) p. 148ff. for a discussion of the Laconia Order (U-boats must not attempt to rescue all survivors) and its US and British equivalents.

16. Conot, *n.* 14 above, p. 160.

17. Ibid., p. 329.

18. 'The Nuremberg Judgement', *American Journal of International Law* 41 (January 1947), p. 172.

19. *Re Krupp and others* (1948), 15 ILR 620.

20. *Re Ohlendorf and others* (1948), 15 ILR 656.

21. Tusa, *n.* 11 above, pp. 421 and 423.

22. See Albert Pierrepoint, *Executioner Pierrepoint* (Harrap, 1974), p. 148.

23. Shawcross, *n.* 9 above, p. 133.

24. John W. Dower, *Embracing Defeat: Japan in the Wake of World War 2* (W. W. Norton, 1999), p. 453. Dower's is the best, and most recent, analysis of the long-term damage done by Hirohito's immunity. He concludes (p. 562) that, 'Even Japanese peace activists who endorse the ideals of the Nuremberg and Tokyo Charters, and who have laboured to document and publicize Japanese atrocities, cannot defend the way the war crimes trials were carried out; nor can they defend the American decision to exonerate the Emperor of war responsibility and then, in the chill of the Cold War, release and soon afterwards openly embrace accused right-wing war criminals like the later Prime Minister Kishi Nobusuke.'

25. Ibid., p. 437.

26. See Yves Beigbeder, *Judging War Criminals* (Macmillan, 1999), p. 72.

27. Ibid., p. 69.

28. Simon Wiesenthal, *'Justice Not Vengeance'* (Weidenfeld & Nicolson, 1990), pp. 91, 208–9.

29. Ibid., ch. 30.

30. Resolution 96(1) of the UN General Assembly (11 December 1946).

31. The debate over the need for linkage is summarized by Stephen Ratner and Jason Abrams, *Accountability for Human Rights Atrocities in International Law* (Oxford, 1997), pp. 45–57; and see the decision of Justice Toohey in the High Court of Australia, *Polyuknovich* v. *Commonwealth* (1991), 172 CCR, pp. 501, 664–77.

32. *Reservations to the Convention on Genocide Case* (1951), ICJ Rep. 15, p. 23.

33. *Barbie* (1988), 78 ILR, pp. 137–40.

34. See the commentary to Article 19 (Prohibition of Genocide) of the ILC Draft Code of Crimes against the Peace and Security of Mankind (report of the ILC on the work of its 43rd session, 1991). The definition of genocide in Article 6 of the Rome Statute of the International Criminal Court is identical to that in the 1949 Genocide Convention.

35. *Prosecutor* v. *Akayeru* (1998), 37 ILM, p. 1399.

36. *Kevin Buzzacott* v. *Hill and Downer*, Federal Court of Australia (1 September 1999).

37. *A-G of Israel* v. *Eichmann* (1962), 36 ILR, pp. 18 and 277; *Extradition of Demjanjuk* (1985), 776 F2d 571.

38. *Ex parte Pinochet (No. 3)* (1999), 2 All ER 97, pp. 108–9 (Lord Brown-Wilkinson). The quotation is from *Extradition of Demjanjuk*, *n.* 37 above.

39. *Filártiga* v. *Peña-Irala* (1980), 577 F. Supp 860.

40. See the Privy Council decision in *Re. Piracy Jure Gentium* (1934), AC 586.

41. *Lotus Case (France* v. *Turkey)* (1927), PCIJ Ser. A, no. 10.

42. *A-G of Israel* v. *Eichmann* (1962), 36 ILR, pp. 28, 26 (District Court), p. 277 (Supreme Court).

43. *Barbie* (1988), 89 ILR, pp. 125, 130.

44. Yoram Sheftel, *The Demjanjuk Affair – The Rise and Fall of a Show Trial* (Gollancz, 1994), p. 216. This account of the case is by Demjanjuk's much-vilified Israeli defence lawyer.

7. SLOUCHING TOWARDS NEMESIS

1. Ernesto Sábato, Prologue to *Nunca Más, Report of the National Commission on the Disappearance of People* (Faber, 1986).

2. See Toine Van Dongen, 'Vanishing Point – The Problem of Disappearances', *Bulletin of Human Rights* (1990), p. 23.

3. *Nunca Más, n.* 1 above, pp. 29–31.

4. Jacobo Timerman, *Prisoner without a Name, Cell without a Number* (Knopf, 1981), p. 148.

5. See Christopher Joyce and Eric Stover, *Witnesses from the Grave* (Bloomsbury, 1991), ch. 12.

6. Van Dongen, *n.* 2 above, p. 29.

7. See Diane F. Orentlicher, 'Settling Accounts: The Duty to Prosecute Human Rights Violations of a Prior Regime', *Yale Law Journal* 2588 (1991), *n.* 227.

8. *Einsatzgruppen Case (US* v. *Ohlendorf and others)*, IV Trials of War Criminals (1950), p. 498.

9. *Batista* v. *Colombia* (October 1995), *HRC* 27 para. 8.6.17; *IIRL* 19, p. 24.

10. UN Doc A/6716 (1967).

11. Collected in Naomi Roht-Arriaza, *Impunity and Human Rights in International Law and Practice* (Oxford, 1995), ch. 3.

12. *Janes Case (US* v. *Mexico)*, 4 Reports of International Arbitral Awards (1926), p. 82.

13. *West Case (US* v. *Mexico)*, 4 Reports of International Arbitral Awards (1927), p. 270.

14. *Velasquez Rodriguez Case* (29 July 1988), *HRLJ* 9, p. 212; and see Julianne Kokott, 'No Impunity for Human Rights Violations in the Americas', *HRLJ* 14, p. 153.

15. See, for example, *Bleier* v. *Uruguay* (1982), UN Doc A/37/40; *Baboeram* v. *Suriname* (1985), UN Doc A/40/40.

16. See Naomi Roht-Arriaza, 'State Responsibility to Investigate and

Prosecute Grave Human Rights Violations in International Law', *Californian Law Review* 78 (1990), p. 451; at p. 481 commenting on *Donnelly* v. *UK* (1976), YB ECHR 84.

17. IAC 66, OAS/Ser L/V/III 29 Doc. 4, and see Padilla, 'Reparations in *Aloeboetoe* v. *Suriname*', HRQ 17 (1995), p. 541.

18. Ian Brownlie, *Principles of Public International Law* (4th edn) (Oxford, 1990), p. 310.

19. *Trajano* v. *Marcos*, 878 F2d 1439 (9th Circuit); *Re. Estate of Ferdinand Marcos Litigation* (1992), 978 F2d 493, 498 (9th Circuit).

20. *Filártiga* v. *Peña-Irala* (1980), 630 F2d 876.

21. The modern position in the British Commonwealth is summarized by the Privy Council in *Lennox Phillip* v. *DPP of Trinidad (No. 1)* (1992), 1 AC 545.

22. *US* v. *Klein* (1871), 80 US 13 Wall 128.

23. *The Federalist* no. 74 (1788) (Bourne edition, 1947), p. 79.

24. *Murphy* v. *Ford* (1975), 390 F Supp 1372.

25. *A-G of Trinidad* v. *Lennox Phillip (No. 2)* (1995), 1 AC 396.

26. *Mustapha* v. *Mohammed* (1987), LRC Const & Admin 16, applied in *A-G of Trinidad* v. *Lennox Phillip*, n. 25 above.

27. HRC, General Comment no. 20 (on Article 7) 44th session (1992).

28. Inter-American Commission on Human Rights, Uruguay Report, *HRLJ* 13, p. 340, paras 21–7; ibid., Argentina Report, pp. 336–9.

29. Inter-American Commission on Human Rights, El Salvador Report (24 September 1992): 'State Responsibility for Los Hojas Massacre', *HRLJ* 14 (1993), p. 167.

30. Naomi Roht-Arriaza and Lauren Gibson, 'The Developing Jurisprudence of Amnesty', *HRQ* 20 (1998), pp. 850–1.

31. Rivera, 'Two Examples of Battling Impunity in Chile', *ICJ Review* 53 (1994), p. 13.

32. *Romo Mena Case* (26 October 1995), Chile Supreme Court.

33. Argentina Supreme Court Decision on the Due Obedience Law (22 June 1987); Kritz, *Transitional Justice* Vol. III (US Institute of Peace Press, 1995), p. 509.

34. International Committee of the Red Cross interpretation of Article 6(5) cited by Roht-Arriaza and Gibson, n. 30 above, p. 865.

35. *Chile in Transition* (Americas Watch, 1989), p. 73.

36. Carlos S. Nino, 'The Duty to Punish Past Abuses of Human Rights Put into Context: The Case of Argentina', *Yale Law Journal* 100 (1991), p. 2624.

37. Belinda Aquino, 'The Human Rights Debacle in the Philippines' in Roht-Arriaza, n. 11 above, p. 231.

38. Richard Carver, 'Zimbabwe: Drawing a Line through the Past', in Roht-Arriaza, *n.* 11 above, p. 252.

39. See generally P. Hayer, 'Fifteen Truth Commissions – 1974–1994: A Comparative Study', *HRQ* 16 (1994), p. 597; David Pion-Berlin, 'To Prosecute or Pardon? Human Rights Decisions in the Latin American Southern Zone', *HRQ* 16 (1994), p. 105.

40. 'Bolivia: A Historic Ruling against Impunity', *ICJ Review* 51 (1993).

41. See 'Chilean Death Squad Chief Faces Arrest', *Guardian* (10 June 1999); 'Pinochet's Legacy: The Reckoning', *Economist* (18 September 1999), p. 76; 'Life Without Pinochet', *Economist* (16 October 1999), p. 82.

42. The El Mozote massacre was first reported by Ray Bonner in *The New York Times*. It was committed by a battalion trained in the US, but Assistant Secretary of State Thomas Enders told a Senate committee it had never taken place. See Mark Danner, *The Massacre at El Mozote* (Vintage, 1994).

43. See M. Ensalaco, 'Truth Commissions for Chile and El Salvador: A Report and Assessment', *HRQ* 16 (1994), p. 664.

44. Panama has become a dumping ground for the political waste of the region. See 'A Refuge for Ex-presidents', *Economist* (18 April 1998).

45. Sábato, *n.* 1 above, pp. 160–1.

46. Quoted by Aryeh Neier in *War Crimes* (Random House, 1997), p. 37.

47. *Azanian People's Organization* v. *The President of the Republic of South Africa* (1996), 4 South Africa Law Reports 637, Ismail Mahomed CJ, para. 32.

48. Desmond Tutu, *No Future without Progress* (Rider, 1999), pp. 24–30. But compare Martin Meredith, *Coming to Terms – South Africa's Search for Truth* (Perseus, 1999), which gives a much more critical and pessimistic account of the Commission.

49. *Weekly Mail* (24 February 1995), pp. 7–8, cited by Parker, 'The Politics of Indemnities, Truth Telling and Reconciliation in South Africa', *HRCJ* 17, p. 1.

50. Jane Perlez, 'Hungarian Arrests Set Off Debate: Should '56 Oppressors be Punished?', *The New York Times* (3 April 1994), p. 10. 'Four in Court for Hungarian Uprising Massacre', *Guardian* (12 October 1999), p. 17.

51. Susanne Walther, 'The Berlin Wall Shootings', in Roht-Arriaza, *n.* 11 above, p. 99. And see 'No Escape from Jail Term for East German Leader', *Guardian* (9 November 1999), p. 14.

52. 'Chief of "Balkan Auschwitz" Gets 20 Years in Jail', *Guardian* (5 October 1999).

53. See Robert O. Paxton, 'The Trial of Maurice Papon', *New York Review of Books* (16 December 1999), p. 32.

54. 'Time Closes Dossiers of the Nazi Hunters', *The Times* (4 September 1999).

55. *IAC Annual Report* (26 September 1986), p. 193, and see Kokoff, 'No

Impunity to Human Rights Violations in the Americas', *HRLJ* 14 (1993), p. 153.

8. THE BALKAN TRIALS

1. 'War Crimes Court Urges Sanctions against Serbs: Goldstone Attacks NATO Inaction', *Guardian* (7 June 1996).

2. Anthony Parsons, *From Cold War to Hot Peace* (Penguin, 1995), p. 230.

3. 'Croatia Angers United Nations with Promotion of Indicted Soldier', *Guardian* (16 November 1995). Blaskić was later surrendered for trial after US pressure.

4. An anonymous example of this argument is 'Human Rights in Peace Negotiations', *HRQ* 18 (1996), p. 249.

5. Charles Lane and Thom Shanker, 'Bosnia: What the CIA Didn't Tell Us', *New York Review of Books* (9 May 1996), p. 11.

6. Report of the Secretary-General Pursuant to Paragraph 2 of Security Council Resolution 808 (3 May 1993), S/25704.

7. 'Effects of Awards of Compensation Made by the United Nations Administrative Tribunal' (1954), ICJ Reports 47.

8. *Tadić Case (Prosecutor v. Duško Tadić)* (1995), International Criminal Tribunal for the Former Yugoslavia, The Hague, *HRLJ* 16, p. 426 (Trial Chamber), p. 437 (Appeals Chamber).

9. Ibid., Appeals Chamber, p. 451, para. 70.

10. *Nicaragua* v. *US* (1986), ICJ 4.

11. *Tadić Case*, *n.* 9 above, p. 458, paras. 96–7.

12. Ibid., p. 469, para. 141.

13. *The Kanyabashi Case* (18 June 1997), *HRLJ* 18 (1997), p. 343.

14. See Lyall S. Sunga, 'The First Indictments of the International Criminal Tribunal for Rwanda', *HRLJ* 18 (1997), p. 329.

15. William W. Horne, 'The Real Trial of the Century', *The American Lawyer* (1996), p. 61.

16. 'Failure to Arrest War Crimes Suspects Marrs Talks', *The Times* (14 June 1996).

17. Statute of the International Criminal Tribunal for the Former Yugolsavia, Article 21 (4) (d). See Judge Vorah's opinion in the *Tadić Case* (27 November 1996), importing the European Convention 'equality of arms' principle.

18. International Criminal Tribunal for the Former Yugoslavia, Rule 89 (c).

19. Ibid., Rule 93.

20. Opinion of Judge Sidhwa in *Rajić Decision* (13 September 1996), IT-95-12-R61.

21. The best example of an international court explaining the danger of convicting upon eyewitness evidence is the Privy Council in *Reid and Dennis v. R.* (1990), AC 363.

22. Lane and Shanker, *n.* 5 above, p. 10.

23. *Rajić Decision, n.* 20 above; *Nikolić Decision* (1998), IT-92-2-R61.

24. *Tadić Case, n.* 8 above, Denial of Defence Motion on Jurisdiction (Trial Chamber), para. 39.

25. Catherine Niarchos, 'Women, War and Rape: Challenges Facing the International Tribunal for the Former Yugoslavia', *HRQ* 17 (1995), p. 649.

26. See Aryeh Neier, *War Crimes* (Random House, 1998).

27. The *Celebići Case: Prosecutor* v. *Zejnil Delalić and others*, IT-96-21-T (16 November 1998), para. 476.

28. *Tadić Case, n.* 8 above, Decision on the Prosecutor's Motion (10 August 1995), Protective Measures for Victims and Witnesses.

29. International UN War Crimes Tribunal for the Former Yugoslavia, Rule 75A.

30. For example, *Kostovski* v. *Austria* (1989), Series A no. 166; *Ludi* v. *Switzerland* (1992), 15 EHRR 173.

31. *Blaskić Case* (5 November 1996), IT-95-14-T.

32. *The Prosecutor* v. *Mile Mskić and others* (3 April 1996), Review of Indictment under Rule 61, Trial Chamber I (*Vukovar Hospital Decision*).

33. *Tadić* judgment (7 May 1997), para. 653. See also the Appeals Chamber judgment, *Tadić Case* (15 July 1999), and its sentencing judgment (26 January 2000).

34. International Law Commission Report (1991), p. 266 (Draft Code, Article 94).

35. *Mauthausen Case* (1946–7), Vol. XI Law Reports, 15.

36. *Gustav Becker and others* (1946–7), Vol. VII Law Reports, 67.

37. *Zyklon-B Case (Trial of Bruno Tesch and others)* (British Military Court, Hamburg, 1946), 1 War Crimes Reports, pp. 93, 103.

38. *The Justice Case (The Trial of Joseph Altstoetter and others)*, Vol. VI Law Reports, 88.

39. International Tribunal First Annual Report (28 July 1994); and see note by Secretary-General to the UN General Assembly (29 August 1994), A/49/342 para. 15.

40. 'Five Croats Jailed for War Crimes', *The Times* (15 January 2000).

9. THE INTERNATIONAL CRIMINAL COURT

1. Quotations in this paragraph are from Amnesty International, *The Inter-*

national Criminal Court – Making the Right Choices Part 1 (January 1997), pp. 76–7. The section on 'defences' continues until p. 88.

2. 'A New World Court', *Economist* (13 June 1998).

3. Jorgen Wouters, 'America v. Its Allies, *ABC World News* (17 July 1998).

4. A point well made by Ruth Wedgwood, 'Fiddling in Rome – America and the International Court', in *Foreign Affairs* 77 (November/December 1998), p. 20.

5. *Yugoslavia* v, *UK*, ICJ (2 June 1999), para. 40.

6. This definition combines the nub of paragraph 1 of Article 7 with subparagraph 2 (a), which clumsily adds to the essential elements of the crime.

7. Kenneth Roth, 'The Court the US Doesn't Want', *New York Review of Books* (19 November 1998), p. 45.

8. Rome Statute of the International Criminal Court, Article 53(3)(b). Even more oddly, the prosecutor may be required to proceed by a chamber comprising only one judge: see Article 57(2).

9. Lawrence Wechsler, 'High Noon at Twin Peaks', *New Yorker* (18 August 1997).

10. See Payam Akhavan, 'Justice in The Hague, Peace in the Former Yugoslavia?', *HRQ* 20 (1998), p. 794.

11. The right to counsel of choice for an indigent accused may mean the right to choose from a list of counsel prepared to act for the moderate payment on offer from the registry. See the Rwanda Tribunal decision in the *Ntakirutimana Case* (1997), *HRLJ* 18 (1997), p. 340.

12. *Edwards* v. *UK* (1992), 15 EHRR 417.

13. Rome Statute, Article 80: 'Nothing in this Part of the Statute affects the application by State Parties of penalties prescribed by their national laws.'

14. William R. Pace, 'The Day Peace Won', *International Criminal Court Monitor* 9 (August 1998).

10. THE CASE OF GENERAL PINOCHET

1. DINA head Mañuel Contreras, seeking parole from his prison sentences for directing the Letelier bombing, has testified that Pinochet gave him verbal orders for this and other assassinations. This chimes with the American prosecutor's case against the DINA operatives who effected the bombing. Lawrence Barcella Jr, 'The Case We Made 22 Years Ago', *Washington Post* (6 December 1998); Richard J. Wilson, 'Prosecuting Pinochet: International Crimes in Spanish Domestic Law', *HRQ* 21 (1999).

2. See Inter-American Commission on Human Rights, Report 36/96 (15 October 1996) and Report 29/98 of 2 March 1998.

3. Judge Juan Guzmán, of the Santiago Appeals Court, seized with all cases against Pinochet, stated, 'I am prevented from issuing any kind of arrest warrant' (*El Mercurio*, 5 August 1998). After Pinochet's arrest in London three months later, the Chile government petitioned the pro-Pinochet Supreme Court to appoint one of its own justices to take the cases over from Judge Guzmán so that the military tribunals could not assert jurisdiction. The court refused, by 13 votes to 3, to permit even this distant possibility of Pinochet standing trial in Chile. According to Roberto Garretón (the distinguished lawyer who was chief human rights adviser to the government of Chile 1990–4) in his evidence for Human Rights Watch in *Ex parte Pinochet (No. 3)*, 'There is virtually no chance that Pinochet would be prosecuted in a Chilean court' (affidavit, 12 January 1999). In July 1999, Chile's Supreme Court allowed that disappearances still unresolved could be characterized as the ongoing crime of 'kidnapping' which continues after, and therefore beyond and outside, the amnesty. Some twenty army torturers and one junta member (Humberto Gordon) have been arrested in consequence: whether these investigations will ever result in trials (or trials in non-military courts) remains doubtful.

4. Richard J. Wilson, *n.* 1 above, p. 927.

5. See Hugh O'Shaughnessy, *Pinochet: The Politics of Torture* (Latin American Bureau, 1999).

6. R. v. *Evans, ex parte Augusto Pinochet Ugarte* (28 October 1998), Divisional Court (Bingham CJ, Collins J (quoted) and Richards J).

7. *Ex parte Pinochet (No. 2)* (1999), 1 All ER 577.

8. Article 1, Montevideo Convention on the Rights and Duties of States (1933).

9. The Papal States were conquered in 1870 by Italy, which by the Treaty of Locarno recognized their traditional claim to sovereignty. There is no reason why any other state should recognize the Vatican, however, any more than the bantustans were recognized as states independent of South Africa.

10. See Malcolm Shaw, *International Law* (4th edn) (Cambridge, 1998), p. 143.

11. See *The South-west Africa Case*, ICJ Reports (1971), p. 16.

12. Borchard, 'Government Responsibility in Tort', *Yale Law Journal*, 34 (1924), pp. 4–5.

13. See J. L. Brierly, *The Law of Nations: An Introduction to the International Law of Peace* (6th edn, 1963), pp. 9–11, discussing J. Bodin, *De Republica* (1576).

14. As one of them, Vattel, memorably put it: '[A] Head of State who commits murder and other grave crimes in the course of war is chargeable with all the evils, all the horrors, of the war; all the effusions of blood, the desolation of families, the rapine, the violence, the revenge, the burnings, are his work

and his crimes. He is guilty towards the enemy, of attacking, oppressing, massacring them without cause, guilty towards his people, of drawing them into acts of injustice, exposing their lives without necessity, without reason, towards that part of his subjects whom the war ruins, or who are great sufferers by it, of losing their lives, their fortune, or their health. Lastly he is guilty towards all mankind, of disturbing their quiet, and setting a pernicious example' (quoted in Quincy Wright, 'The Legal Liability of the Kaiser', *American Political Science Review* 13 (1919), p. 120).

15. *Parlement Belge* (1880), 5 PD 197.

16. See respectively *Porto Alexander* (1920), 1 ILR 146; *Krajina* v. *Tass Agency* (1949), 2 All ER 274.

17. *Trendtex Trading Corporation Ltd* v. *Central Bank of Nigeria* (1977), 2 WLR 356.

18. See criticisms of the 1952 'suggestion of immunity' procedure in *Isbrandtsen Tankers Inc.* v. *President of India* (1971), 404 F2d 1198 (2nd Circuit).

19. See Ian Brownlie, *Principles of Public International Law* (5th edn) (Oxford, 1998), p. 336; and *Littrell* v. *USA (No. 2)* (1995), 1 WLR 82.

20. *Io Congresso del Partido* (1983), AC 244.

21. *The Schooner Exchange* v. *McFaddon* (1812), 7 Cranch 116.

22. *Saudi Arabia* v. *Nelson* (1993), 113 S Ct 1471.

23. *Siderman de Blake* v. *Republic of Argentina* (9th Circuit, 1992), 965 F2d 699.

24. *Al-Adsani* v. *Government of Kuwait* (1996), 107 ILR 536.

25. *Letelier* v. *Republic of Chile* (DDC 1980), 448 F Supp 665.

26. For this reason, a more satisfactory extra-judicial settlement was achieved by negotiation between France and New Zealand over the sinking by French secret agents of the Greenpeace vessel *Rainbow Warrior*, moored in Auckland before a proposed voyage to protest at nuclear tests in the south Pacific. The agreement between the countries provided, *inter alia*, for France to pay $7 million to New Zealand: it had suffered no material damage, other than the insult of having the duties it was owed in international law treated with contempt by the French. The Letelier family was eventually compensated by the post-Pinochet government, after a special commission set up under a 1914 treaty for the resolution of disputes between Chile and the US; see 31 ILM 1 (1992).

27. M. Cherif Bassiouni, *Crimes against Humanity*, pp. 499–508. And on the duty to extradite, see Ian Brownlie, *Principles of Public International Law* (5th edn) (Oxford, 1998), p. 318.

28. UN Doc. A/CONF 157/23 para. 60.

29. 'US Diplomatic and Consular Staff in Tehran', ICJ Reports (1980), p. 3, para. 91.

30. *Kilgour* v. *Windsor*, *International Law Review* (1981), p. 605.

31. *Lafontant* v. *Aristide* (EDNY, 1994), 844 F Supp 128.

32. *In re. Estate of Ferdinand E. Marcos*, US Court of Appeals 9th Circuit (21 October 1992).

33. *Estate of Ferdinand Marcos* (1994), 25 F3d 1467 (9th Circuit).

34. *The Times* (26 February 1999).

35. See Ralph G. Steinhardt, 'Fulfilling the Promise of Filártiga: Litigating Human Rights Claims against the Estate of Ferdinand Marcos', *Yale Journal of International Law* 65 (1995).

36. *Ex parte Pinochet (No. 1)* (1998), 4 All ER 897 at 939–40 *per* Lord Nicholls.

37. UN General Assembly Resolution 95(1) (11 December 1946).

38. Of the six judges in the majority, Lord Hutton clearly agreed with *Pinochet (No. 1)* that it was not a function of a head of state to commit serious international crimes, and this seems to have been the conclusion of Lord Phillips, at least in the case of torture. Lord Millet (who took the broad brush approach that there could be no immunity to charges of crimes against humanity) thought that immunity might attach to purely ceremonial state functions, but not to crimes committed in the capacity of commander-in-chief or head of government. Lords Hope and Saville argued from exactly the opposite premise: that torture was an official act, and the Torture Convention applied to a crime it defined as only capable of commission by officials, therefore the convention itself had necessarily abolished the immunity. Lord Browne-Wilkinson agreed with this argument on a hypothetical basis, but also seemed to think that a crime would fall outside the function of a head of state if it had a *jus cogens* quality and universal jurisdiction had been clearly established. He found that in the case of torture, universal jurisdiction was established by the Convention itself, in its requirement that parties either 'extradite or prosecute' suspected torturers found within their borders. See *R.* v. *Bow Street Magistrates ex parte Pinochet Ugarte (No. 3)* (1999), 2 All ER, pp. 97–192.

39. Sir Arthur Watts, 'The Legal Position in International Law of Heads of States, Heads of Government and Foreign Ministers', *Recueil des Cours* 247 (1994), p. 82.

40. Quoting Sheldon Glueck (1946), *Harvard Law Journal* 59 (1946), p. 396.

41. *Ex parte Pinochet (No. 3)*, n. 38 above at p. 177.

42. Citing *Prosecutor* v. *Furundžija*, Hague Tribunal for the Former Yugoslavia, case no. 17-95-17/I-T, para. 153.

43. Michael Dines, 'Liberia's Gruesome Top 20 Killers', *The Times* (2 November 1999).

44. This common sense solution was referred to by Lord Hope in *Ex parte Pinochet (No. 3)*, although he found no authority in its support. See *n.* 38 above at p. 146.

45. 'Top Cardinal Made Plea for Pinochet', *Sunday Times* (11 February 1999), p. 24.

46. Castro's recent abuses of power fall short of crimes against humanity as strictly defined. But the Cuban gulag was a reality for too many, too long; see Armando Valladares, *Against All Hope* (Alfred A. Knopf, 1987).

47. Lord Justice Simon Browne, *R. v. Home Secretary ex parte Belgium* (15 February 2000), p. 28.

11. GUERNICA PARADOX: BOMBING FOR HUMANITY

1. Tony Blair, 'A New Generation Draws the Line', *Newsweek* (19 April 1999).

2. Hansard (25 March 1999), col. 617.

3. Foreign Policy Document No. 148 (1986), British Yearbook of International Law 56, section 2, para. 22. It did concede that 'the best case can be made in support of humanitarian intervention is that it cannot be said to be unambiguously illegal'.

4. Vattel, cited by Michael J. Bazyler, 'Re-examining the Doctrine of Humanitarian Intervention', *Stanford International Law Journal* 23 (1987), p. 547. See Louis Henkin *et al.*, *Human Rights* (Foundation Press, 1999), p. 708.

5. Report of the International Committee of Jurists Giving an Advisory Opinion upon the Legal Aspects of the Aaland Islands Question, cited in Henkin *et al.*, *n.* 4 above, p. 462. And see Antonio Cassesse, *Self-determination of Peoples* (Cambridge University Press, 1995), pp. 27–33.

6. See Mark Littman, *Kosovo: Law and Diplomacy* (Centre for Policy Studies, 1999), appendix 1: Submissions of Counsel for Yugoslavia to the International Court of Justice.

7. *Nicaragua* v. *USA*, judgment of 27 June 1986, paras. 266–8.

8. Ibid., para. 176.

9. *Yugoslavia* v. *UK*, judgment delivered at The Hague on 2 June 1999, para. 16.

10. *Corfu Channel Case* (1949), ICJ Rep. 22.

11. See Adam Roberts, 'Willing the End but not the Means', *The World Today* (May 1999), pp. 10–11.

12. Richard Butler, 'Bewitched, Bothered and Bewildered: Repairing the Security Council', *Foreign Affairs* (September/October 1999), p. 9.

13. American journalist John Gunther, *Inside Europe* (1940), quoted in Misha Glenny, *The Balkans* (Granta, 1999), p. xxiii.

14. See William W. Hagen, 'The Balkans' Lethal Nationalism', *Foreign Affairs* (July/August 1999), p. 52.

15. Barton Gellman, 'The Path to Crisis: How the US and Its Allies Went to War', *Washington Post* (18 April 1999).

16. Quoted in Littman, *n.* 6 above, p. 16.

17. Edward Luttwak, 'Letting Wars Burn', *Foreign Affairs* (July/August 1999), p. 41; Michael Ignatieff, 'Future War', *The World Today*, vol. 56, no. 2 (February 2000) and *Virtual War – Kosovo and Beyond* (Chatto & Windus, 2000).

18. Michael Ignatieff, *Virtual War – Kosovo and Beyond*, *n.* 17 above, pp. 197–8.

19. Julian Borger, 'Pentagon Kept the Lid on Cyberwar in Kosovo', *Guardian* (9 November 1999), p. 15.

20. George Soros, commencement speech at Johns Hopkins University (27 May 1999), see Open Society Institute newsletter (Autumn 1999), p. 2.

21. Samantha Power, 'Weighing Values in the Calculation of Self-interest', Open Society Institute newsletter (Autumn 1999), p. 7.

22. *The Times* (15 July 1999), p. 46.

23. Elizabeth Sellwood, 'Kosovo: Frustration Grows', *The World Today* (December 1999), p. 9.

24. Timothy Garton Ash, 'Anarchy and Madness', *New York Review of Books* (10 February 2000).

25. Kofi Annan, 'Two Concepts of Sovereignty', *Economist* (18 September 1999).

26. Cassesse, *n.* 5 above, p. 226.

27. See the *Western Sahara Case* (1975), ICJ Rep. 12.

28. Statement by Senator Gareth Evans, Australian Minister for Resources (20 March 1986).

29. *East Timor Case (Portugal v. Australia)* (1995), ICJ Rep. 90.

30. Lynne O'Donnell, 'Jakarta's Final Solution', *The Australian* (17 September 1999).

31. Elisabeth Becker and Philip Shenton, 'With Other Goals in Indonesia, US Moves Gently on East Timor', *The New York Times* (9 September 1999).

32. Michael Binyon, 'The World Wrings Its Hands but is Reluctant to Intervene', *The Times* (7 September 1999).

33. See John Aglionby, 'Indonesia's President Says He will Punish Ex-army Chief', *Guardian* (1 February 2000).

34. 'Ending the Cycle of Impunity', Tapol (Indonesian Human Rights Campaign) Report (24 January 2000).

35. Noel Malcolm, *Kosovo: A Short History* (Macmillan, 1998), p. 25.

EPILOGUE

1. Stuart Hampshire, 'Innocence and Experience' (1989), cited by Michael Perry, 'Are Human Rights Universal?', *HRQ* 19 (1997), p. 483.

2. *Economist* (13 February 1999).

3. 'A Traditional Practice That Threatens Health – Female Circumcision', *World Health Organization Chronicle* 51 (1986), reproduced in Henry Steiner & Philip Alston (eds.) *International Human Rights in Context* (Oxford, 1996), p. 242.

4. Yash Ghai, 'Human Rights and Governance: The Asia Debate', *Australian Yearbook of International Law* 15 (1994), p. 5.

5. Kim Dae Jung, 'Is Culture Destiny? The Myth of Asia's Anti-Democratic Values', 73 *Foreign Affairs* 189 (1994).

6. Bill Clinton, 'Why the Allies Must Fight on', *Sunday Times* (18 April 1999).

7. *The Times* (15 July 1999), p. 46.

8. Michael Ignatieff, *Virtual War – Kosovo and Beyond* (Chatto & Windus, 2000), p. 6.

9. 'In the World of Helms', *The New York Times* (21 January 2000), p. A8.

10. 'Chechens Report Abuses at Russian Camps'. *Washington Post* (18 February 2000), p. A19.

11. Samuel P. Huntington, 'The Lonely Superpower', *Foreign Affairs* (March/April 1999), p. 38.

12. In 1998 the US suffered the indignity of a critical report from the Human Rights Commission's Special Rapporteur on arbitrary executions, who condemned poor representation in capital cases, the sentencing of juveniles to death and the general lack of awareness of prosecutors and judges of the standards in the Civil Covenant. See Bacre Waly Ndiaye, *Mission to the USA*, E/CN.4/1998/68 (22 January 1998).

13. Stephen B. Bright, 'Death in Texas', *The Champion* (July 1999), p. 16.

Appendix A: Human Rights in History

1139	Second Lateran Council forbids the use of the crossbow in wars between Christians
1215	Magna Carta
1648	Peace of Westphalia: protection of religious minorities in Germany Trial of Charles I
1651	*Leviathan* by Thomas Hobbes
1679	Habeas Corpus Acts
1688	'Glorious Revolution' and English Bill of Rights
1690	*Second Treatise of Government* by John Locke
1764	*Of Crimes and Punishments* by Cesare Beccaria
1776	*Common Sense* by Thomas Paine American Declaration of Independence
1789	French Revolution: 'The Declaration of the Rights of Man and the Citizen' (France)
1792	*The Rights of Man* by Thomas Paine Alien Tort Claims Act (US)
1803	*Marbury* v. *Madison*: US Supreme Court asserts power to make laws conform to constitutional guarantees
1807	Abolition of slavery in England
1843	'Anarchical Fallacies' by Jeremy Bentham
1844	'On the Jewish Question' by Karl Marx
1863	The Red Cross founded by Henri Dunant *Lieber Code*: a war law manual for armies in the field
1865	America abolishes slavery
1868	St Petersburg Conference on limiting armaments
1878	Congress of Berlin
1885	Berlin Conference on Africa: ensuing treaty between European states forbids trading in slaves

1898   US declares war on Spain because of its oppression in Cuba

1899   First Hague Conference on arms limitation

1900   US Supreme Court decision in *The Paquete Habana*

1904   Theodore Roosevelt proclaims the right of humanitarian intervention

1907   Second Hague Conference on arms limitation

1919   Versailles Peace Conference

Charter of the League of Nations

1923   Hague agreement to confine aerial bombing to military targets

1925   Geneva Protocol against Use of Poison Gas

1926   Anti-Slavery Convention

1928   Kellogg–Briand Pact

Chorzów Factory Case (Permanent Court of International Justice)

1933   Hitler in power: first League of Nations petition against the Nazis for discriminating against Jews lodged by Franz Bernheim

1935   *Minority Schools in Albania* decision (Permanent Court of International Justice)

1936   London agreement on rules of submarine warfare

1936–8 The Moscow show trials

1937   Draft Convention for the Prosecution and Punishment of Terrorism

1939   Declaration of Second World War

H. G. Wells writes to *The Times* urging human rights as a war aim

1940   *H. G. Wells on The Rights of Man* (Penguin Special)

Darkness at Noon by Arthur Koestler

1941   Franklin D. Roosevelt makes 'Four Freedoms' speech

1942   1 January: Allies declare protection of human rights as a war aim

1944   Dumbarton Oaks: Allied powers determine to establish UN

1945   April: British army enters Belsen and Buchenwald concentration camps

26 June: Charter of UN signed at San Francisco

July: Potsdam Conference: Allies confirm they will hold trials of major war criminals

6 August: Atom bomb ('Fatboy') dropped on Hiroshima

8 August: Nuremberg Charter proclaimed

Animal Farm by George Orwell

1946   30 September: Judgment delivered at Nuremberg

Re. Yamashita (US Supreme Court)

11 December: UN General Assembly Resolution 96(i) recognizes the Nuremberg Charter and Judgment as stating customary international law

1948   10 December: Universal Declaration of Human Rights adopted by
        UN General Assembly, Paris
        11 December: Genocide Convention
1949   *Corfu Channel Case* (International Court of Justice)
        Geneva Conventions I–IV, on treatment of prisoners-of-war and
        civilians during war
        Soviet Union tests atom bomb: arms race begins
1950   European Convention on Human Rights
1950–3 Korean War
1951   Refugee Convention
        International Court of Justice Opinion on Genocide Convention
1953   Death of Stalin
        Electrocution of Julius and Ethel Rosenberg
1956   February: Khrushchev condemns Stalin and show trials at 20th Party
        Congress
        November: Soviet tanks invade Hungary
1960   Massacre at Sharpeville, South Africa
1961   Berlin Wall goes up
        Amnesty International founded
        Trial of Adolf Eichmann
        Bay of Pigs invasion
1962   Cuban Missile Crisis
1964   US bombing of Vietnam begins
1966   Twin Covenants: Covenant on Civil and Political Rights and
        Optional Protocol on Economic, Cultural and Social Rights
1967   First UN sanctions against South Africa
        Seven Day War: Israel settles Gaza Strip
1968   Tehran Proclamation on Universality of Human Rights
        USSR invades Czechoslovakia
        Convention on the Non-Applicability of Statutory Limitations to
        War Crimes and Crimes against Humanity
1969   Convention on the Elimination of All Forms of Racial Discrimination
        (CERD)
        Inter-American Convention on Human Rights
        Vienna Convention on the Law of Treaties
1970   Convention on Return of Cultural Property
        Friendly Relations Resolution, UN General Assembly
1971   Convention on the Suppression and Punishment of the Crime of
        Apartheid

1973   UN General Assembly adopts principles for co-operation in punishment of crimes against humanity

Sakharov's open letter to US Congress calling for trade sanctions on the Soviet Union

Pinochet coup in Chile

1974   *Nuclear Test Case* (*Australia* v. *France*) (International Court of Justice)

1975   UN declaration against torture

Helsinki Accords

1976   Military junta seizes power in Argentina

Ireland v. *UK*, European Court of Human Rights

1977   Charter 77 launched in Prague

UN imposes mandatory trade sanctions on South Africa and Rhodesia under Chapter VII of the Charter

Carter administration adopts human rights as foreign policy objective

Geneva Convention Protocols I and II

Human Rights Committee (HRC) established pursuant to Optional Protocol of the Civil Covenant

1978   Pinochet grants amnesty to death squads and torturers and himself

1979   Convention against the Taking of Hostages

1980   *Filártiga* v. *Peña-Irala*

1 June: CNN begins broadcasting

1981   Convention on the Elimination of All Forms of Discrimination against Women

African Charter on Human and People's Rights

Sakharov exiled to Gorky

1983   US invasion of Grenada

1984   Convention Against Torture

ECOSOC Safeguards on Imposition of the Death Penalty

1985   *Nunca Más: Report of the National Commission on the Disappearance of People* by Ernesto Sábato, followed by trial of Argentinian junta

1986   Sakharov permitted to return to Moscow

Burkina Faso v. *Mali*: the International Court of Justice ignores the right of self-determination

UN General Assembly declares the existence of 'a right to development'

Nicaragua v. *US* (International Court of Justice)

1986–8 Proceedings in Israel against Ivan Demjanjuk
1988   Trial of Klaus Barbie
      Velasquez Rodriguez Case (Inter-American Court)
1989   Convention on the Rights of the Child
      Saddam Hussein uses poison gas on Kurds at Halebja: 7,000 killed
      Massacre in Tiananmen Square
      UN Convention on Recruitment and Training of Mercenaries
      Collapse of communism in eastern Europe: demolition of Berlin
        Wall
1990   Democracy restored in Chile
      Iraq invades Kuwait
1991   Civil war begins in Yugoslavia
      Operation 'Desert Storm' liberates Kuwait
1992   US ratifies Civil Covenant
      Torture Victims Protection Act (US)
1993   *Aloeboetal* v. *Suriname* (Inter-American Court)
      Pratt & Morgan v. *Jamaica* (Privy Council)
      Hague Tribunal for War Crimes in the Former Yugoslavia established by Security Council Resolutions 808 & 881
      Security Council sanctions on Libya
      June: UN Human Rights Conference in Vienna
      October: 18 American peacekeepers killed in Mogadishu
1994   *Trajano* v. *Marcos* verdict
      April–June: 800,000 massacred in Rwandan genocide
      Security Council establishes Rwanda Tribunal in Arusha
      Toonen v. *Australia* (HRC)
1995   Amnesty for General Cedras and others killed in Haiti
      Nuclear Non-Proliferation Treaty
      Lennox Phillip v. *DPP of Trinidad* (Privy Council)
      15 May: Indictment by Hague Tribunal of Bosnian Serb leadership (Karadžić and Mladić)
      July: Fall of Srebrenica: 7,000 massacred
      Beijing Conference on Women's Rights
      Dayton Peace Accords
1996   Opinion on Legality of the Threat or Use of Nuclear Weapons (International Court of Justice)
      Tadić Case (Hague Tribunal, Appeals Chamber ruling on jurisdiction)
      Japan apologizes to wartime 'comfort women'
1997   Dusko Tadić convicted and sentenced

Ottawa Convention on banning anti-personnel land mines

1998   Report of South African Truth and Reconciliation Commission

Death in Kampuchea of Pol Pot, but his chief lieutenants, Khieu Samphan and Nuon Chea, are welcomed back by Hun Sen

17 July: 120 nations vote to approve the Rome Statute for the International Criminal Court

US attacks Osmara Bin Laden bases in Sudan and Afghanistan

Overthrow of President Suharto in Indonesia

16 October: General Pinochet arrested in London

December: *Ex parte Pinochet (No. 1)*: House of Lords rules against immunity from charges of crimes against humanity for ex-heads of state

1999   OECD Convention against Third World bribery

24 March: *Ex parte Pinochet (No. 3)*: Law Lords rule no immunity for ex-heads of state under Torture Convention

NATO bombs Serbia

9 June: Milošević accepts ceasefire agreement

10 June: Security Council resolution providing for Kosovo autonomy

4 September: Result of East Timor ballot: 78.5 per cent vote for independence

12 September: President Habibie permits UN troops to occupy East Timor

8 October: Pinochet ordered to be extradited to Spain to face torture charges

Switzerland returns Maurice Papon to France

November: Appeal court jails Egon Krenz for commanding Berlin Wall shootings

16 December: Carlsson Report condemns UN for complicity in Rwanda genocide

2000   20 January: Senator Jesse Helms addresses Security Council

31 January: UN HRC report and Indonesian HRC report both condemn Indonesian army officers for crimes against humanity in East Timor and call for prosecutions

February: Prosecution in Senegal of Hissène Habré, ex-dictator of Chad

3 March: General Pinochet returns to Chile, irreversibly brain-damaged

General Blaskić sentenced to forty-five years' imprisonment by the Hague Tribunal for crimes against humanity

Appendix B: Universal Declaration of Human Rights

PREAMBLE

Whereas recognition of the inherent dignity and of the equal and inalienable rights of all members of the human family is the foundation of freedom, justice and peace in the world,

Whereas disregard and contempt for human rights have resulted in barbarous acts which have outraged the conscience of mankind, and the advent of a world in which human beings shall enjoy freedom of speech and belief and freedom from fear and want has been proclaimed as the highest aspiration of the common people,

Whereas it is essential, if man is not to be compelled to have recourse, as a last resort, to rebellion against tyranny and oppression, that human rights should be protected by the rule of law,

Whereas it is essential to promote the development of friendly relations between nations,

Whereas the peoples of the United Nations have in the Charter reaffirmed their faith in fundamental human rights, in the dignity and worth of the human person and in the equal rights of men and women and have determined to promote social progress and better standards of life in larger freedom,

Whereas Member States have pledged themselves to achieve, in co-operation with the United Nations, the promotion of universal respect for and observance of human rights and fundamental freedoms,

Whereas a common understanding of these rights and freedoms is of the greatest importance for the full realization of this pledge,

Now, therefore The General Assembly proclaims This Universal Declaration of Human Rights as a common standard of achievement for all peoples and all nations, to the end that every individual and every organ of society, keeping this Declaration constantly in mind, shall strive by teaching and education to promote respect for these rights and freedoms and by progressive measures, national and international, to secure their universal and effective recognition and observance, both among the peoples of Member States themselves and among the peoples of territories under their jurisdiction.

ARTICLE 1

All human beings are born free and equal in dignity and rights. They are endowed with reason and conscience and should act towards one another in a spirit of brotherhood.

ARTICLE 2

Everyone is entitled to all the rights and freedoms set forth in this Declaration, without distinction of any kind, such as race, colour, sex, language, religion, political or other opinion, national or social origin, property, birth or other status. Furthermore, no distinction shall be made on the basis of the political, jurisdictional or international status of the country or territory to which a person belongs, whether it be independent, trust, non-self-governing or under any other limitation of sovereignty.

ARTICLE 3

Everyone has the right to life, liberty and security of person.

ARTICLE 4

No one shall be held in slavery or servitude; slavery and the slave trade shall be prohibited in all their forms.

ARTICLE 5

No one shall be subjected to torture or to cruel, inhuman or degrading treatment or punishment.

ARTICLE 6

Everyone has the right to recognition everywhere as a person before the law.

ARTICLE 7

All are equal before the law and are entitled without any discrimination to equal protection of the law. All are entitled to equal protection against any discrimination in violation of this Declaration and against any incitement to such discrimination.

ARTICLE 8

Everyone has the right to an effective remedy by the competent national tribunals for acts violating the fundamental rights granted him by the constitution or by law.

ARTICLE 9

No one shall be subjected to arbitrary arrest, detention or exile.

ARTICLE 10

Everyone is entitled in full equality to a fair and public hearing by an independent and impartial tribunal, in the determination of his rights and obligations and of any criminal charge against him.

ARTICLE 11

(1) Everyone charged with a penal offence has the right to be presumed innocent until proved guilty according to law in a public trial at which he has had all the guarantees necessary for his defence.

(2) No one shall be held guilty of any penal offence on account of any act or omission which did not constitute a penal offence, under national or international law, at the time when it was committed. Nor shall a heavier penalty be imposed than the one that was applicable at the time the penal offence was committed.

ARTICLE 12

No one shall be subjected to arbitrary interference with his privacy, family, home or correspondence, nor to attacks upon his honour and reputation. Everyone has the right to the protection of the law against such interference or attacks.

ARTICLE 13

(1) Everyone has the right to freedom of movement and residence within the borders of each state.

(2) Everyone has the right to leave any country, including his own, and to return to his country.

ARTICLE 14

(1) Everyone has the right to seek and to enjoy in other countries asylum from persecution.

(2) This right may not be invoked in the case of prosecutions genuinely arising from non-political crimes or from acts contrary to the purposes and principles of the United Nations.

ARTICLE 15

(1) Everyone has the right to a nationality.

(2) No one shall be arbitrarily deprived of his nationality nor denied the right to change his nationality.

ARTICLE 16

(1) Men and women of full age, without any limitation due to race, nationality or religion, have the right to marry and to found a family. They are entitled to equal rights as to marriage, during marriage and at its dissolution.

(2) Marriage shall be entered into only with the free and full consent of the intending spouses.

(3) The family is the natural and fundamental group unit of society and is entitled to protection by society and the State.

ARTICLE 17

(1) Everyone has the right to own property alone as well as in association with others.

(2) No one shall be arbitrarily deprived of his property.

ARTICLE 18

Everyone has the right to freedom of thought, conscience and religion; this right includes freedom to change his religion or belief, and freedom, either alone or in community with others and in public or private, to manifest his religion or belief in teaching, practice, worship and observance.

ARTICLE 19

Everyone has the right to freedom of opinion and expression; this right includes freedom to hold opinions without interference and to seek, receive and impart information and ideas through any media and regardless of frontiers.

ARTICLE 20

(1) Everyone has the right to freedom of peaceful assembly and association.

(2) No one may be compelled to belong to an association.

ARTICLE 21

(1) Everyone has the right to take part in the government of his country, directly or through freely chosen representatives.

(2) Everyone has the right of equal access to public service in his country.

(3) The will of the people shall be the basis of the authority of government; this will shall be expressed in periodic and genuine elections which shall be by universal and equal suffrage and shall be held by secret vote or by equivalent free voting procedures.

ARTICLE 22

Everyone, as a member of society, has the right to social security and is entitled to realization, through national effort and international co-operation and in accordance with the organization and resources of each State, of the economic, social and cultural rights indispensable for his dignity and the free development of his personality.

ARTICLE 23

(1) Everyone has the right to work, to free choice of employment, to just and favourable conditions of work and to protection against unemployment.

(2) Everyone, without any discrimination, has the right to equal pay for equal work.

(3) Everyone who works has the right to just and favourable remuneration ensuring for himself and his family an existence worthy of human dignity, and supplemented, if necessary, by other means of social protection.

(4) Everyone has the right to form and to join trade unions for the protection of his interests.

ARTICLE 24

Everyone has the right to rest and leisure, including reasonable limitation of working hours and periodic holidays with pay.

ARTICLE 25

(1) Everyone has the right to a standard of living adequate for the health and well-being of himself and of his family, including food, clothing, housing and medical care and necessary social services, and the right to security in the event of unemployment, sickness, disability, widowhood, old age or other lack of livelihood in circumstances beyond his control.

(2) Motherhood and childhood are entitled to special care and assistance. All children, whether born in or out of wedlock, shall enjoy the same social protection.

ARTICLE 26

(1) Everyone has the right to education. Education shall be free, at least in the elementary and fundamental stages. Elementary education shall be compulsory. Technical and professional education shall be made generally available and higher education shall be equally accessible to all on the basis of merit.

(2) Education shall be directed to the full development of the human personality and to the strengthening of respect for human rights and fundamental freedoms. It shall promote understanding, tolerance and friendship among all nations, racial or religious groups, and shall further the activities of the United Nations for the maintenance of peace.

(3) Parents have a prior right to choose the kind of education that shall be given to their children.

ARTICLE 27

(1) Everyone has the right freely to participate in the cultural life of the community, to enjoy the arts and to share in scientific advancement and its benefits.

(2) Everyone has the right to the protection of the moral and material interests resulting from any scientific, literary or artistic production of which he is the author.

ARTICLE 28

Everyone is entitled to a social and international order in which the rights and freedoms set forth in this Declaration can be fully realized.

ARTICLE 29

(1) Everyone has duties to the community in which alone the free and full development of his personality is possible.

(2) In the exercise of his rights and freedoms, everyone shall be subject only to such limitations as are determined by law solely for the purpose of securing the recognition and respect for the rights and freedoms of others and of meeting the just requirements of morality, public order and the general welfare in a democratic society.

(3) These rights and freedoms may in no case be exercised contrary to the purposes and principles of the United Nations.

ARTICLE 30

Nothing in this Declaration may be interpreted as implying for any State, group or person any right to engage in any activity or to perform any act aimed at the destruction of any of the rights and freedoms set forth herein.

Appendix C: Ratifications of Human Rights Treaties

(As of 1 March 2000)

Instrument	Number of State Parties
Forced Labour Convention (1930)	150
Statute of the International Court of Justice (1946)	187*
Acceptance of Compulsory Jurisdiction under the Optional Protocol	60
Convention on the Prevention and Punishment of the Crime of Genocide (1948)	130*
Geneva Conventions (1949)	188*
Convention for the Suppression of the Traffic in Persons and of the Exploitation or the Prostitution of Others (1950)	73
Convention Relating to the Status of Refugees (1951)	135
Convention on Status of Stateless Persons (1954)	50
Supplementary Convention on the Abolition of Slavery, the Slave Trade, and Institutions and Practices Similar to Slavery (1956)	118*
Abolition of Forced Labour Convention (1957)	139*
Vienna Convention on Diplomatic Relations (1961)	179
International Covenant on Economic, Social and Cultural Rights (1966)	142
International Covenant on Civil and Political Rights (1966)	144*

* Ratified by the United States

Appendix D: Excerpts from the Rome Statute of the International Criminal Court

Adopted by the United Nations Diplomatic Conference of Plenipotentiaries on the Establishment of an International Criminal Court on 17 July 1998.

PREAMBLE

Conscious that all peoples are united by common bonds, their cultures pieced together in a shared heritage, and concerned that this delicate mosaic may be shattered at any time,

Mindful that during this century millions of children, women and men have been victims of unimaginable atrocities that deeply shock the conscience of humanity,

Recognizing that such grave crimes threaten the peace, security and well-being of the world,

Affirming that the most serious crimes of concern to the international community as a whole must not go unpunished and that their effective prosecution must be ensured by taking measures at the national level and by enhancing international co-operation,

Determined to put an end to impunity for the perpetrators of these crimes and thus to contribute to the prevention of such crimes,

Recalling that it is the duty of every State to exercise its criminal jurisdiction over those responsible for international crimes,

Reaffirming the Purposes and Principles of the Charter of the United Nations, and in particular that all States shall refrain from the threat or use of force against the territorial integrity or political independence of any State, or in any other manner inconsistent with the Purposes of the United Nations,

Emphasizing in this connection that nothing in this Statute shall be taken as authorizing any State Party to intervene in an armed conflict in the internal affairs of any State,

Determined to these ends and for the sake of present and future generations, to establish an independent permanent International Criminal Court in relationship with the United Nations system, with jurisdiction over the most serious crimes of concern to the international community as a whole,

Emphasizing that the International Criminal Court established under this Statute shall be complementary to national criminal jurisdictions,

Resolved to guarantee lasting respect for the enforcement of international justice,

Have agreed as follows . . .

PART 2. JURISDICTION, ADMISSIBILITY AND APPLICABLE LAW

Article 5

Crimes within the jurisdiction of the Court
1. The jurisdiction of the Court shall be limited to the most serious crimes of concern to the international community as a whole. The Court has jurisdiction in accordance with this Statute with respect to the following crimes:
(a) The crime of genocide;
(b) Crimes against humanity;
(c) War crimes;
(d) The crime of aggression.

2. The Court shall exercise jurisdiction over the crime of aggression once a provision is adopted in accordance with articles 121 and 123 defining the crime and setting out the conditions under which the Court shall exercise jurisdiction with respect to this crime. Such a provision shall be consistent with the relevant provisions of the Charter of the United Nations.

Article 6
Genocide

For the purpose of this Statute, 'genocide' means any of the following acts committed with intent to destroy, in whole or in part, a national, ethnical, racial or religious group, as such:
(a) Killing members of the group;
(b) Causing serious bodily or mental harm to members of the group;
(c) Deliberately inflicting on the group conditions of life calculated to bring about its physical destruction in whole or in part;
(d) Imposing measures intended to prevent births within the group;
(e) Forcibly transferring children of the group to another group.

Article 7
Crimes against humanity

1. For the purpose of this Statute, 'crime against humanity' means any of the following acts when committed as part of a widespread or systematic attack directed against any civilian population, with knowledge of the attack:
(a) Murder;
(b) Extermination;
(c) Enslavement;
(d) Deportation or forcible transfer of population;
(e) Imprisonment or other severe deprivation of physical liberty in violation of fundamental rules of international law;
(f) Torture;
(g) Rape, sexual slavery, enforced prostitution, forced pregnancy, enforced sterilization, or any other form of sexual violence of comparable gravity;
(h) Persecution against any identifiable group or collectivity on political, racial, national, ethnic, cultural, religious, gender as defined in paragraph 3, or other grounds that are universally recognized as impermissible under international law, in connection with any act referred to in this paragraph or any crime within the jurisdiction of the Court;
(i) Enforced disappearance of persons;
(j) The crime of apartheid;
(k) Other inhumane acts of a similar character intentionally causing great suffering, or serious injury to body or to mental or physical health.

2. For the purpose of paragraph 1:
(a) 'Attack directed against any civilian population' means a course of conduct

involving the multiple commission of acts referred to in paragraph 1 against any civilian population, pursuant to or in furtherance of a State or organizational policy to commit such attack;

(b) 'Extermination' includes the intentional infliction of conditions of life, inter alia the deprivation of access to food and medicine, calculated to bring about the destruction of part of a population;

(c) 'Enslavement' means the exercise of any or all of the powers attaching to the right of ownership over a person and includes the exercise of such power in the course of trafficking in persons, in particular women and children;

(d) 'Deportation or forcible transfer of population' means forced displacement of the persons concerned by expulsion or other coercive acts from the area in which they are lawfully present, without grounds permitted under international law;

(e) 'Torture' means the intentional infliction of severe pain or suffering, whether physical or mental, upon a person in the custody or under the control of the accused; except that torture shall not include pain or suffering arising only from, inherent in or incidental to, lawful sanctions;

(f) 'Forced pregnancy' means the unlawful confinement of a woman forcibly made pregnant, with the intent of affecting the ethnic composition of any population or carrying out other grave violations of international law. This definition shall not in any way be interpreted as affecting national laws relating to pregnancy;

(g) 'Persecution' means the intentional and severe deprivation of fundamental rights contrary to international law by reason of the identity of the group or collectivity;

(h) 'The crime of apartheid' means inhumane acts of a character similar to those referred to in paragraph 1, committed in the context of an institutionalized regime of systematic oppression and domination by one racial group over any other racial group or groups and committed with the intention of maintaining that regime;

(i) 'Enforced disappearance of persons' means the arrest, detention or abduction of persons by, or with the authorization, support or acquiescence of, a State or a political organization, followed by a refusal to acknowledge that deprivation of freedom or to give information on the fate or whereabouts of those persons, with the intention of removing them from the protection of the law for a prolonged period of time.

3. For the purpose of this Statute, it is understood that the term 'gender' refers to the two sexes, male and female, within the context of society. The term 'gender' does not indicate any meaning different from the above.

Article 8
War crimes

1. The Court shall have jurisdiction in respect of war crimes in particular when committed as a part of a plan or policy or as part of a large-scale commission of such crimes.

2. For the purpose of this Statute, 'war crimes' means:
(a) Grave breaches of the Geneva Conventions of 12 August 1949, namely, any of the following acts against persons or property protected under the provisions of the relevant Geneva Convention:
  (i) Wilful killing;
  (ii) Torture or inhuman treatment, including biological experiments;
  (iii) Wilfully causing great suffering, or serious injury to body or health;
  (iv) Extensive destruction and appropriation of property, not justified by military necessity and carried out unlawfully and wantonly;
  (v) Compelling a prisoner-of-war or other protected person to serve in the forces of a hostile Power;
  (vi) Wilfully depriving a prisoner-of-war or other protected person of the rights of fair and regular trial;
  (vii) Unlawful deportation or transfer or unlawful confinement;
  (viii) Taking of hostages.

(b) Other serious violations of the laws and customs applicable in international armed conflict, within the established framework of international law, namely, any of the following acts:
  (i) Intentionally directing attacks against the civilian population as such or against individual civilians not taking direct part in hostilities;
  (ii) Intentionally directing attacks against civilian objects, that is, objects which are not military objectives;
  (iii) Intentionally directing attacks against personnel, installations, material, units or vehicles involved in a humanitarian assistance or peace-keeping mission in accordance with the Charter of the United Nations, as long as they are entitled to the protection given to civilians or civilian objects under the international law of armed conflict;
  (iv) Intentionally launching an attack in the knowledge that such attack will cause incidental loss of life or injury to civilians or damage to civilian objects or widespread, long-term and severe damage to the natural environment which would be clearly excessive in relation to the concrete and direct overall military advantage anticipated;

(v) Attacking or bombarding, by whatever means, towns, villages, dwellings or buildings which are undefended and which are not military objectives;

(vi) Killing or wounding a combatant who, having laid down his arms or having no longer means of defence, has surrendered at discretion;

(vii) Making improper use of a flag of truce, of the flag or of the military insignia and uniform of the enemy or of the United Nations, as well as of the distinctive emblems of the Geneva Conventions, resulting in death or serious personal injury;

(viii) The transfer, directly or indirectly, by the Occupying Power of parts of its own civilian population into the territory it occupies, or the deportation or transfer of all or parts of the population of the occupied territory within or outside this territory;

(ix) Intentionally directing attacks against buildings dedicated to religion, education, art, science or charitable purposes, historic monuments, hospitals and places where the sick and wounded are collected, provided they are not military objectives;

(x) Subjecting persons who are in the power of an adverse party to physical mutilation or to medical or scientific experiments of any kind which are neither justified by the medical, dental or hospital treatment of the person concerned nor carried out in his or her interest, and which cause death to or seriously endanger the health of such person or persons;

(xi) Killing or wounding treacherously individuals belonging to the hostile nation or army;

(xii) Declaring that no quarter will be given;

(xiii) Destroying or seizing the enemy's property unless such destruction or seizure be imperatively demanded by the necessities of war;

(xiv) Declaring abolished, suspended or inadmissible in a court of law the rights and actions of the nationals of the hostile party;

(xv) Compelling the nationals of the hostile party to take part in the operations of war directed against their own country, even if they were in the belligerent's service before the commencement of the war;

(xvi) Pillaging a town or place, even when taken by assault;

(xvii) Employing poison or poisoned weapons;

(xviii) Employing asphyxiating, poisonous or other gases, and all analogous liquids, materials or devices;

(xix) Employing bullets which expand or flatten easily in the human body, such as bullets with a hard envelope which does not entirely cover the core or is pierced with incisions;

(xx) Employing weapons, projectiles and material and methods of warfare which are of a nature to cause superfluous injury or unnecessary suffering or which are inherently indiscriminate in violation of the international law of armed conflict, provided that such weapons, projectiles and material and methods of warfare are the subject of a comprehensive prohibition and are included in an annex to this Statute, by an amendment in accordance with the relevant provisions set forth in articles 121 and 123;

(xxi) Committing outrages upon personal dignity, in particular humiliating and degrading treatment;

(xxii) Committing rape, sexual slavery, enforced prostitution, forced pregnancy, as defined in article 7, paragraph 2(f), enforced sterilization, or any other form of sexual violence also constituting a grave breach of the Geneva Conventions;

(xxiii) Utilizing the presence of a civilian or other protected person to render certain points, areas or military forces immune from military operations;

(xxiv) Intentionally directing attacks against buildings, material, medical units and transport, and personnel using the distinctive emblems of the Geneva Conventions in conformity with international law;

(xxv) Intentionally using starvation of civilians as a method of warfare by depriving them of objects indispensable to their survival, including wilfully impeding relief supplies as provided for under the Geneva Conventions;

(xxvi) Conscripting or enlisting children under the age of fifteen years into the national armed forces or using them to participate actively in hostilities.

(c) In the case of an armed conflict not of an international character, serious violations of article 3 common to the four Geneva Conventions of 12 August 1949, namely, any of the following acts committed against persons taking no active part in the hostilities, including members of armed forces who have laid down their arms and those placed hors de combat by sickness, wounds, detention or any other cause:

(i) Violence to life and person, in particular murder of all kinds, mutilation, cruel treatment and torture;

(ii) Committing outrages upon personal dignity, in particular humiliating and degrading treatment;

(iii) Taking of hostages;

(iv) The passing of sentences and the carrying out of executions without previous judgement pronounced by a regularly constituted court, affording all judicial guarantees which are generally recognized as indispensable.

(d) Paragraph 2(c) applies to armed conflicts not of an international character and thus does not apply to situations of internal disturbances and tensions, such as riots, isolated and sporadic acts of violence or other acts of a similar nature.

(e) Other serious violations of the laws and customs applicable in armed conflicts not of an international character, within the established framework of international law, namely, any of the following acts:

(i) Intentionally directing attacks against the civilian population as such or against individual civilians not taking direct part in hostilities;

(ii) Intentionally directing attacks against buildings, material, medical units and transport, and personnel using the distinctive emblems of the Geneva Conventions in conformity with international law;

(iii) Intentionally directing attacks against personnel, installations, material, units or vehicles involved in a humanitarian assistance or peace-keeping mission in accordance with the Charter of the United Nations, as long as they are entitled to the protection given to civilians or civilian objects under the law of armed conflict;

(iv) Intentionally directing attacks against buildings dedicated to religion, education, art, science or charitable purposes, historic monuments, hospitals and places where the sick and wounded are collected, provided they are not military objectives;

(v) Pillaging a town or place, even when taken by assault;

(vi) Committing rape, sexual slavery, enforced prostitution, forced pregnancy, as defined in article 7, paragraph 2(f), enforced sterilization, and any other form of sexual violence also constituting a serious violation of article 3 common to the four Geneva Conventions;

(vii) Conscripting or enlisting children under the age of fifteen years into armed forces or groups or using them to participate actively in hostilities;

(viii) Ordering the displacement of the civilian population for reasons related to the conflict, unless the security of the civilians involved or imperative military reasons so demand;

(ix) Killing or wounding treacherously a combatant adversary;

(x) Declaring that no quarter will be given;

(xi) Subjecting persons who are in the power of another party to the conflict to physical mutilation or to medical or scientific experiments of any kind which are neither justified by the medical, dental or hospital treatment of the person concerned nor carried out in his or her interest, and which cause death to or seriously endanger the health of such person or persons;

(xii) Destroying or seizing the property of an adversary unless such destruction or seizure be imperatively demanded by the necessities of the conflict;

(f) Paragraph 2(e) applies to armed conflicts not of an international character and thus does not apply to situations of internal disturbances and tensions, such as riots, isolated and sporadic acts of violence or other acts of a similar nature. It applies to armed conflicts that take place in the territory of a State when there is protracted armed conflict between governmental authorities and organized armed groups or between such groups.

3. Nothing in paragraph 2(c) and (d) shall affect the responsibility of a Government to maintain or re-establish law and order in the State or to defend the unity and territorial integrity of the State, by all legitimate means.

Article 27
Irrelevance of official capacity

1. This Statute shall apply equally to all persons without any distinction based on official capacity. In particular, official capacity as a Head of State or Government, a member of a Government or parliament, an elected representative or a government official shall in no case exempt a person from criminal responsibility under this Statute, nor shall it, in and of itself, constitute a ground for reduction of sentence.

2. Immunities or special procedural rules which may attach to the official capacity of a person, whether under national or international law, shall not bar the Court from exercising its jurisdiction over such a person.

Article 28
Responsibility of commanders and other superiors

In addition to other grounds of criminal responsibility under this Statute for crimes within the jurisdiction of the Court:
1. A military commander or person effectively acting as a military commander shall be criminally responsible for crimes within the jurisdiction of the Court committed by forces under his or her effective command and control, or effective authority and control as the case may be, as a result of his or her failure to exercise control properly over such forces, where:
(a) That military commander or person either knew or, owing to the circumstances at the time, should have known that the forces were committing or about to commit such crimes; and
(b) That military commander or person failed to take all necessary and reasonable measures within his or her power to prevent or repress their

commission or to submit the matter to the competent authorities for investigation and prosecution.

2. With respect to superior and subordinate relationships not described in paragraph 1, a superior shall be criminally responsible for crimes within the jurisdiction of the Court committed by subordinates under his or her effective authority and control, as a result of his or her failure to exercise control properly over such subordinates, where:

(a) The superior either knew, or consciously disregarded information which clearly indicated, that the subordinates were committing or about to commit such crimes;

(b) The crimes concerned activities that were within the effective responsibility and control of the superior; and

(c) The superior failed to take all necessary and reasonable measures within his or her power to prevent or repress their commission or to submit the matter to the competent authorities for investigation and prosecution.

Article 29
Non-applicability of statute of limitations

The crimes within the jurisdiction of the Court shall not be subject to any statute of limitation.

Article 33
Superior orders and prescription of law

1. The fact that a crime within the jurisdiction of the Court has been committed by a person pursuant to an order of a Government or of a superior, whether military or civilian, shall not relieve that person of criminal responsibility unless:

(a) The person was under a legal obligation to obey orders of the Government or the superior in question;

(b) The person did not know that the order was unlawful; and

(c) The order was not manifestly unlawful.

2. For the purposes of this article, orders to commit genocide or crimes against humanity are manifestly unlawful.

Appendix E: Excerpts from the Charter of the United Nations

WE THE PEOPLES OF THE UNITED NATIONS DETERMINED to save succeeding generations from the scourge of war, which twice in our lifetime has brought untold sorrow to mankind, and to reaffirm faith in fundamental human rights, in the dignity and worth of the human person, in the equal rights of men and women and of nations large and small, and to establish conditions under which justice and respect for the obligations arising from treaties and other sources of international law can be maintained, and to promote social progress and better standards of life in larger freedom,

AND FOR THESE ENDS to practise tolerance and live together in peace with one another as good neighbours, and to unite our strength to maintain international peace and security, and to ensure, by the acceptance of principles and the institution of methods, that armed force shall not be used, save in the common interest, and to employ international machinery for the promotion of the economic and social advancement of all peoples,

HAVE RESOLVED TO COMBINE OUR EFFORTS TO ACCOMPLISH THESE AIMS. Accordingly, our respective Governments, through representatives assembled in the city of San Francisco, who have exhibited their full powers found to be in good and due form, have agreed to the present Charter of the United Nations and do hereby establish an international organization to be known as the United Nations.

CHAPTER I. PURPOSES AND PRINCIPLES

Article 1

The Purposes of the United Nations are:
(1) To maintain international peace and security, and to that end: to take effective collective measures for the prevention and removal of threats to the peace, and for the suppression of acts of aggression or other breaches

of the peace, and to bring about by peaceful means, and in conformity with the principles of justice and international law, adjustment or settlement of international disputes or situations which might lead to a breach of the peace;

(2) To develop friendly relations among nations based on respect for the principles of equal rights and self-determination of peoples, and to take other appropriate measures to strengthen universal peace;

(3) To achieve international co-operation in solving international problems of an economic, social, cultural, or humanitarian character, and in promoting and encouraging respect for human rights and for fundamental freedoms for all without distinction as to race, sex, language, or religion; and

(4) To be a centre for harmonizing the actions of nations in the attainment of these common ends.

Article 2

The Organization and its Members, in pursuit of the Purposes stated in Article 1, shall act in accordance with the following Principles.

(1) The Organization is based on the principle of the sovereign equality of all its Members.

(2) All Members, in order to ensure to all of them the rights and benefits resulting from membership, shall fulfil in good faith the obligations assumed by them in accordance with the present Charter.

(3) All Members shall settle their international disputes by peaceful means in such a manner that international peace and security, and justice, are not endangered.

(4) All Members shall refrain in their international relations from the threat or use of force against the territorial integrity or political independence of any state, or in any other manner inconsistent with the Purposes of the United Nations.

(5) All Members shall give the United Nations every assistance in any action it takes in accordance with the present Charter, and shall refrain from giving assistance to any state against which the United Nations is taking preventive or enforcement action.

(6) The Organization shall ensure that states which are not Members of the

United Nations act in accordance with these Principles so far as may be necessary for the maintenance of peace and security.

(7) Nothing contained in the present Charter shall authorize the United Nations to intervene in matters which are essentially within the domestic jurisdiction of any state or shall require the Members to submit such matters to settlement under the present Charter; but this principle shall not prejudice the application of enforcement measures under Chapter VII.

CHAPTER V. THE SECURITY COUNCIL

Composition

Article 23

(1) The Security Council shall consist of fifteen Members of the United Nations. The Republic of China, France, the Union of Soviet Socialist Republics, the United Kingdom of Great Britain and Northern Ireland, and the United States of America shall be permanent members of the Security Council. The General Assembly shall elect ten other Members of the United Nations to be non-permanent members of the Security Council, due regard being specially paid, in the first instance, to the contribution of Members of the United Nations to the maintenance of international peace and security and to the other purposes of the Organization, and also to equitable geographical distribution.

(2) The non-permanent members of the Security Council shall be elected for a term of two years. In the first election of the non-permanent members after the increase of the membership of the Security Council from eleven to fifteen, two of the four additional members shall be chosen for a term of one year. A retiring member shall not be eligible for immediate re-election.

(3) Each member of the Security Council shall have one representative.

Article 27

(1) Each member of the Security Council shall have one vote.

(2) Decisions of the Security Council on procedural matters shall be made by an affirmative vote of nine members.

(3) Decisions of the Security Council on all other matters shall be made by an affirmative vote of nine members including the concurring votes of the

permanent members: provided that, in decisions under Chapter VI, and under paragraph 3 of Article 52, a party to a dispute shall abstain from voting.

CHAPTER VII. ACTION WITH RESPECT TO THREATS TO THE PEACE, BREACHES OF THE PEACE, AND ACTS OF AGGRESSION

Article 39

The Security Council shall determine the existence of any threat to the peace, breach of the peace, or act of aggression and shall make recommendations, or decide what measures shall be taken in accordance with Articles 41 and 42, to maintain or restore international peace and security.

Article 40

In order to prevent an aggravation of the situation, the Security Council may, before making the recommendations or deciding upon the measures provided for in Article 39, call upon the parties concerned to comply with such provisional measures as it deems necessary or desirable. Such provisional measures shall be without prejudice to the rights, claims, or position of the parties concerned. The Security Council shall duly take account of failure to comply with such provisional measures.

Article 41

The Security Council may decide what measures not involving the use of armed force are to be employed to give effect to its decisions, and it may call upon the Members of the United Nations to apply such measures. These may include complete or partial interruption of economic relations and of rail, sea, air, postal, telegraphic, radio, and other means of communication, and the severance of diplomatic relations.

Article 42

Should the Security Council consider that measures provided for in Article 41 would be inadequate or have proved to be inadequate, it may take such action by air, sea, or land forces as may be necessary to maintain or restore international peace or security. Such action may include demonstrations, blockade, and other operations by air, sea, or land forces of Members of the United Nations.

Article 51

Nothing in the present Charter shall impair the inherent right of individual or collective self-defence if an armed attack occurs against a Member of the United Nations, until the Security Council has taken measures necessary to maintain international peace and security. Measures taken by Members in the exercise of this right of self-defence shall be immediately reported to the Security Council and shall not in any way affect the authority and responsibility of the Security Council under the present Charter to take at any time such action as it deems necessary in order to maintain or restore international peace and security.

CHAPTER VIII. REGIONAL ARRANGEMENTS

Article 52

(1) Nothing in the present Charter precludes the existence of regional arrangements or agencies for dealing with such matters relating to the maintenance of international peace and security as are appropriate for regional action, provided that such arrangements or agencies and their activities are consistent with the Purposes and Principles of the United Nations.

(2) The Members of the United Nations entering into such arrangements or constituting such agencies shall make every effort to achieve pacific settlement of local disputes through such regional arrangements or by such regional agencies before referring them to the Security Council.

(3) The Security Council shall encourage the development of pacific settlement of local disputes through such regional arrangements or by such regional agencies either on the initiative of the states concerned or by reference from the Security Council.

Article 53

(1) The Security Council shall, where appropriate, utilize such regional arrangements or agencies for enforcement action under its authority. But no enforcement action shall be taken under regional arrangements or by regional agencies without the authorization of the Security Council, with the exception

of measures against any enemy state, as defined in paragraph 2 of this Article, provided for pursuant to Article 107 or in regional arrangements directed against renewal of aggressive policy on the part of any such state, until such time as the Organization may, on request of the Governments concerned, be charged with the responsibility for preventing further aggression by such a state.

(2) The term enemy state as used in paragraph 1 of this Article applies to any state which during the Second World War has been an enemy of any signatory of the present Charter.

Article 54

The Security Council shall at all times be kept fully informed of activities undertaken or in contemplation under regional arrangements or by regional agencies for the maintenance of international peace and security.

Article 68

The Economic and Social Council shall set up commissions in economic and social fields and for the promotion of human rights, and such other commissions as may be required for the performance of its functions.

Article 92

The International Court of Justice shall be the principal judicial organ of the United Nations. It shall function in accordance with the annexed Statute, which is based upon the Statute of the Permanent Court of International Justice and forms an integral part of the present Charter.

Article 94

(1) Each member of the United Nations undertakes to comply with the decision of the International Court of Justice in any case to which it is a party.

(2) If any party to a case fails to perform the obligations incumbent upon it under a judgment rendered by the Court, the other party may have recourse to the Security Council, which may, if it deems necessary, make recommendations or decide upon measures to be taken to give effect to the judgment.

Article 103

In the event of a conflict between the obligations of the Members of the United Nations under the present Charter and their obligations under any other international agreement, their obligations under the present Charter shall prevail.

Index